ISBN 978-0-332-63688-7
PIBN 10294416

Forgotten Books is a registered trademark of FB &c Ltd.
Copyright © 2018 FB &c Ltd.
FB &c Ltd, Dalton House, 60 Windsor Avenue, London, SW19 2RR.
Company number 08720141. Registered in England and Wales.

For support please visit www.forgottenbooks.com

From the collection of the

San Francisco, California
2006

Planning and Civic Comment

Official Organ of American Planning and Civic Association and
National Conference on State Parks

CONTENTS

MARCH 1962

PLANNING AND
CIVIC COMMENT

Published Quarterly

Successor to: City Planning, Civic Comment, State Recreation

Official Organ of: American Planning and Civic Association,
National Conference on State Parks

SCOPE: *National, State, Regional and City Planning, Land and Water Uses, Conservation of National Resources, National, State and Local Parks, Highways and Roadsides.*

AIM: *To create a better physical environment which will conserve and develop the health, happiness and culture of the American people.*

Second-class postage paid at Harrisburg, Pa., and at additional mailing office.

EDITORIAL AND PUBLICATION OFFICE, 901 Union Trust Building, Washington 5, D. C.

Printed by the Mount Pleasant Press, J. Horace McFarland Company, Harrisburg, Pa.

Planning and Civic Comment

| Vol. 28 | March, 1962 | N ⁷ | No. 1 |

Ladies Who Wear the Uniform of the National Park Service

By ROGERS W. YOUNG, National Park Service

For more than 40 years lady employees of the National Park Service have been wearing its uniform in one capacity or another. Although little known to the public generally, this work by those of the distaff side has been highly skilled and performed by many able and attractive women who have served the public throughout the United States under unusual conditions. So, in 1960, when the National Park Service issued a written statement on the employment of women in uniformed positions, it was not announcing a new policy, but reaffirming and emphasizing a long-established practice to employ qualified women in positions where they could help the public understand and enjoy the parks.

In urging administrative officials to consider fully all qualified applicants for vacancies in the public service, the 1960 statement reaffirms the objective of the National Park Service "to employ in its uniformed positions the best qualified men and women available." While the policy "recognized that women cannot be employed in certain jobs, such as Park Ranger or Seasonal Park Ranger . . . in which the employee is subject to be called to fight fires, take part in rescue opera-

tions, or do other strenuous or hazardous work . . .." it does stress that::

"Participation by women employees in lecture programs, guided tours, museum and library work, and in research programs would be entirely appropriate and very helpful in many Parks. Increased attention may also be given to children's programs in some Parks and to extension work to schools for which women interpretive employees may be even more effective than men."

The National Park Service has no lady rangers today. Yet, a lady ranger, Miss Claire Marie Hodges (now Mrs. Peter J. Wolfsen), served as a Seasonal Ranger in Yosemite National Park as early as 1918. She had duties similar to those of the male rangers of that day, rode mounted patrol in Yosemite Valley and reported directly to the Chief Ranger. The male domain of the Park Ranger was next invaded by the ladies in 1920, when Superintendent Horace M. Albright, Yellowstone National Park, hired Miss Isabel D. Bassett to act as Seasonal Ranger "in guiding people about the geyser formations while performing the duties relating to the protection of those formations."

Mr. Albright, second Director of the National Park Service (1929–1933), recently had pleasant recol-

moted and, following the transfer of the Chief Park Archeologist in 1959, took over as Acting Chief until her promotion in March of 1960, to Chief Park Archeologist . . . While there is nothing unusual in the above, it may be of interest to other women to know that as each change in position took place, the new position was first occupied by a woman, the present Chief Park Archeologist of Mesa Verde.

"Mrs. Pinkley's duties as Chief of the Interpretive Division cover all facets of interpretation, including acting in advisory capacity to the Superintendent, supervising research pertinent to interpreting the park and its features, operation of museums, trailside and roadside exhibits, an integrated visitor-services program, the excavation and stabilization of prehistoric ruins and planning for the future development of the interpretive program of the park."

Two other interesting ladies in Park Service uniforms are described for us by Yosemite and Hawaii National Parks. First, at Yosemite, we find Seasonal Park Naturalist Lorraine Miles, who spends a good portion of her time relating Indian lore and giving nature instruction to children's groups. Then, from Hawaii National Park, we learn about the work of Mrs. Mitsuko T. Shikuma of Hilo, Hawaii, who serves as a uniformed Information-Receptionist at the Park Headquarters and Visitor Center, where she provides information and interpretive data and is most helpful to many of the park's visitors because of her ability to speak Japanese.

In December 1961, the *Philadelphia Inquirer* reported with a flourish that "There's Something New at Independence Hall." It's true! The "something new" is the news that five personable, attractive young ladies are now telling the public the great stories of liberty and independence at Independence National Historical Park. These uniformed ladies are historians and they are pioneers in "an experiment with an idea new to the Service but not new outside the Service—the employment of women on the basis of personality and physical attributes as well as educational qualifications to create a favorable image and to interpret the park story to visitors in a pleasant manner. Reporting on these ladies— Ruth Noble Friday and Joan Riley Emery, both married; and Judith A. Rhoade, Margaret A. Ciborowski, and Elizabeth Brennan—the Superintendent of the park comments as follows on their training and work:

"An extensive training program was developed and put into effect. Wide-scale reading from appropriate volumes in the Park Library, historic structures reports, and other documents provided the foundation for the preparation of talks the young ladies give in Independence Hall. Other aspects of their training included voice counselling by a professional voice (through a grant of the Eastern National Park and Monument Association), practice speaking with the use of tape recorders, and field trips to the United Nations, Rockefeller Center, Colonial Williamsburg as well as to two National Park areas to observe interpretation in practice. The young ladies entered on duty in the Hall in November 1961 and visitor reaction has been most favorable. Indeed, they have already received considerable publicity in the press and on television. Their training in subject matter will continue so that the completeness and accuracy of their presentations will approach that of professional historians. Guided tours will be inaugurated this spring."

From National Capital Parks, in Washington, D. C., we learn of two interesting lady employees of the Service who perform unusual public-service duties either in or out of uniform. The first is Seasonal Naturalist Phyllis Wells, who holds a bachelor's degree in conservation from the University of Michigan.

She spends a great deal of her time walking the woods in the parks in the Washington area, explaining birds, plants, and geological features to adults and school groups. The second is Mrs. Agnes Mullins, Historian in charge of the unusual Colonial cultural demonstrations at the Old Stone House in Georgetown. Her work is directed especially to children who engage in the making or dipping of bayberry candles and are actually taught by Mrs. Mullins to learn by doing the pleasures and secrets of this and other historical arts and crafts.

And what does the future hold for women in the uniformed work of the National Park Service? That the Service's 1960 restatement of its steadfast purpose to employ qualified women in its program of services to the public is not an empty gesture is shown by statements and actions of park administrators throughout the System. For example, the Service's southeastern or Region One Office at Richmond, Va., comments:

"We believe the future definitely holds a brighter prospect for the employment of women in Region One for uniformed positions. With the completion of public-use facilities under the Mission 66 Program, opportunities for uniformed women employees are increasing, but possibly not as rapidly as they should. In Region One . . . there are more jobs arising for which women are especially trained, such as curatorial work in museums and in furnished historic structures."

The Regional Director of the Service's northeastern or Region Five Office at Philadelphia, Pa., in reporting the future for women in a region which contains many historic structures especially suited to the skills of the lady historian, expresses his belief that:

"As evidenced by the . . . reports of several Superintendents, we already have a fairly substantial number of women in uniformed positions in comparison to the number of suitable positions in the Region. One of the two Student Trainee Park Historians hired in Region Five is a female. In appearance, aptitudes, attitudes, and availability for intermittent or part-time employment, women are frequently better prepared than men for uniformed interpretive services. And with equivalent educational qualifications, we believe they can compete on a par with men for research work which does not include strenuous physical exertion or other factors of an environmental nature for which men are better prepared.

"Unless unforeseen conditions change the situation, it seems likely that in the future an increasing number of women in uniform will be employed as we expand visitor facilities such as guided tours."

The Service's midwestern region, at Omaha, Nebraska, reports that it "shall continue to consider women wherever possible for all positions for which they are qualified." Finally, the Pacific Coast headquarters of the National Park Service, at San Francisco, Calif., sums up the prospects in that region for women employees in uniform by observing that:

"So far as the future is concerned it appears likely that Park Ranger jobs will be restricted to men because of the physical requirements of all such positions. Because of expanding staffs in many areas there will be less need to expect interpretive personnel to "double in brass" in the protective role and thus there should be more of an increasing number of positions appropriate for women in such jobs as Park Historian, Park Naturalist, and Park Archeologist.

"There also appears the possibility that more positions such as Receptionist or Guide may be established that will not require a professional background and in many cases would be suitable for women."

Strictly Personal

Albert S. Bard was honored on his 95th birthday at the December luncheon of the Citizens Union of New York City. He is one of the two surviving founders of the Union. Mr. Bard was praised for "a lifetime great in service and distinguished in activity."

———◇———

William C. Arntz of Rockville, Md. has been named Deputy Director of the Open Space Land Branch of the Urban Renewal Administration.

———◇———

Jerome M. Alper, attorney and transportation authority, and Counsel of APCA, has been selected to prepare plans for an agency in Washington which would finance, build and operate a metropolitan rapid transit system.

———◇———

Aaron Levine has been appointed Executive Vice-president of the Greater Honolulu Council and assumed duties on March 1. This newly formed Council of 25 business leaders in Honolulu is devoted to the sound planning of the Island. Mr. Levine has served nearly a decade as Executive Director of the Citizens Council on City Planning in Philadelphia.

———◇———

Horace M. Albright received the gold medal of the Camp Fire Club at its conservation dinner held in January in New York, which he attended as guest of honor.

———◇———

Paul M. Dunn of New York City was elected President of the American Forestry Association for a two-year term 1962–63. Mr. Dunn is director of forestry of the St. Regis Paper Company and has been a director of the American Forestry Association. He succeeds Charles A. Connaughton of San Francisco who was not a candidate for reelection.

———◇———

Clyde Nichols, Jr., member of the Board of Trustees, APCA, sent out an interesting Christmas and New Year's card with news of his family. He has completed his year as national President of the Young Presidents Organization and is now chairman of an effort to improve economic education in the grade and high schools of the United States and Canada.

———◇———

Secretary of Agriculture Freeman announced March 9 the retirement of Richard E. McArdle, 63, as chief of the department's Forest Service. He will be succeeded in the $19,000-a-year post by Edward P. Cliff, a career forester who has been with the service for 32 years.

———◇———

Edmund R. Purves, F.A.I.A. has joined the firm of Chatelain, Gauger and Nolan, architects and engineers, of Washington, D. C. as an associate.

———◇———

Ellis S. Tisdale retired Feb. 1 as executive director of the Interstate Commission on the Potomac River Basin. He has directed the commission for six years.

———◇———

Roger D. Hale, vice-president of the Conservation Foundation of New York City, was named the new

6

chairman of the Natural Resources Council of America at that organization's annual meeting which took place recently in Santa Fe, New Mexico. He succeeds C. R. Gutermuth, vice-president of the Wildlife Management Institute of Washington, D. C., now a member of the Council's executive committee.

———— ◆ ————

Webb & Knapp, Inc., New York real estate and development company, named William Zeckendorf as chairman, a newly created post. Mr. Zechendorf is on the Board of Trustees, APCA. William Zeckendorf, Jr. was appointed president, a post his father formerly held.

———— ◆ ————

Samuel H. Ordway, Jr. has been elected president of the Conservation Foundation succeeding Fairfield Osborn, who resigned to become Chairman of the Board. Mr. Ordway has served as executive vice-president of the Foundation for 14 years.

———— ◆ ————

Laurance S. Rockefeller, Chairman, Outdoor Recreation Resources Review Commission, is to speak at the opening general session on Monday, March 12, on the subject, "Recreational Needs in Years Ahead" at the 27th North American Wildlife and Natural Resources Conference to be held in Denver, Colorado.

———— ◆ ————

Mrs. Edward Waugh has been appointed Chairman of a newly authorized Historic Sites Commission of Raleigh, N. C.

———— ◆ ————

A. Clark Stratton has been named Assistant Director in charge of the National Park Service's design and construction program. He succeeds Thomas C. Vint, who retired at the close of 1961 after 39 years of park work.

———— ◆ ————

Corwin R. Mocine was reelected to the presidency of the American Institute of Planners at its annual meeting in Detroit last November. Mr. Mocine is professor of city planning at the University of California.

———— ◆ ————

Charles W. Eliot, planning consultant of Cambridge, Mass. and Lawrence M. Orton, member of the New York City Planning Commission were given the Distinguished Service Awards by the American Institute of Planners at the Annual Meeting in Detroit.

———— ◆ ————

Leon Zach, Paul A. Goettelmann and Leon Chatelain, Jr. have been named as Consulting Architects, an advisory committee on Highways to the Department of Highways and Traffic of the District of Columbia which is headed by Harold L. Aitken, Director.

———— ◆ ————

Theodore Savage of Pittsburgh, has been named Executive Director of the Washington Housing and Planning Association. Formerly the Washington Housing Association, the organization has new headquarters at 929 L Street N. W., Washington 5, D. C. A three-year grant of funds will enable the organization to study general community problems such as zoning and planning.

Zoning Round Table

Conducted by FLAVEL SHURTLEFF, Marshfield Hills, Mass.

COMPREHENSIVE ZONING PLAN

In a very recent case the Supreme Court of Rhode Island said, "The narrow issue here is whether there is any evidence in the record indicating that the amendment was adopted pursuant to a comprehensive plan." Since the Court found none, it followed that the city council exceeded its statutory authority in enacting the amendment. The record consisted of findings by the trial justice among which the following were most pertinent:

(a) the amendment applied solely to the plantiff's land which before the amendment was zoned industrial, and in which trailer parks were permitted uses;

(b) no evidence was presented showing that other industrial land in the area had been converted to residence use;

(c) because of the nature of plantiff's land, it could not be used for the purpose permitted by the amendment and therefore the plaintiff was deprived of property rights without due process;

(d) the original zoning ordinance was enacted in accordance with a comprehensive plan, but the amendment was a capricious restriction of the plaintiff's property.

The Supreme Court ruled that these findings were supported by the evidence, and the decree that the amendment was void was affirmed.

The plaintiff's property contained 16 acres and was part of a larger parcel which had been zoned industrial since the enactment of the zoning ordinance in 1928. There was other industrially zoned land adjoining, and near by, as well as a residential B district. The plaintiff had bought the land for use as a trailer park in November 1958. The amendment changing the zoning designation of the plaintiff's land only to residence B was enacted January 28, 1959.

The court brushed aside the city's contentions that there had been a substantial change of conditions in the area, and that the size of the plaintiff's parcel justified the amendment. In the absence of evidence that the amendment was drafted pursuant to a comprehensive plan, these arguments had no bearing.

Town and Country Mobile Homes, Inc. vs. Inspector of Buildings—City of Pawtucket. Decided Dec. 8, 1961.

The case leaves one with questions. What evidence would have swung the decision the other way? What constitutes "pursuance to a comprehensive plan?" Is it enough to show houses constructed on the land zoned industrial, or that the plaintiff's 16 acres adjoined a residence B zone?

Certainly comprehensive plans can be and often are amended. Can any rules be formulated for testing "pursuant" amendments? Are changed conditions either in the city or in the area affected by the

8

proposed amendment essential? Would a general statement help to the effect that a comprehensive plan of zoning must be based on a land use plan calculated to satisfy the objectives of zoning,—public safety, health, morals and welfare,—and that unless the amendment is pointed to the same objectives, it will not be valid?

Several Massachusetts cases have clarified the meaning of "financial hardship" which was added as a reason for variance by an amendment to the zoning enabling act adopted in 1958.

In one of the most recent of these cases, Bruzzese *vs.* Board of Appeals of Hingham, the plaintiff wanted to divide a large lot into two lots, one of 12,600 square feet with a frontage of 90 feet and one of 24,000 square feet in a zone requiring a frontage of 125 feet and an area of 20,000 square feet. He was refused a variance, but in the superior court the judge ruled that he suffered a substantial financial hardship in being forced to have so much frontage and area in the neighborhood in which the land was located. The supreme court reversed this ruling on two grounds (1) the deprivation of a potential financial advantage does not constitute a hardship; (2) the land was usable for the permitted use of a residence, and no hardship was suffered because two residences could not be built.

The court pointed out also that "seldom if ever can a judge grant a variance which has been refused by a Board of Appeals", citing

Cefalo vs. *City of Boston* 332 Mass. 178. See also

Vainas vs. *Board of Appeals of Lynn* 337 Mass. 591.

Di Rico et al. vs. *Board of Appeals of Quincy.* .

Cary vs. *City of Worcester.*

Barnhart vs. *Board of Appeals of Scituate.*

From the above citations most of which are reported in the Advance Sheets of the court's decisions, the following considerations apply in deciding the validity of a variance for financial hardship:

1. There will be no relaxation of the rule that variances should be sparingly granted.
2. No variance if the hardship is personal. It must spring from a condition peculiar to the property.
3. The financial hardship must be substantial.
4. All the conditions must be present: (a) peculiar circumstances attached to the property which cause the hardship; (b) no detriment to public welfare and no derogation from the purpose of the ordinance.
5. Where a variance has been denied by the Board of Appeals it can seldom if ever be granted by the trial justice.

Where a street 30 feet wide has been open to the public for over fifty years and most of the lots are occupied by residences, it was held a "taking" to refuse a building permit for residence on a lot which conformed in all respects to the regulations of the zoning ordinance except that it did not front on a public street, for which, as defined in the ordinance, a width of 40 feet was required.

9

All value of the lot was taken away. The owner's only right was "to look at it and pay taxes on it."

Jencks vs. *Building Commissioner of Brookline.* Advance Sheets 1960— page 867.

Commentaries

An attractive book has come to our attention entitled, Britain's National Parks, edited by Harold M. Abrahams. The book marks the tenth anniversary of the British National Parks Commission and describes the ten national parks which have been designated since 1950. Of its thirteen chapters, ten are descriptive essays on the charm of each National Park written by park champions, P. J. Monkhouse on the Peak; Clou h Williams-Ellis on Snowdon and Lady Sayer on Dartmoor. Illustrated, these chapters present some of the finest stretches of the countryside, and readers are pleased that these areas have achieved official recognition and protection. The remaining chapters make clear how long has been the struggle to achieve this recognition and how vulnerable the parks remain to future threats of damaging development. Gallant work is being done by the authorities, plus the growing public opinion behind them. This book should make that public opinion stronger and more vociferous.

As early as 1810 William Wordsworth said that visitors to the Lake District in northwest England thought of it as "a sort of national property, in which every man has a right and interest who has an eye to perceive and a heart to enjoy." Since then awareness of the need to protect unspoiled countryside has grown with the progress of industrialization and has become more and more vocal. In 1949 the National Parks and Access to the Countryside Act was passed and the National Parks Commission inaugurated. Because of the small size of England and Wales, and the limited amount of unoccupied and relatively wild land, space for the recreation of some 46 million people has to compete with more strictly economic needs such as mineral-working, afforestation and the provision of water-gathering grounds, to say nothing of agriculture itself.

The result is that the British National Parks, as they were proposed and as they have come into being, include villages and even towns around the margins of upland areas and in their valleys. It follows that any national view of a Park system must come to terms with the local life of each Park. Not only farming but maybe even industry must flourish in a Park.

❧

The Peninsula Committee for Parks and Planning, based at Hampton, Virginia, is a citizens organization dedicated to the reservation and acquisition of adequate parks, recreation areas and open spaces before the land is preempted for other uses, to the preservation of historic sites and to the conservation of natural resources. The organization envisions the creation of a magnificent Shoreline Drive along the Peninsula's remaining Chesapeake bayside beaches. A public hearing was held to present four sections of Hampton's master plans. The Peninsula Committee issues a mimeographed newsletter and solicits the support, both moral and financial, of interested citizens.

❧

The *New York Times* of January 2 and 3, 1962 published two editorials, Parts I and II entitled: "Needed: New National Parks." The initial statement that the national park system of the United States is an example for the world of how a great nation can set aside outstanding areas of its land, not for commercial or industrial expansion but for the aesthetic enjoyment and physical refreshment of its people, sets the tone of the editorials. It is pointed out that fortunately there are areas still available which would be worth-while additions to the system. These are mentioned individually and the *Times* advocates their addition within the National Park System to preserve in unspoiled state, these superb examples of the extraordinary natural, scenic and historic heritage of America.

☙

The second grant under the provision of the law which created the Open-Space Land Branch of the Urban Renewal Administration will go to the Massachusetts Natural Resources Department. A $46,500 grant from the U. S. government will be supplemented by $108,500 of Massachusetts money to acquire the picturesque 647-acre cranberry bog near Taunton to preserve it as a park, recreation and nature study area. It also contains five small man-made lakes.

Arthur A. Davis, who heads the Open-Space Land Branch in the Urban Renewal Administration, said he has received more than 250 grant applications or letters of notification.

"It already is apparent," says Commissioner William L. Slayton, "that this will be one of our most popular programs."

Congress authorized a $50 million program and appropriated $35 million to get it started.

When Congress approved the program, it said the aim was to help curb urban sprawl and prevent the spread of urban blight and deterioration, to encourage more economic and desirable urban development, and to help provide necessary recreational, conservation, and scenic areas by assisting in preserving open-space land."

☙

LIFE magazine, in a special, double issue, dated December 22, 1961, entitled, "Our Splendid Outdoors—the Land We Love and Enjoy and the Fight to Save It" covers a wide variety of conservation subjects. Secretary of the Interior Udall outlines a program for America to be presented to the American people for rounding out the National Park System. The publishers of *LIFE*

deserve an accolade for this magnificent issue.

☙

John M. Leavens, Executive Director, Citizens Budget Commission of New York wrote an excellent letter to the Editor of *New York Times* under date of December 11, which was published in a subsequent issue, which was a plea for citizen participation. While the letter is geared to the problems of New York, it applies in principle to cities and communities everywhere. Following are quotes from Mr. Leavens' letter, a clarion call for citizen participation:

"The *Times* editorial 'The Lost Citizen' on Dec. 9 should be reprinted daily. You are right when you say that New York needs interested and active citizens. You are right when you say that New York has first-class talent but doesn't always use it. But neither you nor we, nor many other agencies in our great city have yet found a magic formula for awakening interest and action by many of the city's potential leaders who shun civic affairs.

Arousing their interest is a challenge for all of us. We in the Citizens Budget Commission try and we shall continue to try—as we know you will. The greatest obstacle is the fact that so many New Yorkers are not convinced that what happens in municipal government makes much difference to them personally . . .

We agree with you that the appearance of more of our New York leaders in the business and professional world at meetings of the Board of Estimate, City Planning Commission or other public bodies would furnish a healthy stimulant to better municipal government.

We think, though, that there are many well-meaning individuals whom neither you nor we have yet reached who just do not know what to do, or think they haven't time to do anything. We suggest they sign up in the voluntary civic organization of their choice and in this way, at least, get a direct view of what is going on. Maybe this will encourage them to take a personal part in the municipal drama.

There is always room for municipal improvement. We will get it only when and if the latent talent of our city arises from a deep sleep and plays its proper role in municipal affairs. We are optimists, so we urge you to continue to summon these potential civic leaders to do their duty."

❧

America the Beautiful?—an article *The Reader's Digest* reprinted from the *Atlantic Monthly*, is written by Vance Packard, author of "The Status Seekers" and "The Waste Makers" who points out the need for an accelerated effort to clean up our countrysides. Sixteen states now enjoy a measure of protection against billboard blight for their new Interstate Highways. But the country is still plagued by blots of ugliness and disorder. Mr. Packard complains of this in his article and cites examples of desecration of the American landscape which threatens to make a cruel jest of the phrase, "America the Beautiful." He coins a new phrase, *rampant slobbism* which refers to the litter on our roads. "A society as prosperous and ambitious as ours should certainly act against these desecraters."

Reprints of the article may be obtained from *The Reader's Digest*, Pleasantville, N. Y.

❧

Many communities have asked for and received advice from the National Trust for Historic Preservation, which played a direct role in helping with legislation to protect the historic areas of San Francisco and Santa Barbara, Calif.; Litchfield, Conn.; Georgetown, D. C.; Lexington, Ky.; Vieux Carré of New Orleans, La.; Annapolis and Easton, Md.; Beacon Hill of Boston, and Nantucket, Mass.; St. Louis County Mo.; Strawbery Banke of Portsmouth, N. H.; Richmondtown of Staten Island, N. Y.; Winston-Salem, N. C.; Cincinnati, Ohio; Bethlehem and King of Prussia, Pa.; Newport and Providence, R. I.; Charleston, S. C.; and Church Hill of Richmond and Alexandria, Va.

Local planning officials are encouraged to consider the economic and cultural values of conserving historic buildings or areas of their city. In addition to advice, reference sources available through the Trust are *Historic Preservation Law* by Jacob H. Morrison; *Preservation of Historic Districts* by John Codman, published by the American Society of Planning Officials; and *Planning and Community Appearance* by the New York Chapter of the American Institute of Architects and the Regional Chapter of the American Institute of Planners.

❧

A call to arms has been sounded for Californians to resist conversion of the Golden State into "slurbs."

The term was coined by a new nonprofit organization as meaning chaotically developing urban areas—"our sloppy, sleazy, slovenly, slipshod semicities."

A sixty-three-page report prepared by California Tomorrow, a foundation headed by Alfred E. Heller of Nevada City, cautioned this week that the prospective No. 1 state had no master plan to guide its growth.

"A real threat to the economy of California lies in the fact that within the next twenty years the slurbs could take away between one-fourth and one-half of the state's best land from agricultural use.

Samuel E. Wood, executive director of the foundation, formerly was with the Federal Departments of Agriculture and the Interior. Mr. Heller, publisher of *The Nevada County Nugget*, is a son of the late Edward H. Heller, a San Francisco industrialist.

The report noted that California especially needed a plan because 3,000,000 acres of open land would disappear by 1980 under the wave of population growth and 2,000,000 acres of new farmland would have to be irrigated by that time to furnish the newcomers with food and fiber.

Moreover, it said, the state would spend some $55,000,000,000 on public works programs in the next twenty years.

12

National Capital Parks Named as Region Six of National Park Service

National Capital Parks, a unit of the National Park Service in charge of Washington area park lands, was given the status of a region, the Department of the Interior announced January 25.

National Capital Parks will become new Region Six with jurisdiction over 780 park units in the District of Columbia, Maryland and Virginia totaling 32,098 acres of park land.

Conrad L. Wirth, Director of the National Park Service, said that the move had been taken in recognition of National Capital Parks' status in the Nation and in the Nation's Capital because of the increased value and significance of its program and operations during the rapid growth period of this area.

He pointed out that the administration and operation of the Parks' program in the Capital City has reached such magnitude that a more efficient organization is necessary to provide an effective and more economical administration of the park system in the Washington area.

Visitor figures for the Washington area have shown substantial increases over the past few years. These figures for 1961 count jumped nearly three-quarters of a million over the prior year visitor count. All of this, Director Wirth said, involves increased responsibilities in facilities, maintenance, operations and administration.

T. Sutton Jett, superintendent of National Capital Parks, has been designated as the new regional director. His senior assistant superintendent, Robert C. Horne, has been selected to be associate regional director.

Under the reorganization, the new region will have four functional groupings, each under the general supervision of an assistant regional director.

Nash Castro, assistant superintendent of National Capital Parks, has been designated assistant regional director for Administration and will continue supervision over the United States Park Police.

The National Park Service has, for years, operated its far-flung nationwide organization through five regional offices, two major design and construction offices, and its field office of National Capital Parks in Washington, D. C. The reorganization will bring the regions up to six and the design and construction field offices to three.

Region Six, unlike other regions, will have operational as well as staff functions. Under the jurisdiction of the new region will be all national memorials and other park resources of the Capital City, parks and other areas in the region as well as Prince William Forest Park in Virginia and Catoctin Mountain Park in Maryland.

Included in the regional area will be the Washington Monument, the famed Lincoln Memorial, Jefferson Memorial, Lincoln Museum, Custis-Lee Mansion, Rock Creek Park, and the Chesapeake and Ohio Canal.

National Capital Notes

Outstanding Current Planning Issues before the
Nation's Capital

★   ★   ★

A Report to the Congress from the Board of Commissioners of the District of Columbia entitled, "State of the Nation's Capital, 1962" emphasizes the significance of the changing characteristics of the Nation's Capital in relation to the actions that are necessary to meet the problems occasioned by such changes. The general object of the Report is to assist the Members of Congress in exercising their legislative authority over the District of Columbia.

The Legislative Program for 1962 recommended by the D. C. Commissioners is outlined in detail.

An Appendix presents factual analysis of Population and Housing, Health, Welfare, Education, Law Enforcement, Urban Renewal, Highways, Public Works, Finances and Metro Area.

★   ★   ★

Action Plan for Downtown, a far reaching action plan to transform the central business district of Washington, was made public by *Downtown Progress,* the National Capital Downtown Committee. This 48-page printed report was presented at a luncheon attended by nearly 1,000 representatives of all sectors of the Washington public. The sponsoring group is an organization of businessmen set up about two years ago under the joint auspices of the Federal City Council, a group of local businessmen, and the National Capital Planning Commission.

The plan as disclosed is designed to reshape the physical appearance of the main downtown area, revise its traffic pattern, bring in more people to live, work and shop, lead to public and private redevelopment, and thus revitalize the city's whole economy. The plan suggests steps which can be taken prior to employment of urban redevelopment powers.

The main goals include subway and expressway construction; tunneling to provide underpasses beneath the central business area; street-widening and paving; construction of a $5 million Visitor's Center; encouragement of public and private projects to supply new office buildings, hotels and apartments.

Recommended for an early start is a demonstration block to try out under actual conditions test sections of arcades, pavement, landscaping and special street furniture. The revitalization program will be carried out primarily by private enterprise and by private investment within the framework of public improvements to make the Downtown worthy of its role as the heart of the Nation's Capital.

★   ★   ★

Woodrow Wilson's House in Washington, D. C., became the property of the National Trust for Historic Preservation, on December 28, when his widow Edith Bolling Wilson died there on the 105th anniversary of the birth of the World War I president. By terms of Mrs. Wilson's bequest, the house at 2340 "S" Street and contents, together with a $250,000 trust fund, were given to the Trust to "preserve and maintain the said premises in perpetuity, as a memorial in honor of the Grantor's late husband, the Honorable Woodrow Wilson, a past President of the United States of America." The house in the embassy section of the capital is a large Georgian brick structure designed by the late Waddy B. Wood, A.I.A.

★　★　★

Plans of capitals of other nations are of interest to Washington, D. C. The National Capital Commission of Ottawa, Canada, has issued an interesting booklet entitled, the National Capital Commission, an account of the history, legislation and composition of the National Capital Commission together with an outline of the work, projects and other functions of the Commission. Maps and illustrations add to the effectiveness of the report. Jacques Greber prepared a comprehensive Master Plan for Canada's Capital immediately after World War II. His plan known as the "National Capital Plan", was accepted by Parliament in 1952 and has been the Commission's planning guide during the ensuing years. Current

legislation governing the activities of the Commission is entitled the "Act respecting the Development and Improvements of the National Capital Region" in order that the nature and character of the seat of government of Canada may be in accordance with its national significance.

"Canberra After Fifty Years" was the. leading article in *The Geographical Review*, October 1961. It was prepared by Dr. G. J. R. Linge, of the Department of Geography, Institute of Advanced Studies, Australian National University, Canberra. The problems of contemporary Canberra are of particular interest inasmuch as it is fifty years since the Australian federal government, at the beginning of 1911, took over 939 square miles in a sparsely settled area in New South Wales as the territory in which to build the administrative center of the Commonwealth. Dr. Linge's appraisal of the problems of Australia's capital city is most comprehensive and interesting. Maps and photographs illustrate the article.

★　★　★

"Open Spaces for the Washington Region" by Frederick Gutheim, President of the Washington Center for Metropolitan Studies, appeared in the January 1962 issue of *Landscape Architecture*. Mr. Gutheim analyzes the problem which confronts the Washington area with regard to an open-space program which will be in step with agency plans being formulated.

The Civic Trust
An Outline of the Work of an Amenity Society

The British Civic Trust, with headquarters at 79 Buckingham Palace Road, London, S. W. 1, was established in July 1957 as an independent, non-profit-making organization which seeks to promote high standards of architecture and civic planning and to encourage a wider interest in the appearance of towns, villages and countryside.

Its funds have been generously provided in the form of seven-year covenants by leading industrial and commercial companies. The funds and general policy are controlled by a Board of Trustees. Mr. Duncan Sandys is President of the Civic Trust. Men of the highest calibre have set up and are running the organization.

Many people, it was thought, are depressed by the drabness of their surroundings and feel frustrated because they do not know what to do about it. Mr. Sandys asks in one of the Trust's booklets: "Do you care about the appearance of the town or village where you live . . . If so, it is up to you to do something about it. It is no good leaving it all to the people on your local Council or Planning Authority. They are merely your representatives and will take as much or as little interest as those whom they represent . . . If you club together in your district with others who feel as you do, you will soon make your voice heard; and, providing your ideas are sensible and practicable, you will be surprised how quickly you will begin to exert an influence on those who have the power to make decisions."

A society concerned with the improvement of amenities must offer practical suggestions based on local experience and a sound knowledge of the facts. Once it has shown itself to be constructive and well informed, its views are seldom unwelcome to those in authority and are acted upon. This is the premise upon which the Civic Trust proceeds.

The Civic Trust is an independent and unofficial body. It addresses its message to the population of Britain as a whole. Most of its first year was spent in explaining the aims and plans to government departments, local authorities, employers' organizations, trade unions, and professional institutions, seeking their support. Not merely good will, but active collaboration was secured. The Royal Institute of British Architects, the Royal Institute of Chartered Surveyors, the Institution of Civil Engineers, the Institution of Municipal Engineers and the Town Planning Institute together took the step of setting up a special joint committee, to which the Trust could look for authoritative technical advice.

The Trust works with existing societies of all kinds. It carried out the necessary inquiries and compiled a comprehensive record of the names and objects of all groups who would cooperate in the work of the Trust. These societies are provided with publications, lectures and films. The quarterly informational bulletin provides a link with these societies and some 5,000 copies are issued free. The Trust is therefore becoming more and more a center to which both local authorities and independent groups turn for advice on local problems.

In addition to advisory functions, the Trust set out to give a positive lead by means of practical experiments. The object is to show what can be done to improve the appearance of town and country. The first experiment was made in Magdalen Street in the city of Norwich. Like thousands of other shopping streets, it had an uninviting and uncared-for look about it. The buildings had become submerged in a jumble of discordant shopfronts, a clutter of advertisements and traffic signs. The aim of the project was to demonstrate how cheerfulness, dignity and a sense of unity can be achieved at comparatively little cost. Some 80 shopkeepers and other property owners all agreed to play their part. Details of the scheme were worked out by a coordinating architect, selected by the Trust, with the assistance of the City Engineer and five local architects. Properties were repainted, signs were re-lettered and improved; other details contributed to a project which was extensively reported in the press, radio and television and soon other parts of Norwich noticed the "new look" and accordingly decided to give a "face-lift" to their own streets. In the ensuing months, the Trust vigorously exploited this break-through and the idea caught on rapidly.

In its war against ugliness, the Trust undertook a variety of tasks to eliminate existing eyesores. The Piccadilly Circus inquiry was an outstanding example of its influence. They brought out two points in their opposition to proposed buildings—that Piccadilly Circus ought to be redeveloped as a whole and not piece-meal.

Every available medium of publicity has been used to awaken public interest in good architecture and planning. In cooperation with the BBC, the Civic Trust has arranged for a series of 20 minute films to be made under the general title, *"Who Cares."*

In the December 1951 issue of *Town and Country Planning*, an article summarizes the result of two and a half years since Magdalen Street when some twenty further schemes have been completed and about forty are in hand. The article states that it is particularly noticeable that wherever successful schemes have been completed, the idea tends to spread in the locality. It does not seem unreasonable to see in this movement an instrument for changing the whole climate of opinion surrounding civic design in general. So far as the Trust is concerned a number of important central area redevelopment problems have been referred to it as a result of the face-lift proposals. It is thought that the various problems will come to be seen as different aspects of one and the same problem—the preservation and creation of towns that are pleasant to live in.

The Trust is to be congratulated. It has awakened public interest and the progress it has made in various directions is opening up fresh opportunities for fruitful activity.

Eivind T. Scoyen, Associate Director of National Park Service, Retires

Secretary of the Interior Stewart L. Udall announced that Eivind T. Scoyen, associate director of the National Park Service, was retiring on January 7, 1962. Mr. Scoyen has had 46 years of Government service, most of it with the Department's National Park Service.

National Park Service Director Conrad L. Wirth expressed regret that Mr. Scoyen was leaving the Park Service. "Through his devotion to the cause of park conservation," the Director said, "Mr. Scoyen has contributed significantly to the wise use of America's human and natural resources. Among the national leaders in the field of park management and conservation, he is almost unique in having spent virtually his entire lifetime in national parks and related Federal reservations."

Mr. Scoyen was born at Mammoth Hot Springs in Yellowstone National Park, Wyoming-Montana-Idaho, on October 16, 1896.

While a student at St. Olaf College, Northfield, Minnesota, he worked during the summer months in Yellowstone. From 1916 to 1918, he was employed with the United States Weather Bureau in Yellowstone, followed by service with the United States Navy. In 1919, he was appointed a park ranger in Yellowstone and in 1921 was promoted to assistant chief park ranger. He has also served as chief park ranger at Grand Canyon National Park, associate regional director in the Park Service's Region Three Office; and superintendent of Glacier National Park, Sequoia and Kings Canyon National Parks, and Zion and Bryce Canyon National Parks. He has been associate director of the National Park Service since 1956.

Mr. Scoyen has written and lectured extensively on the parks. In 1951, the California Conservation Council presented him with its Merit Award. In 1958, he received the Department of the Interior Distinguished Service Award, and also was awarded the Cornelius Amory Pugsley Gold Medal.

He is a member of the Sierra Club of California, the Potomac Corral of the Westerners of Washington, D. C., and the Explorers Club of New York City.

New Members
American Planning and Civic Association
January, February, March 1962

California
State College Library, Los Angeles
District of Columbia
Edmund R. Purves
Mrs. Robert W. Shackleton
Mrs. William P. Cresson

Massachusetts
Prof. Joseph F. Zimmerman, Worcester
Pennsylvania
Arthur F. Loeben, Norristown
Virginia
Thomas R. Jones, Falls Church

John Nolen, Jr. Appointed Director of Transportation Planning

John Nolen, Jr. has been appointed Director of Transportation Planning in the Office of Transportation under the Urban Assistance Program of Housing and Home Finance Agency. The office was established in connection with Section 701 of the amended Housing Act in 1961 designed to facilitate and encourage the preparation of comprehensive urban transportation surveys, studies and plans to aid in solving problems of traffic congestion, and facilitating the circulation of people and goods in metropolitan and other urban centers. Mr. Nolen will carry out mass transportation and demonstration grant provisions.

The appointment was announced in February by Housing Administrator Robert C. Weaver.

A graduate of the Massachusetts Institute of Technology, Mr. Nolen has been in city planning work most of his life. After graduating from M.I.T. in 1920, he worked for eight years as a civil engineer in Boston, the Canal Zone, Cincinnati, Cleveland, and several Florida cities. He then went to Philadelphia where he served as assistant planning engineer in the development of a regional plan for the Philadelphia–Trenton–Wilmington tri-state district. While there he was in charge of one of the first comprehensive regional transportation surveys in the country.

Mr. Nolen came to Washington, D. C., in 1931 to join the National Capital Park and Planning Commission. He served with it and its successor, the National Capital Planning Commission, more than 26 years as City Planner, Director of Planning, and finally as Director.

Mr. Nolen was director of the National Capital Planning Commission until 1958. He has been a member of the American Planning and Civic Association since 1935. He is the son of John Nolen, distinguished planner, who came into the Association in 1911 and carried on membership until his death in 1937.

William L. Slayton, Commissioner of Urban Renewal Administration, writing in the *Traffic Quarterly*, for January 1962, under the title, "Urban Renewal and Mass Transportation Planning," states that urban transportation is one of the major problems of almost all American cities.

Most of President Kennedy's recommendations on urban transportation were incorporated in the Act of 1961. Federal funds are available for surveys, studies and plans. The planning to be done under the Section 701 program does not permit the undertaking of detailed engineering plans, designs and specifications.

Grants may be made to the following agencies which perform the following functions:

1. State planning agencies, or (in States where no such planning agency exists) to agencies or instrumentalities of State government designated by the

Governor of the State and acceptable to the Administrator as capable of carrying out the planning functions contemplated by Section 701, for the provision of planning assistance.

2. Official State, metropolitan, and regional planning agencies, or other agencies and instrumentalities designated by the Governor (or Governors in the case of interstate planning) and acceptable to the Administrator, empowered under State or local laws or interstate compact to perform metropolitan or regional planning.

3. Cities, other municipalities, and counties which (A) are situated in areas designated by the Secretary of Commerce under Section 5(a) of the Area Redevelopment Act as redevelopment areas or (B) have suffered substantial damage as a result of a catastrophe which the President, pursuant to Section 2(a) of "An Act to authorize Federal assistance to States and local governments in major disasters, and for other purposes," has determined to be a major disaster.

4. Official governmental planning agencies for areas where rapid urbanization has resulted or is expected to result from the establishment or rapid and substantial expansion of a Federal installation.

5. State planning agencies for State and interstate comprehensive planning (as defined in Subsection 701(d) and for research and coordination activity related thereto.

Applications for comprehensive urban transportation planning shall be submitted to the HHFA Regional Office in accordance with current Section 701 procedures and forms. Inquiries and requests for assistance in developing such applications should be directed to the HHFA Regional Office.

Horace M. Albright Conservation Lectureship

Recent developments under the Horace M. Albright Conservation Lectureship at the University of California: Professor Marston Bates, zoologist and naturalist will serve as the first regularly appointed Albright Lecturer during the latter part of April. Prof. Bates will participate in both student and faculty seminars and on April 23 he will give public lecture entitled "The Human Environment", which will be published in the Albright Lectureship series. The published version of Mr. Albright's lecture last year, "Great American Conservationists" should be released in March.

Harland Bartholomew Retires from Planning Firm He Established

It was announced in February that Harland Bartholomew, nationally known planner, former chairman of the National Capital Planning Commission, and Acting President of APCA, is retiring as a full partner of the planning consultant firm, Harland Bartholomew and Associates, which he founded in 1919.

Another partner, Harry Alexander, who has been a partner with the firm since 1938, also has retired. Both Mr. Bartholomew and Mr. Alexander will continue to participate in projects of the firm and will be available for consultation.

Recently the firm established a Washington, D. C. office in the Transportation Building. The main offices will continue in St. Louis with a new location at 1030 Pierce Building, 112 North Fourth Street, St. Louis 2, Mo.

Private Planning Library

An unusual private library is maintained in the Newark offices of a firm of community planning and urban renewal consultants.

The library, one of the largest of its kind in the country, contains more than 6,000 publications relating to housing and city planning. It is owned by Candeub, Fleissig & Associates, consultants, who use it as an information center for their field offices throughout the country.

Housing, planning and architectural experts frequently turn to the library for help, because of its rare historic documents and out-of-print books on city planning and housing. Foreign and domestic government papers not readily available elsewhere are included in the collection, which now is more than ten years old.

Candeub, Fleissig started the collection to supply information to its staff on a multitude of technical subjects in the planning field.

The library was started as a private collection by Isadore Candeub, president of the firm, several years before he established the partnership. The present librarian is Mrs. Joseph Getman, of West Orange, who coordinates the flow of books, periodicals, reports and data received by the firm.

The collection contains comprehensive material on housing and planning matters in each of the fifty states, including comparative census and area data, reports on urban characteristics, and building and zoning standards. It also has detailed traffic and transit regulations, as well as income and market sales data for all regions.

There are 150 subject headings. They are classified for ready reference under master plans, urban renewal, housing, zoning, codes and ordinances, statistics, legislation and general reference.

New material is ordered at the rate of 1,000 publications a year. Mrs. Getman subscribes to more than 145 periodicals and trade journals.

The New Jersey Division of State and Regional Planning is using the Candeub, Fleissig library as a model for a reference library it plans to establish.

N. Y. Times, Feb. 10, 1962

ORRRC Report

A sweeping plan for providing outdoor recreation for coming generations was presented to the President and to the Congress on January 31 by the Outdoor Recreation Resources Review Commission. It is the culmination of extensive study by the ORRRC staff, state and federal agencies, private organizations, and university professors under research contract. The result is an impressive array of facts and estimates concerning existing recreational opportunities for the American public, and a blueprint for future action.

The Commission was established by Congress to develop a policy. It has spent three and a half years, and $2.5 million, in this pursuit. The chairman, Laurance S. Rockefeller, has now presented the final report.

About 90 percent of all Americans 18 and over participated in some form of outdoor recreation in the summer of 1960, according to the report. Pleasure driving, walking, swimming and picnicking were the most frequent of all activities.

Studies showed that the most urgent need of the future lies in providing outdoor opportunities near metropolitan areas. About two-thirds of the people in the U. S. (117 million) live in these areas now. By the turn of the century, some 73 percent (est. 255 million) will reside there. The report states that a huge population generates such an enormous demand for non-recreation as well as recreation uses that recreation may never get its full share of space.

Recommendations of the Commission include a broad national policy, recreation resources management guidelines, expansion, modification, and intensification of present programs, establishment of a Bureau of Outdoor Recreation in the Department of the Interior, and a federal grants-in-aid program to states. A system of classifying outdoor recreation resources is proposed. A clarion call for coordinated, cooperative action is issued to all.

Perhaps the most controversial recommendation is the creation of a new Bureau of Outdoor Recreation within the Interior Department.

Such a bureau would coordinate Federal programs involving recreation or conservation, provide technical aid to States and communities, sponsor research and administer the grant program. Its policy decisions would be made by a council of the Secretaries of Interior, Agriculture and Defense.

Under the direction of the President, proposals will be made to Congress to implement the ORRRC Report.

Copies of this 245-page Report may be obtained from the Superintendent of Documents, Government Printing Office, Washington 25, D. C. Price $2.00.

President Kennedy's Special Conservation Message—Land Purchase Funds Sought

In a special conservation message to Congress, President Kennedy called for the creation of a land conservation fund to acquire recreational areas across the country.

Administration sources estimated buying would total between $800 million and $1 billion over the next eight years. Costs would be paid by people who use existing Federal parks and outdoor facilities, through admission and other fees; by the diversion of unclaimed motorboat fuel tax rebates from the highway trust fund and by receipts from the sale of surplus Federal land.

While those funds build up, President Kennedy recommended a Treasury advance not exceeding $500 million for the eight-year span. He said Congress could make the money available by annual appropriations to the conservation fund and have it replaced by income from the fees and other sources.

Plans are being formulated and an inter-bureau committee has been appointed to arrange for a two-day White House Conference on renewable natural resources. It was first considered for February, but it now appears that the date will be set in March or April. This conference is being planned for government-wide participation of all resource

President Kennedy outlined the plan, fashioned from a study by the Outdoor Recreation Resources Review Commission, in a lengthy message declaring the Nation's conservation effort must cover the entire spectrum of its resources.

In the field of recreation, President Kennedy asked Congress to establish a system of matching grants to help the States develop outdoor programs. He requested an additional $50 million to assist States and cities to acquire open spaces for the recreation of urban area residents. And for the great outdoors, he urged Congress to pass controversial legislation introduced last year to preserve wilderness areas.

To evaluate past progress and plan for the future, President Kennedy announced he would convene a White House Conference on Conservation some time this year.

* * *

agencies, Congress and representatives of national and state organizations and citizen groups. Theme topics will focus attention on conservation goals of the Administration.

To provide for a coordinated framework for natural resources research programs, the President asked the National Academy of

Sciences to undertake a thorough and broadly based study and evaluation of the present state of research underlying the conservation, development and use of natural resources. A Committee on Natural Resources was formed by the Academy last spring, arranged under the Division of Physical Sciences, with Col. Robert A. Cliffe as its staff executive. The committee has been meeting at about monthly intervals and has issued a number of information reports for the use of its members. No date has been announced for the filing of a report.

Academic News in Planning

A doctoral program in planning has been established at the University of North Carolina. It is aimed at preparing people for careers in teaching and research in the planning field. A limited number of fellowships are available for doctoral candidates.

Rutgers Urban Studies Center is offering fellowships in Urban Studies to enable persons holding responsible positions in government and voluntary organizations study in fields bordering upon the problems of urban communities. Applicants must obtain a year's leave of absence to spend an academic year at the Center. Applications are available from the Center, Rutgers, New Brunswick, N. J.

A graduate program in *planning and policy sciences,* leading to the M.S. and Ph.D. degrees, is available at Case Institute of Technology. The program, designed to employ the technical and social sciences in dealing with public policy problems, is divided into two areas: metropolitan development, which includes city planning, regional and urban economics and politics, trans-portation, and urban sociology; and water resources, which includes sanitary and hydraulic engineering, geology, governmental organization and administration, and regional planning and economics. Fellowships and assistantships are available to qualified students.

A course in city planning design for architects, city planners, engineers and surveyors was offered for the first time by University College, adult education division of Washington University, at St. Louis, Missouri beginning February 1.

Local practitioners and teachers will present design problems to the class, and then offer individual criticism of each student's solution. Drawing or drafting proficiency is necessary.

Director of the new course will be William Weismantel, city planner and associate professor of architecture. He said that the sessions will offer practice and criticism in land use planning and the design of subdivisions, shopping centers, street and parking systems and typical site planning assignments.

Ladies Who Wear the Uniform of the National Park Service

Park Historians Rhoade, Ciborowski, and Friday form a personable trio enroute to their day's work explaining the great stories of liberty and independence at Independence National Historical Park at Philadelphia.

Above: One of the First "Lady Rangers". Claire Marie Hodges (now Mrs.
J. Wolfsen) served as a seasonal ranger in Yosemite National Park in 1
She rode mounted patrol in the Yosemite Valley and reported directly t
Chief Ranger.

Below: Only "lady" archaeologist. Mrs. Jean M. Pinkley, Mesa Verde Nati
Park, interpreting Mug House to members of Colorado service organiza
prior to the start of excavation, Wetherill Mesa Archeological Project.

Right: Park Historian Agnes Mullins directs a cultural demonstration for children at the Old Stone House in Georgetown, a unit in the National Capital Parks, Washington, D. C. Here she is assisting the children make or dip bayberry candles in the old colonial manner.

Below: Seasonal Naturalist Phyllis Wells conducts a party of Girl Scouts through historic Fort Washington, a unit in the National Capital Parks, Washington, D. C.

Left: Explaining the hinga Trail, Evergl[National Park, Seasonal turalist Gale Zimmer pa at one of the covered exhi overlooking the evergla slough.

Below: Mrs. Mitsuko T. S kuma, of Hilo, Hawaii, formation - Receptionist, the Park Headquarters a Visitor Center, Hawaii tional Park, provides in mation and interpretive d to visitors.

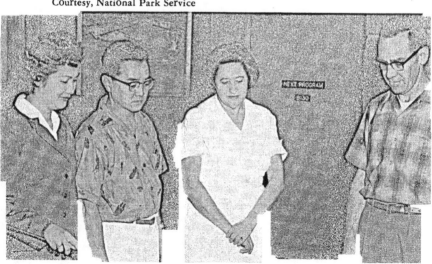

Watch Service Report

The 87th Congress reconvened for its second session on January 10, with its docket crowded with legislation of particular interest. Important conservation proposals, some new and some old, as well as other key matters in the Administration's program, will be under discussion for action. Primary areas of interest to our readers follow.

National Parks

Under consideration are proposals for the following areas: See September issue of PLANNING AND CIVIC COMMENT for descriptive article on areas proposed for national park areas which include Padre Island National Seashore; Oregon Dunes National Seashore; Sleeping Bear National Seashore; Pictured Rocks National Seashore; also S. 1760–H. R. 6873, establishing the Great Basin National Park which passed Senate January 25, 1962; S. 1381–H. R. 5712, establishing the Ozark Rivers National Monument; H. R. 6289, creating the Ozark Scenic Riverways; S. 73, authorizing the Prairie or Grasslands National Park; S. 77–H. R. 4684, establishing the C and O Canal National Historical Park; S. 1981—H. R. 7236, creating the Ice Age National Park in Wisconsin; S. 543, providing shoreline area studies and authorizing grants to states for suitable areas; S. 476–H. R. 2775 and H. R. 3244 to establish the Point Reyes National Seashore in California.

H. R. 9492 (Baldwin, Jr., Calif.) introduced January 10, 1962. Directs the acquisition of two small parcels of property totaling less than nine acres in Contra Costa County, California for the establishment of John Muir National Monument.

Hearings were held in February on Senator Douglas' new bill S. 1797 to establish the Indiana Dunes Lakeshore Park before the Public Lands sub-committee of the Senate Committee on Interior and Insular Affairs.

The C and O Park bill, S. 77–H. R. 4684 authorizes the establishment of a national historical park which would extend from within the District of Columbia for 184 miles along the historic Canal. This would include some 4,800 acres now a National Monument and in Federal ownership. An additional 10,200 acres of adjacent private lands along the banks of the Canal and the Potomac River would be included in the park. The bill passed the Senate in the last session of Congress. Hearings will be held before the House Committee and it is hoped the bill will be brought out of Committee to the floor and passed.

A number of bills relating to historical areas are pending action.

H. J. Res. 449 to provide for the establishing of the former dwelling of Alexander Hamilton as a national memorial.

H. R. 9494, to authorize the establishment of the Theodore Roosevelt Birthplace and Sagamore Hill National Historic Sites.

H. R. 2470. By voice vote the House adopted the conference report on this bill providing for the establishment of the Lincoln Boyhood National Memorial in the State of Indiana and thus cleared the legislation for Presidential action.

Federal City

H. R. 10128 (Hansen) introduced February 7, 1962. Provides for the preservation of the historic waterfront of Georgetown on the Potomac River in the District of Columbia. Identical to H. R. 10015, introduced by Rep. Frelinghuysen, Jr. on January 31, 1962. Referred to Committee on Interior and Insular Affairs.

H. R. 10127 (Hansen) introduced February 7, 1962. A bill to amend sections 2 and 5 of the act entitled "An Act to regulate the height, exterior design, and construction of private and semipublic buildings in the Georgetown area of the District of Columbia" approved September 22, 1950. Referred to the Committee on the District of Columbia.

Wilderness Preservation

S. 174, establishing the National Wilderness Preservation System, has been passed by the Senate. Field hearings were held in the West last fall. The fate of this bill is uncertain.

Department of Urban Affairs and Housing

S. 1633–H. R. 8429. Legislation to set up this cabinet-level Department cleared Senate and House Government Operations Committees. However, Republican opposition to the measure defeated it in the Rules Committee. President Kennedy then announced that he would send Congress a reorganization plan which would consolidate existing housing agencies in a new Department of Urban affairs and Housing and that he would name Dr. Robert Weaver as the first secretary of the new department. The House barred establishment of such a department by a 264 to 150 vote. Under the Government Reorganization Act, defeat of a presidential plan by either House is sufficent to kill it.

Surplus Property

S. 2724 (Bennett) introduced January 23, 1962. Amends Section 203 (j) of the Federal Property and Administrative Services Act of 1949 to permit disposal of surplus property for use in the development, operation and maintenance of state parks and recreation areas. Referred to Committee on Government Operation.

H. R. 10439 (Cunningham) introduced February 27, 1962. To amend the Federal Property and Administrative Services Act of 1949 as amended to permit donation and other disposal of surplus personal property to tax-supported public park, recreation or historic monument agencies. Referred to Committee on Government Operations.

26th World Congress, International Federation for Housing and Planning

The 26th World Housing and Planning Congress to be organized by the International Federation for Housing and Planning, in cooperation with the Confédération Francaise pour l'Habitation et l'Urbanisme, will be held in Paris (France) from September 2 to 9, 1962 (working sessions), with post-Congress tours extending from September 9 until 14.

The present information is given in order to enable attendants to make the necessary arrangements for participation.

Congress-theme: HUMAN ENVIRONMENT AND CIVILIZATION.

A detailed program (working schedule, time-table, registration formalities, hotel accommodation, tours, etc.) will be distributed in early 1962; registration forms and membership blanks will be added, announces the President of the International Federation for Housing and Planning, J. Canaux.

All correspondence, suggestions or requests for information concerning the organization of the Congress should be addressed to the Confédération Francaise pour l'-Habitation et l'Urbanisme 15, Avenue Théophile-Gautier, PARIS XVIe.

Hope for Cameron Hill

The appointment of a technical guidance committee to the Chattanooga Housing Authority, announced in February, is a most commendable and needed step. Two distinguished men in the architectural field have agreed to serve: Henry L. Kamphoefner, dean of the school of design at North Carolina State College, and Paul Heffernan, director of the school of architecture at Georgia Tech.

Other members are DeSales Harrison, president of the Chamber of Commerce; Robert L. Maclellan, president of the Provident Life and Accident Insurance Co.; Harry Miller, financier and civic leader; Marble Hensley, city coordinator, and Billy C. Cooper, director of urban renewal for the CHA.

The purpose of the technical guidance committee is to enhance sound planning, aesthetic and harmonious interrelation, land use and other features.

Both William Zeckendorf, Jr., now president of the far-flung Webb & Knapp organization, and Martin Meyerson, director of the Harvard-Massachusetts Institute of Technology joint urban studies center, for example have voiced reservations during visits here about the cutting down of Cameron Hill. Chattanooga's planners in charge obviously have stood by their feeling that the cut must be made, but citizen interest in these matters is a healthy thing.

Cameron Hill earth has been consigned to freeway construction. However, we believe that the needs in this respect could well be restudied and evaluated in the light of the best over-all use.

Two men of international experience have been placed on the technical guidance committee. The step is of significance in furthering the aim of establishing the new West Side as a vigorous instrument for progress in the whole of Chattanooga.

Chattanooga Times, Feb. 4, '62

New Members
National Conference on State Parks
January, February, March, 1962

California
James M. Doyle, Oroville

Maine
Clyde D. Walton, Augusta

Nebraska
John C. Kurtz, Crawford
Richard A. Wolkow, Waterloo
L. M. Snodgrass, Grand Island

North Carolina
Charles C. Stott, Raleigh

Ohio
John F. Seward, Frazeysburg

Pennsylvania
C. Charles Hollenbaugh, Dayton
William C. Forrey, Camp Hill

Texas
Max Starcke, Austin

Canada
A. Pellegrino, Quebec

Recreational Aspects of Three Nebraska Lakes

By EDGAR Z. PALMER, Director, Bureau of Business Research, University of Nebraska

What is the effect of new reservoirs, in a previously lakeless area, on the recreation habits of nearby residents and on the local economy?

This is the key question to which an answer is sought in this recent study, made by the University of Nebraska for the National Park Service and the Bureau of Reclamation.

The study involves three relatively new irrigation and flood control reservoirs, Enders, Swanson, and Strunk Lakes, in the winter wheat belt of southwestern Nebraska. Recreation facilities are administered by the Nebraska Game, Forestation and Parks Commission.

McCook, with a population of 8,301, (1960), is the "metropolis" of the 19 county region and is located relatively near the reservoirs. People are few and far between in the rest of the area surrounding the lakes—less than seven persons per square mile.

Not surprisingly, most of the visitor days tallied during the year of the study, 1959, are accounted for by residents in or just outside of the 19 county area. A somewhat amazing figure is that as many as 70 percent of the residents of this area have visited one or more of the reservoirs since they were imimpounded. Family groups constituted sixty-eight percent of the visiting parties.

The large majority of visitors, 90 percent, stayed one day or less; 47 percent of local visitors stayed less than two hours.

Surprisingly, visitors registered substantial satisfaction with facilities at the lakes, though many are rustic and some incompletely developed. Ninety percent of the visitors indicated satisfaction with picnic grounds, campgrounds, and supervision, while provision of boats for hire, swimming beaches, and boat docks and ramps received the lowest number of votes.

The study, in attempting to isolate the place of lake oriented recreational expenditures in the local economy, holds some surprises. It finds that $1.4 million is spent annually in connection with the lakes. An additional $1.2 million is spent elsewhere. The $1.4 million generates additional business of up to $2 million in the 19 county lakes area. Dr. Palmer finds that the $1.4 million spent locally constitutes less than one percent of the total retail and service receipts of the lakes area for the year concerned; but, even so, represents a nice dividend to the region.

Approximately 120 workers, or some 300 persons including family members, are supported by the recreation business generated by the lakes.

Footnote:
Reviewed by John H. Eichstedt, Park Planner, National Park Service. The complete study is available from the National Park Service, Region Two Office, 307 Federal Office Building, Omaha, Nebraska.

South Dakota Parks Association

For several years, a small group of South Dakotans wanted to do something to improve the parks in their State. On September 12, 1956, they organized the South Dakota Parks Association with the purpose, as stated in its constitution, ". . . to promote the appreciation, use and development of public parks and other outdoor recreation areas within the State of South Dakota, including areas administered by the Federal, state, county and municipal governments."

When a preorganization letter proposing a Parks Association was first circulated on May 28, 1956, one of the immediate objectives was that there should be representation in the Association from all park districts. Rather than a membership of professional park personnel, it was planned that the South Dakota Parks Association should be primarily a lay organization. One of the main criteria for membership was to be "active participation of park-interested people" since this was believed to be essential for the organization of an effective association.

To assure a unity of purpose between park administrators and the Association as an advisory group, an educational program was undertaken. Under this program, panel discussions among Federal, state, county and city park officials were held to acquaint Association membership with the philosophy behind a state and national park system and the basic difference between national, state, county or city parks. In line with this program, the Association recommended that the Game, Fish and Parks Commission adopt a long-range plan which set forth the Commission's goals, policies, development plans and operational procedures. The Commission has developed an excellent program along these lines.

Its efforts to create a more favorable climate for the development of an outstanding system of state parks in South Dakota were rewarded when the Legislature passed two Association-supported bills in 1957 which separated forestry and park financing from that of game and fish and provided state park and forest operating funds. The Association worked for the establishment of Fort Sisseton State Park new Britton, South Dakota and Bear Butte State Park near Sturgis. Last year, Fort Sisseton became a unit of the State Park System and Bear Butte was authorized by the Legislature. The Commission is acquiring the necessary land to establish this park.

One of the problems faced by South Dakotans was the concentration of state and national parks and forestry areas in the western part of the State and several state parks in the northeast corner of the State. Present planning proposes construction of a number of water-control projects on the James River Valley in eastern South Dakota. The development of a chain of lakes along the Missouri River through construction of several dams along the main stem in central South

Dakota afforded the State an opportunity to diversify its recreation pattern. In addition to scenic areas, the State could now offer parks with water-oriented recreation. The Association also continued to urge broader distribution of parks throughout the State, and stands ready to "go to bat" for state parks when and where needed.

Today, the Association is composed of over 200 men and women and organizations, all of whom are interested in assisting and advising the Forestry and Parks Division of the Game, Fish and Parks Com-

mission so that this agency can obtain sufficient appropriations for its program of improvements and expansion. The Association continues to work with the legislators to sell them on the need for adequate financing to give tourists the needed, attractive park and recreation areas and facilities they expect.

Present officers are: President, R. J. Perry; First Vice-President, Ted Hustead; Second Vice-President, Randall Stensome; Treasurer, Ed English; and Secretary, Warren J. Hobson. R. J. Perry, *President*
Warren J. Hobson, *Secretary*

Weather and City Planning

Dr. H. E. Landsberg, Director of the Office of Climatology, Weather Bureau, U. S. Department of Commerce, spoke recently in Washington to the American Meterological Society on the subject of air pollution. The relationship between weather and city planning is not as obscure as may be thought. Dr. Landsberg traced the importance of major changes which have disturbed atmospheric condition in the mechanized areas of the world chiefly radical alteration of the surface and continuous addition of a wide variety of substances in the air.

Dr. Landsberg said that only fragmented reports and papers exist in the broad general study of city climate, and only a few scattered studies on the atmospheric environment of the 74 standard metro-

politan areas are available. Private enterprise, the planners of the future and intelligent citizens need authoritative and comprehensive reference sources on the mesoclimate of metropolitan areas. The studies remain to be written. He believes that the matter of clean air is as important as clean drinking water and that the study of basic problems of city climate has been neglected.

Dr. Landsberg also dwelt upon heat island effects. This is an important subject and an interesting reference is "The Temperature of Cities" by J. Murray Mitchell, Jr. also of the Office of Climatology published in the December 1961 issue of *Weatherwise*, published by the American Meteorological Society.

Great Lakes Park Training Institute

The sixteenth Annual Great Lakes Park and Training Institute was held at Potawatomi Inn, Pokagon State Park, Angola, Indiana, February 19–23. Registrar Robert D. Starrett reported registration reached an all-time high of 431 persons representing 22 states, the District of Columbia, and .five Canadian provinces. Park and recreation administrators came from California and British Columbia on the west coast, New Brunswick and Maine on the east coast, and Florida and Texas in the south. There were state park people in attendance from Maine, New York, New Jersey, Maryland, Pennsylvania, Ohio, Michigan, Indiana, Illinois, Wisconsin, South Dakota, California and Florida. The Director of the Institute, Garrett G. Eppley, Chairman, Department of Recreation, Indiana University, kept the program moving at a lively pace, aided by Richard W. Lawson, Instructor in Recreation at the University, with the help of an outstanding group of graduate students. Ten park and recreation organizations and agencies acted as cooperating sponsors.

An interesting highlight of the first day was an address by Conrad L. Wirth, Director, National Park Service, on the subject "PARKS FOR AMERICA." Commenting on the ORRRC Report he said that a grants-in-aid program is very desirable, that the Federal government does not do enough for the states and that the states do not do enough for the municipalities and local governments. Mr. Wirth also recommended the creation of a forum on park and recreation services composed of representatives of all agencies concerned.

Reynolds E. Carlson, Professor of Recreation, Indiana University, presided at the Monday evening program, which consisted of a slide talk on "Parks in Western Europe" by John A. Lundgren.

The second day's program was given over to such practical matters as a report on AIPE's "Concession Operators Workshop," and discussions on "How Automatic Vending Machines Can Serve Park and Recreation Departments," "Golf, A Year-Round Program," "Effective Use and Maintenance of Park Equipment," and "The Use of Plastics by Park and Recreation Departments." An interesting and unusual slide talk on the subject "Illumination for Park Beautification," showing the application of this technique in Canadian parks was presented by Maxim T. Gray, General Manager, Niagara Parks Commission, Niagara Falls, Ontario. The evening program consisted of a clever illustrated lecture on "Indiana's First Manufacturing Company."

One of the most informative and interesting sessions of the Institute was held Wednesday morning. This was an explanation by Ernest J. Postal, Sanitary Engineer, Division of Parks and Recreation, Michigan Department of Conservation, of the construction and operation of "Sewage Lagoons." This was followed by a panel on "Municipal Parks and Recreation." Wednesday afternoon a series of eight workshops, organized by Daniel L. Flaherty, General Superintendent, Chicago Park District, were held. The subjects were "Design and Maintenance of Man-Made Sand Beaches," "Soil Data for Park Planning," "Maintenance of Heavily Used Areas," "Buy It or Rent It," "Boating," "Development of Administrative Manuals" and "Tent and Trailer Camping."

An inspiring slide talk on "Playgrounds With a Theme" showing highly imaginative playground developments by the city Parks and Recreation Department of Colorado Springs, Colorado, was given by its Director, James W. Taylor, on Thursday morning. This was followed by discussion on "Recreation Areas as Applied to Sub-divisions," "Ways to Improve Your Business Correspondence," and "State and County Parks." All of Thursday afternoon and Friday morning were given over to the reports on the workshop sessions given by their respective chairman and followed by discussion periods.

The annual banquet was held Thursday night. The speaker, Charles K. Brightbill, Head, Department of Recreation, University of Illinois, gave a particularly fine talk on the subject, "Our Goals." Drawing on his experience in foreign travel and the great need for world understanding of mutual problems, he talked about the readjustment in living habits which is being brought about by technical advances, automation and the vast increase in leisure time. His message was such that it could not fail to inspire in those present a realization that they are engaged in a fine profession which has a tremendous challenge and responsibility in providing opportunities for leadership in the wise use of leisure time.

Garden Club of America Adds to Redwood Grove

In accordance with its continuing policy of purchasing in-holdings and fringe areas to round out Redwood State Parks wherever possible, the Save the Redwoods League recently purchased 40 acres of privately-owned land in the heart of the Garden Club of America Grove in Humboldt Redwoods State Park.

The land, acquired at a cost of $33,000, lies on the headwaters of Canoe Creek in a beautiful park-like basin. On it, there is a stand of exceptionally large, tall redwoods intermingled with Douglas fir which a professional timber cruiser has estimated to contain 1,421,000 board feet, mill cut, of redwood and 344,000 board feet of Douglas fir.

The 40-acre square tract is surrounded on three sides by the Garden Club of America Grove. Privately owned land adjoins it on the fourth side.

Contributions by members of the Garden Club of America in recent years to a fund for the purchase of additional redwoods to round out the Grove, totaling $16,617, were used toward acquisition of the tract.

State Park Notes

Governor Edmund G. Brown announced the appointment of Edward F. Dolder as Chief, Division of Beaches and Parks, California, effective November 14, 1961. He said, "Mr. Dolder's intimate knowledge of the administrative area which will be his responsibility suits him exactly for the job." Mr. Dolder is a career civil servant who has been Deputy Director of the Department of Natural Resources since 1956. He is a native of Alameda, educated in California and received a bachelor of arts degree in economics from the University of California at Berkeley in 1936. After graduation he joined State service in the Department of Natural Resources and held positions as public information editor, public information officer, supervisor of conservation, and chief of conservation education.

Kenneth S. Lowe, editor of *The Marquette Mining Journal*, Marquette, Michigan, was named to the Michigan Conservation Commission December 5, 1961 by Governor Swainson to fill the unexpired term of Joseph P. Rahilly who retired last November after serving 27 years. Mr. Lowe, 40, a graduate of the University of Michigan, has been with *The Mining Journal* since 1948. From 1951–55, he was editor of the *Northern Michigan Sportsman* and has authored a number of hunting, fishing, and conservation articles in national magazines.

R. I. Colburn of Paris, Missouri, has been chosen Chairman of Missouri's bi-partisan State Park Board to succeed the late Harry Wooldridge who died suddenly on December 9 in Jefferson City. Ruby Green, from Kirksville, is vicechairman. William E. Dye, Lexington, was appointed to the Board to fill the vacancy left by Mr. Wooldridge's death.

Ray J. Elliot, formerly a district forester in South Dakota, was appointed head of North Dakota State Park System on November 16, 1961. Mr. Elliot, 41, was born in Hurley, South Dakota and graduated from high school there. He attended Sioux Falls College and South Dakota State College and had been with the South Dakota Department of Game, Fish and Parks since March 1950.

Ernest J. Gebhart, an employee of the Ohio Division of Forestry for 14 years, was appointed assistant chief of the Ohio Division of Parks, effective February 15. In announcing the appointment, V. W. Flickinger, Chief, Division of Parks, said Mr. Gebhart would succeed George T. O'Malley, who is now Director of the Colorado State Park and Recreation Board. A native of Marietta, Ohio, Gebhart is a graduate of the University of Minnesota with a bachelor of science degree in forestry.

Les Berner, Chief of the South Dakota Game Division since 1957, has been appointed special assistant to Walter J. Fillmore, Director, South Dakota Department of Game, Fish and Parks. Mr. Berner, 47, joined the Department in 1948 as a small game biologist. A native of Ledgewood, N. D., he earned his B. S. degree in wildlife at the University of Minnesota and his master's degree from the University of Missouri.

Gov. Price Daniel has named two new members, Max Starcke of Austin and Harry Hornby of Uvalde, to the Texas Parks Board. Mr. Starcke, a native Texan, has been active for many years in civic affairs, both on the local and state level. In 1938 he assumed management of the Lower Colorado River Authority which grew to a giant $150 million project under his guidance and now owns and operates six major dams and power plants on the Colorado River. Mr. Hornby has operated the *Leader-News* since he purchased the newspaper from his father in 1948. As a Uvalde publisher he has favored public dams and lakes and, when the first such project was completed at Utopia, the State Park Board selected him to cut the ribbon at the dedication.

LEGISLATION

An automobile sticker fee for state park users was passed overwhelmingly by the Wisconsin Legislature and signed by Governor Nelson on December 14, 1961. This $2 season or 50-cent daily sticker fee matches the sticker fee now charged by Minnesota and Michigan. Revenue will go to the Conservation Department for the acquisition, development and administration of state parks. The fee is expected to raise about $400,000 between April 1, 1962, when it goes into effect, and the end of this biennium in 1963. Total two-year income will amount to about $900,000. Five historical parks are excluded from the sticker requirements. The other 28 parks and developed picnic and camping areas of the state forests will require stickers for entry. Governor Nelson said the new law "is especially important because it ties in so well with Wisconsin's $50 million resource development program."

MEETINGS

Attendance at the 43rd National Recreation Congress, held in Detroit's Cobo Hall on October 1–6, 1961, was larger than ever before. Approximately 2,265 recreation representatives—professional leaders, board or commission members, government representatives, recreation directors of the armed forces, private agencies and institutions, and distinguished guests from other related fields were present. The Congress was cosponsored by the National Recreation Association and the American Recreation Society, with the cooperation of the

Detroit Department of Parks and Recreation, the Recreation Association of Michigan, and the Federation of National Professional Organizations for Recreation.

There was an awareness throughout the Congress that the recreation field is facing a great challenge in today's new era of leisure and quest for peace with its implications and responsibilities in the national picture. Speakers at the general sessions seemed to agree on the growing importance of recreation in America and its inevitable influence on the citizens of our nation. Mr. Dan Dodson of New York University in his keynote address outlined the new leisure—recreation concept in "The Dynamics of Programing."

Greetings were extended to all delegates by the Hon. Louis C. Miriani, Mayor of Detroit. Joseph Prendergast, NRA Executive Director and chairman of the Congress Policy Committee, presided and read a letter from President Kennedy at the opening session which said, in part, "It is significant that you should be meeting at a time referred to by Secretary of the Interior, Stewart L. Udall, as the 'quiet crisis'. This administration is actively leading a massive and sustained national conservation effort to save—while there is yet time—the few remaining extensive segments of our rapidly disappearing shorelines and wilderness areas. It is our purpose to encourage state and local governments in the timely acquisition of vital needed open space for parks and recreation areas." Gov. John B. Swainson of Michigan told of the broad objectives of Michigan's recreation policy. Other speakers included Martin S. Hayden, Editor of the *Detroit-News*, speaking on "Recreation in a Mobile America"; Leonard Woodcock, UAW Vice-President, talked on the shaping of men's leisure tastes, interests and pursuits; and Donald J. Pizzimenti, American Management Association, Detroit Edison Company, outlined techniques of helping staff develop their fullest potential. Sharing the honors as guest speakers at other sessions were Secretary of the Interior, Stewart Udall, speaking on "The Role of the Federal Government in the Field of Recreation"; Dr. Theodore Forbes, director of health, physical education and recreation for the President's Council on Youth Fitness, who promised wholehearted national backing for any program of "fitness through fun"; and Dr. Donald P. Kent, special assistant for aging, U. S. Department of Health, Education and Welfare, speaking on "The Challenges of Leisure for the Aging Population" proposed a "National Voluntary Service Corps."

Mr. Howard Crowell, general superintendent of the Detroit Parks and Recreation Department, received a citation for outstanding services to the field of recreation from the National Recreation Association. Among the American Recreation Society citations and awards presented, one went to Joseph Prendergast "in recognition of exceptional service to his fellowmen through the medium of recreation." Three other citations and three fellow awards were also presented by the ARS.

Two days before the opening of the Congress, Mr. Prendergast spoke at NRA's 6th Annual Institute in Recreation Administration on "Recreation's Part in the National Economy." He pointed out that, in the midst of our affluent society, millions of Americans—more than one-third of the nation—still require special attention because of the low income and lack of education; thirty-five percent of all American families have incomes under $4,000 a year before taxes. "No city in the country today is spending what it should to provide the creative services and opportunities for this thirty-five percent," he said, and predicted that the $6 annual per capita expenditure which the NRA has suggested as a guide to city spending for recreation must be revised. Preliminary figures, compiled by the Association recently, show a marked increase in spending by cities of all sizes.

Seventy-five park employees attended the 12th Annual Park Managers' Training School at Lake Hope State Park, October 30, 1961. V. W. Flickinger, Chief, Ohio Division of Parks, announced that several out-of-state park officials participated in the program including: Allen T. Edmunds, Chief of Recreation Resource Planning, National Park Service, Region Five; M. W. Wood, U. S. Army Corps of Engineers; and Kermit McKeever, Chief, Division of Parks and Recreation, West Virginia. Also lecturing were personnel from the Ohio Departments of Natural Resources, Highways, Health, the Industrial Commission, Water Commission, and the State Fire Marshal's office. Classes and workshop subjects included safety, sanitation, machinery and equipment maintenance, and resources planning. A new camping area at Hocking State Park was inspected in Hocking County.

The annual conference sponsored by the Michigan Forestry and Park Association in cooperation with Michigan State University, Department of Resource Development, College of Agriculture, and Continuing Education Service was held at The Kellogg Center, East Lansing, Michigan, February 8–9. On February 8 a "Short Course in Entomology" was conducted by James W. Butcher, Associate Professor, Department of Entomology, MSU.

On February 9 Allen T. Edmunds, Regional Chief of Recreation Resource Planning, National Park Service, Philadelphia, gave "A Progress Report on The Great Lakes Shoreline Survey;" Professor Lyle Craine, Chairman, Department of Conservation, University of Michigan, spoke on "Providing Space for Michigan's Recreational Needs." He was followed by speaker David Powell, John Bean Division, Food Machinery and Chemical Corporation on the subject of "Spray Application: Equipment and Materials."

The 34th Annual Conference of the Illinois Association of Park Districts meeting jointly with the Illinois Recreation Association in Springfield, October 11–13, 1961, attracted a large attendance and was considered very successful. The program included an address by Prof. Charles K. Brightbill on "Recreation and Parks—Desirable or Essential in Tomorrow's World,"

Planning and Civic Comment

and "The Art of Living" by Dr. Carl S. Winters; also, panel discussions on the following subjects: "How Can Park and Recreation Agencies Best Coordinate Program and Facilities?", "Methods of Evaluating Summer Playgrounds," "Aquatic Carnivals," and "Preparing Written Reports." Professor Fred F. Weinard of Urbana succeeds L. M. Krause of East St. Louis as Association President.

Over 200 persons representing city, county and state park agencies attended the seventh Southwest Park and Recreation Training Institute at Lake Texoma State Park, Kingston, Oklahoma, February 4–7. The meeting was sponsored by and affiliated with the AIPE and conducted by the Horticulture and Park Management Department, Texas Technological College, Lubbock, Texas. Mr. Mack Burks welcomed the group and Chairman Robert Frazer introduced keynote speaker William Christian. Bill Collins and Dean Gerald Thomas addressed the opening session on "Population Trends in Park Planning" and "Impact on Land." Two subjects of unusual interest at Wednesday's general session were "Cooperative Planning of National Park Service," by Ernest Allen, and "The Texas State Park Survey." Delegates from the eight adjacent States actively participated in discussions of park and recreation problems of mutual interest during four busy workshop sessions on "Using Floodways, Flood Plains, and Other Flood Areas as Parks," "Nature Centers and Nature Parks Within Cities," "Golf Course Operational Problems," "Maintenance of Boule-

vards and Rights of Way," and "Work Reports." Speakers at other general sessions addressed the delegates on "Selling a Bond Issue," "Planning an Arboretum," "Gaining Community Support," and "Training Your Successor."

James W. Taylor, Director, Parks and Recreation, Colorado Springs, Colorado, was elected president and Elo J. Urbahovsky, Texas Technological College, Lubbock, Texas, director.

ARTICLES

"What Citizens Can Do To Preserve Natural Areas," an article with a message directed to the individual citizen in his own community, by the Hon. Stewart L. Udall, Secretary of the Interior, appeared in *The Nature Conservancy News*, October–December 1961. Secretary Udall tells what must be done to meet the crisis of America's rapidly vanishing open space and how local communities, private citizens and citizens groups can be effective forces in halting the rapid loss of open space.

"To perpetuate our American way of life, we need in this Country a variety of public parks and recreation areas—ranging in kind and location from remote wilderness to highly-developed playgrounds near densely populated areas," he said. "I want to see throughout the Nation a system of parks and recreation areas—large and small, local, State and Federal—in sufficient DEPTH to provide all segments of our present and future population with adequate urban and non-urban areas near their homes for frequent day and weekend use, as well as

37

remote areas for vacation use." Citizen support of these national objectives is vital, but state and local objectives are of equal significance. In the case of extensive natural areas and outstanding scenic or recreational values, these open lands may be recommended to the States or to the Federal Government for consideration as State and National Parks. Action on the part of citizens may therefore be limited to reporting the existence of vacant lands to appropriate government agencies or to conservation groups such as The Nature Conservancy. Local communities and private citizens are usually aware of such areas in their immediate vicinity, and that is why action must usually begin on the local front.

In the November 17–22, 1961 South Dakota Department of Game, Fish and Parks *Newsletter*, Robert J. Arkins, State Forester, comments on possible solutions to the growing problem of adequate financing for the State's parks and recreation areas. Mr. Arkins said, "Unless we would nickle and dime park users to death, there is no way to finance South Dakota's parks except by getting the bulk of funds through legislative appropriations. In order to make any park entirely self-supporting, we would have to create a penny arcade atmosphere with meters on picnic tables, meters on fire places and every other thing in a park which is now taken for granted. Either that, or there would have to be an entrance fee so large that many park users would refuse or be unable to pay it." At the present time most South Dakota parks do not have resident caretakers to enforce or collect entrance fees. "Since parks should be properly regarded as a service of government, they cannot be self-supporting," he said.

The January issue of *Parks and Recreation* reports the creation of a "PARK AND RECREATION FOUNDATION" by the American Institute of Park Executives to supplement the work of the AIPE to insure long-range stability in the servicing of park and recreation operations in communities throughout the nation. Millions of acres of park lands are lost to encroachment; vandalism is becoming a major problem; sub-division planning frequently excludes park and recreation areas; city-county parks are merging and many officials deplore the lack of college graduates to fill positions in the expanding park and recreation market.

To meet these needs, the AIPE has founded the PARK AND RECREATION FOUNDATION incorporating it as a separate entity for perpetual succession. It provides a vehicle for AIPE members to build an endowment fund to supplement the Institute's educational program; and to raise money for major projects and research which otherwise would be neglected or postponed. The Foundation is governed and managed by a Board of Trustees consisting of the President, Vice-President, and Executive Secretary and six skilled and experienced business leaders, appointed by the Executive Committee to serve staggered terms of five years each. Since 1898, when the AIPE was founded, its members have been deeply concerned about the direction of the park and recreation movement. An extensive campaign for grants from individuals, business, industry, and other foundations is being planned. But before outside assistance is solicited, members of the Institute will be asked to build up capitalization in the Professional Endowment Fund.

An article entitled "A Plan For Public Park Systems," by U. W. Hella, Director, Division of State Parks, Department of Conservation, Minnesota, given at the Governor's Conference of Metropolitan Problems in October 1961, was published in the Department's November–December 1961 official bulletin. Mr. Hella stresses the importance of overall outdoor recreation planning—Federal, state, and local, and said, "Man's search for outdoor recreation opportunities is not limited by political boundaries. Parkwise on the Federal, state, and local levels these limits are within loosely delineated areas of responsibility on which a certain amount of overlapping is to be expected." The need to provide for recreation opportunities is, however, the responsibility of political entities. He very briefly describes such limits of responsibility as follows:

1. The Federal Government through the National Park System is responsible for establishing and preserving park areas of nationally outstanding scenic, scientific and historic significance. They offer outdoor recreational opportunity of the extensive variety such as camping, hiking, riding, boating, field observations in geology, biology, archeology and history or enjoyment of a superlative natural scene unspoiled by man.

2. The State through its State Park system has a parallel responsibility except that the values preserved therein are significant at the state level. Recreational opportunities provided as in the National Park system are primarily "extensive."

3. The County has a responsibility for establishing park areas of county wide significance. They may provide intensive as well as extensive recreational opportunities. By intensive we mean golf courses, ball fields, tennis courts, artificial swimming pools and the like.

4. The urban communities need to provide formal open spaces, playgrounds, golf courses, tennis courts, stadia, beaches and in some instances relatively large natural areas —catering mostly to intensive types of recreation.

In 1936 the Congress enacted legislation authorizing the National Park Service to cooperate with the individual states in preparing long-range state park system plans. "The need for the metropolitan area to plan and provide adequately now in the way of city and county parks * * * is obvious. One of the most significant pieces of legislation enacted in Minnesota this past season was a model permissive County Park Bill. We hope that the six metropolitan counties which presently do not have a County Park system will take advantage of this law," Hella said. "The need for county park systems is immediate— the opportunities of acquiring suitable county park areas at reasonable prices is diminishing fast. The

State Park System will in itself never fully fill the metropolitan needs for parks and open spaces."

NEWS FROM THE STATES

California. Hearings to consider proposals for a Bond Issue for acquisition of state parks, recreation and historic sites were held in Sacramento, Los Angeles, and San Francisco in November and December 1961. Gov. Edmund G. Brown in early 1960 instructed the State Park Commission and the Division of Beaches and Parks to develop a program for California's beaches and parks which would insure the adequacy of a park program for today and a decade from now. Because a program submitted to the 1961 Legislature must be voted on at the next general election, June or November 1962, the Legislature decided to wait until 1962 when Governor Brown will place the measure on special call. Based on the hearings a decision will be made on the scope of the proposals, the urgency of the need, the amount of the bond issue and its general use.

A lease, signed May 18, 1961, between the United States and the State of California for about 4,000 acres of public land along the lower Colorado River in Imperial County will be developed as a state park. "This lease," Secretary Udall said, "is one of the first major steps to be taken to implement the Department's program for utilization of public lands along the Colorado River from Davis Dam to the Mexico border." The lands heretofore have been administered for reclamation purposes and, in part, as the Imperial Wildlife Refuge.

Florida. Koreshan State Park containing nearly 300 acres of gardens and grounds is the State's 36th and newest park and has an interesting history. The Koreshan Unity, a small religious group, once flourished near Estero, a sun-drenched town stretched briefly along the Tamiami Trail between Fort Myers and Naples. The Koreshan Unity—Koresh is the Hebrew word for Cyrus—came into being in 1888 and flourished in the 1890's when it claimed to have about 4,000 members in the United States and abroad. Only four active members now survive at Estero. Completely debt free and unmortgaged, the property has been deeded to the Florida Board of Parks and Historic Memorials. The Koreshan Unity will continue to have the use of the buildings and other facilities it has erected on the area during the years.

Probably the structure most frequently noticed today by motorists passing through Estero is a wooden building labeled "Art Institute," which houses memorabilia and artifacts relating to the Koreshan sect and its singular beliefs, religious and scientific.

Indiana. Largely due to the enthusiasm, hard work, and interest shown by Dr. Jack McCormick, a former naturalist in the Indiana State Parks, the 595-acre beautiful natural Pine Hills area is now a part of Shades State Park. It was while he spent several years working at the park that he became interested in nearby Pine Hills and realized that its natural features could best be protected if acquired as an addition to the 2,000-acre Shades

State Park. The scenic area, 12 miles southwest of Crawford, with gorges, bluffs, meandering streams, and narrow ridges carved from solid rock, is unparalleled by any other natural formations in the State. The unusual geological features provide a variety of habitats for plants and animals, and the white pine and hemlock forests are considered to be remnants of a sub-arctic type of vegetation.

Pine Hills, also called the "Shades of Death" in allusion to the deep shadows beneath the nearly unbroken cover of forests on broken lands, will be maintained by the Indiana Department of Conservation in keeping with the wording and spirit of the restrictive clause of the deed. Mr. James A. McCormick, Attorney, Indianapolis, father of Dr. McCormick, devoted much time toward handling legal matters at no cost to The Nature Conservancy. Developments will be confined above the 710-foot contour level on the west side of the gorge above Indian Creek and above the 670-foot contour level of the east side of the gorge.

Iowa. To provide all the rural recreation areas the public demanded and to ease the pressure on other recreation facilities, 62 of Iowa's 99 counties have set up locally financed county conservation boards. Since 1955, when legislation was passed permitting counties to establish such boards, 11,000 acres of county parks and recreation areas have been acquired. The program, ranking among the nation's finest, fills the gap between city and state park systems. The counties acquire, develop and administer these recreation areas with funds obtained from a one-fourth to one mill tax on all real and personal property. The State Conservation Commission must approve all land acquisition, development plans, and construction before any action is taken or work initiated. The Commission in 1960 created the Office of Coordinator of County Conservation Activities with two coordinators to aid the county boards in planning and procedural work.

Kentucky. A new Division of Construction and Maintenance has been created in the Department of Parks to oversee construction and maintenance of park facilities. State Park Commissioner Edward V. Fox said the new division became necessary because of the Department's sizable construction program. George S. Lyon, 57, a veteran Highway Department employee and former City Engineer and City Manager of Covington, has been named to head the new Division. The old Division of Planning, Construction, and Maintenance now becomes the Division of Planning with Thomas J. Nelson remaining as Director of that Division.

Maryland. Plans for an open air theatre with seating capacity of 2,000 and featuring an annual large-scale drama based on early Maryland history have been announced by the Maryland Historical Drama Assn. The group headed by Elmer M. Jackson, Jr. has met with Governor Tawes to discuss the project which would be in the Sandy Point

State Park at the western approach to the Chesapeake Bay Bridge.

The committee hopes to start construction next summer. The state is to build the amphitheatre as part of Sandy Point Improvement program and will lease it to the non-profit organization.

A $300,000 construction figure in the capital improvements request of the Department of Forests and Parks has been submitted to the Governor and the State Planning Commission. The Drama Association expects to raise $40,000 for production costs through sale of stock.

The drama to be called "Flame of Freedom," is by Ray Hamby and is based on actual events in the founding of the state. It will have an original score. There will probably be a cast of over 100 actors, singers and dancers performing the piece six nights a week for 10 weeks each summer.

Michigan. Support for public recreation and wildlife values in the lower Detroit River drew a solid vote of confidence recently when the Secretary of the Army denied an application to establish new harbor lines in waters near the mouth of the Huron River adjacent to real estate developments. Approval of the application would have cleared the way for private shoreline owners to fill or build docks and other permanent structures to a harbor line over an approximate 1,400-acre area at the expense of public pleasure boating, hunting, fishing, and waterfowl and fish habitat. State Conservation Department officials filed a written protest against the application, as did a number of conservation groups and local individuals, prior to final action by the Secretary of the Army.

In January the services of Louis F. Twardzik, assistant professor of recreation at Michigan State University, were made available to the Michigan Department of Conservation by MSU as interim consultant for Governor Swainson's new state recreation program. Last year, at the Governor's request, Mr. Twardzik drafted a broad 11-point statement which laid the groundwork for the new program.

The Conservation Commission directed where part of the first bond sale revenue funds will be used when it recently approved land purchase options. These options will permit prompt acquisition of three new state parks and pave the way for further development of three existing sites. Lands to be acquired as new parks include 136 acres on Lake Michigan in Ottawa and Muskegon Counties to be named P. J. Hoffmaster State Park for the Department's late Director; 175 acres on Little Traverse Bay, Emmet County, to be known as Petoskey State Park; and 123 acres on Lake Huron, Chippewa County, to be named De Tour State Park. Approved for addition to existing areas are 101 acres at Cheboygan State Park, 42 acres at Pontiac Lake State Recreation Area in lower Michigan and 71 acres at Indian Lake State Park in the upper peninsula. The sale of a $2 million bond issue was authorized in August and another $3 million in November for capital outlay improvements. Not more than $1 million of the $5 million total may be spent to buy new park lands.

Nebraska. The Nebraska Park and Recreation Association was organized June 29, 1961 to stimulate and increase public interest in the possibilities of the need for and the value of adequate parks and recreation in the State. According to its constitution, other purposes and objectives are to unite in one organization all park and recreation personnel and all individuals, groups and agencies having an interest in recreation in Nebraska; to foster and maintain high standards of park and recreation leadership qualifications; to affiliate and cooperate with similar agencies and organizations and to function in any other manner which will further the interests of the park and recreation movement. There were about 55 people present representing city, state and Federal agencies, the P.T.A., Council of Churches, and public schools. Robert Dula, Lincoln Air Force Base, was elected President; Mrs. Clifford Jergenson, P.T.A., Vice-President; and Mr. Robert McKinnon, Superintendent of Recreation, City Parks, Omaha, Treasurer. Fifty-two charter members were accepted at the first annual meeting last October. Membership is open to all professional and lay people interested in parks and recreation in Nebraska and to persons outside the State by invitation.

New Jersey. Approximately 460 acres of Fort Hancock Military Reservation fronting on Sandy Hook Bay and the Atlantic Ocean have been leased by the Department of the Army to the State for 25 years for park and recreation purposes. The lease which was accepted by Governor Meyner on January 8 provides for administration of the Sandy Hook Peninsula area in Monmouth County by the New Jersey Department of Conservation and Economic Development. This is a portion of the exceptionally fine Seashore area recommended in the National Park Service report, *Our Vanishing Shoreline.*

New Mexico. A crowd estimated in excess of 1,000 attended the formal dedication of Pancho Villa State Park on November 18, 1961, in a ceremony marked by expressions of good will between the United States and Mexico. The principal speakers, New Mexico's Gov. Edwin L. Mechem and Gov. Teofilo Borunda of the Mexican State of Chihuahua, exchanged expressions of international good will.

New York. Acquisition of a 67-acre farm of open space and woods at a cost of $20,800 for the Township of Aurora, under the multi-million-dollar state aid park lands bond issue, is considered a "pilot project" that could go a long way in selling the land-for-parks program in the opinion of officials in charge of this acquisition. "Not the least encouraging aspect of it is that so modest an initial try-out was selected," reports the December 1961 *Park Maintenance.* "Usually 'pilots' are expensive, expansive, and showy. This one seems the direct opposite— a happy change."

North Carolina. The new Water-side Theatre being built on Roanoke Island on the site of the original amphitheatre built in 1937, is scheduled for completion by the time "The Lost Colony" opens next summer for its 25th anniversary season.

The structure is being built by the National Park Service at a cost of about $70,000.

Pennsylvania. Dr. Maurice K. Goddard, Secretary, Department of Forests and Waters, on November 1, 1961, announced a dramatic new park program for Pennsylvania, labeled PROJECT 70, to be presented to the General Assembly at the 1962 session. One part of the program—a proposed $70 million bond issue—requires a Constitutional Amendment which must be approved by the voters after passing two separately-elected legislatures. PROJECT 70 means that by 1970 the State proposes: (1) to establish three large Federal recreation areas in Pennsylvania; (2) to establish through the $70 million bond issue, regional parks and open space—$50 million for land acquisition by the Commonwealth and $20 million to be made available for matching grants to local governmental bodies; (3) to use $5 million of the $50 million for purchase of important fish and wildlife areas threatened by development; and (4) to diversify and broaden recreation facilities in the State's non-urban counties where substantial amounts of public-owned land already exist—"in order to stimulate development of a new American vacationland."

South Dakota. Work done by the National Guard last summer in cooperation with the Department of Game, Fish and Parks at Fort Randall Reservoir State Recreation Area and Lewis and Clark Lake Recreation Area, valued at $100,000, was accomplished with an outlay of less than $4,000 by the Department. Development was accomplished that would otherwise take several years to achieve, at little cost to the taxpayers. Seven and a half miles of new access roads were constructed and graveled; a salvaged steel bridge and two wooden bridges were constructed; and three culverts installed. Cooperation between Forestry and Parks and the National Guard began in 1957.

Texas. The Texas Research League submitted a report to the Texas State Parks Board in October 1961 on the composition, management and financing of the Texas State Parks System. The report was made by Glenn Ivy and John Hargrove of the League's staff at the request of the Board and is based on a year-long study. The League is a privately supported, non-profit, non-political, educational corporation engaged in objective research into the operations, programs and problems of Texas government. Its report will be a companion to the long-range park development plan under preparation by Texas Technological College, reported in September 1961 *Planning and Civic Comment.* J. Harold Dunn, Chairman, Texas Research League. said in his transmittal letter that, "This study and report * * * suggest the groundwork for a new era in the

Texas State Parks System. The long-range development plan now under construction by the Parks Board and the Department of Horticulture and Parks Management at Texas Technological College, should complete the blueprint for future growth." The League staff made four basic recommendations, to each of which the Parks Board has given careful consideration: (1) A set of basic criteria and minimum standards for Texas State Parks should be developed; (2) Park acquisition, development, interpretation and maintenance should be based on a carefully drawn, long-range plan; (3) Personnel standards of the Parks Board staff should be raised, and qualified professional park rangers should be recruited to operate the system; and (4) Park management and concessions operation should be divided. Wherever possible, private concessions contracts for services compatible with the purpose of the parks should be made.

These recommendations have been partially implemented, and the State Parks Board has adopted a set of basic criteria and minimum standards. Three major area categories were established: Historical Parks, Scenic Parks, and Recreational Parks. The Board recently contracted with the Texas Technological College to provide a long-range state park plan, and it tentatively adopted a set of personnel qualifications for all staff members. It also agreed to the principle of separation of parks and concession management. With the League's report and the Texas Tech study, when completed, the Board will be in a position to furnish the Legislature with detailed, documented plans and estimates for bringing the State Parks System to a high standard—"an object of pride for Texans and an attraction to out-of-state visitors."

Wisconsin. The Wisconsin Conservation Commission has authorized the purchase of 2,400 acres of land at a cost of $200,000 and anticipates rapid acquisition of some 63,000 acres for about $3 million under the State's new $50 million recreation and resources development program. By December a total of 4,700 acres had been acquired and options held on 7,000 acres of lands under the new program.

IN MEMORIAM

JAY NORWOOD DARLING

1876-1962

"Ding" Darling *Des Moines Register* cartoonist, who won two Pulitzer Prizes for his cartoons, died February 12 at the age of 85, of a heart ailment at Iowa Methodist Hospital in Des Moines. He had been in poor health for some time.

Mr. Darling served as a member of the Board of Directors of the American Planning and Civic Association from 1935 until the middle of 1939. He attended many meetings during that period.

Mr. Darling was awarded his first Pulitzer Prize in 1924 for a cartoon entitled "In the Good Old USA." It depicted opportunities in this country which permitted such men as President Warren Harding and world-famed engineer (and later President) Herbert Hoover to rise from lowly origins.

His second Pulitzer Prize was awarded for a cartoon entitled "What a Place for a Wastepaper Salvage Campaign" in 1943. That cartoon showed a flood of bulletins, reports and pamphlets coming out of Washington.

Mr. Darling was named the Nation's best cartoonist in 1934 in a poll of the Nation's editors by *Editor and Publisher* magazine.

In 1934 and 1935 his love for the outdoors prompted Mr. Darling to cast aside his $100,000-a-year job as a cartoonist to take an $8,000-a-year post as chief of the United States Biological Survey in Washington, D. C.

There had been a critical drop in the migratory waterfowl population in a cycle of drought years and Mr. Darling decided to help.

While in Washington he secured $17 million in Federal funds for wildlife restoration.

A printer's error led to Mr. Darling's use of the world famed signature, "Ding."

Mr. Darling signed his cartoons with the abbreviation of his last name, D'ing. One day a printer dropped the apostrophe and Mr. Darling so liked the name he adopted it.

It will not be easy to forget his exuberant personality. He leaves a void among laymen who have devoted time and enthusiasm to conservation.

PIERRE M. GHENT

1904-1962

Pierre M. Ghent, well-known Washington planning consultant, died January 9, 1962 at the age of 58.

As chief planner of Pierre Ghent and Associates, he had been a planning consultant in Washington since 1939, and was associated with several large developments in the Washington area.

He was born in Baltimore and received his civil engineering degree from Johns Hopkins University in 1923. He came to Washington in 1934 and worked at American University towards a master's degree in

national resources planning and housing economics.

He was a member of the Committee of 100 for the Federal City, and had been an active member of the American Planning and Civic Association since 1943.

Report

A Preliminary Plan for Scenic Highways in California

A new comprehensive plan for state scenic highways just issued is believed to be the first of its type in the Nation. It is expected that the 1963 session of the California Legislature will pass legislation to implement the program outlined.

The Report was issued upon authorization of the State of California, Senate Concurrent Resolution 39, 1961, under the auspices of the Citizen's Advisory Committee on Scenic Highways, the Interdepartmental Coordinating Committee on Scenic Highways and the California Department of Public Works. Its theme is that the appropriate development of the State Highway System in scenic areas and the preservation of California's great heritage of scenic resources are of

paramount importance for the sound economic growth of the State, and for the continued pleasure and cultural enhancement of its citizens.

It has been recommended that the Advisory Committee be kept in existence for another year to work jointly with the counties and cities to devise improved policies and procedures for scenic conservation and to review the proposals made in this report. Further collaboration is desired between state and local agencies and planners concerned with this program.

The Report is illustrated and its Recommendations are important to all interested in the development of a state-wide system of scenic highways.

Recent Publications

MINNESOTA LANDS. Ownership, Use and Management of Forests and Related Lands. By Samuel Trask Dana, John H. Allison and Russell N. Cunningham. American Forestry Association, Minnesota Landownership Study. 464 pp. $5.00.

THE CASE FOR A DEPARTMENT OF NATURAL RESOURCES. Reprint from the Natural Resources Journal, Vol. 1, No. 2, November 1961. (Author anonymous in order to stimulate attention on the controversial issues involved.)

PUBLIC FINANCE. By Earl R. Rolph and George F. Break. The Ronald Press Co., 15 E. 26th Street, New York 10, N. Y. 586 pp. $7.50.

THE HUMAN SIDE OF URBAN RENEWAL. By Martin Millspaugh and Gurney Breckenfeld. Study under a Fund for Adult Education grant. 233 pp. $4.50.

EUROPE'S NEEDS AND RESOURCES. Trends and Prospects in Eighteen Countries. By J. Frederic Dewhurst, John O. Coppock, P. Lamartine Yates and Associates. The Twentieth Century Fund, 41 East 70th Street, New York 21, N. Y., 1198 pp. Charts, maps and tables. $12.00.

FUTURE GROWTH AND CALIFORNIA ENVIRONMENT. A selection of papers from the Eighth Annual University of California Conference on City and Regional Studies. Department of City and Regional Planning, University of California, Berkeley 4, Calif. $1.00.

DISCOVERY: GREAT MOMENTS IN THE LIVES OF OUTSTANDING NATURALISTS. Edited by John K. Terres. J. B. Lippincott Co., East Washington Square, Philadelphia 5, Pa. 1961. $6.50.

CONNECTICUT'S COASTAL MARSHES—A VANISHING RESOURCE. The Connecticut Arboretum, Connecticut College, New London. 36 pp. 40c.

1961 CONSERVATION DIRECTORY. Educational Servicing Division, National Wildlife Federation, 1412 16th Street N. W., Washington 6, D. C. $1.00.

THE FUTURE METROPOLIS, 1961 (Wesleyan University Press, 356 Washington Street, Middletown, Connecticut); 216 pp., $1.50.

A GUIDE FOR COUNTY ZONING ADMINISTRATORS IN ILLINOIS, James E. Lee (Bureau of Community Planning, University of Illinois, 1202 W. California, Urbana, Illinois, 1961); 32 pp., 50c.

GUIDELINES FOR BUSINESS LEADERS AND CITY OFFICIALS TO A NEW CENTRAL BUSINESS DISTRICT, Institute of Government, University of North Carolina, Chapel Hill, North Carolina, 1961; 150 pp., $3.00.

THE VANISHING NATURAL AREAS OF THE UNITED STATES, 1960. The Nature Conservancy, 2039 K St. N.W., Washington 6, D. C. 33 pp. illus. Available on request.

OUR NATIONAL PARK POLICY: A CRITICAL HISTORY. By John Ise. Published for Resources for the Future by Johns Hopkins Press, Baltimore, Md. 1961. 701 pp. $10.00.

AMERICA'S NATIONAL MONUMENTS AND HISTORIC SITES. By E. John Long. Doubleday and Co., New York, 1960. 260 pp. illus. $4.50.

COMMUNITY DEVELOPMENT THROUGH UNIVERSITY EXTENSION. By Katherine Lackey. Department of Community Development, Southern Illinois University, Carbondale, Ill. 1960. 120 pp. mimeo. $1.00.

COMMUNITY PLANNING. Division of State and Regional Planning, N. J. Department of Conservation and Economic Development, Trenton 25, N. J., 1961. 20 pp.

ANONYMOUS (20TH CENTURY). Leonardo Ricci. Translated by Elizabeth Mann Borgese. New York, George Braziller, Inc. 215 Park Avenue South, New York 3, N. Y. 1962. 254 pp. $5.00.

A FRAMEWORK FOR URBAN STUDIES. An Analysis of Urban-Metropolitan Development and Research Needs. By Coleman Woodbury. A Report to the Committee on Urban Research, Highway Research Board, National Research Council, 2101 Constitution Ave., Washington 25, D. C. 38 pp.

THE UNPLANNED AND THE PLANNED METROPOLIS, 1985. Regional Plan Association, 230 W. 41st Street, New York 36, N. Y. 1961. 20 pp. illus.

Annual Conferences

National Conference on State Parks

1962—Illinois Beach State Park, Zion, Illinois
   September 30 through October 4, 1962
   Headquarters—Illinois Beach Lodge

1963—Washington, D. C.—Joint meeting
   with AIPE
      September 22-26, 1963
   Headquarters—Sheraton Park Hotel

1964—New Jersey
      Dates not determined

Planning and Civic Comment

Official Organ of American Planning and Civic Association and National Conference on State Parks

CONTENTS

JUNE 1962

SECOND QUARTER—APRIL—MAY—JUNE

PLANNING AND
CIVIC COMMENT

Published Quarterly

Successor to: City Planning, Civic Comment, State Recreation
Official Organ of: American Planning and Civic Association,
National Conference on State Parks

SCOPE: *National, State, Regional and City Planning, Land and Water Uses, Conservation of National Resources, National, State and Local Parks, Highways and Roadsides.*
AIM: *To create a better physical environment which will conserve and develop the health, happiness and culture of the American people.*

Second-class postage paid at Harrisburg, Pa., and at additional mailing office.
EDITORIAL AND PUBLICATION OFFICE, 901 Union Trust Building, Washington 5, D. C.
Printed by the Mount Pleasant Press, The McFarland Company, Harrisburg, Pa.

A National Approach to Outdoor Recreation

By EDWARD C. CRAFTS, Director
Bureau of Outdoor Recreation, U. S. Department of the Interior

Recently, President Kennedy received a letter from a little girl in one of our large eastern cities, which read, in part, as follows: "Us kids think we should have parks around our way. Everywhere we go we get chased away. When we play tag we get chased by the landlord so we really have no place to go. We can't even run."

This little girl's letter echoes the plight of millions of children, and as many adults, in the urban centers where most American people are now concentrated and where three-quarters of them will live by the end of this century. Today's city dweller doubtless has heard of Yellowstone and Bryce Canyon National Parks and our extensive national forests and our shorelines; but most are able to visit such places only on rare occasions, particularly if their homes are in the East. The average urbanite is cut off by distance, time, and expense from frequent contact with our seashores, lakes, mountains, forests, and open spaces. In fact, he is fortunate if he can look up each day and see a sky unlaced by wires, or look about him and find grass and trees.

The young lady's letter was referred to me for reply and, of course, I was unable to promise her a park. However, because of the happenings of recent months, I could at least assure her that something was being done about it, and that if she and her friends were patient . . . and lucky . . . they might someday see their dream for readily available outdoor recreation come true.

I do not imply that we have just begun to concern ourselves with the recreational needs of our people. There is a long and brilliant history of concern, marked by many notable achievements. Our Federal Government has created and maintains the most magnificent system of national parks and national forests in the world. Recreation is a vital ingredient in the management policy of both the national forests and parks. Lakes have been built for boating, swimming, and fishing, and beautiful camping and picnic sites have been developed. States and local governments, and many private interests, have demonstrated their interest and concern by establishing recreation centers of various sorts.

Unfortunately though, our recreation resources still do not satisfy our needs. Although there is adequate land physically available, it is not accessible to enough of our people. To twist a famous phrase: Never has so much done so little for so few!

One reason for this is that our efforts to conserve and develop recreation resources have, in numerous instances, lacked coordination. Our accomplishments to date have been those of individual organizations going their individual ways. Such an approach no longer can be expected to do the job that must be done.

The face of America is changing rapidly. Since the end of World War II, increases in population, income, leisure time, and mobility have combined to produce a remarkable upsurge in demand for outdoor recreation areas and facilities. This demand is expected to triple by the year 2000. Nothing short of a well-coordinated nationwide program for outdoor recreation of all kinds can meet America's requirements and, at the same time, anticipate and provide for those of the future.

Realizing this, President Kennedy, in his March 1 message to the Congress on conservation, announced his intention to appoint a Recreation Advisory Council. He also called for establishment, within the Department of the Interior, of a Bureau of Outdoor Recreation, which, within the policy guidance of the Council, would work and consult with the some 20 Federal agencies having recreation resource responsibilities, and cooperate with and encourage State, local, and private organizations working in the outdoor recreation field. In this way, a unified, national plan for outdoor recreation can be developed that will meet America's needs today and tomorrow.

Secretary of the Interior Udall moved swiftly in response to the President's message and, on April 2, the Bureau of Outdoor Recreation came into being. On April 27, President Kennedy by Executive Order established the Recreation Advisory Council consisting of the Secretaries of the Interior, Agriculture, Defense, and Health, Education, and Welfare, and the Administrator of the Housing and Home Finance Agency.

President Kennedy's action, and that of Secretary Udall, stemmed primarily, of course, from what has become widely known in conservation circles as "the ORRRC report." This comprehensive appraisal of present and future requirements for outdoor recreation, based on more than three years of exhaustive study and discussion, laid the necessary groundwork for a national approach to recreation problems.

The Outdoor Recreation Resources Review Commission emphasized the necessity for placing outdoor recreation squarely within the context of American life. The Commission indicated clearly that the States and public and private local organizations must play key roles in developing adequate resources. But it outlined just as clearly the responsibility of the Federal Government to coordinate its own efforts and to cooperate with and assist non-Federal organizations in every way possible.

The Commission also made specific recommendations on how Federal cooperation and assistance can be effectively provided. Federal appropriations are needed, the Commission said, not only to finance increased conservation and development of outdoor recreation resources, but also to assist the States in program planning, and to promote effective coordination of Federal and State programs. Bills providing for such appropriations are now pending in the Congress.

It is important to remember that outdoor recreation means different things to different people. It encompasses a host of activities ranging all the way from a "morning constitutional" to wilderness camping in the High Sierras. Recognition of this fact led the Commission to recommend that all agencies administering outdoor recreation resources adopt a uniform system for classifying recreation lands. Such a system would cover all outdoor recreation resources, ranging from high-density areas already intensively developed and managed for mass use, and general recreation areas that can be developed for a variety of activities, to unique natural and wilderness areas, and the historic and cultural sites so essential to the preservation of our national consciousness. Adoption of an adequate classification system will permit a consistent and logical approach to management and development problems, and will be a significant step in the formulation of a national outdoor recreation policy.

When Secretary Udall established the Bureau of Outdoor Recreation, he assigned it several responsibilities, and the Executive Order of April 27 added others. Chief among these are the tasks of promoting program coordination among the many Federal agencies already active in outdoor recreation, and encouraging and assisting State, local, and private. organizations in their efforts to meet growing demands for outdoor recreation.

In fulfilling the first of these responsibilities—the coordination of Federal programs—we realize that there will doubtless be sensitive areas in the Bureau's relationships with other Government organizations. Nevertheless, we are confident that good will and honest intent will make it possible to achieve the unified Federal effort called for by President Kennedy. Moreover, we believe the Bureau will be able to do a more effective job in meeting its responsibilities because, at the present time, it is not contemplated that the Bureau will be administering land and water areas.

With the experience of ORRRC as a precedent, we can also expect a wholesome attitude in our cooperative dealings with State, local, and private organizations. When legislation now pending is enacted, we intend to do all we can in offering to the States such assistance as they may desire in planning the programs they need for their people.

The Bureau will also have other things to do. A continuing inventory of the Nation's outdoor recreation resources, and research on many aspects of both the supply and demand sides of outdoor recreation, are essential if this use of resources is to be properly meshed with the many other pressures upon the fixed amount of land and water that is available. The Bureau

(*Please turn to page 9*)

Strictly Personal

Dr. Paul A. Herbert of East Lansing, Michigan was reelected to a second term as President of the National Wildlife Federation at the conclusion of the 26th annual meeting in Denver, Colorado.

———◇———

Edwin H. Folk has been appointed new Executive Director of the Citizens' Council on City Planning of Philadelphia. He has been Director of the City Planning Commission of Youngstown, Ohio. He assumed his new duties on March 19 and replaces Aaron Levine who served as Director for the past ten years. Mr. Levine has assumed a new planning post in Hawaii.

———◇———

Lewis Mumford, author and critic, was presented the 1962 Award of Merit on April 12 by the New York Chapter of the American Institute of Architects. The Award is bestowed upon an individual who has distinguished himself by meritorious work in his field. Mr. Mumford was cited for having delighted, inspired and provoked the layman and professional alike through his perceptive and stimulating articles, books and lectures. Although he is neither an architect nor a city planner, Mr. Mumford is a member of leading architectural and planning societies in the U. S. and England. Queen Elizabeth II awarded him a Royal Gold Medal for Architecture last year from the Royal Institute of British Architects.

The Secretary of Agriculture has announced the appointment of Edward P. Cliff, Chief Forester and Chief of the Department's Forest Service. Mr. Cliff was former Assistant Chief in charge of National Forest Resource Management. The appointment was effective March 17. Mr. Cliff succeeds Dr. Richard E. McArdle who recently rounded out ten years as Chief Forester while completing a lifetime career of 39 years in Federal Service. Mr. Cliff is a career professional forester with 32 years of service with the organization. A native of Heber City, Utah, he graduated from the College of Forestry, Utah State University, in 1931 with a BS degree in Forestry. He has served in many capacities in the Forest Service over the years.

———◇———

Sigurd F. Olson of Ely, Minnesota, has been appointed as consultant to the Secretary of the Interior and to the Director of the National Park Service on major problems in the field of wilderness preservation. Mr. Olson is a nationally known naturalist and wilderness "veteran." His duties will concern the policies and practices of the National Park Service relative to the management of the natural and scenic areas of the National Park System.

———◇———

Jack Eisen, Assistant City Editor and staff writer of the *Washington Post*, was cited by the American

Society of Planning Officials at its recent conference, for "excellence in reporting on aspects of city and regional planning." Mr. Eisen supervised the production of the *Post's* 10-part series, "Progress or Decay" and also wrote several of the articles.

◆

Ernest J. Bohn, the first and only Director of the Cleveland Metropolitan Housing Authority, was presented with the Ohio Planning Conference's second annual award for "his matchless contributions to the advancement of the fields of city planning, housing and urban renewal."

◆

A. H. C. Shaw, planning engineer of the Cleveland Board of Zoning Appeals received a round of applause at one of the luncheons of the meeting of the Ohio Planning Conference for having been at the first meeting 42 years ago. Mr. Shaw is the author of a monograph on the history of the Cleveland Mall—considered the best authority on the subject.

◆

William Penn Mott, Jr., a Past President of the American Institute of Park Excutives has been appointed manager of the East Bay Regional Park District which embraces nearly 18,000 acres of essentially undeveloped land atop the coastal range immediately behind Oakland and the neighboring East Bay communities.

◆

Geoffrey Platt, architect, will head New York City's Landmarks Preservation Commission set up in April. Last Feb. 8 the N. Y. Board of Estimate appropriated $50,000 to establish the Commission. The Commission will designate for preservation buildings, structures, monuments and works of historic or esthetic importance, recommend appropriate action on preservation and prepare for the Mayor a detailed legislative program for the effective protection of those portions of designated landmarks that fall within public view. Mr. Platt will serve a three-year term.

◆

Correction. Paul M. Dunn was listed as the new President of the American Forestry Association in our last issue. This was in error— Mr. Dunn was elected President of the Society of American Foresters, the professional forestry organization. Mr. Dunn is a Director of the American Forestry Association.

◆

Samuel H. Kauffmann, president of The Evening Star Newspaper Company of Washington, D. C., today was elected a director of ACTION at its annual meeting in Detroit.

ACTION, the National Council for Good Cities, was launched in 1954 as the American Council to Improve Our Neighborhoods.

◆

August Hecksher, Director of the Twentieth Century Fund, has been appointed to the specially created post of Special White House Consultant on the Arts. Mr. Hecksher will coordinate cultural affairs for the President.

5

Zoning Round Table

Conducted by FLAVEL SHURTLEFF, Marshfield Hills, Mass.

Tax Relief Planning

Communities of all sizes and kinds, especially those in the commuting area of the central city are struggling with the mounting burden of taxation on the home. Education must go on, and at over $3.50 per pupil for this greatest single item in the cost of running the town, the total bill is at an all time high in many places. Where the bill is paid almost entirely by taxes on residential real estate the family is levied a tax on the home twice and often three times as high as in 1950. Widening the tax base is sound financial planning, but how?

The movement of industry out of the central city is apparently going along with the spreading outward of population, and this may be a part of the answer to rising taxes. A study made by the Civil and Sanitary Engineering Department of Mass. Institute of Technology in 1958 of the industrial development of Route 128 and its effect on regional economy has much significant data. Route 128 is a limited access circumferential highway running from south of Boston to Rockport on the north shore at varying distances from Boston but never nearer than eight or ten miles from the business center.

At the end of 1957, ninety-six industrial plants employing 17,000 and representing an investment of 85 million dollars were located at new sites on Route 128. Of the sites vacated by relocated industries, 64 percent were being used, 32 per-

cent were vacant and 4 percent had been taken for new highway construction. The net gain to the region in invested dollars was 81 million, and in employees was 11,700. The fact that 55 percent of the total investment in new sites was interested only in Route 128 or in other suburban locations was significant evidence that there was a definite trend to industrial decentralization. The five most highly rated factors in plant location were given by the industries in the following order of importance:

(1) the need for more land for expansion;
(2) accessibility for commercial purposes;
(3) attractiveness of the site;
(4) the labor market;
(5) accessibility for employees.

In two towns almost exclusively residential up to 1950 the coming of industry was examined with more particularity. Both towns had nearly doubled in population between 1945 and 1957, and the great expansion in municipal services, especially in sewer extension and school building had brought bond issues and a greatly increased tax rate. In Lexington during this period the cost per capita for municipal services had increased from $39 to $142; in Needham from $48 to $127.

Needham developed an industrial center at an abandoned gravel pit which by 1957 had attracted an investment of 17 millions and a new wage force of 2200. New tax revenue from this source amounted

6

to $315,000 and the cost to the town for service to the industries was only $25,000. The area which was but 1.2 percent of the entire area of the town paid 10 percent of the taxes. The savings to an average home owner in taxes each year was estimated to be $45.

Lexington had no industry in 1957 but in 1958 an amendment to the zoning by-law permitted an office building and research center estimated to cost 12 millions. The assessed valuation of the site moved up from $113,000 to $5,729,300. This will yield $420,000 in tax revenue some of which in the first years must go into sewer extension.

The picture is probably not as bright as the figures show. In both towns the sites might have been developed for residence, but more evidence of their fitness for residence use would be needed to make a comparison of any value. The industrial use was a fact—the residential use a speculation.

The other factor which may throw doubt on the complete validity of the figures is residential migration. Whether there will be a considerable movement of workers to the towns where they are employed, and whether their housing and schooling will offset any gains in tax revenue from industries are vital questions which have not been answered by the study. It may be too soon to attempt a reliable answer. In 1957 25 percent of the workers lived in Boston, 55 percent in an intermediate zone within four or five miles of Route 128; 20 percent in an outlying zone. Of the workers formerly employed at Boston locations 37 percent still lived in Boston, but of the new employees 67 percent lived in the intermediate zone. There is reason for the conclusion that almost as many families of workers have moved out of the town of employment as have moved in. If this is true and remains so, the impact of this factor need not be considered.

One definite and outstanding conclusion from the Route 128 study is the importance of a most careful analysis of land use to determine not only the fitness of an area for an industrial location, but its fitness for other revenue yielding uses. Obviously the towns will profit most which have land of presently low assessed value attractive to industry and unattractive for any other use.

Donald B. Alexander Becomes APCA Executive Director

On April 30, Harland Bartholomew, Acting President of the American Planning and Civic Association, announced the appointment of Donald Briggs Alexander as Executive Director of the Association. Mr. Alexander assumed office on May 1.

Mr. Alexander has a broad background in landscape architecture, park planning and fiscal work. He is a graduate of the University of Massachusetts, Amherst, Mass. and holds the degree of BS in Landscape Architecture and Engineering. He worked under Conrad L. Wirth through the CCC program, first in Mr. Wirth's immediate office and later as Regional Officer in the Springfield, Massachusetts office. He was later Assistant Regional Director of Region 2, NPS, Omaha, Nebraska. Subsequently, he served as Director of the Connecticut State Park and Forest Commission.

His most recent experience in government service has been in the fiscal field. He was Chief of the Budget Division of the Veterans Administration, Branch 4 at Richmond from 1946–50; Budget and Fiscal Officer for the Executive for Reserve and ROTC affairs, U. S. Army, stationed at the Pentagon Building, 1950–51; and for the past ten years Special Assistant to the Comptroller at one of the confidential agencies in Washington, D. C.

As Administrative Director of the Connecticut State Park and Forest Commission, he coordinated the Commission's programs and

interests and assisted in the reorganization of the Department. His first professional connection after graduation was with the Akron Metropolitan Park District, where he was in charge of land surveys and mapping which resulted in the acquisition of about 3,000 acres comprising six major Metropolitan Park Areas. For the City Planning Commission of Akron, he performed property record research and prepared a complete set of maps of all city-owned property. He was also assigned to the Board of Zoning Appeals in the enforcement of the City Zoning Ordinance.

Upon assuming his position May 1, Mr. Alexander said: "To come back into this field of endeavor at this particular time is most gratifying. It seems to me that the opportunities for advancing the cause of planning, parks, open space and outdoor recreation are perhaps greater now than at any time in the past thirty years."

Mr. Alexander has been a member of the American Society of Landscape Architects. He is a native of Massachusetts and makes his home in Alexandria, Va.

DORA A. PADGETT RETIRES

On the same day, April 30, Mr. Bartholomew announced the acceptance of the resignation of Mrs. Dora A. Padgett, who has been serving the Association as Secretary and Editor since 1959, and has been connected with the Association for the past thirty years. She became editor of CIVIC COMMENT in 1931 and in 1935 editor of PLANNING AND CIVIC COMMENT, upon the merger with *City Planning* and *State Recreation*. She served as assistant editor of the *American Planning and Civic Annual*.

Maj. Gen. U. S. Grant 3d, then President of the Association, appointed Mrs. Padgett Secretary early in 1959 to carry on the administrative duties of APCA. The Board of Directors of the National Conference on State Parks appointed her Executive Secretary of the Conference in 1960. She also served as Secretary of the Committee of 100 on the Federal City, the active and influential Committee of which APCA is the parent body.

PAST SECRETARIES

Looking backward over the past years of the Association, it is surprising how few individuals have served as Secretary since 1904, when the Association was first established. During the early days of organization, Charles Mulford Robinson, distinguished writer on civic improvement, served as Secretary for a short period, followed by Clinton Rogers Woodruff when the fledgling organization had headquarters in Philadelphia.

It was Richard B. Watrous, prominent in the public relations field, who took over in 1909 and served until 1917. He was actually the first full-time executive officer. Upon his resignation, Miss Eleanor Marshall, who later became Mrs. Albert Lee Thurman, served for a brief period until the appointment of Miss Harlean James as Executive Secretary in 1921. Miss James served until 1957 when Charles A. Phelan, Jr. became Executive Director and served until his resignation in 1959. Miss James retired at the close of 1958.

Mr. Alexander will carry on as Executive Secretary of the National Conference on State Parks, which maintains its headquarters with APCA. Secretariat service has been performed by APCA for the Conference since 1935.

A NATIONAL APPROACH TO OUTDOOR RECREATION
Continued from page 3

plans also to become a central source of information on work under way in the field of outdoor recreation, and on new ideas and methods that can be applied in planning, organizing, developing, and operating all kinds of outdoor recreation activities.

The job of organizing a new Federal agency is a demanding one. For those of us who are trying to make the Bureau of Outdoor Recreation a going concern, there have been long days—and not a few nights—of planning and discussion.

And there have been moments, too, of frustration and weariness. But the conviction remains that this new Bureau can make a meaningful contribution to a vital cause at a critical moment in our Nation's evolution.

We will need cooperation and assistance, and we intend to give unstintingly of both. In this way, we believe that a balanced nation-wide program for outdoor recreation can be developed to meet the needs of all Americans for many years to come.

The Planning Environment of Postwar West German City Reconstruction

By THOMAS GREENE, Washington, D. C.

EDITOR'S NOTE:—We are pleased to present this article which is adapted from a doctoral dissertation for the Department of Politics at Princeton University by the author who is now connected with the Foreign Service Institute of the Department of State. Last year we published some notes by the same author on Reconstruction of Kiel and Trier.

When the smoke cleared from ruined cities in Europe in 1945, it appeared that reconstruction would take generations. Mines and rubble were everywhere. Houses, roads, railroads, harbor installations, bridges, and utility lines were only a few of the material casualties of the war. By whatever yardstick one uses to measure the results of the raids: the total number of raids, the number of bombs and mines dropped, the number of air raid victims, the number of buildings that were destroyed, and the amount of rubble in the cities at the end of the war, the destruction was incredible.[1] With such widespread destruction, indeed, planning everywhere came to the forefront. Here we shall review some of the imperatives that confronted city planners in West Germany, where cities of every description were flattened.

In the Allied air raids against Germany, more than 1,440,000 bomber sorties and 2,680,000 fighter sorties were flown. Almost 2,700,000 tons of bombs were dropped.[2]

The intensity of the bomb fall was so great that fire-fighting efforts were fruitless. As the many fires broke through the roofs of the buildings, there rose a column of heated air more than 2½ miles high and 1½ miles in diameter . . . In a short time the temperature reached the ignition point for all combustibles and the entire area was ablaze. In such fires complete burn-out occurred; that is, no trace of combustible materials remained and only after 2 days were the areas cool enough to approach.[3]

Particularly severely damaged in the air attacks between 1942 and 1945, German cities suffered as well under artillery bombardment in 1945. In Berlin and in many cities, furthermore, house-to-house fighting increased the amount of destruction. No one in Germany in 1945 would have imagined that the cities would rebuild as rapidly as they have.

Amid such extensive destruction, in what measure were city planners able to change the layouts of the cities? Was it possible to superimpose a radically different new map upon the old? Amid the rubble of 1945 and in the lean years immediately following the capitulation the relative value of what little had survived the destruction was so inordinately large in comparison with total wealth available to the municipality that planners found that no clean sweep was possible. Some cities, such as Cologne where perhaps 90 percent of the old city was destroyed, still had an enormous underground investment such as sewage, gas, and water lines. The value of these survivors of the blitz, as Randzio demonstrates,[4] was many times crucial in the planner's de-

10

cision to retain old street lines. Thus did the past evidence itself, even where all buildings had to be rebuilt from the ground up.

Consideration of the replanning of West German cities cannot be limited to building that is, strictly speaking, REconstruction. In the welter of activity in Germany since the war it is not always easy to separate reconstruction from new construction, or to draw a sharp line between reconstruction and the essential rubble clearance which preceded it. Furthermore, changes in the functions of cities have resulted in the construction of buildings that are not replacements of prewar structures. Such are the new quarters for the *Land* governments in Kiel and Hanover, made state capitals after the war. Yet we cannot separate such buildings from general reconstruction, since allocation of space and resources to them has meant not allocating them to other projects.

In postwar German city planning, it is necessary to distinguish between environmental factors relating to policy decisions, and the impact of the environmental factors on the operational results of these decisions.

> With respect to policy-making and the content of policy decisions, what matters is how the policy-maker imagines the milieu to be, not how it actually is. With respect to the operational results of decisions, what matters is how things are, not how the policy-maker imagines them to be.[5]

In the individual city it is the milieu of the planner as he perceives it that is most important. With respect to the results of decisions,

however, what matters is how things are. On this level we shall now review the imperatives—political, legal, psychological, demographic, and economic—which confronted all city planners in West Germany in the years immediately after World War II.

Perhaps the most important political imperative to planning was the fact that no German state existed in the years 1945–49, when far-reaching decisions important to planning might have been taken. The German state disappeared in 1945. The Allied zones of occupation, originally intended to be mere administrative districts for an all-German government, took on governmental functions themselves. Provisional measures of the military commanders took on an air of permanence. City planning was not a field in which the occupying powers were particularly interested, and during these years no all-German reconstruction law was enacted. In 1948–50, when the economy was beginning to revive and when reconstruction materials became available, precious time had to be spent formulating laws which might have been enacted beforehand. In this atmosphere, it was all too easy for people to think that reconstruction laws were missing.

During the Nazi era property in Germany could be expropriated at will. The owners were not compensated and in some cases even were imprisoned. As a result of such excesses, planners in West Germany leaned over backwards not to take away private property after the war. Indeed, everywhere in West Germany this reaction to Nazi ex-

11

cesses was evident. Provisions such as eminent domain and forced sale were not used to the extent that they were in other West European countries. Parcels of land were extremely small in the center of most German cities; sometimes the heirs were not to be found. There were cases where property settlements involving mergers could not be reached because the owner of 1/2048th of a parcel was unwilling to relinquish his share. Each parcel of land represented a bundle of property rights that the planner had to disentangle before he could redesign his city. It is indeed surprising that so much was accomplished in the way of property consolidations to facilitate reconstruction.

The partition of Germany and the separation of the east zone politically and economically from the west has confronted city planners with imperatives on every side. Refugees have poured west. Cities such as Lübeck and Braunschweig are so near the Iron Curtain that firms have hesitated to locate in them,[6] whereas Hanover has become the seat of many industries that formerly were in East Germany. Since 1949 there has been virtually no commerce across the border between East Germany and West Germany except at a few designated crossing points. Thus has the line from Travemünde on the Baltic to the Czechoslovak border become one of the tightest frontiers in the world. The entire West German situation has been affected by this split.

What has been the legal framework of planning in the Federal Republic? On all sides people have claimed that reconstruction laws were in confusing disarray, and that had there been a common national reconstruction law, planning and redesigning urban layout would have been far easier.[7] Laws relating to reconstruction can be divided into four categories: (1) *Land* laws from before 1933, (2) *Reich* laws from the years 1933–45 that are still valid in the Federal Republic; (3) *Land* laws passed since World War II, (4) Federal laws since 1949. All of the West German *Länder* except Bavaria and Bremen have passed reconstruction laws. These laws, complaints notwithstanding, contained more provisions than the city planner could use, if he took existing political and economic limitations into account. Even though the laws concerning reconstruction were somewhat scattered, they were there for the energetic planner to use. True, there were uncertainties as to what statutes should be enforced. The fact remains that all too often complaints about existing laws were a convenient excuse for not taking action that might have been politically unpopular. "It can be said without exaggeration that the paralysis caused by claims that legal provisions were insufficient actually hurt reconstruction more than did the missing links in the laws."[8] Those laws that are needed for general planning can be learned relatively quickly, even though they are scattered in many collections of legal documents. Too often planners perceived the legal situation as making planning impossible because that was the easiest course of action. Some of the most successful reconstruction projects, including the Kreuzkirche project in Hanover, were done without the help of *Land* reconstruction laws.[9]

One heritage of dictatorship that was felt everywhere was widespread indifference toward planning and other governmental activities. This was almost to be expected after an era in which government pervaded all spheres of life as was the case from 1933 to 1945 in Germany. The need for self-preservation, furthermore, in the lean years after the war, was so pressing that immediate material interests were paramount. Small wonder that planners often found it hard to get the public interested in their reconstruction plans.

An essential factor in the present state of the German economy and hence in reconstruction planning has been the presence of a large number of refugees. Germans were forced out of Czechoslovakia (2.4 million), Poland (540,000), other satellite countries, and Silesia (2.7 million), East Prussia (1.4 million), Pomerania (1.2 million), and Brandenburg (130,000), in 1945 and 1946, "with a mercilessness surpassed only by the previous brutalities perpetrated upon many of these countries by the Nazis."[10] This was not the end of refugees, for people from the Russian zone of Germany, now called the German Democratic Republic, have entered West Germany in a continuous stream, averaging a quarter of a million per year since 1952. All these refugees have contributed to the volume of the labor force. They have evinced a willingness to work and a spirit of enterprise that can almost be singled out as the key to West German recovery. The refugees had lost everything, and millions of them worked at low wages and in trying conditions to regain their status and the standard of living of the prewar era. By their drive, in many instances the refugees impelled the natives of a given area to work harder too. The effect of all this on the overall picture of the West German economy should not be underestimated, for the amazing recovery of West Germany no doubt came sooner than would have been the case without refugees.

In June 1948 the currency reform took place in the three western zones of occupation in Germany. The money supply was cut in order to remove the existing disproportion between money and goods. All currency and bank deposits owned by individuals and firms had to be registered; they were converted to the new *Deutsche Mark* at the ratio of ten to one. Likewise all debts were devalued at the same ratio.

On June 21, 1948, goods reappeared in the stores, money resumed its normal function, black and gray markets reverted to a minor role, foraging trips to the country ceased, labor productivity increased, and output took off on its great upward surge. The spirit of the country changed overnight.[11]

This was, it need hardly be underlined, a necessary precondition of urban reconstruction.

The economic atmosphere created by the "Social Market Economy"[12] of Minister of Economics Ludwig Erhard has been of great importance to city planners in West Germany. The economic recovery, helped by German conscientiousness, foreign

13

aid, the Korea boom, and many other factors, have presented city planners with unexpected good fortune. The events of the postwar years culminated in the east-west split, with each side trying to woo its portion of Germany. The flow of Marshall Plan aid was one result of the east-west split; an estimated 3.58 billion dollars was poured into Germany from the United States between the end of the war and 1955.[13] West Germany took advantage of the post-Korea boom with prompt delivery dates and good, reasonably priced equipment on the world market. The increased output of industry improved the immediate environment of the planners at home; it increased Germany's balance of payments position remarkably. Good fortune and good management has naturally enough had repercussions on the cities—on their ability to build more and better buildings, and on their general financial situation. Counterpart funds, furthermore, added considerably to domestic investment. Reconstruction of West German cities can only be understood as part of the general revival of the West German economy.

Having reviewed some of the political, legal, psychological, demographic, and economic imperatives of West German city planning, we should mention a number of permissive assumptions found on the level of individual cities. These assumptions were often explicitly taken into account by planners. One such assumption is zoning: many German cities mix shops, housing, and light industry to an extent unknown in the United States or Great Britain. Furthermore, business firms prefer to locate in their own building rather than to rent space from someone else. The result is often isolated reconstruction, in the desire of firms to have the security in land and buildings in case of another runaway inflation. In matters of transportation, German planners almost without exception underestimated the boom in vehicular traffic, with the result that there is hardly a city in West Germany which has adequate space for parking or even for circulation.

In some cities planners in West Germany have considered planning the preserve of architects and experts. Perhaps planners have even overestimated their own importance. Yet because of the aura of their own position and because of the relatively low level of popular participation in matters of community concern, the West German planner has been given a wider latitude for work than was the case in many countries. In this atmosphere, while the imperatives which we have discussed are felt on every turn, the possibilities of redesigning individual cities left to the individual planner are nevertheless enormous. Thus, in the wake of extensive destruction, if there was local leadership in planning with energy and vision, outstanding city planning concepts could be executed even in the face of great legal, economic, and organizational difficulties.

1. See Leo Grebler, *Europe's Reborn Cities* (Washington: Urban Land Institute, 1956).
2. United States Strategic Bombing Survey, *Over-all Report (European War)* (Washington: U. S. Government Printing Office, 1945), p 1.
3. *Ibid.*, p. 93.

4. Ernst Randzio, *Unterirdischer Städtebau* (Bremen-Horn: Walter Dorn Verlag, 1951).
5. Harold Sprout & Margaret Sprout, "Environmental Factors in the Study of International Politics," *Conflict Resolution* I (1957), pp. 327–28.
6. See Leo Grebler, *Op. cit.*
7. Josef Wolff, *Zeitfragen des Städtebaues* (Munich: Verlag Georg D. W. Callwey, 1955), p. 71.
8. *Ibid.*, p. 82.

9. See Ernest Thomas Greene, "Politics and Geography in Postwar German City Planning," (unpublished dissertation. Princeton University, 1958), Ch. I, Part 8.
10. Henry C. Wallich, *Mainsprings of the German Revival* (New Haven: Yale University Press, 1955), pp. 272–73.
11. *Ibid.*, p. 71.
12. *Soziale Marktwirtschaft.*
13. Henry C. Wallich, *Op. cit.*, p. 273.

Second Annual Scenic Highway Contest

With its May 20 issue, *Parade* will launch its second annual Scenic Highway Contest. The contest commends the highway which best advances the principles of beauty and good design as well as safety and efficiency. Highway agencies throughout the country are expected to participate.

Entries will be screened under the auspices of *Parade* and in early September the judges will get together in Washington to review photographs and entry material. The panel will select one winner and four honorable mentions. Winners will be announced about October 15. Officials of several national groups will serve as judges. The American Planning and Civic Association is represented by Jack Wood, substituting for Harland Bartholomew, Acting President.

New Members
American Planning and Civic Association
April and May, 1962

California
Sacramento State College

District of Columbia
Senator Robert Hale
Soil Conservation Service
U. S. Dept. of Agriculture

Michigan
Richard L. Ross, Detroit

New Jersey
Isadore Candeub, Newark

New York
Howard Bentley, New York

Pennsylvania
Graduate School of Public and International Affairs, University of Pittsburgh

South Dakota
Harold Gray, Watertown

Texas
City Planning Department, Ft. Worth

Washington
John R. Merrill, Vancouver

Commentaries

Selections from Speeches, 1900–1959 of Murray Seasongood, former Mayor of Cincinnati, and long a member of the American Planning and Civic Association, have been assembled by his wife Agnes Seasongood. Knopf is the publisher of the volume.

The first oration was a valedictory to Mr. Seasongood's Harvard class of 1900. In reviewing the book for *Public Administration Review* (Winter 1962, p. 46) H. Eliot Kaplan says that as valedictorian of his class, Mr. Seasongood showed great maturity of intellect. "An outstanding lawyer by profession, Mr. Seasongood has been a true fighter for public righteousness and is still a tower of strength to all worthy public causes," writes Mr. Kaplan. In conclusion he states: "This book is an enjoyable adventure through the trials of a civic 'reformer' and the enjoyments of an inveterate optimist. One closes the volume with an urge to don his armor, unsheath the sword of civic virtue and go forth to help slay the dragon of political evil."

એન્જ

Frank Mann Stewart, author of "A Century of Municipal Reform: The History of the National Municipal League," died unexpectedly on October 17, 1961, four months after he retired as professor of political science at the University of California, Los Angeles.

એન્જ

A Committee to Save the Walt Whitman Building has been formed to restore as a Memorial Museum the historic Brooklyn building where Whitman helped handset and print the first edition of Leaves of Grass in 1855. New York's Housing and Redevelopment Board, in charge of the planning for an urban renewal area called Cadman Plaza, has recommended the demolition of the building on the opinion that it lacks architectural merit. The Committee believes that this would be unnecessary destruction of a highly important historic landmark site. The Committee has issued a Report on the Walt Whitman Building, 98 Cranberry Street, Brooklyn 1, N. Y. under date of March 19, 1962.

એન્જ

The final issue of *Yosemite* Vol. XXXX, No. 6 which has served for nearly 40 years the park and the National Park Service interpretative program, has been published. *Yosemite* has been discontinued as a periodical. A new era will begin in 1962. The Yosemite Naturalg History Association, publisher, will begin a series of publications, "Occasional Papers of the Yosemite Museum." No production schedule will be attempted but it is hoped that at least one occasional paper will be issued each year by the Yosemite Museum. The final issue contains a Bibliography of Yosemite Nature Notes and Yosemite. The announcement of the demise of the publications is one of sadness. It is stated to be a victim of rising costs, diminishing manpower and the changing times.

એન્જ

The United States Department of Agriculture's Centennial Year is saluting American agriculture. The Centennial begins officially on May 15 with a World Food Forum in Washington, D. C. Centennial activities will continue throughout the rest of 1962 and a booklet has been issued with useful material to publicize the 100th anniversary of the establishment of the Department of Agriculture.

એન્જ

Specialists on industrial parks joined 100 Florida leaders in April, sponsored by Rollins College Center to meet at the Central Florida Industrial Park, an 1100-acre development 8 miles south of Orlando. Four other sessions on industrial parks, interregional parks and regional planning councils developed pursuant to Florida statutes were held at Winter Park. Prof. J. Marshall Miller of the School of Architecture, Columbia University, was a discussant. He was the leading proponent of Motor City, a community developed in Ohio. Paul C. Watt, now a member of the Harland Bartholomew Associates office in Washington, discussed the plan for Southeast Florida. Excellent speakers appeared in addition on parks and the motor park concept.

❧

A contract was awarded in St. Louis in March for construction of the Gateway Arch, a long-planned national memorial on the Mississippi Riverfront to stand as a symbol of the Gateway to the West. The arch, designed by the late Eero Saarinen, will tower 630 feet high and will have an outer coating of stainless steel. It will be built just east of the central business district in a national park, the Jefferson National Expansion Memorial. The concept of a national park here to signify the opening of the West originated among civic leaders in 1935. The Federal Government agreed to the project, but twenty-five years elapsed before Federal funds were made available.

The city is contributing $7,500,000 to the park and the Federal share is $22,500,000. The Terminal Railroad Association of St. Louis contributed $500,000 for relocation of railroad tracks. The park is expected to include a visitors' center, a museum of westward expansion, a Mississippi River overlook and other features. The arch, which has been adopted by St. Louis organizations as a symbol of the city's future, is expected to be completed in 1964.

❧

Shell Oil Company, one of the nation's leading outdoor advertisers, has announced plans to discontinue its billboard advertising program. Abandonment of the company's highway advertising program was described in a recent issue of *Harper's Magazine*.

❧

Water Resource Activities by Western States is a report prepared by a joint committee representing the National Reclamation Association and the Association of Western State Engineers. Hugh A. Shamberger, Director, Department of Conservation and Natural Resources for the State of Nevada, served as chairman of the committee.

This is a unique report—the first of its kind that has ever been presented showing activities of the various Western States in the field of water resources. The report for each State was prepared by the State Engineer or the individual in that State having responsibilities in water resource conservation development and use.

❧

The Proceedings of the Community Renewal Program Roundtable, jointly sponsored by the National Association of Housing and Redevelopment Officials and American Institute of Planners, is intended to be the tool by which a city can put into perspective its total renewal, housing, and long-range revitalization and preservation plans and activities. Urban renewal projects should receive, it is thought, a more balanced analysis and treatment. The meeting held last May on the CRP contributed a great deal to a better understanding of the need for and the use of the CRP as a community-wide approach to urban renewal.

Copies are available from the Washington Offices of NAHRO and AIP for the price of $1.00.

❧

Prince Philip, Duke of Edinburgh, was the guest of honor and speaker at a dinner of the World Wildlife Fund at the Waldorf-Astoria Hotel in New York City on June 7. Prince Philip, President of the British National Appeal of the World Wildlife Fund, was joined by *Prince Bernhard of The Netherlands,* president of the World Wildlife Fund.

The American, British and Swiss groups organized as World Wildlife Funds are separate entities with independent Boards, but interested in a common objective to "Save the World's Wildlife."

White House Conference on Conservation
May 24-25

President Kennedy and Dr. Walter W. Heller, Chairman of the Council of Economic Advisers, were the principal speakers at the White House Conference on Conservation in Washington, D. C. on May 24-25.

Dr. Heller sounded the Conference keynote on May 24 and President Kennedy's address climaxed the Conference on Friday, May 25. The President stressed the application of science as the great opportunity in the Sixties. He said that the Nation which develops an economical method of converting salt water to fresh water could do more for mankind than the Nation that is first in space. Conservation, he thought, ties in with the United States policies abroad and its foreign aid. It is important to emphasize to the developing Nations the advantages of dams and other uses of natural resources. He said also that he did not want the entire Atlantic Coast from Boston to Florida to become one vast metropolitan area without some green around it.

The conference, held in the State Department Auditorium, brought together for the first time conservation spokesmen from throughout the country and Federal, State, and Congressional conservation authorities for a discussion of "Conservation for the Sixties."

The program included four panel sessions, two featuring Federal cabinet officers, one composed of the members of Congress and one of State Governors. A question and answer period was part of each panel session.

Panel speakers from the Federal agencies, each discussing aims and objectives of their agencies in "Conservation for the Sixties," were Secretary of the Interior Stewart L. Udall, Secretary of Agriculture Orville L. Freeman, and Robert C. Weaver, Administrator of the Housing and Home Finance Agency, James M. Quigley, Assistant Secretary of Health, Education and Welfare, and Elvis J. Stahr, Secretary of the Army, followed with a panel discussion. Moderator of the morning session was Laurance S. Rockefeller, Chairman of the Outdoor Recreational Resources Review Commission. Gilbert F. White, Chairman of the Department of Geography at the University of Chicago, was the afternoon moderator.

Following the conclusion of the executive department panels, Senator Clinton P. Anderson of New Mexico, Chairman of the Senate Interior and Insular Affairs Committee, took over as moderator of the panel on "Conservation and the Congress." Participating with him were Senator Lee Metcalf of Montana and Representatives Wayne N. Aspinall of Colorado and John P. Saylor of Pennsylvania. Senator Metcalf is a member of Interior and Insular Affairs Committee. Mr. Aspinall is Chairman of the House Interior and Insular Affairs Committee and Mr. Saylor is ranking minority member of the same committee.

18

Friday morning, May 25, prior to the President's address, was devoted to a panel of State Governors composed of Governors Clyde of Utah, McNichols of Colorado, Ellington of Tennessee and Hughes of New Jersey, with Dr. Ira N. Gabrielson, President of the Wildlife

Management Institute as moderator.

Chester Bowles, Special Representative and Advisor to the President on African, Asian, and Latin American Affairs, was the speaker at a noon luncheon on Thursday, May 24, in the Benjamin Franklin Room of the Department of State.

National Capital Notes

★ ★ ★

The April issue of *Holiday* magazine is devoted entirely to Washington, The Nation's Capital, and some of the finest articles on the city have been contributed by an impressive array of today's writers and authors. Those who have written for this issue are: Aubrey Menen, who describes the impact of the city on the visiting foreigner; Carlton Ogburn, Jr., who tells of the birth and growth of this world capital; and many others. The issue is lavishly illustrated with full-color photographs of Washington views and personalities.

★ ★ ★

Walter C. Louchheim has been reappointed a member of the National Capital Planning Commission.

Mr. Louchheim, appointed last year to fill a vacancy caused by the resignation of William C. Foster, was named to a new 6-year term by President Kennedy. He is chairman of the Commission's urban renewal committee.

A financier and stockbroker, he joined the Securities and Exchange Commission shortly after it was created in 1934 and resigned his post of SEC foreign economic adviser in 1953.

★ ★ ★

The appearance of the Federal City was analyzed by Victor Gruen, one of the country's foremost architects, in an address before the second annual Community Appearance Conference in Washington, D. C. on January 5. Mr. Gruen's speech was reprinted in the Congressional Record of March 1 and a supply of reprints is available. We will gladly send copies upon request. This is an important, though controversial, speech.

★ ★ ★

The National Capital Planning Commission will move next July from its present quarters in the Interior Building to a new privately owned commercial building at 1701 Pennsylvania Ave. N. W., where it will occupy the entire third floor. The Department of the Interior now needs the space occupied by the Commission for the past 30 years. Other small government agencies will move to the same building.

★ ★ ★

The *New York Times* published a strong editorial on April 19 which was entitled, "A Threat to Mount Vernon."

Mount Vernon—George Washington's home, a shrine that attracted over 1,100,000 visitors last year—is in danger. The danger is not from freeways or from other encroachments on the 500-acre tract once farmed. The danger arises from the proposal of the Washington Suburban Sanitary Commission to build a sewage disposal plant on the opposite

Maryland shore of the Potomac River. There are alternate locations for that needed facility. The location which the commission has selected will permanently mar one of the most scenic views in America.

In Washington's day as at present, the river view from Mount Vernon was of fields set in a wilderness background. The scene is restful to the eye; its serenity is part of the beauty of Mount Vernon. Once that view is marred by industrial or municipal projects, Mount Vernon loses an important part of its subtle charm.

Two far-sighted citizens—Representative Frances Bolton of Ohio and Dr. Henry G. Ferguson—have acquired about 500 acres of land opposite Mount Vernon, which they propose to give to the Federal Government if the remaining acreage (about 600 acres) is obtained. An appropriation to acquire this land has recently been disallowed on the House side, due to the opposition of Representative Michael J. Kirwan of Ohio. A Senate measure, which would accept the private grants and appropriate the money for the acquisition is now pending before a Senate committee.*

We urge the Senate to restore the stricken provision. If Mount Vernon is to be ringed with structures such as a sewage disposal plant, it will be a mutilated Mount Vernon. The majestic view from Mount Vernon, as well as the property itself, ought to be a national shrine.

*Note: Subsequent action by the Senate Committee recommends that $937,000 be used by the National Park Service to buy the 586 acres in question.

*   *   *

A proposal to preserve Capitol Hill as a historical park has aroused interest. The bill introduced by Representative Kearns proposed to "establish a Capitol Hill National Historical Park for the protection of its historic character, dignity and environment. The proposal, put before the House in March, would empower Interior Secretary Udall to set aside for preservation any structures within an area bounded by G streets, Northeast and Northwest, by the Anacostia River on the east and by Third street, west of the Capitol.

*   *   *

Fine Arts Commission opposition to the $50-million Watergate Towne development in Foggy Bottom has been withdrawn after minor concessions by the developer.

Under an agreement between three architect members of the Commission and representatives of Societa Generale Immobiliare, the Italian sponsor, the buildings will be about 6 percent smaller than originally proposed and building heights will be "modulated."

A start of construction of the apartment, hotel and office building development early next year was promised after last minute agreement revived the almost-abandoned project that will overlook the Potomac River.

The project will occupy a site bounded by New Hampshire avenue, Virginia avenue, Potomac Parkway, and F street.

In view of the massive and repeated opposition of the Commission to the design over a long period of time, the agreement after discussion came as a surprise.

Architects Explore Ugliness

The First Conference on Aesthetic Responsibility was sponsored by the Design Committee of the New York Chapter, American Institute of Architects, with the cooperation of the national Board of Directors of the AIA. The conference was held at the Plaza Hotel, New York City on April 3.

The sponsoring group was designated a Pilot Committee at the 1961 AIA convention, its principal purpose to see what could be done to arouse interest in good architectural design. The one-day conference was the Committee's initial answer to the problem. It featured three panels of six speakers discussing the questions "What Are Our Aesthetic Values?", "What Are the Aesthetic Responsibilities of Government, Business and Institutions?" and "Who is Responsible for Ugliness?"

August Heckscher, Special Consultant to the President on the Arts, was the luncheon speaker.

In his first major address since his appointment by President Kennedy nearly a month ago, Mr. Heckscher told an architectural conference he sees ahead the possibility of "an age of cultural achievement such as our country has never known before.

"The next decade will be a period of vast building and of great physical transformations of the American scene," he said.

"New highways will criss-cross the country, cities will be torn down and rebuilt. The countryside will be made over into new forms of urban and suburban communities."

But he warned that future changes must be well designed if they are to contribute towards national advancement.

"A civilization begins to manifest itself when men and women have begun to take thought about what they construct, and why, and to what end," he said.

The purpose of the sessions was to set up committees "to fight manmade ugliness" in cities throughout the country.

Such "committees on aesthetic responsibility" will include business and professional men, architects, artists and others and will seek to encourage widespread interest in design, planning and other matters affecting the appearance of cities and the countryside.

Special targets will be highway construction, city planning, building design and such details as signs, street lights, automobile graveyards and other examples of "urban ugliness."

Over five hundred participants and eighteen distinguished panelists from almost as many different fields attacked the problem.

Chairman Richard W. Snibbe closed the conference with the presentation of a Plan for Action—a plan which can serve as a guide to the establishment of local level Design Committees throughout the country.

Watch Service Report

Key Outdoor Recreation Bills

S. 3117 (Anderson and others) introduced April 4, 1962. To promote the coordination and development of effective Federal and State programs relating to outdoor recreation, and to provide financial assistance to the States for outdoor recreation planning. Referred to the Committee on Interior and Insular Affairs. A companion bill H. R. 11165 was introduced in the House on April 9, with Aspinall and others sponsoring the same bills with different numbers. These bills authorize $50 million for grants to States for planning comprehensive outdoor recreation programs and vest the new Bureau of Outdoor Recreation with needed authorities for undertaking research coordination, planning and for providing technical and other assistance to the States. The $50 million would be made available to the States over a five-year period with allocations based mostly on populations and with a diminishing level of federal financial assistance through the life of the program. Each State would be required to designate an agency to administer its planning program.

S. 3118 (Anderson and others) introduced April 4, 1962. To provide for the establishment of a land conservation fund. Referred to the Committee on Interior and Insular Affairs. The House companion bill is H. R. 11172 (Aspinall), was introduced April 9. These bills seek to authorize a land conservation fund to buy land within the exterior boundaries of federal parks, forests, recreation areas and for certain fish and wildlife purposes, including lands around Federal reservoir projects. Funds would be derived from user charges, levied by the President on all recreation areas on Federal lands, proceeds from the sale of non-military surplus lands, re-allocation of the 2-cents-a-gallon tax on gasoline and motor fuels used in boats, now refundable, and an annual tax on recreation boats longer than 144 feet. The President has recommended that Congress provide an advance of $500 million to get the program going. Public hearings on these two important proposals have been held by the House and Senate Committees during the current session.

National Parks

S. 4, establishing the Padre Island National Seashore on 88 miles of Shoreline in Texas received a favorable report by the Senate Committee on Interior and Insular Affairs on March 6 (Senate Report 1226). Passed Senate April 10. Referred to House Committee. House bills provide for smaller area.

H. R. 10884 (Addonizio)—S. 2916 (Bible) introduced March 1. Designates the Edison Home National Historic Site and the Edison Laboratory National Monument, together with adjacent parcels donated to the U. S., as the Edison National Historic Site. Referred to the Senate Committee on Interior and Insular Affairs.

S. J. Res. 171 provides for the establishment of the former dwelling house of Alexander Hamilton as a national monument. This house, Hamilton Grange, on 141st Street, New York, is the only home ever owned by Hamilton and the house where he spent the night before his fatal duel with Aaron Burr. Moved from its original site in 1889, it is now scheduled to be moved again to the campus of College of the City of New York, the cost estimated at $460,000. Reported favorably without amendment on March 16 by the Senate Committee on Interior and Insular affairs. Passed Senate March 28 and referred to House. H. J. Res. 449 House Resolution passed April 16. Cleared for the President. Public Law 87-438.

S. 476, creating the Point Reyes National Seashore in California, was reported favorably April 19 by the House Committee on Interior and Insular Affairs, with only minor changes from the version which passed the Senate last year.

S. 2387, providing for the establishment of the Canyonlands National Park in Utah, was the subject of hearings by the Public Lands Sub-Committee of the Senate Committee on Interior and Insular Affairs March 29-30. Controversy on the bill centers upon provisions which permit the continuation of grazing, mining and wildlife management. Field hearings were held in April in Utah.

S. 3007 (Moss) introduced March 16. Provides that the Utah Department of Fish and Game and the National Park Service shall devise a program to insure the permanent conservation of the wildlife population within that portion of the Dinosaur National

Monument situated in the State of Utah. Referred to the Senate Committee on Interior and Insular affairs.

H. R. 10682 to create a pilot Youth Conservation Corps, received a favorable report by the House Committee on Education and Labor on March 29, and is similar to S. 404 which was reported favorably to the Senate last fall and is still pending. The Senate bill would authorize a build-up to a peak enrollment of 150,000 in the Corps, and costs would be greater than authorized in H. R. 10682.

S. J. Res. 183 (Hartke) introduced May 4. Joint Resolution to establish a Commission to formulate plans for memorials to past Presidents of the United States. Referred to the Committee on Rules and Administration.

H. R. 8484 to authorize establishment of the Theodore Roosevelt Birthplace and Sagamore Hill National Historic Sites, N. Y. Passed by House on April 2.

Federal City

S. 3180 (McCarthy)—H. R. 11241 (Kearns) introduced April 11. To direct the National Capital Planning Commission to develop forthwith a plan for the historic Capitol Hill area and vicinity in the District of Columbia which will protect the U. S. Capitol and the surrounding buildings of the Federal Government. Referred to the Committee on Public Works.

Public Works

H.R. 10113, the Public Works Coordination and Acceleration Bill and H. R. 10318, the Standby Capital Improvements Bill, both introduced by Congressman Blatnik were subject to hearings on March 26. The $2 billion emergency program would permit a $750 million increase in district Federal expenditures for projects previously authorized including resource, conservation and other Federal public works; and would authorize $750 million matching grants to State and local governments for public improvement programs; and would authorize a $250 million loan program to State and local governments otherwise unable to finance their share of the costs of projects for which Federal grants are authorized; and provide an additional $250 million to be allocated to any of these three programs as circumstances warrant. All of the projects would have to meet essential public needs and be completed within 12 months.

Open Space and Urban Development

S. 2946 (Williams) introduced March 8. To increase by $50 million the open-space grant authorization under Title VII of the Housing Act of 1961. This increase is in accord with the President's budget request for the program for this year. Title VII called for an open-space program providing $50 million in grants to share 20 and in some cases 30 percent of the cost of acquiring and preserving open-space land in and around urban areas by State and local governments.

General Grant Reminisces

The National Capital: Reminiscences of Sixty-Five Years

Maj. Gen. U. S. Grant 3d, beloved and highly revered Past President of the American Planning and Civic Association, has written an account for the current proceedings of the Columbia Historical Society of Washington, D. C., of memories of his career and experiences in the National Capital. These reminiscences were first given at the 65th Anniversary Dinner of the Society. It so happened that General Grant's first visit to Washington coincided with the founding of the Society.

The personal reminiscences are of great interest but General Grant's activities in connection with the official development of the National Capital are of exceptional value and importance. He was ordered to Washington in June 1925 and assigned to the final design and construction of the Arlington Memorial Bridge. The following year he succeeded Colonel Sherrill as Director of Public Buildings and Parks. He took part in the Public Buildings Commission's preparation and administration of the 1926 Public Buildings project, the principal features of which were the Federal Triangle and Constitution and Independence Avenues.

General Grant's reference to the Committee of 100 on the Federal City is most interesting:

The ever increasing danger from the automobile traffic, which stopped safe use of the streets for play, and the failure of the authorities to acquire land for parks, as recommended by the McMillan Commission, together with the enhanced population that was rapidly filling vacant lots and land with buildings, led to a thorough survey by the Committee of 100 on the Federal City, under the leadership of Frederic A. Delano in 1924. This had the enthusiastic backing by inhabitants of the District and many members of Congress and resulted in the establishment of the National Capital Park Commission in the same year with authority to secure appropriations to buy land "to prevent pollution of Rock Creek and the Potomac and Anacostia Rivers, to preserve forests and natural scenery in and about Washington, and to provide for the systematic and continuous development of the park, parkway and playground systems."

The Commission soon found that it was impossible to perform its mission intelligently and economically without close integration of the purchases made by it in the city street system, the schools and other parts of the city plan. . . . Consequently there were added by Act of April 30, 1926 to the ex-officio members of the Park Commission "four eminent citizens well qualified and experienced in city planning, one of whom shall be a bona fide resident of the District of Columbia" to be appointed by the President. The Commission so enlarged was given the additional mission of revising the city plan and making plans for the environs. Because Washington is the Nation's Capital and of interest to all good Americans, it was possible to secure outstanding professional men from all over the country to fill the four appointive positions . . . The L'Enfant Plan and reports, the McMillan Commission's studies were carefully restudied, as well as the changes in the city which made adjustments of them necessary, and gave the Commission its jump-off line. The Commission's plans and recommendations were presented to the public at a large mass meeting in Constitution Hall. The Commission's proposals were generally received with approval, resulted in the establishment of the Maryland National Capital Park and Planning Commission, and in legislation by Virginia authorizing the appointment of local planning commissions to cooperate with the Federal Commission . . . Finally the Capper-Cramton Act gave legislative sanction to the system of parks, parkways, recreation centers and playgrounds proposed by the Commission.

DONALD BRIGGS ALEXANDER

Newly Appointed Executive Director of the
American Planning and Civic Association
and
Executive Secretary, National Conference on State Parks

25

Forty-Second Annual Meeting
of the National Conference on State Parks

September 30 to October 5, 1962

Headquarters: Illinois Beach Lodge, Zion, Illinois
Host State: Illinois

Illinois Beach State Park, the headquarters of the 1962 National Conference on State Parks, is situated near Waukegan and Zion, in Lake County, Illinois. It contains 1,651.3 acres and its outstanding natural features are dunes and beaches.

The new Lodge, with 106 rooms available for the public, features luxury facilities.

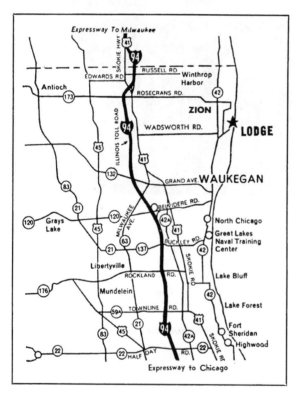

Location of
Illinois Beach
State Park

26

Illinois Beach Lodge, Conference headquarters

The Conference theme for 1962 is State-County Park Relationships. The Program Committee has prepared a tentative program which will feature two days of inspection trips to Illinois State Parks, such as Chain O'Lakes, Starved Rock, White Pines, Cook County Forest Preserve District and Winnebago County Lake.

A boat trip is being arranged at the Great Lakes Naval Training Center. Dinners, with distinguished speakers on park subjects, will be held, Monday, Tuesday and Thursday, when the Honorable Otto Kerner, Governor of Illinois will address Conference delegates.

Roll call of the states, an annual feature of the Conference, will begin on Monday and be concluded Tuesday.

The Program Committee is composed of the following: Chairman—William A. Smith, Superintendent, Division of Parks and Memorials of the Illinois Department of Conservation, David Abbott, V. W. Flickinger, Clinton Johnson, Roman Koenings, U. W. Hella and Gerald O'Connor.

The Exhibits Committee is composed of the following: Chairman— Gerald O'Connor, Arne Kugler, David Abbott and Ed Romilly.

Election of officers and some new members of the Board of Directors will take place at the Members Meeting.

Beach House on the Lake Side

General Grant concludes what he calls his "random reminiscences" with a warning against the effort to tie subsidized hydro-electric power with adequate provision for the water supply of the metropolitan region and build a high dam at Great Falls. He states that Washington is a beautiful city and can still be an example of the best that America has done and can do in city development.

Gratitude must go to General Grant for these additions to the informal history of the National Capital. The outstanding part he played in the development of the city may not be known to all until these reminiscences are read. His great influence is discernable by reading between the lines of the factual statements. One realizes that he was the moving force in most of these Federal operations.

Pittsburgh's Culture Complex

A group of Pittsburgh non-profit institutions have formed a private development corporation to build 1500 acres into "the Nation's first culture complex."

The company, known as Oakland Corporation, has called on the City of Pittsburgh to establish and renew cultural facilities in the community, clean up blighted sections and provide the University of Pittsburgh and other institutions with the room they need to expand.

According to Edward H. Litchfield, chancellor of the University of Pittsburgh, "the project may re-quire an expenditure of $250 million for acquisition of land and construction."

So far, the institutions which have joined in the venture are the University of Pittsburgh, (the corporation's major stockholder), Carnegie Institute of Technology, the Roman Catholic Diocese of Pittsburgh and Mount Mercy College.

The plan will be carried out over a 10-year period and will involve private, city and state agencies.

Recreation Development at Missouri Basin Reservoirs and in Bank Stabilization and Channel Improvement Areas

By JACK D. STRAIN, Chief, Division of State Parks, Nebraska

It has been no secret to those of us in the management end of outdoor recreation in the past few years that these activities have become more and more water-oriented. It comes as no surprise, then, that the recently released report of the Outdoor Recreation Resources Review Commission states in part that "Water is a prime factor in most outdoor recreational activities. The Commission's National Recreation Survey reports that 44 percent of the population prefer water-based recreation activities over any others. Water also enhances recreation on land. Choice camping sites and picnic areas are usually those adjacent to or within sight of a lake or stream, and the touch of variety added by a pond or marsh enriches the pleasures of hiking or nature study."

The observations of each of us, as well as the foregoing excerpt, assume significance when we analyze current outdoor recreational activities and attempt to project future use pressures.

Based on the 1960 Survey, ORRRC reports that the top ten outdoor recreational activities were as follows:

1. Pleasure driving
2. Swimming
3. Pleasure walks
4. Sports and games
5. Sightseeing
6. Picnicking
7. Fishing
8. Bicycling
9. Witnessing outdoor sports events
10. Boating other than canoe or sail

Considering all factors such as increased mobility, income, leisure time, etc., ORRRC considers that by the Year 2000, the top ten will be:

1. Swimming
2. Pleasure driving
3. Sports and games
4. Pleasure walks
5. Sightseeing
6. Picnicking
7. Boating other than canoe or sail
8. Fishing
9. Bicycling
10. Witnessing outdoor sports events

The thing that is particularly significant here is the fact that two water-oriented activities, swimming and boating, are expected to show major gains in popularity with swimming taking over first place from pleasure driving, and boating moving up from 10th to 7th place.

If present trends continue over the next 40 years, we can expect active participant, water-oriented activities to increase at the following rates over existing levels: water-skiing—nearly five times; and boating and swimming three-and-one-half times. During this same time, non-water related activities, such as pleasure driving and picnicking, are expected to increase only about two-and-one-half times.

When we, in Nebraska, and some of the other basin states as well, consider that much of our water development potential in the form of impoundments is poorly located in distance-relationship to populations, we indeed have cause for concern and must, in some cases, look to the river itself for development potential.

In the recreation sense, water has one significant advantage over land: it can be used and reused by a variety of specific interests in a relatively short period of time without re-arrangement of facility and without capital investment.

Thus, in high density situations, and under a time zone management program, the same segment of water can conceivably be utilized by swimmers, boaters, skiers, and fishermen in a 24-hour period in spite of the fact that some of these usages are in severe conflict.

Unfortunately, for users and administrators alike, land generally does not have this same attribute of latitude—a wildlife refuge does not convert well to a week-end organized youth camp situation, and a tennis court is good for very little except playing tennis.

In the average sense, then, we can safely consider that an acre of water will support a higher volume of participant-type recreation than an acre of land, and it logically follows that the nearer these surface acres of water are to population centers, the more valuable they become.

If the points that I have raised in the foregoing are considered only as educated guesses rather than established fact—and I think we must attribute any long-range view at least in part to crystal gazing—we must still conclude that the demand for water-oriented outdoor recreation is going to boom in forthcoming years.

The pertinent question is who is going to provide and develop the necessary water and land surfaces and facilities to meet this demand? Is it to be the federal government—state or local agencies—or private enterprise? None of these, individually, is totally equal to the task. Each must recognize the potentials and opportunities inherent in its area of operation and discharge its full responsibilities if the challenge is to be met.

With respect to meeting water recreation problems, private enterprise can make substantial contributions in the area of facility development. It can do little in the provision of significant additional water-surface acres, necessary access, and public-use lands. Private enterprise has generally been slow to develop the economic potentials of water-based recreation in the Basin and, in many cases, this caution is warranted because of a general lack of public facilities and because of the distance factor. As mobility, leisure and development increase, so also will investments of private capital.

State and local governments manage about 16 percent of the nation's recreation acres, but yield over 50 percent of the total annual visitation. The federal government through its many land agencies manages 84 percent of the recreational acres but accounts for a vastly disproportionate share of the recreational use. Much of the federal land, to quote again from the ORRRC report, is "located where the people are not. One-sixth is in sparsely populated Alaska. Seventy-two percent of the remainder is in the West where only 15 percent of the people live. The Northeast, where one-quarter of the people live, has only four percent of the recreation acreage of the 48 contiguous states."

On the other hand, most of the high density recreational area is managed by state and local governments which is as it should be.

In parallel to the national picture, much of the water recreation potential in the MRB states is not well oriented to populations. Clump and strip population concentrations typify the region and water developments are generally well upstream in areas of relatively sparse population. My own State of Nebraska is a classic example, with not one existing major reservoir within a hundred miles of the center of population.

I am not suggesting that a flood control or irrigation impoundment be located in primary consideration of recreational usages for obvious reasons and because in the ultimate consideration, increased mobility, personal income, and leisure time will tend to overcome the distance factor, particularly with respect to those impoundments that exist, or are planned, on the fringe of day-use capability.

I am proposing that all aspects of recreation be given full considera-tion in the planning and financing of future water projects, and this is an obligation that in spite of a long established need is not being met by the major constructing agencies today.

The areas of deficiency, at present and for some time past, are primarily those concerning lands acquired in public ownership in conjunction with reservoir construction and the level of recreational development at the time the reservoir is completed.

In short, there has not been enough land acquired in recent projects to meet even the recreational needs of the day, far less those of the future; and the development of those facilities necessary to the full enhancement and enjoyment of the recreational opportunities falls far short of reality.

What, then is the answer?

The solution, in my opinion, is one of logical sequence and co-operative effort:

We must all take a firm and realistic look at the outdoor recreation problems that face us today and particularly in the light of the part the MRB states will play in the overall scene in the reasonably predictable future. There are many facets to this task other than those posed by water surface and access needs but the interrelationship is so close that they cannot be logically separated. I know of no better analysis of these matters than the ORRRC Report, and recommend its careful study with an open mind.

Last, but by no means least, each agency concerned must recognize and face up to its responsibilities and execute sound programs toward their fulfillment.

Parks Advisory Board Makes
Recommendations to Interior Department

Following the 46th Meeting of the Advisory Board on National Parks, Historic Sites, Buildings and Monuments held in Washington, D. C., from April 30 to May 3, the Department of the Interior today announced the 11 resolutions adopted by the Board and the names of the new officers who will head the group.

Recommendations sent to Secretary of the Interior Stewart L. Udall included a request that the Secretary take all possible steps to assure that sufficient land is acquired and dedicated to utilize the full recreation potential of the Tocks Island (Penna.-N. J.) Reservoir, "when and if developed," to fill "a vital recreation need in a metropolitan area where 25–30 million people live within a 100-mile radius."

The Board also asked that positive steps be taken to prevent further damage from mining activities to Organ Pipe Cactus National Monument in Arizona.

The Board reaffirmed its belief that a Canyonlands National Park should be established in Utah and amended its previous resolution by recommending that "adverse uses, especially including mining and hunting, should not be permitted in the proposed park."

Other recommendations were that the following areas be authorized and included in the Park System: Poverty Point, Louisiana, and Florissant Fossil Beds, Colorado, as national monuments; and Saint-Gaudens Memorial, New Hampshire, (now owned and administered by the Saint-Gaudens Trustees) and Fort Larned, Kansas, as national historical sites.

It was also recommended that Pecos Pueblo and Mission, New Mexico be accepted as a donation from that State and established "as the Pecos National Monument" and that the "Park System explore with the State of New Mexico the best means of preserving and interpreting the highly significant sites" of the pueblos of Abo and Quarai, which are within existing New Mexico State Monuments.

The Board reiterated its opposition, in principle, to public hunting in National Parks and Monuments and "specifically opposes the provisions of Senate Bill 3007 authorizing such hunting in Dinosaur National Monument", in Colorado and Utah.

The new officers selected by the Board include Harold P. Fabian of Salt Lake City, Utah, as chairman, replacing Frank E. Masland, Jr., of Carlisle, Pa. Mr. Fabian is chairman of the Utah State Park and Recreation Commission and formerly vice chairman of the Advisory Board. The new vice chairman is Dr. Stanley A. Cain, professor and chairman, Department of Conservation, University of Michigan. Dr. Edward B. Danson, Jr., director, Museum of Northern Arizona, Flagstaff, will remain as secretary.

President Kennedy's National Transportation Program

On April 5th, President Kennedy called on Congress to write a basic national transportation policy.

He asked for a program that would emphasize more competition, less Federal subsidization and less regulation of fares and rates on railroads, airlines, trucks and barges.

At the same time, Mr. Kennedy recommended massive Federal aid for developing mass transportation systems in and around cities.

Part II of the Message stated that the President had previously emphasized to the Congress the need for action on the transportation problems resulting from burgeoning growth and the changing urban scene.

He stated that: Higher incomes coupled with the increasing availability of the automobile have enabled more and more American families to seek their own homes in suburban areas. Simultaneously, changes and improvements in freight transportation, made possible by the development of modern highways and the trucking industry, have reduced the dependence of manufacturers on central locations near port facilities or railroad terminals. Many industries have moved to the periphery of urban areas. At the same time the importance of the central city is increasing for trade, financial governmental and cultural activities. One result of these changes in location patterns has been a change in the pattern of urban travel. Added to traditional suburban-to-city movements are large crosstown flows which existing mass transportation systems are often not geared to handle. Also, the increasing use of automobiles to meet the urban transportation needs has resulted in increasing highway congestion and this has greatly impeded mass transportation service. Public mass transportation is geared to older patterns.

To conserve and enhance values in existing urban areas is essential. In less than 20 years we can expect well over half of our expanded population to be living in forty great urban complexes. Many smaller places will also experience phenomenal growth . . . Our national welfare requires the provision of good urban transportation with the properly balanced use of private vehicles and modern mass transport to help shape as well as serve urban growth.

At his request, he said, the problems of urban transportation have been studied by the Housing and Home Finance Administrator and the Secretary of Commerce. Their findings support the need for substantial expansion and important changes in urban mass transportation. . . .

On the basis of this report, he recommended that long-range Federal financial aid and technical assistance be provided to help plan and develop the comprehensive and balanced urban transportation that is so vitally needed.

The President concludes his message by stating that the country cannot afford delay.

The Regional Parks Program in Saskatchewan

By G. G. RATHWELL

The Regional Parks Act was enacted in Saskatchewan in March 1960. The purposes of the Act are threefold:

1. To encourage appreciation and use of natural and recreational resources throughout Saskatchewan.

2. To assist local government agencies in the establishment of regional parks with a view to making some of the natural and recreational resources of Saskatchewan available to every member of the public.

3. To facilitate the establishment of regional parks at such places that every resident of Saskatchewan will be within a reasonable driving distance from a provincial or regional park.

The program was launched in the spring of 1960. Prior to that time, considerable time was devoted to setting up the mechanics of the program which was subsequently incorporated into the Act.

The Regional Parks Program is essentially a shared capital-development program, whereby the Province of Saskatchewan agrees to share 60 percent of the cost of land acquisition and capital development over a period of five years. The remaining 40 percent is to be raised by a group of municipalities who have concluded an agreement to share in the development of a proposed regional park.

Upon approval by the Province of a formal application from the participating municipalities, the Regional Park Authority is created by order-in-council. It is a corporate body which in turn is fully responsible for undertaking development, operation, and maintenance of the park. It is the responsibility of the Authority to see that all moneys obtained from the Province and the money obtained from the participating municipalities are properly expended, and that development undertaken is in the best interests of the public it represents. The planning staff of the Parks and Conservation Branch have been giving assistance in park layout, construction plans, and general information which will assist in promoting better development within a regional park.

At the present time there are fourteen organized regional parks in Saskatchewan, with definite indication of another eight this year. After a year of operation by the various Regional Park Authorities, there is justified reason for optimism for the future of the program. While the members of the various Authorities are lacking in experience, it is surprising how much ingenuity is displayed by many individuals who are interested in a park development for their community. It is worthy of repeating to say that competent planning assistance to each Authority is a must to ensure maximum benefit to the residents of the community.

The Regional Parks Program is the first of its kind in Canada.

Annual Meeting of the Board of Directors of the National Conference on State Parks

The Officers and Board of Directors of NCSP met in Washington for the annual board meeting on March 16 and 17. The meeting was preceded by a get-together dinner on March 15.

Directors in attendance at the meetings were: Frank D. Quinn, Chairman of the Board; Arthur C. Elmer, President; Earl P. Hanson, Vice-President; Ben H. Thompson, Treasurer; Dora A. Padgett, Executive Secretary; Harold J. Dyer, E. Elwood Edey, V. W. Flickinger, Mrs. Ethel W. Harris, Polk Hebert, U. W. Hella, C. West Jacocks, Joseph Jaeger, Jr., Miss Harlean James, Sidney S. Kennedy, Charles Monroe, Thomas Nelson, Gerald W. O'Connor, Jack D. Strain, Lawrence Stuart, Joseph J. Truncer, Robert B. Williams and Conrad L. Wirth. Ira B. Lykes, Chief, Park Practice, attended, as well as William Wells, Joseph Kaylor, Kermit McKeever and Alfred LaGasse, Executive Secretary of the American Institute of Park Executives, who outlined plans for the 1963 joint conference to be held in Washington, D. C. Following the reports of officers and committee Chairmen, plans for the 1962 meeting at Illinois Beach State Park were discussed and the President subsequently announced the Conference Program Committee to be composed of the following: William A. Smith, Chairman, David Abbott, V. W. Flickinger, Clinton Johnson, Roman Koenings, U. W. Hella and Gerald O'Connor.

A review of the ORRRC Report was made by several members present, including discussion of a Bureau of Outdoor Recreation as recommended by the Report, and since carried into action.

The following resolution was presented by Mr. Thompson and seconded by Mr. Strain and adopted unanimously:

The National Conference on State Parks commends the ORRRC for its objective and thoughtful report on *Outdoor Recreation For America.*

The Conference endorses in principle the recommendations of the Committee of Fifteen and the ORRRC that authority be sought for a grants-in-aid program to expedite planning and acquisition of lands for public parks and recreation purposes, thereby facilitating the cooperation of parks agencies at all levels of government in providing adequate parks and related recreation areas for the people of the United States.

The Conference endorses in principle the early establishment of a Bureau of Outdoor Recreation in the Department of the Interior as recommended by the report.

The meeting concluded with a resolution of appreciation of the service of the retiring Executive Secretary, with a rising vote of thanks.

An outstanding event of the meeting was the cocktail party given by Mr. and Mrs. Sidney Kennedy at their home in Bethesda. Mr. Donald B. Alexander, who was at that time under consideration as the new Executive Director of the American Planning and Civic Association and who has since been appointed to that position, was a guest of honor with Mrs. Alexander. It was the occasion for the renewal of many of Mr. Alexander's past friendships in the park field.

Fifteenth Annual Meeting of the Midwest State Park Association

By WILLIAM W. WELLS

Thirty-two members of the Midwest State Park Association, program participants and representatives of the National Park Service met at Effigy Mounds National Monument, McGregor, Iowa, to attend the Fifteenth Annual Meeting of the Midwest State Park Association May 13–16, 1962. Eight member states were represented. This is the first time that the group has met at an area under the supervision of the National Park Service. Registration on Sunday evening was followed by a slide talk on the subject, "Philosophy of the National Park Service," by Kenneth R. Krabbenhoft of the Region Two Office.

On Monday morning the Conference was officially opened by Robert Espeseth, President of the Association, and participants were welcomed by Daniel J. Tobin, Jr., Superintendent, Effigy Mounds National Monument. This was followed by a five-minute capsule report from each state present, and the Region Two, Region Five and Washington Offices of the National Park Service. Highlights of these reports are covered below.

Following the national trend, all states reported a very substantial increase in camping. The Ohio legislature has appointed a committee to study state park admissions and is considering a one-cent tax on cigarettes. Fifty percent would be spent for Departmental lands, mostly impoundments, of which forestry and parks would share. Twenty-five percent would be used for developments on existing lands and twenty-five percent for grants to local political subdivisions. Illinois reported a lake development program underway and rising per-visitor costs.

Michigan has sold the second two million issue of its $10 million revenue bond program and noted a twenty-five percent drop in attendance, twenty percent of which is attributed to the entry-permit fee put into effect in 1961. Less resistance to the charge is apparent this year. Minnesota reported a static attendance figure and the development of a ten-year program aimed mostly at land acquisition. One dollar of each two-dollar entry-permit fee is set aside for buying land with a goal of 50,000 additional acres by 1970.

Missouri had a twenty percent increase in attendance; a very successful legislative program; two favorable bids for the operation of a proposed new lodge facility to be developed with private funds; and a successful pilot inmate labor program. Iowa had a banner attendance year and is developing new campgrounds. Cabin use is decreasing and apparently is being captured by a large increase in camping.

Nebraska has abolished its sticker fee system and is now financed by a .30 mill tax, which has recently increased from .13, based on a projected ten-year development plan. Multiple-use areas are being acquired, and hydraulic replacement lakes created by highway construction are being used for recreational purposes. Wisconsin is embarked on a ten-year $50 million development program based on a one-cent cigarette tax.

Howard Baker, Region Two Director of the National Park Service, reported on the Bureau of Outdoor Recreation, MISSION 66, and a movement underway in North Dakota for a separate state park setup. Peter DeGelleke of the Region Five Office reported on the late winter storm damage to the Atlantic Coast and the Interior Department's recommended conservation zone to help preserve the coastline.

Much of the emphasis of the program was on the subject of interpretation. Superintendent Tobin presented two different types of automatic interpretive slide talks used in the park visitor center— one informational and the other inspirational. These were followed by a trail hike to the Effigy Mounds and later by a panel on Interpretive Programs by Don Lewis of Minnesota, Leonard Haslag of Missouri, and M. E. Beatty of the Park Service. A panel on "Uses and Problems of Insecticides," chaired by Fred Bender, was especially well handled by Dr. Ralph Glasser of the Shell Oil Company and Dr. John George of the Branch of Wildlife Research, Bureau of Wildlife and Sport Fisheries.

The classification and zoning of Wisconsin lakes was an interesting part of Mr. C. W. Thrienen's talk on the "Recreation Use of Waters." This was followed by a tour of the Pikes Peak State Park, Iowa, and Wyalusing and Nelson Dewey State Parks in Wisconsin.

At the business meeting the following officers were elected for next year: Donald Sheldon, Ohio, President; Fred Bender, Missouri, Vice-President; and James McMillen, Illinois, Secretary-Treasurer. Illinois was selected as the host state for next year.

William W. Wells of the National Park Service spoke on "The Impact of the ORRRC Report on State and National Parks" at the Annual Dinner.

A tour of Villa Louis Historic Site and the Museum of Medical History in Prairie du Chien followed the Conference meetings.

New Members
National Conference on State Parks
April and May, 1962

New York
    Lester J. Nimsker, Warsaw
Pennsylvania
    Conrad R. Lickell, Harrisburg

Australia
    Shellharbour Municipal Council, Albion
    Park, NSW

Workshop on Interpretive Programs

By MARC SAGAN, Park Planner Branch of State Cooperation Region One Office,
National Park Service

The 8th Annual Workshop on Interpretive Programs was held April 5–8 at the Outdoor Education Center, Glen Helen, Antioch College, Yellow Springs, Ohio.

Sponsoring organizations were: The Association of Interpretive Naturalists, The American Institute of Park Executives, The Interpretive Committee, National Conference on State Parks, Indiana University.

About 100 participants from 13 states and Ontario represented 42 organizations and institutions. Conservation education was the unifing interest of the various federal, state, county, municipal and private agencies represented.

The group was welcomed to Antioch by Dr. Kenneth Hunt, Director of the Outdoor Education Center.

In an interesting opening program Charles Mohr of the Kalamazoo, Michigan Nature Center discussed the status of interpretation of caves. Of some 150 caves in the United States now open to the public, all but a few are privately operated. Inadequate interpretation at most of these "commercial" caves fails to help visitors understand and enjoy their underground experiences. Operators also lose opportunities to encourage conservation of irreplaceable cave formations and rare cave life. The group was asked to encourage establishment of adequate interpretive programs and to assist cave operators in setting them up.

William Colpitts of the Forest Service, U. S. Department of Agriculture gave an informative summary of his agency's Visitor Information Service Program. The aim of the program is to increase the enjoyment and enrich the experience of National Forest visitors. Pilot projects in the Nicolet, Clark, and other National Forests will provide the basis for interpretive programs in National Forests across the nation. Among the services and facilities offered are self-guiding interpretive trails, multiple use demonstration areas, miniature forest demonstration areas, visitor information centers, restoration and interpretive management of historic sites, mobile visitor information service units, roadside exhibits, conducted campfire programs, and conducted tours of interpretive forest sites. In the development of these new programs the Forest Service has enjoyed an excellent cooperative relationship with the National Park Service and other agencies.

Outlining the origin and aims of the Interpretive Programs Workshops, Dr. Reynold Carlson of Indiana University related the steadily increasing annual workshop attendance to growing interest and activity in the field of nature interpretation and conservation education.

A Panel on the role of the naturalist in the total park program was chaired by Walter Tucker, Director of Columbus, Ohio, Metropolitan Parks. It was emphasized that naturalists should serve not only regular park users but have a particular responsibility to the uninitiated and uninterested members of the community. Selling parks to these people, teaching them skills which will enable them to use, enjoy, and appreciate natural areas may well determine passage of bond issues or legislation to acquire or preserve these areas.

A high point of the meeting was a thought-provoking discussion of the relationship between interpretation and the preservation of natural area values. Roland Eisenbeis of Cook County, Illinois, Forest Preserve, moderated the panel. The following classification of land was suggested:

Primary value of use of area
  Scientific research (outdoor museums)
  Scenic-esthetic
  Educational
Degree of preservation required
  Greatest protection—least possible disturbance
  Somewhat greater disturbance permissible
  Less protection—greater disturbance permissible

The key to the apparent conflict between preservation and use of natural areas is land use classification. While some areas can concurrently support scientific, recreational and interpretive uses without conflict, others permit only a single use compatible with the need to protect primary values. The answer to increasing use is often not more facility development and reclassification of existing areas, but more areas.

Interpretive techniques were reviewed on afternoon field trips through Glen Helen. The trips included inspection of the Glen's trailside museum and use of self-guiding interpretive trails.

Director E. J. Koestner of the Dayton, Ohio, Museum of Natural History told of the museum's success in using young volunteer staff members. Youngsters are encouraged to pursue their natural history interests and to advance through a series of graduated stages from junior naturalist to junior curator, volunteer staff member and, in a few cases, regular staff member. Several young people who accompanied Mr. Koestner to Glen Helen demonstrated their projects and skills with impressive enthusiasm and competence.

"Are we naturalists doing the job?" asked Dr. Charles Dambach of Ohio State University in a talk designed to stimulate realistic self evaluation.

The workshop closed with a business meeting of the Association of Interpretive Naturalists. The 1963 workshop will meet again at Glen Helen during the first weekend in April.

State Park Notes

Effective April 1, Wilbur A. Rush, who has been coordinating county conservation activities for the Iowa Conservation Commission, was named Director of County Conservation Activities; Raymond R. Mitchell succeeded Mr. Rush as Chief, Division of Lands and Waters; and Joe W. Brill, former District Park Supervisor, succeeded Mr. Mitchell as Superintendent of State Parks.

William Penn Mott, Jr., 51, will be the new General Manager of the California East Bay Regional Park District. Mr. Mott's 15-year career as superintendent made Oakland's city park system nationally famous. He will assume the $20,000 a year post not later than July 1, to fill the vacancy created by the resignation of Richard Walpole.

Dr. E. L. Clark, 54, who served since 1959 as the first Director of Colorado's Natural Resources Board, died suddenly of heart trouble March 9.

Harold Schick has been appointed as Superintendent of State Parks in Oregon to succeed Mark Astrup who is now heading the Highway Commission's Landscape Section.

The region reports that Mr. Schick, age 40, "holds a Masters Degree in Park Management from Michigan State University; has been City Forester, Pontiac, Michigan, City and County Park Director, LaCrosse, Wisconsin; State Extension Specialist in Park Management at East Lansing and has advised Michigan cities and counties on park management."

LEGISLATION

The supplemental $25 million bond issue for land acquisition, passed by the recent session of the New York Legislature, will be placed before the voters for ratification in November.

The Pennsylvania Legislature passed with only five dissenting votes a $70 million bond issue for acquisition of park and recreation lands, including matching grants to local governments. It will become effective if passed again by the next legislature and ratified by the voters.

A $150 million bond issue has been enacted by the California Legislature and will be placed before the voters for ratification on June 5. It provides (1) $95 million for acquisition and development of

41

roads, parking facilities, reservoirs, water and sewage systems, boat launching ramps, permanent buildings, and beach restoration at state beaches, parks, recreation facilities and historical monuments; (2) $45 million for grants to counties for regional and joint county-city day-use recreation facilities; (3) $5 million for expenditure by the Wildlife Conservation Board for recreation purposes; and (4) $5 million for expenditure by the Division of Small Craft Harbors of the Department of Parks and Recreation. Payment of principal and interest will be provided by annual legislative appropriations.

A ten-year $100 million land acquisition program under consideration by the Ohio Legislative Service Commission to meet future requirements for water management and recreation will be submitted to the 105th Ohio General Assembly not later than January 15, 1963. In April 1960 the Department of Natural Resources, with the approval of the Governor, initiated a comprehensive study of the need for a program of land acquisition to provide open space for outdoor recreation activities and in February 1961 its report, "Public Land Needs For Water Management and Recreation" was presented to the Governor and all members of the General Assembly. Herbert B. Eagon, Director, Ohio Department of Natural Resources, on April 2, 1962 submitted the Department's report entitled "A Study of Possible Methods of Financing Land Acquisition for Water Management and Recreation" to Representative Robert E. Holmes, Chairman,

Water Management and State Park Study Committee, Legislative Service Commission. This legislative group is making a statewide survey of parks and recreation facilities and will report its findings and recommendations to the next General Assembly.

MEETINGS

The 40th Southwest District Recreation Conference sponsored by the National Recreation Association, Santa Fe Recreation Department, and the New Mexico Recreation Association was held at Santa Fe, New Mexico, April 10–13. The conference was well attended by members and national, state and city leaders in recreation; its theme: "Leadership—The Key To Success." Howard M. Isham, Director of Recreation, Santa Fe, New Mexico, was Chairman of the "Kick-Off Session"; and Professor Frank E. Papcsy, President, New Mexico Recreation Association, Chairman of the Opening Session. Mayor Leo T. Murphy welcomed the assembly and Gov. Edwin L. Mechem, State of New Mexico, greeted those present. Miss Lou Hamilton, Superintendent of Recreation, San Antonio, Texas, gave the keynote address on her "Philosophy of Recreation" and speakers at other sessions and workshops were concerned with the following subjects: "Basic Principles of Leadership; Expanding the Scope of Recreation Programs through Introductions to the Fascination and Beauty of Our Natural Surroundings; Physical Fitness Through Recreation; The Armed Forces Recreation Program; Arts and Crafts in Recreation; the

Performing Arts as Recreation; Professionalism in Recreation; Bond Issues; Fees and Charges; Budget and Finance; and Teenage Problems and Special Events."

Over 250 delegates from state, county and municipal agencies from eight midwest states registered for the Midwest District Recreation Conference held on April 17–20 at Wichita, Kansas.

Dr. Arthur S. Daniels, Dean, School of Health Education and Recreation, Indiana University, talked on the physical aspects of fitness. Dr. C. Kermit Phelps, Chief of Psychology Service, Veterans Administration, Kansas City, dealt with mental aspects of fitness, and Joseph Prendergast, Executive Director, National Recreation Association, New York City, spoke on the general fitness for America.

Mr. Prendergast stated that it is at the grass roots level where the average citizen does most of his recreating, and that interest must be cultivated there. He said, "Until the people become interested enough to prevail upon the state legislators to do something, the progress within the state will be slow." He claims the real need is development on the local front, which in turn will strengthen support on the state level, and that both fronts, the state and local, must be worked simultaneously for the best and fastest results.

Robert L. Black, Park Planner, National Park Service, Region Two, Omaha, Nebraska, talked on "A Look To The Future" and the Federal Government's role in recreation services to the various subdivisions of government.

It was encouraging to note that some 60 park superintendents attended the workshop session on maintenance at this Conference. Most of them had never attended a recreation conference before. At the close of their meeting they suggested a two-, instead of a one-day maintenance workshop. The facilities and equipment of the Wichita Park and Recreation Department did, of course, afford an excellent opportunity to see a well-run modern department in action.

The Seventh Annual Southeastern Park and Recreation Training Institute was held February 27 through March 2 at North Carolina State College, Raleigh, North Carolina. As in past years, the Institute was conducted by the Department of Recreation and Park Administration of the School of Education and the College Extension Division. Cooperating Sponsors were: Association of Southeastern State Park Directors; Alabama Recreation Society; Georgia Recreation Society; Kentucky Recreation and Parks Society; North Carolina Recreation Commission; North Carolina Recreation Society; South Carolina Recreation Society; Tennessee Recreation Society; Virginia Recreation Society; and West Virginia State Recreation Society.

Charles C. Stott of the faculty of the Department of Recreation and Park Administration was Director of the Institute and Harry H. Wilkerson, Recreation Specialist, Tennessee Valley Authority, was President.

This year's Institute differed from previous ones in that it was attended by three sets of groups: recreation and related interest groups, state parks and related interest groups, and industrial and related interest groups. Attendance was sponsored by the Association of Southeastern State Park Directors to provide in-service training to state park workers in the states included in the Association.

The program included both separate sessions for each group and joint sessions attended by all groups. Sessions specifically for state park workers were held on state park philosophy, state park design, interpretive programs and maintenance of facilities. Subjects presented in the joint sessions included maintenance equipment, public relations, research progress, family camping and principles of personnel relations. A highlight of the meeting was an address entitled PARKS FOR AMERICA, delivered by Conrad L. Wirth, Director of the National Park Service.

A wide variety of agencies participated in the Institute. Representatives of county and municipal parks, state parks, the American Recreation Society, National Recreation Association, American Red Cross, Corps of Engineers, United States Forest Service and the National Park Service were among those who appeared on the program.

O. W. Sapp, Director of Recreation, Lumberton, North Carolina, and Co-Chairman of this year's Institute, was elected President of the 1963 Institute.

Over 200 delegates and exhibitors attended the AIPE sponsored second Annual Revenue Producing facilities Conference at Oglebay Park, Wheeling, West Virginia,

March 11–14. National, state, city and county members came from such faraway places as San Diego, California; Miami, Florida; and Montreal, Canada. A diversified program provided information on every facet of revenue producing facilities in parks and zoological departments. Bernard G. Memmel, Administrative Assistant, Milwaukee County Park Commission, Milwaukee, Wisconsin, served as chairman, and Charles D. Harris, Chief, Field Operations, Michigan Department of Conservation, Lansing, Michigan, was program chairman. Martin A. Janis, President of the Toledo Zoological Society and member of the Ohio House of Delegates gave the Keynote Address, and three days of busy sessions were devoted to such topics as leased operations, fees and charges, souvenirs and gifts, food sales, employee accountability, and fiscal policy. They toured Wheeling's Park System and chose Charles Harris Chairman for the third annual conference, and Paul Douglas Green, Supervisor of Service, Niagara Park Commission, Niagara Falls, Ontario, Canada, program chairman for 1963. Certificates were presented to six committee members for their work on the 1961 committee; Bernard Memmel received a citation for his work as Chairman of the 1962 conference and Joseph Bissonnette, for coordinating and acting as chairman of the 1961 conference.

Over 100 representatives of city, county, state and federal park and forest areas established residence in group camps at O'Leno State Park, Florida, for the Thirteenth

Annual Park Short Course, April 2-6. The course was conducted by the General Extension Division of Florida in cooperation with the Florida Association of Park Personnel, Florida Park Service, National Park Service, American Institute of Park Executives, and University of Florida.

Members of the Park Short Course faculty from outside the State of Florida-were Assistant Director Daniel B. Beard, National Park Service, and Frank Vaydik, Superintendent of Forestry and Landscaping, Department of Parks and Recreation, Detroit, Michigan. Each gave two courses during the five-day session.

Presiding at the sessions were: Dr. Robert L. Fairing, General Extension Division; J. W. Rogers, Jacksonville City Parks; Frank Vaydik, Detroit, Michigan; Gene Lidden, Park Superintendent, Gainesville; James Blackledge, Barco, Inc., Lake Worth; E. A. Colquitt, Parks Department, Fort Lauderdale; John R. McCormack, Dade County Parks; C. Raymond Vinten, National Park Service, St. Augustine; Robert A. Harper, U. S. Forest Service.

The subjects were varying and included soils, horticulture, maintenance, planning, personnel training and supervision, programs for elderly, adult, and children groups, natural history, and present and future park planning and objectives. Anyone interested in the development of these Park Short Courses can get detailed information and sample programs by writing to Dr. Robert L. Fairing, General Extension Division of Florida, 908 Seagle Building, Gainesville, Florida.

It was the opinion of all who attended that this was the best of all the thirteen annual training sessions.

All Short Course sessions are traditionally held at O'Leno State Park. Mid-year sessions of the Florida Association of Park Personnel, the principal cooperating agency for the Short Course, were designated for Miami in the fall of 1962, and for Tampa in the fall of 1963.

NEWS FROM THE STATES

Six states have acted to implement land acquisition recommendations contained in the 1959 National Park Service Atlantic Coast and Great Lakes Survey report as follows:

Illinois is enlarging its Illinois Beach State Park holdings on Lake Michigan; Michigan has acquired five new areas and added Great Lakes shoreline frontages to four existing areas; New York has acquired, or is in the process of acquiring, virtually all of eight areas on Lake Ontario; Ohio has recommended that six areas on Lake Erie be included in the State's long-range conservation program; Pennsylvania has recommended acquisition of the Elk Creek area fronting on Lake Erie; and Wisconsin has acquired two of the recommended shoreline areas and three more are under negotiation on Lakes Superior and Michigan.

Alaska. This past year a poll conducted by the Division of Lands among the 550,000 visitors at its 59 wayside areas to determine whether tourists and their friends will return in 1962 has influenced to a great extent its present plans to establish 10 new campgrounds in 1962. A note in the Division's Newsletter said, "This system of camping areas is far more important to the State than the amount of money so far expended on it would indicate." The $160,000 anticipated expenditures for fiscal year 1962 will exceed the actual expenditure for 1961.

Florida. Another new state park has been added to the park system. The 160-acre Falling Waters State Park, situated three miles south of Chipley on Florida 77A, was deeded to the Florida Park Service by the Washington County Commission on April 12.

Acquisition of the property had been in progress for some time through the efforts of the Washington County Development Authority. One of the main attractions of the park will be a stream that flows through the area and disappears into an 80-foot sink hole. The ground within the park is honeycombed with limestone caverns and caves. This area is also the site of the first attempt to find oil in Florida. The legislature appropriated $31,000 for improvements for the 1961–1963 biennium.

Kansas. The Kansas Forestry, Fish and Game Commission has transferred the administration of recreation at Cedar Bluff Reservoir to the Kansas State Park and Resources Authority, except for administration of wildlife.

Kentucky. In April, the State issued revenue bonds in the amount of $9.9 million for expansion of its state park system. This supple-

ments the $10 million made available through issuance of general obligation bonds authorized in 1960.

Maryland. Nine miles of Assateague Island, which lies between the Atlantic Ocean and Sinepuxent Bay, will become Maryland's first state-owned ocean recreation area when park lands have been acquired by the Board of Natural Resources at a cost of approximately $2.5 million. Already, the State has underway condemnation proceedings to take 680 acres at the upper end of the island just south of Ocean City.

Joseph F. Kaylor, Director, Department of Forests and Parks, plans to stabilize the beaches with trees and ground-cover plants and provide camping areas and bathing facilities. A new bridge is planned by the State Roads Commission near Assateague which will provide a southern entrance to the park. To the south of the proposed park area lies the privately owned Ocean Beach development which extends southward on the island to the Virginia border where the Fish and Wildlife Service has established a wildlife refuge.

New Mexico. A major expansion of the state park system can be expected soon if minimum financing and maintenance costs can be met, said E. R. Smith in his January 12 annual report to Gov. Edwin L. Mechem. The state legislature slashed the current biennium 1961–62 budget to $430,000, compared with $775,750 for 1959–60 and the State Park Commission is in a fund pinch, the report indicates. Two new state parks were added in 1960 and the acquisition of recreation areas on Valdo Lake, Pine River and east of Tucumcari are planned.

Oregon. A proposed 450-acre state park at Nestucca Spit between the Pacific Ocean and Nestucca Bay and River in Tillamook County, south of Pacific City, is being purchased by the State Land Board. Gov. Mark O. Hatfield, Chairman of the Board, may grant high priority for development of the area. The ocean shoreline, sheltered bay, large sand dunes and facilities for boating, camping and picnicking will form one of the most attractive areas on the Oregon coast. The State Parks and Recreation Division plans to stabilize the sand dunes, provide day-use facilities, overnight campsites, boat ramps and other boat facilities.

Tennessee. Gov. Buford Ellington, on January 16, proclaimed the year 1962 the "Silver Anniversary of Tennessee State Parks" and invited all citizens to visit and enjoy the State's parks. Moreover, he requested schools, youth and adult organizations to make a special effort to devote programs to promote a greater appreciation and utilization of the state parks program. Establishment of the system gained support in 1934 during the CCC and other recovery cooperative programs and in 1937 the Division of

State Parks was created in the Department of Conservation. Beginning with five leased areas in 1938, the system now includes 20 areas with recreation facilities within 50 miles of each resident of the State.

Texas. Members of the Texas Outdoor Writers' Association, comprising most of the outdoor recreation specialists on Texas newspapers, have a new committee working to help improve the status of the state parks, according to its president, Ed Holder. The writers named Dick McCune, Outdoor Editor of the *Dallas TIMES HERALD*, as chairman to work with the State Parks Board to create more interest in and improvement of Texas state parks. Mr. Holder, Outdoor Editor of the *Port Arthur NEWS*, a dynamic fellow and one of the most vigorous proponents of a broader outdoor recreation format, said, "I believe that Texans need only to realize that they have such an inadequate parks system to stir them to action. That includes backing the needed financing." The $1 per car fee, already endorsed by several substantial groups, would raise about $5 million annually.

IN MEMORIAM
ANSEL FRANKLIN HALL

Ansel Franklin Hall died suddenly in Denver, Colorado, March 28, 1962. He was in his 68th year. He is survived by his widow, six children and their families. He was an officer of the National Park Service for twenty years. Since 1937 and until his untimely passing, Mr. Hall was the executive head of the Company that operates the concession in Mesa Verde National Park, Colorado, for furnishing accommodations and services for the travelling public in that Park.

Ansel Hall entered the National Park Service as a ranger upon graduation from the University of California in 1917, the first year of the existence of this new bureau. He immediately attracted the attention of Director Stephen T. Mather and his associates by his high intelligence, his great energy and efficiency in carrying out his assignments, his versatility in undertaking and solving technical problems, and his abiding interest in the protection and interpretation of the natural features of the parks.

World War I interrupted his national park activities and he became an officer in the 20th Engineers and saw active service in France. As the war drew to an end he was assigned as an instructor in forestry at the A. E. F. University at Beaune, France.

On returning to civil life, Mr. Hall was enthusiastically welcomed back to the National Park Service. He was assigned to Yosemite National Park where he soon began the collection of objects for museum display—specimens of the minerals, the plants, the fauna, and Indian artifacts of the Park. He personally built large scale models of the Yosemite Valley and other natural features. His interpretation program won the attention of Chauncey J. Hamlin, President of the American Association of Museums, and, together, they submitted the Yosemite Museum project to the Laura Spelman Rockefeller Memorial. It was approved and a grant of $75,000 was made for the construction of the museum in Yosemite Valley which today is one of the most complete in the West.

Mr. Hall wrote excellent guidebooks of Sequoia and Yosemite National Parks, particularly the Giant Forest and Yosemite Valley, as well as numerous magazine articles on the national parks and monuments and conservation of natural resources.

His outstanding achievements in Yosemite Park naturally led to his promotion to Chief Naturalist, Chief Forester and Chief of the Field Division of Education of the National Park Service with headquarters first at the University of California in Berkeley, California, and later in a specially designed building near his home in North Berkeley. In these higher and more general assignments of leadership, Mr. Hall travelled extensively through the national park system. He assembled a large personal library of national park and forest literature. He did much of the planning of the museums in Yellowstone and Grand Canyon national parks and other parks and monuments.

Besides the museums, the libraries, the nature trail systems and other interpretative features of national park administration were greatly advanced by the vision and genius of this great naturalist and forester. With emergency funds available during the 1930's, he organized and directed a large staff of artists, writers, museum exhibit preparators and research specialists, and produced publications, museum

exhibits and other interpretative tools and devices on a vast scale.

Mr. Hall's dynamic personality and that of his charming capable wife made them outstanding members of the National Park Service organization, and later concessioners of extraordinary popularity.

His death was a loss of monumental proportions to his friends and the many organizations to which he belonged. Besides this, to the writer of this brief sketch of a fine career in public service, Mr. Hall will always be remembered as the most versatile man he has ever known.   H.M.A.

ROBERT WOODS BLISS
1875-1962

Robert Woods Bliss, a former Ambassador to Argentina and Minister to Sweden who served in diplomatic posts for more than thirty years, died on April 19 in his home at 1537 Twenty-eighth Street, N. W. He was 86 years old.

Mr. Bliss is survived by his widow, the former Mildred Barnes.

Mr. Bliss rose to the rank of Ambassador to Argentina after more than thirty years of service in posts in the United States consular and diplomatic service.

He was appointed Ambassador in 1927 and served in Buenos Aires until 1933, when he requested his retirement.

In World War II Mr. Bliss was called back from retirement to act as a consultant and then as special assistant to the Secretary of State. He retired again from government service in 1945.

He was born in St. Louis, on

Aug. 5, 1875. He graduated from Harvard in 1900.

In 1940, the Blisses donated to Harvard University their historic estate, Dumbarton Oaks, and a research library and art collection covering the medieval and Byzantine period. Dumbarton Oaks, one of the largest late Georgian estates in the District of Columbia, later was the scene of the international conference that led to the creation of the United Nations.

Mr. Bliss was a life member of the American Planning and Civic Association and active in the Committee of 100 on the Federal City. He served as Chairman of the Joint Committee on the National Capital for a number of years.

The Nation's Capital has sustained a great loss in the death of Mr. Bliss who had exerted a great influence by his active participation in civic groups.

JAMES LAWRENCE HOUGHTELING
1883-1962

James L. Houghteling, former U. S. Commissioner of Immigration and Naturalization, died after a short illness at the age of 78.

A native of Chicago, Mr. Houghteling was graduated from Yale University in 1905 with a bachelor of arts degree. Four years later he joined the family banking firm of Peabody, Houghteling & Co. and in 1919 became its vice-president.

During World War I, Mr. Houghteling served as a captain in the 103d Field Artillery and took part in the Argonne and Meuse offensive. He was assigned a position as a special attache to the American Embassy in Petrograd, Russia, (St. Petersburg) and was there during the Russian Revolution of April 1917. The next year Mr. Houghteling published "A Diary of the Russian Revolution," based on his observations of the struggle.

In 1920, after returning to this country, he entered the newspaper business, joining the staff of the *New York Evening Post*. The next year Mr. Houghteling joined the *Chicago Daily News*, leaving soon after, however, to become chief editorial writer for the *Chicago Evening Post*.

On July 22, 1937, Mr. Houghteling was appointed Commissioner of Immigration and Naturalization, coming to Washington to accept the post.

In 1917, Mr. Houghteling married Laura Delano, daughter of Frederic A. Delano, uncle of President Franklin D. Roosevelt.

He maintained a membership in the American Planning and Civic Association, in addition to that held by his wife, who has also been active on the Committee of 100 on the Federal City.

H. PAUL CAEMMERER

H. Paul Caemmerer, who served as Executive Secretary of the Commission of Fine Arts for 32 years, and retired in 1954, died on May 13 after a long illness. He had written many historical articles on Washington, and several books including the "Life of Charles Pierre L'Enfant," published in 1951, a biography of the first planner of Washington.

Mr. Caemmerer was elected President of the Columbia Historical Society in 1947, a post he held for three years.

He received a masters degree from George Washington University, a law degree from Georgetown University and a doctorate from American University.

For thirty years he carried membership in the American Planning and Civic Association which he held until his retirement.

He had a highly specialized knowledge of Washington and his research into area history has been a valuable contribution.

JACK E. HAYNES

As we go to press, we have learned of the death of Jack E. Haynes, historian, photographer and conservationist, often called "Mr. Yellowstone."

In our next issue Mr. Horace M. Albright, will present a tribute to his old friend, Jack Haynes.

Mr. Haynes died on May 11 and friends from Montana, Idaho and many other states gathered in Bozeman to attend funeral services.

Yellowstone officials were pallbearers and honorary pallbearers included Conrad L. Wirth, Director of the National Park Service, Washington, D. C.; Horace M. Albright, former Director of the National Park Service and Superintendent of Yellowstone National Park; Edmund B. Rogers of Denver, former Yellowstone Superintendent, and many others.

M.I.T. Announces Special Summer Session on City and Regional Planning

The twenty-fourth in the series of annual two-week Special Summer Programs in City and Regional Planning will be held at the Massachusetts Institute of Technology, in Cambridge, from Monday, July 16, through Friday, July 27, 1962.

As in former years, the Program will include a comprehensive review of the principles of city and regional planning and of the administration of planning programs. Special emphasis this year will be placed on the types of public regulatory controls over land development which are available and the ways in which they can be used to carry out major elements of a comprehensive planning program. The Program is expected to have special interest for those directly concerned with city and metropolitan planning or planning for rapidly developing areas, including practicing professionals and others with a strong interest in the relationships of basic land uses and circulation. It is oriented toward the individual who lacks formal professional training or advanced professional experience in comprehensive planning.

During the two weeks of the Program, seminars will be held each week-day morning and afternoon, and there will also be two evening sessions each week. On Saturday, July 21, there will be an all-day field trip to some significant developments in suburban Boston.

Seminar leadership will be provided by members of the faculty of the Department of City and Regional Planning and guest speakers selected for their ability to make a special contribution to the subjects under discussion. Tuition is $250, due and payable upon notification of admission. Academic credit is not offered. The planning seminars will be under the general direction of Frederick J. Adams, Professor of City Planning, M.I.T., Cambridge, Massachusetts.

Recent Publications

DESIGN OF WATER-RESOURCE SYSTEMS. New Techniques for Relating Economic Objectives, Engineering Analysis, and Governmental Planning. By Arthur Maass, Maynard M. Hufschmidt, Robert Dorfman, Harold A. Thomas, Jr., Stephen A. Marglin and Gordon Maskew Fair. Harvard University Press, 79 Garden St., Cambridge, Mass. 1962. 660 pp., tables, figures, charts. $12.50.

WATER POLLUTION; ECONOMIC ASPECTS AND RESEARCH NEEDS. By Allen V. Kneese. Resources for the Future, 1962. Distributed by the Johns Hopkins Press, Baltimore 18, Md. $1.75.

CRUSADE FOR WILDLIFE. By James B. Trefethen. The Stackpole Company, Harrisburg, Pa., 1962. 377 pp. (The role of the Boone and Crockett Club, organized in 1887) $7.50.

RECREATION AND PARK YEARBOOK. National Recreation Association, 8 West Eighth St., New York 11, N. Y. 1962. $5.50.

PROCEEDINGS OF THE FIFTH WORLD FORESTRY CONGRESS. 1,386 pp. in English, 234 in French and 180 in Spanish. Fifth World Congress, P. O. Box 7265, Apex Station, Washington 4, D. C. 1962. $25.00.

ECONOMIC BASE SURVEY OF THE POTOMAC RIVER SERVICE AREA, 1957–2010. Supt. of Documents, Government Printing Office, Washington 25, D. C. 55c.

PLANNING RESEARCH, a Register of Research for all concerned with Town and Country Planning. The Town Planning Institute, 18 Ashley Place, London, S. W. 1, England, 1961. 18 shillings and sixpence, plus postage and packing 1/6.

CONSERVATION OF RESIDENTIAL AMENITIES. By Oscar Sutermeister, consulting City Planner, for Lake Barcroft Community Association. 5923 Johnson Avenue, Bethesda, Maryland.

HOUSING, PEOPLE AND CITIES. By Martin Meyerson, Barbara Terrett and William L. C. Wheaton. McGraw-Hill Book Company, 330 West 42nd Street, New York 36, N. Y., 1961. $9.75.

A NATIONAL PROGRAM OF RESEARCH IN HOUSING AND URBAN DEVELOPMENT. The Major Requirements and a Suggested Approach. By Harvey S. Perloff. Resources for the Future, Inc., 1775 Massachusetts Ave. N. W., Washington 6, D. C. September 1961. 50c.

LANDSCAPE ARCHITECTURE. By John Ormsbee Simonds. F. W. Dodge Corporation, 119 West 40th Street, New York 18, N. Y. 244 pp. $12.75.

AMERICAN ARCHITECTURE AND OTHER WRITINGS. By Montgomery Schuyler. Belknap Press, Harvard University, 1961. Two volumes, illus. $12.50.

COMPARISONS IN RESOURCE MANAGEMENT. Six Notable Programs in Other Countries and their Possible U. S. Application. Edited by Henry Jarrett. The Johns Hopkins Press, Baltimore 18, 1961. 271 pp. Illus.

MY WILDERNESS: EAST TO KATAHDIN. By William O. Douglas. Doubleday, 1961. Illus. 290 pp. $4.95.

A NATURALIST IN ALASKA. By Adolph Murie. Devin-Adair, New York, 1961. 302 pp. Illus. $6.50.

COMPLETE BOOK OF CAMPING. By Leonard Miracle and Maurice H. Decker. Harper and Bros., New York, 1961. 594 pp. Illus. $4.95.

THE NEXT TWENTY YEARS. A General Plan for the Development of the Charlotte Metropolitan Area. Charlotte-Mecklenburg Planning Commission, Charlotte, N. C. 1961. 39 pp. illus., charts, tables.

MONTEREY COAST MASTER PLAN. County of Monterey, California. Sections I and II. Skidmore, Owings & Merrill, San Francisco, Calif. 1960. 26 and 42 pp. respectively.

WORLD URBANIZATION; EXPANDING POPULATION IN A SHRINKING WORLD. Technical Bulletin 43. April 1962. Urban Land Institute, Washington, D. C. $3.00.

GREEN BELTS AND URBAN GROWTH. English Town and Country Planning in Action. By Daniel R. Mandelker. University of Wisconsin Press, Madison, Wis., 1962. $5.00.

PLAN TO ATTEND

42nd Annual Conference
National Conference on
State Parks

Illinois Beach State Park

September 30   October 4, 1962

/5+T

Planning and Civic Comment

Official Organ of American Planning and Civic Association and
National Conference on State Parks

ß

CONTENTS

SEPTEMBER 1962

PLANNING AND
CIVIC COMMENT

Published Quarterly

Successor to: City Planning, Civic Comment, State Recreation

Official Organ of: American Planning and Civic Association,
National Conference on State Parks

SCOPE: *National, State, Regional and City Planning, Land and Water Uses,
Conservation of National Resources, National, State and Local Parks,
Highways and Roadsides.*
AIM: *To create a better physical environment which will conserve and develop
the health, happiness and culture of the American people.*

Second-class postage paid at Harrisburg, Pa., and at additional mailing office.

EDITORIAL AND PUBLICATION OFFICE, 901 Union Trust Building, Washington 5,
D. C.

Printed by the Mount Pleasant Press, The McFarland Company, Harrisburg, Pa.

Planning and Civic Comment

| Vol. 28 | September, 1962 | No. 3 |

Report on the First World Conference on National Parks, Seattle, Washington, June 30-July 7, 1962

By PAUL THIRY, F. A. I. A.

EDITOR'S NOTE:—Mr. Thiry is a member of the American Planning and Civic Association and was its official representative at the Conference.

The colorful First World Conference on National Parks, which opened its first formal conclave July 2 in the Century 21 Exposition (Seattle World's Fair) Playhouse with greetings from governmental officials and other dignitaries before moving to convention headquarters at the Olympic Hotel, Seattle, gave all the outward appearance of a United Nations gathering with representatives of 71 nations (160 delegates) participating as well as guests and interested observers monitoring the meetings.

The high level conference organized under the direction of the International Union for Conservation of Nature and Natural Resources and sponsored by UNESCO, the Food and Agriculture Organization of the United Nations, United States National Park Service and The Natural Resources Council of America, began its discussions almost immediately on the theme of statements such as: "we recognize the need for sanctuary for birds and caribou, why not men?"; and that like agriculture, there should be no need of a defensive attitude about conservation and preservation; and "wildlife preservation is necessary for the sanity of mankind." The thought was advanced for "islands in space."

Harold J. Coolidge, chairman of the Conference and executive director of the Pacific Science Board of the National Research Council, pointed out the conference—first in history to focus international attention on the importance of National Parks—is designed to promote the interchange of technical information primarily through discussion groups. These discussions ran all the way from the subject of protecting the African snail, a food source for Ghanians as well as gourmets internationally, to the establishment of maintenance of National Parks throughout the world, and to educating and providing the needed technical aid and assistance such enterprises require.

The global role of parks was emphasized by many speakers and with particular eloquence by Conrad L. Wirth, Director of the U. S. National Park Service. He warned that in this "chaotic and complex world" resources must be preserved before they are gone. "We as individuals have use of the natural resources of this earth while we live

Planning and Civic Comment

here. We cannot take them with us. We have inherited the right to use them, but do not have the right to misuse them, depriving future generations." With equal feeling, Stewart Udall, U. S. Secretary of the Interior, called for a common market of conservation knowledge. Secretary Udall warned, "Time is fast running out. Few opportunities for conservation prospects of grand scope will remain by the year 2000. In an era of noise and pollution and jostle and blight, it is not hard to predict that our children will place as high a value on the right of solitude in the out-of-doors, and the right of access to places of natural beauty, as they now accord the right of free speech and the right to a trial by one's peers." He warned of a threat to conservation posed by growing industrialization and expanding populations. "The hour is late, the opportunities diminish with each passing year, and with each day that passes the natural world shrinks as we exert greater artificial control over our environment."

Others who spoke for preservation were Dr. Jacques Verschuren, Arusha, Tanganyika, Biologist of the National Parks of the Congo and Ruanda-Urundi; Theodore Monod, France, L'Institut de l'Afrique Noire, Dakar, Senegal; and Paul Brooks of Houghton-Mifflin Publishing Company, Boston, the latter making the salutary statement, "Year by year we whittle away the priceless heritage of wilderness forgetting that it is possible for an environment, as for a species of animal, to become extinct."

The discussions carried into the subject of wildlife. Lee M. Talbot of the University of California pointed out over 100 kinds of mammals and nearly 100 kinds of birds have become extinct since the time of Christ, and another 600 mammals and uncounted birds are now verging on extinction because of man's activities. He referred to the heavy toll as a result of outright killing, misuse of fire, excessive livestock grazing, flooding and such apparently innocuous actions as drainage, heavy cultivation and urban expansion.

Alain Gille, of France and UNESCO's Department of Natural Sciences pointed out the needs of international cooperation. "We are speaking of problems requiring supranational organizations, but what we have are loose international ones." The problem as pointed out was to the effect it is impossible to cope on a national level with migrating birds which are protected in one country and shot in the next, with animals unable to recognize frontiers or parks boundaries and with a world population which seems increasingly indifferent to its own possible extinction, let alone that of animals. Similar statements were made by Major Ian Grimwood, Chief Game Warden of Kenya, and others.

Perhaps one of the most far reaching and thought provoking statements was made by Dr. Carleton Ray, member of the New York Zoological Society and Secretary of the Bahamas National Trust, which manages the Exuma Cays Land and Sea Park in the Central Bahamas. Dr. Ray described the gigantic expanse of the ocean's 340 million cubic miles of water and the necessity of setting aside unmolested study areas in the sea, "parks" where all life would be protected. He called for an "extension of the ideas of land and fresh water conservation to the marine environment with all that this implies . . . parks, sanctuaries, management and regulations to control man's behavior in relation to marine resources."

He emphasized it is the shallow seas near centers of civilization that are most in need of protection, although they are "the most productive areas on earth." Estuaries, inlets, bights and marshes, the nurseries of the sea, are fast disappearing through development, filling, drainage, bulkheading and pollution.

Other aspects of National Parks not often mentioned or thought of were brought out by David P. S. Wasawo of Uganda, East Africa, who pointed out that properly conducted tours of parks "can do much to broaden the bases of education in our society." Dr. Boonsong Lekagul of the Association for Conservation of Wildlife in Thailand, pointed out the religious significance—"In Thailand, where the people believe in Buddhism, national parks promote the teaching of religion, the people are able to witness wild animals contentedly leading their lives freely in natural surroundings. This atmosphere expounds one of the most important precepts of Buddhism; not to take life."

"Panel papers" were available to those attending the Conference. Reading these gave further opportunity to reflect on the nature and the depth of content of the panel discussions and the meetings themselves.

Panel paper by Dr. Maria Buchinger, Forestry Advisor, Institute for Forest Research, Argentine National Forest Service, contained a total verbiage of factual material which enunciated clearly that "wilderness must be protected because of its value for scientific research."

Further, Dr. Buchinger stated, "Modern man cannot be considered a part of the biotic circle, he brutally upsets the balance" and as an observation on this point—"The ideal balance, in the Antarctic was spoiled when man arrived. Apart from the inevitable killing of some animals for food supply, or samples for research, there were other and quite unnecessary disturbances. A helicopter flying over a penguin rookery when the young are small, or the egg unhatched, causes panic among the parents, who crush and stamp upon the helpless young, destroying most of them. A ship pumping oily bilges near a rookery may destroy thousands of parent birds returning from the sea with food for their young ones." And amplifying the point, "Near a small base in the Antarctic all lichens disappeared within a year or two due to air pollution. These lichens, with their high capacity to resist extreme climactic conditions are valuable phytogeographic indicators, especially in polar regions, where no higher plants can be found . . ."

Arturo Eichler, Institute of Geography and Conservation, University of Los Andres, Merida, Vene-

3

zuela, writes "The complex conditions that result from precipitate development in regions whose economy is just getting underway tend to delay the arrival of a clear concept and a just appreciation of the vital importance of nature conservation. Primeval nature is not a sign of backwardness."

A paper by M. A. Badshah, Wildlife Officer, State of Madras, India, and C. A. R. Bhadran deals with the urgent need for the establishment of more national parks to usefully serve man, who is becoming more and more urbanized and artificial in his outlook at the sacrifice of a balanced way of life in tune with nature.

Messrs. Badshah and Bhadran remind us "Natural resources all over the world are inter-related, the depletion of natural resources in one part of the world can have serious repercussions on another;" they refer to migratory birds as an example and in warning, "The ever-growing population of the world has been appropriating large slices of well-clothed land for human habitation and agricultural and industrial undertakings. The forests are cut down ruthlessly, and streams dry up. The giant trees wail as they fall, the denizens of the forest are driven out either to face the bullet or die for want of shelter and food. In short, all the good soil of the earth is being drained and exposed to the sun and the winds. The desolate and barren Sahara, once the granary of Rome, is man's handiwork . . . Experts have estimated that only about two percent of the earth's entire surface is fit for habitation, the rest being covered by

mountains, deserts, water and eternal snow."

John S. Owen, Director of National Parks, Arusha, Tanganyika, pertinently referred to a common opportunity. "There are still several areas in Tanganyika which abound in wildlife and which are not under the immediate threat of settlement by human beings. It is essential that the best of these be made into National Parks as soon as possible while they are unencumbered by human rights and before poachers exterminate the game. We have three such areas now under consideration and there are others yet to be surveyed."

Proceedings of the conference were broadcast through transistor intercoms which were available individually to those attending the sessions. Translations were in English, French and Spanish, which made it easy to follow all speakers except some of the speakers from the British speaking nations. One sort of hoped these talks could have been translated into U. S. A. English as well as in French and Spanish.

The conference members were entertained with a number of events —noteworthy from a Pacific Northwest standpoint was a salmon bake and boating excursions on Puget Sound and Lake Washington. Irving Clark, Jr., was chairman of the local reception committee.

In review, perhaps what was said of India could be understood and given world meaning. It was said India, in spite of its 438,000,000 population, has not lost sight of natural reserves and wildlife con-

Please turn to page 6

4

Common Market of Conservation Knowledge Urged by Udall at World Parks Conference

Mounting population pressures makes the sharing of conservation knowledge imperative throughout the world, Secretary of the Interior Stewart L. Udall told the First World Conference on National Parks at Seattle.

Speaking before delegates representing more than 60 countries, Secretary Udall said:

"The hour is late, the opportunities diminish with each passing year, and we must establish here a Common Market of conservation knowledge which will enable us to achieve our highest goals and purposes."

The conference is sponsored by the International Union for Conservation of Nature and Natural Resources, with UNESCO, the National Park Service and the Natural Resources Council of America as co-sponsors and hosts. Delegates included representatives from Switzerland, France, Thailand, Poland, Africa, Australia, Belgium, Japan, the United Kingdom, Mexico, and more than 50 other countries.

"So great is the power of men and nations to enlarge the machine-dominated portion of the world, it is not an exaggeration to say that few opportunities for conservation projects of grand scope will remain by the year 2000," Secretary Udall said. "With few exceptions the places of superior scenic beauty and the spacious refuges for wildlife that our generation saves will be all that is preserved."

The Interior Secretary pointed out that the world population will double every 35 years, adding:

"In an era of noise and pollution and jostle and blight, it is not hard to predict that our children will place as high a value on the right of solitude in the out-of-doors and the right of access to places of natural beauty as they now accord to the right of free speech and the right to trial by one's peers."

Secretary Udall urged creation of an exchange program of "conservation thinkers and planners," including land management specialists, biologists, foresters, and hydrologic specialists to advise on efficient methods of land and water utilization.

Increased use of the Peace Corps as well as the development of technical schools to teach the techniques and rationale of land management for immediate application in the field also were recommended.

The Interior Secretary paid tribute to the strides taken in the world park movement, pointing out that where prior to 1945 England had no national parks, today there are 10. In West Germany 24 more national parks are planned, and significant progress has been made in game preservation projects in Africa.

"Yet, as we look ahead in this country and yours, we are faced with the fact that during the adult life of our children the demand for municipal parks and playgrounds will increase fourfold . . . and the demand for wilderness and seashore parks will be an estimated 10 times greater," he said.

"I would like to think that this conference strikes a wholesome note of sanity in a troubled world," Secretary Udall told the conference. "It is a sign that men are questioning the false gods of materialism, and are coming to realize that the natural world lies at the very center of an environment that is both life-giving and life-promoting. There is hope in this meeting, or so it seems to me, that the values of the spirit are reasserting their primacy—and this in turn gives fresh hope in other vital areas of human endeavor."

REPORT ON THE FIRST WORLD CONFERENCE ON NATIONAL PARKS, SEATTLE, WASHINGTON, JUNE 30-JULY 7, 1962

Continued from page 4

servation. India now has 79 sanctuaries and 5 national parks covering an area of 6,206 square miles, sheltering most species of wildlife, both rare and common.

The conference seemed to reconfirm the need for a common language when it comes to describing common problems and objectives and that uniform laws should and must be created to conserve the resources of, not only the land, but also the sea and the air as well. The relation of one place to the other was forcefully expressed as speakers and delegates unfolded their specific problems and areas of interest. The parks and preserves of Africa and Asia became a part of a common responsibility as they spoke.

The conference closed on Saturday, July 7, with final discussions and conclusions—foremost of these was a resolution to the effect "structures such as dams and reservoirs should not be allowed in National Parks" which after murmurs of dissent from the delegates was amended to read "dams and reservoirs for hydroelectric and other purposes which would in any way be prejudicial to the purpose of the park . . ."

Other final actions revolved around recommendations to the effect, wherever appropriate, the administration and control of National Parks and equivalent be vested in an autonomous statutory organization charged with the duty of permanent trusteeship—and resolutions with reference to saving specific wildlife now threatened with extinction.

This "observer" was not privileged to attend all sessions and consequently has not included all presentations or proceedings. The foregoing for the most part, however, reflects the nature of the conference, which we trust is only the beginning of such gatherings geared to mutually acceptable standards and ideals.

There is no question this was a most enlightening conference and the subjects covered were of prime importance to the people of the world.

Address By Conrad L. Wirth, Director, National Park Service

EDITOR'S NOTE:—Although Mr. Wirth's address as well as Mr. Beard's (P. 27) will be published in the proceedings of the First World Conference on National Parks we feel that both are of such timely significance as to warrant them being made available to the membership at once.

Fellow delegates and colleagues from around the world: It is a great pleasure and an honor to extend greetings to you from the National Park Service of my country, and to express my personal gratitude and appreciation for this opportunity to meet all of you and discuss our mutual interests. Many of you have traveled from afar to attend this milestone conference—from lands of many tongues and many ages. As have I, you brought with you mental pictures of your parks, your forests, your streams and ocean beaches, your trails and camps in their settings of beauty and quiet. There are stories to tell of these places, and ideas and dreams to compare. That is why we are here.

In preparing for my opening remarks, I have tried to search deeply into the philosophy of national parks; deep into my own soul as to why we, the human branch of the creatures of this earth, are gathered here to talk, compare notes, and advance our thinking on how all peoples can better enjoy the great natural areas on the planet on which we have been destined to live.

I have struggled with myself emotionally, to a certain extent, but have also tried to retain a practical approach or an approach that makes sense and is usable and can be understood by all. I say this for, while we are all citizens of this world, we have different problems due to circumstances often beyond our control, yet we have certain basic things in common and which, again may I say, are often beyond our control.

What are these common denominators? *First*, regardless of what political subdivision of this world we come from, we all depend on the soil, the water, and the air, and the things they produce for our existence, our enjoyment and spiritual and cultural well being. *Second*, we as individuals have use of the natural resources of this earth while we live here. We cannot take them with us. We have inherent right to use them, but do not have a right to misuse them, so that generations that follow will be deprived of the benefit of their use. *Third*, as human beings we all have a body and all the organs that make it click, regardless of our individual religious beliefs as to our origin and hereafter. Further, due to our economical, social, and cultural developments and growth in population, nationalities have been intermingled to such extent, whether we like it or not, that many of us have close relatives in two or more countries.

I was born in the United States of America and am deeply proud of my country and want to serve it to the best of my ability. However, on my father's side, I represent the first generation born in this country and between our small family of six, including two daughters-in-law, we have close blood relatives in five other nations. We are not an unusual family in my country, and I am sure the same thing prevails to a greater or lesser extent in the countries represented here today.

What I am trying to say in making these three points is that we have basic interlocking common denominators that affect us all. One of them is the conservation of certain of our natural resources for that part of our life on this earth that will satisfy our cultural, spiritual, and enjoyment need. We are here to better understand these things and to improve our management of these types of resources which many have termed National Parks.

As we meet and talk with our counterparts from distant lands, great questions will come to the minds of all of us. As we explain our individual country's concern for its parklands and exchange thoughts, we will in turn ponder the problems we face in meeting the challenges of a world whose affairs have become more chaotic, more complex, and yet more in need of the values of which we speak than ever before. This, too, is why we are here.

This first World Conference on National Parks is long overdue. The world of radio and television, of planes that race the sun, has done much to bring all Nations closer together. We see photographs of far-off parklands with strange and inviting names and hear of techniques of management solutions

to problems that stimulate our curiosity and arouse in us the desire to know more. But there is no substitute for personal liaison and a face-to-face exchange of information and ideas. This also is why we are here.

The National Park concept is but an extension of an older and basic human need, one that has been with us since man first saw and wondered about the colors of an ancient sunset, or joined his companions in marveling at the symmetry of a flight of geese as they winged their way to a distant nesting ground. These first fleeting moments of perception, or wonder and a sense of reverence, were the beginning. When a distant cousin planted a row of tiny seeds and watched them day by day as they grew and supplied food and fiber for his family, it showed him, whether he realized it at the time or not, that he had the power to bend his environment to his wishes. He also learned that his power was not supreme, that other factors, myriad natural laws that give order to our universe, were constantly at his elbow. Recognizing them and working with their magic represented man's first steps toward growth as an intellectual force.

Perception and receptivity were an integral part of this wisdom. Where man had once taken his environment for granted, and had accepted its blessings with oftentimes callous indifference, there now came time for reflection. With it came the practical realization that man's once abundant natural storehouse had limits and that his material existence would be decided by his

8

stewardship of the land. With proper husbandry he might withstand time; without it he would, in the end, perish. Conservation of natural resources became a national and world doctrine.

National parks and the preservation of the natural landscape with all its creatures, plants and geology are a cultural, social and spiritual expression of enlightened conservation. They are a vital part of a complete land ethic. The concepts they embody do not necessarily assure a complete and whole ethic, yet there can be no balance unless they are present.

National parks are one form of the realization that while man has it within his power to change the face of the Earth, the Earth and its bounties have had, and still retain, that sometimes-mysterious ability to shape the destiny and aspirations of man. Thomas Jefferson once said: "The face and character of our country are determined by what we do with America and its resources." While our forefathers were carving a civilization from the wilderness, the land in turn made enduring inroads into their minds and thoughts. Jefferson saw qualities of perseverence, independence, and initiative developed and refined as the American character was shaped on the vast stretches of virgin prairie, beside rolling rivers, and in lonely mountain passes.

It is in the National Parks that these contributory elements can be maintained and kept pure, so that this and future generations may know and feel, and benefit from, the same wonderous exposure that our forefathers experienced.

The forms of a National Park program vary from nation to nation. Circumstances may warrant a particular approach here, a variation of it there. But always the motivation, the goal, remains the same: perpetuation of those natural and historic values of the land in such manner as to provide a country's people visual and tactile contact with the natural environment. This was the compelling motivation behind establishment of our first National Parks before the turn of the century; this is the guiding principle before us in the present drive to establish and develop new parks, while there are still suitable areas available.

Over the years, this country has added certain refinements to this basic concept as it applies to our particular needs. National Parks, for example, are the "crown jewels", representing the finest and most superlative scenic wonders we can offer. On an equal level, but contributing to the perpetuation of different values, is the great array of National Monuments, established to protect features and objects of nationally significant scientific, archeological or historic importance. Outstanding natural scenery is not a requirement for this category, although many of our national monuments contain landscapes that compare favorably with those found in the National Parks. We also have National Parkways, which are elongated parks with a studiously landscaped highway, for the pleasures of scenic travel. These roadways are closed to commercial traffic and free from local access.

Our historic heritage, those golden links with the past that give meaning and a sense of continuity to events of today and tomorrow, have not been overlooked. Events that shaped the destiny of our country, and the men who guided them, are well represented.

Independence Hall, where on July 4, 186 years ago, our founding fathers signed the Declaration of Independence and later the Constitution of the United States, stands today much as it did in 1776. It is, in the words of Carl Van Doren, ". . . a shrine honored wherever the rights of men are honored . . . a shrine cherished wherever the principles of self-government on a federal scale are cherished." The Hall, and other historic landmarks in the City of Philadelphia, are preserved in the Independence National Historical Park.

From what I have said one would almost be tempted to suppose that the road leading to this country's present National Park System has been a smooth one, paved with unanimous public approval and support, and with scarcely a bump or rough spot to prevent us from moving ahead with great speed. You must surely know from your own experiences that such is not the case. The responsibility for the Nation to provide appropriate park lands for its people also carries with it the responsibility for the Government to assess and weigh all factors pro and con, to consider standards and feasibility, and at all times keep in mind the broad national interest. This involves widespread public understanding of the values that may be lost, as well as those that are to be gained, by establishment of a public park, and a workable means of resolving conflicting and divergent viewpoints concerning competitive land uses.

Although there was a time when a vast stretch of wild country could be set apart for park purposes with scarcely a glimmer of public concern or opposition, this abundance of free land died with the American frontier. But the demise of the frontier also brought with it the realization that its contributions to the American dream of greatness had been immeasurable and that somehow, somewhere, vestiges of this element should be protected and perpetuated. With the need for a strong National Park System becoming more evident every day, and the diminishment of available and qualified land, the stage was set for conflict. These conflicts are being met today with increased understanding and with greater vigor. They will be settled, I am sure, to the benefit of all mankind. I believe it would be desirable in order to help this conference for me to outline very briefly the growth of the National Park System in the United States, so you can compare it with your experience in your own country.

The first action by the Congress of the United States to set apart some of the public lands for man's inner needs came during the Civil War. In 1864, the Congress granted to the State of California the Yosemite Valley upon the express condition:

". . . that the premises shall be held for public use, resort, and recreation; shall be held inalienable for all time."

In those quoted words are to be found the seed of an idea and the beginning of a new national public-land policy. A policy that recognized the need for the holding of land in public ownership in perpetuity for other than material gain or riches.

The Act of Congress coming as it did during a period of internal strife, when the founding principles and ideals of the Nation were at stake, was more than fate or a coincidence of history. While the kinship might be hard to prove, the strange phenomenon has repeated itself in subsequent periods of adversity. Strange too, is the fact that the action was taken at a time when a large portion of the country was still unknown and untamed wilderness.

The action of Congress looked beyond the period of a divided government to a day of internal unity—to a day when the wilderness would be tamed and there would no longer be an abundance of virgin land and natural resources—to the time when the original creations of nature would be sought and revered by mankind for their re-creational benefits alone. Little time was lost in translating the vision into recommended actions.

In 1865, the Board of Commissioners appointed by the Governor of California to assist with the management of Yosemite Valley, prepared a report defining the policy

that should govern the management. The report is still a classic treatise on public-park philosophy. The report was written by Frederick Law Olmsted, a member of the Commission and first superintendent of Central Park, New York City.

In a broader sense the report developed the basic philosophy for publicly owned parks and laid the groundwork for the national park idea. The philosophy is best expressed in the following extracts from the report:

"Thus, unless means are taken by government to withhold them from the grasp of individuals, all places favorable in scenery to the recreation of the mind and body will be closed against the great body of the people. * * * To simply reserve them from monopoly by individuals, however, it will be obvious, is not all that is necessary. It is necessary that they should be laid open to the use of the body of the people.

"The establishment by government of great public grounds for the free enjoyment of the people under certain circumstances, is thus justified and enforced as a political duty."

A few years later those thoughts found expression in the action of a group of men exploring the Yellowstone country. They decided that the natural wonders they had seen should not be exploited for the benefit of a few individuals but held in public ownership for the benefit of the many.

That idealism brought into being the first national park and has been characteristic of each succeeding one. In 1872, Yellowstone National Park was authorized by an Act of Congress. That Act defined a policy and purpose that has been reaffirmed each time the Congress has authorized an additional national park. The significant passage in the Act setting forth the policy reads as follows:

"* * * is hereby reserved and withdrawn, from settlement, occupancy or sale under the laws of the United States and dedicated and set apart as a public park or pleasuring ground for the benefit and enjoyment of the people."

No charter for establishment of a public institution was ever stated so meaningfully and explicitly as that for the first national park. The words "reserved and withdrawn from settlement, occupancy or sale," emphasized the departure from the traditional public land policies and uses. The establishment of a new category of public land and a new form of land-use was defined in the words "dedicated and set apart as a public park or pleasuring grounds."

Park land was to be used "for the benefit and enjoyment of the people" not the production of material goods or commodities. The natural curiosities and wonders of the park were to be the resources of enjoyment, the source of the benefits. That they were to be so managed was made expressly clear in the authority given the Secretary of the Interior to establish rules and regulations.

In establishing rules and regulations the Act specified the conditions to be met in the following words:

"Such regulations shall provide for the preservation, from injury or spoilation, of all timber, mineral deposits, natural curiosities or wonders within said park and their retention in their natural conditions."

The Act of Congress that established the National Park Service in 1916 did more than provide for a unified administration. It defined a purpose that gave form and substance to a specific type of land-use that in turn decreed the management philosophy for park lands and their resources. The particular passage in the Act that has guided the actions of the National Park Service for the past 46 years read as follows:

"The Service thus established shall promote and regulate the use of Federal areas known as parks, monuments, and reservations hereinafter specified by such means and measures as conform to the fundamental purpose of the said parks, monuments and reservations, which purpose is to conserve the scenery and the natural and historic objects and the wildlife therein and to provide for the enjoyment of the same in such manner and by such means as will leave them unimpaired for the enjoyment of future generations."

That passage is the most quoted and mis-quoted of all the laws applying to National Parks. All too frequently only a portion is quoted and by so doing, the intent and meaning is distorted. The philosophy expressed in the quoted passage represents almost a half century evolution.

It is interesting to note that the man credited with writing that important section of the Act, Frederick Law Olmsted, Jr., a landscape architect, was the son of the man who wrote the report on Yosemite Valley in 1865.

The political and social reforms of the past century coupled with a technological and scientific revolution have contributed much to the betterment of mankind. Science has discovered and developed new resources, and substitutes have been developed that ease the drain on natural resources. Despite all of those advances, no satisfactory substitute has been developed for the joys and pleasures of the outdoors. The need for land for the production of that particular product increases rather than diminishes with the advancement of civilization.

The resurgence of public interest in the outdoors is revitalizing the ideas, strengthening the ideals and broadening the vision of the past. It is taking such tangible forms as legislation leading to the acquisition of additional public parks, greater use of all public lands for recreation, greater accessibility, and increased financing of improvements.

All levels of government—Federal, State and local, are participating in the revival of interest. Crowning the revival of interest are the wilderness and outdoor recreation resources bills now being considered by the Congress.

The bill to establish a national wilderness preservation system declares it to be:

"The policy of the Congress of the United States to secure for the American People of present and future generations the benefits of an enduring resource of wilderness. * * * to be administered for the use and enjoyment of the American people in such manner as will leave them unimpaired for future use and enjoyment as wilderness."

The bill to promote the coordination and development of effective Federal and State programs relating to outdoor recreation states:

"That the Congress finds and declares that the general welfare of the Nation requires that all American people of present and future generations shall be assured the availability and accessibility of such quantity of outdoor recreation resources as are desirable and necessary for the

physical, spiritual, cultural, recreational, and scientific benefits which such outdoor recreation resources provide; and that timely and coordinated action is required by all levels of government on a nationwide basis to conserve, develop, and utilize such resources for the benefit of the American people."

Those two expressions of national policy are a fitting tribute to the fruits of a century of internal unity and hold forth great promise of new heights yet to be achieved in the general welfare. The welfare of mankind is deeply rooted in our philosophy of government. It is the motivating force behind park legislation and the activating spirit of the park philosophy of management. It is best expressed in the words,—"for the benefit and enjoyment of the whole people."

A National Park is a natural land composition, spacious in extent, of such outstanding natural character, wonder and beauty that it has been dedicated and set apart as a public park by the Congress of the United States to preserve the distinctive quality and resources of the composition and their inherent capacity to provide enjoyment and inspiration for the benefit of the people of this and future generations.

National Parks are a specific form of land use. The distinguishing characteristic is the nonconsumptive use of natural resources. The product of park lands is not a commodity that can be moved to the market place. Instead, the consumer—the park visitor—must move to the park. There, through the knowledge and skillful guidance of park management, the benefits are derived without consuming the natural resources. Only through the harmonious blending of land-management and consumer can the benefits of national parks be realized in any significant measure. Without all three elements, National Parks would be but a meaningless term.

The National Parks are a priceless part of the American heritage. They are a national resource—a scientific resource—an educational resource —a recreational resource. They are all of those because they are so used.

National Parks symbolize democracy in action. They are born of the people for the use of the people. Public-spirited men and women conceive a proposal and give of their time and talents to bring it into being. There are those who support and those who oppose the development of the proposal, each guided by his own sincere convictions. It is the Congress that makes the final decision. They must weigh the national interest against the local interest and decide whether the national welfare is best served by foregoing material gain for eternal

spiritual values. The cyle is completed by those who use the Parks, partake of their benefits, and pass judgment on their efficacy.

In closing, let me again express my appreciation for the opportunity this conference affords us all to become better acquainted personally, and to discuss and compare techniques, problems, and advances in the National Park field around the globe. We have much to learn from each other and I am sure that out of this conference will come new inspirations we will all want to take with us and rely on in the months ahead. In so doing let us heed the good words of Daniel Burnham, the architect and planner, who said:

"Make no little plans; they have no magic to stir men's blood, and probably themselves will not be realized. Make big plans; aim high in hope and work, remembering that a noble, logical diagram once recorded will never die, but long after we are gone will be a living thing, asserting itself with evergrowing insistency. Remember that our sons and grandsons are going to do things that would stagger us. Let our watchword be 'order' and our beacon be 'beauty'."

Horsky Named to White House Post

President Kennedy has appointed Charles A. Horsky to the newly created position of Special Assistant for District of Columbia Affairs. Mr. Horsky, an active member of the American Planning and Civic Association, and of its Committee of 100 on the Federal City, is an attorney and Washington metropolitan area civic leader.

Never before in the history of the commission form of District of Columbia government has a President had an expert in the White House to coordinate Federal city functions. Mr. Horsky's experience qualifies him to bring together diverse planning, highway, transit and housing interests.

Zoning Round Table

Conducted by FLAVEL SHURTLEFF, Marshfield Hills, Mass.

What Control Over Subdivisions?

From the viewpoint of the planners the accomplishments of subdivision control have been spotty and in some states definitely disappointing. In the two most active subdivision states in New England, the most recent decisions of the highest court seem restrictive in the interpretation of the authorizing statutes and in contrast with decisions under zoning enabling acts, much less liberal.

The early decisions involving plotting and subdivisions may have given false hopes. In Ridgefield Land Co. vs. Detroit* decided in 1928 the Michigan Supreme Court upheld the requirement in the ordinance of Detroit of a seventeen foot dedication of land in addition to the usual thirty-three feet where the plot abutted on a major thorofare. The ordinance was authorized under the platting statute of the state, and the unusually large dedication was approved as a proper exercise of the police power in a well considered decision.

The New Jersey Supreme Court in Mansfield and Swett vs. Town of West Orange,** decided in 1938, established the validity of subdivision control as a police power regulation although the specific exercise of the power by the town planning board was set aside as beyond the authority given by the town's regulations.

But in New England, more than twenty-five years after the Detroit case, the reverses came. In 1954 the highest court of Connecticut agreed unanimously that it was beyond the power of the planning board to base a rejection of a subdivision plan on the town's financial inability to provide a school for the expected increase in population due to the proposed subdivision.*** There was nothing in the statute or in the regulations adopted by the planning board to justify the rejection. There was no doubt that Milford's financial situation called for a drastic remedy, but even if the right had been contained in the regulations, would the court have supported it as a police power regulation?

Then in 1959 the Supreme Court of Massachusetts in the Daley case† said that the words "securing adequate provision for water" in the statute must be read with the basic purpose of subdivision control as expressed in the statute. This was the lay out and construction of adequate ways of access to the lots in a subdivision. Consequently an adequate system of water pipes would satisfy the statute, not an adequate water supply. Even though the subdivision's requirements of water might create a water shortage, this would not justify the rejection of the subdivision. The plan as proposed by the subdivider

*241 Mich. 468 and 217 N. W. 58
**120 N. J. L 145 and 198 Art. 225
***Beach vs. Planning and Zoning Commission of Milford, February 1954, 103 Atlantic 2nd 814.
†Daley Construction Co. vs. Planning Board, 340 Mass. 149

15

fully met the requirements of the statute and the regulations.

This decision was doubly disappointing to the planners. They had hoped after the lower court approved the action of the planning board that an effective check on too rapid subdivision growth would be possible. The supreme court's ruling was a blow, but there was an added sting in the language of the decision. "*Overzealous planners* had attempted to extend their authority beyond the intent of the framers of the law," and the result was "more arbitrary action by planning boards than was consistent with the ideals of constitutional government."

The Pieper case‡ decided by the same court soon after reversed the action of the planning board in rejecting a plan because "we feel it essential to have a master plan available before approving any further subdivision of properties." Such a plan would be ready in seven months at a cost of $40,000. The court said there was no provision in the statute authorizing the planning board to delay its decision beyond the forty-five days specified therein.

Finally in April 1962 the Castle case†† continued the strict interpretation of the statute. The planning board had approved a subdivision plan subject to three con-

‡Pieper *vs.* Planning Board, 340 Mass. 157
††Castles Estates Inc. *vs.* Park and Planning Board. Adv. Sheets 1962, P. 769

ditions—(1) a suitable water distribution system must be installed and connected with the public water supply system; (2) a drainage easement must be obtained over land in other ownership; (3) the sanitary system must be approved by the board of health. The Massachusetts Supreme Court said that the record showed no recommendation by the board of health that the plan should be disapproved or approved conditionally, and that neither the water supply or drainage conditions could be imposed, since neither the statute or the regulations authorized such action. The language of the court is significant. "The subdivision control law attached such importance to the board's regulation as to indicate that they must be comprehensive, reasonably definite, carefully drafted so that the owners may know in advance what standards and procedures will be applied to them."

There may be a ray of hope in this decision. If a code is written similar to a zoning by-law setting out with precision the regulation of utilities which have a substantial relation to public health, a violation of the code in a proposed subdivision might be supported as the basis of a rejection. But such a code would be carefully scrutinized by the court for the reasonability of its regulations.

Ozark Rivers National Monument —A Proposal

EDITOR'S NOTE:—This is the first in what is planned as a series of articles, descriptive in some depth, on the several proposed additions to the National Park System. Succeeding subject areas will be selected for publication as they appear to have some degree of timeliness. This article was prepared by the National Park Service at our request.

Through the mellow Ozark hills in southeastern Missouri flow rivers that are clear and pure, and relatively free from that industrious meddler known as "Progress." Waters from giant springs create and feed the rivers, waters that have hollowed a wondrous Ozark underworld of caves. The streams spill over hard ledges, cut the softer rocks into picturesque cliffs and course in broader valleys between hills wooded by oaks and hickories.

And down these free-flowing rivers float the canoes and indigenous John-boats of vacationists—fishermen, most of them—who seek to catch the fighting bass for which these waters are renowned. They also catch contentment.

We speak often in these times of outdoor recreation resources—places where Americans can enjoy and appreciate their heritage of the natural world. Such resources include a number of kinds of parks: seashores, mountain and forest preserves, deserts and grasslands. Free-flowing streams are of equal importance. They provide a dimension of park experience that no other resource can substitute for. That is the satisfaction of knowing and enjoying a river as it was created, strong, alive and clean.

A river world is compounded of currents and eddies, swift water and calm, light and shadow, and an ever-changing environment of rock and strand, tree and plant, animal, bird and fish. A river has a life of its own, and countless other lives flow with and around it. Man instinctively likes to join in that flow and add it to his experience.

Unspoiled rivers, unobstructed, unpolluted and uncivilized, once veined our country everywhere, but such are few in number now. Most are so altered and hedged about by developments that at best they can give only a poor reminiscence of their once clean and natural flow. To protect the few that are left, especially those which are still relatively near to centers of population, is of urgent necessity in present-day conservation programs.

Thus, it is that a proposal is being considered to preserve three outstanding rivers in an Ozark Rivers National Monument: the Current, its tributary Jacks Fork, and the Eleven Point River not far away. In total some 190 miles of free-flowing waterway would thus be preserved in a beautiful landscape.

Conservation measures for these three outstanding rivers have been a long-standing recommendation of the State of Missouri, supported by Federal agency reports, and in 1959 the state requested legislation to create a national recreation area within these watersheds. Following the further study that was necessary the National Park Service proposed

Planning and Civic Comment

an Ozark Rivers National Monument to encase the three streams in a 113,000-acre preserve. Senators Symington and Long and Representative Ichord of Missouri are sponsoring legislation to authorize the national monument. Representative Curtis of Missouri has introduced another bill to create an Ozark Scenic Riverway to be administered by the U. S. Forest Service, which now administers as part of Clark National Forest some of the acreage recommended for the national monument. The Department of Agriculture has reported favorably on the national monument bill, and some Senate and House hearings have already been held.

The 113,000-acre monument proposed would include 117 miles of the Current River—84 miles of it in one continuous stretch—39 miles on Jacks Fork and 34 miles on the Eleven Point. Within the boundaries would be 13 named caves, 11 interesting geological sites, more than 40 archeological sites, a number of fine ecological areas, and a great many springs. Six springs, each having a flow of 65 million gallons or more per day, are included within the proposed monument boundaries or in adjacent state parks, while there are 13 others of considerable size and many smaller ones also included. The monument would be administered to provide for heavier public use in areas best suited to accommodate large numbers of visitors so that the wild character of other portions of the area would be better protected.

As proposed, the Ozark Rivers National Monument would comprise five sections. The upper Current Section would begin adjacent to Montauk State Park near Salem and would follow the Current River's course for nearly 40 miles to a point below Round Spring State Park. This 21,000-acre tract would include such notable features as Round Spring Cavern, Ashley Cave, Welch Spring, the Sunkland and the Sinks. Developments would be kept few and simple here, preservation of the outstanding scenic area and the wilderness atmosphere being the paramount objectives. The state parks adjacent to and surrounded by the monument would continue as state parks to serve the public as major developed areas.

The Cardareva Section would continue the national monument another 45 miles down the Current River to a point just above Van Buren and would include the largest block of land composing the monument: some 49,800 acres adjoining the state's Peck Ranch Wildlife Management Area. This exception to allowing the river course to control the land area reservation was adopted in order to include a typical sample of Ozark hill country. Special features of this section would be Blue Spring, Rocky Falls, Cardareva Mountain, Paint Rock, Big Creek, Chilton Creek, and the juncture of the Current with Jacks Fork.

Below Van Buren, national monument lands would resume, adjacent to Big Spring State Park, with 32 more miles of river. The river is broader here and offers much boating activity. The monument lands

18

would end a few miles north of Doniphan.

Separated from the Current River portion of the proposed national monument by an area surrounding the town of Eminence, the Jacks Fork Section of the proposal would protect approximately 39 miles of that wild and scenic stream in a 17,160-acre reservation. Management plans envision preserving the wild character of this valley, particularly above adjoining Alley Spring State Park, though Jam-Up Cave, one of the most striking and unique features of the monument, would be a point of considerable public interest.

The Eleven Point Section, lying in a different drainage, would be somewhat separated from the other four. This 14,000-acre tract would protect some 34 miles of that river, which has characteristics similar to Jacks Fork and the upper Current. Attractive Greer Spring and Mill, historic Turners Mill, and Blue Spring are notable features there.

If the Ozark Rivers National Monument is authorized, it will be the first unit of the National Park System established primarily to protect and feature a natural waterway. It may also be the first step in the establishment of a system of national rivers, a concept recommended by a number of conserva-

tion leaders. Already another river reserve has been proposed to include the Allagash River and its headwaters lakes in northern Maine to preserve the wilderness character of that famed north woods canoeing water. Other rivers, too, are under study for possible national protection.

The urgency of setting aside in public ownership still-unspoiled portions of rivers and shorelines has become ever more apparent and is beginning to receive long-due recognition. The urgency is part of what Secretary of the Interior calls the "quiet crisis in conservation" as the Nation's population grows and the search for outdoor recreation intensifies. Even today the Ozark Rivers are within a comfortable day's drive of more than 20 million people. These unspoiled rivers represent a park resource that has dwindled alarmingly during the years and a type of outdoor recreation opportunity that cannot be duplicated in other kinds of areas. Yet the health and pleasure derived from streams like the Current and Eleven Point become increasingly important to us as our industrial, urban world denies us the simple refreshment and understanding experienced in following clean, free-flowing rivers in America.

Strictly Personal

S. R. DeBoer, of Denver, Colorado, was presented a beautiful bronze plaque by President S. W. Driftmeir of the Colorado Nurserymen's Association, for outstanding achievement in horticulture. In his response, Mr. DeBoer told about his early work for the City of Denver including the grading and planting of Cherry Creek Boulevards and the many parks that were laid out at the time. He stressed the importance of trees in the city plan and said our present plans are too mechanical and do not provide sufficient attractiveness and liveability. He felt we need a positive program of planting trees instead of cutting them down. The meeting was held at the Rolling Hills Country Club, near Golden.

———◆———

James S. Pope, former Executive Editor of the *Louisville Courier-Journal*, has been named Chairman of a Committee that will review Ford Foundation-supported projects in urban research, education and extension.

———◆———

James S. Schoff has been elected President of The Regional Plan Association at New York. He succeeds Amory H. Bradford, Vice-President of the *New York Times* who had served for three years. Mr. Schoff, President and Managing Director of Bloomingdale Brothers, has served as a Vice-President of the Association since December 1959. He is also Vice-President of Federated Department Stores, Inc., a Trustee of the Union Dime Savings Bank and a member of the Board of the Better Business Bureau.

———◆———

R. A. Wilhelm has retired from the National Park Service and now has a private practice in Landscape Architecture and Civil Engineering in Gatlinburg, Tennessee.

———◆———

William B. Marquis, Partner of Olmsted Associates, retired from the partnership in April 1962 and will continue with the firm as Consultant. Artemus P. Richardson and Joseph G. Hudak, remaining partners, will continue the firm's practice from the established address of 99 Warren St., Brookline, Mass.

———◆———

Ralph D. Ford has been appointed Director of the Mississippi State Park Commission. Mr. Ford was born at Brookhaven, Mississippi April 29, 1927, received an LL.B. degree from Jackson School of Law, is a former field investigator, Mississippi Public Service Commission and served two and a half years as Executive Assistant to Governor Ross R. Barnett of Mississippi. He is married and the father of two children.

———◆———

Kenneth McElroy, Columbus, is the newly-elected president of the Ohio Parks Association it was announced in Cincinnati at the conclusion of the association's annual meeting. McElroy is the landscape architect for the Ohio Division of

Parks, and works in the Development Section. He has been an employee of the division for 17 years.

◆

Sigurd F. Olson of Ely, Minnesota, past president of the National Parks Association and a member of the Advisory Board on National Parks, Historic Sites, Buildings and Monuments, has been appointed consultant to Secretary of the Interior Stewart L. Udall and to the Director of the National Park Service on major problems in the field of wilderness preservation. Naturalist, author, lecturer and wilderness veteran, Olson will examine policies and practices of the National Park System relative to the management of the natural and scenic areas of the System, giving particular attention to those situations which have aroused spirited controversy as to methods of management and control.

◆

H. Raymond Gregg, Superintendent of Hot Springs National Park, Arkansas, has been named Superintendent of the Jefferson National Expansion Memorial, St. Louis, Mo., National Park Service Director Conrad L. Wirth, Department of the Interior announced recently. Mr. Gregg succeeds George B. Hartzog, who resigned to accept employment with Downtown St. Louis, Inc. Director Wirth said that Hartzog was an outstanding park man whose career began in 1946, and that his services will be greatly missed.

Mr. Wirth said that Supt. Gregg's extensive background in interpretation and knowledge of Service policies, as well as his dynamic personality were important factors in his selection for the Memorial post.

Mr. Gregg has been superintendent of Hot Springs National Park since November 1959. During his 29 years with the National Park Service, he has served in Naturalist positions at Rocky Mountain and Hot Springs National Parks and in the National-Capital Region as well as the Washington Office of the National Park Service. Prior to taking the post of superintendent of Hot Springs National Park he served for four years as Regional Chief of Interpretation in the National Park Service Midwest Regional Office, Omaha, Nebraska. Mr. Gregg is a native of Fayetteville, Arkansas. Before entering Federal service he had six years experience as a school administrator in Arkansas.

Mr. Gregg was on military duty with the U. S. Navy from October 7, 1942 until November 25, 1945. He served as a recruiting officer in Denver and also at the Philadelphia Navy Yard, where he acted as liaison officer between the fleet and shore training activities. He has an A.B. degree in English from Hendrix College, Conway, Arkansas.

In the June issue of *Historic Preservation*, the Dedication of the James Monroe Library in Fredericksburg, Va. is graphically presented, as a fitting tribute to the author of "The Monroe Doctrine." The Rembrandt Peale Portrait of Monroe is described. In the garden there is a bust of President Monroe by Margaret French Cresson, daughter of Daniel Chester French. Mrs. Cresson is a member of our Committee of 100 on the Federal City.

◆

In June Horace M. Albright received an LL.D. from the University of New Mexico.

This was the 50th anniversary of the Class of 1912 at the University of California. Among the well known members were Mr. and Mrs. Horace M. Albright, Newton B. Drury, and Earl Warren.

◆

Sidney S. Kennedy, long-time official of the Department of the Interior's National Park Service, has been named Chief, Division of Cooperative Services, of the Department's new Bureau of Outdoor Recreation, Secretary of the Interior Stewart L. Udall announced.

Mr. Kennedy's responsibilities will include providing technical assistance in outdoor recreation planning and operation to States and their political subdivisions. Technical assistance and services available include all phases of recreation planning and management. Involved are policies, practices, objectives, protection, area selection, interpretation programs, concessions, and legislation.

In addition, he will be responsible for making recommendations to the General Services Administration on disposal of surplus real properties for park, recreation and historic monument purposes.

Mr. Kennedy's work with the National Park Service began with the Civilian Conservation Corps in 1933 when he served in Ithaca, N. Y., as a landscape foreman, serving successively as CCC camp inspector, and assistant regional officer.

He transferred to Washington, D. C., as a park planner, and since that time his work has involved providing cooperative assistance to other Federal, State and local agencies, including consultative and advisory assistance on all aspects of park and recreation area programs, reservoir planning and management, park practice programs, making investigations and recommendations on surplus Federal properties requested by State and local agencies for park, recreation and historic monument use.

Prior to joining the National Park Service, Mr. Kennedy worked with an Ithaca landscape architect and with the Finger Lakes and Genesee State Parks Commission in Ithaca and Castile, New York.

He is a native of Mount Pleasant, Michigan. He attended Central Michigan University and received a bachelor of science degree from Michigan State University in 1923. In 1928, he was graduated from Harvard University, School of Design, with the degree of master of landscape architecture.

Mr. Kennedy is a fellow of the American Society of Landscape Architects, a professional member and director of the National Conference on State Parks, and a fellow of the American Institute of Park Executives.

◆

Robert W. Ludden, career employee of the National Park Service, has been named Chief, Division of Planning and Surveys, in the Department of the Interior's new Bureau of Outdoor Recreation, Secretary of the Interior Stewart L. Udall announced.

Director Edward C. Crafts of the Bureau of Outdoor Recreation stated that Mr. Ludden's division will be responsible for compiling and keeping current a nationwide outdoor recreation plan. This plan will take into account the existing and proposed private and commercial programs in outdoor recreation as well as present and planned activities of Federal agencies, the States and their subdivisions.

In addition, Mr. Ludden's division of the Bureau of Outdoor Recreation will be responsible for certain special projects assigned by Secretary Udall. These will involve study and evaluation of outdoor recreation needs and potential in specific areas.

One such project now underway includes Middle Atlantic seacoast areas which were heavily damaged in the storm of March 6 and 7.

The Bureau of Outdoor Recreation's new division chief joined the National Park Service during the early days of the Civilian Conservation Corps program in 1935. He worked in several capacities in the recreation and land planning field for the Park Service.

As Chief of the Division of Recreation Resource Surveys, he directed the Service's park, parkway and recreation area study program. Mr. Ludden coordinated the seashore surveys of the Atlantic, Gulf and Pacific coasts and the Great Lakes shoreline which the National Park Service undertook between 1955 and 1959.

Mr. Ludden is a native of Schenectady, New York. He holds an LL.B. degree from the National University of Law in Washington, D. C., and is a fellow of the American Institute of Park Executives. During World War II he served with the 15th Air Force in Africa and Italy.

Look How Open Space Can Hold Down Your Taxes

By RUTH RUSCH, Peekskill, N. Y.

EDITOR'S NOTE:—Mrs. Rusch, who lives in Peekskill, N. Y., has been in conservation work for about 10 years. She is a graduate of Barnard College and taught American History and Government at Scarborough School, Scarborough-on-the Hudson, N. Y. She writes a column on nature subjects and conservation for Hudson Valley newspapers. She participated in the Open Space Survey known as Park, Recreation and Open Space Project of the Tri-state New York Metropolitan Region conducted by the Regional Plan Association.

If there is some green open land in your community, you're lucky. Take a good look at it because the City Fathers are probably making plans to use it for garden apartments or a subdivision of split-levels.

Perhaps if you move fast enough you can save it by getting into their hands facts and figures to prove that keeping it just the way it is will provide a buffer against rising taxes. There is mounting evidence to support the claim that open space can save the hard-pressed taxpayer money, at the same time supplying him and his children with a place for healthy recreation and enjoyment of the out-of-doors.

In many communities open space has been completely swallowed up by urban growth, even to the little corner lots where the kids used to play baseball. The "put it on the taxroll" complex has so dominated official thinking that the sight of a patch of green in a municipal park has been enough to prompt special meetings of the local Council to explore ways of "putting it to better use."

The village of Mamaroneck, New York, found out the hard way that building a large post-war garden apartment on vacant land resulted in higher taxes for property owners.

The development paid $42,415.00 in school taxes in 1960. However, based on Board of Education figures, it cost $107,800.00 to educate the children living in the apartments. The taxpayers paid the difference.

Municipal officials too frequently lose sight of the fact that the profit from a piece of property on the tax-rolls is the revenue received *less* the cost of services rendered. Those services include utilities, streets, sewage disposal, garbage removal, drainage, police and fire protection, plus the cost of educating the children that live there.

The planning firm of Frederick P. Clark Associates completed in 1958 a land study in the Town of Yorktown, Westchester County, New York, reported by the Regional Plan Association. It was found that each dwelling pays $100 less in real estate taxes than it receives in municipal services. The staff calculated that the acquisition of a public park including the loss of tax revenue from the vacant land and the purchase and maintenance costs, would result in a 15 percent lower annual cost to the Town than if the land were developed with houses.

When State Park Commissioner Robert Moses announced plans to purchase the 1426 acre Marshall

Field estate at Lloyd Harbor, New York, protests arose from residents of the area.

The village board hired a firm of planning consultants to determine the effect of the park on the tax structure. It was found that the creation of the park would raise the tax rate from $14.33 to $16.91 but if homes in the $35,000 class were built on two acre minimum plots, they could expect a tax rate of $21.64.

A study of open land made in the Town of Lexington, Massachusetts, by Roland B. Greeley, a member of the planning firm of Adams, Howard and Greely, underscores the advantages to the taxpayer of retaining open space. Mr. Greeley found that if the Town were to buy up, over a period of a few years, about 2000 acres of undeveloped land, selecting the areas least accessible, least easy to service, least desirable for residence, the net saving over the cost of providing municipal services for the same areas would amount to a quarter million dollars annually.

Assuming that the land would cost a million dollars, based on present land values, Mr. Greeley estimated that this sum spread over a twenty year period should not exceed $75,000 per year, including loss of tax revenue from the raw land.

On the basis of Lexington's postwar experience, each new home pays about $400 per year in taxes. Assuming that such homes average only 1½ school age children per family, the cost of schooling alone would be equal to or exceed the taxes paid during the first 15 or 20 years of the dwelling's existence. Thus the cost of school construction, sewers, drainage, street maintenance and even some health and welfare expenses would have to be met by the Town as a whole. Hence the cost of servicing these homes, if they were built, would add up to far more than the $75,000 per year which the Town would spend to keep the land undeveloped.

"As communities become urbanized the amount of undeveloped land that can be taxed to subsidize the essential running costs of the community decreases and eventually vanishes", states Richard H. Pough, President of the Natural Area Council, who has made studies of the effect of open space on the economic life of urban areas.

"In fully developed communities real estate taxes simply prorate the cost of services among the residents based on the size of the house and lot or the apartment a man chooses to live in. The only subsidy left is what can be obtained from business establishments that contribute school taxes without sending any children to school."

Mr. Pough points out that many a "bedroom" community does not have this cushion. In a typical "bedroom" community near New York City where virtually all the costs of running the community and its schools are borne by the homeowners, they run as follow per capita:

Streets, water, sewage, waste disposal.................. $19.59
Judiciary, police and fire protection. 23.89
Schools.......................... 65.77
Administrative and other expenses.. 29.39

Total: $138.64

The idea that per capita costs will drop if the population density increases is contrary to all actual experience, according to Mr. Pough's findings. "In fact these costs do just the opposite—they increase", he states. To substantiate this, he refers to the per capita taxes of New York City where a fair share of business establishments help carry the load:

Streets, water, sewage, waste disposal....................... $17.46
Judiciary, police and fire protection. 47.13
Schools........................ 20.95
Administrative and other expenses.. 77.81

Total: $165.35

As a guide for civic groups and public officials wishing to analyze their local tax problems in relation to available open space, Mr. Pough suggests the following outline:

Name of Community
Period covered
Population
Number of School Children
Number of Residential Units
Total area of Community in Acres
Open Space Acreage

Annual Cost of Government and of Services provided:
(including capital expenditures, debt service, maintenance, running expenses)

	Total	Per Family	Per Capita
Streets, water, sewage, waste disposal		....	....
Judiciary, police, fire		....	....
Parks, recreation		....	....
General Expenses (administrative, legislative and financial)........		....	....
Miscellaneous......		....	....
Total			

Sources of Funds to Cover Above Expenses:

	Total	Percent of Total
Residential structures and lots....	....	
Business establishments and land...	....	
Productive land.... (crop land, forest, watershed)	..	
Undeveloped unproductive land.....	....	....
Miscellaneous......	....	....
Total		

In his presentation of the tax study made of Lexington, Massachusetts, Mr. Greeley pointed out the added advantage of open space in helping to retain the rural charm of a suburban community and in providing outdoor areas for recreation. Residents are afforded ample elbow room for outdoor activities— intensive sports and games as well as quiet relaxation and rest in the open air. Keeping the "old swimming hole" and the corner lot for the neighborhood kids may end up being not only a contribution to the community's recreation program but a sound financial investment promising future savings as well.

Address By Daniel B. Beard, Assistant Director, National Park Service

ENJOYMENT AND UNDERSTANDING OF NATIONAL PARKS IN THE UNITED STATES OF AMERICA AS PROVIDED THROUGH INTERPRETATION

The key word, mentioned over and over again in national park legislation in the United States is "enjoyment": national parks have been and will be created so they may be enjoyed by people now and in the future. The National Park Service, an agency of the United States Government, was established in 1916 to see to it that the opportunity to enjoy national parks would be provided and continued in perpetuity. This was and still is a very attractive idea. Some say it has been a miracle that the idea has lasted in the face of constant buffeting by those who believe that every acre of land should produce materials of some kind. Yet, the idea has been so attractive and so well accepted by the people that almost 23 million acres of this Nation containing outstanding scenery, archeological remains, historic sites and structures and related things were, and will be, set aside from other uses for enjoyment. Of course, a great natural phenomenon must be protected and preserved if it is to continue to be appreciated and enjoyed. Enjoyment of parks stems from the thing to be enjoyed and not from any artificial development. And, furthermore, it must be recognized that a national park has many auxiliary benefits to the community and to the nation at large.

When the National Park Service sets out upon its mission of seeing that the opportunity to enjoy the parks is provided and preserved, it plunges into a whole realm of activities: protection of people, planning, construction, fire protection, research, maintenance, land acquisition, and so on. Yet, these activities, necessary though they may be, are incidental because enjoyment is really an emotional experience.

Very early in the history of the National Park Service, various people recognized that a national park can be enjoyed better, appreciated more fully if one has an opportunity to learn more about its features. But, whose duty was it to impart this knowledge and how was it to be done? Did the public coming to see the wonders of the parks want to be educated, and if so, by whom?

It all started simply enough in our national parks here. Men, such as Dr. Harold C. Bryant and Ansel Hall, took such park visitors as were interested on nature walks. They pointed out trees, birds, flowers, and rock formations. The opportunity was being provided in a modest way for those who cared to accept it. This was called "nature guiding."

It quickly became apparent that nature guiding was a popular program and the idea spread to other

27

national parks. It was frankly admitted from the beginning that this was an educational activity and should not be considered some sort of entertainment. So, by the time Dr. Carl P. Russell took over leadership of the program almost twenty years later, it was a successful and well accepted activity in all national parks. Russell popularized the word "interpretation" and the name of the whole program was changed accordingly. It was finally defined in 1957 by Freeman Tilden in his book *Interpreting Our Heritage* as: "An educational activity which aims to reveal meanings and relationships through the use of original objects, by firsthand experience, and by illustrative media, rather than simply to communicate factual information."

Tilden said that the chief aim of interpretation is not instruction but provocation. The good interpreter uses the tools and techniques of his profession up to a level of interest and curiosity, then steps aside.

Walt Whitman must have had the same thought in mind when he wrote:

"You must not know too much or be too precise or scientific about birds and trees and flowers . . . a certain free margin, and even vagueness—perhaps ignorance, credulity—helps your enjoyment of these things."

No man can leave the Grand Canyon, the Rain Forest of Olympic, or the silent ancient cities of Mesa Verde and be the same as when he came in. Visitors who enter the awesome groves of giant sequoia trees are often so profoundly moved that they instinctively remove their hats. But that

is not enough for many. At Grand Canyon, if one knows and can get into conscious perspective the tremendous span of the earth's history that the grinding river has laid bare before his eyes, the spectacle takes on greater meaning; his enjoyment of the park and his whole life experience as well has been enriched. The function of the interpretive program is to give such an opportunity to learn to those who want it.

Park interpretation is dependent upon a continued flow of knowledge that comes from research or investigation. The park itself must be studied by qualified specialists to provide the basic knowledge for interpretation and for intelligent management of the park resources. The park visitors and their use of and reaction to the interpretive program must be continually studied. Knowledge gained elsewhere may be used in an interpretive program. Let us say, for example, that a geologist in Europe or Asia finds that the climate during the Jurassic was entirely different than previously supposed. This would or should have an immediate effect upon the interpretive program of Dinosaur National Monument in Utah which features the story of Jurassic dinosaurs.

In our experience, some research by interpreters is helpful because the men and women of the National Park Service who are the interpreters, have various professional backgrounds in biology, archeology, history, and geology. It is often suggested that this is unnecessary because "anybody can learn to give a talk on any subject." That is

28

true enough, but unless one knows his subject, has enthusiasm for it, and is enriched with a depth of knowledge, he is likely to be a poor interpreter. To this line of argument can come the rebuttal that a scientist is not necessarily a good interpreter, that the very fact that he is a scientist indicates he is not interested in people. That, too, can be and often is true. The aim then is to obtain professionally trained people who have an aptitude for good human relations. They must be able to pitch interpretation to the frame of reference of the person to whom they are speaking. This cannot be done by instinct alone. It is not enough that our interpreters have a thorough professional background, that they like people, and that they have a flair for teaching. They have to be alert to changing conditions and some of them at least must be able to appraise the changing needs of park visitors and to imaginatively plan and develop interpretation to fit modern needs.

This evening, in parks throughout the United States, people will emerge from campgrounds, hotels, and other places to attend outdoor campfire programs conducted by naturalists. Some of these programs are in amphitheaters that will attract hundreds of people and are equipped with stage and projection and sound equipment. Others will be attended by no more than a dozen or so seated on logs or on the grass.

At most of these gatherings there will be a campfire, reminiscent of man's more intimate dependence on and association with nature, to warm the hearts if not the bodies of

an audience. The evening gathering of park visitors provides an opportunity to further orient them and to suggest what to see and do on their own and to invite them to attend interpretive activities.

The talk is the most important part of the program. This is what the audience comes to hear. In education there is no adequate substitute for the teacher and the same is true of the educational activity we call interpretation. A "live" interpreter is far better than a mechanical or inanimate one. It follows that the "live" interpreter must be skillful at his trade because a poor speaker is little more than nothing at all. This does not mean that the speaker must be an outstanding orator or an actor of some kind. The good interpreter is a teacher who presents facts in an interesting manner so that his audience is stimulated to know more about the subject. His job is to interest and not to entertain. Above all, he must be accurate. The competent interpreter is always in short supply so he must be used where he will be most effective. The campfire program is such a place. Given a versatile interpreter, the outdoor evening program is a highly successful medium of interpretation. It provides an opportunity to meet large audiences of park visitors under favorable circumstances for increasing interest, enjoyment, and appreciation of the national parks.

Tomorrow, in caves and caverns, on forest trails, along ocean beaches, across mountain glaciers, in prehistoric Indian ruins, and in historic houses throughout the Park System, naturalists, archeologists, and historians, will lead groups of visitors and interpret to them the features that are seen. Like the campfire program, the conducted trip also is a traditional method of interpretation in the parks. It is regarded as the most effective kind because the subject matter is close at hand and can be seen and touched while the interpreter is talking.

There is no other practical way for some of the park features to be seen and interpreted than by the conducted trip. The delicate formations of caves and caverns would soon be lost if visitors were permitted to go by themselves. Nor would it be safe for the visitors. In Glacier National Park, naturalists lead visitors across crevassed glaciers where it would be unsafe for them to go alone. Some park features cannot be adequately interpreted by any other means. Some archeological ruins, and historic buildings need the live interpreter to give them meaning.

Under some conditions, a demonstration serves very well. It is a teaching method that is as old as man. In park work it is best used in historical interpretation: a horse-drawn barge on an old canal, Indian dancers, handicrafts, the firing of an old musket. No number of signs, diagrams, pictures or books could tell it as well. For instance, one of the most delightful places along the Blue Ridge Parkway is Mabry Mill, which creaks and groans through the years as it turns out "water ground corn meal." The rushing water turns the mill wheel just as it did in great-grandfather's day. Inside this old mill the smell and sounds are exactly the same so that (as if by some ledgerdemain) the

visitor is himself back in the days when pioneer settlers lived in the Blue Ridge Mountains.

Soon after the National Park Service was established, the late Ansel F. Hall, a park ranger at the time, conceived the idea of converting an old artist's studio in Yosemite National Park, California, into a museum and a focal point for the naturalist program that was just beginning to be developed there.

The American Association of Museums became interested as park after park began developing some type of exhibit. According to Dr. Carl Russell, former Chief of Interpretation, "It was Dr. (Harman C.) Bumpus (of the Association) who originated the 'focal point museum' idea so well represented by the several small institutions in Yellowstone, each one concerned with a special aspect of the park story, and so located as to tell its story while its visitors were surrounded by and deeply interested in the park features outdoors. Site museums is another name for them, although this name is quite new."

Most of the museums in the parks can be rightfully called site museums, although the term applies most obviously to museums at historic and archeological sites. The trailside exhibits now commonly used in many national parks and first tried at Obsidion Cliff in Yellowstone were an outgrowth of the focal point museum idea.

In my own remembrance, which goes back to park museums of the 1920's, exhibits and collections differed but slightly from those found in city museums. Park museums tended, however, to feature objects from the area itself rather than from all over the globe, and park museums were developed by ingenuity and little else. City museum exhibits were more elaborate because they were better financed. But the very simplicity and obvious "labor of love" gave park museums a tremendous appeal. Somewhere along the line, resemblance to the city-type museum became very tenuous. People did not come to national parks in order to visit museums full of stuffed bears, deer, and birds that could be seen in the wild nearby. In fact, even the name "museum" connotating such things was beginning to be looked upon with disfavor. The museum was, after all, not the goal but merely one of the tools of interpretation.

When someone said: "The park is the museum" then the naturalists, historians, exhibit planners and others, began to develop a different perspective of the function of the park museum as an integrated part of the interpretive program. "The park as a whole may be regarded as an exhibit and the museum as an explanatory label. This concept underlies all park museum work."

Within the last few years, the idea of a "visitor center" has become prominent in our parks: a structure designed to provide the visitor with information, and interpretation in a centralized location.

It came upon the scene as a method, if you will, of meeting the impact of a great many more park visitors than ever before. Personal contact and friendly little museums could no longer meet the public needs. Park entrance stations, clogged with traffic, were no longer able to serve as information booths.

The typical park visitor center is more attention getting than the traditional structure. It asks to be seen and beckons one to enter. It fails in its purpose if it hides. An early stop at a visitor center enables the visitor to get the information necessary to make the best use of his time in the park according to his interest. Inside the buildings, the same welcome is incorporated into the lobby where a uniformed naturalist or information receptionist is normally available at an information desk. In a relaxed atmosphere, carefully and purposely developed, the visitor can see exhibits on the park which stimulate his interest while increasing his knowledge. He may talk to the uniformed representatives, ask questions and receive accurate answers. Most visitors will want to attend the audio-visual "show" in a little theater-like room in the visitor center. As a general rule, it will be an automatic program with color slides and professionally taped narration. Quite often, a "picture window" in the visitor center lobby opens on a prime park view which the exhibit may interpret.

The visitor center, if it does its job, is a pause in the park visit. It sends the visitor into the park in a mood to enjoy it more. He knows he is welcome, he knows where he is going. And, most important of all, he has made the transition from the world outside to the park. He can see, enjoy, understand and appreciate.

Visitor centers are not cheap. Space, exhibits, audio-visual equipment and facilities, and good architecture cost money. So far, 63 visitor centers have been completed by the National Park Service. Sixteen are under construction and 66 more are programmed between now and 1966.

This year, areas administered by the National Park Service will receive about 80 million visits. To meet this influx, interpretive services, will have about 844 historians, archeologist, guides, information specialists, etc., over half of whom are seasonal employees. As can be readily understood, all interpretation cannot be handled by personal contact alone. Considerable reliance must be placed upon the various devices and techniques which are not manned, such as self-guiding trails and tours.

Self-guiding facilities along park roads and trails are on 24-hour duty seven days a week. No other interpretive medium can reach so many people. Not only that, they provide interpretation at the most favorable places—the sites of features or events. It would not be desirable even if it were possible, to have a live interpreter at every important park feature.

Self-guiding interpretation along roads and trails is more important today than it was years ago because visitors do not stay as long. It suits the convenience of visitors who are in a hurry. At Mesa Verde National Park, for instance, the average length of stay 30 years ago was 2–3 days. Now it is ¾ of a day.

Signs and wayside exhibits have been used for many years to interpret features seen in proximity to park roads. Until quite recently, these were often "targets of op-

portunity" rather than a carefully planned, interrelated and integrated program. Although not universally applicable, many park roads are so situated that a self-guiding tour is an excellent interpretive method. In fact, roads are now designed for that purpose.

Interpretive signs are difficult to develop. There can be nothing casual or haphazard about them if they are to do their job. Facts must be accurate and text pertinent. Freeman Tilden gives us an example of a good one. He saw it in New Hampshire and this is the thought it conveyed:

THE BASIN
Over a period of centuries
a pothole was formed by the
action of a large stone
turning and spinning
under the pressure of rushing
whirling water, in a depression
of the granite stream bed

How much better that is than saying: "This is a pothole in granite!"

Nature trails are well accepted and widely used in this Country. They follow two set patterns without much overlap. The earliest nature trails employed little signs that described features encountered in place. Most popular now are the trails with booklets keyed to numbered stakes or stations. The latter system is beginning to be questioned as to its actual value in use because in numerous instances, investigators have found that people soon tire of reading a section of a descriptive pamphlet at each numbered station. It seems possible that a combination of the two systems is indicated or perhaps someone will think up an entirely new approach. One of the greatest sins in park interpretation is to say too much—to say more than the visitor will read. Perhaps this is the difficulty with some of our self-guiding trail booklets. Obviously they are not effective if they are not used.

The National Park System of the United States when completed will contain the outstanding examples of our landscape relatively intact with plants and animals in normal relationships. Most of our great historic sites will be in the System. So, taking it as one thing—one system—we can see that it is an educational resource that has scarce-

ly been tapped. It has the capacity to do much more than it has in the past to enrich the lives of our people and those who come to visit us from other countries.

It seems to me that national park management has matured through the years, and that one very good index of this process has been the growth of our interpretive program.

Techniques of interpretation will change as new means of communication develop. I predict that in twenty-five years the interpretive programs of the National Park Service will constitute the major activity of this agency.

Laurence S. Rockefeller Addresses Izaak Walton League

Speaking before the 40th Annual Convention of the Izaak Walton League of America at Portland, Oregon, Mr. Rockefeller told the delegates that "the report (of the Outdoor Recreation Resources Review Commission) was only the top of the iceberg."

"In addition to the research work of its own staff the Commission initiated a number of special studies and it went far beyond the conventional recreation channels to get the right people for the job," he declared. "These studies they produced, were not only a foundation for the Commission's own report, they are individually a mine of information and new ideas," said he.

After reviewing the action taken

following completion of the report—The President's Conservation Message to the Congress, the convening of the White House Conference on Conservation and the establishment of the Bureau of Outdoor Recreation in the Department of the Interior—Mr. Rockefeller went on. "—Senator Clinton Anderson, a Commission member, introduced legislation, S 3117, to strengthen the Bureau with matching grant funds for helping the states' comprehensive planning." "The bill has received strong bipartisan support" he said, and added "it seems likely that it will be followed by further legislation providing grant funds for acquisition and development."

Design Opportunities in Urban Planning

By PAUL OPPERMAN, AIP

EDITOR'S NOTE:—Paul Opperman, AIP, a Board Member of the American Planning and Civic Association made the following remarks as a panel member discussing "New Dimensions of Architectural Knowledge" at the 94th Annual Convention of the American Institute of Architects at Dallas, Texas. The Editor, AIA Journal, has given permission for reproduction of Mr. Opperman's remarks.

Everyone knows that the architect does not in fact today shape the urban environment. Neither, I am more than willing to admit, does the planner—even the most effective among us. Most of us, most of our adult life, have been keenly and often painfully aware that the way our cities were being built gave us no real gifts of delight!

Do we know who shapes the environment? Any answer is surely compound, never truly simple. Some would say science or technology or the machine determine how our cities are built and what kinds of cities they are. Partly true. Others would need only a single pregnant word to supply their answer: This word would be "money." Then there are the most general of the general thinkers who may be expected to say that it is society or the community or government that is the builder of cities—its "architect" in fact. As a general thinker myself, I would have to say cities are the product and the reflection of the general culture of a people— and run the risk of receiving a blank stare from most questioners.

Meanwhile, as we wait for better answers, in each of these current years, something more than a million dwellings are erected, perhaps fifty billion dollars worth of industrial construction is built, and many billions out of another fifty billion for national defense are also spent for construction. This is only a substantial part of the enormous volume of environment-shaping building that goes on in the cities and urban regions of the country. Regardless of how we judge it on design criteria, and irrespective of whether the architect is having as great a hand in the total effort as his protagonists might wish, the American environment is being shaped— and how!

An important amount of this tremendous volume of the nation's building is residential in character. Here the homebuilders take over. Architects are not asked for much help, as yet, and in this area there should be a greater contribution by them.

"Architecture hath firmness, commodity and delight." As to firmness and commodity—or, if you will, structure and utility for the purposes of the client, public or private —in these aspects, the building product of today doubtless provides a vastly better answer to the building problems and needs of our society than the building product of the country did a generation ago. Indeed, it may be a vastly better product of its kind than ever before in history.

One thing is certain, however, and that is that the better-built houses, the better-built factories, office buildings, hospitals, and schools, do not together constitute

34

well-designed, well-built, firm, useful, and attractive communities.

Meanwhile, there is a whole literature of more and more critical analysis and commentary on what the American people have done and are doing to their environment, urban and non-urban. An obvious question to be directed to such a panel as ours is not only how under the sun did we get into the pickle we are in affecting design, but how in the world can we get on a more defensible and agreeable course?

I believe I have made my point that without the architect—and without the architect not simply as an ordinary producer of firm and useful buildings which many others can plan as well or better than he, but as a creator, in a planned context, of firm, useful, and delightful, yes, beautiful, buildings—we can expect to *have* no urban design.

It seems all too clear that a scattered few well-designed buildings will not leaven the whole urban lump. It may only result, as much of the townscape appears to testify, in making the urban lumps conspicuously lumpier by the contrast it affords.

The conditions for building have been changing fast and the prospects for further change are clearly present. Among important challenges to those concerned with design in an urban planning framework are some established but still fairly recent examples.

Present and tangible opportunities for "new dimensions" in architectural scope and practice offered in any proper list surely would include the following:

The redesign, both functionally and esthetically ʻof the central business district.

Design of the integrated shopping center of regional, district or neighborhood character; integrated recreation complexes of hotels, motels, marinas, private and governmental, on new patterns.

Factories in-the-field and offices in the countryside.

College and university campus redesign, and entirely new campuses on new land-sites and the whole wide range of educational facilities.

Research and administrative centers of the defense establishment and for private industry.

Redevelopment of economically depressed communities and regions.

New towns on new sites or planned and balanced expansion of existing towns within a new towns program concept.

Urban renewal across the nation slowly beginning to move ahead.

Conservation and rehabilitation —a different but major concern. All of these are of the largest consequence both to planners and to the architectural profession, requiring "new dimensions" in planning as well as architectural practice. They raise pertinent questions relating to the AIA-proposed "expanded services" concept. This is a matter which must be resolved, of course, in appropriate ways which are consonant with the profession's traditions, its ethics, its present and future areas of competence.

The guiding physical frameworks, the comprehensive plans, based on research and analysis—demographic, economic, and fiscal, functional, spatial, social and cultural, have

35

utmost relevance to design. Architects and planners must work together in all jurisdictions today—and the design aspect of these environmental opportunities depends on an effective relationship of the two professions.

These large-scale developments are complicated and expensive. They require large amounts of teamwork and the assembly and coordinated management of varied and various skills and competence, from mature and senior professionals to workaday technicians, secretaries, and clerks.

How can we get on a more sensible and agreeable course? How might the architects take the initiative in restoring to the profession a strategic role in urban design? A few suggestions:

Recognize the planning profession.

Not only "support" planning, but insist on it.

Insist also on referring all architectural projects to the plan. When there is no plan, insist on knowing why there isn't and when there will be.

Procedures with promise that directly relate to the design opportunity in urban planning might include examples like those which follow:

A very large office-building complex, which was recently proposed for several contiguous central city sites, made its first public appearance recently with dramatic effect. Its impact, however, was rather promptly diminished because the separate site schemes, not having been given the benefit of design coordination, were vigorously and effectively subjected to public criticism.

The plan commission of the community proposed a coordinated scheme of identical scope, providing a superb opportunity for design integration of the several related but separate proposals.

In another city, the city plan has provided excellent "project area" frameworks within the master plan for a number of urban renewal projects. The redevelopment agency and the planners together and in unity have stressed excellence in architectural effectuation of all urban renewal.

With the assistance of the local chapter of The American Institute of Architects, the city has carried through with evident conviction, utilizing specific procedures and requirements affecting design. These include the continuing use of architectural review and administrative controls to achieve coordination of site arrangements with structures, of structures with each other (both public and private), and of site plans with the city's master plan.

In his book, "The Image of the City," Kevin Lynch suggests "a method whereby we might begin to deal with visual form at the urban scale," and offers some first principles of city design.

Philip Lewis, now with the Wisconsin Department of Conservation and Resources Development, has applied a similar method to the regional landscape—that is to say, at the scale of the metropolitan area, or even larger.

Another highly promising procedure is the interdisciplinary approach to city and regional research proceeding in an increasing number of universities, through urban institutes and study programs, aided by foundation grants.

In conclusion, let me point quickly to two planning developments which architects concerned with urban design should give special heed to. One is the new Federal urban posture represented by the proposal for a Department of Urban Affairs, through new and vigorous administrative processes supporting coordination of local planning and development at the metropolitan level, and through efforts to close the gap between Federal, state, and local relationships, effecting the planning of urban growth and development.

Another planning development to watch is my own preoccupation, metropolitan planning. Of 225 census-designated areas, about one-third have established metropolitan planning commissions.

These agencies are developing broad, guiding planning frameworks for central cities, suburbs, and their fringes, based on research and multiple purpose planning for land use, transportation, flood control, open space and other functional requirements of metropolitan areas.

Within these great frameworks there are—or will be—design opportunities of every kind, ranging from central city redevelopment, to regional, shopping centers, industrial and residential parks, and wholly new educational, recreational and health facilities.

There is no doubt about the challenge. There should be none about the response!

Bureau of Outdoor Recreation-Declarations of Intent

Edward C. Crafts, Director, Bureau of Outdoor Recreation, Department of the Interior, speaking at the 40th Annual Convention and Conservation Conference of the Izaak Walton League of America, Portland, Oregon, June 21, 1962 issued sixteen declarations of intent which he said will be the Bureau's guiding principles. Dr. Crafts said, "These are my personal creed. They are what I believe. They are the policies I intend to pursue."

1. Outdoor recreation needs to be vigorously advocated across this land and in chambers where policy is made. I hope to be one of those advocates and to balance enthusiasm with realism. Sometimes a tinge of evangelism may even be in order. My old Dean and mentor Sam Dana of the University of Michigan, once told me that the trouble with me was that I was all logic and no emotion. I hope to prove him wrong.

2. There needs to be national and nonpolitical leadership in recreation. The Bureau of Outdoor Recreation as a career service should provide that leadership. It should be intellectual leadership, not bureaucratic aggrandizement. There needs to be effective articulation that reaches the public heart and mind. This we shall try to do.

3. There needs to be public understanding that recreation is not only a renewing experience but also serious business. It is serious national business both because of its economic impact and its beneficial effect on the physical, cultural, social and moral well-being of the American people. It is a partial solution to the social problems created by urbanization and leisure time. It is a solution, at least in part, to the fact that man is not wholly suited physiologically to meet the technological demands placed upon him. Most of the hospitalizations in the country today are emotionally based. In this vein I like to think of the new organization as the Bureau of Outdoor Re-Creation. We have heard much of ORRRC. Now I like to think in terms of BORC for the Bureau of Outdoor Re-Creation.

4. The recreation business is the great hope for economic improvement of certain rural portions of this country that are otherwise depressed. Further the manufacture and marketing of recreation equipment and provision of recreation facilities have a major impact on our economy. Think for a moment of what is involved in the manufacture, use and operation of sporting arms, fishing tackle, camping equipment, pleasure boats, winter sports equipment, pleasure

trailers, recreation roads, resort hotels, motels, lodges and dude ranches, and the recreation press. All of this we recognize in the new Bureau.

5. There is need to professionalize recreation education in our colleges and universities and with the broad gauge orientation which I am now trying to describe. Those currently engaged in the work of providing recreation for others are made up of a multitude of disciplines —geographers, foresters, landscape architects, zoologists, physical education majors, engineers, and so on. I look forward to the day when recreation conservation may be recognized professionally as fully as forestry is today.

There is the other side of the coin too, namely the education of those who wish to partake intelligently and effectively of recreation opportunities. I think more is being done in this field than in the education of the professional technician in outdoor recreation.

6. This Bureau is and should continue to be small in terms of personnel and money. My hope is that though it be small in men and dollars, it may loom large in policy and in contribution to the welfare of the American people.

7. There will be no empire-building in this Bureau. We have no intention to place the clammy hand of restraining bureaucracy on the initiative of other Federal bureaus, States, or the private sector.

The primary emphasis of the Bureau should be on assistance to the States, to local instrumentalities of government, and to private enterprise. We hope to facilitate, to aid, and to be a catalytic agent.

8. This Bureau will not be a land-managing agency. Its duties will be policy, planning, long-range programs and coordination. As it gains stature my hope is that it might function in the Federal heirarchy somewhat as an appellate court in the field of recreation. The emphasis should be on the quality not quantity, improvement of standards and facilities, attraction of better personnel, and broadening of vision.

9. An unfortunate fact of life is that most of the people are where the land is not. This was dramatically impressed upon me recently as I flew nonstop from Anchorage to Chicago over Alaska and northern Canada with its tremendous scenery and millions of lakes but without a sign of human habitation or encroachment. Recreation opportunities need to be brought close to people, so much of the emphasis of the Bureau will necessarily be in the East and on the West Coast where our population concentrations occur.

10. In the Federal area the Bureau function will be coordination, programing, and promotion of Federal acquisition of certain properties needed for the furtherance of the recreation

aims of our National Forest and Park Systems, our Wildlife Refuges and Game Ranges, and the Federal reservoirs.

11. "Coordination" is a difficult word and in many ways an onerous one. No power has been conferred on the Bureau by statute or by Executive fiat, to impose its will on any other government entity. "Correlation" is perhaps a better word. This objective of correlation or coordination may be achieved through legislative review, budgetary review, conference, consultation, and the respect and stature which the Bureau may gain over a period of time as well as the force of public opinion which may develop behind it.

12. This Bureau is by no means another National Park Service or another Forest Service. Its orientation, its scope, its approach and objectives are quite different from any existing agency of government, Federal or State. It is in a very real sense a new experiment in government.

13. There should be, in my opinion, a Citizens Advisory Council to the Bureau and it is my hope to recommend one soon to Secretary Udall.

14. The emphasis of this Bureau needs to be on the needs of the people whereas too often in the past the emphasis in outdoor recreation has been on the utilization of a resource.

15. During the few years that I shall be Director of this Bureau I intend to push vigorously for the legislation, funds and policy that to me are in the public interest. There will be no "pussy-footing" around; but by the same token political expertese will be involved here and the meshing of goals with the art of the possible.

16. Finally, I should say I have little patience with plans that do not lead to action. I have no desire that this Bureau engage in academic or stratospheric planning which finds its use only in the libraries and with doctoral candidates. Planning and programming to me are primarily significant in direct relation to the results stemming from them.

In conclusion, let me remind you of two points which the President made in his talk at the recent White House Conference on Conservation. In emphasizing the need to apply science to conservation, the President said that the successful application of science to conservation may result in a great deal more lasting benefit to a particular country than being first in space. He also said: "I don't think there is anything that could occupy our attention with more distinction than trying to preserve for those who come after us this beautiful country which we have inherited."

New Federal Architectural Policy to Enhance Washington

President Kennedy has appointed a 10 member Advisory Council to advise members and staff of the National Capital Planning Commission on a project to turn Pennsylvania Avenue into the city's most outstanding ceremonial thoroughfare.

Secretary of Labor Goldberg, who played a major role in developing the project welcomed the members of the new Advisory Council at a White House meeting and said it would be their job in advising on the project to "balance" the important aspects of the Avenue. "Pennsylvania Avenue is the bridge between Congress and the Executive, and in addition is a great thoroughfare for the city," said he.

Mr. Goldberg said that all over the country "there is a tremendous interest in the Capital that is increasing" and it is time, he declared, "to recapture the original spirit" of the city.

The group is headed by Nathaniel Owings of San Francisco and the other members are: Minoru Yamasaki, Detroit architect; Paul Thiry, Seattle architect; William Walton, Washington artist; Douglas Haskell, New York, editor *Architectural Forum* magazine; Ralph Walker, New York architect, member Fine Arts Commission; Daniel Kiley, Landscape architect; Frederick Gutheim, head of Washington Center for Metropolitan Studies; Daniel P. Moynahan, Special Assistant to Secretary Goldberg; Charles Eam, Los Angeles, famous for the Eams chair.

Planning Commission staff work on the project will be carried out under the direction of William E. Finley, staff director. Polly Shackelton, formerly an official of the American Institute of Architects will serve as Secretary to the Council. Announcement of the Council's membership at the White House carried out a recommendation made several weeks ago by a cabinet-level committee for redevelopment of the north side of the Avenue from the Capitol to Fifteenth Street, N. W. This proposal was to transform the Avenue into the "Grand Axis" envisaged in the original plan for Washington, conceived by Pierre L'Enfant and also included broad guidelines of a new Federal architectural policy to insure that the vast program contemplated would enhance the beauty and dignity of Washington as the seat of government.

The Planner, The Council and The Citizens' Organization

By E. A. LEVIN, Director Community Planning Branch,
Saskatchewan Department of Municipal Affairs

EDITOR'S NOTE:—This article was adapted from an address given during an extension course in planning at the University of Saskatchewan. Reprinted from *Community Planning Review* by permission of its Editor.

In broad terms, the objective of physical planning might be described as the creation of the ideal physical environment. Having said that, one is immediately involved in such embarrasing questions as "What is ideal?" and "Ideal for whom?", and so on; questions which it is not the purpose of this paper to deal with.

However, among the many qualities which together would make up the concept of the "ideal" physical environment as conceived by most reasonable people, would be the quality of orderliness. And, accordingly, one of the most obvious functions of the planning process is to create an orderly environment.

Involved in this process of realizing, or bringing into being, the orderly pattern of the environment—are three principal agencies—the professional planner, the elected council, and the public at large; and as things stand at present, there is a great deal of confusion about the status, the role, and the interrelationships of these three elements.

One of the basic conceptual difficulties underlying this confusion arises out of the ambiguity of the word "planning" itself. There are, of course, many different kinds of planning, and many different kinds of planners, and the distinctions between them are in great need of clarification. The kind of planning we are discussing here is that which deals with the *physical* environment, but even within these limits there is ambiguity about objectives, and disciplines. Physical planning is also known by a variety of other names such as community planning, city planning, urban planning, and so on. By the addition of such qualifying adjectives it is intended to convey the idea that the function is concerned with physical matters, that is with the physical environment, and in particular with the urban physical environment.

This seems like quite a simple and straightforward proposition: Planning is concerned with the ordering or arranging of streets, and buildings, and parks and playgrounds, and railway tracks, and all the other elements that together comprise the physical surroundings within which urban dwellers lead their lives; and it is not very much concerned with the "social environment" which the sociologists have in mind when they speak of the "environment," or with problems of social values.

Unfortunately it is not as simple as that. Planning implies objectives. In fact, *planning is simply the making of arrangements in the present to achieve objectives in the future.* But objectives imply values: a thing is sought after because it is valued more highly than that which is not sought after. We zone for single family dwellings because we believe that children will somehow grow up "better," and that property will be more "valuable" in a residential area free from industries or commercial activity, than in one with a mixture of these uses; we devise extremely complicated and expensive traffic circulation systems because we value the private automobile as a means of transportation more than we do public transit. Any measures for ordering the physical environment express, implicitly or explicitly, a value-judgment, so that willy-nilly, planning becomes involved in the value-system of society and cannot restrict its interest to the purely impersonal, physical aspects of the environment.

Now this in itself would not present any very serious problem, were it not for two unfortunate circumstances. One of these is that the planner's idea of what is "good" and what is "bad" doesn't always correspond with the public's ideas on these questions; the other is that, for a number of reasons which we shall look at in a moment, the planner is often put in a position where his notion of what is good or bad becomes the final authoritative basis for action.

We hear these days all sorts of warnings about the dangers of government by the expert. One of the basic concepts in our political system is that social goals are set by the people and decisions are made by them through their elected representatives. The usurpation of these functions by the expert is regarded as a threat to our way of life. Moreover there is, in such a

situation, a very real possibility that the expert's personal value-system will become confused with that of the public at large. And apparently this is happening, not just in planning but in other fields as well.

The public of course can react quite violently in such circumstances. Planners have often been roasted in the local press. They are frequently charged with trying to ram their ideas down the public's throat, or acting in a dictatorial, arbitrary or coercive manner. And yet, in most cases, the charges arise out of matters of policy, rather than administration; it is a reflection on the confused relationships existing today in the planning process, that these policies should be identified with a paid employee—even though he is an expert—rather than with the political authority which is ultimately responsible for matters of policy.

Part of the reason for this confusion may be the currently prevalent system of planning by appointed commission. Council is removed from the actual planning process except insofar as it gives final approval to the proposals which the commission has worked out. But of course most of the proposals originate with the planner, and accordingly tend to become identified with him, not only in the mind of the public, but also in the mind of the planner himself. This arrangement may have a tendency to diffuse the relationship within the planning function, and obscure the clarity of responsibility. Moreover it may even be argued, with some justification, that under the Planning Commission arrangement, it is quite proper for the planner to assume initiative and responsibility for planning proposals, since he is not an employee of Council in the strict sense. But this merely underlines the potential for ambiguity of responsibility in the commission system.

Undoubtedly the planner has an important contribution to make toward the solution of our urban problems because of his training and skill. But because of that very training and skill, in other words because he is an expert, his notion of what is desirable and what is not desirable often varies quite radically from the view of the general public on these questions. This is a common dilemma in the relationship between the public and the expert and may be found not only in planning, but in any activity which seeks to influence people's views and habitual attitudes.

The problem is to distinguish between the two questions: "What would we like to achieve?" and "How shall we best achieve it?" Like that of all experts, the planner's professional function lies in the realm of "How shall we best achieve it?" But it is often difficult, if not impossible, to separate the two. Moreover, the planner probably has some worth-while things to say about what we ought to be striving for. If the planner is in private practice then his problem is somewhat modified inasmuch as he is responsible only to himself, and he can therefore champion a particular point of view with all the force and partianship he can muster. If, however, the planner is a public employee, as in most cases he is, he

cannot, with the same freedom, advocate measures or ideas which are not subscribed to by the public or the authority which employs him. This is so, not simply because he is not likely to remain an employee for very long under these circumstances, but because it is a fundamental principle in our kind of society that social goals should be determined by the people, and not by government or its employees. In practice, of course, the distinction can never be clearly maintained. Obviously there must be ideas and influences flowing in both directions. But in principle, it is of fundamental importance to distinguish the primary role of the planner, that is the role of expert adviser on "How best can we achieve our objective?" from his secondary role —that of an informed member of society, advocating particular social objectives.

I personally do not believe that the planner's job, *as planner* is to formulate social objectives. I do not think, for example, that it is his job to say whether it is best for people to live in row houses or apartments or single family dwellings. It is not his job to say that people should ride in public transit vehicles rather than their own private cars, or that central areas are preferable to the suburbs as a place to live. In short, I do not believe that it is the planner's job to tell people how they ought to live. He must of course be aware of the various possibilities, and he must know the technical implications and consequences of all the choices, because his basic job is to advise council about these things. He can even have strong personal views on all these matters and hold them with great conviction; but his primary role is not that of social critic. As a planner he ought not to mistake his personal attitudes for universal or objective truths, or to assume that they represent the general point of view, or even that they are necessarily preferable to alternative viewpoints; and he certainly ought not to base his technical proposals on his own private scheme of values.

But, unfortunately, there is often no other scheme of values available to him as a basis for his planning proposals. He is often *forced* into the role of social critic and advocate of his own special views because the community has no clear views of its own about its physical environment. And this is probably the central problem which besets the planning function and the relationships of the various elements within it.

The evidence is all about us, everywhere, that the public is *not aware* of the physical environment as something which has capabilities of beauty, convenience, order and economy. Land and space, landscape and buildings are simply not thought about in these terms by the public at large. But the planner *must* think about them in these terms, and he must frame his recommendations about the physical environment in these terms.

It seems then, that until such time as the community provides the planner with a clearly articulated image of the kind of environment it wants, the planner will have to go on providing one for himself. This is unfortunate because, for the

reasons we have seen, the public should participate in the planning process, and should have a clear idea of the objectives it wishes to achieve. But it must be *a public that is informed and aware.* In my view nothing could be farther from the truth than to assume that the public can make a valuable contribution to the planning of the physical environment simply because it has the political right to say what it wants. It has that right of course. But it also has the responsibility which is part of that right—the responsibility to become informed and aware, and to understand the implications of its choice.

One cannot expect everybody in a community to have carefully thought out and clearly articulated ideas about the kind of town he wants. One can't expect everybody to be interested in the physical environment and community planning, any more than one can expect everybody to be interested in service clubs, or international trade, or politics, or the problems of education. The fact is that the human being seems to have a limited capacity for interest. Most of us simply do not have sufficient curiosity and intellectual equipment to be interested in everything, or even a wide range of things, nor sufficient energy to be able to devote ourselves to a variety of interests. If we manage to sustain an active interest in one or two fields beyond our vocation, that usually requires all the curiosity, brains and energy that we can muster.

However, there are always groups of people who *do* have the same interests in common, such as service clubs, for example, or parent-teacher associations, or people interested in penal reform, and so on. It is these groups of people who manage to articulate objectives, and to stimulate action in the fields in which they are interested. And it is these groups who become, in fact, the spokesmen for the entire community on the problems which they have chosen as their particular field of interest.

Much could be done to resolve the major problem we are discussing, if the many voluntary organizations which have some interest in civic development could be brought to the point where they performed the role of crystallizing and articulating the community's physical development goals. Such organizations as the Community Planning Association of Canada, the Junior Chamber of Commerce, the Kinsmen, Rotary, and others who have some partial or specific interest in civic growth, could well be the ones to undertake this task.

However, it will take a great effort on the part of these individuals and groups to bring their perception of the environment, and their awareness of its potential, up to the point where they can make a responsible contribution. But I think it is worth the effort, not merely because it is unfair that

the planner should have to take the responsibility, and blame, for conceiving the form of the environment without having the benefit of the community's own self-image, but also because we are not likely to make any significant progress towards the creation of an "ideal" environment until there is a general understanding of what this means, and a general desire, based on such an understanding, to achieve it.

If it is important for the public at large to develop an understanding and an awareness of the physical environment, it is perhaps even more important for members of Council to have a heightened perception of the physical aspects of the community. The business of local government is in large measure concerned with the physical environment, and until the political power and responsibility of members of council is matched by their perception and understanding of their environment, it is likely that policy decisions affecting physical development will continue to be made on almost any grounds except those concerned with the orderliness and beauty of the surroundings; and the planner will likely have to continue in his ambiguous and awkward role of social critic, image-maker, technical adviser and whipping-boy.

Three New Members Appointed to National Parks Advisory Board

Three new members of the Advisory Board on National Parks, Historic Sites, Buildings and Monuments were appointed by Secretary of the Interior Stewart L. Udall. They are: Mrs. Marion S. Dryfoos (Mrs. Orvil Eugene Dryfoos) of New York City; Dr. Earle Wallace Stegner, Los Altos, Calif., and Dr. Melville Bell Grosvenor of Washington, D. C. The Board, created by the Historic Sites Act of 1935, is composed of 11 non-salaried members appointed by the Secretary of the Interior. Other members of the Advisory Board are: Dr. John A. Krout, Vice-President and Provost, Columbia University, New York City; Sigurd F. Olson, Ely, Minn., Earl H. Reed, 343 S. Dearborn St., Chicago, Ill., Dr. Robert G. Sproul, President Emeritus, Univ. of California, Berkeley, Calif., and Dr. Robert L. Stearns, Citizens Committee on Modern Courts, Inc., Denver, Colo.

National Park Service Regions Now Designated Geographically

The six National Park Service regions, heretofore known by number, have now been designated by geographic location. The new nomenclature, which takes effect immediately, was announced July 10 by the Department of the Interior.

Region One now becomes Southeast Region, with its regional office in Richmond, Va. as before. Region Two, which covers the northern part of the Plains and Rocky Mountain States and is administered from Omaha, Nebraska, is changed to Midwest Region. Santa Fe, New Mexico remains headquarters for Southwest Region, formerly Region Three. Western Region is the new name for Region Four, which includes the Pacific states, as well as Alaska and Hawaii, with its regional office in San Francisco. Region Five becomes Northeast Region, which is administered from Philadelphia.

The National Capital Parks, which includes park land in the District of Columbia and nearby Maryland and Virginia, was briefly known as Region Six, from January 12, 1962. It is now National Capital Region, with headquarters in Washington, D. C.

Commentaries

Baltimore County is losing its low, rolling skyline.

The new skyline will be dotted with high rise apartments and tall office buildings, according to the prediction by Malcolm H. Dill, Baltimore County's planning and zoning director.

Where will this occur? Mr. Dill points to the county's major centers of population, Towson, Dundalk, Pikesville, Catonsville, and those towns building now, or not yet built.

Since World War II, Baltimore County's farmland and woodland have become practically nonexistent in a strip from 5 to 10 miles wide-east, north and west of Baltimore city. During this period all new buildings held to the low, rambling style of suburbia. The schools, shopping centers and industry stayed within the 50 foot elevation limit.

But now the county zoning regulations permit office buildings to go higher. New zoning regulations now under consideration would allow greater flexibility in determining the height of elevatorybuildings in apartment zones. Mr. Dill says these high rise apartments would be allowed only in such areas as heavily populated Towson, Dundalk, Pikesville and Catonsville.

Now that the exploding population has used up most of the land, Mr. Dill sees large areas for expansion above that 50 foot mark.

❧

The Illinois Board of Economic Development has adopted a positive role in promoting community planning. No longer will it wait for communities to become acquainted with the development programs and with the available sources of funds for community planning and development purposes.

The Board has taken this position because there is a strong correlation between state and local economic development and community structure. Industries and businesses are increasingly attracted by sound community development, planning and management. Communities with adequate water resources, local comprehensive planning, far-sighted zoning, and effective law enforcement, to say nothing of civic beauty and cultural and educational institutions, have found them to be assets when present—and damaging liabilities when absent—in attracting industry and business to their community.

Planning acceptance by local communities is increasing and has an accelerating snow-ball effect. As more communities become actively associated with planning, the activity becomes increasingly attractive to others. This means not only stronger, more prosperous, individual communities but, through the combined effect of individual improvement, a better state as well.

❧

The National Academy of Sciences will study the feasibility of an expanded natural history research program under an agreement with the National Park Service, the Department of the Interior announced recently.

The agreement between the National Academy of Sciences and the National Park Service grew out of a request from Secretary of the Interior Stewart L. Udall asking that a comprehensive and coordinated long-range research program be initiated on behalf of the National Park Service.

The National Park Service has long recognized that broad ecological knowledge is indispensable to the integrity and general welfare of the national parks. This undertaking will explore how comprehensive and coordinated research will be able to provide the National Park Service with a continuous flow of knowledge about the characteristics of the national parks and monuments, the nature of the normal and man-imposed forces at work within them, and the relationships of park visitors to the natural environments.

48

This knowledge is necessary to back up park planning, development, protection and interpretation.

One of the country's most distinguished botanists and a member of the National Academy of Sciences, Dr. William J. Robbins, will serve as chairman of the committee to recommend an expanded natural history research program in the National Park Service.

It will be the job of the Academy committee to set forth findings and recommendations for a research program designed to provide the data required for effective management, development, protection, and interpretation of the national parks, and to encourage the greater use of the national parks by scientists for basic research. After the completion of the study and evaluation, recommendations will be given to Secretary Udall.

❧

An arrowhead insignia, showing in vignette a giant sequoia tree, a snow-covered mountain, a lake, and a bison, has been approved by the Department of the Interior as the official emblem of the National Park Service.

In an item published in the Federal Register, Assistant Secretary of the Interior John A. Carver gave notice that "whoever manufactures, sells, uses, or possesses this symbol without authorization from the United States Department of the Interior is subject to the penalties prescribed in Section 701 of Title 18 of the United States Code." The notice is designed to protect the official emblem of the Service from misuse and commercialization.

The arrowhead "trade mark" of the National Park service symbolizes the scenic beauty and historical heritage of the country. The history and prehistory of the U. S. is recognized in the arrowhead shape of the shield. A tall tree in the foreground implies vast forest lands and growing life in the wilderness. The small lake on the shield is a reminder of the role of water in scenic and recreational resources. Behind the tree and lake towers a snow-capped mountain typifying open space and the majesty of nature. Near the point of the

arrowhead is an American bison as the symbol of the conservation of wildlife.

❧

Keep America Beautiful, Inc., the national public service organization for the prevention of litter which has recently intensified its efforts through an expanded campaign is guided by an Advisory Council that includes representatives of 54 national public interest organizations and 11 agencies of four federal government departments. It is supported by business firms, labor unions and trade associations representing nearly every major industrial category in the United States. KAB, Inc., 99 Park Ave., New York City serves over 7,000 communities in all 50 states.

❧

Montgomery County (Ohio) Planning Commission's Director, B. E. Clark in announcing plans for a survey of open space said, "Shall our children and grandchildren, when they reach adulthood, struggle to secure areas suitable to fill their community's need for open space and open air recreation?" They need not. Plans can and are being devised that will pinpoint the future as well as present open space needs.

Although it has been slow in getting started, an open space study, encompassing all of Greene and Montgomery Counties is scheduled to begin on the first of July and be completed by Christmas.

This study, being financed out of local government funds and conducted on a do-it-yourself basis, will pinpoint presently available areas and present needs, determine future needs and pinpoint suitable areas and recommend methods for financing, acquiring, developing, and maintaining open space areas for future generations. Participants in the study include both the Greene and Montgomery County governments, plus the Dayton, Kettering, Oakwood, Vandalia, Xenia and Yellow Springs governments.

The Open Space Plan resulting from the unified efforts of staff personnel from these participating agencies, will show us where areas should be preserved for open space needs and if the plan is properly supported, our sons and daughters will be assured of having adequate, properly located open space areas, without having to go through costly condemnation and clearance procedures to supply their communities' need.

❧

For the outstanding quality of their "citizen action", eleven communities each year are awarded the coveted title of All-America City. The competition now in its 14th year, is co-sponsored by the National Municipal League and *Look* Magazine. It is open to any U. S. community which has made exceptional strides through the resourceful activity of its citizens.

If your city has an alert citizenry now at work on major improvements, you are invited to enter it as a contestant in the 1962 competition.

The rules below, and the thumbnail sketches of last year's winners, will give you a good idea of whether your city may be a candidate for entry. Discuss with other members of your community, and analyze your city's progress in terms of what has been done by the citizens themselves rather than by government officials.

RULES OF ELIGIBILITY

1. A city must show outstanding civic achievements of benefit to the community as a whole.

2. It must give evidence that these achievements resulted from "citizen action" that is, the initiative and effort of a substantial number of citizens acting to improve their community.

3. Any size city or town may enter. Population and resources will be taken fully into account in judging a city's achievements.

4. A city need not be a model community. Dynamic citizen leadership, not perfection, is the criterion. But because an All-America city is looked up to, nationally and internationally, as an example of good citizenship, any critical problems still outstanding might lead to disqualification unless steps have already been taken toward their solu-

tion. These residual problems might include continued inadequacies in local government and municipal services, unchecked slum blight, school segregation and other problems of racial relations, insufficient health and recreational facilities, lack of plans for future development.

5. To qualify for consideration, a city must be formally entered as a contestant by one of its citizens, citizen groups, or public officials.

❧

The King County, Washington Park Department's recreation program for handicapped children was started in the summer of 1958. Since that time the participation has increased from 65 to over 600 registered in the various programs this year. About 80 percent of these children are mentally retarded and about 20 percent are physically handicapped.

As a general policy the purpose of the program is to teach the participating children the fundamentals of recreation and group behavior. An effort is made to include brothers and sisters of a handicapped child and, in some cases, neighborhood children. When handicapped children have progressed to the point where they can benefit from, and compete in, regular recreation programs, they are encouraged to join them.

During the school year a swimming program is carried out in cooperation with several districts. These are Highline, Bothell, Kirkland and Bellevue. The children are transported to and from the activity in school buses and parents and school teachers frequently assist in the program.

Three pools are used during the school year and a fourth is added for the summer program. During the school year, the Park Department hires ten instructors on a hourly basis and uses five volunteer instructors. About 260 handicapped children participate each week.

In the bowling program, lessons are given to handicapped children without charge. However, the children, or their parents, must pay a small charge for the use of the facilities. A part-time instructor, usually a high school student, is hired on an hourly basis to assist in the program.

The recreation programs include a wide variety of activities. Held in activity centers in various parts of the county, the recreation periods include games, sports, arts and crafts, story telling, dramatics and the use of playground equipment. In the past, fees have not been charged for this program, but parents will be requested to pay an $8.00 fee for the program this summer, which will be used to defray the cost of part-time instructors.

༄

The Ventura, California County Zoning Ordinance has been completely revised to make it more effective in guiding the rapid growth according to the various elements of the General Plan. To encourage more homogeneous urban areas, an exclusive rather than pyramiding type of ordinance was developed. By use of this technique, the zones are mutually exclusive, for example, residential uses are eliminated from the commercial zones, and commercial uses are not permitted in the industrial zones. The number of zones was reduced from 24 to 17. This will permit more flexibility in administration, and aid good planning principles. Several zones were combined, and new zones were established for harbor, airport and mobilehome park developments. Mobilehome parks should be located in areas where multi-family residences would logically exist. They have the same impact as multi-family housing, and if properly landscaped and managed, can be an attractive asset to the community.

SIGNS. Signs, in the Zoning Ordinance, have been classified into 11 different types and have maximum sizes allowed for each type. In addition, the ordinance gives by zone the type of signs allowed, and in some zones, the number of signs allowed.

It is one consideration to have these regulations in an ordinance but to enforce them is quite another. Generally the zoning inspectors only take action when a complaint is made. In the control of signs, a different approach is taken. A survey of all the signs in the County was made to determine what signs were illegal or non-conforming uses. Courtesy letters were then sent to owners notifying them that their signs were illegal and giving them 30 days to comply. The owners of non-conforming signs are also notified by letter 30 days prior to the 3 year expiration date. The good cooperation and excellent public support being experienced with the sign program is primarily because of use of the 30 day courtesy letters and the approach of being impartial to all sign owners.

COMMUNITY PARK CLAUSE. The portion of the ordinance that is satisfying is that which allows the County to obtain park sites in subdivisions without actually having to purchase the land. The ordinance allows the subdivider to decrease his lot size slightly in order to provide the additional space for a park site. Lots of 8,000 square feet may be reduced to 7,000 square feet and 7,000 square feet may be reduced to 6,500 square feet if a community park is incorporated in the design. The ordinance does not allow the subdivider to use this procedure if it results in lot sizes of under 6,500 square feet. The location and size of parks are usually determined in the review and redesign of the subdivision plat. However, some subdividers are including a park site in their initial plat. The subdivider may, if he chooses, donate park space outside the subdivision if such a site fits into the park plan. This was done in one case in which the developer donated 5 acres to an adjacent regional park.

Even though the ordinance is new, 8 local parks have been dedicated to date through this procedure. A direct result has been the formation of two park districts which cover the entire Simi Valle and the Camarillo-Pleasant Valley area and a third district near finalization which comprises the Conejo Valley.

State Park Notes

State Park Statistics—1961

State Park Statistics—1961 reveal significant progress over the previous year in all categories, as follows:

Total Attendance	273,484,442	increase	5.6 percent
Tent and Trailer Campers	18,562,533	increase	14.5 percent
Cabin, Hotel and Lodge Guests	2,229,808	increase	31.4 percent
Total Expenditures	$110,101,338	increase	26.0 percent
Expenditures for Land	$ 13,035,245	increase	7.9 percent
Expenditures for Improvements	$ 36,085,225	increase	89.6 percent
Total Funds Available for Expenditure	$133,672,787	increase	1.7 percent
Revenue from Operations	$ 23,363,524	increase	3.2 percent
Personnel	18,126	increase	3.4 percent
Total Number of Areas	2,792	increase	4.8 percent
Total Acreage	5,799,057	increase	3.5 percent

Returns were submitted by 101 agencies in 50 states. During the seven-year period, 1954–1961, the number of reporting agencies increased 22 percent and the salaries and wages increased 94 percent. Day use, which accounted for 91.1 percent of visitor attendance, increased by 4.5 percent, while overnight attendance increased 11.8 percent. Actual expenditures for park improvements were more than twice as much as in any year prior to 1956.

Eighty-one additional areas were reported as acquired during 1961. This acquisition includes 156,485 acres, which, considering the disposal of 3,972 acres and acreage revisions by certain states, gives a total state park acreage of 5,799,057.

———◆———

News from the States

Florida. The Governor's Committee on Recreation Development presented its "Interim Report" to Gov. Farris Bryant on February 4. Many public and private agencies have participated in the studies and in the collection of data since last April when the Committee was appointed. Chairman William R. Kidd said, in the report, that the enthusiasm and devotion of field personnel and various conservation agencies have encouraged the committee to redouble its efforts to produce a program which will meet the demands of an ever changing Florida. There is among the people a growing awareness of the urgent need for a revaluation of their conservation effort and for the maximum utilization of state owned lands. Some of the facts revealed in the report are as follows: Of the 1,016.36 miles of usable sand beach on the Florida Coast, only 309.62 miles, or less than one third, is still publicly owned; only 256 miles, or 25% is in accessible public ownership; and only 23.7 miles of this lies within state parks. Of the 114.5 miles of sand beach owned by the Federal government, approximately 62 miles are open to public use. Indications are that Florida will experience a population increase of around 44% during the next ten years and must double its present facilities. Industrial and urban growth is already pressing hard against existing natural resources, and unless active steps are taken to alleviate the problem and plan for the future, the state can be expected to lose much of her attractiveness to residents and tourists alike. Walter Coldwell, Director, Florida Park Service, and active member of the Governor's Committee, welcomes comments or suggestions from fellow conservationists regarding the report.

Illinois. The Sid Simpson State Park near Quincy is the Department of Conservation, Division of Parks and Memorials' newest state park, named for the late Congressman Sid Simpson. It is the first state park in the area to make use

of the Mississippi River and is comprised of acreage obtained by local purchase and a $40,000 state appropriation.

The Illinois state park system will soon have another new site. It will be the William G. Stratton State Park located near Morris in honor of the former Governor. The park, on the Illinois River near the former Governor's hometown, was authorized by the general assembly early last spring and approved by Gov. Otto Kerner.

Michigan. The Conservation Commission voted in June to acquire 495 acres in Alcona and Alpena Counties within an area cited by the National Park Service as one of Michigan's top 40 Great Lakes shoreline sites remaining for public recreation. Near South Point, the property includes 4,300 feet of Lake Huron frontage of which 1,800 feet is a fine sand beach. Adjacent land, which lies within the boundary of Alpena State Forest, is currently under study by the Department of Conservation for possible dedication as Alpena State Park.

Missouri. Vandalism costs the people of Missouri thousands of dollars every year, according to Joseph Jaeger, Jr., Director of Parks. "We have always done our utmost to curb vandalism in state parks," he said. "Now with teeth in our law and with violators being punished severely, we expect more results." The last session of the state legislature gave state park superintendents the power to arrest for vandalism and rowdyism in state parks. In a number of cases, those arrested for these crimes have paid fines and court costs. At Lake Wappapello State Park on July 3 two men were arrested, jailed and at their trial pleaded guilty to disturbing the peace, careless and reckless driving, and were fined $25 and $35 plus court costs. At Washington State Park recently two men pleaded guilty to malicious damage charges and were fined $10 each plus $12 court costs for vandalism, and at Alley Springs State Park a man arrested for disturbing the peace and destroying property was fined $75 plus $20.75 in court costs.

New Hampshire. Plans for a 3,000-acre new state park and recreation area unequaled elsewhere in the state, and situated almost in the middle of the most densely populated southeastern section, are at the enactment stage, according to the July *Park Maintenance* magazine. Financing of the park has been tentatively earmarked under a $9 million recreation bond issue, with Russell B. Tobey, Director of Recreation, proposing $375,000 to be set aside for the proposed Pawtuckaway State Park. The property is now owned by the Water Resources Board. The first step toward processing the 809-acre Pawtuckaway Lake and the 820 acres of land adjacent to it, is to designate the Recreation Division as manager of the properties. Three access roads are possible and planned improvements include extensive swimming areas, with parking nearby; boat launching sites; picnic and camping areas. In addition, more than 30 small islands afford picnic spots which may prove attractive to boating parties. Miles of hiking trails offering a varied terrain will be opened to park visitors and proposed additional ski trails will be considered if a study reveals the necessity. Another important factor being considered within the park is setting aside a "primitive area" as a wilderness preserve on the Bay of Fundy. About 65 percent of the state's more than 606,000 residents live within a 31-mile radius of Pawtuckaway.

Ohio. City and county officials in Toledo plan a joint purchase of 330 acres along Swan Creek for a park and recreation area. Purchase cost is $500,000 and under the plan the county will provide $122,000, the city $228,000, and the Federal government $150,000. The project will qualify for a 30 percent Federal Grant since the Toledo Metropolitan Park Authority will develop the land. The city of Toledo's share will come from proceeds of parklands lost to the expressway programs. Approximately 80 acres of city parkland is expected to be taken for the expressway, so that the new Swan Creek Park should be considered as a replacement.

Total attendance at Ohio State Parks during the first 11 months of fiscal year 1962 was 17,061,879, an increase of more than two million from the previous year, according to V. W. Flickinger, Chief, Division of Parks. The 2,085,574 park visitors in May represented a new attendance mark for that month since 1949 when the division became a part of the Department of Natural Resources. Total attendance for the fiscal year ending June

54

30 was a record 20,648,956 persons, more than double the state's population. No new parks were opened this year, so the 10 percent gain over the previous year's attendance was all counted at the 50 existing state park areas.

Washington. The North Beach Trailer Association and Grays Harbour County trailer park operators have complained about competition from trailer facilities in state parks. More than 50 persons attended an open hearing called by the State Parks and Recreation Commission June 10 in Seattle to air the charges. Spokesmen for trailer owners' groups, however, argued at the hearing that Washington would become a "backward state" if it abandoned trailer facilities for tourists at the state parks. The parks department staff advised the Commission that a survey of 56 travel trailer owners and campers at Ocean City and Twin Harbors State Parks on June 9 showed that they would not have come to the areas if public facilities had not been available. State Parks and Recreation Director Clayton E. Anderson has said the department will not back down in its policy to allow trailer camping at its parks, according to the July

issue of Mobile Home Park Management.

The State Parks and Recreation Commission has approved two more salt water state parks. The acquisition of 92 acres and 1,827 feet of waterfront at Jones Beach, near Olympia, and 32 acres with 950 feet of waterfront at Scenic Beach at Seaquest on Hood Canal for park sites was approved at its July 16 meeting. Estimated cost is $182,000.

Wisconsin. Gov. Gaylord Nelson is sponsoring a large financial program to acquire recreational areas before they become industrialized or privately owned. While advocating acquisition of land for public use, he recently said it was his opinion that zoning is even more important than acquisition in maintaining the state's reputation as a scenic and recreational attraction. His main objective is to maintain as broad a recreational environment as possible, and to do this he has recommended the purchase by the state of easements on privately owned property as another way to control and curtail destructive use of the land. Wisconsin has already obtained scenic easements along 50 miles of highways overlooking the Mississippi River for an average cost of less than $700 per mile.

Jack Ellis Haynes—A Tribute

When, on May 12, 1962, Jack Ellis Haynes passed away in Livingston, Montana, after a brief illness, there was a loss of monumental proportions suffered by his family and friends, and by the entire National Park Service in general and the organizations—public and private—in Yellowstone Park in particular.

Jack Haynes was not only the Dean of national park concessioners, he had been rated for nearly a half century as one of the best of all the individuals engaged in furnishing travel facilities, accomodations and services in the national park system. The high regard in which he was held by Government officials and fellow concessioners was the natural appraisal of a man who placed public service—and service to the public—above personal interests—profit and prestige. His father was already in business in Yellowstone National Park when he was born in Fargo, Dakota Territory, Sept. 27, 1884. Of his long and successful life, Jack Haynes spent 75 of his 77 years in the Park. His love of the Yellowstone was a part of him from earliest childhood.

He was ever ready to aid the Park as he was to safeguard his family and his business. No man in business in a national park was ever more cooperative, more generous, more unselfish.

He was educated as a mining engineer, graduating from the University of Minnesota in 1908, but he was a born artist, historian, explorer, author and business man. He was a talented musician. Photography was a skill attained early in life. Following in the footsteps of his father, whom he adored, he continued the famous Haynes Guide to Yellowstone National Park, improving it year by year, always keeping it up-to-date and constantly seeking new features to make it indispensable to park visitors who seriously sought information that would enable them to get the utmost enjoyment out of their trips. Long ago, the Haynes Guide was declared to be the Official Guide of the Yellowstone. Jack was also the author and editor of other important publications on the Park.

Following the trail his father blazed for him, he continued the collection of books, pamphlets, souvenirs, artifacts and other memorabilia of Yellowstone National Park, and the pioneer days of the surrounding country. No item was too small or too insignificant for Jack's attention if it had historical, archaeological or anthropological value.

When the museums were being established in Yellowstone National Park, Jack Haynes acted as director of the one at park headquarters and devoted much time even in the midst of busy tourist seasons to the planning and installation of exhibits. And he generously contributed not only essential pictures but many objects from his own collections for the museum displays. He also, as a consultant, without any compensation advised the Park Service naturalists and museum specialists who later developed the museums in other sections of the Park.

He loved to explore the wilderness Yellowstone and probably no man, except a few rangers and old-time scouts, covered more of the remote parts of the Park by horse and packtrain, boat and even afoot than Jack Haynes. He heartily supported the proposed boundary revisions and extensions of the Park, and the creation of the Grand Teton National Park. In these legislative programs, his pictures and material from his collections were important aids to the Interior Department and the National Park Service officers.

When landscape restriction policies and new building programs were adopted by the National Park Service, the Haynes shops and their grounds were promptly rebuilt to meet the new conditions. When other concessioners failed to respond to a plan for tourist facilities at Tower Falls, the risks were assumed by Haynes as a public service without much hope at the time that they might ultimately be profitable.

The Haynes Picture Shops at all points of interest in the Yellowstone have been outstanding for the variety and quality of the objects offered for sale, and for the superb taste with which Mr. and Mrs. Haynes planned the exhibits.

Jack Haynes' personality naturally contributed to his success and great popularity as a business operator, and as a personal friend to all of us who were privileged to know him. He was a kindly, gentle, soft-spoken man. His wit enlivened parties of all kinds whether they were at home, on a pack trip, or "cook-outs" of the "Scientific Committee" or just riding or walking along with this charming fellow.

Jack's father, F. Jay Haynes, who had been in business in the Yellowstone since the very early 1880's, died in 1921, but he had succeeded the founder of the House of Haynes in 1916. The previous year—1915— I had the opportunity to meet Jack, but it was the year that he was taking over the management of the photographic business that I came to know him well. The stage coaches were still on the Yellowstone roads. My first trip with Jack was in an automobile and I recall our observing the special rules governing auto travel to avoid the horse-drawn coaches. There were times when we just had to sit and wait for the time to move on the tight schedule, and it was then—46 years ago—that I came to appreciate the fine qualities of Jack Haynes. Every year since then my interest in him and my affection for him has continued and grown stronger.

I shall always be grateful for the opportunity accorded me to act as master of ceremonies at the dinner in tribute to Jack Ellis Haynes in Yellowstone Park, Sept. 3, 1959, when our friend approached his 75th birthday. A host of Jack's friends were present and spoke in praise of his life and work. Among them were Director Conrad L. Wirth, former Assistant Secretary of the Interior Wesley D'Ewart, Lon Garrison Yellowstone's superintendent, Edmund Rogers, his predecessor. It was a great night for Jack, but in his mind it was by no means his last birthday party.

He had helped organize the celebration of the 50th anniversary of Yellowstone Park's creation in 1922, and the similar recognition of the 75th anniversary in 1947. At his 1959 dinner, Jack made many of us promise to be at the big party he was planning for March 1, 1972 when Yellowstone National Park will be 100 years old.

Like Jack, some of us won't be there. However, there will be tributes to Jack Haynes, eloquently expressed along with those paid to Hedges, Langford, Clagett, Jackson, Hayden, President U. S. Grant and others responsible for the creation of Yellowstone National Park and the marking of the beginning of the World's greatest national park system.

—Horace M. Albright

IN MEMORIAM

MRS. EDITH GRANT
Wife of U. S. Grant 3rd

Mrs. Edith Grant, 82, wife of Major General Ulysses S. Grant 3rd, (U. S. Army, retired), a prominent Washington civic leader and former chairman of the Civil War Centennial Commission, died May 22 at the family home in Clinton, N. Y. Mrs. Grant, who was the daughter of the late Secretary of State, Elihu Root, had been confined to her home on College Hill, facing the campus of Hamilton College, for the past year. A native of New York City, Mrs. Grant attended Brearly School, a private institution in that city. She lived in Washington during the several times General Grant was stationed there. She also traveled with him on his military assignments. In addition to her husband, she leaves three daughters, Mrs. John Sanderson Dietz of Syracuse, N. Y., Mrs. David W. Graffith of Arlington, Va. and Mrs. Paul E. Ruestow of Malverne, N. Y.; a brother, Elihu Root, New York City attorney and 10 grandchildren.

JOHN DE LA MATER

John De La Mater, 85, the first Secretary of the Committee of 100 on the Federal City and a member of the Washington Board of Trade for 27 years died July 1 while visiting his daughter in Hopewell, Va.

He became traveling secretary to the general manager of the Chicago, Burlington and Quincy Railroad in 1903. Later he handled special assignments for the Federal Reserve Board's division of bank operations.

During 1948–58 he became Secretary of the Corporation of Union Commercial Insurance Agency in Cottage City, Maryland. He was a member of Calvary Methodist Episcopal Church here and while on the Board of Trade was active on the harbor improvement committee as well as in the Committee of 100 on the Federal City. He was a member of the Mt. Pleasant Citizens Association and of the Association of Oldest Inhabitants.

Book Reviews

THE NATIONAL PARKS OF THE UNITED STATES
By LUIS A. BOLIN

A few years ago, the distinguished diplomat, world traveler and conservationist, Luis A. Bolin, of the Embassy of Spain, in Washington, our Nation's capital, wrote a book on our national parks which was published in the Spanish language and which has had a wide circulation.

Recently, this excellent book has been translated into English and published by Alfred A. Knopf who has brought out many of the most important volumes on the American national park system, including Robert W. Shankland's "Steve Mather of the National Parks" and Freeman Tilden's "The National Parks; What They Mean To You and Me," etc. As in the case of all Knopf's productions, this translation of Mr. Bolin's brief book is most attractive for its fine printing and clear, sharp illustrations selected with great care.

Mr. Bolin's book is titled "The National Parks of the United States." It contains a brief history of the National Park system establishment and the creation and development of the National Park Service which governs it. There follows a discussion of policies relating to the management and protection of the parks based largely on the codification of policy declarations by the National Parks Association made some years ago, which, of course, are not in all cases currently practiced by the National Park Service, but which are com-prehensive and which are employed and enforced where applicable under current operating conditions.

Then Mr. Bolin reviews the concessions policy of the National Park Service and outlines the facilities available to the visitors to its areas both scenic and historic. He enthusiastically describes the opportunities the visitor and his family have to enjoy themselves freely according to their own inclinations, calling attention to camping, fishing, hiking, riding, following nature trails or merely relaxing in the wilds. He emphasizes the wilderness character of these great reservations. He is obviously delighted with the interpretative programs. The book contains brief descriptions of all the national parks. Finally, Mr. Bolin adds an interesting commentary pointing out the "Traces of Spain" especially in the park areas of Florida, Puerto Rico and our Southwest.

This book has some errors of fact, doubtless due to the complications of correspondence and translation, and one can regret that the translation was not carefully reviewed by the National Park Service, but the inaccuracies can easily be corrected in another edition. However, they do not detract seriously from the book as a whole which gives the reader a large increment of knowledge pleasingly presented about our national parks by a writer from abroad who is obviously devoted to them, and he makes this presentation in a beautiful book quickly and easily read. Add the touch of the Spanish influence and one has here a book of special value. It can be a nice and valuable ornament to any section of a library on our national parks.

HORACE M. ALBRIGHT

* * *

UNIQUE CHARACTER OF SEATTLE SHOWN IN NEW BOOK

Ink sketches, from houseboats to skyline panoramas, depict the unique character of Seattle in a new book by architect Victor Steinbrueck. In *Seattle Cityscape: Sketches and Observations* the author seeks to portray through 275 pen drawings and critical commentary the color of Seattle's physical environment. He emphasizes the present and associations with the past.

Topics include impressions of early and new buildings, homes, street scenes, parks, waterways, vistas, and such characteristic spots as Pioneer Square, Pike Place Market, the University of Washington campus, and the World's Fair site.

While not intended as a guidebook, *Seattle Cityscape* is probably the most comprehensive pictorial representation of places to see that has yet been produced. It may well spur the city's pride in its environment and help to provide a basis for future planning through the author's value judgments. Publisher is the University of Washington Press.

The image the book gives of the city should interest Seattleites and visitors as well as planners and architects. Victor Steinbrueck is Professor of Architecture and Urban Planning at the University of Washington and a practicing architect.

* * *

A SECRET OF JAPANESE GARDENS

Norman T. Newton, FASLA, Professor of Landscape Architecture, Graduate School of Design, Harvard University, says of this fascinating work, "This booklet consists mainly of illustrations with brief notes that suggest in their quaint yet lucid way the thoughts and purposes underlying Japanese gardens of various types. To a western eye and ear even the names of some of these types, rendered quite literally into English, are both fascinating and informative: there are the Boating-Pond Garden, the Stroll-Pond Garden, the Viewing-Pond Garden, the Dry-Up Water Garden. The Flat Garden differs markedly from the Tea-Ceremony Garden; the Condensed Scenery Garden is not the same as the Borrowed Scenery Garden. From the illustrations of these and other types, comprising about half of the booklet, the viewer can readily perceive the varied techniques involved. The second half is devoted to illustrations of ways in which different materials and constituent elements are used."

National Capital Notes

The Committee of 100 on the Federal City has been busily engaged in recent months in informing the Commissioners of the District of Columbia and members of Congress on the various committees dealing with affairs of pertinent interest of the views of the Committee of 100 and the American Planning and Civic Association.

Several hearings of various Congressional Committees have been attended by Admiral Phillips (USN, ret.) Chairman of the Committee of 100 on the Federal City as well as by a number of its members to testify on zoning, highways, transportation, the FDR Memorial and other matters.

★ ★ ★

The new Central Maintenance Headquarters of the newly created National Capital Region of the National Park Service was recently dedicated by Assistant Secretary of the Interior, John A. Carver, Jr. The two-story building which occupies nearly a square block at 515 New York Ave. N.E. cost $1.7 million according to T. Sutton Jett, Regional Director who presided at the dedication. Besides blacksmith and other workshops, the building also houses air-conditioned offices, a cafeteria and a large storage area.

★ ★ ★

The tree-shaded streets bordering historic Lafayette Square would retain a Federalist flavor if new plans, recently authorized, come to fruition. Earlier plans, which would have placed two large Federal buildings on the Square, have been discarded and a fresh look is being taken by the newly employed architectural firm of John Carl Warnecke and Associates of San Francisco. The San Francisco firm's job is to map a master plan for the square relating "complex factors of architectural and landscape design to its historic character." It is expected that many of the famous old structures surrounding the Square would be preserved to the end that a "quiet and dignified setting for the White House" would result.

Recent Publications

SEATTLE CITYSCAPE: Sketches and Observations. By Victor Steinbrueck. 292 pp., 275 illus. $4.75; Paper, $3.95. 1962.

TRANSPORTATION AND URBAN LAND. By Lowdon Wingo, Jr. Study relating the largest use of urban space—residential land for households—to the organization and technology of urban transportation. Supplies framework for analyzing and projecting urban arrangement through a theoretical model. 144 pages. $2.00.

WATER POLLUTION: ECONOMIC ASPECTS AND RESEARCH NEEDS. By Allen V. Kneese. Reconnaissance study of water pollution problems that, in recent years, have reached critical national proportions. Examines physical, economic, and social aspects of the pollution problem in order to pinpoint areas where more information must precede intelligent planning and sound political decision-making. 120 pages. $1.75.

A NATIONAL PROGRAM OF RESEARCH IN HOUSING AND URBAN DEVELOPMENT. By Harvey S. Perloff, with the RFF staff. Study prepared at the request of the Administrator of the Housing and Home Finance Agency, Robert C. Weaver, and made generally available for the first time in the fall of 1961. 36 pages. 50c.

A SECRET OF JAPANESE GARDENS. By Prof. P. Takuma Tono, Tokyo. The Mitsuo Onizuka Press, 65 pp. From Harold Merrill, 5700 32nd St., N.W., Washington 15, D. C. $1.00.

WASHINGTON: Village and Capital 1800–1878. By Constance McLaughlin Green. The Washington that greeted federal legislators in 1800, when they first streamed into the recently chosen capital, was little more than a few buildings and roughly indicated roads on the bank of the Potomac River. This volume describes the growth of the capital during the first three-quarters of the nineteenth century.

In the second volume of this history of Washington, D. C., the author will study the growth of the city from 1879 to 1941. 445 pages. $8.50. Princeton University Press.

Watch Service Report

Canyonlands National Park

S. 2387 authorizes the establishment of 332,292 acres of rugged canyon country in southeastern Utah as the Canyonlands National Park.

The Public Lands Subcommittee of the Senate has held hearings on S. 2387 in both Washington and the field.

The National Parks Subcommittee of the House held hearings on H. R. 8573 on May 28, 1962.

Chesapeake and Ohio Canal National Historical Park

S. 77 authorizes the establishment of the Chesapeake and Ohio Canal National Historical Park to include the present Chesapeake and Ohio Canal National Monument and such additional lands in the vicinity of the Canal as the Secretary deems desirable for the purposes of the park, but not to exceed 15,000 acres including land already in Federal ownership.

S. 77 passed the Senate on August 2, 1961.

Grand Canyon National Park, Orphan Mining Claim

Public Law 87-457 was approved by the President on May 28, 1962. This law authorizes the Secretary to accept on certain specified terms conveyance of title to the Orphan Claim, a mining claim of about 20 acres on the rim of the Grand Canyon, provided that the grantor releases any extralateral rights that it may have. The deed to the United States shall be subject to certain conditions, the most important being that all mineral rights are to be reserved to the grantor but the exercise of the rights is to be limited to underground mining.

Great Basin National Park

S. 1760 provides for the establishment of Great Basin National Park on over 123,000 acres in eastern Nevada. The characteristics of the Great Basin are not now represented by any unit in the National Park System. The area includes 14 peaks above 10,000 feet and six of these stand a mile or more above the adjacent lowland deserts.

The Lehman Caves National Monument, established by Presidential Proclamation on January 24, 1922, lies within the proposed park boundary. Under this bill it would be abolished as such and become a part of the Great Basin National Park. The Cave is one of the most beautiful in the world and would be an outstanding feature of the park.

S. 1760 passed the Senate on January 25, 1962. Hearings were held by the National Parks Subcommittee of the House on July 27 and 28, 1961, on H. R. 6873.

Hamilton Grange National Memorial

Public Law 87-438 was approved by the President on April 27, 1962. This law authorizes the establishment of the former dwelling house of Alexander Hamilton (commonly known as The Grange), situated in New York, New York, as a National Memorial.

Ice Age National Scientific Reserve

This proposed legislation provides for the preservation, interpretation, and maintenance of representative examples of continental glaciation in Wisconsin.

The Department's proposed substitute bill for the original bills introduced in Congress was introduced by Congressman Reuss on July 9, 1962. This bill provides for the establishment of an Ice Age National Scientific Reserve administered by the State of Wisconsin and its political subdivisions with cooperation from the Secretary of the Interior. The Secretary's cooperation would consist of (1) formulating, within two years, a comprehensive plan for preservation of the outstanding examples of continental glaciation in Wisconsin; (2) assisting the State and its political subdivisions in acquiring additional lands needed in the Reserve; and (3) assisting in providing interpretive facilities for the Reserve and in maintaining all physical facilities for the visiting public.

Planning and Civic Comment

Indiana Dunes National Monument
On August 28, 1961, Senator Douglas introduced amendments in the nature of a substitute (S. 1797) to establish Indiana Dunes National Lakeshore.
The Department's report on S. 1797 was signed February 23. Hearings were held by the Public Lands Subcommittee of the Senate on February 26, 27, and 28, 1962.
No action has been taken on either the Hartke bill (S. 2317) or the Saylor bill (H. R 6544).

Oregon Dunes National Seashore
S. 992 introduced by Senator Neuberger authorizes the establishment of the Oregon Dunes National Seashore Recreation Area consisting of about 35,650 acres along the Oregon coast as a unit of the National Park System. About 14,000 acres of this is Federal land within the Siuslaw National Forest.
The Department sent a proposed report to the Bureau of the Budget on July 6, 1961, but it has not been cleared for release.
H. R. 6528 introduced by Congressman Durno authorizes the establishment of the Oregon Dunes National Shorelands to be administered by the Secretary of Agriculture as a part of the Siuslaw National Forest.
The Department has not reported on H. R. 6528. No hearings have been held.

Ozark Rivers National Monument
Companion bills H. R. 5712 and S. 1381 provide for the establishment of the Ozark Rivers National Monument in the Current and Eleven Point Rivers area of Missouri with an area of not to exceed 113,000 acres.
Hearings were held on H. R. 5712 by the National Parks Subcommittee of the House on July 7, 1961.
Hearings were held on S. 1381 by the Public Lands Subcommittee of the Senate on July 6, 1961, in Washington, and on July 23, 1962, in Van Buren, Missouri.

Padre Island National Seashore
S. 4, which passed the Senate on April 10, 1962, provides for the establishment of Padre Island National Seashore along an 85-mile stretch of Padre Island, Texas.
S. 4 was reported with amendments by the House Committee on Interior and Insular Affairs.

Point Reyes National Seashore
S. 476, authorizing the establishment of the Point Reyes National Seashore, passed the Senate on September 7, 1961, and passed the House on July 23, 1962.
This legislation provides for an area of approximately 53,000 acres; however, within a zone of about 26,000 acres no parcel of more than 500 acres shall be acquired without the consent of the owner so long as it remains in its natural state, or is used exclusively for ranching and dairying purposes.

Prairie National Park
Companion bills S. 73 and H. R. 4885 authorize the establishment of 60,000 acres of land in Pottawatomie County, Kansas, as the Prairie National Park. Enactment of this legislation would preserve representative portions of the grasslands and native wildlife of the prairie which at one time comprised a vast and unique region of plant and animal life between the eastern forests and the Great Plains.
No hearings have been scheduled in either the House or Senate.

Theodore Roosevelt Birthplace and Sagamore Hill National Historic Sites
Public Law 87-547 was approved by the President on July 25, 1962. This law provides for the preservation of the Birthplace of Theodore Roosevelt at 26 and 28 East Twentieth Street, New York City, and Sagamore Hill, the Roosevelt Estate on Long Island.

Sleeping Bear Dunes National Recreation Area
S. 2153 introduced by Senator Hart and Senator McNamara authorizes the establishment of the Sleeping Bear Dunes National Recreation Area in Michigan. Over 20,000,000 people live within an easy day's drive of the area.

Field hearings were held on S. 2153 in Traverse City, Michigan, by the Public Lands Subcommittee of the Senate, on November 13, 1961.

On July 11, 1962, Senator Hart introduced a revised bill, S. 3528, to establish the Sleeping Bear Dunes National Lakeshore. Under the provisions of this bill the Secretary's authority to acquire land is greatly restricted.

Virgin Islands National Park

S. 2429 would revise the boundaries of the Virgin Islands National Park to include about 5,650 acres of adjoining submerged lands and waters. This bill would also authorize the Secretary to acquire, with appropriated funds, lands within the boundary as it now exists and as revised by this legislation.

S. 2429 passed the Senate on June 29, 1962.

S. 2429 was reported out by the House Committee on August 13, 1962.

Tocks Island National Recreation Area

The Corps of Engineers has recommended the construction of Tocks Island Dam across the Delaware River at a point approximately six miles upstream from the Delaware Water Gap. S. 3530, H. R. 10522, and H. R. 12246, authorize the establishment of a National Recreation Area at the location of this reservoir project in Pennsylvania and New Jersey.

The water based recreation opportunities afforded by this project are of exceptionally high quality. Moreover, there are 30,000,000 potential users within a 100-mile radius.

Hearings are scheduled by the Public Lands Subcommittee of the Senate on August 16.

Land Conservation Fund

S. 3118 and H. R. 11172 authorize the establishment of a land conservation fund to be dedicated for the acquisition of lands and interests in lands for the National Park System, the National Forest System, and Wildlife Refuges, but the fund will be available only in the amount determined by the appropriation acts. The proposed legislation authorizes advance appropriations of $500 million to the fund to be used for an 8-year program (through fiscal year 1970) to permit the acquisition program to be initiated without delay.

The four revenue sources proposed by the bill are:

1. Proceeds from entrance, admission and other recreation user fees on Federal land and water areas.

2. Proceeds from the sale of Federal surplus non-military real property.

3. That portion of the gasoline excise tax for gasoline used in boats which is now refundable under existing law.

4. Revenues from a new system of annual Federal user charges on recreation boats.

Hearings were held by the full House Interior and Insular Affairs Committee on July 11 and 12 and by the full Senate Interior and Insular Affairs Committee on August 14.

Planning Assistance

S. 3117 and H. R. 11165, to promote the coordination and development of effective Federal and State programs relating to outdoor recreation and to provide financial assistance to the states for recreational planning.

S. 3117 passed the Senate August 9, 1962 and H. R. 11165 was reported out of Committee August 10, 1962.

Wilderness Preservation System

S. 174 passed by the Senate on September 6, 1961, provides for a National Wilderness Preservation System to be composed of portions of the National Park System, wildlife refuges, and game ranges administered by the Department of the Interior and portions of the national forests administered by the Department of Agriculture. The portions of the National Park System to be included in the National Wilderness Preservation System will be selected and included in the system over a 10-year period in accordance with prescribed procedures set forth in the bill.

Hearings were held by the Public Lands Subcommittee of the House on May 7 through May 11.

Proceedings of the

1962 National Conference

on State Parks

will be issued as a Supplement

to the December Quarterly

JY 1

Planning and Civic Comment

Official Organ of American Planning and Civic Association and
National Conference on State Parks

CONTENTS

DECEMBER 1962

Planning and Civic Comment

Vol. 28   December, 1962   No. 4

Land Utilization Planning in Metropolitan Calcutta

By CHITTAPRIYA MUKHERJEE

EDITOR'S NOTE :—The author, in preparing this article, has done a substantial amount of research. The manuscript, as received, was copiously annotated and carried a section of thorough documentation and statistical tables. For obvious reasons these have been omitted, without detriment, we feel, to the text.

Why,—after successful completion of two Five Year Plans,—are we thinking of having a separate plan for Greater and 'better' Calcutta? What are the problems peculiar to Calcutta which necessitate a 'plan within a plan?' Is it for removing the inadequacies of 'minimum' civic amenities which city-dwellers throughout the world are entitled to?—What are our requirements?—Better houses for all and sundry? Removal of the eyesores—the Bustees? More of filtered water? Better and cheaper transport? More parking space for cars? More schools and hospitals? More open space? Less of unemployment? More cinema houses? What are we aiming at? . . . If these are inadequate, is it because more people live in the city than it can hold, or because the City administration has failed to provide us with what should have been given?

Why do we want to live in Calcutta? Because of better living conditions or because of better opportunities to earn our living?

If the 'standard' of amenities is to be raised, who will be the beneficiaries? Those who pay for the improvements or all those who are destined to, or have a right to, live in this City?—if we cannot pay for all the improvements, who is going to pay for us, and who will repay it?

If the *present* City-dwellers are willing to have a better standard of living, are not the rural folk living around the city entitled to even a fraction of the amenities enjoyed by the City-dwellers? If the 'pull' of Calcutta further impoverishes the surrounding villages, have the villagers not the right to come to and seek shelter in the City? . . .

Recent report of the sale, by auction, of a plot of land, by the Calcutta Improvement Trust, at Rs. 75,000/-per 'cottah' (720 sq. ft.)[1] has, as is evident from a series of discussions in current papers, created much surprise and deep concern amongst a large section of the residents of Calcutta; grave doubts have been expressed in some quarters about the possible repercussions of this trend on the reconstruction programme of the city.

[1] Converting Indian Rupees to U. S. Dollars at the official rate of Rs 476 to $1.00 and "cottahs" (720 sq. ft.) to acres (60.5 cottahs per acre), the price per acre would be $9,532.38.

Fantastic though this price may seem to be, it is the inevitable manifestation of an old and deep-rooted system inherent in our existing economic structure; price of a scarce 'commodity'—and so scarce a 'commodity' as land in an over-crowded city,—when determined solely by the time-honoured 'law of demand and supply' puts a new meaning to the theory of the 'survival of the fittest.'

With control over only a small fraction of the total land in the city, the Calcutta Improvement Trust (which, incidentally is contemplating a revision in the procedure of sale by auction that pushes up the land price in times of boom) has its arguments for having followed this course so far; auctioning of smaller parcels of land than that acquired at 'market price' and developed, hardly covered the entire capital layout in the past allotment to the 'highest bidder' always kept the Trust above criticism of yielding to pressure from vested interest people.

The man-in-the-street, himself pushed away to the suburbs, has the satisfaction of living in a city that once enjoyed the place of pride as the 'Second City of the British Empire' and is now, again, coming forward to be ranked as one of the 'First Three' or the 'First Five' big cities of the world!!

In the context of the proposed long-term and comprehensive measures for reconstructing Calcutta, this question of land price and land utilization,—not only in the city but in the entire area coming within 'metropolitan influence' — assumes particular significance.

If our predecessors had, with a myopic vision, failed to look ahead of their generation and left behind a congested, unplanned city, we (now that we are citizens of a free and Welfare State, and are free from the invidious discrimination of having to live in the "Black Town") are surely determined to take steps of far-reaching effects so that our posterity may not blame us of "doing too little, too late."

Judged by the developmental measures taken, and various restrictions imposed, in the past which have made Calcutta what it is today, it has to be conceded that, however short-sighted or half-hearted such measures might have been, the problem of Calcutta has not been so much of a lack of planning for the City as such; it has always been, as has been put so aptly, "a race between the problems and the solutions"!!

Apart from the post-Independence influx of about four hundred thousand uprooted people that has practically washed away all the good work done in course of the last fifteen years, Calcutta has never had a balance between its physical capacity, and the number of people, —from adjoining and remote districts of Bengal as well as from other States,—forced out of their occupation at home, and huddled in 'Bustees' or even pavements of Calcutta. If there is any point of similarity between the urbanization of Europe or America and that of India, it is surely not the economic reasons at the background, but the 'modern' civic amenities imported by us. Disparity of male and female population and increasingly larger proportion of immigrants over 'natural' population,—reflections of that social and economic disintegration which is not a phenomenon entirely originating in Calcutta,—assumed quite a serious proportion even as early as in 1901.

If, in spite of all improvements in the city's amenities brought about since the days of John Company, almost continuously, the problems of Calcutta have appeared again and again in worse and more acute form, it is surely due more to the problem inherent in the economic set-up of the country as a whole than in the city itself. The prob-lems of Calcutta, in order to be tackled effectively, have inevitably to be related more to the problems elsewhere than within the city or its suburbs.

If the Welfare State,—working within the framework of a democratic set-up,—now proposes to grapple with the problem of Calcutta then (apart from the more fundamental issue of 'regional dispersal' now accepted as a part of National Planning) it is perhaps imperative that, so far as land utilization planning within Calcutta *and* in the region coming under 'metropolitan influence' is concerned, the old policy of 'intelligent compromise with the inevitable' has to be given up . . . Broadening the streets, pulling down uninhabitable buildings, providing more supply of filtered water, beautifying the parks, removal of 'bustees,' constructing under-ground railways,—all these are no doubt essential parts of city planning; but the problem ultimately boils down to one basic question, viz.,

Consistent with the fiscal capa-bilities,—not of the city alone or its conurbation but of the benevolent Central Government and our benefactors abroad,—to what extent the 'modernization' of the city would be feasible or desirable? If a part of the 'modernization' is removal of bustees from the heart of the city, past experiences possibly show that the 'eye-sores' do not disappear, they only shift their venue just beyond the jurisdiction of the city planners, till the city's area is widened and the Bustee dwellers are pushed further away. If these people have a right, or are being compelled by circumstances, to earn their livelihood in the city, their daily movement from the outskirts of the city encroaches on their time and adds to their transport cost, and strains the inadequate transport services of the city.

If the price of land within Calcutta is soaring up, it is conceivable that, the area to be brought under 'Greater Calcutta' having been declared, land price within the radius is not remaining static; land in a developing metropolitan area is now a better investment than even gold! Opening up of the Barasat-Basirhat railway, electrification of Kharagpur-Howrah line, installation of the giant Thermal Power Station at Bandel, or, for that matter, all other measures to connect places within the radius of sixty or seventy miles, and to improve living conditions in Greater Calcutta, are offering golden opportunities to investors to hold on and to reap a rich harvest in the near future. While the "long-term" plan takes shape, series of "short-term" plans make their headway in every corner; constitutional protection being in favour of all those myriads of claimants to land-use (with different, conflicting, interests in land values) who effect a lawful purchase of land, the State,—when it finally enters the 'land-market',—does not have the final say either in respect of land-price or in land-utilization pattern. Equipped though the State is with powers to acquire, either a vacant or occupied land in 'public interest,' the process is prolonged; 'fundamental rights' may stay the hands of 'bureaucracy' for an even longer period; "reasonable" price that has to be paid as compensation from the National Exchequer may yield an 'unearned' and windfall income to the last owner of the land. Ultimate land-use pattern has thus been a conglomeration of pulls of innumerable sectional interests; those with weak bargaining power have invariably succumbed, and the State, —being just one amongst many parties in the market, has not so far, generally speaking, assumed the role of the final determinant of land use.

Instances of the State selling or leasing out land to 'private sector,' both within Calcutta and in the reclaimed lands in agricultural areas, are not new; in every case the net result was not what had been expected. Explanation for failure of such piece-meal and half-way measures, is not difficult to trace. Recent enactments abroad and to some extent in our country show a growing awareness of the need for *comprehensive* State control over land-price and use. Repugnant though, to the 'private sector,' the idea is, of 'bureaucracy' having the last word

in land utilization and price, this is surely the *starting point* for Greater Calcutta planning; failure to do this now (when the Welfare State is planning for the 'people') would amount to postponing the evil day and inviting it later with more virulence and further complications.

Though the net result may be quite feeble, a move in the desired direction is to be found in the decision of the State Government to sell land in the reclaimed Salt Lake area or in Kalyani, at a reasonable price, to middle class people for residential purpose. Expensive though it is, reclamation of Salt Lake was no doubt an urgent necessity irrespective of cost; although opinions may differ as to the relation between the paying capacity of middle-class people and the minimum price fixed by the State, the 'open market' price as well as the use-pattern would certainly have taken a less desirable course if left to 'private sector.'

As compared, however, to the total area likely to come under 'metropolitan influence,' in course of a few years, the area under direct State control so far is infinitesimally small. Instead of letting things drift and allowing the sprawling city of Calcutta to cover many times larger area in the fashion of other big cities (which, in spite of all planning, have followed so far a laissez faire policy), it is perhaps imperative on our part to (a) put an immediate ban on land speculation, (b) make all transactions in land and construction of buildings, subject to the approval of a central high power organization and (c) chalk out a comprehensive land-use policy for

4

the districts of Howrah, Hooghly, 24 Parganas, and parts of Burdwan, Nadia and Midnapore with restrictions on permanent or semi-permanent immigration from areas outside the radius.

While the area of influence of the city stretches far beyond this area, it is conceivable that,—given adequate machinery to implement an over-all plan,—if the gradual 'urbanization', with all its effects on the economy and the society, could be halted, the long-term result would not be altogether undesirable.

If the entire area cannot be adequately brought under the purview of the Metropolitan Authority, the other choice possibly lies in narrowing down the area to corridors of, say, ten-mile width along the existing rail routes and roads and in such areas where rail or road may (or should) be opened up in near future (Kolaghat-Contai for instance).

This being taken as the starting point, we are invariably brought to another question: to what extent the city,—or for that matter, other urban areas within the radius,—should be allowed to expand, and what should be the degree of disparity in "standards" of amenities between the urban and rural areas? In spite of the urban area, or the Calcutta conurbation having so far been restricted to a relatively small portion along the River, its impact on the economy of the whole region has increasingly been detrimental to a balanced growth. Although there are patches of regions where agriculture, small industries, and supplementary cash income to the people travelling to and working in

Calcutta, have maintained a balance, the general picture is one of over-saturation point in agriculture and inability of non-agricultural sources to maintain the surplus population; this 'spill-over' population from rural areas have concentrated in urban areas with the desperate hope of eking out their existence. The population has . . . not grown according to space available but according to where it can find the means of sustenance . . . Density selects only particular small areas for its growth to the comparative neglect of other larger areas. These select areas of extraordinary rapid growth in density will show what a searching nature a population, dislodged from traditional agriculture, or squeezed out by the pressure of land, has in finding sustenance elsewhere. Recent trends show an increasing proportion of migration from other urban areas as well.

If Calcutta is allowed, or so designed, to spread over a wider area either for industrial or residential purposes, existing problem will all the more be aggravated; encroachment on the agricultural land, which already shows signs of stagnant productivity, would hardly be compatible with present day concepts of balanced growth; (and we are surely not expecting such rise in land productivity as to allow, like U.S.A., a phased reduction of agricultural land and diversion of the same to non-agricultural purposes). Ever since the railways were opened up, mostly in the last century, stagnant rural areas got a fresh lease of life; agricultural products got their ready market in the city and cash money flowed to the villages. Increasing concentration of population within the city on the one hand, slow but steady impoverishment of agriculture on the other, and increasingly brisk wholesale purchase by middlemen in the villages gradually soaked not only the 'surplus' but almost the entire agricultural products; this contributed to the sapping of the vitality of surrounding rural areas.

Further expansion of the area of Calcutta will,—it may be argued— mean more capital-investment in houses, roads, sewerage and other amenities for which money would have to be raised either by loan or by the beneficiaries themselves (and number of beneficiaries is likely to be less than the number of people obliged to find shelter elsewhere); recurring cost to the 'commuter' population in terms of time lost in transit and transport fare would again, cumulatively, be a loss to the nation which can ill afford to spend more of its coal, petroleum, or other 'derived' sources of power, on moving passengers daily, when more urgent use of power is being held up.

It would further be argued that,— apart from the few low-density non-industrial urban areas which continue to maintain a balanced link with the rural areas,—'urbanization' as is understood in the context of the 'Calcutta Industrial Belt,' would only result in increased social complications, and would tend to create so-called 'urban' habits amongst rural folk, which would, to say the least, not be conducive to the interests of the rural areas directly brought under 'metropolitan influence' . . . Arguments against a sprawling city, or rather in favour of a well-knit Calcutta city have, no doubt, many strong points. If fiscal capability of the city-dwellers is a point to be reckoned with, it is better to concentrate,—as the argument goes, on improvements to existing arrangements in the city and on schemes already drawn up or implemented in part; this may still make Calcutta, at a lower cost, a city worth living in. Municipal services,—if pulled up from the present deplorable condition,—can indeed bring about much environmental changes; Durgapur Gas Grid will soon help in removing the 'smog' nuisance; more stringent regulations for stoppage of misuse, or utilization of unused land, renovation of dilapidated houses, remodelling,—and not necessarily removal, —of Bustees, improvements in public transport converging in and within the city, supply of more filtered water (together with measures for conservation of the huge quantity of filtered water that goes to waste every day!) will make living condition better than what it is now. If we cannot strike at the root of the problem that has created the present dichotomy, we have hardly any justification for having a more 'modern' city, with its Tube Railway, when conditions all round are not really 'modern' enough. Instead of investing foreign money worth crores of rupees for a 'better Calcutta,' can't a plan, with the same amount of money, be chalked out as would be less spectacular, but discourage distress immigration to the city and help the people all around to stand on their own resources in rural areas? Continuing the arguments in favour of confining the

6

abnormal swelling strictly within the present area, it would be said that there should be a sort of a 'ban' (either by restrictive measures on industrial expansion within, or by ameliorative measures outside the 'Industrial Belt') on further inflow of population; those who would prefer staying outside the city limits, and to be amongst the 'daytime population' within the city, would have the facility of constructing their residential buildings on *State-owned land,* purchased at controlled price, and availing of the fast transport now being provided.

Comparing, however, the congestion of Greater Bombay, Calcutta City, London or New York with that of Calcutta, it cannot perhaps be denied that, if not on economic, then on social grounds, dispersal of population is an urgent necessity. Bustee-dwellers,—and a large number of 'lower-middle-class' people though in many cases living with their families, are creating problems of their own and inflicting worse problems on the society as a whole; 'houseless' people are yet another source of problem to the civic life of Calcutta. Humanitarian considerations demand that all of them should have adequate housing facilities; judged by present-day concepts of good living conditions, it is not difficult to assess how many acres of land would be required for the purpose. But, then again, there are millions of villagers around Calcutta,—socially and economically a completely different group of people,—who live under worse conditions; moreover what they lack is the civic amenities of city life,—filtered water, good roads,

electricity,—which are at the disposal of even the slum-dwellers (mostly migrants from other states) of Calcutta.

If the State has an obligation to the city's bustees—the present day "Black Town,"—it cannot possibly fulfil it at the expense of or in disregard of, the living conditions of the villagers around Calcutta; these villagers are contributing to the prosperity of Calcutta, if not directly then by denying themselves the food produced in their midst.

If dispersal of the population of Calcutta is a necessity, it would surely have to be harmonised with the economic, geographic and social conditions prevailing in the surrounding areas; we cannot possibly afford to repeat the errors of earlier days by focussing entire attention on the city dwellers' problems in utter disregard of rural people.

Assuming that dispersal of existing cluster of factories is ruled out and that establishment of new factories within the radius (except under considerations of larger 'national interest') is restricted by the Central Metropolitan Authority, the problem will be one of moving the residential population to places wherefrom they can attend their daily work without loss of time. Though the transport system around Calcutta is as yet 'toylike' compared to that of London or New York the existing network has no doubt helped dispersal to a considerable extent. Improvements to transport now under implementation will help movement of a larger number of people.

Here comes in the problem of finding residential accommodation for the (i) *existing surplus* population of Calcutta and its conurbation; (ii) *local* people of the places where such constructions would be contemplated; (iii) *future* increase in population (and this future is rather uncertain if immigration either from the other states or from across the border cannot be effectively regulated).

With extension of 'urban' housing to the interior, apart from the possible clash with agricultural land, strange and undesirable reactions may be reflected on 'rural' housing as well as on rural habits.

Multi-storeyed tenements with better amenities for the residents (for economising the use of land, construction of 'luxury' suburban villas will certainly be prohibited or restricted to the minimum) in the midst of, or surrounded by thatched huts with all the disadvantages of villages, will, collectively speaking, hardly improve matters. 'Urbanising' all the houses—both for the overflow of Calcutta people and the local rural people—will, economically, not be feasible. Larger the area of 'urban households,' further away will be pushed back the poorer rural folk not entitled to, and without having the means to live in better houses. All that they will derive is 'cash compensation' for the land taken away, or land in an inferior location.

Secondly, there is the question of relating place of residence with the place of earning. So far as 'local' people are concerned, widening the scope of non-agricultural means of livelihood, for supplementing the agricultural source would, of course, be an imperative necessity. What-ever the characteristic products (in addition to agriculture) of the different localities may now be, growing pressure of population on diminishing return from land demands a radical change for the better in respect of the means of livelihood for the rural people. By the time the far-reaching damages to the agricultural areas done in the previous century are rectified, now problems are creeping in, and notwithstanding all current measures through Community Development Project and emphasis on 'cooperation,' recent trends show widening of the area of 'urbanization' and concentration of economic power in fewer hands.

On the other hand further dispersal of population from Calcutta would require extension of the facility of transport to an extent as would maintain, over a foreseeable period, a balance between the carrying capacity and the number of 'commuter' population. Taking lessons from the experiences of London or New York and the present trends in our big cities as well we shall have to decide not only on the extent to which such extension of transport facility would have to be stretched but also on the mode of transport. While it is agreed that railways (to choose between surface and under ground railway it is presumed we shall prefer the former if the total cost is lower) and automobiles have their strong points in respect of capital cost, operating expenditure, supply of fuel, carrying capacity and employment potential (which we do not discuss in the present article) we can hardly afford the luxury of following a laissez faire policy in

8

favour of private automobiles. Protagonists of "peoples' cars" would no doubt consider this to be an unwarranted encroachment on their freedom; purchasing power only should, in their opinion, be the ultimate determining consideration for owning a private car. If the same consideration had led to the spectacular ratio of one car for every third man in U. S. A.—(a country, rich in mineral oil, and having the affluence in all other natural resources as well as in surplus land for more and wider roads!)—it would be worthwhile to see what a section of the people of U. S. A. say about it. "In the monumental effort that has gone into the planning of our 'American way of life,' one thing has been forgotten. That is travel convenience for the millions who work, shop, make professional calls and seek recreation in the central areas of down-town America . . . ; when a city is faced with an epidemic—infantile paralysis for example—we rally as a unit and do something about it, even if it means curtailing the personal privileges of freedom of some citizens. Today the epidemic is *traffic paralysis*, as fatal and crippling to the city as infantile paralysis is to human beings."—It would surely not fit in with the planning of a welfare State with poor resources, to permit this sort of growth in our cities.

Ultimate success of 'Greater Calcutta' planning depends on our willingness and determination to combine and co-ordinate the needs of the 'urban' and the rural areas. If Calcutta city,—like other cities elsewhere—attained its present growth under an economic set-up already outmoded, then the solution lies not in 'urbanizing' the entire area of 'metropolitan influence' but in so spreading the means of livelihood and the population as would reduce the economic disparity between the city and its surrounding villages and would enable the villages to retain their characteristics. Availability of cheap electric power to every village, rigid control over land utilization, house construction, and land price, restriction on unfettered growth of big industries, expansion of cheap public transport with maximum carrying capacity, together with radical changes in legislations on land tenure system, and on landed properties may, in the long run, bring about a balance between 'industrial urban centres' and 'agricultural rural areas' and break the vicious circle that has created present day Calcutta and is creating the Calcutta of days to come. 'Rural' housing will find its own solution if means of livelihood is widened. 'Urban' amenities would, on the other hand, have to be curtailed to a level that would be in conformity with the spending capacity of the nation . . . If the entire process is more difficult to achieve, the result is likely to be more lasting.

If we have decided to rebuild Calcutta, it is time that we choose between "profitable jobs, publicity, lavish expenditure for engineering and public works," and a radical re-orientation in our approach to the fundamental relationship between the city and the village.

9

Anti-Uglies, Unite!

A Proposal for an American Civic Trust

EDITOR'S NOTE:—This editorial by Grady Clay, Editor, *Landscape Architecture* is reprinted by permission, with our feeling that the thoughts expressed should focus our attention on the problems and, hopefully, stimulate some positive action toward their solution. Mr. Clay is a Board Member of the American Planning and Civic Association. Two letters To THE EDITOR (*Landscape Architecture*) which follow indicate some of the immediate reaction to this thought-provoking editorial.

A significant change is taking place in the American public's attitude toward its physical environment. A look at the federal highway program offers both a clue to this change, and a positive suggestion for the future.

The passage of the Federal-Aid Highway Act in 1956 caused most of us to welcome this big solution to urban and interurban traffic. The future appeared serene, once all those "41,000 miles of tomorrow" were laid in concrete.

But as expressways quickly began cutting through communities, doubts appeared. Many highway officials showed themselves little better than legalized free-booters armed with public money and power. Many citizens, while enjoying the roads, began counting the costs.

In San Francisco there occurred the now-famous "freeway revolt" in January, 1959. Public protest against freeways of insensitive location and ugly design caused that city's Board of Supervisors to adopt an official policy "opposed to the construction of all freeways contained in the San Francisco Master Plan." Only after bitter controversy did the highway developers begin to concede to the importance of good design.

None of these local "revolts" could halt the national program, but cumulatively they caused deep concern over the lack of civic awareness of many highway developers, and the poor quality of many final designs.

Slowly, the highway construction industry is waking up to the criticism which its works have generated. Its conferences, including the recent Hershey, Pa., sessions called by Automotive Safety Foundation, show signs of welcome soul-searching. The same kind of critical self-examination now flourishes in urban renewal. In many another field it is long overdue.

These years since 1956 have been most educational. The first lesson is obvious: the rebuilding and physical expansion of our country has only begun. We are certain to get more new towns and suburbs, new transport and movement systems, their tributaries and terminals; urban and rural reclamation projects and new dwellings at a rate approaching 2,000,000 units per year; conversion of land to city uses at something like 2,000,000 acres per year . . . All this at a speed of execution, and on a geographic scale never seen before.

What is now needed—what has been lacking in the immediate past —is the voice and pressure of a strong national citizens' organiza-

10

tion to encourage and to insist on well-planned and beautifully executed public works; and to sponsor private demonstrations. At present, those who oppose an unsightly or ill-considered project are weak and divided. Usually they fight strong national or locally-organized special interest groups. Occasionally they include fanatics (how else do protest groups survive?). Often they are too late, inept, and emotional. Sadly lacking in positive suggestions or programs of their own, they often are cast in the unpopular role of being "aginners."

The significant lesson we can learn from all this is that the time has come for positive, rather than negative action. The time is ripe for a national alliance of citizens with these goals:

To preserve, enhance, and improve this nation's great bounty of natural and man-made beauty; to conserve irreplaceable natural and scenic resources; to encourage and publicize superior design in landscape architecture, architecture, and urban development; to prevent blight, neglect, and uglification; and to develop an educated public vigorously supporting these goals.

That is quite an order. Yet the accomplishments of the Civic Trust in England, our National Trust for Historic Preservation, Action, Inc., and, in an earlier day, the American Planning and Civic Association, show clearly the possibilities. The Civic Trust's demonstration projects, such as the Burslem Market Place renovation described in LANDSCAPE ARCHITECTURE in July, 1961, are fine examples.

We have much to build upon: a host of existing groups with common interest in improvement. We have leagues for the preservation of worthy institutions, scenes, and objects; for the wider use of art in everyday life; for renewal, remodeling, restoration. The American Society of Landscape Architects and the American Institute of Architects have fought significant battles, and will continue in the forefront.

They have hundreds of potential allies: garden clubs and neighborhood improvement societies eager to venture beyond arranging flowers and annual picnics, downtown improvement leagues, citizens' associations for planning, open space committees, local renewal societies, most of them with no national affiliations, their efforts and funds often dissipated in driblets. Many would gladly cooperate in a common cause.

They need a clearinghouse, a reference center, a source of guidance, advice and help. Thus they can rise above local partisanship, remain above self-seekers, overcome public apathy, fight uglification, and help create a more beautiful America.

———————◆———————

To THE EDITOR:

I'm all for preserving and improving the nation's bounty of natural and man-made beauty. So is everyone else. I'm all for eliminating beer cans, billboards, dump heaps, auto junk yards wherever they appear on the landscape, and I would gladly join any organization that promised to do something effectual about them. And I'm also all for eliminating slums, urban blight, industrial plants which belch smoke and dust and filth over their surroundings.

Would I join an organization that promised to eliminate them for aesthetic reasons? I doubt it. And would I join an organization that campaigned for better-designed freeways and better-designed high-rise housing developments? But suppose I disapprove of *all* freeways and *all* high-rise housing developments? What then?

I am not saying that I do, but as I understand it, the assumption back of the proposed Civic Trust is that the only thing that matters is the aesthetic effect, and that the really essential traits of the American landscape are to be decided by someone else. And as a matter of fact this is pretty much the case: government and business do all the deciding for us; we laymen are lucky and count it a triumph when we manage to dissuade the bulldozers and cement mixers from overrunning one or two acres for every hundred they *do* overrun.

You know of how little account widespread local protest has been in the past when it is a matter of dissuading highway engineers or urban-renewal experts. And I admire your determination to try to alter this state of affairs by other than revolutionary means. But I fear it can't be so easily done: You can wash the child's face, but it takes something more radical than soap and water (and good will) to alter his expression. Still, there is this to be said for a clean child: it allows us to give serious thought as to how to make it smile.

And since you ask for comment I would say that the anti-uglification movement should start at precisely the lowest, simplest soap-and-water level: by block and neighborhood clean-up, paint-up campaigns, campaigns for cleaner streets, cleaner parks, cleaner rivers, less smoke, less litter, more greenery, more household and civic self respect.

All this enthusiasm would get just so far before the grass-roots reformers were confronted by the facts of life, and then perhaps would come something like an earnest national self-examination: Why *can't* we have a harmonious environment in spite of all our attempts at tidying up? What forces are there, collective as well as individual, which stand in the way? Do we really have a coherent, reasonably widespread standard for landscape beauty? If not, how do we go about formulating one?

This is when the Civic Trust could come into action, but not, it seems to me, before. The small immediate job of beautification comes first; not because it would be effective, but precisely because it would be ineffective and reveal to the public that ugliness, like beauty, is more than skin deep, and that if America is to look healthy it must *be* healthy.

J. B. JACKSON
Editor, *Landscape*
Santa Fe, New Mexico

———◆———

TO THE EDITOR:

There is no doubt that formation of an American Civic Trust, or some similar organization, would prove of inestimable value in creating increased awareness of the need for

(Continued on page 50)

12

Zoning Round Table

Two recent zoning decisions of the Massachusetts Supreme Court have been much discussed. The chief criticism of the first case cited below has been that the distinctions are thin and the reasoning more legalistic than realistic.

Zoning by contract

Sylvania Electric Products vs. City of Newton* decided in May 1962 presented a new question to the court. The plaintiff company at the suggestion of the city planning board subjected a parcel of land containing 153 acres to restrictions in the use of the site, and the city council changed the zoning classification of the site by amendment of the ordinance from single family residence to light manufacturing.

The issue was the effect of the action of the company on the validity of the amendment. The court cited decisions on this issue in the highest state courts of Florida, Maryland and New Jersey which held that the rezoning of land on condition that the owner would impose restrictions on its use was invalid. Since the conditions were not generally imposed on all land in the same zone, it was "spot zoning," and not in accordance with the comprehensive plan. In coming to the opposite conclusion the Massachusetts court conceded that the restrictions on the use of the land induced the city council to amend and that the restrictions were induced by the probability

*Adv. Sheets of 1962, Page 883

that the council would make the amendment. However, the amendment was upheld. The court said that this was not a case where the amendment restricted the use of the locus. This had already been done by the voluntary action of the company, and the restrictions were in the interest of general public policy.

The facts seem very similar to those which in other states have been struck down as "zoning by contract." The company was very likely assured that the planning board was speaking for the city council before it placed rather extensive restrictions on its land. It may not have been relying on a definite promise of favorable action, but was taking little chance that the action would be adverse, especially where the restrictions were in the public interest, and a very considerable increase in taxable property would result.

It must be concluded that the court was swayed by the evidence of a probable increase in the general welfare of the city and consequently found a way to overcome the invalidity of "contract zoning." If the case is good law, it points the way to hurdle the obstacles in a zoning ordinance and throws into question its protective value.

One judge wrote a strong dissenting opinion.

Non-Conformity

In the Chilson case* also decided in May 1962 the Board of Zoning Appeals in the city of Attleboro

*Mass. Advance Sheets of 1962, Page 855

13

granted permission to build a modern, masonry, two bay service station 46 feet long by 27 feet wide to take the place of an old, shabby cement block structure 30 feet by 25 feet in floor area which for several years had been used as a filling station. This use was non-conforming.

The issue as defined by the court was the extent to which a zoning ordinance may make provision for property because it has had a non-conforming status. The pertinent words of the statute are in Section 5 of Chapter 40A of the General Laws, "a zoning ordinance or by-law shall not apply to existing buildings . . . nor to the existing use of buildings . . . or of the land to the extent used at the time of adoption of the ordinance, but it shall apply to any change of use . . . and to any alteration which would amount to reconstruction." The court pointed out that this language does not prohibit special provision in a zoning ordinance or by-law for such situations. It says only that if changes are made which destroy the right to exemption, the validity of the new use must be determined under provisions of the ordinance "other than those which state the exemption."

Alternatives to changes in non-conforming uses would be for the owners to hold on to run down premises, and conditions might well be so bad as to be a serious deteriorating influence in the neighborhood. Consequently a non-conforming site has a "special aspect," and invites a special treatment. This has been recognized in ordinances which permit enlargement of non-conforming buildings or the substitution of new business uses, providing the enlarged building or the new use "is not more detrimental to the neighborhood."

In the case of Dobbs vs. Board of Appeal* the local zoning ordinance permitted a change in the non-conforming use, "if the new use were not more detrimental or objectionable to the neighborhood or substantially different in character." The court ruled that the proposed new use must satisfy both requirements, and that a beauty parlor as proposed was different in character from the existing grocery store.

Seekonk vs. Anthony** had a similar provision and a similar decision. In the early case of Cochran vs. Roemer*** the erection of additional buildings was allowed by the court where a similar provision to the above was in the local ordinance.

Without some such provision in the local zoning regulations clearly a change in the non-conforming use is barred except to a conforming use, but in the cases cited and in the present case each site which has been non-conforming falls into a special class for which criteria may be set up in the ordinance. Evidently no exact line can be drawn. The court will judge the reasonability of the criteria, but will hesitate to upset a decision by the Board of Appeal. In this case the improvement and modernization of

*339 Mass. 684 (1959)
**339 Mass. 49 (1959)
***287 Mass. 500 (1934)

(*Continued on page 19*)

Minnesota Defines Incorporation Policy

Proliferation of small units of government unable to finance their own services or solve their own problems will sap the vitality of local government.

In recent decisions on village petitions to incorporate, the Minnesota Municipal Commission eloquently expresses its understanding and its policy on this subject.

Under Commission guidelines on incorporation in metropolitan areas, approval of a new municipality will be withheld until there is reasonable proof that the proposed entity "has an adequate tax base, a reasonable prospect of providing necessary services when it is completely organized, is not a part of a large entity which can more adequately sustain municipal responsibilities, and would not be served better by annexation." In the public interest there must be better reason for incorporation than a wish to avoid annexation, or to protect special interests, e.g. land use and liquor licensing, from regulation by municipal government.

The Commission was created by the Minnesota legislature to introduce order in the creation of new municipalities. In doing so, it considers methods of providing municipal services efficiently and economically without confusing existing boundaries.

In a recent case where a village sought to retain its separate identity to avoid being engulfed by the tide of metropolitan population moving south from Minneapolis, the Commission, denying the petition,

observed that the village would be unable to devote the equipment and funds to road construction and maintenance that present township service provides and that the proposed budget was unrealistic, one-quarter of it depending on revenue from liquor licenses.

A tax base adequate for the provision of economical and effective municipal services and utilities was lacking. The Commission felt that local residents, and the metropolitan area, would be better served by seeking a larger solution which would permit the development of broader and integrated land use patterns.

In a decision on the petitions of four townships each seeking separate incorporation, the Commission indicated its preference for a total incorporation of one community in the major area involved. The towns lie in a formerly agricultural portion of Dakota County, separated from Minneapolis and St. Paul by the Minnesota and Mississippi Rivers. They will be in the line of heaviest population growth in that area in the coming decades. The Commission suggests that the towns look beyond their present borders, take counsel with one another, and perhaps produce a unified plan for future urban development.

The Commission is concerned with the continuing fragmentation of local government and the diffusion of tax sources in the metropolitan area. It has not hesitated to say that remaining unincorporated land within

(Continued on page 19)

15

"Private Property--Please Come In"

EDITOR'S NOTE:—This article is reprinted in its entirety from The Izaak Walton Magazine because it deals with a relatively new practice in the field of Outdoor Recreation, provision of facilities to the public by private land owners.

This Alabama firm spent half a million dollars to build a recreation area, then opened it not only to employees but to all who seek wholesome outdoor family recreation.

Believing that healthful outdoor family recreation strengthens not only the people but the economic health of the community as well, The Russell Manufacturing Company of Alabama has gone far beyond normal responsibility to its employees and has provided extensive facilities for wholesome recreation for all the people of Alexander City and surrounding area. What this progressive industrial firm is doing may be the pattern to solve the growing outdoor recreation problem that can no longer be thrust entirely upon government nor confined to publicly owned lands.

The Russell family, owners of the company that employs 3,500 persons in its textile operations in Alexander City, feels it has a civic responsibility which cannot—or, at least, should not—be delegated to local, state or Federal government as long as the resources for its fulfillment are within the capability of private enterprise.

Several generations of wise management and economic necessity have provided the company with the facilities—mostly suitable land. These include forest land but, probably more important, Elkahatchee lake that provides the industrial water supply. Supporting the policy of multiple use, this lake and the forested area are developed fully for recreation activities and to carry out the well accepted principles of conservation and good wildlife management.

Most spectacular of the company's public service operations is Wind Creek park located on Lake Martin near Alexander City. The company spent half a million dollars to provide this 2,000 acre site with improved shore-line recreation facilities along its entire 8 miles of lakeside, including 5 man-made beaches, boat launching ramps, 450 barbecue pits with picnic tables, fishing piers, shower-dressing rooms, covered pavilions and health-department approved water and sanitation provisions. Except for a small fee for overnight camping, everything is free and enjoyed by thousands of families in the East Alabama and West Georgia area. Not only the construction expense, but the entire operating loss is borne by The Russell Manufacturing Company. This is in addition to other company public service operations such as the building and financing of schools, athletic teams, youth activities of various kinds and many other constructive diversions.

Lake Martin, on which Wind Creek park is located, is a 50,000 acre body of water created by building Martin Dam and serving as a reservoir for the electric power system of the Alabama Power Com-

16

pany. The park itself is within 8 miles of Alexander City and less than 40 miles from Montgomery. Columbus, Georgia, site of the Army's huge Fort Benning, is less than one hour away, and Birmingham is no more than a two hour drive. Personnel of the Air University at Maxwell Field, Ft. Benning and Gunter Air Force Base find this spot ideal for off-duty pleasure.

What the Russell company has accomplished here would not be possible without a broad appreciation of human values in a community's economy—a factor which industry ranks highly when discussing theory, but pushes down to a low priority when carrying it out. What is unique about the Russell community service enterprise is that it has been put into operation with the same zeal that other companies devote mainly to the acquisition and use of the best operating sales and advertising technics. In addition to that, the budget is adapted to the recreation needs, not the needs to a tightened down budget.

One more thing is important. What is being done today and what has been accomplished even in this generation would not have been possible without the means of accomplishing it which, in turn, had to be acquired during generations past. This is another way of saying that worthwhile outdoor recreation resource development is a long term operation and can be carried out only by people of vision.

The Russells will tell you that their apparent altruism is not inconsistent with profitable operations but, on the other hand, it cannot be planned for if day-to-day—or even

annual—profits are the controlling motives. Therefore, half-million dollar Wind Creek park, built and operated for the public with private corporation funds, had its beginnings with Benjamin Russell, founder of the company who saw far into the future in both economic opportunities and in anticipation of the needs of the people of his home area. We might well study his thinking, for it is men of his type today who will provide the broad needs of the next generation.

Mr. Russell, a University of Virginia law graduate, dropped the practice of law soon after his graduation when he saw a more pressing need for a local bank in Alexander City than he did for his services as a lawyer. It was his continued ability to foresee needs that characterized his future success.

In 1902, Banker Russell recognized a need for more employment for the people of the community. You may say he saw a need for more employment for customers and potential customers of his bank, if you care to. It is a fine point of distinction to determine where good business stops and good human relations starts— if they do stop and start. "Join" might be a better word—or "overlap." It is the point of this story that they do overlap and it is the mission of this article to prove this to others who are employers.

Altruistic or businesslike—or both —Banker Benjamin bought 12 second-hand knitting machines from a mill that had closed in Georgia. The knit cloth was made into garments by the wives of the former farmers who had now becomed skilled knitters. The increasing demand for the products of The Russell Manufacturing Company dictated expansion into the spinning of local cotton into yarn, and then followed weaving, and finally a complete finishing plant for locally produced textiles as well as for other mills in the Southeastern area.

The community prospered and Ben Russell saw a variety of needs. He started a newspaper, a laundry, a bakery, a creamery, and many other services when he saw that such services were not being adequately supplied to the area. To offset a lack of employment opportunity for men leaving the farms, he built a soil-pipe foundry and, although these interests since have been sold, his enterprising action was the beginning of three successful foundries now located in Alexander City.

In the early 20's, the Alabama Power Company built Martin dam on the Tallapoosa River, flooding Kowaliga and Elkahatchee creeks and surrounding fields and creating Lake Martin. Looking thirty years ahead Russell saw the importance of sound conservation practices in soil cultivation and woodlands management, as well as the potential future of Martin lake as a recreation area. He began to buy thousands of acres of land around the lake.

He had planted several thousand acres in improved cotton. But the red clay hills covered with flint rock were not ideally suited for cotton growing, and during the 30's it was learned that this was not a profitable venture. However, this type of land was well suited for growing slash pine, and much of this area had a good stand of timber already

growing. Gradually cotton fields were abandoned, and pine trees were planted on every foot of available land.

As the years went by, scrub trees needed to be thinned to leave sufficient growing space for the healthy trees. These were sold for pulpwood and scientific cutting practices and reforestation policies developed the muddy, rocky acres into beautiful timber lands.

The recreation possibilities that Ben Russell had envisioned after Lake Martin was flooded did not develop immediately. The water was muddy and unsuitable for fishing and water sports.

But the reforestation program of The Russell Manufacturing Company and the Alabama Power Company checked soil erosion and held back the deposit of silt. The water began to clear up and suddenly Lake Martin became one of the beauty spots of the South with clear blue waters lapping its extensive shoreline.

When he died in 1941, Benjamin Russell's eldest son, Benjamin C., became president of the company. Benjamin Jr., died in 1944 and the second son, Thomas D. became president and has held that position ever since and another brother, Robert A. is executive vice-president.

The Russell brothers, and their sister Elizabeth, also a part owner of the company, watched Lake Martin grow in popularity. In the past 10 years, hundreds of summer homes have been built there and the demand for more houses is insatiable. Thousands of people filled the beaches and park every day during the summer months and, even in the

18

wintertime, fishermen and wildlife enthusiasts criss-crossed the lake and tramped through the woods.

But the Russells realized that everybody could not have a home on the lake and there was need for a great deal more recreation space. Following in the family tradition of acting to meet the need, they determined to create a recreation spot that would be readily accessible to all people. It would be a restful, clean, orderly, family outing spot that would provide all the needed facilities but without any commercialized or carnival atmosphere.

There are broad paved roads leading into the major areas of the reservation but one quickly becomes surrounded by pine trees and native Southern hardwoods. The 30 or more fishing piers are in secluded spots where it is hard to choose between fishing or napping. Skillful arrangements of native shrubs and flowers give a delightful touch of color, and the remnants of early farms have been converted to park use. Field stone chimneys left abandoned for years by departed settlers have been converted into large barbecue pits. An old farm silo has been magically changed into an observation tower without disturbing the natural beauty of the setting.

There is not a comparable park in the Southland. It is beautiful because it is natural. It is unique because it is privately financed and owned, but dedicated to public use.

The park doesn't make any money but The Russell Manufacturing Company does. This may provide an incentive for other industries to follow!

❧

ZONING ROUND TABLE

(*Continued from page 14*)

the property and its effect on the neighborhood were factors in the decision. The new service station would contain the cars serviced inside the building. The old station was so small that unsightly conditions resulted.

The court must decide in this situation between extending nonconformity which gives a preference contrary to the intent of the zoning law and continuing an undesirable condition.

MINNESOTA DEFINES INCORPORATION POLICY

(*Continued from page 15*)

metropolitan districts should be annexed to existing cities and villages as the need for municipal services arises. An exception would occur when one unified portion of the metropolis experiencing rapid population growth could provide an adequate economic base so that the resulting newly created municipality could furnish government services as effectively and efficiently as they could be furnished through annexation.

Good Housing Design Competition

This year, the Ministry of Housing and Local Government, London, England in collaboration with the Royal Institute of British Architects, conducted a competition in the field of Housing Layout and Design. With many local authorities busy redeveloping slum clearance areas and with wornout areas of towns and cities being redeveloped, the competition sought the schemes with the best layout and design. Schemes of 20 or more dwellings were eligible for consideration and could include shops, offices and other development, provided housing predominated. Improvement to the urban scene as well as quality of design were taken into account in the judging.

In commenting on the competition the Ministry said, "Pressure for development in rural areas means infilling and expansion of many villages and it is particularly important that new development should blend with the old and proper attention be paid to landscaping of new houses.
. . . The main emphasis in judging will be on successful reconciliation of old and new building and on sympathetic landscaping, but account will also be taken of the design of individual buildings and of the treatment of particular features such as fences, walls, gates, garages and pathways."

National Council on Architecture and Urban Design

Just before the adjournment of the 87th Congress in October of this year, Senator Harrison A. Williams Jr. of New Jersey introduced a bill which proposed the establishment of a temporary National Council on Architecture and Urban Design to "preserve and promote the pleasing appearance and the livability of community environments . . .," and ". . . conduct a comprehensive study to appraise the level of architectural and urban design attainments of the Nation and formulate goals thereto . . .."

In a speech entitled "America the Beautiful?" Senator Williams stated that the bill ". . . represents what I hope is at least one appropriate way of meeting this twofold task: One, to encourage a positive architectural and design responsibility on the part of the Federal Government with respect to those programs it enacts and administers; and two, to promote greater understanding and leadership on the part of public officials and private citizens and organizations throughout the country."

This is a very broad gauged proposal with far-reaching implications and is most consistent with the aims and objectives of the American Planning and Civic Association.

This proposal will be re-introduced when the 88th Congress convenes in January 1963.

National Capital Notes

The National Capital Transportation Agency published, on November 1st, its "Recommendations for Transportation in the National Capital Region, Finance and Organization." The document is a Report to the President for transmittal to Congress. The following statements are quoted from a summary of the report, "Congress established the Agency in 1960 to prepare a transportation program for the National Capital region and, subject to Congressional approval, to construct and provide for the operation of mass transit facilities."

"The region's transportation problem springs from the fact that the population is rapidly expanding and that most people working downtown have no satisfactory alternative to using their automobiles. The result is serious congestion of streets and highways and this will become steadily worse unless a decided improvement is made in transportation facilities."

———————◇———————

A $29 million plan for restoration and construction on both sides of Lafayette Square was recently given a red-carpet unveiling at the General Services Administration.

Work on the vast project will begin next year, and architect John Carl Warnecke of San Francisco said much of the cost can be paid out of the 1962–63 budget. Construction will be finished in 1965, he said.

All existing buildings will be retained—and revolated—except the Belasco Theater and some office buildings on Jackson Place.

A new Executive Office Building and new Court of Claims and Court of Customs Appeals Building will occupy the centers of both blocks, rising above the facades of the old buildings.

Belasco Theater will be replaced by a four-story building in keeping with other old architecture.

Dolly Madison and Tayloe Houses on Madison Place will be restored, and so will the old Court of Claims Building on Pennsylvania Ave. at 17th St.

The old Carnegie Building, at Pennsylvania Ave. and Jackson Place, will be joined to the Blair and Lee Houses. More space is needed for entertainment of foreign VIP's, Mr. Warnecke said.

Tree-shaded courts will flank the new large buildings, and entrance to each will be inconspicuous, through the restored frontages on Jackson Place and Madison Place.

Mr. Warnecke also proposed that Lafayette Square itself should be greatly improved, perhaps to include fountains.

A letter from President Kennedy expressed satisfaction with the plan. The Square had been a subject of controversy for many years—the Government once had planned to tear down the old buildings and replace them with Federal office buildings.

———————◇———————

Report on Downtown Progress

Six major new buildings are now under construction. A comparison between construction activity in Downtown and west of 15th Street, N. W., was compiled for the November Report. This will provide both an indication of development potential and a means for gauging the progress of revitalization.

Savings and Loan Associations: Construction and renovation activities by savings and loan associations provide some measure of the increased interest in development in Downtown. During the past year and a half, four such associations have undertaken new buildings or major remodeling efforts. Enterprise Federal Savings and Loan Association occupied its enlarged and remodeled office building in October 1962; Republic Savings and Loan Association opened a new office in a completely remodeled building in April 1962; Columbia Federal Savings and Loan Association is now adding five floors to its main office building constructed in 1948; and Prudential Building Association has started construction of a new building on G Street.

21

Strictly Personal

William E. Finley, Director, National Capital Planning Commission, has resigned to become Vice-President of the James W. Rouse Co. and Community Research and Development, Inc. of Baltimore, Washington and Pittsburgh.

———————◆———————

The Washington Planning and Housing Association recently announced the election of Reuben Clark as its new president. Mr. Clark, a partner in the law firm of Wilmer, Cutler and Pickering, succeeds **Charles A.** Horsky who resigned his WPHA post last July when he became President Kennedy's Advisor on National Capital Affairs.

———————◆———————

Mrs. Thomas Terry Stevens of Miami, Florida, a member of the Board of Trustees of the American Planning and Civic Association, was honored recently by the South Florida Chapter of the Planning and Zoning Association of Florida. A former Chairman of both planning and zoning committees, she was instrumental in the planning of Coral Gables.

———————◆———————

Bill **M.** Collins has recently resigned his position as Executive Secretary-Director of the Texas State Parks Board.

Tracy **B.** Augur, assistant commissioner for urban planning in the Urban Renewal Administration since 1957, has been appointed special assistant to URA Commissioner William L. Slayton.

In his new post, Mr. Augur will serve as URA adviser on urban planning and community development. He also will handle special assignments on State and local planning in areas adjoining major Federal installations and will provide liaison between the agency and many groups concerned with planning and urban development.

———————◆———————

Samuel A. King, a veteran National Park Service employee and native of Ashland, Wisconsin, took over the newly established position of project manager for recreation planning, development and administration at the Whiskeytown Reservoir Area, near Redding, California, on September 17. With the signing of a Memorandum of Agreement with the Bureau of Reclamation and the National Park Service, the Service assumes responsibility on an interim basis. The 7,000-acre area, about evenly divided between land and water, is eight miles west of Redding and is a unit of the Trinity River Division of the Central Valley Project being developed by the Bureau of Reclamation. The Bureau of Outdoor Recreation has under study the entire Whiskeytown complex.

NCSP Elects National Officers

The Board of Directors of the National Conference on State Parks elected EDWARD J. MEEMAN, Chairman of the Board, at its 42nd Annual Meeting at Illinois Beach State Park, October 2, 1962.

Mr. Meeman is editor emeritus of *The Memphis Press-Scimitar*, a Scripps-Howard newspaper, of which he was editor for 31 years.

He was born in Evansville, Indiana. Immediately after graduation from the Evansville High School, he took a job as cub reporter on the *Evansville Press*, which had been started by the Scripps organization. He intended to earn money so that he could go to college, but he became so fascinated with newspaper work that he never did go to college. He helped to establish the young newspaper and become its managing editor.

In an expansion period of The Scripps-Howard newspapers he was invited to go to Knoxville, Tenn., to start a newspaper in 1921. The venture was successful, and *The News* bought its competitor, *The Sentinel*, from Gen. L. D. Tyson in 1926, and Mr. Meeman became the editor of the combined newspaper, *The News-Sentinel*, in 1926.

As editor of *The News* and *News-Sentinel*, Mr. Meeman was one of the leaders in the movement which established the Great Smoky Mountains National Park. His paper's crusade for better government led to the establishment of council-manager government in Knoxville and that nonpolitical government was an outstanding success. Mr. Meeman battled the effort of the power trust to get possession of the dam sites in the Tennessee River and as a result these sites were in public possession and ready for later development by the TVA.

Mr. Meeman moved to the larger field of Memphis in 1931 as editor of *The Memphis Press-Scimitar*. Here he continued his work for conservation. In 1933 he saw the large state forests of Europe near the cities and asked, "If Europe can have these natural parks close to their cities, why cannot my country?" He initiated and led to successful conclusion a project which created Shelby Forest State Park, a natural forest area of 12,500 acres only eight miles from the city limits of Memphis. He helped to organize the Friends of the Land and the Wolf River Watershed Association. His paper for years conducted the Save-enrich Our Soil Contest which encouraged and rewarded the efforts of farmers in conservation thruout the Mid-South area.

He was a member of the United States delegation to the Atlantic Congress in London in 1959.

He lives on a farm next to Shelby Forest where he raises cotton, cattle and timber and practices soil conservation.

His writings appear not only in *The Press-Scimitar* but in other Scripps-Howard newspapers and in magazines.

Mr. Meeman is also a Vice-President of the American Planning and Civic Association.

23

The Conference elected the following officers:

President—EARL P. HANSON of California

Vice-President—JACK D. STRAIN of Nebraska

Vice-President—POLK HEBERT of Louisiana

President HANSON is a career employee of the California Division of Beaches and Parks, being its Deputy Chief. He was born in Oakland, California, attended the local schools and received his B. S. degree in Forestry from the University of California in 1936.

Mr. Hanson held various technical and administrative positions in the parks, recreation and conservation fields in California before attaining his present position.

He is a member of the Society of American Foresters, California Alumni Foresters Advisory Committee and Citizens Advisory Committee of Sacramento County.

He is married and has three children.

————◆————

Vice-President STRAIN is Chief, Division of State Parks of Nebraska. He was born in Nebraska, attended public schools and received his A.B. degree in Education with the science major.

Mr. Strain served five years in World War II including overseas duty in the Southwest Pacific area.

He was employed by the state of Nebraska Game, Forestation and Parks Commission in 1947 and has administered State Parks since 1951. Elected to the Board of Directors of the National Conference on State Parks in 1958, Mr. Strain has also served as President of the Midwest State Park Association.

He is married and has four children and resides in Lincoln, Nebraska.

————◆————

Vice-President POLK HEBERT attended the public schools in Jeanerette, Louisiana and later attended University of Southwestern Louisiana; University of Texas where he studied Business Administration; Tulane University, Safety Engineering and Louisiana State University, Real Estate Appraisal.

Mr. Hebert has engaged in a wide range of civic activities including leadership positions in the Boy Scouts, Rotary Club, Chamber of Commerce and others. He is a former member of the Board of Directors of the National Conference on State Parks.

He is currently engaged in private business, owning and directing Industry Service Inc. of Hammond, Louisiana and spends considerable time in real estate appraisal.

Canberra, Standards for Civic Design

By J. W. OVERALL, National Capital Development Commissioner, Canberra, A. C. T., Australia

Canberra, Capital of Australia with a population approaching 60,000 and now Australia's largest inland city, has, in the post war years, grown in status as well as in size.

Canberra has won acceptance for its role as National Capital and is fulfilling the function envisaged by the statesmen who first conceived the city—it has become a true "working symbol of federalism."

Most of the Australian Federal Government departments now have their headquarters in Canberra and the transfer of the remaining departments from Melbourne is proceeding at a steady, planned rate. As well as being the seat of government, Canberra is diplomatic headquarters for the nation and is becoming increasingly important as a centre of academic and cultural life.

At the same time the city is growing in its own right as a commercial and regional centre.

As an outstanding example of a fully planned city, Canberra is also taking on a role as a planning pilot for the rest of Australia. The standards of civic design and planning being set in Canberra will increasingly become the yardstick by which the standards in other Australian cities, and even in overseas cities, will be judged.

The building of a new city dedicated to the purpose of government has many examples in modern history. Washington, D. C., New Delhi in India and, more recently, Brasilia, in Brazil, are three examples.

When, in 1901, the six Australian States agreed on Federation, the leaders of Federation decided that "the seat of government of the Commonwealth shall be determined by the Parliament and shall be within Federal Territory."

The Australian Commonwealth Parliament in 1908 selected the Yass-Canberra district as the site for the future capital and on January 1, 1911, an area of some 910 square miles was transferred to the control of the Commonwealth, which set about securing a plan for the new city.

The original Canberra plan was designed by Walter Burley Griffin, a landscape architect of Chicago. This plan, with some subsequent modifications, has been followed in laying out and building the city.

A key feature of the Griffin plan was the proposal to construct a series of ornamental lakes across the centre of the city. By this means two problems were to be solved: the flood plain of the Molonglo River would be virtually eliminated and the city's two sections, north and south of the river, would be integrated by the beauty of a striking water feature.

Progress in the actual building of the city, however, was slow in the initial stages.

World War I, the world wide economic depression of the 1930's and the Second World War interrupted the city's growth.

Since the World War II, the tempo of Canberra's development

25

has greatly increased. The rate of population increase in Canberra is now over 10 per cent yearly compared with the overall Australian figure of about 2½ per cent. In 1911 the population of the whole of the Australian Capital Territory was 1,900. In 1921, when building was resumed after the First World War, there were 1,200 residents in the Canberra City District. The population had risen to 13,500 by 1935 and reached 15,000 in 1947. In 1961 the 55,000 mark was passed and, it is estimated, the population will be 100,000 by 1969 and 250,000 by the end of the century.

Rate of Growth Poses Problems

This rate of growth poses many problems. The body charged with responsibility for them is the National Capital Development Commission, a planning and construction authority staffed by architects, engineers and town planners and headed by the Commissioner.

The Commission was established by act of Parliament and began work in 1958 to develop Canberra both as the National Capital and as a city in which increasing numbers of people will live.

The greater part of the building boom that is rapidly changing the face of Canberra is, of course, concerned with housing and other community projects. At the same time, a start is being made on features which will help considerably to confirm Canberra's identity as the National Capital.

The Commission spends at least 95 per cent of its annual allocations on normal municipal requirements.

In a city in which the population is increasing at the rate of 10 per cent each year, the provision of housing and engineering services necessarily accounts for a very large part of the total expenditure.

At the same time, work has been proceeding on projects of a significant national nature. These projects, while accounting for only 5 per cent of the Commission's expenditure, are of vital importance to Canberra's role as National Capital.

One of these projects of National significance is the Canberra Lake. The Lake, always an integral part of Canberra's planning, will be a unifying agent, drawing the two halves of the city together. In the long term it will make possible the creation in Canberra of a central area panorama which will rank with the most beautiful in the world.

The lake scheme provides for a dam on the Molonglo River at Woden, near Government House, four miles downstream from Canberra City. The dam, now under construction, will create, by the end of 1963, a lake of some 1,740 acres in surface area and of an average depth of 15 feet. The lake will be 6.8 miles long, will have a width of from 1,000 to 4,000 feet and a shoreline of some 26 miles.

The engineering aspects of the lake are being handled by the National Capital Development Commission with consultative assistance of G. Maunsell and Partners, William Holford and Partners and the Australian Commonwealth Department of Works.

Contractors for the lake dam, a 65 feet high, 800 feet long structure, are Citra (Australia).

Two major bridges are to be built across the lake within the present planning future. Construction of one of these, Kings Avenue Bridge, neared completion early in 1962. This bridge is a dual carriageway structure carrying four lanes of traffic. The first of the carriageways is already in use. Designed on "slim" lines, Kings Avenue Bridge, in elevation, resembles a "taut bow" stretched 950 feet across the lake.

The second bridge, Commonwealth Avenue Bridge, will be a heavier construction, 1020 feet between embankments. It will also have dual carriageways but will carry six lanes of traffic.

Of Engineering Interest

This bridge is to be completed by 1963, and is of particular engineering interest.

Unlike Kings Avenue Bridge, in which supported pre-stressed beams are used as basic units for the deck, the Commonwealth Avenue Bridge deck will consist of about 200 post-tensioned small deck units supported on only four piers between the two abutments.

The 200 units will each be some 37 feet long, 10 feet high and 10 feet wide and weigh 40 tons. They will be lifted on to a timber falsework and adjusted to their final position with gaps of three inches between each.

When all the units are in place, mortar will be inserted in the gaps and high tensile steel strands will be placed through the units from one end of the bridge to the other. No

conventional steel reinforcement will pass through the mortar points. Very high tensions will then be applied to the steel strands and the 200 box units will come together like beads on a string.

In the design of these two bridges consultants to the Commission have been Maunsell and Partners and William Holford and Partners.

Supervision is being carried out by the Commonwealth Department of Works. Contractors for the bridges are Hornibrook McKenzie Clark and Hornibrook-Kaiser.

As these projects go on, planning and design work for the remainder of the Central Areas is continuing. Recently the Commission announced the appointment of Mr. Walter Bunning and Mr. T. E. O'Mahony, both of Sydney, as consultant architects for the new National Library. The library, to stand on the lakeshore adjacent to the site for the future permanent Houses of Parliament, will be one of the most important buildings in Canberra.

In urban planning, the Commission is finalizing detail plans for the development of Woden Valley as the city's next major residential area.

By 1963, the present Canberra City District will be built out. Residential development emphasis will then shift to the Woden area—southwest of the present Canberra city District—where 11 new neighbourhoods are planned with ultimate total population of some 60,000.

The new southern neighbourhoods will have their own schools, shops and recreation facilities. Many of the people living there will work in (*Continued on page 28*)

Pattern for Park Planning and Acquisition

Anticipating the need for a park system many times larger than the one existing at the time the citizens of Aurora, Colorado, a residential community which abuts the eastern city limits of Denver, requested the City Planning Department to prepare a master plan for parks as one section of the advance planning program then underway.

The final report showed there were only 85 acres of land devoted to park and recreational use. Added to the 60 acres of similar facilities provided by the school district it was determined that 200 additional acres for the present population and an additional 600 acres to provide the total of 1000 acres needed for the projected 1980 requirement should be secured.

The master plan showed that the cost of this land would have been substantially less had it been acquired before the steep upward curve of growth and cost occurred. However, the report also indicated that the price of this land would probably continue to rise in the future and that if the city did not acquire it, building might soon begin and the land would be lost or become prohibitive in cost.

After a few months of meeting with a citizens' committee and the city council, a $400,000 bond issue was proposed. In the one month remaining before election the story was carried to the voters by means of 5,000 brochures distributed through the schools and civic organizations. Talks illustrated with colored slides before various civic groups also spread the word.

At the election, the voters approved the project by a vote of four to three. This vote was especially favorable since a $1.9 million school bond issue had recently been passed and a $2.0 million hospital bond issue appeared on the same ballot. Planning does pay dividends, as do promotions.

———◆———

CANBERRA, STANDARDS FOR CIVIC DESIGN

(Continued from page 27)

Canberra City but provision will be made for sites for Government institutions, private offices and service industries to provide a proportion of employment close to the residential areas. Road access to Canberra—from three to six miles away —will be provided by three arterial links. Within the Woden Valley an arterial road will provide access to all the new neighbourhoods and to their shopping and employment centres. The rest of the road system will consist of collector, distributor and residential access roads.

Planning such as that being finalized for the Central Areas of Canberra and that for the new urban areas is catching the imagination of Australians in all States. Where once, not so very many years ago, Australians tolerated Canberra as a "bush capital" and did not expect much from it, they are now showing positive enthusiasm for the virile development of their planned capital.

New Towns

A Proposal for the Appalachian Region

Earlier this year a proposal entitled "New Towns for the Appalachian Region" was published. Sub-titled "A Case Study Located in Eastern Kentucky" the proposal was prepared under the auspices of the Kentucky Research Foundation by the Department of Architecture of the University of Kentucky of which Charles P. Graves is Head.

In acknowledging the proposal Governor Bert Combs of Kentucky said, "I am most interested and gratified in the ambitious and visionary—but practical—proposal to carry out the study and planning for a NEW TOWN program in the Appalachian Region . . . I want to express my support and encouragement. You may count on the cooperation of state agencies in your endeavors and I wish you full success."

John D. Whisman,* Executive Director of the Eastern Kentucky Regional Development Commission, following review of the proposal by the Commission declared "The Eastern Kentucky Commission has discussed the NEW TOWNS proposal with great interest.

"The Commission, as you know, is convinced that only a most comprehensive special regional development program can deal with Appalachian and Eastern Kentucky problems. As key elements in such a regional effort, there will have to be great projects, comprehensive in

themselves, dealing in a special way with special problems. Among the list of categorical problems of the region—transportation, water resource development, education, or others—none occupies a higher priority than the overall problems of community development.

"The Commission sees, with you, the opportunity to deal with the essential nature of this problem for all communities of the region, as well as the very real possibilities for a successful and highly significant NEW TOWN project itself, in carrying out your proposal. Your work in this regard is most encouraging to us at a time when we are, for the first time, seeing realistic action by state and federal government and others, shaping up, to bring a complete Appalachian Regional Development Program into being.

"The Commission will endorse and encourage your work with sincere appreciation and with high hopes for the contribution you will be making in the face of a crucial need for improvement by the people of our region."

In a stimulating PREFACE Grady Clay* had this to say:

"Stretching almost 1,000 miles across the face of America lies a national problem; an axis of poverty from Alabama into New York State. Here is a problem from which water and people flow with equal speed, leaving behind poverty, erosion and semipermanent depression.
"This is Appalachia, one great region which has remained outside the mainstream of American economic growth. It spreads through twelve states, but it in-

*Both Mr. Whisman and Mr. Clay are members of the Board of the American Planning and Civic Association.

State, County and City Park Relationships
Speaking for The City

By DANIEL L. FLAHERTY, General Superintendent, Chicago Park District.
(Delivered by Mr. Shultz in Mr. Flaherty's absence)

At the outset of my remarks permit me to congratulate your Program Committee on undertaking this problem of relationships between the State, County and City park systems. Forging relationships of this kind in effective terms is long overdue. We have too long remained in our own individual corners, maybe suspicious of one another, and certainly at the cost of efficient coordination and good planning.

It is essential in these times that our respective agencies work together, due to the tremendous growth of population and the sporadic urban development, not only in our older existing metropolitan areas but also in the new coming metropolitan areas. We are witnessing a time when farm population is on the decline and urbanization is increasing at a rate never before reached in this country. Unfortunately, even at a time when our skills and knowledge of planning are actually at an all time high, land speculation and the competition for land has never been greater.

In this particular situation which concerns most of us, more especially in city parks to a greater extent than those of you in the now urban parks, we are encountering tremendous demands for our services. These demands are being created by an increasing leisure for people with more money to pay for their play. The demand upon city and county parks are being conditioned by more enlightened appetites in terms of parks and recreation services. People are no longer satisfied with mere picnic space; they now seek a beach or a pool with all the sanitary appurtenances that our modern science can develop. They not only seek a place to walk through the woods, but they seek a golf course with tees, fairways and greens kept up to almost professional standards. For those of us in the city, our people not only expect playgrounds but they desire fieldhouses with gymnasia, craft shops, theaters for dramatics and enough services to take care of people from the cradle to the grave.

These tremendous growing demands are naturally not accompanied with tremendous increases in our revenues. I think I should leave our own Illinois State Park people to discuss that question with you. And, speaking as a city park superintendent, I want to point out that our tax levy has been held level for the past two years, although we have been fortunate that a number of our bond issues have been approved. We have been a little more fortunate than other cities in that our bond program has produced a very significant increase in park facilities.

However, our bond program has gone on without coordination with the county and state park systems. There is no doubt in my mind we are now at the point in our growth, especially when we consider land, that we must look to the county and the state park systems to acquire acreage for our growing population.

It is certainly timely that we begin to define our respective roles and secure the funds necessary to fulfill the land requirement that would be spelled out with the new goals that we jointly develop.

There are several trends that are certainly helping us, the work begun by Resources For The Future and The Outdoor Recreation Resources Review Commission. These various studies that have been completed, dealing with natural features and the recreational opportunities they afford will go far to accommodate our highly mobile urban population. The unified action of the various federal agencies cooperating with state government are bringing about fruitful results. It is my wish that these studies will stimulate more detailed planning by state park departments to help not only the counties and county park systems, but also to bring within the reach of our cities more adequate facilities, particularly for weekend patrons.

Another phase of planning initiated in Chicago that would be of interest to this audience is our Northeastern Illinois Metropolitan Area Planning Commission, under the leadership of Paul Oppermann. This agency has attempted to bring all metropolitan area planning into a single focus and has done a very admirable job in getting started. This agency, too, has recently completed a study for The Outdoor Recreation Resource Commission which I am sure will be helpful to all of us in the Chicago Metropolitan area.

The difference between this study and some of those that we have reviewed in other states is that it has been aimed at the goal of preservation of open space. I am sure that Paul here will be happy to relate for you the study and its implications. I want to congratulate him and his Commission for its adoption of a policy on open space that I hope will serve to guide all of us in Chicago on the use of our land and that will give us assurance of ample recreation space, both for state parks, county parks and city parks. Incidentally, there are other cities in the metropolitan area that will need these planning guides over and beyond the City of Chicago.

Now I would like to go on to the definition of roles that Paul has asked me to give you from the city park department's viewpoint. Naturally, our park planning, for those of us in the city, must be premised on the natural values that surround our cities. Climate, native forests, lakes, rivers, topographic features are characteristics that will condition planning. The next responsibility that we have to meet is that of serving millions of people living in a relatively dense urban setting. This kind of living means that their children will have to have places to play, that mothers and housewives will have places to go and things to do. And that the teen-agers in their after-school hours, will

EARL P. HANSON

PRESIDENT

NATIONAL CONFERENCE ON STATE PARKS

JACK D. STRAIN
VICE-PRESIDENT

POLK HEBERT
VICE-PRESIDENT

NATIONAL CONFERENCE ON STATE PARKS

33

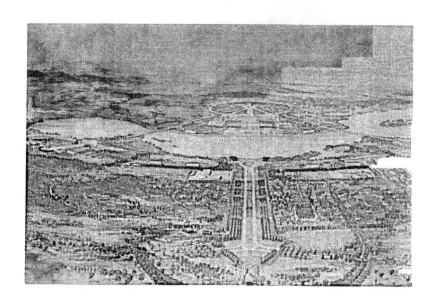

CANBERRA TOMORROW

ABOVE—HOW THE LAKES SCHEME WILL TRANSFORM
THE CITY OF CANBERRA

BELOW—HOW THE REDESIGNED PARLIAMENT HOUSE
AREA WILL EVENTUALLY LOOK

Taming Urban Giant

Metropolitan planning needs to be a working partnership of various levels of government.

By C. DAVID LOEKS

EDITOR'S NOTE:—Mr. Loeks is director of the Twin Cities Metropolitan Planning Commission at St. Paul, Minnesota. This article is Mr. Loeks' address before the National Conference on Government of the National Municipal League, December 1, 1961, Miami Beach, Florida. This is reprinted from the *National Civic Review* by permission of the Editor.

The hard question facing metropolitan areas in this country is this: Can the big issues confronting urban America, which are more and more coming to be recognized as being of multigovernmental concern, be solved in a manner which will satisfy the diverse interests which operate in the metropolitan area? If not, where and how is a compromise to be struck? Metropolitan planning as it is practiced today has as its core principle voluntary intergovernmental cooperation.

Traditionally, planning in American government is by definition advisory. It has been identified as having all the power of a suggestion. Planning at the metropolitan level, which has no single policy-making body to which it can relate, is a particularly chancy game if one is to adopt as a criterion for success the fact that there must be a demonstrable relationship between effort and results. As a consequence, metropolitan planners in this country are laboring under formidable odds. They have been given a dictaphone, a calculator and a fist full of prisma color pencils and have been directed to sally forth and slay the giant of urban disorder. Unlike the original David—who had something quite tangible with which he rendered his Goliath *hors de combat*—the contemporary metropolitan planner must be content to throw ideas, suggestions and proposals. All of the foregoing, of course, poses a paradox: If "a soft answer turneth away wrath" how come everybody is mad at the planners?

Perhaps the explanation of the paradox can be found in the observation that those who criticize planning are departing from the wrong premise. This isn't a case where planning has been tried and found wanting but wanted and found trying—very trying. This observation is not intended as a reflection on planning. Rather, it is a commentary on the intellectual orientation of those who would have the American public believe that planning calls the tune at the urban development dance and that therefore it must be blamed for all the ills that beset our environment. Following that logic, we should blame the doctors because people get sick!

All this should not be interpreted as being deprecatory; it is intended rather to give perspective to how we look at metropolitan planning. I believe that such planning is potentially one of the most significant tools developed for achieving urban progress. My involvement in metropolitan planning has led me to a deep conviction concerning the need to look at this tool realistically, to recognize it for what it is, essentially a new device the full potentialities of which are yet to be realized.

It is entirely appropriate that we should ask: What is metropolitan planning as it is being practiced today? What are its strengths and its limitations? What should we legitimately ask of it in the way of results? How can the probability of its achieving its objectives be maximized?

Before dealing with these questions in specific terms, I would like to present a few ideas which will help in establishment of a needed conceptual framework within which we can think about metropolitan planning in relationship to the numerous other activities that also deal with urban problem solving.

"POLYKINETICS"—GREASE FOR THE SQUEAKING WHEELS OF METROPOLITAN PROGRESS

It is no secret that efforts to reorganize local government along metropolitan lines have not been greeted with unqualified enthusiasm. This may be due in part to the fact that they tend to put the governmental cart before the environmental horse. People are being asked to trade their old familiar government machinery for a shiny new model with no clear idea as to what it is to accomplish in terms of an improved living environment.

Bloody Mary had enough native intelligence to know that "you can't make a dream come true without first having a dream." The American urban dweller also has enough native intelligence to know that the key function of local government is to provide the framework whereby a good environment for living can be produced. Perhaps they are beginning to suspect that it would be a good idea first to develop a consensus concerning what is wanted in the way of environment (the dream) before designing the governmental machine to make it come true.

The effectiveness of current efforts to achieve metropolitan progress seems to be blunted by the fact that the urban community is made up of well meaning but diversified groups, each of which is convinced that its particular approach will provide the answer. No doubt in most cases each of these approaches has significant advantages. Unfortunately, when pursued outside the context of other approaches, it often exhibits a fatal weakness. Some examples:

1. *The Conservative Approach,* which has been somewhat whimsically identified as the "diligent pursuit of the status quo," argues that change for the sake of change makes no particular sense, that the desirable qualities of the existing situation should be identified and protected and relinquished only in the face of irrefutable proof that new courses of action would indeed produce better results. Pursued to its extreme it seems to be based on the assumption—which is open to question—that virtually none of the problems of the metropolitan area are so tough that they can't be solved with existing governmental tools if they are sharpened up and applied with skill.

At its best the conservative approach re-enforces the validity of the principle of intergovernmental co-operation which, without a doubt, must serve as the key element in all governmental attempts to deal with urban problems. At its worst, this approach provides a refuge for the congenital "aginers" and plays out as an essentially defensive response to proposals for change. Those who pursue this position often fail to come up with counter-proposals or more acceptable alternatives to the proposals which are opposed. The result is a sort of dynamic equilibrium in which the big issues go begging and nothing is accomplished.

2. *The Governmental Reorganization Approach.* Those who pursue this attack on urban problems have come to the conclusion that the challenges posed by the growth situation confronting American cities cannot be solved completely within the framework of existing governmental institutions. Responses coming under this category are premised on the valid proposition that you can't do much about the problems of urban development unless you have adequate governmental machinery to carry out the programs needed for their solutions.

However, as mentioned above, if governmental reorganization precedes comprehensive urban planning, it can lead to the same kind of problem as that confronting the man who had a suit of clothes made without first having his measurements taken. Efforts at the metropolitan scale coming under this heading range all the way from "creeping ad hocism" ("special au-

thorities will do the job") to "metro uber alles" ("everything must be under one governmental roof").

3. *The Metropolitan Planning Approach* argues that in the long run progress can best come from a consensus concerning the environmental results that are desired, that is, a plan. This provides the framework within which the multitudinous urban development activities can be related to one another in a coordinated fashion.

Metropolitan planning, which by and large is still in its infancy, is at present still raising more questions than answers. Paramount among these is the question of implementation. The fate that befell many early attempts at city plans must be avoided if metropolitan planning is to succeed. Will we have a situation where many well thought out metropolitan plans will be prepared and then "each in its crypt forever laid," primarily because the question of creating really effective machinery for carrying them out has not been thought through?

These three approaches are taken as examples. There are, of course, several others. The point is that each pursued in an isolated context may have inherent virtues but also often has fatal defects. The plain truth is that there is no single approach which, taken in itself, will do the business. This suggests that there is no single road to urban progress, that there are many routes and that columns should be dispatched along each. The trick is to make sure that the multiple actions that such an operation entails will be mounted in such a way that no single column gets too far out ahead or out of synchronization with the others.

In summary, this poses a challenge to our nation's civic and political leadership to encourage a variety of legitimate approaches, pursued in a complementary and harmonious rather than a conflicting and competing relationship. This idea isn't particularly new. As a matter of fact, the principle may have been an integral element of urban progress for centuries. The Greeks probably applied it when they built the Acropolis. If they did, chances are, being Greek, they had a word for it. I'll bet a drachma or two that they'd have called it something like *polykinetics*.

METROPOLITAN PLANNING—PROMISE, PERFORMANCE, POTENTIALITIES

Recently the American Institute of Planners appointed a Metropolitan Conference Committee, of which I was a member, which conducted a three-day workshop attended by twenty professional planners, fourteen of whom were directors or other staff members of metropolitan planning agencies, who worked out a mutually acceptable statement on the role of metropolitan planning. Because it is a consensus it by no means expresses the full view of the individual participants. For that reason, it is important as a working statement on a relatively new activity which lacks and merits authoritative definition. The following are some direct quotes of some of the more important ideas which emerged from this conference.

Definition and Role

Metropolitan planning is comprehensive planning applied to areas containing a large urban concentration where dominant economic, social and physical factors may overarch local and even state boundaries. The function of metropolitan planning is to contribute to the formulation and implementation of optimal public policy for the metropolitan area.

Metropolitan planning functions at a new level in the governmental hierarchy, one which, however, includes fundamental roles for governments at all levels. On the one hand, metropolitan planning serves as a framework and a vehicle for the coordination of the planning of municipal, county, and other local units of government and for relating these plans to the desirable development of the metropolitan area as a whole. On the other hand, planning at the metropolitan level seeks to integrate local and metropolitan plans with the plans of the state and of the nation.

Long Term Policies for Metropolitan Planning Agencies

The metropolitan planning agency should seek the development of a unified plan for land use, density and design, provision and correlation of public facilities, services and utilities, and the preservation of open space and natural resources. It should strive to coordinate local planning, both public and private, with planning at the metropolitan level; similarly, the metropolitan plan should be coordinated with state and national plans—particularly those affecting transportation, public facilities and natural resource programs and functions that are metropolitan in scope. To this purpose, the agency should review the content, conformity or compatibility of all proposals affecting the metropolitan area plan.

Metropolitan Planning Functions

The range of metropolitan planning functions will differ from area to area. There are certain basic functions, however, which the metropolitan planning agency should perform in any metropolitan area. These are: Research, planning cooperation and coordination, and advice and assistance.

1. *Research.* The planning agency must undertake or sponsor the research effort required to provide and assemble the essential data on land use, population, economic base and other foundation elements necessary to the preparation of metropolitan area plans.

2. *Planning.* The metropolitan planning agency should seek establishment and acceptance of goals, both long-range and immediate, for the metropolitan area's physical development (with due regard to economic and social factors). These goals should be the basis for the formulation of the comprehensive metropolitan area plan —and that plan, in turn, should serve as a framework within which may be coordinated the comprehensive plans of municipalities, counties and other units of government in the metropolitan area.

Comprehensive metropolitan plan should be expressed in fiscal and budgetary terms and should be realistically related to the fiscal and programming capacities of the municipal, county and other governmental units affected. Incorporated in such metropolitan plans should be (a) an outline of necessary steps to be taken in implementing them and (b) provisions for their periodic review and updating.

3. *Cooperation and Coordination.* The metropolitan planning process involves coordination of objectives, proposals and plans at various levels among governmental units affected and depends upon the cooperation of those units and of informed and interested civic organizations and individuals.

The type of coordination sought by the metropolitan planning agency—whether formal or informal, voluntary or mandatory—will depend upon legislative conditions affecting the particular metropolitan area and upon the success of local leadership, governmental and civic, in diagnosing metropolitan problems and prescribing metropolitan and local remedial actions.

4. *Advice and Assistance.* The metropolitan agency should provide other planning agencies and local governmental and nongovernmental organizations with advice and assistance, including technical information, research data, handbooks, manuals, organizational help and information on plans, projects, proposals and policies of other governmental agencies.

The agency should establish standards for planning regulations and should encourage their adoption and proper administration by local units of government.

Organization for Metropolitan Planning

Where there are two or more independent governmental units serving the same metropolitan area, a coordinating planning agency is desirable and necessary. This coordinating body, which should be identified as the metropolitan planning agency, should take the initiative in seeking to establish intergovernmental relationships and responsibilities in order to coordinate physical planning at the metropolitan level.

The principal instrument of metropolitan planning should be a professionally staffed, official planning commission. It is recognized, however, that a voluntary association or an independent privately sponsored metropolitan agency may well serve as a forerunner to an official planning agency.

It is further recognized that there is an urgent need to enlist continuing support and participating of the elected and appointed public officials, civic and social agencies, private individuals and groups, and to encourage and develop among these agencies and individuals a metropolitan-wide point of view as regards the planning process.

One method of achieving metropolitan-wide participation is the establishment of technical advisory committees composed of qualified authorities, both governmental and nongovernmental, to provide the planning agency with information and advice necessary in the development of plans, projects and suggested policies. These technical committees will not only help in formulating plans but will aid in the process of implementation. The informal crossing of governmental echelons is justified by the scope of the metropolitan plan and the coordinative role of the metropolitan planning agency.

Legislative Objectives for Metropolitan Planning

Metropolitan planning has need of legislative enactments, both for established planning programs and for those that are being established. The following legislative objectives are recommended:

1. The states should adopt broad enabling statutes outlining general objectives and functions for metropolitan planning, thereby strengthening the ability of the metropolitan areas to deal with their own urban development problems.

2. Legislation should be enacted granting to metropolitan planning agencies broad coordinative powers dealing with mandatory referral of local development plans, the review of capital improvement programming and the establishment of standards.

3. The geographic jurisdiction of a metropolitan planning agency should be adjustable according to definite criteria of growth that are established by state statute or, in the absence of

statutory definition, are developed by the agency itself as a guiding policy.

4. The metropolitan planning function should be supported by the provision of an adequate and stable budget programmed through a routine governmental source or sources.

5. State action should be taken establishing a greater degree of coordination in the administration of state programs affecting metropolitan areas.

6. Federal action should be taken establishing a greater degree of coordination in the administration of federal programs affecting metropolitan areas.

There are a number of things about this statement that bear elaboration and comment. The significant note it strikes is that, properly developed, metropolitan planning operates in working partnership with planning at all levels. Essentially, it supplements local planning, it does not supplant it, and to work effectively all members of the partnership must do their share. Because the objectives of metropolitan planning are basically carried out by the multilateral activities of constituent units of government and other interests, it follows that sound and healthy local government which must concern itself with the specifics of the physical environment that people can actually see and react to, is a fundamental condition of successful metropolitan planning. Conversely, to the measure that metropolitan planning offers a means of solving problems which would overwhelm local governments if they were left to their individual devices, it in turn may be regarded as an essential condition for strong and effective local government.

It is also clear from this statement that a cross section of the metropolitan planners in this country do not, as a matter of consensus, look at metropolitan planning as the "thin edge of the wedge" for metropolitan government. Although as individuals they have varying attitudes about this question, metropolitan planning to be effective must consider the existing structures of government as its clients. The basic mission is not to reform government but to service it, recognizing that by its very nature government is in a continual process of evolution and change. To the measure that metropolitan planning can provide a clearer image of the pros and cons of major alternatives available in the development of the physical environment, it will certainly contribute to the enlightenment whereby the continuing process of governmental change is played out.

In conclusion, it should be emphasized that metropolitan planning should stress the identification of the legitimate alternatives available in the development of the environment and not be content merely to predict the inevitable and then attempt to cooperate with it. Wyndham Thomas, executive secretary of the Town & Country Planning Association of England, said, after viewing Los Angeles, "I have seen the future and it doesn't work." He may just possibly be right and the observation is probably valid in many other metropolitan areas here and abroad as well. (Although after walking from Piccadilly Circus to Trafalgar Square during the five o'clock rush I had to inform him that "I have seen the past and that doesn't work either.")

(Continued on page 56)

40

Open Space Policy
Montgomery County, Pennsylvania

EDITOR'S NOTE:—This is a Basic Policy Statement approved by the Montgomery County (Pennsylvania) Planning Commission, January 1962.

In order to preserve and enhance the suburban open country type of life desired by many of the county residents a program to acquire tracts of land to be preserved as open space will be initiated. The rate of growth of population with its accompanying growth of buildings, roads, streets, and other facilities is consuming land at a significant rate. There is a need to implement a program during the 1960's to acquire tracts of land of all sizes with some designated for immediate use as recreation facilities and others to be set aside as part of the open space reserve.

RECOGNITION OF THE NEED

The need for such a program has been recognized by all levels of government. Some of the municipalities in the county have been and presently are setting aside open space areas. The county, has in the past, acquired a number of areas preserved as parks or open country. The county government now operates a park system of four sites totaling 852 acres. The State government operates two State parks in the county, and is considering "Project 70", a $70 million bond issue which will build a third state park and will also provide funds for the county and the 62 municipalities on a matching basis for acquisition of open space.

Finally, the Federal Government has recognized the need for pre- serving open space in urbanized areas and the Congress passed the Housing Act of 1961 which authorizes matching grants of either 20 or 30% for the acquisition of open space tracts. In view of all this activity it is time for the County Government to take the initiative to establish policy and to implement a program for all of Montgomery County.

THE PROGRAM

The Montgomery County Open Space Program for the decade of the 1960's is a three part program.

1. *A New Large County Park.* The County will acquire and operate a 1500 acre multi-purpose county park providing facilities for swimming, boating, fishing, picnicking, walking, sports and games, and most importantly overnight camping for children's groups on short stays.

2. *Grants in Aid for Municipalities.* The County will provide grants in aid for municipalities to encourage and stimulate the acquisition of open space tracts predominately for neighborhood and local use. These grants may be used to supplement grants from either or both the State and Federal Government, or they may be used solely to supplement local municipal funds.

3. *Acquisition of the County Open Space Reserve.* The County will acquire and maintain larger blocks of land as open space. In most cases no specific recreation use will be

41

planned for the immediate future other than the preservation of woodland or other landscaping with walking or riding trails. These areas will constitute the county's open space reserve. Some areas may be improved for immediate use as recreation facilities but they will not normally be multi-purpose recreation facilities.

FINANCING THE PROGRAM

The county government will finance this program in two different ways.

1. *The New County Park.* The County will join with six water supply companies in the construction of a reservoir on the East Branch of the Perkiomen Creek, and a 1500 acre county park will be developed around the reservoir. The full details of this multi-purpose project are explained in a report prepared by a consulting engineering firm in conjunction with the County Planning Commission. The report will be published by March 1962. The cost of the project will be apportioned among the water companies and the county. It is anticipated the park and reservoir will be ready for use by 1972.

2. *Grants-in-Aid and the County Open Space Reserve.* The county government will appropriate $200,000 per year for 8 years from 1962–1969 for these two programs. For the first year it is proposed to provide the funds from a bond issue but in subsequent years it is hoped that the fund can be provided for from general revenue.

During the first year it is proposed to allocate $60,000 of the

$200,000 to the grant-in-aid program with a maximum of $10,000 to any one municipality per year; and that sum to be 20% or less of the total cost of the proposed project. All municipal projects will be submitted to the County Planning Commission for review and approval prior to final action of the Board of County Commissioners.

The remaining $140,000 will be spent in acquiring larger areas of open land to be set aside in the county open space reserve. The County Planning Commission will make specific site recommendations to the Board of County Commissioners as this program develops.

ADMINISTRATION OF THE PROGRAM

The program is to be effective with the final approval of the 1962 Budget and it will be administered by the Director of the County Planning Commission.

PROGRAMS FOR OPEN SPACE PRESERVATION

Federal Grants for Open Space

Title VII of the 1961 Housing Act authorizes a program of $50,000,000 in Federal grants to states and local public bodies to assist in the acquisition of permanent open space land. A grant may be made to a state, regional, metropolitan, county municipal or other public body which is authorized to acquire open space land. The amount of a grant should not exceed:

1. 20% of the total amount paid for acquiring title to or other permanent interest in open space land; or

2. 30% of the total amount in the case of a public body securing open space responsibilities for an urban area as a whole.

State Grants for Open Space

The Pennsylvania State Planning Board has proposed a new plan entitled *Project 70*. The Planning Board has recommended a state-wide bond issue by the General State Authority of $70,000,000 for the purchase of open land. Of the $70,000,000,; $20,000,000 would be available for matching grants to local governing bodies for their Open Space and Parks Programs. This Open Space Program would have to be approved by the people through a state-wide referendum as well as by two State Legislatures.

County Grants for Open Space

In the 1962 budget, the Montgomery County Commissioners have allocated $200,000 for the preservation of open space. Grants from the County Commissioners for open space would be channeled through the Montgomery County Planning Commission. During the first year of the program $60,000 of the $200,000 would be allocated for municipal open space. A maximum of $10,000 could be granted to any one municipality per year. The remaining $140,000 would be spent in acquiring larger areas of open space as part of the County Open Space Reserve.

Municipal Implementation

Under existing enabling legisla-tion municipal governing bodies are permitted to adopt ▪zoning ordin-ances, subdivision regulations and establish such areas as historic dis-tricts. Through these measures a municipality can provide the mech-anism necessary to preserve open space, establish exclusive recreation districts, preserve the integrity of an historic area, etc. Detailed in-formation on these measures can be obtained from the offices of the County Planning Commission.

Private Open Space Implementation

It is important not to forget the other side of the coin; that is, pri-vate endeavors to preserve open space. The establishment of such a facility as a golf course, a large educational institution or some simi-lar land use is in reality a tool for the implementation of open space. Effort should be made by all levels of government to encourage this type of development.

SUMMARY

The above listing, of course, does not exhaust all possibilities for the preservation of open space. It is only a brief summary of basic con-siderations regarding the tools avail-able for promoting open space in Montgomery County. The County Planning Commission has on hand more detailed information on each of the above paragraphs and will be very happy to provide interested persons with more data or informa-tion.

The World Need for More Parks and Recreation Facilities

By J. AUSTIN SMITH

EDITOR'S NOTE:—In August 1962, the author, an industrial executive, of the Flxible Company, Loudonville, Ohio, journeyed to London to observe the Conference, later going on to Rome and Paris to see their park operations.

For many years, Mr. Smith operated as a public relations consultant, including missions for the State Department, for a division of the Canadian government and a department of the Mexican government. During the second World War he did liaison work for the Chaplain's Corps. In the early days of commercial air travel he was employed to build public confidence in this mode of transport. In the process he conceived the automatic insurance vending machine which led to the first of his several patents, some of which are related to the recreation industry.

London, 8. 6. 62: With delegates from England's Lands End to John O'Groats and from 23 overseas countries, a variety of languages were spoken at this second world conference of park officials but when simultaneously translated they expressed the same universal need for more parks and recreation facilities as also a striking similarity of administrative problems.

This need, as one speaker put it, is rooted in the want of the vast majority of men and women for a link with the land. The industrial revolution, he said, is only a century away and the ingrained habits of our forebears are still strong within us, adding that "environment does affect human behaviour and we neglect this fragment of man's search for his soul at our peril."

The uplifting sight of flowers, trees and green places to city dwellers is a refreshment of mind and body, it was pointed out, "that can create a feeling even the Abbey cannot transcend," and all this, with playing fields for youngsters, "can put a little star in motion."

Parks as a Colourful Backdrop of Life

In a moving appeal for rededication to purpose and resurgence of effort, one conference speaker quoted the Chinese proverb that "If you have two pennies, spend one for a loaf and one for a flower. The bread will give you life; the flower a reason for living."

"What an exquisite epitomy," he added, of the endeavours of park executives everywhere as they "hold the colourful backcloth against which people work out their lives. Let no one underestimate the benefits of the green leaf and gay flowers on the jangled nerves and jaundiced eye of the denizens of the brick and concrete deserts we call our cities."

A Beautiful House But No Kitchen

But the barbered lawns, manicured flower beds and colourful trees—beauty alone—however desirable, is not enough.

"To provide a city with only monuments to amenity," as another speaker said, "is akin to building a beautiful house with no kitchen. In our changing times the

44

need is for more of "the true amenities for our enjoyment by all of our senses; not merely our eyes, and for all our time, not merely in our leisure."

As to the word "leisure," it is questioned here at the conference as a contradiction that sounds like suspended animation: "A well ordered society has no leisure or unoccupied time, but will have time to use at its discretion. Our task is to constructively direct the exercise of discretion."

Failure in this task, the speaker continued, "can direct people to damaging activities with dire results for civilization and progress. And time is not on our side."

A British writer summed it up in these words: "By 1966 it is estimated there will be 800,000 more in the 15–19 year age groups than there are now. 25,481 more babies were born the last 12 months than the preceding 12 months. This suggests the upward trend continues, so we cannot waste time, and with land bringing such fantastic prices, we cannot waste space either."

The figures, of course, would vary with communities. But regardless of size or of country there was complete agreement on the urgent need for more parks, green places and woods; and for more recreation facilities and always for the same reason—a more responsible citizenry, growing from a common means.

The Universal Land Problem

While the space problem is present everywhere, it seems to be more acute in England. About the same area as New York state, which has

some 14,000,000 inhabitants, England has 51,000,000.

Greater London itself, with an 8,250,000 population in 720 square miles would seem better off, spacewise, than metropolitan New York with 7,800,000 persons crowded into 315 square miles.

But this would not suggest an uncrowded London, for New York has built vertically while London has built horizontally.

Actually, there are at least three Londons—the Lord Mayor's London (called "Old London") with one square mile, the London County London of 117 square miles and a population of 3,250,000; and finally the overall greater London of 720 square miles and 8,250,000 people.

The Lord Mayor is the boss of his London. The London County Council with 126 councilmen (39 are women) and 31 aldermen (9 are women) administer the county area under the chairmanship of a council-appointed chairman. The surrounding areas are administered by local authorities.

The parks and related activities in London County are administered by a committee composed of 15 council members. Under this administrative authority and by its cooperation with other authorities, Londoners have available for actual and reserved recreation use 45,600 acres of land—or just over five acres for each thousand persons. The programme is to raise this to seven acres for each thousand persons.

Planning and Civic Comment

A Green Belt to Break Urban Sprawl

27,600 acres of this land is in a "Green Belt" around greater London. Further expansion of the city through new building must be beyond this belt. The belt is permanently protected against the bulldozers and tree destroyers of real estate developers. Its desirability is attested by Paris's already advanced Green Belt, and also attested by green belts around some American cities, as was pointed out by one of the 120 American delegates in a group sponsored by the American Institute of Park Executives.

Outside the London Green Belt, there are 8,000 other restricted acres for all Londoners to enjoy; Epping Forest and Burnham Beeches being the two most important of these resorts.

The London County Council controls and administers 7,500 acres of parks and open spaces with every kind of recreational activity, including 1,500 performances a year by orchestras, ten per cent of which are symphonic. The cost of administering this activity is in excess of $9,000,000 a year with revenue around $1,000,000.

London County has an overall of 2.5 acres of parks, green places and playing for each 1,000 of population. The areas are decentralised and dispersed so as to "take the parks to the people." In the programme to raise the present per capita acreage, 638 additional acres are in process of development.

Apart from all this are the superb Royal Parks in the heart of London —8 of them embracing 1,700 acres.

Parks Fine Enough to be Museum Pieces

Except Hyde, the Royal Parks were once private. At least one was a King's hunting ground. Today, as one writer puts it, "What had been the delights of the lords are now the delights of the people."

A paper handed out at one of the conference meetings imaginatively but effectively describes the feelings one gets in the Royal Parks, in these words:

"There is always drama as though history was waiting in the bushes or behind trees to spring out with some outrageous and valiant story along with an exquisite sound of distant trumpets. Perhaps this is because of a great city, with 2,000 years of turbulent history. Or perhaps it is a little more than that; for indeed battle has raged across these parks, people have assembled in revolt against tyranny in them . . . Kings have walked with their people in them; in the palaces set within them a nation's destiny was framed, and Empires grew from them . . . Surely one's emotions are given a finer edge when, in Greenwich Park, one hears in imagination the guns of Wyatts rebellion against Queen Mary I thundering across Green Park and the echo of Mary's guns from Hyde Park Corner; remembers the girl princess Victoria in a Kensington Park palace woken in the early morning to Empire and 60 years of reign; sees Charles I walking across St. James Park on a frosty January morning to execution in Whitehall . . . William of Orange, his horse stumbling in a mole-hill, losing his life in Hampton Court . . . Jane Seymour's pathetic ghost walking the Queen's apartments in which she dies giving birth to Henry VIII's son, Edward . . . Catherine Howard's terrified ghost running wildly along Haunted Gallery to deny her supposed infidelities to that same inexorable Henry who had her beheaded on the chopping block . . . Hyde Park with gentility fighting duels at one end while highway robbers were taking King George II's purse at the other end . . . and Orator's Corner in Hyde Park where free speech had its early beginnings and is still practised on soap boxes as gusty winds that do no harm."

So much of the city is like that in its remindful power to set off the imagination: For example, on the boat ride along the Thames it is easy to see in the mind's eye George II in his great swan-shaped barge going to parade with his court in the then enclosed and still magnificent Kew Gardens—and his court waiting with powdered wigs, jewels and gold buckles to stroll with him in what can hardly be called, even today, less than an enchanted place, now open and beautifully maintained for all to enjoy. Little wonder that Britishers are so proud of their heritage.

Gravestones, or Growing Things and Life?

While London was congratulated upon the foresight which has provided the land it has for recreation and relaxation, its officials pointed out that the goal is far from reached and the need not yet wholly supplied. And from all that was said by delegates from other countries, their need for land is perhaps even greater than London's need.

A suggestion was put before the conference that one source of land would be to convert old cemeteries and church yards to grassed over areas of usefulness.

With more demands for open places, one speaker said, "there seems hardly room for more and more cemeteries and authorities are encouraging cremation or the location of burial grounds outside cities."

It was stressed that many church yards in densely populated areas are studded with old and neglected gravestones with undecipherable names; that it is but a matter of time till the stones themselves will disintegrate and that all the names on a bronze placque would more fittingly serve the memorial amenities while releasing the grounds for open places of beauty and inspiration instead of desolation and sorrow.

A London delegate reported that after 10 years of effort conversion of one of London's cemeteries had been authorised. It will be grassed over and bedded for flowers, then used as an open place of contemplation and relaxation.

The point of sacrilege and of "walking on the dead" was answered by delegates who cited the kings, famous men of history, and religious leaders now resting under the floors and aisles of edifices like Westminster Abbey, St. George's Chapel at Windsor Castle and St. Peters at Vatican City.

The debate closed on a point of arithmetical inevitability: If 18 square feet of ground surface is set aside in perpetuity for each person born into that part of the world which buries its dead, then the day will surely arrive when all the land surface will be occupied by graves.

Better Town Planning

There was evident a clear determination to exercise some control over new real estate developments so that, just as land is now required to be set aside for streets, in the future land must be set aside for open spaces on a yet to be determined percentage of the total house-occupied area; and, further, that it be dispersed in a decentralised way for ease of access by all.

The restricted use of too many school playgrounds to a few hours a day, with no use during the summer recess period of greatest need, was deplored and a suggestion made for a study of unison between school and park administrators.

While there was a recognition that all this would take time, there also was a sense of urgency and a dedicated determination that these moves must be made and successfully carried out.

And a look at what determined men and the centuries have produced in the open spaces of beauty in London, Rome and Paris, leaves no doubt about the wisdom of action now by men who look at the past and think of the future.

Only God Can Make A Tree

Men, imbued with the spirit of Joyce Kilmer, were on their feet for the most animated discussion of the entire congress when a speaker, obviously unintentionally, made a disparaging remark about trees.

The meeting hall rang with phrases such as "Stop tree slaughter . . . stop lopping off limbs . . . mutilated trees look as uncomfortable as limbless people . . . stop encroachments upon the rights of trees."

"He who plants trees, plants for posterity; give them care and respect; nurture them through the adoloscent stage; at maturity give them the timely attention that will bring them to noble figures through the prime of life . . . and when old age approaches, their inevitable demise can often be delayed by a little skilled surgery."

"Trees are not just here today and gone tomorrow and their departure can leave a gap that only a lifetime can rectify."

As to vandalism of young trees ". . . it is better to plant a tree three or four or five times than to give up to thoughtless youngsters and admit we are not capable of educating them to love and care for beautiful things. To give up is to display lack of faith in the future of man and ourselves."

Just as Britain produced the Magna Carta to preserve the Rights of Man, from this eloquent and spontaneous defense of trees, one could believe that the 23 nations represented at this congress are ready now to produce a Magna Carta for the Rights of Trees.

If justification for all this is needed, it may be seen in the beauty of downtown London's tree-lined avenues . . . in the noble trees on so many of Rome's ancient streets . . . in the splendour of the trees on the avenues of Paris and along the stately drives at St. Cloud, Versailles and Fontainbleau . . . and in the magnificent Bois de Boulogne and Bois de Vincennes, both still in their natural state and inside Paris city limits.

The debate prompted one of the 120 American delegates to wonder whether we of a young America will wait until our cities, like these cities, are centuries old before we awaken to the balding effects of a scorched earth indifference toward trees which is practised by all too many of us.

The One-World Nature of Vandalism

Next to the word trees, it would appear that the word vandalism was mentioned most often. The attitude was not one of despair but of hopeful confidence.

Nor was the blame placed on the youth of today as distinguished from those of an earlier day. As one delegate said, "The youth of my day did not break up play equipment in parks. This was because we had none."

While deplouring a diminishing quality of discipline, programmes described to "get the adults before the children" and to generate parents' interest in parks and games, with strong and sound appeals for family togetherness.

One park official reported that vandalism on trees and shrubs stopped quickly when the parks department obtained a half holiday for school children, then provided each with a metal tag with his or her name on it for the adoption of a tree or shrub. "Thereafter we had only occasional fights when one tree grew faster than its neighbour," he said.

It was not unusual to hear a report from a country where nature studies and "responsibility to nature" are taught on released school time, with credits as an extension of education, including regular games and coaching.

In other reports the importance of "belonging," including pride of ownership, was emphasized as a means of enlisting the constructive help and support of young and of creating a sense of responsibility.

These included the appointment of youth committees with specific tasks of a continuing nature . . . the naming of teams after an area or street . . . the appointment of patrol leaders . . . and play leaders . . . the placement of responsibility followed by guidance and by deliberately planned and sustained effort to create a feeling of pride in something owned at a price instead of something given without price or responsibility.

Challenge Youth;
Don't Just Give, Get

On this latter point, delegates cited the discipline and lack of vandalism in privately owned summer camps where a stiff admission price is charged, and to decreased vandalism in public places where a use charge is made for special facilities.

*"Children can and do spend freely for what they want," said one speaker, "including a reported average (in Britain) of $2,500 a year for pocket money purchases. I see no reason why sport centers should not be self-supporting, and I see no reason why anyone should expect free use of them. If people feel they

49

are part owners, and that they are contributing personally out of their own pockets on a pay-as-use basis, then they take pride in their possessions."

In all of these ways, it was claimed, doors are opened not only to an awareness of civic responsibility but to career opportunities as well.

This was spelled out by one organization which provides apprenticeships in gardening to boys and girls under 18. The course, which includes lectures and practical training, leads to examination for certificated gardeners.

Successful candidates are certified at the age of 21. Other youngsters can enter the service as young labourers between the age of 15 and 21. After two years' practical horticultural experience they may take a proficiency test to qualify them for the grade of uncertificated gardener and after five years experience they are eligible to take the examination to qualify as certificated gardeners.

All the entrants, it was reported must go to day release classes and evening school until they reach the age of 18, and are encouraged to continue evening classes even longer.

In these ways "young stars are put in motion," new doors opened, civic pride and responsibility stimulated from within youth groups, and future park administrators are put in training.

The discouraged youngster without the means or prospects to head for Eton and Oxford has opened to him a door to an equally stimulating experience with a professional career in an uncrowded field as the reward. The depth of his knowledge may not match that of college-degree professional horticulturists.

But we Americans, whose forefathers carved from a wilderness the foundations from which our nation grew to greatness, well know that lack of formal education, instead of causing defeatism, can become a challenge that spurs man to a realisation of his highest aspirations.

*Correction. This section should read: The youth of England "Spend between 800 m. and 900 m. pounds sterling a year on drink, tobacco, clothes and cosmetics. They can and do spend freely for what they want."

———◆———

ANTI-UGLIES, UNITE!

(*Continued from page 12*)

careful planning and good design in public works. We have demonstrated in Cleveland with the University Circle Development Foundation, and other groups across the country have also shown, that group action is often the only way to achieve needed results. As you point out, local groups often have their hearts in the right place but "need a clearing-house, a reference center, a source of guidance, advice, and help."

A national Civic Trust could have maximum impact by encouraging the formation of effective state and local organizations. There is no substitute for local strength.

NEIL J. CAROTHERS
President, University Circle
Development Foundation
2009 Adelbert Road
Cleveland 6, Ohio

Downtown Renewal in the Small City - - Problems, Resolved and Unresolved

By ISADORE CANDEUB

EDITOR'S NOTE:—Mr. Candeub is President of Candeub, Fleissig and Associates, New Jersey. This statement was prepared for presentation at the Workshop Conference of the National Association of Housing and Redevelopment officials at the University of Oregon, School of Architecture and Allied Arts, Eugene, Oregon, July 1962.

Main Street, U. S. A., is in trouble. In the tug-of-war between the central city downtown areas and the highway regional shopping centers, Main Street as a shopping area furnishes neither the intensity of excitement and diversity of services that can be found in the big city nor does it have the convenience, attractiveness and facilities for the shopper offered by the highway center. But, this is only one phase of the problem affecting the Main Street areas of our smaller cities. They are almost uniformly characterized by obsolescent layout, deteriorated buildings, apathetic property ownership, traffic congestion and parking problems.

The physical layout of the downtown areas of our small cities show many common characteristics. To begin with, Main Street as a shopping area is ordinarily located on a strip of from four to eight blocks along a state highway or on a major street intersecting with a state highway. It generally runs in depth for two blocks on either side of Main Street, with the outer reaches consisting of a conglomeration of retail and non-retail activities. Except where the regional topography is quite flat, Main Street is located in a valley, frequently alongside a small river. Along the river's edge will be found the main line of a railroad and an industrial fringe, with factories and warehouses crowding in behind the retail center. On the other side of Main Street at a higher elevation, residential uses crowd in and are largely intermixed with the secondary commercial uses behind Main Street.

At one or two of the entrances to the shopping area you may encounter a bridge or a railroad underpass. Traffic flow concentrating at these key access points frequently make them the major points of congestion into and out of the business district.

In our typical town, Main Street still retains some of its characteristics as a highway shopping area, including an excessive number of filling stations, a local diner, and a number of signs identifying the ubiquitous "guest house." Otherwise, it is predominantly a local shopping area with maybe one or two large, independent junior department stores, two or three chains and, mostly, a miscellaneous grouping of small stores many of which seem to have bought their interior furnishings some time in the 1920's. The buildings are old and also old-fashioned. Many of them have two or three floors of residential uses above the stores on the ground floor. If one investigates further, he would find that these properties have been in the same hands for as much as

51

50 years and are now tied up in estates or being held by absentee land owners who may not have seen the properties for years. As commercial properties, the individual store fronts are too small, the stores are too shallow, and the uses or collection of uses are frequently inappropriate. The camera shop, shoe shop, barber shop and dress store will be mixed with the delicatessen, a newsstand, the local bank and the shoeshine parlor without rhyme or reason and in contradiction to all of the theories of good, commercial grouping.

Main Street, U. S. A., is remarkably lacking in any of the amenities that would be considered as essential in any well-designed shopping center. One or two major parking areas are located at some distance from the center of the retail strip on property which became available for sale for one reason or another. One may have been an old lumber yard and the other may have been an old movie house. Other smaller lots, privately held and servicing either local banks or some of the more important stores, will be squeezed in at various locations adjacent to the properties they serve. Typically, there will be no bus terminal and not even a minimum shelter area to serve people waiting for a bus. Sitting areas, park areas, or facilities for children may or may not be available, depending upon the original layout of the town.

Main Street's decline as a shopping area began in the late 40's with the first new major retail outlets along the highways. These new outlets took some of the bloom off the post-war prosperity of Main Street but the real shock was yet to come. With new highway improvements, in quick succession, many of the Main Street areas found themselves faced with competition not only from the highway stores but newly created regional centers providing for a variety in the scope of sales and services exceeding those in the older centers. This competition was not taken lightly. Out of emergency sessions of the merchants division of the local Chamber of Commerce or its equivalent, a rapid succession of programs were put into effect including parking lots, better street lighting, night shopping, and a larger budget for promotional activities. In recent years, planters have been placed along some of our Main Streets with flower beds and shrubs, new signs have been installed pointing to parking areas, parking accreditation systems have been instituted, and experimental "stunt days" and even pedestrian malls have been tried as measures of fighting the highway centers.

Some of these programs work, others do not. In the final analysis, Main Street is fighting a losing battle in terms of the type of programs carried out during the 50's. These programs have been virtually entirely shopping-oriented. They have not dealt with the critical matters of the design and function of downtown areas of our smaller cities. They have not secured the involvement of the community as a whole nor received the endorsement of any major segments of the community other than the merchants. They have been oriented to a salvage operation rather than to a program of reconstruction and renewal, looking to the future and to a service function for the community as a whole.

To initiate a sound program of revitalization of our small city downtown areas, as a first step we should recognize that the prime purpose of this program cannot be merely the salvaging of the Main Street merchants. This is far too limited an objective for the community as a whole. It is certainly not one which the average taxpayer will enthusiastically support with his tax dollars and, in the final analysis, it is questionable whether all of the merchants need to be salvaged. The dynamic and progressive businessman on Main Street has, in all probability, already established himself quite strongly in the highway centers or has gone to rather considerable expense to refurbish his store on Main Street and provide it with parking facilities. He is not particularly in need of being salvaged since he is quite capable of taking care of himself and has probably already taken the leadership in getting major renewal programs instituted in the downtown area. The marginal merchant or, more realistically, "storekeeper," with limited resources and abilities, is in need of many types of assistance most particularly in terms of merchandising advice and financing. In the face of sharp competition without the benefit of modern merchandising methods, major investment in fixtures, and a scale of operations larger than his present scale, he stands little chance of competing effectively in the modern merchandising race.

The theme for downtown renewal must, therefore, not be "salvage" but reconstruction for greater service to the community, for greater importance to the region as a whole, in terms of a multiplicity of functions and activities to be carried out in the downtown area. This is the only type of program worthy of the time, effort and funds that will be required to reconstruct these downtown areas.

The procedure that must be followed in undertaking this reconstruction is quite clear. To begin with, the overall traffic pattern in relation to regional highways must be resolved. This means that the traffic function of Main Street must be settled once and for all. It cannot serve equally well as a major highway and as a focal point of shopping and pedestrian activities. The conflicts between these two activities must be resolved. This will require a comprehensive traffic and highway plan, cooperation with the state highway department, new bridges, underpasses, grade crossing eliminations and other improvements of this type. However, these improvements should not be undertaken on a hit or miss basis. Until the traffic situation can be thoroughly resolved, no successful plan for development can be undertaken.

Secondly, we should not delude ourselves about the nature of the buildings in these downtown areas. In many cases, block after block of buildings are obsolete, unattractive, and in need of comprehensive reconstruction. Here, again, half-way measures will not be adequate. While many buildings can be saved, the majority of the old-type of structure going back 70 to 80 years should be acquired and demolished. Property lines must be redrawn to provide for large sites for new stores and services in the downtown areas. New blood is sorely needed to provide the excitement, services and higher standard of merchandising than is presently available in the downtown areas.

Thirdly, the land use pattern of our downtown areas must be completely reconsidered. It is highly questionable in this day and age whether the sprawling lumber yards, the used car lots, the plumbing fixture warehouses, and trucking and repair services have to be in the downtown area. Our goal should be to make downtown a high-density urban nucleus providing a combination of shopping, apartments, churches, schools, government offices, regional offices, small parks, bus terminal facilities, eating places, and entertainment and recreational facilities. Through imaginative designs, these downtown areas can capture some of the urbanity, gaiety and charm that was traditionally found in the old, medieval towns.

Fourthly, we should recognize that this type of reconstruction cannot be carried out through one or two urban renewal projects. What will be required for the successful development of such downtown plans are general plans setting up a schedule for the effective execution on a project by project basis of the various elements of the plan.

I cannot emphasize too strongly that this is the only type of approach that has long-range meaning to the downtown areas. This ap-

proach is in sharp contrast to the typical program for the downtown area, with the pedestrian mall on Main Street and the acres of parking surrounding the shops. Not only are these designs generally exercises in futility because of the high cost of executing them, but they are basically false in concept. Main Street cannot afford to cut itself off from the body of the community by this type of isolation. In separating itself from the rest of the community, it loses all of the natural advantages it has over the highway shopping center and it lessens its functions to the community as a focal point of community activities and interests.

Our smaller cities are now beginning to approach their downtown problems with some degree of understanding. The merchants have exhausted their resources in running through the various devices and promotional efforts they have used in the past decade to cope with the competition of the shopping centers. With the problems of traffic still unresolved, with extensive blight on the fringes of the downtown areas and on Main Street itself, and with the recognized need for sites for new development, the smaller cities are turning evermore to urban renewal for aid. If at this point, as planners, we can assist them in redesigning our downtown areas as sound, functioning units serving the community as a whole, these areas can, in years to come, once more become a vital force in their communities.

Growing Use of University Services in Urban Problems

EDITOR'S NOTE:—This statement is from *News from the Ford Foundation.*

The universities are dealing with two major sets of urban problems.

One concerns the physical and governmental problems of metropolitan areas, which comprise complex political, economic, and sociological factors. In one sense, therefore, "the urban scientist is an educator, with the entire community as his class," says Dean Thurman White of the College of Continuing Education at the University of Oklahoma. "He should be in a position to assist his constituents by providing them with information and, on more complex issues, directing them to the authority in this particular area. He should be able to explain the methodology, the procedures, or the techniques by which a city or town can go about solving its own problems."

The other set of problems concerns the social consquences of urban sprawl. Thus, one of the three demonstration areas selected by the University of Wisconsin urban-extension program is predominantly rural Columbia County. The University's urban experts want a better picture of the background of migrants to the state's urban areas and are also studying the effect of depopulation on rural communities.

The University of Delaware is studying the assimilation of recent migrants to Wilmington, to determine the factors that promote or impede adjustment to city living.

Many urban-extension activities on the social aspects of urbanization are reminiscent of agricultural extension work.

As the home-demonstration agents helped farmers' families raise their living standards, urban agents are working with urban families—particularly the low-income racial minorities flooding into deteriorating city neighborhoods that have been largely abandoned by middle-class white residents.

In a steel-making community in the Calumet, Indiana, region, Purdue University has set up a staff of family-service agents that provides technical assistance on housing, budgeting, and homemaking services. The University's program in one low-income apartment project includes establishment of a play program for pre-school children, a sewing class for mothers, and in-service training for parents.

In Pittsburgh, four universities are cooperating with ACTION-Housing, Inc. in a program centering on the revitalization of older neighborhoods. Prior to the grants, a "self-help renewal" project was conducted in a built-up, predominantly Negro, neighborhood of low- and middle-income families. University researchers conducted field surveys in cooperation with local residents. Leadership training courses and teen-age block clubs were established. Volunteer teachers were

55

trained to assist in homemaking instruction. A program for yard and garden care was set up. With the grant, this program will be extended to other neighborhoods in Pittsburgh and Allegheny County.

In general, the urban-extension programs reflect the close interrelations between the physical, governmental, and social aspects of urban problems.

Rutgers' new Urban Studies Center is conducting surveys on all aspects of community life in Bayonne, Newark, New Brunswick, and Trenton.

The University of Wisconsin's urban-extension center in the Fox Valley, a region marked by rapid industrialization and complex governmental jurisdictions, is working with neighborhood associations and with individual families on their economic problems. In Milwaukee the University's urban agents are encouraging research by existing agencies—health, highway, public-welfare departments, a committee on the aging population, the state association of county boards, and others. The University is also setting up such agencies as a bureau of economic research and a bureau of social research to handle unmet local research needs.

The educational aspects of the programs center on graduate-level training of urban specialists and generalists. Rutgers, in addition, has established a series of fellowships to permit able persons from the community—journalists, younger executives, and civic leaders—to spend a year at the University studying urban affairs and participating in its extension activities.

TAMING URBAN GIANT

(*Continued from page 40*)

The hard questions posed by metropolitan growth are without a doubt going to require some hard answers. Developing these answers is a complex, tough and at times agonizing experience. It is no job for the cynical, the lugubrious, the fainthearted, or those lacking in essential optimism concerning man's capacity to develop his environment in a creative way. And we'd best get on with it.

NEW TOWNS

(*Continued from page 30*)

ways in the world—this nation should not fail to attempt to build truly livable, efficient, and handsome New Towns. Our purpose here is to suggest how it may be done in Kentucky."

GRADY CLAY
Louisville, Kentucky.
May, 1961.

It occurs to us that this proposal represents the type of study and planning that should be applied to many other "depressed" areas.

D. B. A.

Commentaries

NEW ORLEANS*

The descriptions in a year-old copy of the newsletter of the National Trust for Historic Preservation of violations in the New Orleans French quarter of the ordinance governing area architecture are of interest to San Antonians getting acquainted with Mr. Jacob Morrison, the man responsible for translating into law the concern of Louisianians for their heritage.

One of the Vieux Carre violations cited in the newsletter involved a pair of 18th century Spanish structures on St. Philip Street. The owner was charged with failure to preserve the structure, permitting it to decay and become unsafe, and refusing to make repairs—constituting "demolition by neglect" under the statute. He had won a series of delays through various court devices, but the New Orleans preservation law has already been upheld by Louisiana's Supreme Court, and any demolition would be accomplished by defiance of the statute.

The other violation involved a restaurant on St. Peter St., Pat O'Brien's, built in 1817. Its courtyard and street facade with "Egyptian" capped pilasters and distinctive fenestration, are among its notable features. Without the required prior approval of the Commission, the original street windows were replaced with single large sheets of plate glass which in turn were covered with heavy ornamental cast iron grilles. The owners claimed that this did not fall within the regulations of the ordinance which covers exterior features visible from the street.

As beloved old San Antonio buildings crumble from neglect are bulldozed away, or altered beyond recognition, those who can see the need for legislation for historic preservation look with envious respect to New Orleans. The care and foresight which have saved so much of old New Orleans have brought the new New Orleans rewards both aesthetic and economic. Lovely old buildings bring more tourists than do gas stations and parking lots.

*From San Antonio Conservation Society Newsletter.

Who is a park superintendent and what are his duties? These are questions that cannot be answered in one sentence. However, during my short time with the Tennessee Division of State Parks, I have run across numerous definitions of a park superintendent, and I have found out that his duties are not always the customary ones.

The following is a list of some of the things a superintendent is, and some tasks he is called on to perform, which might explain the worried look he possesses most of the time . . .

1. A park superintendent is, first of all, a leader. He is the head of all activities in the park.

2. He is at times a   ic speaker. Community functions call for his help in this regard on many occasions.

3. He is always an adept public relations man, trying to keep the park guest happy.

4. He is a patient and courteous host, even when being called on in the middle of the night to register some guest or hear some problem.

5. He is a master of self control, because he is the sounding board for any complaint about the park.

6. He is a diplomat in handling all personnel problems.

7. He is a business manager, lawyer, laborer, babysitter, electrician, restaurant operator, planner, accountant, janitor, secretary, policeman, grounds-keeper and judge all in one.

The list could go on and on and still not include important everyday situations a superintendent encounters.

K. H.

57

Planning and Civic Comment

QUOTE

". . . We are ruining our landscapes as we have already ruined our cities, by permitting the destructive blight of ugliness to spread without check. The creeping, crawling hideousness of so many of the newer housing developments is justified on the ground that they get people out of the even more hideous city slums, as if they were not our deliberate creation too. The nauseous dumps, the automobile graveyards, the polluted air, and the all-too-frequent atmosphere of carelessness and neglect have turned much of a beautiful state into a monstrosity of ugliness. Someone must declare open war on this ugliness.

"The chief reason for all this is sheer insensitivity, and I firmly believe that insensitivity is amenable to education. In our educational programs we assume that insensitivity to falsehoods and unreason is not incorrigible, and that we can induce receptivity to moral and ethical values. Is there any reason to assume that we cannot induce receptiveness to beauty as the first step in our assault upon ugliness?

". . . Our first technique should be to encourage the receptiveness to beauty by every educational means that we can employ. The second should be to demonstrate the sheer impracticality of being willing to settle for drabness and ugliness. And the third should be to throw our full support behind every measure which will enhance and preserve the natural beauty that is ours. I personally feel that an important first step is support of the referendum to buy parklands and preserve thereby the green acres that now exist. But more than this we must give our fullest cooperation to all the planning activities in the State which share these objectives. And above all we must use all the means at our command to remind our neighbors that beauty, so far from being an added and inessential attraction, is at the very heart of the kind of life we want to live. These I believe are highly proper functions for the state university in its role as the cultural conscience of the State. . ."

From a Commencement Address
by Dr. Mason W. Gross
at Rutgers University on June 7, 1961

In spite of repeated pleas from historians and developers to save Boston's India Wharf building, designed by Charles Bulfinch c. 1805, it was demolished in June. Abbott Lowell Cummings, of the Society for the Preservation of New England Antiquities, called the India Wharf building "probably the only existing important commercial building on the Eastern Coast by so important an architect." He contended that the structure was as important to Boston's economic history as Faneuil Hall to its political structure. Pointing out that India Wharf was the only remnant of India-China trade left in Boston, Walter Muir Whitehill said that the demolition was a case of "Temporary financial interests predominating over the interests of the city . . . I think it's the greatest misfortune that could have occurred to the waterfront. No other single thing could have been more detrimental to the development of that region." The building's 34 stores were filled during the 19th century with porcelain, fabrics, ivory, tea—products of Boston's East Indies trade.

A blueprint for preserving the beauty of Monterey County's (California) scenic coast was recently approved after a spirited public hearing. Five years in the making, the plan will guide development of the 72 miles of coast line between Carmel Highlands and the south county line. Its adoption had long been

(Continued on page 60)

IN MEMORIAM

Harvey Hiram Cornell, prominent Santa Fe landscape architect and civic leader, died September 9, 1962 at the age of 69, after an extended illness.

He attended school in Iowa, receiving his advanced education at Grinnell College, Iowa State College and Harvard University from which he obtained his master of landscape architecture degree in 1921. Following several years practice of his profession he taught courses in landscape architecture and planning at the University of Minnesota.

Mr. Cornell joined the staff of the National Park Service in 1933 and directed CCC work in parks in Oklahoma, Texas and Louisiana. In 1940 he was promoted to the Santa Fe regional headquarters as chief of planning and later moved up to become Assistant Regional Director.

In 1955 he went to the National Park Service office of design and construction at Philadelphia where he served as chief landscape architect for all work throughout the eastern half of the United States. He retired in September 1959.

Returning to Santa Fe, Mr. Cornell became a principal member of the firm of Franke and Cornell, city planners and landscape architects.

He was a member of the American Society of Landscape Architects, the National Trust for Historic Preservation, the American Planning and Civic Association and the Santa Fe Chapter of Rotary International.

———◆———

The untimely passing of California Congressman Clem Miller came as a grievous shock to his host of friends and admirers. An ardent conservationist as well as an able legislator, the Point Reyes National Seashore legislation which he wrote, introduced and piloted to successful conclusion was perhaps Clem Miller's greatest single legislative achievement. He had been a member of the American Planning and Civic Association for several years.

———◆———

Charles A. Phelan, Jr., former Executive Director of the American Planning and Civic Association and Executive Secretary of the National Conference on State Parks, was almost instantly killed early Saturday, October 13, 1962 when his car collided with a truck as he was returning home to Warm Springs, Ga. from a business meeting in Atlanta. He is survived by his wife and three sons.

Book Review

The State Parks, Their Meaning in American Life. By Freeman Tilden. Alfred A. Knopf, New York, N. Y. 496 pp., 80 photographs and 5 maps. $5.50.

Here is a book which fills a long felt need. It puts together in fascinating style all the history and romance of the State Park movement to date and will, in our opinion, become the basic authority on the subject.

Particularly impressive is the author's enlightened treatment of the many facets of State Park philosophy, principles and policy during the formative years.

Mr. Tilden follows the evolution of the acquisition, planning, development and use of State Parks and related areas, offering recreation in its many forms, through their various phases, the early beginnings, the Civilian Conservation Corps period and the post World War II years.

To those intimately associated with the early history of the State Park movement the author's account of it will give a feeling of pride, not to mention a twinge of nostalgia; to those who have become associated later it should serve as an inspiration and a challenge.

The publisher says of this book, "In the course of preparation for his book Mr. Tilden traveled over 40,000 miles and visited hundreds of state parks. The result is this authoritative study, designed to be both useful as a guide for the tourist, traveler and vacationist and a compendium of detailed information to more than 180 of the most important state parks. Mr. Tilden's remarks on the natural endowment, the historical background, the native flavor of many of the parks are both detailed and comprehensive.

By example and anecdote the author brings alive in intimate terms the state park systems as well as the social credo that informs them and the policies that gave them initial expression.—Here, in a variety of perspectives, is the definitive study of a part of our American heritage as it is preserved unspoiled clear across the land."

D. B. A.

COMMENTARIES

(Continued from page 58)

urged by scenic conservationists to keep the rugged stretch of shoreline from being spoiled by the encroaching touch of civilization. Key features are the banning of construction within 100 feet of both sides of Highway 1 throughout the area and the prohibition against heavy population development in the southern section. Implementation of these controls awaits the adoption of a precise zoning map on which the planing department will begin work soon.

The 87th Congress and Conservation

Major advancement in water pollution control, the establishment of three national seashores, and modest progress in the preservation of waterfowl wetlands were features of an otherwise undistinguished conservation record compiled by members of the 87th Congress, who adjourned the Second Session "sine die" on Oct. 13, 1962, and went home.

The 1962, or Second Session, was the longest period the Congress has remained in Washington, D. C., since 1951 and it was marked by frustration as several important conservation measures were brought near enactment only to fail of final passage. The 88th Congress convenes Jan. 9, 1963.

Bills Enacted Into Law ·

High among accomplishments of the Second Session was creation of the Point Reyes National Seashore in California (Public Law 87-657) and the Padre Island National Seashore in Texas (Public Law 87-712). Point Reyes (Report No. 38, page 257) will consist of 53,000 acres on a peninsula some 30 miles north and west of San Francisco. Padre Island (Report No. 41, page 277) will consist of an 80-mile, 47,000-acre seashore off the Texas coast. In the First Session last year, the Congress established the Cape Cod National Seashore in Massachusetts (Public Law 87-126) and funds were granted to initiate land acquisition. An effort was made to secure $5 million to start acquisition at Point Reyes but the supplemental appropriation failed to pass shortly before adjournment.

Many proposals to create new national parks or monuments or natural areas of special designation were introduced and some received favorable attention in one of the two bodies. None cleared, however, although boundaries of the Virgin Islands National Park were enlarged by Public Law 87-750 to include 5,650 acres of additional submerged lands (Report No. 42, page 287). A few new national historic sites and memorials were established. The Congress last year had created the Hawaii Volcanoes National Park from a portion of the Hawaii National Park (Public Law 87-278).

A major step in preserving migratory waterfowl was taken in the First Session with enactment of Public Law 87-383, which authorized an advance loan of $105 million over seven years for the Bureau of Sport Fisheries and Wildlife to initiate a "crash" program of wetlands acquisition. Enthusiasm was somewhat dampened this year, however, when the Bureau was refused the necessary permission to buy or lease land in the critical "pothole" country of North Dakota and South Dakota. Only the amount of $7 million of the emergency fund was appropriated for fiscal 1963. Bills which would have redistributed income from wildlife to the counties and allegedly meet objections in the Dakotas failed to pass.

Federal subsidies for wetlands drainage was halted at least temporarily in Congressional action this year. The Agriculture Appropriations bill contains language which prohibits, for one year, financial or technical assistance for the drainage of certain wetlands of high value to wildlife. Then, Federal cost-sharing for drainage of wetlands in the Dakotas and Minnesota would be denied under certain conditions by Public Law 87-732 (H. R. 8520) if the Interior Department says the practice is harmful to wildlife (Report No. 39, pages 259–60).

Outstanding progress in water pollution control legislation was recorded by the 87th Congress. The so-called "Blatnik Bill," enacted into Public Law 87-88 in the First Session, not only strengthened Federal law enforcement but provided increases in grants for waste treatment plant construction, state programs, and research. The construction grants limitation was upped from $50 million to $80 million for 1962, $90 million for 1963, and $100 million thereafter for each of the following four years. The maximum appropriations were allowed in both sessions. The Senate last year also approved of the U. S. acceding to the International Convention for the Prevention of the Pollution of the Sea by Oil and, subsequently, the legislation necessary to implement the Treaty was approved by the Congress and signed into Public Law 87-167.

Also passed by the Congress this year were these important items of natural resources legislation:

H. R. 8181, establishing a National Fisheries Center and Aquarium in the District of Columbia, P. L. 87-758 (Report No. 42, page 285).

61

S. 901, providing for a comprehensive, long-range, and coordinated national program in oceanography (Report No. 41, page 280).

H. R. 1171, providing for incidental or secondary use of refuges and hatcheries for public recreation, P. L. 87-714 (Report No. 41, page 277).

S. 455, providing for public hearings on air pollution problems of more than local significance and extending authorizations under the Air Pollution Control Law, P. L. 87-761 (Report No. 41, page 279).

H. RES. 489, offering p o ec ion for the golden eagle, passed October 12, 1962 when Mr. O. C. Fisher (Texas) withdrew an objection based upon a letter from the Under Secretary of the Interior who said the Secretary's regulations will provide for recognition of a 20-county area in southwest Texas "by not requiring that individual permits will be required to control golden eagles that are damaging livestock" (Report No. 42, page 285).

Also of interest are these: H. R. 6682, exempting fowling nets from duty, P. L. 87-770 (Report No. 41, page 282); S. 3431, allowing additional states to join the Pacific Marine Fisheries Compact, P. L. 87-766 (Report No. 41, page 281); S. 3504, providing for alternate representation on the Migratory Bird Conservation Commission, P. L. 87-812 (Report No. 41, page 281); H. R. 9728, doubling Federal participation in the Cooperative Forest Management Act, P. L. 87-680 (Report No. 41, page 282); H. R. 12688, providing assistance for States in forestry research P. L. 87-788 (Report No. 41, page 283); and H. R. 12434, updating and clarifying several laws relating to administration of national forests (Report No. 42, page 287).

Important bills passed by the 87th Congress in the First Session last year included: P. L. 87-152, authorizing use of surplus grain for the emergency feeding of wildlife, and P. L. 87-119, establishing the new Wyandotte National Wildlife Refuge in Michigan.

Conservation in Other Bills

Natural resources were inseparably involved with other programs.

H. R. 12391, Public Law 87-703, the "Food and Agriculture Act of 1962," contains provisions for a pilot outdoor recreation program (Report No. 40, page 275). Last year, Public Law 87-112 for the first time authorized Federal cost-sharing for wildlife practices under the ACP program.

S. 2965, The Standby Public Works Acceleration bill, Public Law 87-658, gives the President authority to spend up to $900 million to accelerate public works programs in economically-depressed areas and $400 million was appropriated for the program in fiscal 1963 (Report No. 39, page 264). There are early indications that a large chunk of this money will be used for water pollution control grants for waste treatment plant construction.

Passed late in the Second Session was H. R. 12135, the "Federal-Aid Highway Act of 1962" which, among other things, provides for these contract authorizations: forest highways, $33 million each for 1964 and 1965; forest development roads and trails, $10 million for 1963, $70 million for 1964 and $85 million for 1965; public lands development roads and trails, $2 million for 1964 and $4 million for 1965; park roads and trails, $22 million for 1964 and $25 million for 1965; parkways, $16½ million for 1964 and $15 million for 1965; Indian reservation roads and bridges, $16 million for 1964 and $18 million for 1965; and public lands highways, $6 million for 1963 and $9 million each for 1964 and 1965.

Appropriations for Resource Agencies

Interior Department agencies fared comparatively well in appropriations granted by the Congress through H. R. 10802, P. L. 87-578 (Report No. 32, page 230). The Bureau of Sport Fisheries and Wildlife was granted $27,112,000 for management and investigation of resources, as compared to the budget estimate of $26,572,000, but the staff for administration of the migratory bird conservation account was limited to 200 persons. The Bureau of Commercial Fisheries was allowed $15,225,000 for management and investigation of resources, about the same as the budget request of $15,213,000, and $8,473,000 for construction. The National Park Service was allocated $25,525,000 for management and protection, including "not less than $1,101,096" for transfer to the new Bureau of Outdoor Recreation, and $40,775,500 for construction. The Bureau of Land Management was granted $41,510,200 for management of lands and resources, less than the $43,252,000 requested, and the agency's important information program was cut to

Planning and Civic Comment

the bone. The Bureau of Indian Affairs received $34,300,000 for resources management and $16,000,000 for road construction. The Geological Survey was appropriated $56,100,000 for surveys, investigations, and research while the Bureau of Mines got $26,075,000.

The same bill allowed the *Forest Service* $139,400,000 for forest land management, a bit less than the $140,740,000 requested but considerably above the $128,000,000 appropriated last year. The Service also was allocated $24,835,000 for forest research, $15,830,000 for State and private forestry cooperation, and $2,000,000 for access roads. The sum of $2,000,000 was allowed to complete wilderness canoe area purchases within the Superior National Forest.

H. R. 12648, making appropriations for the Department of Agriculture for 1963 (Report No. 40, page 275) was the subject of strenuous disagreement over authority of the two bodies to originate legislation. The bill finally was passed October 11, 1962. The Agriculture Research Service received $174,443,500; the Cooperative State Experiment Station Service $38,207,000; and the Extension Service $75,344,500. The Soil Conservation Service was allowed $90,705,500 for conservation operations, $60,585,000 for watershed protection, $25,000,000 for flood prevention, and $12,250,000 for the Great Plains conservation program. The Agricultural Stabilization and Conservation Service received $685,973,000 for acreage allotments and marketing quotas, ASCS expenses, the Sugar Act program, ACP, and the Conservation Reserve.

One of the last bills to be cleared by the Congress before adjournment October 13, 1962 was H. R. 12900 (Report No. 41, page 277), making appropriations for Public Works. The Army Corps of Engineers was appropriated $1,041,358,000, of which $792,845,500 was for construction. The Bureau of Reclamation was allowed $333,687,000 of which $158,218,000 was for construction and rehabilitation and $107,808,000 was for the Upper Colorado River fund. This bill also contains the $400 million for Public Works Acceleration.

In addition to providing the maximum authorized amounts for waste treatment plant construction grants and state program grants, the Congress granted funds through H. R. 10904, or P. L. 87-582, for three of seven regional research laboratories authorized in 1961 (Report No. 32, page 231) and two water quality laboratories. Over-all, the Division of Water Supply and Pollution Control was granted $24,505,000.

Conservation Disappointments

The 87th Congress produced its share of conservation disappointments and several were associated with consideration of the Wilderness Bill.

S. 174, The Wilderness Bill was passed by the Senate last year and referred to the House Committee on Interior and Insular Affairs. The Public Lands Subcommittee of the House Committee on Interior and Insular Affairs conducted western field hearings late in 1961. After delays purportedly for the purpose of awaiting an Outdoor Recreation Resources Review Commission report, hearings then were held in Washington, D. C. Late in the Second Session, the Committee ordered reported a substitute bill but directed it be brought to the House floor under procedures which would not allow debate or amendment. The Speaker denied a request for this procedure. The Committee then refused to meet, at least a quorum of members could not be obtained, and the Chairman left the city. As a result, these important proposals died within the House Interior Committee along with the Wilderness Bill: S. 1988, to promote the conservation of wildlife in the Tule Lake-Klamath area of Oregon and California; H. R. 11165 and S. 3117, establishing the Bureau of Outdoor Recreation; S. 543, providing for shoreline area studies; and S. 77, establishing the Chesapeake and Ohio Canal National Historical Park along the Potomac River. Shortly before final adjournment, printed copies of the Committee's report (House Report 2521) on the Wilderness Bill finally became available. With minority views filed by Mr. John P. Saylor (Pa.), the Report covers 138 pages.

Then, in the closing days, the Congress adopted a conference report upon H. R. 13273, the Omnibus Rivers and Harbors-Flood Control bill, and sent it to the President. Among other things, the bill authorizes construction of the controversial Bruces Eddy Dam and Reservoir on the North Fork of the Clearwater River in Idaho, a project long opposed by conservationists. The final version of H. R. 13273 (Report No. 41, page 276) contained authorizations for 207 projects and a total monetary authorization of $2,260,220,000.

Other projects in the Columbia Basin which were authorized: Asotin Dam on the Snake River, Idaho and Washington; Strube Reregulating Dam and Reservoir, South Fork, McKenzie River, Oregon; Gate Creek Dam and Reservoir, Oregon; Fern Ridge Dam and Reservoir modification, Long Tom River, Oregon; Cascadia Dam and Reser-

63

Planning and Civic Comment

voir, South Santiam River, Oregon; Ririe Dam and Reservoir, Willow Creek, Idaho; and Blackfoot Dam and Reservoir, Idaho.

The Conference Committee's report upon H. R. 13273 included the following: "In taking its action authorizing Bruces Eddy Dam and Reservoir, North Fork, Clearwater River, Idaho, the conferees were aware of the objections that have been made to this project by numerous groups interested in fish and wildlife conservation. It is the intention of the conferees that the Secretary of the Army shall adopt appropriate measures to insure the preservation and propagation of fish and wildlife affected by this project, and shall allocate to the preservation and propagation of fish and wildlife, as provided in the act of Aug. 14, 1946 (60 Stat. 1080), an appropriate share of the cost of constructing this project and of operating and maintaining the same." The action came despite a report released by the Fish and Wildlife Service August 22, 1962 which indicated the Bruces Eddy Dam would have a highly adverse effect upon anadromous and resident fish populations and elk and deer herds.

During a meeting of the Conference Committee, it was agreed that the House Committee on Public Works would hold public hearings as soon as practicable as the 88th Congress convenes on the following projects which were held out of H. R. 13273: Cape Fear River Basin, N. C.; Flint River, Ga.; the South Fork of the Cumberland River, Ky. and Tenn.; Knowles Dam and Reservoir, Montana; Burns Creek Dam and Reservoir, Idaho; Waurika reclamation project, Oklahoma; Savannah River-Duke Power Company, S. C. and Ga.; and Trotter's Shoal Reservoir, Savannah River.

Appropriations bills contained some disappointments. As in previous years, no funds were allowed to protect the Rainbow Bridge National Monument in Utah from waters of the new Glen Canyon Dam on the Colorado River. Still cut off without funds are the Arctic and Izembek Wildlife Ranges in Alaska. The controversial fire ant eradication program in the South is continued at about the same level of $2.5 million annually. Failure of a supplemental appropriations bill to pass in the closing hours of the Second Session not only denied $5 million for emergency land acquisition at the new Point Reyes National Seashore but cut off $500,000 in salaries and expenses for the new Bureau of Outdoor Recreation.

Resource Bills Which Failed

Among the other proposals which failed of final passage were: proposals which would have applied the principles of multiple use management to properties administered by the Bureau of Land Management; authorization for a Water Resources Planning Act; establishment of a Youth Conservation Corps; designation of the Salmon River in Idaho as a fish sanctuary to be kept free of impoundments; and making State wildlife agencies eligible to receive excess Federal property.

❧

STATEMENT OF OWNERSHIP, MANAGEMENT, CIRCULATION, ETC. REQUIRED BY THE ACTS OF CONGRESS OF AUGUST 24, 1912, AND MARCH 3, 1933 OF PLANNING AND CIVIC COMMENT published quarterly, at Harrisburg, Pa. for October 1, 1962, Washington, D. C. as:

Before me, a Notary in and for the State and county aforesaid, personally appeared Donald B. Alexander, who, having duly sworn according to law, deposes and says that he is the Managing Editor of the Planning and Civic Comment, and that the following is, to the best of his knowledge and belief, a true statement of the ownership, management, etc. of the aforesaid publication for the date shown in the above caption, required by the Act of August 24, 1912, as amended by the Act of March 3, 1933, embodied in section 537, Postal Laws and Regulations, printed on the reverse of this form, to wit:

1. That the names and addresses of the publisher, managing editor and business manager are: Publisher: American Planning and Civic Association and National Conference on State Parks, Inc., 901 Union Trust Building, Washington 5, D. C.; Managing Editor: Donald B. Alexander; Business Manager: None.

2. That the owner is: American Planning and Civic Association and National Conference on State Parks, Inc., 901 Union Trust Building, Washington 5, D. C.

3. That the known bondholders, mortgages and other security holders owning or holding 1 percent or more of total amount of bonds, mortgages, or other securities: (If there are none, so state.) None.

Donald B. Alexander
Managing Editor

Sworn to and subscribed before me this December 20, 1962

(My commission expires Feb. 14, 1964)

Regina C. McGivern
Notary Public, Washington, D. C.

Official Organ of American Planning and Civic Association and
National Conference on State Parks

Selected Papers from the 42nd Annual
Meeting of the

NATIONAL CONFERENCE ON STATE PARKS

Sept. 30—Oct. 4, 1962

ILLINOIS BEACH STATE PARK
Zion, Illinois

❀

National Conference on State Parks
901 Union Trust Building
Washington 5, D. C.

DECEMBER, 1962

SUPPLEMENT — PART II

Planning and Civic Comment

Vol. 28   December, 1962   No. 4

42nd Annual Meeting of the National Conference on State Parks
Host State: Illinois

Welcome Address by Governor Otto S. Kerner

As governor of the host state for your 42nd meeting I take genuine pride in extending you a hearty welcome. I understand this is the second time Illinois has had this honor, although we were once co-host with our sister state of Indiana at a meeting held at our Pere Marquette State Park.

We welcome you, not only to Illinois Beach State Park, but to Illinois—the crossroads of the nation. Fortunately you will have the pleasure of visiting at least a part of our state—the Morton Arboretum, especially beautiful at this time of year; the outstanding Cook County Forest Preserves; Starved Rock and White Pines Forest State Parks; and one of our new conservation areas which I dedicated only a few weeks ago, the Winnebago County Conservation Area.

Illinois Beach is unique among the Illinois state parks since it is the first to offer public bathing along a lake. Its uniqueness also includes its great natural interests, and, of course, this magnificent lodge.

South of here a short distance is an area long known as "The Flats" which is entirely different from any found in other Illinois parks. It is one of the great natural reservoirs of plant life, and back in 1893, at the time of the Chicago World's Columbian Exposition, this area was visited by the curator of the famous Kew Gardens of England. After seeing the flats and nearby ravines, the gentleman said that here grew a greater variety of trees, flowers and shrubs than at any other locality of the known world.

We are preserving this rare heritage and at the same time making it available to interested visitors. And I note that your program will permit many of you attending this meeting to visit this great nature area.

This lodge—the only state recreational facility to be constructed in the last 20 years—is a most delightful building incorporating the newest ideas in contemporary architecture and design. Yet, it is difficult to find the proper people to operate a property of this size and do those things which the scarcity of state funds makes impossible. Fortunately for Illinois, for the first time in our history, private capital is being spent to develop this state-owned property for the people of Illinois. These developers have such confidence in the future of this lodge that they are investing more than $400,000 of their own money in the swimming pool you see under construction, new meeting rooms, tennis courts, winter ice skating rink and other improvements.

Illinois is proud of its parks, memorials and conservation areas, but our continuing dilemma, as Director Lodge and Superintendent Smith will tell you, is the fact that we do not have enough of them for our expanding population. However, we do hope within the next few years to expand and develop many more of these recreational areas.

We have been ordained by nature as a prairie state and, as such, have few mountains, wilderness areas, nor a multitude of natural lakes. We are, however, developing the best of our resources as you will see when you visit Starved Rock, White Pines Forest and the Winnebago conservation area.

Starved Rock is our most popular park. Last year its 846,000 visitors topped Lincoln's New Salem, our greatest historic park, by nearly 10,000. Outside of swimming, Starved Rock offers everything desired in a park.

White Pines Forest with its stately pines, delightful lodge and excellent recreational facilities ranked fourth in attendance last year. Its popularity is attested to by the trainloads of Boy Scouts from the Chicago area who visit it annually.

West of Illinois Beach, not many miles, is the Chain O'Lakes area— Illinois' only cluster of natural glacial lakes. Here the state's thousands of acres attract great numbers who enjoy fishing, boating, picnicking, camping and hunting.

The rest of the state must depend largely on man-made lakes, which in many cases also provide municipal water supplies, and our parks and conservation areas for their recreational opportunities. Winnebago County Conservation Area is typical of the state lakes. Over the state we have 20 of these conservation areas and a number will become state parks when fully developed.

In addition to these, are 10 state lake areas. At a number of these, work has begun on clearing sites and building dams for artificial lakes. Half of these sites are in the southern half of the state which we believe will become the great natural playground of the Midwest.

This section has the large Shawnee National Forest, wilderness of great beauty, unusual geological formations, plus some of the best lakes and parks in the state. Add to these the development of Rend Lake, Carlyle and Shelbyville Reservoirs and other undertakings and you see the bright promise of not only a recreational paradise, but a restored regional prosperity as well.

Our new Board of Economic Development's Division of Tourism Development and Promotion is working closely with these various projects.

With its vast array of Lincoln shrines, memorials, historic sites, nature areas, scenic wonders, and conservation and recreational areas, Illinois should be able to build tourism into a major industry.

Superintendent of Parks Bill Smith and his committee have worked out a fine program for your meeting and I am sure you will go home richer in knowledge and inspiration. I cordially invite you to return to Illinois soon. There is much we would like to show you.

Nature's Classroom
By Mrs. DOROTHY J. BENNETT

Mrs. Dorothy J. Bennett of Everett, Washington, the dinner speaker on Monday, October 1, whose subject was "Nature's Classroom" provided one of the highlights of the Conference program.

In 1948 Mrs. Bennett launched a unique summer classroom in Mount Baker National Forest in Washington. Camp Silverton-Waldheim consists of a few tents, a rough lodge and 45 acres of rain forest along the Stilloquamish River. She is proud to have had a hand in educating some 7,500 children of fifth and sixth grade school age in woodland lore. She says "I don't believe any Silverton graduate will ever start a forest fire." The small fee charged for her vacation—education—curriculum is termed the cheapest insurance against nature wrecking in the United States.

Federal-State Relations
In Outdoor Recreation

Address by EDWARD C. CRAFTS, Director, Bureau of Outdoor Recreation,
Department of the Interior

I was reared as a boy on the west side of Chicago in Austin and Oak Park. My love and appreciation of the outdoors first began to take shape during boyhood days spent in the Cook County forest preserves, particularly those along the Des Plaines River. Also many a happy hour was spent on Lake Michigan beaches.

The only point of this personal reminiscence is that the occasion today is somewhat like home-coming. It is familiar and feels good to be in the Chicago area once more.

This is my first meeting with the National Conference on State Parks and I trust not the last. Many of my friends are here. But to those of you whom I do not know, I want to get acquainted and trust the reverse is true.

In the past few months, there have been talks before the Western States Land Commissioners, the Izaak Walton League, the American Institute of Park Executives, the Association of State Foresters, and the American Forestry Association. Then there is your conference here, and later this week, the National Recreation Congress in Philadelphia.

This sounds like a lot of talking. It is and perhaps too much, but fall is the meeting time and the speaking time. There is a purpose to be served in these public statements of policy, philosophy, and intent. We satisfy your curiosity in part at least about the Bureau and its leadership.

From our standpoint, we are trying to take advantage of these opportunities to develop a series of statements that will set guidelines, clarify purposes and help public understanding. In the process we are learning a lot, crystalizing our ideas, and seeing many new faces.

Before coming here today, my staff briefed me on your organization. I am told there are about 1000 members, including most State park administrators, numerous local and Federal officials, and many lay persons. I know something of the origins of the Conference in 1921, the active role played throughout its history by the National Park Service, your publications, your objectives, and your close liaison with the American Planning and Civic Association. I have been privileged to ee the galley proof of Freeman Tilden's forthcoming book on State pasks.

Be that as it may, the main point is that you as State park administrators, and the Bureau of Outdoor Recreation as a focal point in the

Federal Government for outdoor recreation, are in this business together. We can and must support and help each other.

First of all, let us never be defensive or apologetic about our mission and profession in outdoor recreation. You and I know full well how difficult it is to compete personnel-wise, budget-wise, and organizationally with activities that are related to the external defense of our Country. Yet we must be defended internally as well as externally.

It has been said before that leisure can be the curse as well as the blessing of a successful civilization and that many thoughtful Americans are uneasy about our current use of free time. We recognize that man is not wholly suited physiologically to meet the technological demands placed upon him and that outdoor recreation is a renewing experience that helps to solve this problem.

We know, too, that there is ingrained in the American tradition a Puritan philosophy of hard work and materialism. There are many many Americans who still do not realize the impact of outdoor recreation on the American way of life, who still tend to think of it as somewhat frivolous and who fail wholly to recognize it for what it is—a necessity to man's internal well-being both physically and emotionally.

In short, recreation needs status in the American way-of-life. We who are in this business are status-seekers for our work.

We can snow under the dubious ones and Doubting Thomases with impressive statistics on the extent and impact of outdoor recreation. Unfortunately, statistics don't do much convincing of those who have preconceived viewpoints, nor do they contribute much to leadership.

We need in this field of outdoor recreation the cumulative effect of personal experiences by millions of people, effective organizations which make their impact felt on policy-makers, recognition in the curricula of higher institutions of learning, and most of all talented leadership that carries with it not only the sober conviction of the mind, but the emotional conviction of the heart.

May I commend to you two recent books, a 20th Century Fund publication, "Of Time, Work and Leisure" and a new book by Walter Kerr, "The Decline of Pleasure." To quote briefly from the cover flap of the latter book, the author suggests that we "Rediscover the gifts we lost during the century in which man's genius was totally directed toward freeing himself from hunger and physical burdens: the gifts of playfulness, of contemplation; gifts of being pleased, of experiencing joy, of recreation that refreshes and truly recreates, for it is not virtue but joy that is its own reward and only by divorcing it from the concept of usefulness can we obtain it."

You and I are well aware that 90 percent of all Americans engage in outdoor recreation annually and that there are some 4½ billion recreation experiences each year. Do we realize equally well that there are a quarter billion acres of public land involved and an almost equal acreage of private land; that consumers spend 20 billion dollars annually on outdoor recreation experiences; that governments—Federal, State and local—spend a billion dollars a year in supplying recreation, and that 40 States now have more than half their population living in urban zones?

The Bureau of Outdoor Recreation recognizes that State governments must play a key and pivotal role. They occupy the middle level in our system of government between Federal and local·public agencies. In many ways they are more advantageously situated than either local units or the Federal government to deal with public recreation.

Many States are moving forward actively. Among these are New York, New Jersey, Pennsylvania, California, Oregon, Wisconsin, Massachusetts, and others. There are over 3000 State parks but these cover only 3.6 million acres or 11 percent of all State land in designated recreation areas. Three-quarters of the State land available for outdoor recreation is administered by State forest and fish and wildlife agencies. Another interesting fact is that 80 percent of the 20,000 State recreation areas are small, being under 40 acres in size. Yet half of the 32 million acres of State land available for outdoor recreation is in some 60 tracts averaging well over 100 thousand acres.

Further, if the recent report of the Outdoor Recreation Resources Review Commission is correct, most State park programs are in difficulty due to inadequate funds, limitations in personnel, and insufficient planning. Back of this lies what I have already mentioned—the lack of well developed civic and political support.

Other than a number of specific recommendations as to State activities regarding organization, planning, acquisition and development, use of regulatory powers, financing, and assistance to local governments, the ORRRC reports did not go into State activities in detail. One study report is a directory of State organizations concerned with outdoor recreation and its very variety and massiveness underscores a main weakness in State activities. This is the lack of a focal point of responsibility for outdoor recreation within the States.

The 50 States have about 500 offices with some responsibility for outdoor recreation. This is an average of 10 per State and the range is from 4 to 26.

Some 17 States have one Department or overall agency handling parks, fish and game and forestry. Almost an equal number, or 14 States, have separate, co-equal Departments for each of these three major breakdowns. Nine States have forestry and parks in one Department but a separate one for fish and game. Three States have just the reverse, with forestry and fish and game in one Department but a separate department for parks. The seven remaining States have still other combinations.

Furthermore, some 15 to 20 States have State or regional planning boards or commissions engaged in outdoor recreational planning and some 25 States have economic or resource development offices which almost without exception are concerned with tourism or other aspects of recreation.

Practically all States have highway or road departments which deal with wayside picnic areas or parks.

Regardless of the reasons such a situation exists, the very fact of wide dispersion of recreation responsibility among a multitude of State organizations greatly weakens the likelihood of progress. State-Federal relations are made more complex as are inter-State relations and relations between States and local governments and between States and the private sector. For example, with what State agency would the Federal Government deal in connection with financial grants-in-aid for recreation planning, or for acquisition or development of State recreation areas, or for technical assistance in recreation?

In unity there is strength, and I think the wide dispersion of outdoor recreation activities among so many State agencies helps to explain the difficulties that have been experienced historically in obtaining civic and political support; until some adjustment is made, recreation in certain State departments will tend to continue its historic role of being an incidental and accidental benefit of State administration of natural resources.

Turning to private organizations for a moment, there are forestry organizations, wildlife and fish and game organizations, park organizations, wilderness organizations, climbing and hiking organizations, and general recreation organizations. At first blush, there would appear to be a multitude and there are many. But if I may say so, the forestry, wildlife, fish and game and wilderness organizations act more aggressively, are perhaps better financed, and consequently have greater impact on civic consciousness and in gaining support than do either park or general recreation groups. Also the latter have been oriented mainly toward urban recreation.

To be more specific, it is my belief that the American Institute of Park Executives, the National Conference on State Parks, the American Recreation Society, and the National Recreation Association, have been less effective in making their views known to key officials in both legislative and executive branches of government, than have such groups as the Wildlife Management Institute, National Parks Association, National Wildlife Federation, International Association of Fish and Game Commissioners, Association of State Foresters, Wilderness Society, and the Sierra Club.

It is my further belief that there is no organization that effectively represents the views and needs of the great body of campers, picknickers and swimmers who use public outdoor recreation facilities.

If outdoor recreation is to be recognized as I think it must and should be, it is my earnest hope that these situations within State governments and private organizations which I have just mentioned, will in due course, be improved.

The Bureau of Outdoor Recreation, as most of you know, is a new conservation bureau within the Federal government, organized last April as a result of one of the basic recommendations of the Outdoor Recreation Resources Review Commission. It has been placed in the Department of the Interior but it has government-wide functions and has been assigned responsibilities for promoting coordination of Federal programs, assistance to States, research, recreation resource surveys, preparation of a nationwide recreation plan, and encouragement of inter-State and regional cooperation.

There also has been created by the President a Cabinet-level Recreation Advisory Council made up of the Secretaries of Interior, Agriculture, Defense, Health, Education and Welfare, and the Administrator of the Housing and Home Finance Agency, with a rotating chairmanship which rests first with the Secretary of the Interior. The Bureau of Outdoor Recreation will serve in part as staff to the President's Recreation Advisory Council.

In the Executive Order which established the Council, the Secretary of the Interior was instructed in consultation with Council members, to develop procedures for encouraging better inter-agency coordination in carrying out National outdoor recreation policies and programs.

I hope before the National Recreation Congress in Philadelphia later in the week to outline a preliminary program for the Bureau of Outdoor Recreation as we see it now. But the primary emphasis of the Bureau will be policy, planning, coordination, assistance and research. The orientation will be to stimulate activities of the States, local governments and private enterprise and to promote coordination of Federal activities.

Our relationships will be with all State agencies concerned with outdoor recreation. However, at some point it probably will become necessary for Governors of the respective States to designate a focal point of contact for the Bureau of Outdoor Recreation.

I believe that in the next Congress legislation may be proposed that would create a conservation fund and would authorize its use for Federal financial assistance to the States in recreation planning, in the acquisition and development of State recreation areas, and in the acquisition of certain Federal recreation lands. Other types of recreation legislation may be offered. One proposal would be to give certain basic organic authorities to the Bureau of Outdoor Recreation much along the lines of Title I of H. R. 11165 of the 87th Congress. Another possible proposal is a technical assistance program in recreation to be administered by the States, through State employees, for the benefit of the States and to provide aid to local governments and the private sector. Financing would be partly by the States and partly by the Federal Government.

There is one other point I wish to emphasize with respect to concepts and scope of the Bureau of Outdoor Recreation. Our concern is much broader than State parks. Our scope is the same as that of the Outdoor Recreation Resources Review Commission which considered all phases of outdoor recreation. Also our orientation is toward meeting needs of people rather than toward resource management per se.

I have not spoken today of the functions of the Bureau of Outdoor Recreation in promoting coordination within the Federal government, other than to mention it. There are some 20-odd Federal agencies engaged in one way or another with outdoor recreation, and there has been little coordination. The recreational use of Federal facilities has grown very rapidly as have those of the States. There is no National policy on recreation. Outdoor recreation has not been defined. Often it is the consequence of or incidental to some other activity. Intra-Federal coordination is extremely difficult because of bureaucratic allegiances, historical situations, and supporting clientele. We are engaged now upon request of the Recreation Advisory Council in developing recommendations for a system of user fees for recreation on Federal properties, in drafting a proposed National policy on outdoor recreation, in defining criteria for National recreation areas, in exploring the feasibility of a National system of scenic roads and highways, and in trying to develop procedures for promoting coordination. Such procedures will include program, legislative and budgetary review.

I think the Bureau is fortunate in having attracted talented men to its executive staff. We have assembled men with a variety of disciplines and backgrounds. The Associate Director is Lawrence Stevens, a geographer by profession and Deputy Director for Studies of the Outdoor Recreation Resources Review Commission. He brings to us all the knowledge and experience acquired during the several years existence of that Commission.

The two assistant Directors are John Shanklin, a forester by training and a long-time staff advisor to the Secretary of the Interior, and Heaton Underhill, a biologist who was most recently director of the New Jersey Division of Fish and Game and the chairman of the Executive Committee of the International Association of Fish and Game Commissioners. Prior thereto, he had experience in both New York and Massachusetts.

Among the Division Directors, we have Sid Kennedy, whom I think all of you know. He has been your Vice-President and recently on your Board of Directors. Sid is in charge of our division of cooperative services, and brings to us his wide experience with the National Park Service. In charge of our division of planning and surveys is Robert Ludden who was with the Park Service for about 30 years and who had charge of somewhat similar work in that Service.

With me here today is Louis Reid who is Director of our Education and Interpretation division. Louis is a newspaper man from Texas with wide experience in journalism. He has served on a number of farm journals. I particularly hope that you will have an opportunity to get acquainted with Louis during this meeting.

The director of our division of Federal coordination is Howard Ball who is a specialist in public administration and comes to us from the State Department with prior experience with the Federal Aviation Agency, the Bureau of the Budget and TVA. We have not yet staffed our research division.

Finally, let me say that we in the Bureau of Outdoor Recreation are trying, with you, to find a compass to guide us through. I think we are idealists without illusions. We intend to be vigorous proponents, certainly not passive brokers. Our intuitions are positive rather than negative. Among our beliefs is a proper respect for privacy and, indeed, the recognition that private enterprise rather than government, must contribute the most to outdoor recreation. At the same time, we are trying to save our outdoors for the many rather than for the privileged few.

Address of George L. Collins

President, Nature Conservancy

(Delivered by Edward J. Meeman, in Mr. Collin's absence)

The Nature Conservancy welcomes this opportunity to come before such a gathering of park men.

We of the Conservancy are engaged in the exacting and highly disciplined work of supporting, privately, the preservation of parks and equivalent reserves.

Our primary concern is with land and other resources that exemplify plant and animal community relationships and are essential in preserving ecological balance.

Often a community, county, state or Federal land-use agency will not be in a position to act quickly enough to save a certain place, of real value to natural history, from the axe, or the bulldozer, or from some other industrial or competitive purpose. The Conservancy tries to be alert to critical situations of such a nature. We try to serve as an intermediary and negotiator in holding off the "commitment to oblivion" of the values to science or recreation, and to ultimate public cultural good. We can speak out sometimes to owners and others interested where the representatives of governmental agencies are unable to do so.

Occasionally the Conservancy will option a property, or even buy it, for a public agency, such as a park authority. The purpose is to take advantage of bargains if no one else can do so. We are not anxious to buy and hold properties indefinitely, generally preferring to act in favor of ultimate ownership by the public. However, the Conservancy does at times reach out to preserve some place or other without knowing at the time what its final disposition may be.

There is an area in Northern California of some 3,800 acres that is in this category. It may one day become a fine State park, but the Conservancy is in no great hurry to decide its ultimate destiny except that the area must be preserved because it has invaluable nature, virgin wilderness qualities. Until someone comes along who can do a better job than we can with this place we will continue to hold it.

Another place of real significance is a plot of about 3 acres in the heart of a busy residential section. It contains at least one plant that no longer is found anywhere else. Dr. Herbert Mason, noted botanist, expressed the view that it is encumbent upon the Conservancy to see to it that every possible effort be made to save any species from extinction. While it may not be very dramatic or spectacular to do so the Conservancy fairly often finds itself in the position of chief advocate of a common, garden variety area that may, for all anyone knows at the moment, eventually prove of inestimable worth. Dr. Mason offers a number of examples to show the validity of this understanding.

That the Nature Conservancy enjoys the "grass roots" public relations of the Soil Conservation Service, the Forest Service, the Corps of Engineers always appears to me to be more appealing than the public relations at the grass roots at least, of the park men.

If that is true, it is because most other major conservation undertakings involve construction, rebuilding, or redoing in the American tradition of progress. We are only beginning to understand as a society of exploiters that it is as incumbent upon us to let some of our resources alone—in our Nature Conservancy State Park case as strict nature reserves in some instances as it is to utilize many of the others commercially or industrially.

Last summer, at the First World Conference on National Parks, we heard of the growing realization in some of the newest countries that saving their wildlife habitat, or a large amount of it, so that people can see game, may be a more economically useful procedure than starting right out to redo the landscape in order to put every possible acre to work producing food and fibre.

Some of us at that Conference were surprised indeed to find park men representing such far off places as Antarctica, Asia and Africa who are very well informed on American parks and forests because we have supplied their chief examples. It was a little disconcerting to have some of them, from countries so new in their own right that we could barely recognize or pronounce their names, warn us of the dangers of overuse of our own parks. But they did. And perhaps we park men in our country can take heart from that kind of an experience with contemporaries from other lands who know us well and respect our initiative more than we realize.

We are in the lead, and on the spot to do a perfect job of it for ourselves and for The World interest in parks and equivalent reserves.

The Nature Conservancy joins with the National Conference on State Parks and with those others who are working toward greater perfection in all phases of conservation. We have our work on the side of private responsibility in fostering the growth of the park and recreation movement here and abroad. We will endeavor to broaden the base of local responsibility by inducing more individuals, more communities, more counties, more educational institutions to function cooperatively with you.

We will continue to seek a stronger balance—a better equilibrium in parkmanship.

While we are not especially the champion of the underdog we do not shun the little places, or the folks in the small community. They so often are tremendously understanding and responsive once they know what we are doing to save something—a remnant of woods, a rare plant, a bird, or a scenic view—which, as is true with all of us, they might have overlooked. As we all know, great things frequently are too close to be seen. As the Rodgers and Hammerstein song says, "a hundred million miracles are happening every day, right before our eyes."

It is not incumbent upon conservationists to save everything. Industry, subdivision, highway building should not be looked upon blindly as the enemies of parkmanship. A balance of values has to be achieved. Arousing private citizen interest in this viewpoint, so that the individual becomes more aware of his personal responsibility to the arts and sciences of saving good samples of each type of landscape, each habitat, is the Conservancy's role. We are not afraid of overdoing it, but we are concerned with the establishment of an equilibrium in which the necessity for parks and equivalent reserves will be recognized in every American Community.

State, County and City Park Relationships
Panel Discussion:

Chairman, PAUL OPPERMANN, Executive Director, Northeast Illinois Metropolitan Area Planning Commission

Members, V. W. FLICKINGER, Chief, Ohio Division of Parks

KENNETH L. HALLENBECK, Director Huron-Clinton Metropolitan Authority

HOWARD GREGG, General Manager, Milwaukee County Park Commission

DANIEL L. FLAHERTY, General Superintendent, Chicago Park District

As discussion leader Mr. Oppermann performed very ably and after introducing the general subject with appropriate comments of his own, presented the other members of the panel whose papers are reproduced herewith. Following each speaker's presentation Mr. Oppermann summarized and coordinated their remarks so that the entire discussion was enthusiastically received by those present.

State, County and City Park Relationships
Talk presented by V. W. FLICKINGER, Chief, Ohio Division of Parks

Your panelists this morning, while representing various levels of government in recreation development, are by no means strangers. Our panel moderator, Mr. Oppermann, on September 12 participated in the 5th Annual Metropolitan area conference having as its theme "Toward Land and Water for 1980." The conferees discussed items which were of interest and concern to us. Would that we, in this session might have some of the highlights of this conference in his summation.

The rest of us are fraters in frater of the Great Lakes Park Training Institute. It has not been my privilege to meet Mr. Gregg at Pokagon, though he has appeared on that program several times. Due to schedule conflicts our paths have not crossed. My personal knowledge of the system he represents is considerably outdated. In 1942, just prior to the Round Table Conference in Chicago, I was privileged to guest visit his system under the guidance of Director Jerome Dretza and Superintendent George Hanson. At that time the operation was outstanding and without question has been materially expanded and improved in the ensuing years. As for Messrs. Flaherty and Hallenbeck, our sharing of ideas and experiences has been more recent.

·Ordinarily my responsibilities are confined to those at the state level in contrast to those in the various echelons of government above and below the state level.

Due to the ever-increasing role of state governments in both local and federal affairs it seems appropriate at this time to limit my remarks to state-local relationships, leaving the state-federal discussion to Doctor Crafts.

Objectives of my discussion will be to outline, as I see them, the responsibilities of the various levels of local governments; to point out our conception of State responsibilities in public recreation by what we have done, or are doing, in Ohio to fulfill that concept.

As administrators of our respective systems we are all confronted with the same problems of land acquisition, finances, development, operations and maintenance. Our methods of attack and solution may be varied but we end up with the same basic philosophy, that of "serving the people."

There is, I believe, general agreement within our profession that our most urgent and complicated problem is the competition we are in for open space; land acquisition. There are several crucial factors which affect the acquisition of land for outdoor recreational purposes, but the major obstacle for many is of a financial nature although some States are in the process of solving this dilemma by bond issues for land purchase. Some of the other factors are a constantly growing population (it was noted in Newsweek of August 13, there is a slight decline in the baby crop due to economic conditions); urban expansion; industrial development; highways; forestry; water supply; and, recreation. Further discussion of these factors is inappropriate at this time as I am certain you are fully aware of the influence each factor has on our efforts in land acquisition.

Each of us will undoubtedly have a different connotation of the term 'recreation.' A precise definition, acceptable to all interests is an arduous task. Each has his own interpretation, but it is possible that we can all concur in the same end point: *Land Use*.

Outdoor recreation may originate with the homesite, estate, or farm, and run the gamut in all levels of public areas and facilities. The homesite cookout, gardening, lawn mowing, or whatever suits the individuals fancy is actually recreation. However, we in parks are not concerned with this phase.

At this juncture, government enters the scene. Neighborhood playgrounds, where the small fry and teenagers participate in age group activities, also beckon to adults who on occasion gather to visit and supervise the younger people at play. Here may be found the park-school complex such as we have in Columbus, which is becoming an ·

increasingly attractive and successful program. This is a part of the neighborhood development and complements the school program.

The municipal park system—village, town and city—usually has a program of multiple use, (see ORRRC report No. 17 for details) which is a concept of management. These provide areas for both passive and active recreation such as picnicking, bird watching and nature study with small bodies of water for boating, fishing and bathing.

There is also a special category, which in larger industrial cities cannot be overlooked. These are recreation areas provided by industry to serve its employees.

Next in order are county or metropolitan parks. In some instances these are, by agreement, combined. In Ohio, the oldest of these is the Cleveland Metropolitan Parks. Created under the provisions of law in March 27, 1917 and recodified in 1953 to Chapter 1545, Ohio Revised Code, over 14,000 acres are now administered by this board, with more being acquired. More recently is the Iowa County Park Board Act, Chapter 111 A, Code of Iowa, which has as its purpose the creation of a county conservation board and to authorize counties to acquire, develop, maintain, and make available to the inhabitants of the county adequate areas and programs for public recreation. Although my information may be in need of revision, I believe 66 of 99 counties in Iowa are participating in this recreation program.

Beyond the two previous categories—city and county—are those which are usually termed as regional or state. These may be state parks, forests, memorials, historic sites, conservancy districts, or other public domain. They may vary from roadside rests to large areas of thousands of acres.

As an example, Ohio is fortunate to have had a federal flood control program originated in 1935 by the United States Army Corps of Engineers, which provides 10 water impoundments of 16,030 surface acres, with 29,417 acres of land for recreation purposes.

The Engineers are responsible for all flood control operations, while the Muskingum Conservancy District, a political subdivision without tax income, operates the state park-like facilities thereon. These lands and waters are located in a section of the state which would not otherwise be developed by the state for the recreation they now provide.

Above the State are the Federal levels.

According to the ORRRC report of date, there are 283 million acres of land used primarily for outdoor recreation of some form or another.

During my years of park service, involving city, state, and federal service, it has been and continues to be my opinion, that four levels of government are concerned in this discussion. These are: City, County, State and Federal, each level being concerned with and having influence on other governmental echelons responsible for public recreation.

At the risk of repetition, but for purposes of clarity, a brief resume of these various levels seems appropriate. Some of my fellow panelists may not concur in my statements, but this is as I see it from my level.

The City, having its areas within the confines of corporate limits receives the first impact. Its neighborhood playgrounds, school parks, swimming pools and larger open spaces are reached by "shanks mare," bicycle, private or public transportation. These are primarily day use areas, although limited overnight use may be permissible if area size allows.

County parks receive the second impact because of the larger, more natural areas. They can accommodate larger visitor loads with facilities similar to city parks and they are more appealing to the visitor. Transportation is generally by private vehicles or chartered buses. There are perhaps some areas which may be reached by public means. Limited overnight use is being considered by some county park administrators.

State areas are those beyond the city and county parks in scope and distance, which receive the third impact. Similar facilities are provided on a larger scale, with less intensive overall development. Overnight accommodations ranging from camping, to deluxe inn and cabin installations are accepted facilities. Transportation is generally by private car. Visitor stay is longer.

Federal areas are, in many instances, too far away from centers of population except the Midwest, to serve a short time need. Facilities are similar to those in state parks but distances from urban populations require that most citizens must utilize a minimum of two weeks travel and vacation time to use them. Transportation is by private vehicle, charter trips, by rail or air to a terminal for pickup by livery service.

Operational procedures vary with each administering agency, but we are all confronted with the ever present maintenance problem, sometimes referred to as janitor service. Acquisition of lands and development thereof are problems similar in nature.

Since we are fraters in the field of recreation, all striving to the common goal of 'serving the public,' what is our problem and how can we improve our relationships?

We all accept the fact that our facilities are severely overcrowded, that the limits of the visitor load for which these facilities were designed are constantly exceeded, thereby destroying many of the esthetic values we have labored to create and must now seek to maintain wherever they exist.

Who is responsible to formulate ways and means of mitigating this ever-increasing public demand for outdoor recreation with subsequent area overuse?

If natural outdoor recreation is to be available for future generations in the manner it is now provided, and if the predicted future attendance figures are accurate, then immediate attention must now be given to planning, cooperating and coordination at all levels of government. In view of the unprecedented population growth, cultural changes in our living, improved highways, faster automobiles, higher income, and a trend toward shorter working hours with a consequent increase in leisure time, we cannot conscientiously delay—LAND IS DISAPPEARING OVERNIGHT to other uses and once gone for another purpose reclamation for recreation is virtually impossible.

This becomes a public problem for all of us. Adequate outdoor recreation for all cannot be left entirely to private and industrial interests, neither should it be reserved for a certain select few who can personally afford it.

Since it is in the public interest, there must be general public cooperation to cope with this situation. Too often State park people in general have evidenced an attitude of desiring to solve this problem by their efforts alone. We have been prone to resist and exclude the interest and help of dedicated lay people. In the situation which we now find ourselves, we should re-examine our present thinking, discard old ideas and form new concepts that are in line with trend of the times. We as public agencies, might catalyze the action and request the help of interested private groups, i.e., suppliers of recreational needs, industry, labor unions and civic groups, all of which have a stake in outdoor recreation. Their interest in the improvement of living conditions in their community, state, and nation is of vital concern to them since these facilities are primarily for their benefit.

The development committee of greater Columbus endorsed both the city and county development programs which passed and included capital improvements for both city and county, and an operating levy for the county. Public support, properly controlled, can do much to assure the success of any program as evidenced by the above action. An interested citizenry with ambition can do things which the professional cannot do.

Concerted action is plagued by several problems, first of which is incomplete information on the part of the general public and private leadership regarding the extensive and critical need for natural resources; second, the resultant indifference of the public to the seriousness of the land acquisition problem; third, the complex nature of our common problem 'competition for open space.'

There are solutions to negate those problems if we are willing to cooperate. As a beginning we must first, coordinate the planning at all levels of government: city, county, state, and federal. We are all aware of the Federal Government role in planning and development at the national level and will become more informed on federal progress when Dr. Crafts speaks to us on Tuesday.

The need for the state to assume the responsible leadership in recreation was recognized in the 54th annual meeting of the Governors Conference at Hershey, Pennsylvania on July 2, 1962. There it was resolved that the Governors conference urge each state to prepare a long range plan for the development of outdoor recreation opportunities, and that each state take the lead in working with local government to attain a balanced state-local outdoor recreation plan. Just prior to the establishment of the Bureau of Outdoor Recreation, the State of Ohio had submitted a request to Secretary of the Interior Udall for a study of recreation resources in Ohio. In reply, Assistant Secretary John A. Carver, Jr., indicated that it would be considered as soon as the Bureau was established. We would hope that the survey will be sufficiently broad to include a complete land use plan to determine the best and most practical type of outdoor recreation facilities.

New Jersey, New York, and Wisconsin have approved major open space programs; Pennsylvania has its "Project 70" scheduled for referendum; California's failed by a slight majority. Each of the programs makes provisions for the lower echelons of government participation.

Dr. H. G. Wilm, Commissioner of Conservation, New York State gave the case history of the New York State recreation plan before the 40th annual convention of the Izaak Walton League of America at Portland, Oregon. In a paper entitled "The Roles of States in Recreation Development" he stated "it is our conviction that the major role of state government is in conduct of regional, statewide, or inter-state affairs; and in providing assistance to local governments where these are not financially or socially able to meet the problem." He also issued a warning to the State—which is right and proper—by saying "in providing state leadership, guidance, or assistance, the higher level of government needs to be meticulous to provide only minimum standards and guidelines for local action and to avoid any semblance of domination."

In October of 1960 representatives (5 each) from the following professional park organizations, The American Institute of Park Executives, The National Conference on State Parks and the National Park Service, met in Washington, D. C. to discuss a program of parks at all levels of government. This program was given the name "Parks of America." One of its recommendations being that Federal Funds be made available on a matching basis for the purchase of recreation lands. In the event funds became available, how should they be handled with the secretary's office? It was agreed by those in attendance representing the city and county level, that they would prefer to have the state park agency assume the responsibility for handling their share of whatever funds might be available. This was predicated upon the basis of meeting the requirements of planning, coordination, etc., as prescribed by the secretary.

In Ohio, it is being proposed that the tax on cigarettes be increased 1 cent per pack. This would result in $12,000,000 annual revenue earmarked for land purchase and development as follows:

50 percent for the purchase of state lands for water impoundment sites and recreation,

25 percent for the development of existing lands,

25 percent to cities and counties on a matching basis.

We are hopeful of favorable action by the General Assembly early next year.

Within our respective states it is imperative that we communicate, each with the other, to keep each level generally informed. It is imperative to effect greater liaison in coordination, planning, study and action between all city, county and state and federal agencies. By so doing, we could avert waste and duplication, but more important would be the development of integrated, multi-purpose planning and development of available resources.

Planning coordination in Ohio at the state level is being handled by our Department of Industrial and Economic Development, which is limited in the functions it may legally perform. In the Division of Parks planning assistance is given on a voluntary request basis.

We maintain liaison with the various county park boards and numerous regional planning boards. We share mutual information and data. This relationship could be improved. Our Water Commission and State Division of Water, have had watershed resources studies long underway.

Many state park administrators have expressed a reluctance to become interested or involved in local park-like programs. Many believe they should concern themselves with non-urban lands only, leaving the urban problems to the cities and counties. Outdoor recreation does not limit itself, people are no longer concerned where the facilities are located, what today is rural becomes urban tomorrow. If the State is in accord with the Governors Conference resolution of balanced state-local outdoor recreation programs, it would appear that the conference must seriously consider deleting the word 'non-urban' from its constitution if we, as administrators, are to continue active support of this program. Outdoor recreation recognizes no man-made boundaries or barriers.

Perhaps the most important facet, is the one most often overlooked, that of research. Lack of research is apparent not only in the conservation, planning and land use fields, but in the recreation field as well. These are listed in ORRRC Study Report #13, page 66.

What facilities are most needed and what type of recreation is most desired? Most of all, we must know more about human behavior. I personally hope that someone, once and for all, could place a dollar valuation on the intangibles of outdoor recreation, its aesthetic stimulation, its health and moral value to the public who seek it.

Granted that the ORRRC reports have given us all valuable information, there is much research to be completed with the public by those skilled in human relations. While it may loom large in our minds at the moment and require time, money, and effort, it will be useful to us in future planning and development programs.

In summation:

1. Parks at all levels of government are essential. This may appear axiomatic. One level cannot hope to meet the needs alone. Sharing will make the load easier, if we all work together toward the common goal.

2. We must coordinate, plan and develop facilities for the maximum use without impairment, being ever alert to avoid duplication of effort and expenditures. Multiple-use, a form of land management, should be encouraged at all levels.

3. One level must not be allowed to dominate the other. Minimum standards and guidelines must prevail at all times.

4. Institute a research program; in which we all share the effort, as well as the results.

It is to be hoped that in the various aspects of outdoor recreation in its broadest sense, that we each may find a common denominator wherein we can all continue to plan and develop outdoor recreation facilities for those whom we serve.

State, County and City Park Relationships

By KENNETH L. HALLENBECK, Director,
Huron-Clinton Metropolitan Authority

For many years the metropolitan area of Detroit held the unenviable position of providing less park area per capita than any other district of more than 500,000 population in the whole United States. A survey conducted in 1941 showed that the Detroit area had only 2.65 acres of publicly owned park land for every thousand people living in the area. The same survey showed that Buffalo had more than twice as much with Boston and Cincinnati nearly three times as much; and Cleveland, New York and Chicago ranging from four to five times as much as the Detroit area.

These comparative figures are not intended to imply that our district should follow the lead of any other district, nor that any other district has the perfect proportion of recreational land to population. They do show, however, that the Detroit district was lagging far behind the leaders in recreational services on whatever basis the comparison is made.

The State of Michigan, with its hundreds of miles of Great Lakes shoreline, is widely known as one of the greatest recreational states in the Union. Its recreational industry is the second largest in the State, being surpassed only by the automobile industry. At the time of the 1941 survey most of the recreational facilities, many of them privately owned, were far away from the metropolitan area of Detroit, and were not available for the everyday use of its concentrated population. Only a comparatively small percentage of the metropolitan population had the time, or the funds, to escape to more distant regions where recreational facilities are abundant, such as they are in Northern Michigan.

The southeastern part of Michigan is studded with inland lakes. There are about 1,200 of them, but on only 25 of them could the public gain access through small pieces of shoreline that were in public ownership. There are also 600 miles of streams in the same district, possessing scenic and recreational values, but only 14 miles were in public ownership.

The county of Wayne, in which is located the City of Detroit, is for the most part very flat, and its topography does not lend itself well to the development of recreational facilities in natural surroundings. However, the four counties which partly encircle Wayne County are much more fortunate in that respect. Within these counties lies a belt of high moraines with ranges of rough hills. Interspread between the hills are numerous lakes, streams, swales and forests. In many respects, it is an area ready-made for providing fishing, hunting, swimming, boating and other normal forms of recreational activities.

Within this belt, there existed enough unused acreage to provide ample area for the development of public parks for the hundreds of thousands of people living in the congested areas in and around Detroit.

This briefly describes the conditions which existed during the late 1930's and prior to the creation of the Huron-Clinton Metropolitan Authority.

An enabling Act was passed by the Michigan Legislature in 1939 which carried a referendum to permit the electors of the five counties to create a Metropolitan District for "Planning, Promoting, and/or for Acquiring, Constructing, Owning, Developing, Maintaining and Operating, Parks, Connecting Drives, and/or Limited Access Highways."

The Act stated further that its purpose should be carried out, either acting alone or in cooperation with the Department of Conservation, the State Highway Department, any Board of County Road Commissioners, or any federal or other state or local body having authority to construct and maintain parks or highways.

This proposition was voted upon in November, 1940 and was passed in all 5 counties by an overwhelming majority.

Cooperation over many years, or if you would prefer to use the Conference Theme, the excellent relationships between two recreation agencies can best be illustrated by describing what occurred to bring our 4,500 acre Kensington Metropolitan Park into realization.

The Michigan Department of Conservation and the Huron-Clinton Metropolitan Authority made a joint survey in the early 1940's to determine what lands in southeast Michigan would be desirable and available for public recreation.

Among the areas selected is the aforementioned Kensington Park which Huron-Clinton agreed to purchase and develop and Island Lake State Park which adjoins Kensington Park downstream on the Huron River which the Conservation Department agreed to purchase and develop.

Engineering studies determined the best site for the dam to form the 1,200 acre lake would be in the proposed Island Lake State Park area but the greater part of the lake would lie in Kensington Park. Therefore by mutual agreement and full cooperation between these two public agencies, Huron-Clinton secured from the Conservation Department a 99-year lease on the land for the dam, constructed the dam with its funds and for several years this lake has actually been shared by two agencies without any actual or implied conflict, all of which has been in the public interest.

I have been delving a bit into history but can as honestly state that these relationships have continued to this moment not only with our State Department of Conservation but with a great many units of government in our five-county area—and there are many—as you might well know.

I would be painting a false picture if what I have said so far or by inference leaves the impression that all has been tea and crumpets in every conference or discussion with every governmental unit. There have been and will continue to be many differences of opinion, a goodly number of arguments, and even misunderstanding not all of which has been resolved by any means. We are admitting our shortcomings over the years which has been mostly errors of omission in that too many times we unthinkingly did not request an audience with, say, the township board, to discuss with them even our short-range plans which without question would involve them. Well, you know what happened and I'll be happier not refreshing my own memory.

Contributing in no small measure to the transition from too few conferences to almost too many, has been the establishment of legally constituted planning boards or commissions at practically all levels of government with guidance usually being offered by professional planners as consultants.

Those of you from states which have had planning boards or commissions for many years may be surprised to learn that in Michigan the first legally constituted County Planning Commission was not organized until 1947 in Ann Arbor. By a strange coincidence I was honored to be one of the charter lay-members. There remain many counties and an untold number of townships without such Board or Commission.

Working very closely with us as they are with others in southeastern Michigan is the Detroit Metropolitan Area Regional Planning Commission. This Commission completed in 1960 a Recreation Lands Plan and immediately directed its Staff to take steps to implement the plan through the development of a coordinating council representing those agencies and units of government involved in recreation and conservation.

Many of you know Paul Reid the Executive Director of the Regional Planning Commission who, at the first meeting of the Coordinating Council last June said—"The major purpose of the Council is to seek implementation, through various operating and policies agencies, of a recreational lands plan on a regional scale. The Commissions 1970 plan for recreational lands can be utilized as a guide for longer-range planning and for progressive steps in the acquisition and development of large parks and recreation areas in the 7-county southeastern Michigan region. Common concern and mutual cooperation on the part of the operating agencies and policy bodies provide the basis for a united and sustained program along these lines. Before us is a dynamic opportunity and a real challenge to develop cooperatively in this southeastern Michigan region a meaningful, adequate and effective regional recreational lands system."

The development of the above Recreation Lands Plan consumed many months and was carried on under the guidance of a Recreation Advisory Committee. The membership of about 20 persons came not only from all levels of government but also from industry and labor.

It is much too early to even guess what the outcome will be for all of the hard work and thought which contributed to the plan but I can say of my own knowledge that it has been of material benefit to us at Huron-Clinton inasmuch as we had underway at about the same time an updating of our Master Plan. We executed a contract over a year ago with the Regional Planning Commission to develop for us a recreational lands plan to 1980 and to single out that portion of the plan which we should undertake.

I also know first-hand that subsequent to the presentation by Regional Planning Commission's Staff of the Lands Plan to each of the operating agencies that each of them have taken steps—admittedly some are long and some short—but steps they were toward implementing the plan.

I hope that I haven't spoken this morning more as a Planner than as an administrator, but however it has been, I tried to thread throughout this paper my concept of "State, County and City Park Relationships" as they appear to be in Southeastern Michigan.

State, County and City Park Relationships: "The County"

By HOWARD GREGG, General Manager, Milwaukee County Park Commission

The "Conference Theme of State—County—City Park Relationships" is most timely and, as we all agree, most important!

The competition for the tax dollar is very fierce these days, and it is important that all levels of government work together to produce the most efficient and economic service possible.

My purpose today is to discuss the County aspect of our theme. In order to do this, I shall outline the organizational structure, some of the policies and methods of inter-governmental cooperation of the Milwaukee County Park Commission.

As the result of a public referendum, most all park areas in Milwaukee County were placed under our jurisdiction in 1937. Some of the units of government retained facilities, such as school playgrounds and playfields. The Village of Whitefish Bay on the north shore retained a small Lake Michigan beach, and the City of Milwaukee held their boulevards and social centers. But, in total, a large consolidation was effected in order to develop a more economic, efficient and effective park system.

At that time about two-thirds of the area of Milwaukee County was unincorporated; that is, was under the township form of government. Today we have no unincorporated lands within the County.

The Park Commission was established in 1907 under the State Law. We have seven non-salaried commissioners who serve seven-year terms and are appointed by our County Executive and confirmed by the County Board of Supervisors. This commission has considerable independent authority for park administration. For example, no land acquired for park purposes can be put to any other use, or disposed of, without the consent of the Commission. In recent years this has been a most valuable authority in preventing the many efforts to put park lands to other uses.

At the present time we have over 11,000 acres of parks under our jurisdiction. Fortunately, we have enjoyed fine cooperation of our County Board in that it has given us approximately one million dollars in each of the past four years for land acquisition. Our program calls for the same amount each year for the next five years.

Now to discuss our methods of cooperation and coordination with:

1) OTHER MUNICIPALITIES

2) OTHER COUNTIES

3) STATE GOVERNMENT

1. COOPERATION WITH MUNICIPALITIES—

A great deal of our coordination effort involves the City of Milwaukee, because it covers about 40 percent of the County's area.

In order to eliminate duplication and to produce more effective recreational programs and facilities, we maintain three important committees:

I. Committee on Recreational Policies—

This group is composed of representatives of the Milwaukee Common Council, Milwaukee School Board, Milwaukee County Board of Supervisors, and the Milwaukee County Park Commission. In addition, the technical staffs of each unit are made available. This committee meets periodically to discuss mutual problems.

II. Milwaukee School Board Site Selection Committee—

The members represent the School Board, the City and County planning agencies, and the Park Commission.

Through this group careful study is given to expansion of existing sites and to the acquisition of new ones, and also coordination is obtained in locating playgrounds in a most effective and economic manner. Duplication of facilities is eliminated with resultant budgetary savings.

III. The "Big 11" Committee—

This committee is comprised of recreation leaders of eleven governmental units within the County.

Here again mutually beneficial discussions are held regularly through which areas of responsibility are established and a firm coordinated plan is developed and followed.

In addition to these committees we operate under a formal Two-Part Agreement with the Milwaukee School Board.

Part I—Program of Activities

Part II—Facilities

As a policy matter the Park Commission applies this agreement to all other units of governments within the county.

2. COOPERATION WITH COUNTIES—

In this area the County Park Commission has had periodic meetings with Park and Planning Agencies in adjoining counties. Continued liaison is had between the technical staffs also.

The recently formed Southeastern Wisconsin Regional Planning Commission has provided us with another fine opportunity for coordination, although that agency has not as yet been able to study the region's recreational problems. This agency covers the seven counties surrounding Milwaukee. Several of our staff members are serving on study committees within the region, dealing with natural resource and watershed management.

3. COOPERATION WITH STATE—

We have no formal program as yet, but we have had several informal conferences with representatives of the State Conservation and Park Departments. A formal program will be set up in the near future.

This area is most important as the State has acquired land and is planning to acquire more lands as part of the Kettle Morain State Park which is located from twenty to thirty miles from Milwaukee County.

We feel that our County and State recreational departments should establish a closer liaison and develop an agreement in areas of responsibility. Such activities as horseback riding, overnight camping, nature and hiking trails, etc., can be more effectively accommodated within the large State Park and Forest lands. By following our existing co-operative procedures and developing additional ones, we feel that a most economic and beneficial recreational program can be obtained for the residents of our Metropolitan Area.

State, County and City Park Relationships
Speaking for The City

By DANIEL L. FLAHERTY, General Superintendent, Chicago Park District.
(Delivered by Mr. Shultz in Mr. Flaherty's absence)

At the outset of my remarks permit me to congratulate your Program Committee on undertaking this problem of relationships between the State, County and City park systems. Forging relationships of this kind in effective terms is long overdue. We have too long remained in our own individual corners, maybe suspicious of one another, and certainly at the cost of efficient coordination and good planning.

It is essential in these times that our respective agencies work together, due to the tremendous growth of population and the sporadic urban development, not only in our older existing metropolitan areas but also in the new coming metropolitan areas. We are witnessing a time when farm population is on the decline and urbanization is increasing at a rate never before reached in this country. Unfortunately, even at a time when our skills and knowledge of planning are actually at an all time high, land speculation and the competition for land has never been greater.

In this particular situation which concerns most of us, more especially in city parks to a greater extent than those of you in the now urban parks, we are encountering tremendous demands for our services. These demands are being created by an increasing leisure for people with more money to pay for their play. The demand upon city and county parks are being conditioned by more enlightened appetites in terms of parks and recreation services. People are no longer satisfied with mere picnic space; they now seek a beach or a pool with all the sanitary appurtenances that our modern science can develop. They not only seek a place to walk through the woods, but they seek a golf course with tees, fairways and greens kept up to almost professional standards. For those of us in the city, our people not only expect playgrounds but they desire fieldhouses with gymnasia, craft shops, theaters for dramatics and enough services to take care of people from the cradle to the grave.

These tremendous growing demands are naturally not accompanied with tremendous increases in our revenues. I think I should leave our own Illinois State Park people to discuss that question with you. And, speaking as a city park superintendent, I want to point out that our tax levy has been held level for the past two years, although we have been fortunate that a number of our bond issues have been approved. We have been a little more fortunate than other cities in that our bond program has produced a very significant increase in park facilities.

However, our bond program has gone on without coordination with the county and state park systems. There is no doubt in my mind we are now at the point in our growth, especially when we consider land, that we must look to the county and the state park systems to acquire acreage for our growing population.

It is certainly timely that we begin to define our respective roles and secure the funds necessary to fulfill the land requirement that would be spelled out with the new goals that we jointly develop.

There are several trends that are certainly helping us, the work begun by Resources For The Future and The Outdoor Recreation Resources Review Commission. These various studies that have been completed, dealing with natural features and the recreational opportunities they afford will go far to accommodate our highly mobile urban population. The unified action of the various federal agencies cooperating with state government are bringing about fruitful results. It is my wish that these studies will stimulate more detailed planning by state park departments to help not only the counties and county park systems, but also to bring within the reach of our cities more adequate facilities, particularly for weekend patrons.

Another phase of planning initiated in Chicago that would be of interest to this audience is our Northeastern Illinois Metropolitan Area Planning Commission, under the leadership of Paul Oppermann. This agency has attempted to bring all metropolitan area planning into a single focus and has done a very admirable job in getting started. This agency, too, has recently completed a study for The Outdoor Recreation Resource Commission which I am sure will be helpful to all of us in the Chicago Metropolitan area.

The difference between this study and some of those that we have reviewed in other states is that it has been aimed at the goal of preservation of open space. I am sure that Paul here will be happy to relate for you the study and its implications. I want to congratulate him and his Commission for its adoption of a policy on open space that I hope will serve to guide all of us in Chicago on the use of our land and that will give us assurance of ample recreation space, both for state parks, county parks and city parks. Incidentally, there are other cities in the metropolitan area that will need these planning guides over and beyond the City of Chicago.

Now I would like to go on to the definition of roles that Paul has asked me to give you from the city park department's viewpoint. Naturally, our park planning, for those of us in the city, must be premised on the natural values that surround our cities. Climate, native forests, lakes, rivers, topographic features are characteristics that will condition planning. The next responsibility that we have to meet is that of serving millions of people living in a relatively dense urban setting. This kind of living means that their children will have to have places to play, that mothers and housewives will have places to go and things to do. And that the teen-agers in their after-school hours, will have games, sports and cultural activities to occupy their leisure; that there is a certain opportunity for the average adult to participate in community activities and to enjoy friendships and social functions; and finally, the senior citizens will not only be served with a pleasing environment but with things to do to make their later years more satisfying.

This means that our urban services will of necessity be more complex. The services will require a wide variety of resources and skills. This means that we will require more personnel trained in a large variety of professional disciplines. In terms of land and land use, it may mean less land used more intensively with a concomitant increase in maintenance cost.

From our city point of view, the county parks might well fill in certain gaps we are forced to leave open, especially in offering such recreational services as golf courses, beaches, picnic groves, swimming pools, nature trails, day camp centers and so on. Certainly, the state parks should continue in their present course of setting up large areas to entertain our people over weekends and long holiday periods. The preservation of naturalistic areas, sites with historical importance, lodging and camping facilities, development of waterways, the conservation of lakes, rivers and streams should continue a state and federal function. In defining these roles there should be more adequate detailed planning with goals frequently brought up to date and more adequately financed. In this way there can be real coordination between our respective systems.

In closing, I want to again pay tribute to the committee who has brought about this rather historic occasion. The opportunity for our three or four levels of park management to get together and outline our direction cooperatively is a most urgent need. To me this is a great professional achievement and it has been a real pleasure to have been here with you. Thank you very much.

Roll Call of the States

Due to the sheer volume of the written material submitted, plus the notes recorded from the oral presentations, much of which is repetitious of written material, and because to edit (cut) this material down to manageable proportions would almost totally destroy its significance, it has been decided not to print it. This will also cause the saving of several hundred dollars, a significant sum.

A different method of making such material available to the membership in the future is being considered and will be presented at the March 1963 Board Meeting for discussion.

Planning and Civic Comment

Official Organ of American Planning and Civic Association and
National Conference on State Parks

CONTENTS

MARCH 1963

PLANNING AND
CIVIC COMMENT

Published Quarterly

Successor to: City Planning, Civic Comment, State Recreation

Official Organ of: American Planning and Civic Association,
National Conference on State Parks

SCOPE: *National, State, Regional and City Planning, Land and Water Uses, Conservation of National Resources, National, State and Local Parks, Highways and Roadsides.*
AIM: *To create a better physical environment which will conserve and develop the health, happiness and culture of the American people.*

Second-class postage paid at Harrisburg, Pa., and at additional mailing office.

EDITORIAL AND PUBLICATION OFFICE, 901 Union Trust Building, Washington 5, D. C.

Printed by the Mount Pleasant Press, The McFarland Company, Harrisburg, Pa.

Planning and Civic Comment

Vol. 29   March 1963   No. 1

Chesapeake and Ohio Canal
National Historical Park

EDITOR'S NOTE:—This is the second in the series of articles on proposed National Park Service projects, prepared by the Park Service at our request.

So near and yet so far!

In park conservation that familiar adage is perhaps most applicable to the Chesapeake and Ohio Canal. Those who know and love it best and those who realize the urgency of park conservation in America today profoundly hope that a Chesapeake and Ohio Canal National Historical Park will not be far but soon a reality. Loyal and enthusiastic sponsors of authorizing legislation, Senator Beall and Representative Mathias of Maryland, Senator Douglas of Illinois and others, have reintroduced C&O park bills early in the 88th Congress—in ample time, if public interest supports them, to authorize the park at last.

So near and yet so far—three Congresses have almost passed the legislation. Each time the Senate passed the bill but the measure failed, often narrowly, in the House of Representatives. Legislative bottle-necks, cost considerations, fear that a park might interfere with river development each time tripped the measure short of enactment. Now, however, there is time. The price tag of some $1.5 million keeps the proposal one of the most moderately priced of all comparable park measures being considered by Congress. And the legislation specifically recognizes that Congress can still provide for other river uses if it sees fit. So the way seems clear and hopes are high for realizing this extraordinary park opportunity.

So near. The old C&O Canal, following one of the few major river valleys in the East not already committed to industrial and urban use, is literally at the doorstep of 18 million Americans—nearly one tenth of the nation's population. This means it is at the doorstep of cities and suburbs, places where a park of any kind means so much in outdoor recreation opportunities.

These factors alone would make the C&O Canal an important state or regional park project. But this monument to transportation history, this link that bound East to West in the critical years of the Republic's youth, is of national significance as the finest relic of America's great canal-building era. That is why this park opportunity in the back yard of the Capital City is a national inheritance.

It was George Washington who first recognized the significance of this canal route to a nation growing westward and vitally in need of transportation ties. "Nature has declared in favor of the Potomac," he wrote to Thomas Jefferson, "and through that channel offers into our lap the whole commerce of the western world." Washington initiated the first canal company, and although the C&O Canal is of later date (John Quincy Adams turned the first spadeful of earth), it remains as tangible evidence of George Washington's vision.

A trip along the canal route and a glance through the pages of history would reveal how much history is spun into this long transportation thread that winds along the Potomac for 185 miles from Washington to Cumberland, Maryland, and rises by means of 74 locks some 600 feet from tidewater to the Alleghenies. The canal's structures survive today as outstanding examples of early American engineering. The concept and project of a canal along the Potomac valley marked nearly a third of America's history. Indeed, the C&O Canal is history woven among history, for along its route are the sites of Indian towns, French and Indian War forts, Civil War battlefields.

To compound the importance of the C&O Canal, its route is through one of the most scenic and unspoiled valleys in the United States, a valley characterized by wild and natural beauty and features of unusual biological and geological interest. These values positioned near so many people make evident the tremendous potential the canal possesses as a recreation resource. There, close to the homes of millions, is a place not only to study and appreciate history, social and natural, but a place to hike, to camp, to enjoy boating, fishing, bicycling and other forms of outdoor recreation difficult to find today in the crowded East.

Fortunately the core of this park resource is already in public owner-ship. The Chesapeake and Ohio Canal itself together with whatever adjacent property belonged to it, a total of some 5,200 acres, was purchased by the Federal government in 1933. The lower 450 acres of the canal is administered as a part of National Capital Parks, and there the canal has been re-watered and canal structures restored, while the rest—about 4,800 acres—has been designated as a National Monument.

With the canal publicly owned and already given national recognition, it might seem that the C&O park proposal was superfluous, but 4,800 acres stretched over the 165 miles from Great Falls to Cumberland constitutes a park resource so tenuous that it is of little practical value for park use. Adverse developments crowd in on the historic canal structures, destroying the atmosphere which would make them pleasant and interesting to visit. There is little space to camp, to picnic or even to park along this thin ribbon of ground, in places so narrow that only the canal bed and towpath are Federal property, and where scenic and historic values cannot be protected.

The Chesapeake and Ohio Canal National Historical Park legislation, therefore, calls for the acquisition of approximately 10,200 additional acres. Even this is minimal. The addition of this land would boost the average width of the canal property from the present 30 acres per mile to only about 94, which is still substantially less than the 125 acres per mile which Congress in the past has provided for national parkways. But with a total of 15,000 acres a Chesapeake and Ohio National Historical Park can be established that will protect the outstanding historical values and serve the public with a good public use area. Of course, a uniform width for the park is not planned. The additional lands would be purchased in areas where they are needed for protection of park features or development facilities. Thus the park would be wide in some places and narrow in others depending upon circumstances. The legislation now being considered by Congress would grant a five-year period during which actual park boundaries could be worked out. Subsequent development plans would ascertain sections of the canal that could be rewatered, would stabilize and restore canal structures and provide needed outdoor recreation facilities.

The entire Potomac River basin from the broad waters of its estuary to the scenic mountain valleys in its upper reaches, represents an exciting opportunity for conserving major recreation resources. It is a challenging opportunity, of course, fraught with many problems, pollution and water supply among them. The Chesapeake and Ohio National Historical Park proposal represents a first and major step in the conservation and protection of this great valley and all its historical and recreational values for public enjoyment. The Interstate Commission on the Potomac River Basin has pointed out that by the year 2000 some 10 million visitor days are expected to be spent by recreation seekers in the Potomac each year—25 times the number

now. As the *New York Times* pointed out in an editorial on the park proposal, "the Chesapeake and Ohio Canal National Historical Park may well prove to be the Central Park of the eastern seaboard's coming megalopolis."

IN MEMORIAM

Robert W. Ludden, 53, Chief of the Division of Planning and Surveys of the Bureau of Outdoor Recreation, U. S. Department of the Interior, died Sunday, February 24, 1963 at the Washington, D. C. Hospital Center.

Mr. Ludden, a native of Schenectady, N. Y., joined the National Park Service during the early days of the Civilian Conservation Corps in 1935 and worked in several capacities in the recreation and land planning field. As Chief of the Division of Recreation Resource Surveys he directed the National Park Services park, parkway and recreational area study program.

With the establishment of the Bureau of Outdoor Recreation in the spring of 1962 Mr. Ludden was transferred to the position he held at the time of his death. He was responsible for compiling and keeping current a nationwide outdoor recreation plan.

Mr. Ludden leaves his wife, Cornelia Nugent Ludden of Washington, D. C. and his mother, Mrs. Nelson Van Wie of Schenectady, N. Y.

He was a member of the American Planning and Civic Association and the American Institute of Park Executives.

"Milestone in Conservation Progress"

EDITOR'S NOTE:—The following letters are reproduced in their entirety due to their significance in the field of public policy.

THE WHITE HOUSE
WASHINGTON

January 31, 1963

Dear Mr. Secretaries:

I was greatly pleased by your joint letter describing the new conservation policy your Departments are adopting to help implement our outdoor recreation programs. This is an excellent statement of cooperation representing a milestone in conservation progress.

I know that there have been many vexing problems over the years in relationships between the Departments of Agriculture and Interior but your joint statement indicates that these are well on the way to resolution. This achievement in settling major jurisdictional issues between the two Departments, in outlining the principles of cooperation that will guide them in the future, and in proposing joint exploration of the North Cascade Mountains in Washington is most significant—it is clearly in the public.interest.

Sincerely,

(Signed) John F. Kennedy

The Honorable Orville L. Freeman
   The Secretary of Agriculture

The Honorable Stewart L. Udall
   The Secretary of the Interior

January 28, 1963

Dear Mr. President:

We are pleased to advise you that the Department of Agriculture and the Department of the Interior have developed a new conservation policy to help implement the outdoor recreation program of the Administration.

We have reached agreement on a broad range of issues which should enable our Departments to enter into "a new era of cooperation" in the management of Federal lands for outdoor recreation. This agreement settles issues which have long been involved in public controversy, we have closed the book on these disputes and are now ready to harmoniously implement the agreed-upon solutions.

The decisions reached will do much to further development of Federal recreation resources, eliminate costly competition, promote cooperation, and recognize the major role that the Departments of Agriculture and the Interior both have in administering Federal lands under their jurisdiction for recreation purposes. We have agreed upon the following principles of cooperation:

1. Mutual recognition is accorded the distinctive administrative functions and land management plans used by the Forest Service and the National Park Service in administering lands under their jurisdiction.

2. Except for existing Administration proposals, those covered in our agreement, or routine boundary adjustments, jurisdictional responsibility will not be disturbed among the agencies of our two Departments which are managing and developing lands for public recreation.

3. Neither Department will initiate unilaterally new proposals to change the status of lands under jurisdiction of the other Department. Independent studies by one Department of lands administered by the other will not be carried on. Joint studies will be the rule.

4. Likewise, each Department, with the support and cooperation of the other, will endeavor to fully develop and effectively manage the recreation lands now under its administration.

In furtherance of the above principles of cooperation, and in recognition of the growing demand for outdoor recreation, we plan to recommend to you the establishment of two new Federally administered National Recreation Areas. These areas are planned to help meet existing and foreseeable outdoor recreation needs.

The Recreation Advisory Council, established by Executive Order 11017, has been considering the need for National Recreation Areas and criteria for their selection and establishment. We expect that the Recreation Advisory Council will soon recommend to you the creation of a limited system of National Recreation Areas along with criteria to guide their selection and establishment. The proposals for National Recreation Areas contained in this letter have been reviewed

and are concurred in by the other members of the Recreation Advisory Council.

National Recreation Areas would be established only by Act of Congress and would be administered by the Department of the Interior, the Department of Agriculture, or other Federal agencies or departments having responsibility in outdoor recreation as may be recommended by the Executive Branch and determined by the Congress. National Recreation Areas would be administered primarily for recreation but with utilization of other resources permitted, provided such use is not incompatible with and does not unduly interfere with the basic recreation purpose. Advice of the Recreation Advisory Council will be sought with regard to qualification of particular areas, priority for establishment, and jurisdictional responsibility.

National Recreation Areas will be in addition to national parks, national monuments, or other special categories of land administered by the National Park Service, and to the wilderness system or other special categories of land having recreation significance now administered by the Forest Service. In our judgment as well as in the judgment of the other members of the Recreation Advisory Council, these two areas will conform fully with the National Recreation Area criteria, now in the final stages of formulation.

Subsequent to the adoption of these criteria, we shall recommend to you that the Administration submit legislation to establish:

1. Whiskeytown - Shasta - Trin-

5

ity National Recreation Area of about 280,000 acres in north central California. This area will consist of three non-contiguous units, surrounding reclamation reservoirs. The areas around Shasta Lake and the Trinity-Lewiston Reservoirs are within the exterior boundaries of the Shasta-Trinity National Forests. These will be recommended for administration by the Forest Service. The 50,000 acre Whiskeytown unit lying outside the National Forest will be recommended for National Park Service administration.

2. The Flaming Gorge National Recreation Area in Wyoming and Utah. This is an area of about 160,000 acres lying upstream on the Green River from the Bureau of Reclamation dam under construction at Flaming Gorge within the Ashley National Forest in northeastern Utah. The two Departments have agreed that the 40,000 acre area within the National Forest boundary will be administered by the Forest Service, and the larger area of about 120,000 acres lying primarily in Wyoming and outside the National Forest boundary will be administered by the National Park Service.

We have agreed further that:

1. An Oregon Dunes National Seashore should be recommended consisting of about 35,000 acres primarily of sand dunes along the central Oregon coast. This land for the most part has been under the protection and management of the Forest Service. Administration

would be by the National Park Service under the same criteria as for National Recreation Areas.

2. A joint study should be made of Federal lands in the North Cascade Mountains of Washington to determine the management and administration of those lands that will best serve the public interest. These lands for the most part have been under the administration of the Forest Service as National Forests for many years. A study team should explore in an objective manner all the resource potentials of the area and the management and administration that appears to be in the public interest. The study team will consist of representatives of the two Departments and will be chaired by an individual jointly selected by us.

Recommendations of the study group will be submitted to us and we in turn will make our recommendations to you.

We believe these agreements represent a major improvement in National Conservation policy. We earnestly hope you will approve them.

Respectfully yours,
(Signed) Orville L. Freeman
Secretary of Agriculture

(Signed) Stewart L. Udall
Secretary of the Interior

The President
The White House
Washington 25, D. C.

Bulldozers on a Leash

By RUTH RUSCH

It was a beautiful stand of mixed woods that topped a gentle slope among the green-clad foothills of the Hudson Valley. In spring native wildflowers bloomed beside the trails that had been trodden by many feet over the years. Birds nested in the branches overhead, deer hoofprints showed in the soft mud, raccoons made their homes in the hollows of the old trees. In autumn the crimson and bronze of the oaks mingled with the gold of the maples to form a tapestry of color. Many came for rest and relaxation, to wander beneath the trees, to search out birds with binoculars, to catch the brilliance of the fall foliage on color film.

Then one day the bulldozers moved in. It took less than two weeks to fell all the trees, a few more days to uproot the shrubs and seedlings, to shove the remaining patches of moss and ground covers and wildflowers into heaps of crushed and broken things. Where a venerable oak had stood a house went up; the trail became a macadam highway, the patches of ladies' slippers the site of a split-level; the laurel thickets gave way to more homes.

And so it goes, in the green woodlands of New England, the river valleys of the Mississippi Basin, on the sandy shores of Florida and the open plains of the far West. At least a million acres are taken every year in the United States for new homes, highways, industrial plants, schools and other needs of our rapidly expanding population.

The frightening power of motor-driven machines to change the face of the earth is cause for growing alarm and dismay among those who view natural communities of living things as treasures beyond price. A crew with chain saws can fell an acre of virgin timber in a few hours. It takes a man with a tractor a matter of minutes to plow an acre of prairie. In many places there are no remnants of wilderness left to preserve intact for future generations the indigenous species of plants and animals.

In a world where the frantic pressures of urban growth seem to leave scant room for any thought of the countryside's beauty, the occasional exception noted here and there gives rise to the hope that the beginnings of a different trend might be setting in. Breaks in the pattern occur in scattered instances. Surrounded by vistas of monotonous sub-divisions, ribbons of asphalt and the gaudy trappings of roadside commerce, bits of living green stand out in welcome relief.

Springvale-on-the Hudson is one of these.

This planned apartment community for senior citizens in the Town of Cortlandt, New York, has been carefully designed to fit the landscape rather than forcing the contours of the land to conform to an architect's drawings. Rectangular shaped buildings of natural wood siding are grouped about the thirty-five acres of rolling countryside, that is dotted with large old trees, patches of young woods, scenic rock outcroppings and thickets of broad-leaved evergreens. Apartment units have been located to afford residents sweeping panorama views of the Hudson.

Springvale is the realized dream of Mitchell Berenson and Lawrence Schnall who have successfully combined their love of the outdoors with their interest in providing restful country living for older citizens.

Only six per cent of the total acreage is occupied by the buildings. Roads and parking areas have been neatly fitted into a pattern of green that has suffered a minimum of disturbance. In many cases mature shade trees are standing within a few feet of the buildings. An old sassafras was painstakingly spared, its massive trunk only two feet from the wall of an apartment. Great care had to be taken in shingling the building as the workmen were required to dodge around the spreading limbs.

The roads through Springvale wind with true rural flavor, avoiding old oaks and maples, clumps of birches, picturesque rock formations. In one case a retaining wall was built on a wide curve at considerable extra expense, to bypass an old maple. Relics of the days of gracious living on what had been an old estate, have been carefully preserved. These include a water tower, rustic summer houses and a watch tower that looks as though it might have stood guard against Indians.

That portion of the tract which slopes steeply toward the Hudson is heavily wooded and has been left untouched. Where man-made slopes were created in the land clearing operations, nurserymen have been called in to advise on the planting of suitable trees and ground covers. Small tree farms are planned for the open areas to grow replacement trees as old ones die, and to provide protection against soil erosion.

The original estate was liberally planted with dogwoods. Great care was taken to save as many of these as possible. Building foundations were planned to avoid large trees wherever feasible. Smaller ones were picked up in the power shovels and moved to new locations.

Protective stone wells were sunk in the ground around trees close to the edge of the road. Some of these are two feet or more in depth. Where large trees are growing on slopes and give evidence of losing moisture around their roots, drainage holes are drilled, to be filled with crushed stone. Tree surgeons are hired to treat trees scarred by construction work.

A graceful clump of birches was in the way of a parking area. Rather than sacrifice the trees, the planners left them intact and the asphalt encircles them at a safe distance back of their low brick wall.

The result gives the impression of a successful effort to combine modern equipped apartments with the charm of a rural countryside. Windows look out upon shade trees, rhododendron thickets, birches and rock gardens. Rustic farm fences line shrubbery borders. Bird feeders hang from branches of trees and porch railings. Trails lead up the wooded slopes to rustic summer houses and shaded picnic tables.

In Montrose, New York, Thurber's Meadows is an illustration of a subdivision where the bulldozers have been held in check with refreshing results. Newly completed homes with front lawns not yet graded, boast of large shade trees in the back yards and a fringe of shrubbery along the property lines. Residents that move in during the warm weather months can enjoy a picnic in the shade of their own trees on the first day in their new home.

This startling departure from the usual method of wholesale land clearing is due to the efforts of Francis Thurber, home builder and amateur botanist. To Thurber a patch of lobelia or arrowhead is something more than a worthless clump of weeds and before his bulldozers move in, he transplants the less abundant wildflowers to a safe place.

Numerous native plants have been moved by Thurber during his building operations. A few years ago he gave a six acre wooded swamp in Ossining, New York, to the Sawmill River Audubon Society as a memorial to his son, Tommy. The Tommy Thurber Memorial has received many acquisitions of wildflowers and seedlings that have been transplanted from home building areas in the path of the bulldozers.

Of Thurber's Meadows the developer states, "In order to retain some of the rural character of this development, I am trying to preserve as much of the plant growth as possible. To keep the destruction of natural planting to a minimum, I protect all the homes I build with a restrictive clause in the deed which provides that no trees or shrubs growing naturally within fifteen feet of the property lines may be cut down, removed or destroyed for three years without my permission." It has been Thurber's experience that after city dwellers have lived for several months with their trees and shrubs, they become as reluctant as he to cut them down.

To stimulate interest in botany among school age children, Thurber proposed at a public hearing on his development plans, that a narrow strip of swamp along the edge of the entrance road be preserved as a natural area. He pointed out that the species of wet-loving plants already growing there could be added to from time to time by class planting projects. He has offered the deed to the little strip to any local nature study group interested in maintaining it as a nature preserve.

Those communities that do not number careful planners among their developers can achieve these results through the adoption of local ordinances and development procedures which provide for the preservation of natural features and open space in subdivisions.

Some municipalities have incorporated in their site plan regulations a provision which authorizes Planning Boards to require that old trees, groves, picturesque rock outcroppings, brooks and similar natural features of esthetic value, be preserved untouched in new subdivisions. The City of Peekskill, New York, has adopted such regulations.

9

North Castle, New York and Summit, New Jersey have ordinances to prevent the heedless destruction of existing trees in large subdivisions wherever the trees do not interfere with proposed building foundations. The typical approach is to first bulldoze the sites clear of all trees under the mistaken belief that this reduces construction costs. However it has been the experience of Summit that developers soon find the saving in tree removal costs offsets the cost of building on a wooded site.

The Regional Plan Association recommends that all municipalities in the New York Metropolitan Region, especially those in the process of development, enact ordinances prohibiting the cutting of trees over a reasonable minimum thickness, in private subdivisions.

The idea of raising density in one portion of a development in order to have open space set aside in the remainder has been accepted by a growing number of communities. Under provisions in the New York State Town Law, Sec. 281, Village Law Sec. 179-P, the state gives municipalities authority to allow this procedure known as clustering. Local regulations permitting it have been developed in Sloatsburg, East Greenbush, the City of New York, the City of Rye. Examples in other states include Radburn, New Jersey, Chatham Village in Pittsburgh, Baldwin Hills Village in Los Angeles. In Smithtown, New York, 42 per cent of a subdivision was dedicated as a park in exchange for reduction in lot size from one acre to ½ acre.

Efforts on the part of individuals and communities to retain scattered bits of their natural environment for esthetic enjoyment acquire added significance in the light of recent studies of human illnesses. Convincing evidence of the close relationship between health and environment in contained in a report made by Drs. Hinkle and Wolff of Cornell University Medical School in April 1958 to the American College of Physicians. After an analysis of five groups involving more than 3,000 individuals, these doctors concluded that the evidence indicates the reaction of man to his environment plays a significant role in at least ⅓ of all episodes of illness.

"The complexities of modern life involve us all in tensions which, if not relaxed from time to time, can impair our physical health," states Richard H. Pough, President of the Natural Area Council. "In our failure to reserve more open land in our communities, are we not depriving future generations of one of the best ways of countering the tensions of life in what seems likely to be an even more difficult and congested world than the one we live in?"

The fact that there are individuals and communities which have recognized this need and have taken steps to meet it realistically, gives reason to hope that an aroused public opinion in other areas may be able to stimulate appropriate action before it is too late. Success in creating a desirable environment in the sprawling suburban complex will depend on the extent to which the bulldozers are held in check.

Zoning Round Table

Border-line Cases

Decisions in border-line cases may or may not make bad law, but they are often based on reasoning which is unrelated to zoning principles, and they may result in harmful precedents.

In the December 1961 issue two cases were cited which illustrate the difficulties. In both cases zoning amendments were adopted which were challenged in the court by nearby property owners as violations of basic zoning principles and of the mandates of the zoning enabling act. In both the changes were from single family residence zones, in one case to business, and in the other to five story apartment houses. The new multi-family zone was a three acre parcel bordering on an attractive pond. The new business zone occupied sixteen acres and consisted of an extension in depth varying from 1000 to 1200 feet of a business zone partially occupied by retail business. In both cases the vote of the approving legislative bodies was apparently swayed by the expected considerable increase in the town's taxable assets due to a several million dollar apartment house development and an equally costly shopping centre.

In the shopping centre case a superior court judge has decided that the action of the town council was valid. His reasoning is most interesting in showing the fine line of these cases. He might have relied on the doctrine of debatability and said, as other judges have said in many such cases, that the action in setting up a new business zone could not be held unwarranted under all the facts. Instead, he met the claims of spot zoning and breach of the comprehensive plan by a clear cut finding to the contrary. On the spot zoning issue, "This is an extension of an existing business area. Courts have rarely termed an ordinance which does no more than extend an existing commercial area as spot zoning", and "no island can be said to have been created and certainly no small area is involved."

The comprehensive plan issue took a little more explaining. The judge found that the original zoning ordinance "disclosed a plan of limiting business uses to ribbons or strips of 300 feet in depth along arterial highways" but that this plan could be amended. Otherwise zoning would be frozen, and the community would be static. The great depth of the business extension evidently bothered him, but he seized upon the one extension from 300 feet to 600 feet in depth at the only shopping centre in the town as showing that extensions in depth must be considered as proper amendments to the original plan. Otherwise "rigidity would place the Town Council in a legal strait jacket, and would have assured the existing shopping centre a virtual monopoly in its type of business."

"In the opinion of the Court, the original zoning plan seems to indicate a comprehensive intent to develop business enterprises along the main highways of the town *without specific limitation as to depth*."

This conclusion seems unwarranted. The other shopping centre extended not from 1000 to 1200 feet in depth, but 600 feet. It was at the business centre of the town, and had no residences near it. On the contrary it was entirely surrounded by land and buildings in actual commercial use. But above all it was, as the judge admitted, a non-conforming use when the zoning ordinance was adopted. Including its 600 feet in depth in the business zone was a recognition of this non-conformity and an adjustment of the zoning plan to it, rather than a sweeping consent to *any* future extension in depth.

How can the development of the town be considered stable, when as the judge concluded, there is no specific limitation to the depth of extension to business zones?

Decisions in border-line cases are not all made by city councils, town councils, or town meetings. Applications for variances present often the same difficulties, and these must be decided usually by the Board of Appeal. The issue is whether the facts make out a case of substantial hardship peculiar to the land of the applicant. A vital difference from a change in zone in the variance situation is the outspoken opposition of the highest state courts to the grant of variances.

An interesting application was recently before the Board of Appeal in a Massachusetts town. The purchaser of church property consisting of three-fourths of an acre of land on which were a chapel and a rectory, petitioned for a variance which would allow him to make over the chapel into a residence. This section of the town was zoned for single family residence on lots of at least one acre. The petition was opposed on the ground that there was no peculiar hardship which would justify the variance which would result in two houses on less than an acre.

Petitioner's attorney pointed out that the one acre restriction made any profitable, or even any practical use of the chapel impossible, that properties on one side were nonconforming homes occupying less than an acre of land, and that the neighborhood would be improved by the plan for another residence. The property was bounded on two sides by open land or woodland.

For the opposition the fact that the chapel was marketable and movable was urged against the hardship claim. Petitioner might make more profit out of a renovation, but he could sell "as is", and in fact an offer had been made for the building. Conceding that the neighborhood would not be harmed by another house on the lot, substantial and peculiar hardship was denied. In this contention the Board of Appeals agreed, feeling it unwise to establish a precedent which might affect the integrity of the one acre residential zoning. Another Board of Appeals might have come to a different conclusion, and the neighbors might have been advised not to appeal.

Clearly the adoption of a zoning ordinance is hardly more than one good step toward orderly development. Unwise zoning changes and liberal variance grants can wreck a sound ordinance.

Financing National Forest Recreation

By KEITH A. ARGOW

EDITOR'S NOTE:—The author is Research Forester, Branch of Forest Recreation Re_search, Forest Service, U. S. Department of Agriculture, Washington 25, D. C.

The renewable resources of the National Forests and National Grasslands are managed to provide water, timber, recreation, forage, and fish and wildlife. Their management is financed by appropriations and under special Congressional authorizations. The Federal budget, submitted by the President to Congress each year, includes funds for the various activities involved in the development and management of these multiple resources.

Following the close of World War II, the early stages of the boom in outdoor recreation and the need for expanded National Forest recreation facilities became apparent. At that time, several members of Congress and other groups proposed that Forest Service funds for recreation be increased. When their efforts to secure more appropriations proved unsuccessful, a long series of attempts to provide funds by special legislation were to follow.

Between 1949 and 1959, 42 bills to finance recreational development and operations on the National Forests were introduced. None of these passed either the House or Senate. A review of the proposed laws may be timely, as Congress and many State legislatures are now seeking additional income to finance recreation projects.

The 42 bills fall generally into three classes: (1) making available a percentage of National Forest receipts for recreation, (2) selling recreation use licenses, and (3) receiving contributions from public and private sources. Most of the bills were introduced between 1953 and 1957 in the 83rd, 84th, and 85th Congresses.

Congress:	House	Senate
81	1	1
82	2	1
83	7	3
84	13	3
85	9	0
86	2	0
Total	34	8

The first of the recreation financing bills was H.R. 2419 introduced in 1949 by Congressman Tackett of Arkansas. It proposed that 10 per cent of all National Forest receipts (from timber sales, grazing fees, etc.) be made available to the Secretary of Agriculture for development, maintenance, and operation of National Forest recreational resources and areas, including wildlife resources. The bill was referred to the House Committee on Agriculture for study and recommendation. At the Committee's hearings, considerable support was expressed by wildlife and conservation organizations who noted the proposed legislation was similar in concept to the present law authorizing the expenditure of 10 per cent of National Forest receipts for roads and trails within the National Forests. A report of the House Agriculture Committee also recommended that part of the receipts from the National Forests be set aside for improvement and operation of recreation facilities. Official testimony by representatives of the Department of Agriculture was in sympathy with the intent of the legislation, but pointed out the Bureau of the Budget opinion that financing recreation development by earmarking receipts was not sound budgetary procedure. The Agriculture Committee, however, reported the bill favorably to the House, but there it was passed over without prejudice and not voted upon. This was the farthest any of the 42 bills went toward becoming law.

After H. R. 2419 and its companion Senate Bill, S. 2409, failed in the 81st Congress, similar measures with minor modifications were introduced in both houses of the 82nd Congress (1951–1952). Considerable support was again voiced by witnesses representing a range of interests, and the Bureau of the Budget reaffirmed its opinion that earmarking of receipts was not sound budgetary procedure. Neither bill was reported favorably out of committee.

Succeeding Congresses saw 29 more bills introduced that would, if passed, have made available a percentage of receipts for expenditure on National Forest recreation facilities. Two of these increased the amount to be earmarked, and one dropped it to 5 per cent. Most of the later bills kept more authority in Congress than earlier proposals had by specifying that none of the funds could be expended until appropriated each year. One proposed giving the counties an increased share of National Forest receipts

to be expended by county officials for recreation purposes on National Forest lands. This would have been in addition to the 25 per cent share of receipts that the counties now get for public schools and roads.

The last proposal to make available a percentage of receipts was introduced early in the 86th Congress (January 1959). Like many of its predecessors, no hearings were held and the bill died in committee.

Between 1952 and 1955, five bills which would require National Forest recreationists to purchase "use" licenses were introduced. The first of this type, H.R. 7000, provided for the purchase of an annual license for the use of National Forest lands and facilities for such purposes as camping, picnicking, swimming, skiing, hunting and fishing. At the time this bill was introduced (early in the 82nd Congress), it was considered in hearings along with one similar to H.R. 2419 (the Tackett bill). The idea of recreation use licenses failed to generate much support. At the time, proposals to use a part of National Forest receipts for recreation were popular. The bill was not reported out of the House Committee on Agriculture.

Later, shortly after the 83rd Congress convened in 1953, a second user fee bill was introduced. This one provided for the issuance of an annual National Forest campfire permit at $1 per year. Although essentially a rewrite of H.R. 7000 with the word "campfire permit" substituted for "Recreation use license," it was carefully reviewed for its merits. Testimony presented to the Committee indicated that it might not be advisable to incor-

14

porate the revenue provisions of this bill with the already established free fire permit system, the primary purpose of which was fire prevention. Neither this bill nor later proposals for charge campfire permits or recreation use licenses was reported out of committee.

Bills of the third group of proposals for financing National Forest recreation were first introduced in the 84th Congress (1955–1956) and again in two succeeding Congresses. If passed, they would have authorized the Secretary of Agriculture to enter into cooperative agreements with public and private parties in order to encourage them to contribute to the development of recreation facilities on the National Forests. None of the bills in this group was reported out of committee, because such authority already existed. Agreements of this type between the Forest Service and local governments had been in effect for a number of years at certain heavily used National Forest recreation areas.

By January 1957, 39 special bills aimed at financing National Forest recreation facilities and operations, plus 15 similar proposals relating to lands under the Bureau of Land Management, had been referred to House and Senate Committees. Only one, the Tackett bill in 1949, was favorably reported. In 1957, however, the Congress approved a program for accelerated development of recreation facilities on the National Forests. This was called "Operation Outdoors." When it

became apparent that more adequate funds were to be available through appropriations, interest in specific legislation dropped off quickly. Only three more bills, each identical to earlier proposals, were introduced.

This was the last of special fiscal legislative proposals for recreation until April 1962, when seven bills were introduced in the 2nd session of the 87th Congress to establish a Land Conservation Fund. Each of these would permit a total Treasury advance appropriation of $500 million over an 8-year period to the Departments of the Interior and Agriculture for the acquisition of land or interests therein for public outdoor recreation and other conservation uses within National Forests, Parks, Wildlife Refuges, and other Federal areas. Such funds were to be repaid with anticipated recreation user fees, proceeds from the sale of surplus nonmilitary Federal real property, a tax on recreation boats 14 feet or longer, and proceeds from refundable taxes paid on special motor fuels or gasoline used in motorboats. Hearings were held in both Senate and House Interior Committees, but none of the bills was reported prior to the adjournment of the 87th Congress.

The Bureau of Outdoor Recreation in the Department of Interior has started studies of alternative sources of revenues for recreation. Bills to establish a Land and Water Conservation Fund have been introduced in the 88th Congress, S. 859 and HR. 3846.

Connecticut Conservation Conference
"Priorities In Open Space"

EDITOR'S NOTE:—The following item is from "Connecticut Woodlands" and states the theme of the 13th Annual Connecticut Conservation Conference. A very worthy purpose indeed.

Must we allow our urban wealth to destroy the wealth of our natural heritage? This is the clear issue that must be faced up to in the next few years. The present growth rate of urbanization is known and the limit of our land resources is recognized. If we are to preserve any part of our natural environment, action must come now.

In order to attempt to salvage vital land areas from the flood of urbanism, an open space program for the State of Connecticut has been proposed. This program recognizes that undeveloped areas play as important a part in the life of our communities as do the streets, sidewalks and parking lots. The program proposes to make State funds available for both State and local purchase of land to be kept in open space.

Recognizing the limitations of funds available for any land purchasing program and the necessity of adequately meeting the demands of urban expansion, the Natural Resources Council will explore the subject of "Priorities in Open Space" at its annual meeting on December 10, 1962 at the Waverly Inn in Cheshire. Well known experts will discuss the value, the need, and the danger of loss of various kinds of open space under four panel headings: Open Space in Salt Marshes and Other Wetlands; Open Space for Soil, Forest and Water Management; Open Space for Outdoor Recreation; and Open Space in Metropolitan Areas. A fifth panel, Open Space and Your Taxes, will discuss the relationship between open space programs and individual taxes and municipal tax structures.

Leaders of the Natural Resources Council point out that "Priorities in Open Space" is one phase of a broad topic. At the last annual meeting of the Council, open space was discussed in its broad implications and last March Attorney Shirley Adelson Siegle addressed the Connecticut Federation of Planning and Zoning Agencies as to various methods of preserving open space. Undoubtedly, other conferences on open space will be forthcoming but the Natural Resources Council feels that it is most appropriate for the Council, with its broad representation of natural resource interests, to thoroughly explore the subject of what land should appropriately be saved in open space and for what purpose. "Somewhere along the line," a spokesman for the Council stated, "there is going to have to be a decision on what land should be given priority. We need to keep land in open space for its benefit to wildlife, for the protection of watersheds, for outdoor recreation and a multitude of other purposes. Problems in some of these areas are acute and must be acted on immediately; in others we must be able to recognize the needs of the future."

Effect of Taxation on Character and Type of Urban Land Use

EDITOR's NOTE:—Reprinted from URBAN LAND.

Wealthy estate communities and industrial suburbs generally enjoy distinct tax advantages, while World War II housing projects and densely-settled, blighted cities are in the poorest tax position, according to the recently published research monograph of Urban Land Institute titled "Changing Urban Land Uses as Affected by Taxation."

According to the monograph, edited by Dr. Jerome P. Pickard, research director of ULI, America's best residential "tax havens" are above average communities with recent industrialization or with stable populations and good management. This is particularly true in counties fragmented into many small political units. One reason for this is that the favored localities are not burdened with disproportionately heavy public service costs.

These findings are based on a series of ULI-sponsored study conferences to examine the impacts of taxation on new urban development, maintenance of existing city properties, and redevelopment of deteriorated urban areas. The monograph summarizes conference discussions held in Washington, D. C., covering the national picture, and in Boston, Newark and Pittsburgh.

Dr. Pickard's monograph points out that one "great paradox" of the current property tax system is the discouraging effect it can have on the improvement of land and buildings in blighted areas. Frequently when a major improvement is made in an old building the assessment goes up. Thus the local property tax often puts a premium on neglect and discourages investment.

The ULI publication notes that Boston, having the highest property tax level of any major American city, has been forced to make tax arrangements to attract new commercial and industrial construction. Observing that Boston's downtown had "unusual stagnation" in building, it was pointed out that, without new buildings, present tax rates would be under continuing pressure to increase. Tax exempt property had grown to 39 per cent of the city's tax base in 1959.

Over-assessment of commercial and industrial property within city limits was found to be widespread while residences were under-assessed. The reverse is frequently true in the suburbs. The problems of the central business district are additionally aggravated because property values have dropped faster than tax assessments, the ULI tax-land use study points out.

The conferees agreed that Federal taxes, investment return, and local property taxes, all affect both the quality and character of land use. Tax "angles," principally concerning Federal levies, are often the determining factor in deciding whether or not a specific project should be undertaken and by what type of investor.

(Continued on p. 22)

Impressions of Foreign Suburbia

By BROCK DIXON

EDITOR'S NOTE:—The author is Assistant Dean of Faculty at Portland State College, Portland, Oregon.

When one is thrust into a foreign culture, it is normal enough to attempt reorientation by reference to one's own field of knowledge as observed or practiced in the foreign land. So it was that I, an admitted if not acknowledged expert in local government especially in its problems at the edge of rapidly growing cities, found myself wandering through the suburbs of Guadalajara within hours of my arrival in that lovely city. Naturally I formed many impressions rapidly and shared them eagerly with such English-speaking people as could be persuaded to listen.

Weeks later as my circle of acquaintances grew and my knowledge of Spanish expanded to the point where I could ask an intelligent question even though I might not understand the answer, some of the preliminary observations had to be revised. It seems to me that the nature and extent of my errors is worth recording—partly because of relevance to the common and important contemporary "problem of suburbia" and partly because we need to become more conscious of the limitations of our "experts" when they suddenly cross a culture barrier. Come with me if you will, and share a few of those first impressions, modify them with me as new observations demand, and finally, follow me to some quite unforeseen conclusions. It will take only a few minutes and it will not

so satiate you with the pleasures of Mexico that you cannot enjoy a visit of your own in some happy future.

Guadalajara, famous in tourist lore for mariachis and jacarandas, is truly a delightful city. The crust of wealth and culture over the pie of poverty and ignorance is thick enough so that one can ignore as much of the pie as comfort demands and conscience allows. My own interest in the suburbs led me inevitably away from degradation and toward a standard of living to which I'd like to become accustomed; for the suburbs of Guadalajara—excluding of course some old towns which the city has grown out to meet—embrace no semi-rural slums or shacktowns.

There is a general appearance of very tight zoning and planning. A developing sub-division may typically look something like this: Wide streets are completely paved and curbed. Sidewalks and sewerage are provided. The streets are lit brilliantly by lights of the most modern design. Trees are planted along the curbs and some of the trees are fifteen to twenty feet tall. The continuity of streets is broken from time to time by traffic circles— "glorietas," they say in Mexico— and the standard planning technique of curving residential streets is observed. The glorietas commonly contain beautiful fountains, some with colored lights, and each sub-

18

division has its own little park or parks. The total effect is so appealing that one is tempted to stop at the tract office and talk to a salesman.

The temptation is, of course, a function not only of obvious good planning but also of the residences which have already been built. In some older areas perhaps ninety-five per cent of the lots are in use, but the average is so much lower that probably 80 per cent vacant lots is not uncommon. And such houses! The architecture is almost universally modernistic, whatever that means. Structure is just as commonly of solid brick covered with plaster inside and out. Dramatic use of concrete, steel, glass, and tile is seen in every block. A very small suburban residence will contain 2,000 square feet, and a solid brick and plaster wall will surround the whole lot even if it is a full block square. Most lots will be narrow and deep, and the finished house quite often fills the entire gap from one side wall to the other. When the vacant lots are filled, a neighbor's house may touch one's own. A horse-back appraisal would value these places if located in the U.S.A. at $17,000 to $50,000 or more. More would fall in the upper part of that spectrum than in the lower.

This, then, is the first impression. These people have been phenomenally successful in sub-division control. They provide a full complement of urban services to the first house-holder who settles in the area. Here is a situation a growing Norte American city might envy and emulate.

And then came the second thoughts and the later observation. The local *Municipal Gazette* publishes the budget and one is shocked to note that the salary of the fire chief in a city of over 700,000 is only a little more than the rent paid by a visiting professor on sabbatical. The mayor would have to pay one-quarter of his salary for a pleasant little one-bedroom apartment in one of the newer sections of the city. Who lives in these beautiful suburbs if such people, assuming dependence on salary and that is assuming too much, cannot? Let us look at a few possible residents. A friend tells me that you can put a first-rate young physician on your payroll for a year for less than the U.S.A. price of a new Chevrolet. We price a very modest suburban dwelling on a small lot. It comes to about $10,000 U. S. or in Guadalajara roughly 4,160 days of wages for a union-scale brick mason, 125 months of the fire chief's salary, or over 3½ years' salary in the case of a resident civil engineer in charge of one major sub-division. In most sub-divisions lots starting at $4,000 and $6,000 are not uncommon. Two thousand square feet of housing (which will cost about $4.50 per square foot) is a bare minimum and, as a guess, most suburban dwellings must represent a cost in excess of $15,000 exclusive of land. The middle class as I have known it doesn't live in these suburbs. Civil servants, school teachers, skilled production men, small entrepreneurs, young physicians, and young lawyers are all excluded by the iron law of economic reality.

Then a few details hitherto unnoticed begin to obtrude. I have

19

mentioned my first impression of zoning. Between two houses which would cost $30,000 each in the states I see a carpenter shop featuring methods not unlike those of a certain carpenter shop in Nazareth twenty centuries ago. "Prior use," I explain to my wife. In a very classy neighborhood there seem to be more corner groceries than the market requires, and I wonder about the wisdom of the planners or councilman in allowing so many deviations from the zone pattern of single family dwellings. Early one morning I am awakened and surprised by the sound of roosters crowing and on my morning walk I discover a chicken ranch of some size surrounded by homes of considerable luxury. It is reasonably clear from appearances that this is not an old chicken ranch, and my glib explanation of zone deviation with the phrase "prior use" falls flat on its face.

At a little party one evening, there is considerable talk about a prominent physician who has been jailed for some illegal operations—in real estate, not bodies. He and his associates have developed one of the city's finest new residential areas, but the cost of putting in all the services that are required by law before lots can be sold has pushed him to the wall financially. Now it becomes clear that the complete set of public services which we have noted in the suburbs is the responsibility of the development company or sub-divider and not of local government. I remember the area in question with hundreds of acres of prime residential land, vacant except for a few homes of great distinction. It is especially impressive at night with fine-looking street lights flooding the vacant landscape. The law requires the sub-divider to keep the area lit, we are told later. Well, it seems that our doctor has been so pressed for pesos that he has sold a few lots which were originally dedicated to some public use, schools or parks or something. Even this person of prominence has been unable, it would seem, to "fix the rap." I remember the salaries paid to public officials and wonder how any decision or sentence could be insulated from the power of money.

A certain misplaced sympathy for the person in jail leads to a consideration of the plight of the sub-divider forced to make such huge investments and wait so long for a return. I think of the happy sub-dividers in the states who have to deal primarily with regulation and who can depend on government to provide many of the basic services which urban living requires. If the control of the city becomes onerous, the carefree sub-divider can frequently escape the heavy hand of control by moving his operations outside the city limits, incidentally forcing the creation of numerous and overlapping special purpose districts as the new residents develop needs for urban services. Why don't these people in Guadalajara simply sub-divide farther out?

A trip to the airport, 8 or 10 miles from downtown, gives no answer. I see a "finished" suburb way out there—a few houses, many acres, all improvements.

The language barrier is frustrating. There are so many questions.

That usually false prophecy, "Wherever you go you'll find people who speak English," is almost always false if one means "speak English and talk intelligently about specialized problems and concerns." One's compatriots in exile are efficient at recommending restaurants and places to shop but only a few of them have learned anything important about the country they live in.

A bright young man at the U.S. consulate proves to be most helpful and some other informants, both Mexican and Norte-American, aid in filling out the picture. According to them, and I have some considerable confidence in their judgment even though experience and mistakes have chastened me, the observation of good zoning is largely illusory. This was my primary observation. The apparent zoning is a fact of economics, not an evidence of strong and effective codes. It is even alleged that land use control codes are all planned to favor the individual owner's decision to use his land as he sees fit. The law, it is said, desires to protect him from oppression on the theory, perhaps, that individual right rather than community right must be the basic doctrine, since individual rights must be afforded timely protection and early protection or their protection will not be a fact at all. Everyone knows that "the little man" is unlikely to win in a long series of court battles with powerful adversaries. "So," say my informants, "don't be surprised to see an occasional carpenter shop or chicken ranch or corner grocery in a plush neighborhood."

Under normal circumstances the high cost of land keeps people from using these properties for objectionable purposes unless of course the objectionable purpose is notably profitable. A night club next to a fine new residence is a case in point. One can speculate, however, that the custom of building high walls around one's property makes a next door night club relatively more tolerable than at home

The high cost of land is partly attributable, it would appear, to general scarcity and thus generally high prices. And then there is the cost of money to consider. Land purchases are normally amortized over a six-year period at 10 per cent interest. Furthermore, it should be remembered that Mexico is a land-conscious country, partly because other forms of investment have been both scarce and risky. Thus the last decade shows a tremendous inflation in land values. One study reports a 1700 per cent increase in the value of urban land in Mexico City between 1947 and 1957. More important, however, is the cost of public services, streets, sewerage, lights, etc., which must be complete before lot sales begin. It is clear that there is no escape in going outside city limits either. This power of sub-division control is a power of state and nation, not city, and it goes out into the hinterland. The artificial and trouble making concept of "city limits" is not for Mexicans, who conceptualize and legislate for the whole "urban area."

I had thought about the natural artistry of the people, so beautifully exemplified in the simple things of life, bowls and fabric and bottles. I thought of an almost instinctive love of beauty reflected in a pure and childlike pleasure in cool, clean, colorful, well-proportioned fountains. However, my friend at the consulate loaned me some Mexican government planning documents and pamphlets wherein I learned (1) that the fountains are almost all relatively new, (2) that Guadalajara has had a water supply adequate for its needs for only a few years, (3) that as recently as 1953 some sectors of the city were supplied by venders selling small quantities from tin cans attached to a burro's pack saddle; and (4) that the fountains are a functioning part of the recirculation and aerating system. I insist, however, that they are nonetheless things of

beauty and that the people do take an obvious pleasure in them.

The suburbs, likewise, are no less delightful because of a few little misapprehensions. Whether for economic or other reasons, the effect of good zoning is maintained. The planning and architecture catch the eye and one applauds. Of course, it's no great feat to bring good planning, good design, and pleasant living conditions to the wealthy in New York City, Pierre, South Dakota, or Oakland, California. My fundamental error in Guadalajara was, I suppose, an initial failure to think of the suburbs as one-class suburbs and extremely high-class suburbs at that. I had been used to messier suburbs which catered to a broader clientele.

EFFECT OF TAXATION ON CHARACTER AND TYPE OF URBAN LAND USE

(Continued from p. 17)

A wide range of opinion was expressed regarding the desirability of coordinating and using taxes to attain planning objectives, comments Dr. Pickard. The Institute calls for a better understanding of tax-land use relationships. The ULI Conference study conducted over the past two years, is the first published report in its program to obtain this objective. The monograph brings together material on both taxation and urban land use in order to examine their interrelationships.

Property taxation in urban and metropolitan counties is highest in the Massachusetts-Connecticut-New

York-New Jersey area; the Upper Midwest extending from Wisconsin to Montana and south through Nebraska; and in California and Arizona. A large low property tax region extends from Pennsylvania through the entire South with the exception of Texas.

Copies of Research Monograph Six, "Changing Urban Land Uses as Affected by Taxation," are available on order from Urban Land Institute, 1200 18th Street, N. W., Washington 6, D. C. The monograph carries a special price of $2.00 to ULI members and libraries; otherwise copies are $4.00.

Big Cypress tree, 14 ft. in diameter. Estimated to be 1500 years old. Near Austin, Texas on a tributary of the Colorado River.

Columbus Dispatch Photo

According to the **National Capital Downtown Committee**, response to its proposal for a National Visitor and Student Center has been uniformly favorable from members of the Congress, other public officials and private citizens in Washington. Good reactions are also reported from other parts of the country. Legislation will be required to establish the Center, the avowed purpose of which would be to help provide Washington's annual millions of visitors with "an enriching understanding of our American heritage." The Downtown Committee states that descriptive brochures are available in reasonable quantities for distribution to individuals and to organizations.

As we go to press, the **House District Committee** has not yet taken positive action on S. 628, the Senate-passed bill to permit the use of urban renewal in Downtown Washington.

In an unequivocal note in the November issue of *Architectural Forum*, **Douglas Haskell**, Editor, offers some salient ideas about Art Commissions:

"Nobody is to be congratulated on being named to one. The most that can happen is that the city itself can be congratulated on those who are appointed to art commissions. Their job is thankless and in a sense always too late. Art commissions, if good, are composed of those who could have done better on most of what comes before them if they had designed it in the first place, but they have not much chance to initiate. All they have a chance to do, usually, is to review and suggest improvements, if not to disapprove altogether."

Those sharing Mr. Haskell's misgivings are alert to practical suggestions for preventing efforts of such groups from becoming abortive. Already, a practical way by which the work of the National Capital's **Commission of Fine Arts** can become more meaningful has been proposed by the **Committee of 100 on the Federal Cit**y and was reported in the September issue of *Planning and Civic Comment*. Now, from Mr. Haskell comes another practical suggestion for Art Commissions in general:

"The idea does occur that an alert art commission might well propose quite a few city beautification ideas and thereby gain the right to nominate the architects to make more specific proposals. Thus a commission unable to initiate designs itself could get good directions initiated."

The **Committee of 100 on the Federal Cit**y recently expressed strong support for S. 1920, a bill authorizing construction of an Annex to the Library of Congress on a government-owned site just south of the present Library. In so doing, the Committee's **Chairman, Rear Admiral Neill Phillips, USN (Ret.)**, urged that the "tendency to extravagant outlay for monolithic memorials" be checked and that something be done to bring "order and plan into Federal construction on Capitol Hill."

In Perspective

Uprooted from the mountains and the plains and scurrying from the villages, we—millions of us—are drawn, as if by magnet, to the greatest cities the world has ever known.

Once here, we boast of possessions literally beyond the dreams of kings of yesteryear. Yet, caught up in the vastness of the modern city, all too few of us sustain the compelling pressures of city life well enough to ask if *these* are the things we really want.

Why *are* we here?

What *do* we seek?

The chances of coping with the pressing mass problems of the American city today are intricately bound with these simple, basic questions—and, unless each of us, as individuals, answers them with a fair degree of certainty, the best of planners could well plan in vain.

Why are we here?

We, who were yesterday's miners, have watched the mines close down. Who once were farmers, with our hands deep in the good loam of the earth, know that the machine does well the work of the man formerly behind the plow. Whose fathers were foresters, have knowledge of the stepped-up yield of the power saw and the meaning of the diesel engine at the front of the log train.

Our motive for coming to the city? The most compelling in the world—to earn our daily bread—quite often in the city's expanding construction projects. It's a motive over-riding the deep-down desire of a man to live in any location he wishes—whether or not it be close to the earth.

Those, who aspire to plan for the future, need to take note of these men—for the stern hand of necessity has forced them to stake out claims in a *milieu* totally unfamiliar to them. Deeply uncertain, in many cases, they are still feeling for the groove of city life and finding it a little spongy.

These are the men who find the jar and tedium of traffic snarls even more irksome than others, who find the "fenced in" feel of city life constricting, who do not understand the green of a quiet, spacious park as an "amenity" but have literally been accustomed to something very much like it as a way of life. Though here, they have not, as yet, set down unyielding roots in the metropolitan community.

Others of us have come to the city willfully seeking the advantages and opportunities the city has traditionally offered. The atmosphere of our time has fostered it. The vast movements of our people, both in and out of the Armed Services during World War II and the Korean War—the most extensive mass movements in history—gave untold numbers of us a persistent taste for that exciting something just across the horizon. Anyone within earshot of G. I. Joe during the fiery days of trial remembers his sustaining dreams for the "future" which is now the present. In many cases, he, with numerous others, is here today—seeking.

Seeking economic opportunity,

C and O Canal, Between Great Falls and Chain Bridge.

Restored Lock on C and O Canal.

Photos by Abbie Rowe
Courtesy National Park Service, U. S. Department of the Interior

The Indiana Dunes—Birthplace of Ecology

EDITOR'S NOTE:—This article is presented in the hope that it will stimulate conservationists everywhere to urge all-out efforts to preserve the Indiana Dunes area. It was prepared by the National Park Service at our request.

Poet Carl Sandburg has said of the Indiana Dunes: "The Dunes are to the Midwest what the Grand Canyon is to Arizona and Yosemite is to California. They constitute a signature of time and eternity: Once lost the loss would be irrevocable."

The Great Lakes Shoreline Survey, conducted by the National Park Service in 1957–58, also recognized the Indiana Dunes as one of the important remaining undeveloped shoreline areas on the Great Lakes. Earlier, in 1916, Stephen Mather, the first Director of the National Park Service, recommended establishment of an Indiana Dunes National Park. At that time, the site under consideration contained a 25-mile strip of tree-covered dunes and wildlife marshes. Steve Mather, then, believed that 9,000 to 13,000 acres of dune lands could be secured for around $200 per acre.

Recently, an offer of well over $100,000 for 10 acres of dunes was turned down near Chesterton, Indiana. In haste, it should be mentioned, that the owners founded the "Save the Dunes Council" and did not want to sell to industrial interests. "How much are you willing to sacrifice for the Dunes?" was the headline of the article in the *Chicago Sun-Times* of November 2, 1962, telling of the rejection of the offer. The owners of this property prefer to give or sell at a moderate price their dunes to the Government in the event that proposed legislation to make the region a national lakeshore is passed by the 88th Congress.

OUTDOOR RECREATION FOR AMERICA, the report of the Outdoor Recreation Resources Review Commission to the President and to the Congress, further highlights the great necessity for recreation areas, such as the proposed Indiana Dunes National Lakeshore.

The report emphasizes the pressing need for acquiring additional public shoreline areas and advises that the "highest priority should be given to acquisition of areas located closest to population centers and other areas that are immediately threatened. The need is critical—opportunity to place these areas in public ownership is fading each year as other users encroach."

The proposed Indiana Dunes National Lakeshore suits to a shoreline this description of an area in need of preserving for the 9.5 million people living within a 100-mile radius. The Dunes, besides being a botanist's paradise, are only 40 miles from the center of Chicago—an hour's travel by train or car.

The Dunes are the best available recreational space for the millions of people who live in the industrial and metropolitan complex which stretches across three State lines from Gary, Indiana to Milwaukee, Wisconsin. This is the third most populous metropolitan area in the country. The need for outdoor recreational facilities is particularly acute for the residents of southern Cook County, Illinois and Lake County, Indiana. About one-fifth of Indiana's citizens live within 50 miles of this shoreline.

The proposed Indiana Dunes National Lakeshore, as described in S. 650 and H.R. 3344 would be located on the undeveloped Lake Michigan shoreline in Porter County, Indiana. The proposed lakeshore encompasses 5½ miles of shoreline backed up by some 9,000 acres of beach, dunes, woodland and marshes.

The Indiana Dunes area, without question, is one of the most famous dune areas in this Nation. In 1913, a group of scientists representing several European nations named the Dunes area as one of the four most interesting spots in America, as far as nature studies are concerned.

Botanists and biologists consider the Indiana Dunes area as an outstanding scientific laboratory. Serious biological researches in this area were already in full swing by the 1890's. The science of plant ecology —the relationship between organisms, and between them and their environment—was founded on studies made at the dunes by Professor Henry Chandler Cowles, University of Chicago botanist. The Cowles Bog, owned by the SAVE THE DUNES COUNCIL, INC., is one of the outstanding natural features here. In all, over 1,000 different flowering plants and ferns may be found in the Dunes, including 75 kinds of trees and 26 members of the orchid family. In this diversified area more than 100 species of birds have been found nesting and 30 or so different kinds of land mam-

mals live here. These natural features, in short, make the Indiana Dunes unusually high in both scenic and scientific interest.

Over 60 years ago Professor Cowles wrote that "the dunes of Lake Michigan are much the grandest in the entire world" with "contrasting types of plant life . . . from bare dunes to magnificent primeval forests."

Secretary of the Interior Stewart L. Udall has written of the dunes: "Preservation of these remaining natural features is important not only because of their great scientific value and interest but because of the vital need for additional recreation space to serve the densely-populated Chicago and Northern Indiana metropolitan area. The area contains a combination of lakefront, dunes and hinterland that is ideally suited to meet some of the recreational and open space needs for the people of this region. Moreover, its scenic and scientific features would attract people from all over the Country."

The Dunes are ideally suited for outdoor recreation. Nowhere on the Great Lakes are factors more favorable aligned for combined recreational use of the water, waterfront and the hinterland. Here the water is warm enough for pleasant swimming; the wide, clean beach provides ideal conditions for the sunbather and the beachcomber; and the combination of wooded dunes and sheltered marshes afford ample opportunity for scenic solitude, nature study and appreciation of outdoor living. Other recreation activities enjoyed in the Dunes area include hiking, picnicking, camping,

28

horseback riding, photography, painting, boating and fishing. Skiing and tobogganing are also enjoyed in the winter. Millions of people have visited the area and recreation use at Indiana Dunes State Park (largely acquired by voluntary contributions—many from Illinois residents) is already high and often excessive.

The broad beach contains clean, white, fine sand and varies from 100 to 300 feet in width. Behind the beach lies a zone of exceptional sand dunes reaching back a mile from the shoreline and rising to heights of 200 feet in a series of "blowouts," ridges and valleys, simulating miniature mountain ranges. "Blowouts", or moving dunes, are fairly common, and occur when dunes subjected to prevailing winds lose their scant vegetative cover. The forest cover consists principally of open oak stands, but such northern species as white and jack pine, tamarack and white cedar are found in the area. There are also a number of marshes, bogs and swamps with their related flora and fauna.

Another significant aspect of this area concerns its geologic history. Following the recessions of the last Wisconsin ice lobes, barrier dunes were built by wave action parallel to the shoreline of the receding edge of glacial Lake Chicago. When the waters of Lake Chicago fell to the level of present-day Lake Michigan, and the waterline became stable, the main series of wind-built dunes were formed. These are much higher than the older barrier dunes and are characterized by their jumbled topography.

Here natural forces and a steadily receding shoreline had conspired during the 12,000 years since the melting of the continental glaciers, to set up a gigantic, controlled experiment, unique in the world. One could reconstruct the history of this plant succession because the whole series of dunes could be roughly dated. The dune ridge forming on the beach today is young; the ridge farthest inland is oldest. To traverse an ideal cross section from the beach inland would be to pass from the sand-binding grasses and cottonwoods of the foredune, through pine dunes, then oak dunes, finally into rich, moist forest—its foot-thick soil testifying to 10,000 years of plant decay.

The area's recreational, scenic and scientific importance is apparent. It appears that the remaining segments of relatively undisturbed beaches, dunes and marshes offer a remarkable opportunity to combine the two major purposes of preserving the outstanding natural features of this area and, at the same time, provide for desirable recreation use. The need is great for both the preservation of the scenic and scientific assets of the Dunes area and the provision of additional recreational space within a few miles of this large metropolitan region.

Conservationists believe that the Indiana Dunes area is of national significance, and should be preserved in Federal ownership for the benefit and enjoyment of all Americans.

We recognize that there are conflicting views concerning the highest

(Continued on p. 33)

29

Strictly Personal

Smith Appointed Chief Engineer for National Park Service Eastern Design and Construction Office

The appointment of H. Reese Smith as chief engineer for the National Park Service's Eastern Office, Design and Construction, has been announced by the Department of the Interior. Smith, who has been superintendent of Cape Hatteras National Seashore, North Carolina, since early last year, will enter on duty in Philadelphia in February.

A civil engineer by profession, he joined the National Park Service in 1932, and served successively as park ranger, assistant chief park ranger, and civil engineer at Colonial National Historical Park, Yorktown, Virginia.

In 1938, he transferred to the Natchez Trace Parkway, Mississippi-Alabama-Tennessee, to serve as assistant superintendent and later as parkway engineer in charge of maintenance and operation of all physical improvements on the parkway.

He was promoted to assistant superintendent of Great Smoky Mountains National Park, Tennessee-North Carolina, in 1954 and in 1956 transferred to the position of regional chief of operations, Southeast Regional Office, Richmond, Virginia, where he remained until his transfer to Cape Hatteras National Seashore in 1962. In the regional office, he supervised the operation and maintenance activities for all national parks in the Southeast.

Prior to his employment with the National Park Service, Smith worked with the Virginia Department of Highways and the U. S. Bureau of Public Roads.

A native of Virginia, he is a graduate of Virginia Polytechnic Institute, Blacksburg, Virginia. From 1942 to 1946 he was on duty with the Corps of Engineers, United States Army.

———————◇———————

Cox Named Park Superintendent at Oakland

Eugene S. Cox was recently named Superintendent of the Park Department, Oakland, California. He has been employed in the department for nearly thirty years and as Forester received recognition for his contribution to the development of Oakland's nationally acclaimed official street tree program. He served as Infantry Officer during World War II receiving two battle stars for action in the Mediterranean area and the General Commendation medal for his work as Personnel Officer at the Oakland Army Base.

———————◇———————

Nading is Fort Wayne Park Superintendent

Martin M. Nading has been appointed to the newly created position of Superintendent of Recreation and Parks for the city of Fort Wayne, Indiana. Since last spring there has been a major change in the reorganization of the city park system and Mr. Nading will assume full administrative re-

(Continued on p. 33)

The Cypress Tree

By THOMAS F. WOOD

EDITOR'S NOTE:—The author of this fascinating story, Thomas F. Wood, of London, Ohio, is a Life Member of the National Conference on State Parks. Through years of research and travel Mr. Wood has become an expert. He has been referred to by the Columbus (O.) Dispatch as the Johnny Appleseed of cypress trees. A retired Madison County (O.) grain dealer, industrialist and philanthropist, Mr. Wood has been interested in cypress trees as a potential replacement for disease-threatened timber crops for over 50 years. He raises and distributes cypress seedlings as a hobby.

When I was a young man of 21 in the year of 1912, I was sent to Newport, Arkansas, to take up—that is, to grade and load,—seventeen carloads of lumber. There, for the first time, I saw the Bald Cypress tree in all its gigantic and majestic glory. These trees towered above all the other trees in the forest.

The Cypress tree is one of the oldest forms of tree vegetation that exists today. It is probably a direct descendant of the gigantic tree-like ferns that covered the earth's surface millions of years ago. Nature endowed it with a resinous protection that has enabled it to withstand the attacks of insects and disease all these centuries.

People think of the Cypress tree growing only in swamps and in water. This is not true. The Cypress tree grows far better on good, moist land and not in the water. The reason we see them only in swamps is that the woodsman could not get to the few in the water to cut them down for lumber.

From the time man settled North America he wanted to use Cypress lumber because it is the most rot resistant of all the woods, and because of the resin termites will not attack it. In Charleston, South Carolina, there are many houses with cypress siding two hundred years old and without paint; the lumber is still good.

One day in London, Ohio, near the creek and about three feet above the water I saw a huge tree that looked like a Cypress—and sure enough it was. That tree is 44 inches in diameter and was planted about ninety years ago. On looking around Madison and Clark Counties I found several large and beautiful Cypress trees. Looking around some more I found that there are about one thousand large Bald Cypress trees in the State of Ohio. Every one of these trees has been brought up from the south as seedlings and planted by someone who was curious to know if the Cypress would grow this far north. They will, without doubt, if planted in good, damp ground.

Seeing these Ohio trees started me on a strange hobby—trying to find out what I could about the Cypress tree. After traveling more than ten thousand miles on at least two dozen of the big river systems of the Southern States—from the Roanoke of Virginia, the Everglades of Florida, the Colorado River of Texas, and up the Mississippi to St. Louis, I have come to the conclusion that the original Cypress forest was really a huge affair.

One aspect of this majestic tree,

I have noted, is its tremendous north and south coverage. It begins in the north tropics of Mexico, extends through the orange belt of central Florida, the tung nut belt of northern Florida, the pecan and live oak belt of the South, on through the long leaf and short leaf yellow pine belt into the red oak, the red gums and hickorys of northern Arkansas, and still on through the poplars, cottonwoods and sycamores of Indiana, southern Illinois and Missouri. It grows well in the burr oak country of central Ohio and in the eastern Ohio soil at Dawes Arboretum near Newark, Ohio, as well as in the Appalachian soils of the southeast. There are some Cypress trees southwest of Lake Erie and I know of a few that are doing fine in the old white pine belt of Michigan, two hundred miles north of the Ohio line. Very few plants or trees could take the variation of soil and temperature that exists in 1600 miles north and south.

Why is there no Cypress forest north of Evansville, Indiana? This is the reason. The seeds of this tree are water borne, that is, they float on the flood waters of rivers and streams and when the water goes down they start to grow. If you stop to think, every drop of water east of the Rockies and south of the Great Lakes divide flows south. The glacier killed all the Cypress trees to the Evansville line and the Cypress tree has not been able to fight its way north. Because of this birds that carry other seeds far and wide will not touch the resin of the Cypress seed and rodents will not carry them either. Also the tree

takes about 210 frost free days for the seed to be fertile. The cone and seed in Central Ohio fully develops but the catkin the part that does the pollinating is as green as grass when the frost kills the leaves.

The seed of the Cypress is in a nut-like ball about one inch in diameter, with about 14 triangular seeds in each ball. These seeds are coated with a sticky resin. The tree is self-pollinating and it looks something like a pine tree. However it loses its fine leaves in the fall. The interior of the first log up on many Cypress trees looks like the wood had been wormeaten and honey combed. This is pecky Cypress. Nature evidently used this way to protect the tree from the terrific hurricanes that blew millions of years ago. If the wood were solid it would compress and splinter. Pecky Cypress is in great demand for decorator finish in many fine homes.

Cypress growing in water and in places subject to a great deal of flood waters send up from their roots several cone-like objects called knees. These knees usually go above the height of the average flood and the tree is supposed to breathe through these knees. I have seen Cypress knees seven feet high.

The best Cypress lumber comes from trees that grow in and along rivers that have tide water from the sea. Direct contact with the sea kills the tree.

The trees that grow in the water in the northern part of the Cotton Belt do not seem to do so well as the trees on land. I suppose the water is too cold. Witness—at Reelfoot Lake in Tennessee there

32

was an earthquake in 1808. Fifty thousand acres of virgin Cypress forest was submerged in from five to twenty feet of water. Some of these trees stood upright and after 154 years are green and healthy, but have made no apparent growth.

About five years ago a man in Franklin County, Ohio, planted ten six-foot trees in a pond having about two foot of water in it. Seven trees died and the three that are living are green and healthy but made no apparent growth. Whereas some trees of this same lot planted at two feet above the water are all living and are fifteen feet high and doing fine.

The Cypress trees will do well in Ohio if planted in good, deep soil in a valley or any low place that gets plenty of moisture. They do not grow well on hills, rocky ground or high ground. Cold weather does not seem to hurt them.

The largest Cypress tree in the United States is in Florida. It is nineteen feet in diameter. The largest one in the world is at Monterey, Mexico. It is over 150 feet around.

There is a tree growing near Ashville, North Carolina, at an elevation of 3100 feet.

Yes, following the trail of the Cypress tree has been a lot of fun, and instructive too. I have seen the huge valley of the Upper Delta of the Mississippi just south of Memphis with its thousands of square miles of unbelievably rich soil, soil that has been washed down the Ohio, the Illinois, the Missouri and a thousand tributaries. I have crossed the broad and fertile valleys of the White River, the Arkansas, the Black, and the Red Rivers of the South and a score or more of others. I have been in strange and out of the way places and seen strange sights that most northern folks do not ever get to see. All this has made the Cypress tree a worthwhile hobby for me.

THE INDIANA DUNES

(*Continued from p. 29*)

and best use for the remaining dunes on Indiana's lake shore. Wise decisions must reconcile strong differences. The critical eye of history will be our judge. Unlike a building or a billboard, once destroyed, these dunes cannot be replaced— at least not for 12,000 years—if then. We, therefore, urge prompt action to preserve forever as much as possible for this vanishing shoreline.

STRICTLY PERSONAL

(*Continued from p. 30*)

sponsibility for the park program. He was first appointed park director of recreation in 1947 and has served as secretary of the Board of Park Commissioners at Fort Wayne; as president of the Indiana Park and Recreation Association; and has been cited for distinguished service by the Governor's Conference on Recreation. He is a graduate of Indiana University and the National Recreation School in New York City.

APCA Board Meeting

The Board of Trustees of the American Planning and Civic Association held a meeting on January 18, 1963 for the following purposes:

1. To hear a report of progress on negotiations with the Taconic Foundation of New York regarding the future program of the American Planning and Civic Association.
2. To elect officers.
3. To amend the Constitution and to reorganize the Board of Trustees.

A letter received from the Foundation granted modest support to the American Planning and Civic Association for 1963 and contains the following significant statement ". . . The Trustees (of the Foundation) have given full approval to an active exploration with the American Planning and Civic Association of possible programs which might be pursued with substantial support from Taconic and aimed toward achieving a more attractive and better designed urban environment in the United States."

The Board elected the following officers: President—Harland Bartholomew, Vice President—Edward J. Meeman, Vice President—C. McKim Norton, Treasurer—C. F. Jacobsen, Executive Director—Donald B. Alexander.

Article IV of the Constitution was amended for the following purposes:

1. To reduce the number of Board members from 75 to 24, which shall include all officers, except the Treasurer.
2. To bring to an end the membership of the existing board.
3. To permit the Foundation to have a free hand in the selection of a new Board.

Article XIII of the Constitution requires the amendment to be confirmed by a majority of the members voting either at a meeting or by mail. The slate of new Board members was also listed on the mail ballot.

All of us engaged in these new developments are very much encouraged about the future of the American Planning and Civic Association. We are anxious to resume members meetings as soon as possible but since there are no current plans for such a meeting it was necessary to use the mail ballot. The returns are pouring in and with more than a third of the ballots received, only two dissenting votes have been cast.

Civic Centers

EDITOR'S NOTE:—Summary of a talk presented by Werner Ruchti, Director of Planning, City of Long Beach, California, at a meeting of the Southern California Planning Congress, January 10, 1963.

Most people think of the civic center as we know it today as being a relatively recent development. Few realize that the basic idea had its origins in the distant past. In ancient Greek times, for example, the "agora" or market-place was the meeting place of the community, and the center for transacting business, both public and private. The Roman forum was the outgrowth of the Greek agora. In the Roman forum the idea of the community or civic center reached practical fulfillment.

The forum was a central open space in the heart of the city, used as a meeting place, market place, rendezvous for political demonstrations similar to the Italian "piazza," the French "place," or Trafalgar Square. The forum reflected not only the commercial and religious life of the Roman city, but was also the center of the corporate and legal functions. In the greatest period of Roman history the principal public buildings, which were grouped around the forum, must have been imposing indeed! These forums of Roman times are early examples of well-developed town planning, and were found in every place that Roman conquest and culture had penetrated.

Coming to modern times, the Chicago World's Fair in 1893 gave a great impetus to monumental and imposing structures represented by the evolution of the "City Beautiful." Civic centers became a popular "cliche." Each city tried to outdo its rivals in constructing costly municipal buildings, many of which represented financial investments far out of keeping with the cities' abilities to pay for them. In many cases the buildings were not located or designed for efficient operation. Problems in connection with transportation and circulation were not even considered as having an influence on the location and proper functioning of municipal structures.

How then do civic centers of today compare with older obsolete centers of times past? Several factors should be considered in studying this problem.

First of all, we should recognize that the civic center is the municipal business and cultural district, the government business district. As the center of public administration, the contents, location, and functions should be carefully considered, if we are to plan wisely and well. Any level of government required to furnish services to its citizens will find it necessary to have buildings or structures from which the services can be rendered conveniently and efficiently. Thus, we find a variety of public buildings such as administrative offices, courts, libraries, fire stations, hospitals, utility buildings, museums, and schools. Each serves a different function, and consequently a desirable location for one type of structure may be wholly unsuitable for another.

Every type of public building

35

must be analyzed as to its function and located where it can be operated to carry out that function most effectively without being in conflict with surrounding uses.

To a great extent the size of the city will determine what buildings and functions are to be included in the civic center. Obviously, a city like Los Angeles or San Francisco will need to provide more facilities in the civic center than a small city. The largest cities may provide a city hall, public safety building, including police, jail, fire and juvenile facilities; court house, law library; county offices; state office building; federal office building; post office; main library; health facilities; board of education administration building; public utilities building for water and gas services; and a central heating plant serving all buildings. Optional structures of a cultural nature may be included. These might be opera house, veterans building, museum or art, music center, civic auditorium, drama center.

A medium size city might find a need for a city hall; public safety building, including police, fire, juvenile, and jail facilities; a main library; courts and county offices; post office; state offices, and public utilities building. A museum of art and a civic auditorium are optional cultural buildings that might be added.

Small cities might find a need for only the following: city hall, police and fire headquarters, main library, post office, and community center.

It is obvious that a civic center should be provided with adequate off-street parking for the needs of the general public who do business in the civic buildings. On the periphery of a civic center might be located such semi-public buildings as churches, public service organizations such as the Red Cross headquarters of the community; charitable and philanthropic organizations; private clubs; a mass transportation center, or terminal and other similar facilities.

There are divergent opinions as to just where in the city the civic center should be located. Some feel that it should be located in the geographic center, others prefer the center of population. Still others are of the opinion that it should be located near the center of business activity—in other words, near the central business district. An examination of just what some cities have done may lead us to a conclusion on this aspect of civic center planning.

Several years ago, in the Long Beach Planning Department a study of many cities was made. By far the largest number of cities in this study had the civic center located adjacent to the central business district, but not in the path of future expansion of the business district. Among cities in this category are Buffalo, Chicago, Cincinnati, Cleveland, Detroit, Kansas City, Milwaukee, Oakland, Omaha, Portland, Oregon, Saint Louis, and Seattle. In these cities people are able to combine business in the civic center with other personal or business interests. The public transportation system serves the business district and the civic center also, if it is located in close proximity to the business area. Shoppers and others are able to plan one trip downtown to shop and complete business in the civic center with most efficiency. The business and professional office concentration in the main business district also benefits by being located close to the civic buildings. Many professional people have almost daily contacts in one or another of the public buildings, and for this reason seek a location near the municipal center. Another advantage of having the civic center adjacent to the central business district is the joint use of off-street parking facilities serving both uses. This is not only true of daytime business uses, but it is also true for uses in operation in the evening hours, such as the main library, civic auditorium, museum of art, or a music center.

In a few cities such as San Diego, San Francisco, and Santa Monica the civic center is separated from the main business district. This is disadvantageous to both areas.

Having decided to embark upon a program of civic center development, the problem of acquisition of land is paramount. The city must be realistic in its appraisal of future needs, being neither too generous or optimistic as to hoped-for annexations or population increases, nor too niggardly with regard to costs as to be limited for space in buildings or land to provide sites for the structures. Land is expensive, and in addition, as the sites for needed buildings are acquired, the city or other public agencies will find that the cost of future acquisitions will rise by reason of location in the municipal center. Land around the civic center will also go up in value.

The question then, is "How much area is actually needed for a civic center?" This question has no definite answer, no measurable standards to apply—each city is different. Each city's needs, desires, and economic limitations will have a bearing on the ultimate civic center plan. It should be apparent that under ordinary circumstances, a small city would have a smaller civic center than a medium or large size city. The city should not try to crowd as many buildings or structures on a limited site as possible. The center as a whole should present an uncrowded appearance—parklike, in a beautiful setting. Each building should be properly related to the others as to function and appearance, presenting a unified, cohesive composition.

The actual area required will vary according to the specialized needs of the different cities. Oftentimes, a city may find it advantageous to add more stories to a building rather than to acquire more land for needed expansion. It is necessary, however, to anticipate probable or potential expansion, and to plan for it so that if and when the need arises, the expansion can be orderly and systematic in accordance with the over-all plan.

In summary, it might be stated that public ownership alone is not a sufficient reason to group all public buildings in one area. Cultural facilities might be grouped away from the civic center area. In the civic center, the buildings or functions should be grouped according to their intended use. For example, the Assessor's office, tax collector,

(Continued on p. 42)

State Park Notes

North Dakota. John G. Hewston, public relations chief for the past seven and one-half years, has resigned from the North Dakota Game and Fish Department to return to Utah State University this fall to work for his doctor's degree in Fish Research. He is a graduate of Pacific Lutheran University and earned his M.S. degree at Oregon State University. No successor has yet been named.

Maine. Former Gov. Percival P. Baxter of Maine recently announced that he had purchased from the Great Northern Paper Company an additional 7,700 acres to be added to Baxter State Park. The park area, including the newly deeded lands, now totals 201,013 acres in ten townships, embracing the State's most scenic mountain areas. Definite conditions in the deeds of gift and in separate legislation require that the park must be preserved as a natural wilderness. Recreation will be provided for those who wish to find it in natural surroundings.

Montana. Approval of a $610,000 biennial budget item for expanding the state park system has been announced. A $300,000 per annum figure, about three times the 1961–62 yearly figure, will be used to meet increased use of park areas. In addition to the new funds which will start the 10-year state park program, Park Director Ashley C. Roberts wants to use unclaimed boat gas tax refunds or one per cent of the State's gasoline tax revenue for park purposes. By agreement with the U. S. Bureau of Reclamation all recreation lands around the Clark Canyon Dam reservoir will be administered by the state park commission.

Planning Funds

Good news about a loan program for recreation and community facilities is contained in an article in the September issue of *Recreation* entitled "Do You Need Funds for Planning?" by Sidney H. Wollner, Commissioner, Community Facilities Administration, U. S. Housing and Home Finance Agency, 1626 K Street, N. W., Washington, D. C. Under the program, money is advanced by the Agency to a community to plan a public facility, and the funds are repaid when construction of the project starts. Many communities and public agencies do not have the necessary specialized staff to draw up plans for projects. Among the recreation

38

facilities for which CFA has made these planning advances have been community parks, a sports arena, a public golf course, recreation facilities included in water and hydroelectric development projects, and public libraries.

California. Angel Island State Park in San Francisco Bay with its rugged terrain, plant and animal life and abundant birdlife has a rich historical background. Located in the largest of a group of islands in the Bay, it is perhaps the most unique State park in the California State Park System. The rocky island with steep terrain, rising sharply from sea level to more than 700 feet, is accessible by boat only. It was here that Don Juan de Ayala landed his Spanish packet in 1775, the first ship to enter and explore San Francisco Bay. He named the 640-acre island "Isla de Los Angeles" or Angel Island, and it has since had an unusual history. Smugglers and pirates used the island as a point of rendezvous until it was turned into a cattle and sheep ranch. Even after the United States took possession in 1848, it was a prison, an immigration station, a U. S. Public Health quarantine station, a fortified harbor defense, an Army fort and overseas military staging area. Before law came to the Bay area it was the scene of many duels, the most famous in 1858 when State Senator William S. Ferguson died in a gun duel with George P. Johnson over the slavery question. Today, ancient buildings are overgrown by sub-tropical and other vines and trees. There are old military garrisons, three active U. S. Coast Guard stations, and boat slips now provide access to State park facilities at Ayala Cove. The 781-foot Mount Caroline S. Livermore, within Angel Island State Park, is the highest point on the island. Present plans are to increase the size of the park from 221 to approximately 300 acres by including adjacent North Garrison, an abandoned military station.

Missouri. A state coordinating body for recreation was proposed by Governor John M. Dalton at the First Missouri Governor's Conference on Parks and Recreation in Jefferson City recently.

The Governor pointed out that 12 state agencies are concerned with recreational services to Missouri citizens. He suggested that a State Inter-Agency Council for Recreation might have representation from the 12 agencies as the most economical method to provide and take responsible action for recreational services in the interest and welfare of all.

All recreational fields were represented at the First Governor's Conference on Parks and Recreation which was sponsored by the Missouri Park and Recreation Association. It was the first such conference to be held in the state.

Growing from the Conference was a plan to register and certify qualified recreation personnel in Missouri. The proposal would be voluntary, according to Joseph Jaegers, Jr., State Director of Parks and President of the Missouri Park and Recreation Association. He said it would, however, establish standards for professional leadership and identify leaders engaged in the recreational field.

The registration plan would provide that present recreation workers in Missouri be certified without examination or qualification if they had at least three years of experience in the field in the last five years. After one year, all applicants would have to be a college graduate with a major in recreation and pass an examination as established by a board.

In other action, the Association told Congress it favored legislation which would prohibit the use of park lands for highway purposes. This was deemed necessary, the resolution said, to preserve open spaces, natural greenery and recreation areas.

West Virginians get first choice of Park-Forest reservations. The Parks and Recreation Division of the Department of Natural Resources has announced that applications for park or forest cabin reservations sent in by West Virginia residents prior to February 15 will be given preference over all others.

A spokeman for the Parks and Recreation Division said that this arrangement is carried out every year. This gives West Virginians who submit applications prior to this date first choice of reservations over all other applicants. Reservations may be made for any dates that are open during any part of the coming season.

After February 15, all applications, whether from West Virginians or from out-of-state tourists, will be treated on a first come, first served basis.

The division also announced that the facilities at Cabwaylingo State Forest would rent at reduced rates throughout the entire season this year. For more information concerning this bargain, write to the Division of Parks and Recreation, Department of Natural Resources, Charleston 5, West Virginia.

Minnesota. Today the State Park system constitutes 73 units comprising an authorized 137,000 acres. The Division is charged with the preservation of their outstanding scenic, historic and scientific values and providing opportunity for recreation consistent with preservation.

Visitations in 1961 *exceeded 3,200-000* for a 9.5 per cent increase over the previous year or an average annual increase since 1942 of 7 per cent. An excess of one million annual visitations to Itasca exceeded visitations to 15 of the 29 National Parks. *Even more significant 342,000 registered tourist camper days statewide represent an increase of 534 per cent since 1954.* Childrens group camping amounting to 47,000 camper days are limited by facilities available.

Division administration is functionally divided into "Field Operations," "Revenue Operations," and "Interpretive Services."

● *In field operation,* minor park units are actively administered by a Park Manager of a major unit in the vicinity. Three staff member District Supervisors—each administering one-third of the State—are charged with maintenance and operational standards, enforcement, budget allocations, operational procedures and improvements and expediting authorized capital improvement programs.

● *Revenue Operations* are administered by a staff Supervisor who is responsible for the annual purchase of $150,000 of resale items, fiscal accountability, merchandising methods and operations of revenue producing facilities including Douglas Lodge. Gross Revenues in 1961 exceeded $424,000 compared with $191,000 in 1954—for an increase of $233,000 in a period of 8 years.

● *Interpretive services* are presently inadequately administered in varying degrees by all staff members. A new position of Chief of Interpretive Services is needed. A Naturalist Service is sponsored jointly with the University of Minnesota Museum of Natural History and constitutes seasonal Naturalist services at five parks, and self-guiding nature trails at 8 other parks. There were over 451,000 incidents of park visitors participation in the Naturalist Program over the last year. The Historical Society has provided speakers on special occasions. Interpretive devices are practically non-existent. Informational literature is also lacking.

What about the Future?

· On the basis of three different standards—independent of each other, *we are short 40,000 State Park acres in meeting present needs.*

To correct this deficit, we are recommending the establishment of *36 new State Parks* and strategic land acquisitions to 38 existing State Park units.

There is a demand for *well defined canoe routes* comparable to those established by Wisconsin.

There is a need to *preserve the scenic beauty* of the roadside for the enjoyment of the motorist.

You may or may not be aware that we worked closely with the National Park Service in helping to establish the "*Grand Portage Monument*" and that we are presently working with them on a possible "*Voyageurs National Park*" in Rainy Lake Region.

In the last session of the Legislature, we recommended a *County Park Law* which was a composite of the best of this type of legislation nation-wide. It was passed and as a result at least two outstate counties are presently engaged in planning county park systems.

We are also recommending that the widely acclaimed and accepted *Interpretive Programs on History, Geology, and Biology* of the Parks be expanded.

The needs for *outdoor recreational opportunities* for our citizenry and visitors have been pointed out over and over again in surveys and studies conducted both at the federal and state level. No other state is as richly endowed to provide for this opportunity as ours. The hour is late—the need for action is now! —U. W. Hella, director, Division of State Parks.

THE ASSOCIATION OF SOUTHEASTERN STATE PARK DIRECTORS held its 21st annual meeting at Williamsburg, Virginia, November 5 to 9, 1962. Eleven of the twelve states of the southeastern region were represented along with the National Park Service, the Bureau of Outdoor Recreation, and the Old Dominion Foundation. The host for the meeting was the state of Virginia and Colonial Williamsburg. The general theme of the meeting was interpretation. The Association was welcomed to the state of Virginia by Lieutenant Governor Mills E. Godwin, Jr. In his remarks, he impressed upon those in attendance the historical significance of the Williamsburg, Yorktown, Jamestown area as related to the formation of our country. Mr. Godwin expressed satisfaction with the job that was being done at Colonial Williamsburg and with the job being done by the National Park Service and the State Park System of Virginia. He also emphasized the importance of preserving our heritage that we might not only use it in our time but that we might preserve it in such a way that it will be here for others to profit from and to enjoy.

CIVIC CENTERS

(*Continued from p. 37*)

and treasurer should be located close together. The civic center should be located adjacent to the main business district, and off-street parking can be provided to serve both types of uses.

One final point should be emphasized: that of community appearance and civic pride. The importance of this factor should not be overlooked, and can be summed up in a quote from Local Planning Administration, Chapter 10, Public Buildings and Community Appearance. *"Perhaps the strongest argument for the grouping of public buildings in a civic center is the increased importance, dominance, and aesthetic significance gained by each building when it is an integral part of a harmonious composition. This consideration is important to the city because a harmoniously designed group of buildings is more easily recognized as an aesthetic asset than is a single building. The group therefore becomes an attractive and well known feature of the city and one of its cultural assets."*

Gordon Whitnall sums it up this way: "There are few public enterprises that do so much to engender justifiable community pride as does a well conceived civic center. And there is no more valuable community asset than justified community pride."

42

Campaign to Preserve the Buffalo River

By Ozark Society to Save the Buffalo

EDITOR'S NOTE:—The preliminary reconnaissance study of the Buffalo River was made by the National Park Service in early 1962. The report which followed indicated the wisdom of proceeding with more work in the area, including an economic study to be undertaken by the University of Arkansas. This has been done and a draft of the economic study is currently being reviewed at the Southeast Region of the National Park Service. A Specific Area Report on the Buffalo River is undergoing final revision for submittal to higher authority.

The National Park Service is interested in the Buffalo River to the point of undertaking these more comprehensive studies. They are nearly complete. However, the findings have not yet been evaluated nor conclusions reached.

An intensive campaign to preserve the magnificent Buffalo River, in north central Arkansas, is gaining momentum which may lead to introduction of Federal legislation to save this free flowing stream from two high dams which would inundate it for almost its entire floatable length, destroying innumerable aesthetic and scientific values, and to develop it into some type of National area.

Legislation for the two dams, Lone Rock, near the mouth, and Gilbert, 59 miles upstream, was introduced in the 87th Congress but the bill did not come up for consideration. Proponents of the dams continue to agitate for this legislation.

The Buffalo is the last free flowing river of consequence in the entire region. In its present state it offers more than a hundred miles of quiet floating in a spectacular natural setting, an activity which is being rapidly curtailed on the American scene and which is known and loved by thousands of individuals and a number of organized groups, not only within Arkansas, but in neighboring states and beyond. Justice William O. Douglas, who floated the river in the spring of 1962, called the Buffalo

"Unique; magnificent; a thing to be preserved forever."

Recently a group of conservationists, principally from Arkansas but including all the surrounding states, have organized the "Ozark Society, Inc., To Save the Buffalo River," centered in Fayetteville, Arkansas.

During the past two years the National Park Service has made field studies to evaluate the significance of the river and its region, its suitability and feasibility for preservation as a National area.

The attention of the National Park Service was focused on the Buffalo River through a communication to Secretary Udall from Senator J. William Fulbright. As a consequence of the generally optimistic report on the Buffalo as a recreation area in this preliminary study, it seemed wise to proceed with more exacting studies. It is expected that the report on these more complete studies will be made public in early spring of this year.

Ozark Society, Inc., believes the Buffalo and area in their natural state are a priceless part of our national heritage. Numerous organizations, among them the Arkansas Wildlife Federation, State League

(Continued on p. 46)

43

Commentaries

Centennial Conservation Education Conference Set

In a recent announcement, Governor W. W. Barron officially set the date for the Governor's Centennial Conference on Conservation Education. The one-day conference is slated for April 3, 1963, at the Daniel Boone Hotel in Charleston, West Virginia.

Theme for the Centennial Conference is "West Virginia's Natural Resources Over Next 100 Years." Governor Barron said that he called the conference in an effort to "Develop an effective and far-reaching conservation education program." The Governor also stated that West Virginia's conservation education programs "need to be improved and generally expanded, thereby providing the opportunity for youth and adult citizens of West Virginia to gain an understanding, knowledge and appreciation of the importance of all our natural resources."

The Conservation Education Conference will be co-sponsored by the Governor's advisory committee on Conservation Education, and by the West Virginia Conservation Education Council.

In preparation for the conference, Governor Barron has asked that two reports be prepared prior to next year's meeting. The first of these is a report by the State Superintendent of Schools concerning what is being done at present regarding conservation education in the schools. The second report will concern a summary of the role of natural resources in the 100 years of our State, their present status, and prospects for the future. A combination of the two reports should give attending members at next year's conference a basic idea of what needs to be done for the betterment of conservation education in the State.

There is an Urgent Need in Michigan

Today, in Michigan, as elsewhere, there is an increasing interest in outdoor recreation, together with a trend toward greater leisure time on the part of many. These combine with the expansion of population and the growing ease of travel, both into and within the state, to place a mushrooming pressure upon our present recreational facilities.

Within the State of Michigan there exists a great wealth of sweeping shorelines, secluded streams, towering dunes, verdant forests, and picturesque vistas, and of scenes hallowed by over three centuries of history. All of this wealth is ideally suited to the re-creation of the people.

There is an urgent need to ensure NOW the provision of this recreational wealth for the enjoyment of all people for all time. The continuing failure in recent years to provide adequate support has already permitted many invaluable sites to pass by default forever out of public use. Other choice areas

are in serious jeopardy from encroaching private developments. And those areas which have been acquired are in too many cases most inadequately developed, if at all.

THE PROMPT ACQUISITION, DEDICATION AND WISE UTILIZATION OF THESE SCENIC AND RECREATIONAL RESOURCES IS A PARAMOUNT PUBLIC NECESSITY!

The Michigan Parks Association calls alike upon the people of Michigan and upon their elected officials at all levels of government to take immediate and vigorous steps to ensure that the needs for public recreational areas will be adequately met, while there is yet opportunity to do so.

The Association seeks to encourage both the donation of private contributions and the timely expenditure of public funds to meet this need. Its members pledge themselves to work zealously toward this goal, and invite all other interested citizens to join with them.

Planning and Civic Comment

1962-63 Renewal Surveys Under Way

Four thousand families in six neighborhoods are being interviewed in an intensive survey launched by the New York City Department of City Planning as the study phase of the 1962–63 Urban Renewal Study Program reaches peak activity.

The survey focuses attention on a large sample of the 140,000 people who live in these six areas, and will supplement other surveys now in progress to develop data concerning the structure and condition of residences, the layout of living quarters, and questions of ownership and existing mortgages. •

Residents are being interviewed and buildings inspected in the Fort Greene Market and Children's Museum Areas in Brooklyn; the Corona-East Elmhurst Area Extension in Queens; the Bronx Park West Area in The Bronx; and the St. Nicholas Park and Cooper Square Areas in Manhattan. Five of these areas were selected by the City Planning Commission for the 1962-63 Urban Renewal Study Program primarily because they lend themselves to rehabilitation and conservation. The sixth, Cooper Square, also contains a section being considered for major redevelopment. The surveys will be completed by the end of December.

Information secured in this massive effort, the largest ever undertaken in the City, will provide basic grassroots knowledge that will have important meaning to the future of rehabilitation and renewal operations in New York. Findings will serve as the basis for further discussions with the communities before specific renewal proposals are advanced for public hearings.

In many of the areas local citizens have volunteered to assist wherever possible in describing the surveys to their neighbors and alerting them to the importance of full cooperation. James Felt, Chairman of the City Planning Commission, expressed gratification for these early signs of an enthusiastic response.

"Especially where rehabilitation work may be contemplated," Mr. Felt continued, "it becomes doubly important to establish strong 'people to people' contact, and to assess the practical possibilities for success. These surveys are an important aspect of that process. The results of these surveys will play a major role in telling us how we can best assist our citizens to improve their homes and neighborhoods."

Information is being sought as to family size, income, rents, occupation of the head of the household, distance travelled to work and length of residence in the area.

In addition, three other surveys are being carried out. The first consists of a thorough inspection of sample buildings in the areas. Professional estimators are checking walls, ceilings, floors, plumbing and other critical structural elements to determine construction and condition. Defects will be tallied, and an estimate prepared as to the cost of making improvements. The list of defects will serve as a basis for determining the range of possible renewal treatment.

A portion of these buildings is being selected for further, more intensive study by an architect-engineer team. In this second survey, the team will develop alternative ways of improving the buildings. They will prepare full case histories on the structures, including detailed suggestions as to the kinds of materials which might be used, and design changes which could be incorporated in future rehabilitation work.

The final survey will deal with the general mortgage structure. Particular attention will be paid to the number and the kind of existing mortgages, and the availability of new mortgages. In addition, projections will be advanced as to the impact of future renewal and rehabilitation work on the area's general mortgage and financial structure.

Planning and Civic Comment

From The Christian Science Monitor

"Here in Florida not long ago I asked a state park superintendent if he could give me a list of some of his problems. He smiled wryly and said that would be easy. The next time I saw him he gave me a neatly typed two page list entitled, "Why Park Superintendents Go Wild."

Here is a partial list of the "suggestions" he constantly receives:

Burn the area to kill off all the snakes.

Kill off all the hawks.

Drain the area to combat flooding conditions in other sections.

Kill off all the older gobblers to promote better and more turkeys.

Open the park to cattle grazing.

Lend, lease, trade or sell portions of the park to special projects of real estate developers.

Permit unrestricted hunting and fishing.

Permit hunting of alligators because they are destructive.

Make an exercise area for training hunting dogs.

Permit egg and rare specimen collectors free rein at all times.

Let amateurs dig into the Indian mounds in the park.

Permit free access to all areas of the park.

Encourage road building and utilities to cross park at will so as not to stand in the way of progress.

Be lenient with all poachers for they are helping to keep the alligators, wild pigs, snakes, old bucks, old gobblers, etc. in balance. They would soon die anyway and someone should get the use of them.

And on and on, each suggestor grinding some ax of his own. Let's hope the Wilderness bill is passed this session. Or we might well soon be sighing, "Ah, Wilderness," with the sure intonation that it is something we will never see again."

CAMPAIGN TO PRESERVE THE BUFFALO RIVER

(*Continued from p. 43*)

of Women Voters, Conservation Federation of Missouri, Arkansas Chapter, The Nature Conservancy, Arkansas Federation of Garden Clubs, Ozark Wilderness Waterways Club (headquarters, Kansas City), and Arkansas Audubon Society are supporting preservation of the Buffalo. Press support has been forthcoming in Little Rock, St. Louis, Fort Smith, Kansas City, and Memphis, and in several national publications.

In spite of this, the situation in regard to the Buffalo River remains critical. Proponents of the dams argue for the economic benefits of more impoundments and offer as a compromise the one-third or less of the river which would remain as a natural area.

Ozark Society, Inc., recognizes the irreplaceable values of the region and of the entire river as a free-flowing stream—the last of its kind in the Arkansas Ozarks. The Society hopes, through increasing public support to terminate this threat to the Buffalo River.

National Capital Notes

Congress is being asked again to create a screening agency to protect Federal park lands in the Nation's Capital from invasion by a hodgepodge of statues, monuments, and other memorial structures, Secretary of the Interior Stewart L. Udall announced recently.

He said his Department has resubmitted the same draft legislation he urged the last Congress to enact to establish a National Capital Parks Memorial Board. That bill was not passed.

Secretary Udall said he had advocated such a measure when he served in the House of Representatives. Now the situation is critical, he added, and the need for legislation is urgent.

In a letter transmitting the new draft to Congress, the Department said:

"Memorializations place a constant demand on park land of the Nation's Capital. There are 96 memorials of the monument or statue type already existing on land in the National Capital Parks System. A number of others have been authorized but not yet constructed. In the 86th Congress alone seven public laws were enacted authorizing the construction of memorials. At least 17 bills

were before the 86th Congress and eight before the 87th Congress to authorize the construction of memorials on park lands in the Nation's Capital.

"It is evident that, if the concept of open space and dignity which contribute so much to the beauty of the Nation's Capital is to be preserved in the face of constant pressures to use the land for memorials, sound guidelines for the control of this use must be formulated, a comprehensive plan must be developed, each proposal must be carefully evaluated, and sound criteria must be steadfastly followed.

"In fact, such a plan offers the only assurance that sites will be available for future memorials that in all respects merit a location in the parks."

Secretary Udall's proposal would establish a nine-member board composed of five persons appointed by the President of the United States; the Chairman of the Fine Arts Commission; the Chairman of the National Capital Planning Commission; the President of the Board of Commissioners of the District of Columbia; and the Director of the National Park Service. The members would serve without compensation, but would be reimbursed for travel expenses.

Recent Publications

AMERICAN CITIES IN PERSPECTIVE, with special reference to the development of their fringe areas. By Dr. G. A. Wissink. This study attempts to give a more or less synthetic picture of the development of American cities, especially of their fringe areas. It ties many loose ends together. There is a great deal of comparison with non-American cities. Fringe development is traced to its historical origins. The Humanities Press, Inc. 303 Park Ave. South, New York 10, N. Y. 320 pp. $7.50.

THE NEW EXPLORATION, A Philosophy of Regional Planning. By Benton MacKaye, University of Illinois Press, Urbana, Ill. 243 pp. $1.75.

CITIES IN THE SUBURBS. By Humphrey Carver, University of Toronto Press. 120 pp. $4.95.

ENVIRONMENTAL ENGINEERING & METROPOLITAN PLANNING, Edited by John A. Logan, Paul Oppermann and Dorman E. Tucker. Northwestern University Press. 265 pp. $7.50.

LAND USE CLASSIFICATION MANUAL, developed by the Land Classification Advisory Committee of the Detroit Metropolitan Area. Public Administration Service, 1313 East 60th St., Chicago 37, Illinois. 53 pp. $5.00.

SITE PLANNING, by Kevin Lynch. The M. I. T. Press, Cambridge, Mass. 248 pp. $8.00.

THE PLACE OF THE IDEAL COMMUNITY IN URBAN PLANNING, by Thomas A. REINER. In this work the author centers his attention on the designs— and their physical aspects especially— of the past seventy years. University of Pennsylvania Press, 3436 Walnut St., Philadelphia 4, Pa. 194 pp. $8.50.

Watch Service Report

The following listed bills are of particular interest and will be reported on from time to time.

S. 1	Youth Conservation Corps. Senator Humphrey and others.
H. R. 1	Youth Conservation Corps. Rep. Blatnik and others.
S. 4	National Wilderness Preservation System. Sen. Anderson and others.
H. R. 930	National Wilderness Preservation System. Rep. Saylor. Hearings Feb. 28.
S. 7	Conservation of Open Space. Sen. Williams, N. J.
S. 20	Bureau of Outdoor Recreation, Organic Act. Sen. Anderson and others. Hearings were held Feb. 5.
H. R. 1762	Bureau of Outdoor Recreation, Organic Act. Rep. Aspinall. Hearings were held on H. R. 1762 Feb. 12 and 13.
S. 33	Establish Coal River National Recreation Demonstration Area, in W. Va., Sen. Byrd.
S. 77	To establish the Chesapeake and Ohio Canal National Historical Park in Maryland. Sen. Beall.
S. 606	To establish the Tocks Island National Recreation Area in Pa. & N. J. Senator Clark.
H. R. 2632	To establish the Tocks Island National Recreation Area in Pa. & N. J. Rep. Saylor.
S. 650	Establishment of Indiana Dunes National Lakeshore. Sen. Douglas and others.
H. R. 1126	Burns Waterway Harbor, Ind. (Dunes Area) Rep. Roush. This bill would adversely effect preservation of the Indiana Dunes.
H. R. 993	Preservation of Shoreline Areas. Rep. Giaimo.
H. R. 1015	Allegheny Parkway in W. Va., Ky., and Md. Rep. Siler.
H. R. 1096	Ice Age National Scientific Reserve, Wisc. Rep. Johnson.
H. R. 1803	Ozark National Rivers. Rep. Ichord.
H. R. 2884	Ozark National Rivers. Rep. Karsten.
H. R. 1841	Dams on Buffalo River, Ark. Rep. Trimble. This bill would adversely effect the desired preservation of Buffalo River.
S. 47	Valle Grande National Park, New Mexico. Sen. Anderson
H. R. 1941	Valle Grande National Park, New Mexico. Rep. Morris.
H. R. 2400	Sleeping Bear Dunes National Park. Rep. Griffin.
H. R. 2857	Chemical Pesticides Coordination Act. Rep. Dingell.

1963 *State Park* *Conference*

National Conference on State Parks

in conjunction with

American Institute of Park Executives

and the

American Association of

Zoological Parks and Aquariums

PLACE: WASHINGTON, D. C.

HEADQUARTERS: SHERATON-PARK HOTEL

DATE: SEPTEMBER 22-26, 1963

Planning and Civic Comment

Official Organ of American Planning and Civic Association and
National Conference on State Parks

CONTENTS

JUNE 1963

PLANNING AND CIVIC COMMENT

Published Quarterly

Successor to: City Planning, Civic Comment, State Recreation

Official Organ of: American Planning and Civic Association,
National Conference on State Parks

SCOPE: *National, State, Regional and City Planning, Land and Water Uses,
Conservation of National Resources, National, State and Local Parks,
Highways and Roadsides.*
AIM: *To create a better physical environment which will conserve and develop
the health, happiness and culture of the American people.*

EDITORIAL BOARD

HARLEAN JAMES   FLAVEL SHURTLEFF   CONRAD L. WIRTH

CONTRIBUTING EDITORS

HORACE M. ALBRIGHT   NEWTON B. DRURY
HARLAND BARTHOLOMEW   V. W. FLICKINGER
GEORGE L. COLLINS   JOHN NOLEN, JR.
KENNETH R. COUGILL   F. A. PITKIN
S. R. DeBOER   FRANK D. QUINN
CHARLES DeTURK   BEN H. THOMPSON

EDITOR

DONALD B. ALEXANDER

ASSISTANT EDITOR

ETHEL J. SWING

Second-class postage paid at Harrisburg, Pa., and at additional mailing office.
EDITORIAL AND PUBLICATION OFFICE, 901 Union Trust Building, Washington 5,
D. C.

Printed by the Mount Pleasant Press, The McFarland Company, Harrisburg, Pa.

Planning and Civic Comment

Vol. 29   June 1963   No. 2

The Cityscape

By

GRADY CLAY, Real Estate and Building Editor, *The Louisville Courier-Journal,*
and Editor, *Landscape Architecture.*

Condensation of a Paper from *Planning 1962,* the National Planning Conference
of The American Society of Planning Officials, Atlantic City,
New Jersey, April 29–May 3, 1962.

The chief yardstick used until the 1950's in the United States to determine what would be done with city land was its price. If a man wanted a downtown corner bad enough, he paid a high price, then built a tall building hoping for high rents to repay his investment with profit. Nothing worked so well as the free market in determining how land would be used. Price was umpire, mediator, arbiter and ruler. Price was impartial, objective, relentless. You paid your money and took your choice. Land was worth what a willing buyer would offer and a willing seller would accept. The "highest and best use" of land was whatever would produce the highest rent or maximum sales price. The lesson of the market place was: If you can't pay the price, stay out of the game.

The market place for urban land in America has periodically been invaded by new influences and a variety of manipulators. Congress manipulated the price of land in many cities by selling land wholesale to speculating companies who laid out cities, sold lots, and established the basic pattern of land use and development. The Ordinances of 1784–87 helped carve the wilderness into negotiable squares of land.

Once the government's help in making land available to the market was no longer needed, the market place took over.

Since 1950, however, thousands of parcels of land in redevelopment areas have been appraised, bought, cleared, sold, leased, or designated for future action as part of the urban redevelopment process. It is a massive exhibition of intervening in the market place for land.

Not only is price of such land determined by a formal process requiring professional appraisal and possibly court action, but the land is put to new uses which may have little to do with the maximum dollar value of the land. Price is not so much what a willing seller will accept, but the amount an unwilling seller is forced to take under threat of condemnation. Future use is determined not so much by the buyer's anticipation of profits, but by his knowledge that he will turn it over to a third party at a loss. The buyer —i.e., the city through its redevelopment agency—is acting as middleman. The third party will not only make a profit but must obtain that profit by using the land strictly in a manner previously determined by the mayor, city council, redevelopment agency, and a host of other individuals in public office and outside as well.

In sum, the "highest and best use" of land—and therefore its price—is no longer necessarily what the market place says it is, but is being prescribed by what public officials and specialists outside the market place think it *ought* to be.

In Washington, the planners on the staffs of William Zeckendorf and the Redevelopment Land Agency decided the Potomac Riverfront south of the Mall "ought" to have a handsome public promenade, although the market had decided long ago it should be used for docks. In Pittsburgh, the planners decided that land at the point where the Allegheny and Monongahela Rivers come together to form the Ohio "ought" to be a public park, although the market long ago had ruled it was best for railroads, industry and warehouses. In England, the London County Council now says that the public "ought" to enjoy a full view of St. Paul's Cathedral from afar, although the free market had shut off that view with profitable buildings ever since the Great Fire of 1666. And the rebuilding plan for the precinct of St. Paul's is carrying out the new concept.

In San Francisco, a man offered the city $8,000,000 for 16.7 acres of the old produce market district on the Embarcadero. The market place said, "Take it; he's offering the top dollar." Instead, the city turned around and sold it to a man offering only $6,000,000 plus "extras" on which the market had great trouble putting a price tag. The key word in all this is

"ought." Hitherto, it had mattered comparatively little what some mayor or planner thought "ought" to happen on a particular piece of land. The price a buyer was willing to pay generally determined what *did* happen.

In the Land of Ought, where price is no longer king, the market place has thus been invaded by a number of new pressure groups, lobbies, professional societies, and civic organizations. The voice of the dollar is somewhat muted. Each newcomer has its own version of how land "ought" to be used; each has its spokesmen and contestants who seek to dominate the market place of ideas, and thus influence the use, price and disposition of land as it goes through the process of development.

This offers a great opportunity to make our country a better place in which to live and work. By June 30, 1961, 30,000 acres of urban land were undergoing advanced planning or had actual renewal construction under way. It now appears likely that this total will be close to 300,000 acres of urban land by 1972.

My ideas concerning the disposition and rebuilding of this public domain are based partly on prejudices, and on visits to some 30 or 40 projects in the last three to four years. As a practicing pedestrian, I offer these yardsticks:

1. No redevelopment project ought to be too big. The yardsticks for deciding what is too big, I submit, should be the human being, his stride, his vision and his voice.

No project should be so large that you cannot walk across it in three minutes, or escape from the middle

2

of it in a minute and a half. A three-minute walk, at a soldier's pace of five miles per hour, is equal to the distance of 1,314 feet or 438 yards, or a quarter-mile total width.

Another yardstick is found in human vision and is based on the visibility of the human face. Most people can recognize one another up to a distance of about 465 feet. This is the point at which objects of a half-inch can be seen under reasonable daylight conditions, and a dimension of a half-inch is roughly the size of the main features of the human face. (Thiel, 1960.)

When Camillo Sitte wrote his monumental work, *The Art of Building Cities,* he concluded that the average dimensions of the great public squares in old European cities were 190 by 465 feet, which coincides in its largest dimension with the visibility of the human face.

From personal experience, I would add one other dimension: The audibility of the normal human voice. Somewhere between 400 and 600 feet is the limit for understanding what somebody is shouting at you. Where there are competing noises of heavy traffic, the distance is less.

The size of a project is as important to the individual citizen, and to the entire community, as it is to the developer. If the project is too big, the average citizen can't find familiar, ordinary cues for estimating distance and space.

Once you get into many of the new redevelopment projects you are literally at sea; the experience is somewhat like being on a desert, or in unfamiliar mountain territory. The greenhorn almost always misjudges distances. The ordinary

space cues for perceiving spaces and distances just aren't there. All the more reason, then, for projects to be only so big as to let you see out to recognizable, familiar buildings and neighborhoods on the ouside; or to walk out, or in, quickly.

2. Projects ought to merge with, and connect easily with, the surrounding community. No project should be isolated by man-made, or man-emphasized barriers which seal off new neighborhoods from old. There ought to be visual, as well as functional, connections specified in the community's plans and specification for new developments.

The ancient landscape art of establishing visual connections between points of topographic or architectural importance is too often forgotten, merely because nobody—from the planning commission down to the private developer—bothers to insist on it.

Two examples from the competition for The Farm redevelopment site in Brookline, Mass., will illustrate this point. The Farm was a low-lying piece of land covered with old three-decker residences in a shallow valley. It was bounded by a highway, a parkway and park, and a steep bank.

Nothing in the community's requirements specified that the project should be connected closely with the neighborhood shopping district across the highway, nor to the neighborhood at the top of the steep bank. Consequently, most of the proposals disregarded these neighbors. One developer, however, did propose a handsome pedestrian bridge across the highway. It hung there in his sketches, a lovely architectural promise without visible means of administrative support. Without it, the project would be isolated from the shopping district.

As is often the case, a geographic barrier—in Brookline, a steep bank with a difference of about 35 feet in elevation—separated the project from the hill neighborhood next door. Most of the development plans disregarded the hill, as though it were not there, and made no connections to join the old and new. This could easily have been required by the community in its specifications for completion.

3. *All projects should be so designed (and the program of competition so written) that the project will have maximum beneficial effect on neighborhoods around it.* The Toronto City Hall and Square competition, held in 1958, offers a case in point. Five hundred and twenty competitors from 42 countries submitted designs in this two-stage competition. The jury unanimously chose Viljo Rewell of Finland as the winner.

There were strong differences of opinion within the jury, however. Out of these came a minority report by two distinguished Englishmen, Sir William Holford, currently president of the Royal Institute of British Architects, and Gordon Stevenson. They recommended that the winning design be changed because its two great curved towers would present blank concrete walls 356 and 290 feet high to the surrounding streets and buildings. The minority report said that these "might have an adverse effect on the future development" of neighboring streets, "whereas the new City Hall could otherwise be expected to spark off a number of surrounding projects." (City of Toronto Planning Board Synopsis of Competition, December, 1958.)

From late reports, the building is to be built without this change recommended by the minority report. Yet, the report points to a fundamental consideration: The proper relation of new buildings and projects to their surroundings. This emphasis on proper relationship should, in my opinion, be the most important consideration throughout the whole process of planning and achieving new redevelopment projects.

4. *New standards of open space ought to be embodied in new projects, especially to those occupying crux or leverage positions in the city's basic structure.* Wherever possible, we ought to aim at modifying the monotonous grid pattern of most cities, without getting rid of it altogether. We should aim for new public open spaces, new openings and, on occasion, tight little passageways, crooked arcades, interior courts, alleys and other pedestrian channels which create a fine contrast with the larger spaces to which they connect.

Narrow spaces often seem to work better than square spaces, just as narrow shopping streets are more enjoyable than broad ones. And for many of the same reasons—you can look across to what's on the other side. Narrow spaces give people a variety of choices compared with square spaces. This is not to suggest that every square be converted into a long and narrow

(*Continued on page 37*)

4

Conservation Strength through Unity of Action

From the Remarks of Conrad L. Wirth, Director of the National Park Service, and President of the American Institute of Park Executives, at the 15th Annual California and Pacific Southwest Recreation and Park Conference, San Diego, California, February 19, 1963.

As park people, we are witnessing an unprecedented surge of interest—a renaissance—in outdoor recreation.

The President has sent to Congress legislation proposing the establishment of a Land and Water Conservation Fund which would be administered by the new Bureau of Outdoor Recreation and would be supported by a wide range of recreation user fees, revenues from boat fuels and other sources.

The Land and Water Conservation Fund, the Interstate Highway Program, and the proposed Youth Conservation Corps are all instruments of conservation progress for the States and for the Federal agencies. We are indeed riding the crest of the conservation wave. The question remains: Are we in a position to take advantage of our good fortune? Are we properly united?

We park and recreation people attend many conferences. For example, we have planned the September, 1963 joint Conference of the American Institute of Park Executives, the National Conference on State Parks, the American Association of Zoological Parks and Aquariums, and a representative group of National Park Service people.

The delegates to this Conference will represent park and recreation people at the municipal, county, state, and federal levels. To my knowledge, this will be the first time, or at least one of the few times in recent years, when park and recreation people, representing this broad scope of Government, will meet together to discuss a program. The Conference has been developed to afford this body of park and recreation people the opportunity to discuss its program with officials of the Executive and Legislative Branches of the Federal Government.

While I firmly believe this Conference with representatives from throughout the United States at three levels of Government, together with the participation of Federal authorities whose work has an indirect and direct relation to park and recreation responsibilities, will contribute much and give great weight to the park and recreation movement over the years to come, in my judgment, this is still not enough.

Some way must be found to bring together all professional people working in the park and recreation field in such a way that their unanimous voice can be sounded in support of sound park and recreation programs.

I know that some members of the American Institute of Park Executives feel that such a large organization, coupled with the loss of identity of each of the composite groups, would not be in the best interest of all concerned. Yet they speak up for an ever-increasing cohesive membership of recognized park and recreation administrators with a high professional standard.

Perhaps we should take a leaf out of industry's book and create some form of hierarchy which would make possible the preservation of the identity of each group, and, at the same time, bring to bear the voice of all. As an expression of what we want and need, it might resemble a sort of United States Chamber of Parks and Recreation.

Whatever we call our united effort, remember the cause must be just and of a benefit to the citizens of our United States; basic objectives must be agreed upon, unity of purposes must be secured; and we must act with one main objective.

Assuming for the moment that we have already achieved this unity of purpose, unity of voice, and unity of action—what are some of our specific objectives? What can we do immediately?

Probably the three most significant and timely instruments of conservation progress are those mentioned above.

There is the land and water conservation fund. Because of the special consideration given to planning and development, in addition to land acquisition, this is a most important measure for the States and their divisions of governing bodies. It is no less important for the Federal Government—although the funds for Federal agencies would be limited to land acquisition only. This is something the so-

called U. S. Chamber of Parks and Recreation could support.

A second important instrument of conservation is one that is already on the books but one which the States have done little about, perhaps because most people are not aware of it. It is the Interstate Highway Program which already gives park development programs considerable leeway for landscaping work, including the construction of scenic overlooks, picnic areas, roadside parks and other amenities to make driving a pleasure. Unfortunately, this authority is scarcely being utilized at all.

It is my earnest hope that in the near future the coordinated effort needed for this park and landscape work can be brought about through closer cooperation with local, state and national programs. A large group of people using our highways are recreation bent. Again, I believe this is something that the U. S. Chamber for Parks and Recreation could express itself about—and it would be appreciated by those in charge of the program.

The third significant instrument of conservation is one that is very close to my heart—the Youth Conservation Corps. It is an important conservation measure which not only would contribute to the beauty of our country and the conservation of our natural resources. It is important, also, for what it could teach our young people in dealing with nature and preserving our wildlife.

Some may consider it as sort of a "relief program," to youth at loose ends, but I definitely do not. In my opinion, it has a definite place in our form of government as an opportunity for all the youth of our Nation to learn and give something to the country in the conservation field. In my opinion, to give one's services to the conservation field can be just as important as to be ready to serve in the military forces. This, I am sure, the United States Chamber of Parks and Recreation would be very much interested in.

From first-hand experience as an administrator with the Civilian Conservation Corps during the 30's, I know what such a program can accomplish. Today many of our leaders in all walks of life can look back to their CCC days with pride.

Perhaps one of the greatest accomplishments of the Civilian Conservation Corps, however, was that it brought to the minds of the people of this country the need for and value of a sound and active conservation program.

It is estimated that the work accomplished by the CCC youth in the park conservation field alone during the ten years of CCC was equal to what might have been expected in fifty years without its assistance. The CCC was not just a pick and shovel project. It contributed tremendously to the Nation's thoughts on parks and recreation.

It was soon realized that one of the first requirements for adequate programs, both immediate and long range, was a comprehensive survey and study. In 1936, Congress enacted the Park, Parkway and Recreation Study Act, and pursuant to this Act, forty-six of the States and the Territory of Hawaii participated with the National Park Service in the conduct of statewide studies.

The 1936 Act is now the basis for the establishment of the new Bureau of Outdoor Recreation in the Department of the Interior, following the recommendations of the President's Outdoor Recreation Resources Review Commission that such a coordinating planning agency be established as an independent Bureau.

There was in 1933—and there still is—a real need to give nationwide attention to the conservation of our natural resources—so vital to the existence and progress of the Nation.

In terms of the contribution the Corps could make to a better America, Secretary Udall recently made the following observations:

A Youth Conservation Corps would conserve and develop the capacities of our two most precious national assets—our youth and our natural resources.

For youth, a soundly operating Youth Conservation Corps will provide employment on useful work that gives dignity to those performing it.

It will develop constructive work habits.

It will provide, informally, on-the-job training in use of a variety of tools and simple machines.

It will offer an opportunity for additional classrooms and other training and education outside of work hours.

It will provide a living experience of established merit in helping young men get along with others and with themselves.

7

It will instill an appreciation of the natural world and an understanding of the land and our dependence upon it.

It will build strong bodies.

For the Nation, a soundly operating Youth Conservation Corps will yield a high percentage of young men better equipped to earn and maintain a useful place in society.

It will help spread public understanding of our natural resources and conservation.

It will help ease the explosive combination of young men concentrated in urban areas with nothing constructive to do.

Finally—and this is the value that elevates the Corps to high levels of usefulness—a sound Youth Conservation Corps, under the supervision of experienced Federal and State conservation agencies, can provide the American people with more enjoyable park and recreation lands, more productive forests, more fish and game, cleaner streams, better protected watersheds. In short, a Corps can help provide over the years, even decades, a more abundant and more enjoyable life for us and for generations to come through the conservation of natural resources.

There are tremendous conservation forces at work in the Nation today which, like the Youth Conservation Corps and the Land Conservation Fund, all blend together into the overall purpose of protecting and beautifying the American landscape—both private and government. And they all deserve public recognition and support.

To accomplish this master plan for America it will take the continued cooperative efforts of every civic and governmental group—National, State and local. Working together will produce a common overall "voice" that will speak for us all consistently, positively, clearly and effectively.

California Park System To Receive Gift

It is expected that the State of California will soon receive into the Park System an outstanding area of some 9,750 acres, located in Santa Cruz County, and known as the Aptos Forest.

The area, practically all of which is vested with second growth redwood, is to be established primarily as a wilderness area.

Its acquisition was made possible through the offer of Herman, Andrew and Agnes Marks who gift deeded some 9,000 acres. The remaining 750 acres will be purchased by the State but the area to be gift deeded is valued at many times over the price to be paid for the remainder.

The Nature Conservancy has played a very prominent part in making this area available for public recreational purposes.

Towards A Conservation Ethic

Excerpts from an article by George E. Brewer, Jr., Vice-President
The Conservation Foundation, appearing in the January 1963 issue,
Teachers College RECORD.

Can we, today, gauge the future with greater accuracy than our forebears did a century ago?

In many ways we can. Although our knowledge is far from complete, we know infinitely more about the sciences of agriculture, forestry, hydrology, and, more recently, ecology. As a result, we should have a far greater fore-knowledge of the consequences to our environment of our behavior.

But if the science of ecology can be said to have one basic premise, it is that the biotic world is a single community—that the land is *one* organism of enormous complexity.

In *The Phenomenon of Man*, Pierre Teilhard de Chardin sums up this concept of unity in imaginative words:

The last molecule is, in nature and position, a function of the whole sidereal process, and the least of the protozoa is structurally so knit into the web of life that, such is the hypothesis, its existence cannot be annihilated without, *ipso facto*, undoing the whole network of the biosphere.

This is a humbling thought, suggesting that man endures as only one interdependent unit in a system of awesome complexity and precision. If one accepts this concept, then the inescapable conclusion follows that man cannot stand aloof and alone from the rest of the natural world and from the moral principle that he should not attempt to manipulate the biotic community without understanding the far reaching ecological effects of his behavior.

Unfortunately, such understanding is not commonly shared by "the man in the street," and yet it is the man in the street—the teacher, the industrialist, the banker, the Congressman, the city planner, the engineer, the advertiser, and the building developer—anyone of whom may be president of his local Chamber of Commerce—who is actually making the controlling decisions which shape and alter the landscape.

Up to now, these decisions have produced two diametrically opposing results. They have given Americans the highest levels of *material* prosperity ever to be achieved by any people in this world, and they have also profoundly *degraded* our environment.

Twenty centuries of "progress" have brought the average citizen a vote, a national anthem, a Ford, and a high opinion of himself, as Aldo Leopold at one time pointed out, but not the capacity to live in high density without befouling and denuding his environment. Nor has he the conviction that such a capacity, rather than mere density, is the true test of whether he is *civilized*.

No creature, including man, remains unaffected by the condition of its environment. Ugliness, blight, congestion, and noise affect the health of the spirit as surely as contaminated air and water affect the

9

health of the body. None of us who have reached even middle life can fail to have noticed a steady erosion of the values which make for contentment and satisfaction in man's relation to man.

In spite of enormous cultural and economic advantages and opportunities, the growing impersonality of life in our over-crowded cities, even in the huge apartment houses where so many of us live, has resulted in a loss of neighborliness and even of common courtesy.

Mounting tensions and pressures are unhappily reflected in the appalling increase in the numbers of emotionally and mentally disturbed persons being treated in our psychiatric clinics. The mass flight of families to the suburbs is essentially a flight of desperation, an attempt to escape the inhuman and intolerable conditions of modern urban living.

One cannot escape the disquieting notion that of late we have become so isolated from the natural world, with our gadgetry and mechanization, that we have dulled our capacity for wonder and reverence, our sensitivity to grandeur and beauty. If this has happened at all, it has happened very recently. Part of our heritage, these attitudes run through literature and art from pre-Christian times onward.

No one pondered the mysteries of nature more profoundly or more humbly than David, the Psalmist:

"When I consider Thy heavens and the stars which Thou hast ordained, what is man that Thou art mindful of him or the son of man that Thou visitest him?"

To David the mystery was unending:

"Thy way is in the sea and Thy path in the great waters, and Thy footsteps are not known."

And where would a man such as David turn when he felt the desperate need for inner tranquility and peace?

"I will lift up mine eyes unto the hills whence cometh my help.'"

It was the wilderness and the mountains to which he turned in times of trouble when he needed to recreate his thoughts and spirit.

We call it recreation, and it will be a dreadful day for us when we too seek the wilderness to find inner peace only to discover there is no wilderness left.

Space is the one natural resource for which there is and can be no substitute. Privacy and periods of solitude and silence are necessary to refresh battered and jaded nerves and to nourish the creative impulse. But privacy is fast becoming an expensive luxury, and solitude is increasingly difficult to come by.

The time has now come to pose ultimate questions: Will the world of tomorrow present a fairer face, or will urban and rural slums continue to spread blight? Will the total environment of earth, air and water suffer from further spoilage and poison, or will improved land practice prevail and the general process of contamination be halted and reversed?

Zoning Round Table

Conducted by FLAVEL SHURTLEFF, Marshfield Hills, Mass.

CLUSTER ZONING

It is usually assumed that for suburban and rural living openness of development is a desirable objective and that it is attainable through the proper use of zoning regulations. The method which is most familiar is the requirement of oversize lots in residential zones of higher classification, and an increase in the size has been a notable trend of the last ten years. An acre minimum is not unusual, and its validity as a zoning regulation has been affirmed in decisions of the Supreme Court in several states. Even higher requirements have been sanctioned by the courts, two acres in New York, three acres in Missouri, four in Connecticut and five in New Jersey.

Clustering is another method of securing open development. As applied to zoning, it permits the developer to take something off the requirement for residential building lots, but only if the reduction is handed over to the community as land to be kept open. In a residential development of 50 acres, located in a zone restricted to lots of one acre, the developer may be permitted to build on a lot of 30,000 square feet, and the more than 13,000-foot reduction, or that part of it found to be fit for the purpose, might be used by the community for public recreation. This option to the developer would, in most cases, be handled in the zoning ordinance as a highly conditioned exception, and certainly one of the conditions would be the submission by the developer of a plan for the approval of the planning commission or other specified community agency. The fitness of the land to be deeded to the community is an essential in the success of the clustering method of securing open development.

Whether cluster zoning will appeal to developers is yet to be proved. They may save something in road construction. They may produce a more interesting residential pattern, and one more attractive to buyers. There may be an advantage in house frontages on open land instead of the more conventional frontage on roads.

The first court test of the validity of cluster zoning was discussed in the February 1963 zoning bulletin of the New York Regional Plan Association. This was a Superior Court case in New Jersey* involving land in South Brunswick Township, located about halfway between New York and Philadelphia. In 1962, prompted by a doubling of the population between 1957 and 1960, the township adopted an amendment to its zoning ordinance "to provide a method of development of residential land which will provide desirable open spaces, school sites, recreation and park areas, and land for other public purposes." At the discretion of the planning board a subdivider would be allowed to reduce a minimum lot size

*Chrinko vs. So. Brunswick Township Planning Board, 187/Atl. 2nd, 221.

11

requirement in excess of 20,000 square feet 20 per cent, and a minimum frontage requirement by 10 per cent, if he donated 20 per cent of his tract to the township, and if his donation was 30 per cent, he could reduce the lot size 30 per cent and the frontage 20 per cent. Among the conditions which the subdivider must accept were: 1) The land deeded to the township must be "located, shaped, and improved as required by the Planning Board;" and 2) the deeded land must be "at least a usable single five-acre tract."

The amendment was attacked on the ground: 1) That it violated the requirement of uniformity of regulation within each zone; and 2) that it did not serve the purpose for which zoning was authorized, but rather was for the special benefit of a subdivider.

In sustaining the validity of the amendment, the court held that "although the state zoning law does not in so many words empower municipalities to provide an option to developers for cluster or density zoning, such an ordinance advances the legislative purpose of securing open space, preventing overcrowd-ing and undue concentration of population." There was also a specific finding that uniformity of regulation was accomplished "because the option was open to all developers within a zoning district." To the claim of special benefit to developers, the court said that any such benefit other than a saving in street construction was obscure, and cited the great weight of authority in support of the doctrine that otherwise valid legislation is not nullified because it gives an incidental benefit to one or more individuals.

We are not told whether an appeal was taken, but rulings are to be expected either in New Jersey or in other states by the courts of last resort on the specific question whether securing public open space through cluster zoning is a valid objective under the zoning law.

Cluster zoning does not guarantee permanence of open space. In time it could be filled up with buildings for community purposes, but since these purposes might contribute to public welfare, the validity of cluster zoning as a proper objective might not be successfully challenged.

It's An Old, Old Problem!

"The prophet Isaiah said a long time ago, 'We continue to place house against house and field against field until there is no place in the world to be alone.' From then until now, we have continued so to place and have done little about the resulting confusion."

—Charles A. DeTurk, Director,
California State Department of Parks and Recreation

Dispersal of Population and Reorganization of Transport System—Calcutta

By CHITTAPRIYA MUKHERJEE

EDITOR's NOTE:—This paper complements the article entitled "Land Utilization Planning in Metropolitan Calcutta," published in the December 1962 issue of PLANNING AND CIVIC COMMENT.

The city of Calcutta, like many other cities of comparable size and contemporary origin, inevitably combines within its fold several functions:

a) that of a major port with all the attendant commitments to serve and to draw upon its hinterland;

b) the seat of the Government, nerve-centre of commercial houses and of educational institutions;

c) a large part of the city proper is inhabited by millions of people directly or indirectly dependent on the city for their livelihood. These inhabitants still consider—in spite of all the problems of housing scarcity, traffic congestion, water-logging of streets, 'smog', and lack of fresh air and all that— the city as a better place to live in than the rest of Bengal and even the suburbs of Calcutta.

If, for argument's sake we assume that as a result of the Hooghly drying up or changing its course, the city eventually loses its attraction as a major port, it is not altogether inconceivable that

a) as a result of the momentum the city has gathered over centuries,

b) due to ever-increasing pressure of population,

c) due to changes in locational factors influencing existence of a city in the present day,

the city will, unlike the old cities of Tamluk, Bandel, Adi Saptagram, Hooghly etc., continue to retain its usefulness as a leading industrial and business centre.

And this possibly explains the present move to rebuild Calcutta irrespective of what happens to the Farakka Barrage Scheme or the Haldia Port Scheme.

Consistent with our accepted policy of "regional dispersal" of economy with which the Metropolitan Planning has, in some way or the other, to be integrated, it has to be ensured that the city, which had in the past thrived—in total disregard of its impact on the rural economy—as a "parasite" to the rest of Bengal, should grow in a manner which would not create further imbalance in the total economy of the country.

If the city has to rebuild itself— and re-build it must—either within the present "municipal limits" or within the "industrial belt" or within what is called "Greater Calcutta," it has possibly to be decided:

a) what portion of our national resources—whether by borrowed capital and technique or by tapping of indigenous help —should be diverted or utilized for the purpose,

b) whether the proposed re-or-

13

ganization would provide for a "minimum decent living" for the entire existing population or for the *expected increase* in population.

c) if geographical and other factors are not conducive to planned reclamation, at a reasonable cost, are we left with no other choice than more intensive utilization of land within the present municipal limits—by having underground railways on the one hand, and multi-storied skyscrapers on the other?

d) the aggregate capital and maintenance cost that the nation would have to pay for such an intensive land utilization is surely a factor to be reckoned with; our resources being scarce, we can hardly invest more for a small area to the exclusion of the rest of the country. Can we not think of creating conditions which would encourage the resident population of the city to stay in planned "satellite" towns and villages, even sixty or seventy miles away, and at the same time to have the facility of moving within the city in the shortest possible time?

Visualizing future Calcutta as the nerve-centre of industry, could we relieve the congestion of resident population within the city limits? While the people gainfully occupied in some sort of work in Calcutta itself have to move in and out of the city, those dependent on the economically active members, have no par-

ticular point in staying within the city.

Assuming that this is a feasible proposition and that the aggregate capital layout as well as recurring cost would be less (with suitable State intervention on land transfers and housing schemes, a large part of the capital expenditure may be left to the private sector) it presupposes —in addition to the creation of appropriate conditions for revival of impoverished villages and construction of planned "satellite" towns with better social environments—introduction of fast-moving and frequent electric train services (I do not discuss at all the need for supplementing railway service with a net-work of good roads), in a manner to bring the working population within the city in, let us say, less than an hour's time from the farthest points of the radius. (With this, of course, has to be combined long-term measures to discourage continuously increasing immigration of the future working force to the surrounding areas).

Scarcity of land within Calcutta, and influx of additional population from other places during the postwar years have no doubt multiplied the suburban population, but the fact remains that the *total loss of time on the way* deters many inhabitants of Calcutta from moving out of the city.

Working out a scheme on the suggested lines would pre-suppose:

a) immediate imposition of *ban on land transfer or speculation* and *pegging the price of land*, both within the city and in the proposed radius;

(Continued on page 16)

14

Gold Medal for Community Improvement Is Awarded

Midtown Plaza has earned for Rochester, New York, the Ward Melville Gold Medal for Community Improvement for 1962. The Plaza was selected by a committee of judges as the best development among large cities and also as the most outstanding among all entries for the year.

To Cambridge, Massachusetts, for Technology Square, has gone the Silver Medal awarded to the winner among intermediate size cities. A winner among small communities was not named.

The Medal for Community Improvement program, now in its fourth year, was established "To encourage the development of the cultural, aesthetic and economic values of our cities, towns and villages—and to recognize outstanding accomplishments in this vital phase of the health and vitality of our nation."

Ward Melville, Chairman of the Board of Melville Shoe Corporation, says: "One of the most critical problems facing our nation is the restoration of its cities, towns and villages to prosperous, pleasant places to live and work. The awards are intended not only to give recognition to outstanding accomplishments in community improvement but also to provide guides to other communities with similar problems."

He further points out, "Despite the attention being focused on the problem by federal and state governments and various national organizations, the basic problem remains one for the individual community and the people who live and work there."

Under the program, any city, town or village in the United States or its territories may be nominated for recognition on the basis of improvement which may have been completed at any time within five years prior to the calendar year of the award.

The improvement need not involve an entire community, but it must benefit directly a majority of the community's population. It need not be fully completed at the time of nomination but should be sufficiently advanced to offer evidence of its nature adequate for judging.

The nomination may be made by any adult citizen of the United States, whether or not a resident of the community in question, with the consent of the principal elected or appointed official of that community. Three size categories of communities are considered separately by the judges: Cities over 300,000 population; those from 50,000 to 300,000; and those under 50,000.

The closing date for 1963 nominations is June 30. Nominations and all supporting materials should be sent to: Ward Melville Gold Medal for Community Improvement, Room 914—342 Madison Avenue, New York 17, N. Y.

DISPERSAL OF POPULATION AND REORGANIZATION OF TRANSPORT SYSTEM—CALCUTTA

(*Continued from p. 14*)

b) evolving a procedure that would, consistent with a comprehensive land-use policy, give priority to people, particularly those who live in sub-human conditions of Calcutta city, to buy land for residential purpose outside the city limits. [This would, at the same time, call for setting up machinery to buy or acquire the land and buildings available within the city, to be utilised for better purposes.]

c) restriction of further immigration of people from places outside the radius.

Even if this is considered to be a practicable proposition, the rigidity that would have to be enforced to make it effective, is perhaps hardly compatible with our democratic approach to planning, or for that matter with the existing law of land acquisition and similar legislation.

d) Construction of separate railtracks for suburban services, as in Bombay, in order to ensure frequent and quick movement. (It is assumed that underground railway is not proposed to be constructed outside the limits of the city.)

I suggest that we consider moving *railway lines*, either at one point or at several points, within the city so as to enable all suburban trains to *converge at a place near the Dalbousie Square or the maidan or the Eden Gardens* and to have, if possible, small halt-ing stations at convenient places within the city itself. If the present peak-hour pressure on trams, buses, and other vehicles gives us an idea of their carrying capacity and of the total requirement, it can perhaps be assumed that while short distance journeys would no doubt be covered largely by buses and trams, a major portion of the working population could make use of the train service, thus relieving, to a considerable extent, the present load on trams and buses. (Separate tracks for trams, or three-carriage trams, or even trolley buses will hardly be adequate to meet the present chaotic traffic conditions.)

As to feasibility of moving the suburban train services within the city, the choice lies between underground and surface railway system. (The third alternative may perhaps be a combination of surface lines and "skyways" or elevated lines at certain places).

Underground railway system would undoubtedly be the last answer to the problem of traffic congestion within the city. Soil conditions of Calcutta having been found to be similar to those of Leningrad, we are thinking afresh of having a similar underground railway system here.

Some arguments in favour of underground, in preference to surface railways, are:

a) difficulty of *re-alignment of roads*, lanes and by-lanes in

(*Continued on page 18*)

Plan To Revitalize Downtown Buffalo

Downtown Buffalo, New York, will be revitalized and revamped with one of the most advanced building developments of any major eastern U. S. city, under a "supersquare" plan put forward by Charles Luckman Associates, New York and Los Angeles planning and architectural firm.

The concept envisions consolidation of retail stores, offices, banks, a hotel, a transportation center, and spacious parking facilities within a network of malls and covered pedestrian walkways. The planned development is sponsored by Greater Buffalo civic and business leaders, headed by President Edward L. Hengerer.

The project, designed to make multiple use of the 17-acre site in the core of the city's business district, represents a reversal in recent trends in urban development which have been aimed at a decentralization of facilities.

Buffalo's "supersquare" development utilizes a plan its architects call "designed density." As applied here it provides a centralized complex of facilities that draw together many of the city's activities for mutual business interest.

Its aim is to meet the problem of high land costs—a roadblock to so many U. S. urban renewal programs—by making the greatest use of all property in the city's vital downtown core.

"The design will promote the expansion of already existing government offices and commercial operations and relate them to greatly increased provisions for Buffalo's economic vitality," according to John T. Stofko, a vice-president in Luckman's New York office and partner-in-charge of the project.

As planned, the "supersquare" project will in effect be three-dimensional.

Its "base" will contain an underground bus terminal as well as parking facilities for 4,000 cars.

A two-story "platform" at ground level will provide space for retail stores, restaurants, banks and other commercial outlets.

Four steel-and-glass towers, offering 2,200,000 sq. ft. of office space, will be extensions of existing facilities.

A fifth, centrally-located tower, will be a 600-room hotel, providing a 24-hour-a-day tenant for the complex. The hotel is considered another planning "plus" since it makes overnight accommodations available in a heavily-populated business area.

"We deliberately included a round-the-clock hotel in this development as a means of keeping the section alive after the evening rush hour when most downtown areas normally die down," Mr. Stofko pointed out.

Outdoor plazas and terraces will enhance the outward appearance of this modern midtown development. The entire area—buildings as well as public facilities—will be interconnected by enclosed shopping malls, and arcades and bridges will span existing streets to protect pedestrians from vehicle traffic.

DISPERSAL OF POPULATION AND REORGANIZATION OF TRANSPORT SYSTEM—CALCUTTA

(*Continued from p. 16*)

case of surface railway lines;
b) cost of *compensation* for the inevitable demolition of several houses for construction of surface railway lines;
c) possible interruption to *movement of large ships* in the Calcutta Jetties, in case the only site for construction of the second bridge (with railway line from the other side of the Ganges) is found to be somewhere between the Shalimar Railway Station and the present Howrah bridge;

These arguments seem to suggest that it would perhaps be wiser and more economical to incur the heavy *capital* expenditure for underground railway and to suffer the comparatively heavy *maintenance* cost.

If Leningrad, with the vast mineral resources and scientific ingenuity of the USSR at her disposal and the high per capita wealth, is an example to us, simply because of its similarity of soil conditions, it would perhaps not be irrelevant to enquire:

(i) if the construction *and* maintenance costs are not too heavy for a country like ours, which would either have to depend heavily on foreign imports for all the complicated machineries, or would have to raise the domestic industrial base to a level to enable us to bear the heavy maintenance cost and to keep the system in a working condition;

(ii) if any other European or North American city (whatever may be the difference in their economic or other conditions with those in India) is remodeling its suburban rail transport system on lines different from those of Leningrad and if any such city offers us an example of preference for surface railways;

(iii) if, with all the geographical, historical and economic differences, Bombay suburban railway system offers us an example that we can draw upon with some advantage.

Just as the electrification of Bombay's suburban train system has some historical explanations, so also the logic for the existence of tram tracks within the city of Calcutta, and termination of steam-driven railways on the outskirts of Calcutta, can be traced to such historical and economic reasons which may not hold good now. If trams had once served Calcutta very efficiently and are even now serving well, it cannot be denied perhaps that in certain congested roads like Chitpur, Dharmatala, Harrison Road, trams, in present day conditions, are more a hindrance than a facility. In absence of a better arrangement we cannot, in spite of the inconvenience it creates, think of doing away with the tram. (The Howrah Bridge, constructed hardly twenty years back, evidently did not—by only providing for tram lines instead of train lines—visualise the future as

(*Continued on page 45*)

PROJECTS IN REVIEW

The Potomac River Basin Report

The Potomac River flows through a land filled with names of legendary places and events—Harpers Ferry, Gettysburg, Antietam, Manassas, Bull Run, the C. & O. Canal, Great Falls, the National Capital, Mt. Vernon. The Potomac has carried the people's commerce, its depths and banks have supplied them food, it has furnished them water to drink.

Thus is the river characterized in a recent report presenting a plan of development for water and related land resources of the Potomac River Basin. Specific projects for immediate authorization are recommended in the plan which has been prepared as a guide for the orderly development, conservation and utilization of the Basin's resources to meet the needs of the next half century.

In a preface to the report, Col. Roy S. Kelley, District Engineer, says:

"Proper development of the water resources of the Potomac River Basin has been the subject of study and discussion for a long time. Nature has been kind to provide this planning margin. But time for discussion has run out. It is time for decision."

The report is the product of a coordinated study, initiated in 1956 and carried out through the efforts of every Federal agency with water and related responsibilities. Included were the Departments of Agriculture, Health, Education and Welfare, Interior, Commerce, and the Federal Power Commission.

The Potomac River drains 14,670 square miles in an area which constitutes the eastern slopes of the Appalachian Mountains in the mid-Atlantic region of the United States. The present population of the Basin totals about three million people, and the population growth rate of the area has been greater than that of the Nation. Employment opportunities are expected to continue to grow at a rate somewhat greater than the national rate over the next fifty years.

But according to the report, attainment of growth in the Potomac River Service Area is tied to the development and control of the water resources of the basin. It points out that the natural dependable flow of the river is the key to relating river capabilities to water needs, and the flow of the Potomac is notoriously variable.

The flow becomes woefully insufficient during many hot, dry, summer periods and produces destructive floods at other times. However, says the report, the Potomac River and its tributary system have enough water to meet all the water needs far into the future provided the water can be made available in the right quantities—not too much, not too little—at the right times and places, and with the right quality.

In arriving at a final plan, the report states that complete fulfillment of *all* desires for water was considered neither feasible nor economically justified. It points out, "Flood damage cannot be completely prevented; some risk must be accepted."

According to Brig. Gen. John C. Dalrymple, Division Engineer, "The recommended plan includes 16 major reservoirs, one of which is already authorized; 418 small headwater reservoirs; three small flood control projects already authorized; and land management and conservation measures to reduce erosion and rapid localized runoff."

It is estimated that the plan will provide for all water supply and water quality control needs, generally, to the year 2010, flood damage reductions of about 63 per cent and recreation opportunities for up to about 16 million visitor-days per year.

The report is available at various public libraries in Maryland, Pennsylvania, Virginia, West Virginia and Washington, D. C. Everyone is urged to become familiar with the proposals contained in it to the end that the best interests of the area may be served. Particular attention should be directed to that section of the report which states that, under the recommended plan, a portion of the historic C. & O. Canal and some natural recreation potential would be destroyed. It is also pointed out that local impact due to relocations, temporary tax losses and changes in the economic base would be severe in some areas.

Interested parties may send written views on the report to the Board of Engineers for Rivers and Harbors, Washington 25, D. C.

Missouri River— Fort Peck to Fort Benton

Some two hundred miles of the wild Missouri River and adjacent land areas are currently of special citizen interest.

Much of the area, which includes the reach between Fort Peck Reservoir and Morony Dam above Fort Benton, Montana, is wild and rugged, sparsely populated, and largely inaccessible by modern means of transportation.

Since, inevitably, the resources of such an area will not remain largely unused, the Congress has recognized that extensive studies are necessary in regard to it. To that end, the U. S. Army Corps of Engineers and several bureaus of the Department of Interior, including the National Park Service, the U. S. Fish and Wildlife Service, the Bureau of Land Management and others, are investigating the opportunities for water and related land resources development in the area.

Eleven alternative plans for development have been formulated and were published recently in an Information Bulletin. Brig. Gen. Robert F. Seedlock, U. S. Army Engineer Division, and Harrell F. Mosbaugh, Regional Coordinator, Missouri Basin Region, point out that all the plans are physically capable of accomplishment but differ in the emphasis placed on specific purposes and in the means of achieving them.

Holding a prominent place in the planning has been a National Park Service proposal to preserve for all

(*Continued on page 44*)

Commentaries

Tomorrow: "A hundred years from now students will ask their history professors, 'Well, did it ever stop—all this building and growing?'

"I know the answer will be, 'No, it never stopped.' They were bold, ambitious, enterprising people—these energetic citizens of the sixties. They went right on building their schools and their homes and highways and playgrounds.

"But they were not so consumed with their own destiny—their own needs and ambitions—that they forgot about ours.

"They left us their spirit—they left us their natural resources—they even left us some of their wilderness as a reminder of our past and our heritage. This they inherited from those who went before them. This they preserved for us. This we must preserve, too."

—From remarks by Mr. John F. Shelley, Congressman from California, *Congressional Record*, April 8, 1963, who introduced H. R. 5246 on March 28, 1963, "to establish a national wilderness preservation system for the permanent good of the whole people of our Nation."

☙

New Brochure: "Land patterns of the future are being decided today."

The statement is made by Secretary of the Interior Stewart L. Udall in a foreword to a new National Park Service brochure, *Future Parks for the Nation.*

The brochure proposes 34 areas of national significance that might be acquired for use as Federal, State, or local park and recreation areas. They are located in 26 States and extend from the Allagash in Maine to Whiskeytown-Shasta-Trinity in California.

According to Secretary Udall, "Man faces the new dimensions of outer space with courage and faith. But he is still rooted to the earth. . . . The most we can do at this late date is not enough. The least we can do—before our land patterns are inalterably fixed—is to preserve the few remaining extensive areas of natural open space, now, while there is still time."

•   ☙

An Aim: What is the big objective of the National Conference on State Parks?

The question was recently put to Polk Hebert, vice-president of NCSP, by Eldon Roark, columnist for the *Memphis Press-Scimitar.* Mr. Hebert's answer, as reported by Mr. Roark:

"Education. The public must be educated to the importance of a long-range program for parks, and educated to the wisdom of keeping the program out of politics."

The greatest need of our state parks today, in Mr. Hebert's opinion, is more camping areas. He points out that people are finding fun in "roughing it" —although with modern camping equipment "roughing it" isn't as rough as it used to be. If the trend continues, Mr. Hebert thinks private enterprise may find it profitable to develop camp areas near state parks.

☙

A View: "The man who towers above the crowd makes an excellent target. So does the building which towers above its neighbors . . . And the design and placement of a multi-storied building carries with it some really grave responsibilities."

That's the position of The Better Housing League of Greater Cincinnati which recently published a timely discussion of "The High-Rise And The City of Cincinnati."

"Ironically enough," says the League, "every time we erect a tall building in our community we are actually creating a view—a man-made mountain so to speak which can be seen for miles around, and whose appearance as a consequence is of enormous concern."

The League acknowledges that it is of great visual importance in the development of the city that the urban landscape be varied—"vertically varied,

21

as well as varied in plan. This is particularly true as renewal begins to involve larger and larger areas."

Cincinnati has recently enacted a view-zoning ordinance which, among other objectives, attempts to keep builders from locating structure so as to obstruct recognizably attractive and commonly shared views."

❧

Campus Architecture: Many colleges are now in action, producing some of the best contemporary architecture in America, according to a recent issue of *Architectural Forum.*

"The change started slowly some 20 years ago," says the Forum, "when colleges began recruiting outstanding architects for their building programs."

❧

Apartment Building: Again, in its April issue, *Architectural Forum* takes a critical view of the architectural quality of most U. S. apartments built over the past 40 years. An article on "The Apartment Boom" says:

"Indeed, some of the solid apartments of the 1920s look better than their notably less solid neighbors of the 1960s. Still, the outlook is not all black: more discriminating tenants, more discriminating builders, somewhat improved financing, more economical methods, better mechanical equipment—plus a more realistic design approach on the part of some architects—all this has produced a new promise of better design."

❧

Urban Renewal: "Colleges and universities are becoming increasingly involved these days in urban renewal projects to get more elbow room and to upgrade their immediate surroundings."

This development was reported recently by Stanley Penn in the *Wall Street Journal.* Continues Mr. Penn:

"The schools' interest in urban renewal is the result of two worsening problems: Insufficient space to meet mounting enrollments, and the encroachment of slums which frequently create physical dangers for teachers and students and almost always deprive the institutions of the decent adjacent housing required to attract and hold a high-quality faculty."

❧

Unity: The inter-dependence of our natural resources is ably emphasized by D. A. Anderson, Head of the Information and Education Department, College Station, Texas, in a recent issue of *Texas Forest News.*

In an article on "Conservation—A Way of Life", Mr. Anderson says:

"Of our total resources, the renewable resources which comprise soil, water, animal life and vegetation, can be maintained indefinitely under wise-use management.

"Each of these renewable resources is dependent upon the others. Soils cannot produce crops without water; water as run-off, cannot be stored in the ground without grasslands and forests. Animal life, in all forms, makes the soil productive and plays an important role in the life cycle of many plants. Cover by trees and other vegetation provides protection to the soil against the erosive force of wind and water.

"Weaken one link and the whole life-supporting chain is placed in danger."

❧

The Elderly: Two concepts now in the forefront of American thinking are likewise receiving emphasis in England. They are the attempt to encourage excellence in architectural design through the holding of contests and the belated search for appropriate housing for the elderly.

From the Ministry of Housing and Local Government in London comes the report that part of its competition in 1963 for "Awards for Good Design" will be devoted to the needs of older persons. The announcement points out that since the special requirements of elderly persons have for some time attracted great interest, the Minister has decided to devote a part of the 1963 competition "to schemes designed for this purpose."

In Perspective

What some of us feel has long needed saying in this time of diverse conflicts has been given effective expression in the March issue of *Fortune* magazine. Under the title, "Business Men Who Love The Land," *Fortune* makes a telling point:

"U. S. industrialists have traditionally been cast as the villians in the nation's early conservation battles, and a good many of them played the role convincingly. But if the century-long battle to preserve the nation's resources, wildlife, and natural beauty is on the way to being won, it is because other determined business men have fought on the side of reform— and are still fighting."

Tracing the conservation effort from the formation of the first national parks in the latter half of the nineteenth century, *Fortune* points out that Nathaniel P. Langford, a Minnesota banker, became the leading propagandist for the creation of Yellowstone National Park and was appointed its first superintendent in 1872.

In 1897, an inspiring family tradition, which was to come to mean much to America, began when John D. Rockefeller, Sr. gave the land and funds for a park along Doan Brook in Cleveland, an important early step in the formation of Cleveland's model park system. At a later day, John D. Rockefeller, Jr. was to contribute greatly toward the preservation of such monuments as Yellowstone, Yosemite, the California redwoods, Great Smokies, Shenandoah, Grand Teton, and the Hudson River Palisades.

In 1908, a Boston banker, John W. Weeks, first a Massachusetts Congressman and later a U. S. Senator, introduced a bill in the House "for protecting navigable streams and promoting navigation." Passed in 1911 after long controversy, the. Weeks law gave the government unprecedented power to acquire vast forest lands.

And in 1916, came formation of the National Park Service, with Stephen T. Mather, a San Francisco-born chemical manufacturer, as its first director.

Carrying the saga to our own immediate day, *Fortune* chooses seven business men who are currently active in conservation and related efforts and uses full-page, color photographs to help depict some of their activities. Among them are Horace M. Albright, director of the National Park Service from 1929 to 1933, a past president of the American Planning and Civic Association and currently on the APCA Board of Trustees, and Laurance S. Rockefeller, also a member of the Board of Trustees. The other five are:

Fred Smith, president of Oakland Corporation of Pittsburgh and consultant to the Prudential Insurance Co. who directs the Council of Conservationists which he founded in 1952.

Elting Arnold, general counsel of the Inter-American Development Bank, who is secretary of the Nature Conservancy.

Ross L. Leffler, former assistant to the executive vice-president for operations of U. S. Steel, who is now general counsel of the International Association of Game, Fish, and Conservation Commissioners.

Bernard L. Orell, vice-president of Weyerhaeuser Co., who administers its public affairs program.

Paul Mellon, a director of Mellon National Bank & Trust, who is founder of the Old Dominion Foundation.

The editors of *Fortune* and their staff have performed a real service in setting an important aspect of American growth and development in true perspective. Through their

courtesy and for our members—many of whom are old hands at this exciting business of conservation, some of whom have newly joined us —we reproduce in the picture section following the pictures of Mr. Albright and Mr. Rockefeller, together with accompanying text as it appeared in the March issue.

This we do in tribute to the leadership which these men have given our association throughout the years. We are sure they are in complete accord with us in saying their efforts are indicative of the earnest efforts of men, everywhere, who, in by-gone years, in our own day, and in the time to come, will ever unite in—

A voice of praise for the land we love—

And a determination to cherish it for generations yet unborn.

Save the Redwoods

The Save-the-Redwoods League recently contributed $1,000,000 toward acquisition of land at Bull Creek in the Humboldt Redwoods State Park, California.

The State of California and the League have been working since 1955 to save the redwood forest which has been threatened with destruction by erosion and tree death. Says California's Governor Brown:

"New acquisitions by the League will greatly assist us in saving these great trees which truly are one of the wonders of the world. The League has led the fight to save these trees and the people of California are indebted to them."

Proposed Prairie National Park, Kansas. General view in vicinity of Carnahan Creek.

Proposed Prairie National Park, Kansas. An area of great beauty and scientific and historic interest, this region was selected after many years of study by the National Park Service, with the assistance of eminent grassland ecologists.

Courtesy National Park Service, U. S. Department of the Interior

Prairie National Park—A Proposal

EDITOR'S NOTE:—This is the third in the series of articles on proposed National Park Service projects, prepared by the Park Service at our request.

Men look to mountains as symbols of their Nation's majesty, but another symbol of strength and beauty for Americans is that great grassland called the Prairie.

The Prairie was a challenge, a fascination, a treasure, a sea of grass to be crossed or a vast garden to be grazed and tilled. Most important, this grassland, one of the most fertile areas on earth, gave the United States of America the capacity for greatness.

The once-vast Prairie, which has had such enormous economic and political effects on our country and the world, stretched across or touched 12 states—from Indiana to the eastern Dakotas and southwest to Texas. Yet the Prairie was a unity in composition and in mood. In essence it was "a way of life" between the wetter forest areas of the east and the drier Great Plains to the west, a complex community of highly competitive yet balanced plant and animal life controlled by soil and climate in a way that made grass dominate.

Like any refined mechanism, however, the Prairie was susceptible to modification by other than normal influences, and the White man on learning how rich was the deep dark prairie loam and how lush its grass, set about with all his power to break the Prairie to his needs.

The plow began it; roadways, powerways, reservoirs, the spread of urban life is finishing the job. But the Prairie belongs to this country's heritage. A portion of it should remain as part of our environment. Its influence on the past and present, its plants, its animals, its aspects and moods should be kept a part of the American scene and in the understanding of the American people.

Hence, there is a proposal, under consideration since 1961, to preserve a 57,000 acre remnant of the Prairie in the Flint Hills region of Kansas as a Prairie National Park.

This area is one of the finest remaining remnants of Prairie left in the United States, located in typical "blue stem country" in Pottawatomie County near Manhattan, Kansas. The park proposal culminates a quarter-century of growing interest in Prairie preservation, in an area selected after studies of the finest grassland tracts remaining in the Prairie States.

The proposed park is roughly 7 by 13 miles in size. The eastern portion consists of gentle rolling lands. The western half, through which most of the major drainages flow, is comprised of unusual grass covered hill formations, which appear as long narrow flat fingers meandering generally north and south. Attractive wooded growth is found in the drainages, and the streams add much to the area's beauty and interest. Despite its relatively small acreage, it has the appearance of vastness, and there are vantage points from which this is strikingly evident.

Adjacent to the proposed park on the west is Tuttle Creek Reservoir, a flood control project now under construction by the Corps of Engineers. The reservoir will offer water-based recreation, will not detract from the park, if established, and will be helpful to wildlife resources of the park.

Bills to authorize a Prairie National Park were considered in the 87th Congress and have been reintroduced in the present Congress, sponsored by Kansas Senators Pearson and Carlson (S. 986) and by Representative Avery (H.R. 4424), who represents the district in which the proposed park is located.

In addition to the cooperation of the Corps of Engineers, from which the bill would authorize a transfer of reservoir shoreland, the park proposal enjoys the support of the Governor and Legislature of Kansas as well as the Kansas State Highway Commission which administers a highway right-of-way through the area.

However, the people of Pottawatomie County, have shown concern over the loss of tax base, homesites and grazing lands. There is also a desire on the part of some groups to develop the reservoir shore on the park side for private recreation, an objective incompatible with the purposes of the park.

If established, planning for park facilities and administration would require deftness in insuring that park developments always have an adequate background of undisturbed Prairie. To reduce the natural Prairie environment, or allow obvious intrusions, would destroy the quality and atmosphere of the park.

The park road system, a prime requisite for visitor use of the area, should therefore consist of small roads conforming to the topography as much as possible and designed to allow for unhurried appreciation and understanding of the area. Trails would supplement the roads, and the entire northwestern portion of the park could remain roadless to provide an extensive area where experiencing the Prairie environment could be enjoyed at a walker's or horseman's pace, just as it was in pioneer times. Campgrounds and picnic areas for motorists, horsemen and walkers would be provided, and an interpretive program adequate to this area of high ecological interest would center at a headquarters site. Private enterprise would be relied upon to supply visitor services outside the area.

Important to the park plan would be protecting existing wildlife species, such as the prairie chicken, and also the reintroduction of animals originally native to the area, at least as far as it is practicable to do so. Such reintroduced species might include bison, elk, antelope, and perhaps wild turkeys. The exterior boundary would be fenced so that the larger grazing animals could not wander out, and yet within the park they would be free to roam naturally.

Many people now hurry across the Prairie and Plains, heading east or west without being encouraged to stop to understand what the Prairie has meant and means as a life community, a landscape, and as an influence upon personal and national life. Evident in a Prairie Park would be the complex and

(Continued on page 47)

30

State Park *Notes*

Texas. The establishment of Padre Island national seashore was recently assured by an over-whelmingly affirmative vote of the Texas legislature. The state bill complements legislation already passed by the U. S. Congress, providing for development of the fringe of land skirting the lower Texas coast as a national seashore area.

The State action climaxed several years of work by supporters of national seashore status for the 80-mile sandy island that runs along the coast between Corpus Christi and Brownsville. The bill as finally approved gives the state and federal governments joint legal jurisdiction within the legend-steeped park area. It also contains a nominal reverter clause dealing with privately owned lands in the area.

Of Padre Island, Ed Kilman, Editor Emeritus of the *Houston Post,* and a member of the State Parks Board says:

"It is rich in history and legendry, of pirates, wrecked ships, Indian fights and buried treasure, dating back about three centuries.

"Chief among its attractions, aside from its scenic and historic allure, are its excellent fishing and extraordinary bird life. The island is near the deepest area in the Gulf of Mexico, an area known as Sigsbee's Deep, approximately 300 miles long, 100 miles wide, and 12,000 feet deep. The balmy climate of Padre and the bountiful marine life are attributed to the proximity of this vast body of deep, blue water. Several years ago a piscatorial authority reported that there were 272 varieties of salt-water fish around Padre beach—a greater assortment than in any other resort waters in the world."

Other recent action of the Texas legislature included passage of a bill to consolidate the Texas Game and Fish Commission and the State Parks Board.

The bill would abolish the present nine-member Game and Fish Commission and the six-member State Parks Board and put functions of both agencies under a new three-member Parks and Wildlife Commission to be appointed by the Governor. The measure was strongly opposed by members of both the Fish and Game and Parks and Wildlife Commissions.

California. In a special message to the California legislature, Governor Brown has called for a long-range beaches and parks program to be financed by establishment of a nineteen million dollar fund now and a one hundred fifty million dollar bond issue later.

The proposed bond issue, under the Governor's plan, would be submitted to the voters at the 1964 general election.

The Governor urged that California save what is left of its natural resources before it is too late. With the price of land throughout the state increasing at the rate of 10 per cent a year, he said acquisition should get under way before the state is priced out of the market.

The proposed nineteen million dollar fund would be used in 21 specific areas, with priority to beach property in the central and southern areas of the state. With only one exception, these projects represent acquisition of private lands.

New York. Governor Nelson Rockefeller has signed into New York law a legislative bill allocating $25,000,000 additional bond funds for a state program of purchasing land for parks and other recreational sites. The additional borrowing, which raises to $100,000,000 the total for the program, was approved by New York voters last November.

The increased allocation will raise the total for purchase of state park lands from $20,000,000 to $30,000,-000. Five million has been designated for general outdoor recreation —camp sites, fishing, hunting, boat-launching sites, winter sports facilities and preservation of scenic areas. The measure also authorizes cities to use funds under the program to establish small neighbor-hood parks for use by children and the elderly.

Missouri. Dedication of a protective shelter for the famous petroglyphs, or Indian rock carvings, at Washington State Park, Missouri, was held recently.

The petroglyph sites in the State Park are believed to have been ceremonial grounds of prehistoric American Indians. Represented by the rock carvings are arrows, squares, ovals, circles, footprints, claws, human figures, and the thunder-bird symbol which is usually associated with rain in the religion of the early Indians.

The newly dedicated shelter and a newly constructed cyclone fence are designed to protect the rock carvings from the weather and vandals.

Principal speaker at the dedication service was Dr. John M. Corbett, Chief Archaeologist of the National Park Service. Joseph Jaeger, Jr., Director of State Parks and a member of the Board of Directors of NCSP, was master of ceremonies.

Nevada. Creation of a state park at Lake Tahoe, Nevada has been provided by newly enacted legislation in that state. The director of the State Conservation and Natural Resources Department is authorized to spend up to $500,000, with the Governor's approval, in the next two years, to purchase land options, to accept land donations or to accept financial grants earmarked for park purchases from various private individuals and charitable foundations.

(Continued on page 46)

National Capital Notes

The Committee of 100 on the Federal City—the oldest planning body in Washington and an affiliate of the American Planning and Civic Association—has opposed the requested rezoning of a 29-acre tract of land adjacent to Fort Washington.

Granting the request would permit construction of high-rise apartment buildings close to the Potomac River.

In a letter to the Prince Georges County Commissioners, Upper Marlboro, Maryland, Rear Admiral Neill Phillips, USN (ret.), Chairman of the Committee of 100 on the Federal City, said:

"There can be no doubt that the people of the metropolitan Washington area and of the country as a whole are strongly opposed to this sort of development. The matter involved is of national concern—a proposal which threatens the basic plans for the nation's capital."

Stating that high-rise apartment buildings close to the Potomac will inevitably destroy the natural beauty of the river, Admiral Phillips explained:

"One of Washington's chief natural assets is the Potomac River. The shores of the Potomac above and below Washington remain today much as they were a century ago. This natural and unspoiled river valley is a unique feature of the city—one of the aspects of Washington which set it apart from other American cities, helping to make it a worthy capital."

The letter of opposition pointed out that granting the request would establish a precedent and said:

"It will then only be a matter of time before high-rise apartment buildings form unbroken walls along both sides of the river."

      ✦   ★   ★

A report, prepared by the Washington office of Doxiadis Associates, Inc., under the direction of *Downtown Progress*, calls attention to a significant aspect of Washington's development and offers appropriate recommendations.

Called "Downtown Streets and Places," it points out that the circles, the squares, the tree lined streets, and the grand diagonal avenues are the visible reminders of The L'Enfant Plan commissioned by President Washington in 1791. It continues:

"As the city has grown and changed over the years, many of the special streets and places designated by L'Enfant have not developed, or have been eliminated, or have become indistinct."

The report makes effective use of drawings to illustrate recommendations for the design and treatment of the streets and places of Downtown Washington "to evoke the heritage of The L'Enfant Plan, and to provide identities for all of the streets and places in Downtown consistent with their functions."

Says the report, "Downtown Washington lacks identity."

      ★   ★   ★

33

The D. C. Civil War Round-table recently presented its 1963 Gold Medal to Conrad L. Wirth, director of the National Park Service, a member of the National Capital Planning Commission, and a member of the Board of Directors of the National Conference on State Parks.

The award was presented by Maj. Gen. U. S. Grant 3rd, former chairman of the U. S. Civil War Battlefields and a member of the Board of Trustees of the American Planning and Civic Association.

The award was made under the Mission 66 program, launched by the National Park Service several years ago. Under the program, a number of commemorative events have been scheduled to coincide with anniversary battle dates in various areas.

★　★　★

A complete plan for the renewal of a mile-long stretch of Pennsylvania Avenue may be completed by the end of the year, according to the National Capital Planning Commission.

In the immediate offing, should Congressional appropriations make it possible, is construction of a working model of the portion of the Avenue between the Treasury and the Capitol.

★　★　★

Ingenuity has been brought to play by the Maryland-National Capital Park and Planning Commission in its effort to get broader citizen understanding of its activities. Free bus tours for groups of thirty or more people cover parks, existing and proposed highways, subdivision layouts, zoning and other aspects of the Commission's functions.

★　★　★

In common with many other cities, Washington is awakening to the fact that too many of its street shade trees are on the sick list. Sycamores and elms, in particular, are dying all over town.

Street trees do more than provide shade and color, of course. They also help reduce the glare of reflected light from the walls of buildings, deaden noise, and, perhaps, reduce dust.

Washington seems to be beyond the zone where the sugar maple, with its brilliant fall colors, will thrive on city streets. Hence, the question is pointing up: What must be done to preserve the National Capital's reputation as the "City of Trees?"

Commission of Fine Arts

The Commission of Fine Arts is undergoing basic personnel change with the resignation of David E. Finley as Chairman and, in addition, expiration of the terms of five of the seven Commission members.

In accepting Mr. Finley's decision to retire "with great regret," President Kennedy said: "You and your colleagues have left Washington a more beautiful city, and our community and our Nation stand deeply in your debt."

The Commission, though it sits only to advise, plays a pervasive role in the design and development of the Nation's Capital. By statute, it is composed of three architects, one landscape architect, one painter, one sculptor and one lay member, all of whom serve without financial remuneration.

Mr. Finley was first appointed a member of the Commission of Fine Arts by President Roosevelt in 1943 for a four-year term. He was reappointed by both Presidents Truman and Eisenhower, and was elected chairman by the members of the Commission in 1950. He was director of the National Gallery of Art for 18 years, leaving the post in 1956.

Strictly Personal

Joseph F. Kaylor, newly appointed assistant to the director of the Department of Interior's Bureau of Outdoor Recreation, will help administer all phases of the Bureau's work, with special emphasis on State-Federal relations and the program of assistance to the states.

He will assist in the coordination of Federal outdoor recreation programs, the administration of the proposed land and water conservation fund, the encouragement of interstate and regional cooperation, and surveys of proposed national recreation areas.

A veteran of nearly 36 years of service in recreation and natural resource conservation, Mr. Kaylor has been director of the Maryland Department of Forests and Parks since 1942. From 1936 to 1941, he was inspector of Civilian Conservation Corps projects, largely outdoor recreation facilities, throughout the Nation.

Mr. Kaylor has been a member of the Board of Directors of the National Conference on State Parks. In addition, as president of the Association of State Park Directors, his activities and accomplishments need little introduction to NCSP members. He is to be congratulated on his selection to his present important post.

———◆———

George B. Hartzog, Jr., recently appointed Associate Director of the National Park Service, has an outstanding record in parks management and civic leadership.

Secretary of the Interior Stewart L. Udall says, "His varied experience and talents as a leader will give new strength to the National Park Service at a crucial period in its history."

Mr. Hartzog, who succeeds Eivind T. Scoyen as Associate Director, was a career employee of the Department of Interior from 1946 to 1962. He left the National Park Service in August, 1962, where he had served as superintendent of the Jefferson National Expansion Memorial in St. Louis, to become executive director of Downtown St. Louis, Inc., an organization of civic and business leaders devoted to developing and promoting the downtown area of St. Louis.

Mr. Hartzog became assistant superintendent of Rocky Mountain National Park, Colorado, in 1955 and assistant superintendent of Great Smoky Mountains National Park, Tennessee, in 1957. He went from the latter position to the Jefferson National Expansion Memorial.

In 1956, he received a Meritorious Award Certificate from the William A. Jump Memorial Foundation for exemplary achievement in public administration and, in 1962, the Distinguished Service Award from the Department of Interior.

———◆———

William R. Ewald, Jr., a member of the APCA Board of Trustees, has announced the opening of a consulting practice at 3706 Ingomar Street, N.W., Washington 15, D. C. His specialities will be urban

35

renewal, area development, community conservation and design projects, programming, and communications.

Planner, designer, and administrator, Mr. Ewald is a former Assistant Commissioner of the Urban Renewal Administration and Senior Vice-President of Doxiadis Associates, Inc. He is author and illustrator of a children's book on city planning, "Neighbor Flapfoot, the City Planning Frog."

———◆———

Kenneth C. Landry has been named director of the Division of Public Services for the American Institute of Architects. He succeeds Matthew L. Rockwell, newly named deputy director of the Northeastern Illinois Metropolitan Area Planning Commission.

———◆———

Fred E. Morr, formerly Director of the Ohio State Department of Agriculture, was recently appointed Director of the State Department of Natural Resources.

Mr. Morr, a law graduate, aged 40, is married and the father of three children. He has a background in the conservation field.

———◆———

Morton Hoppenfeld, civic designer with the National Capital Planning Commission, Washington, D. C., for the past two years, has resigned. After helping set up a department of urban design at the University of California, he will go into private practice.

Trained in both architecture and city planning, Mr. Hoppenfeld is perhaps best known in Washington for his proposal that more pedestrian arcades be included in commercial areas.

———◆———

Foy L. Young was recently named by Secretary of the Interior Udall to be first superintendent of the newly established Bent's Old Fort National Historic Site, Otero County, Colorado. A career National Park Service employee, Mr. Young has been management assistant at Rocky Mountain National Park and Shadow Mountain National Recreation Area, Colorado, since January 1959.

———◆———

Donald Carrier has been named Park Officer at Wild Cat Den State Park near Muscatine, Iowa, according to a recent announcement from the Iowa State Conservation Commission.

———◆———

Kittridge A. Wing, assistant superintendent of Shenandoah National Park, Virginia, has been named superintendent of Gettysburg National Park, Pennsylvania. He succeeds James B. Myers, who recently became superintendent of the Cape Hatteras National Seashore, North Carolina.

Mr. Wing brings to Gettysburg seven years experience in the supervision of Park Service areas. He has served as assistant superintendent at Shenandoah National Park, assistant superintendent and superintendent at San Juan National Historic Site, Puerto Rico, and superintendent at Fort Union National Monument, New Mexico.

(Continued on page 49)

THE CITYSCAPE

(*Continued from p. 4*)

strip, but it does appear that this kind of space works in quite a different manner from the square.

I am for more spacious cities, but this does not mean endless parking lots; for new public squares, parks and plazas in the middle of our cities, but this does not mean creating vast deserts of concrete with outcroppings of grass.

In spite of what Jane Jacobs has written about urban open space in *The Death and Life of Great American Cities,* most of the American population west of West Greenwich Village believes in open space and is not afraid of it. The "ideal" neighborhood density, over 100 families to the acre, in West Greenwich Village, is not very useful when you look at the typical American community. For the typical American family believes in open space, pays tremendous prices for it, goes into personal debt for it, and labors incessantly to care for it, plant flowers and trees in it, cut the grass off it, and spray it with fertilizer, weedkiller, affection, and occasional curses and maledictions.

The need for new open space in American cities was not dreamed up by a Fancy Dan collection of European planners, as Mrs. Jacobs' book alleges. It is deep-seated, and springs from the historic American experience in opening up the West, developing the countryside, and maintaining contact with the good rich soil. It springs from such natural and widespread instincts as a mother's desire to sit outside the kitchen door while her child plays in the sand; from a man's itch to dig in the garden. It comes from a deep affinity for nature which cannot be dissipated by even the most brilliant of arguments.

Open spaces can often outperform buildings themselves in creating a new neighborhood structure for better life. Open spaces offer a theme upon which many a neighborhood can be redesigned; they are often the cheapest building material available for the job of renewal.

We can still believe in cities while wanting them to be properly spacious; it is not "anti-people" or "anti-city" to insist on the quality of our open spaces, as well as the quality of new buildings. Some parts of cities need more open space than we can now afford, even with the financial gimmicks of redevelopment.

5. New standards of mobility and circulation must be applied to all proposals for redevelopment. We must recognize the automobile, not merely by saying "Keep Out." Whenever a railroad is involved in or near redevelopment areas, we should figure out ways to use the railroad and not abandon it.

Two illustrations from recent redevelopments: The first comes from the competition for the Elephant and Castle district in South London held in 1959. The project is now under construction, a combined multi-level shopping center—London's first—with an enclosed air-conditioned mall longer than a football field, with a skyscraper office building rising from one end.

Planning and Civic Comment

The developers very carefully located their shopping mall directly over the carriageway of an abandoned shopping street—one which lingered in the memories of everybody in South London, even though the Germans had blasted and bombed it out of existence in the 1940's. Now, some 23 years later, that familiar old circulation path will come alive again.

The cross-mall will connect the street out front, with its 31 bus routes making 200 stops per hour, to the suburban railroad station out back. Underneath the front of the center are two subway stations. When the London County Council set up the redevelopment plan, it specified the proper interconnections of all these transportation routes. The final plan, which won the competition, did a superb job of weaving the project into this network.

Another example from the competition for the Portal Site in Washington: One of the three designs submitted proposed an ingenious use of a transportation resource already running along one edge of the site—a commuter railroad station for the Pennsylvania Railroad. This proposal represents the kind of multiple-mobility thinking which redevelopment needs.

6. *The redevelopment plan ought to achieve several purposes and not merely one.* These purposes should be both public and private, but it is the obligation of the responsible planning authorities to insist that broad planning goals be achieved by each project. Redevelopment is multi-purpose reclamation of city land and people. Each plan should be judged with this in mind. Even when multi-purposes are not spelled out in the plan, all final project proposals should be considered in this light. All else being equal, the proposal which achieves the widest variety of purposes should get the prize.

7. *Redevelopment projects should incorporate as much of the old city as possible into the new.* This ought to be written firmly into the specifications. The magnificent and often irreplaceable collections of 18th and 19th century architecture, both commercial and domestic, which distinguished many of our older urban neighborhoods should not be junked, even though economically they may be "ripe for redevelopment." They should be recognized by incorporation, not by obliteration.

When you destroy a building, the loss is absolute. We may still enjoy great paintings in reproduction, even after thieves have stolen the original. But architecture cannot be fully enjoyed in photographs; it cannot be experienced in history books. It can only be experienced positively by walking in and around it.

It is easy to say this, but the devil's own task is to incorporate old buildings into a new project, using traditional contractors and attitudes. At the moment, most contractors will propose competitive prices for working on a totally cleared tract of land; when you ask them to incorporate new and old buildings, they throw up their hands. Up to now, too many planners and redevelopment agencies have accepted this sorry situation, but something can be done about it.

At the very least, every community ought to classify its architectural heritage, and seek every way possible to incorporate it into the new projects.

This has to be done far enough in advance so that architectural and historical preservation can get written into the specifications for the project. Not only buildings, but the topography, the existing trees, cobblestones, ancient springs, granite or limestone slabs of the sidewalks—these assets should be catalogued and incorporated as part of the required process for getting Federal approval of a redevelopment plan.

8. Beware of the street, and straight lines, as project boundaries. Most of the projects I have seen are rectangular; the boundaries are straight; there is nothing loose or unexpected. You look at the plan and you know it'll be more of the same as before—this time, with elevators.

The middle of a city block generally is a better project boundary than a street, even though it's not so easy to describe in a city ordinance. Too many project plans destroy the street frontage. When you tear out one side of a street, you destroy the street as a social and economic organism.

9. Both the redevelopment plan, and (in competitions) the winning proposal ought to provide as many multiple choices as possible. Over the past couple of years I have been walking through quite a few projects, counting the choices open to the average human being. They are remarkably few. As you approach many new projects, you discover

there is only one doorway per block, only one gate into the promised land. You can enter from many directions with your eyes, but not with your feet. Often you cannot even see in. The eyes of the public are screened out.

We are getting long stretches of vacuumatic townscape: Blank walls, fences and barriers in place of lively sidewalks. Walk through the typical "project" and you find parking lots, grass plots, and buildings with the one entrance always, so it seems, on the opposite side of the block.

Whenever anybody proposes a project, this is an important civic question: Where do you get in, how many places can you enter, how many choices are there of things to do, doorways to enter, turns to make. The element of multiple choices should not be written out of the townscape.

Summary

The clash and clatter of conflicting opinion and controversy form the testing-ground for every redevelopment plan. This is as it *ought* to be. We ought to institutionalize competition; build it into the planning process; guarantee that every plan and proposal be subjected to the generative process of criticism, comparison and competition.

Too many plans pass in the night, like a gaggle of geese high in the sky, rustling away on their paper wings, with a scornful honk.

Planners who say the public is "not interested" are merely confessing they haven't done their job well. In my experience, the public is *always* interested, once they know the score, once they get the chance to see what plans really mean.

39

Now, one can say "This gives the mob, the common people, just another whack at our beautiful designs. They'll kill it. They always do. We must protect it *against* the mob." I cannot agree, for the American public is growing better educated, more sophisticated every day. Millions of people are raising their expectations of a better environment; more often than not, this includes a conscious desire for new aesthetic experiences. Secondly, out of this subterranean shift in expectations is coming a new willingness to experiment. I believe the aesthetic experimenters have a big slice of the public on their side.

If you put the question to the people, "Which do you prefer: a new million-dollar wing on Children's Hospital, or a million-dollar Museum of Contemporary Art," they will still choose kids over painters. But put the choice to them another way, and they will show a surprisingly sophisticated willingness to include beauty in the municipal budget, even at considerable financial sacrifice.

But, first the public must be given an opportunity to choose in a valid and responsibly organized manner. It is up to the planning profession, and to all those involved in redevelopment, to provide that opportunity.

Urban Design

"This is a good time to be concerned with urban design. It's not too late. For one thing, the urban renewal process is really just beginning to produce sites for developers, and we've had enough samples to know what we have yet to learn. For the other, the dominant factor of our future, the doubling of the U. S. population within the next 40 years, is now being translated into the real terms it means. It is far more significant in scale than what urban renewal can ever do.

"We won't be building subdivisions anymore. We'll be building whole communities, be they articulated nodules concentrated on transportation arteries or whatever pleasant way you choose to picture them. For the next 40 years, for every home that exists now we'll build another. For every factory, another factory. For every school, another school and so on. We need some strong philosophies of urban design to handle this scale opportunity in a human way."

—Excerpt from a paper by William R. Ewald, Jr., *Planning* 1962, the national Planning Conference of The American Society of Planning Officials, Atlantic City, New Jersey, April 29–May 3, 1962.

Seminars, Conferences and University Notes

M.I.T. The twenty-fifth in a series of annual two-week Special Summer Programs in City and Regional Planning will be held at the *Massachusetts Institute of Technology,* in Cambridge, from July 15 through July 26, 1963.

As in former years, the program will include a comprehensive review of the principles of city and metropolitan planning and of the administration of planning programs. Special emphasis this year will be placed on the relationship of the community renewal program to general comprehensive planning for urban areas. The material will be oriented toward the individual who lacks formal professional training or advanced professional experience in comprehensive planning.

Seminar leadership will be provided by members of the faculty of the Department of City and Regional Planning and guest speakers. Tuition is $275, due and payable upon notification of admission. A limited number of scholarships are available to defray, in part, the tuition of members of teaching staffs of other educational institutions. Academic credit is not offered.

The planning seminars will be under the general direction of Dr. Frederick J. Adams, Professor of City Planning, M.I.T., Cambridge, Massachusetts.

The Ohio Conservation Laboratory for school teachers, "the nation's oldest conservation-education workshop," is scheduled to begin a five-week session June 17, 1963 at the new Outdoor-Education Center, Antioch College, Yellow Springs, Ohio.

The laboratory is sponsored by *Kent, Miami, Ohio* and *Ohio State Universities* and the *Ohio Department of Education.* Dr. C. J. Johnson, O.S.U., is director and Robert R. Finlay, supervisor of Conservation and Outdoor Education, State Department of Education, associate director.

Subject matter includes the natural-science and socio-economic fields, including conservation problems of unglaciated Ohio and natural resource problems of cities.

Historic Preservation. A seminar to review the history and clarify the philosophy of the preservation movement will be held in Williamsburg, Virginia, from September 8 to 11, 1963, under the sponsorship of the *National Trust for Historic Preservation* and *Colonial Williamsburg.*

Attendance is limited to persons professionally or actively engaged in the preservation movement and approximately two hundred leaders in this field have been invited.

An announcement of the conference states that the advance of city planning and urban renewal projects has emphasized creating historic districts in living cities and saving important historic buildings by putting them to adaptive uses as homes, offices, shops, and community centers. "It is this complex nature of preservation today that will be examined and discussed throughout the Seminar."

Michigan State. A newly revised curriculum in Park and Recreation Administration has been announced by the Park Management Section, Department of Resource Development of *Michigan State University*. Its aim: To turn out administrators "versed not only in the natural sciences and accompanying skills in managing and maintaining park lands, but also in the social sciences and humanities." A brochure with details points out that park and recreation administration as a specialized profession is a comparative newcomer in the field of public service and states that government agencies are the principal employers of graduates in park and recreation administration.

At Michigan State University, demand for graduates has consistently been greater than the supply. The rapid growth of smaller cities and the blossoming of new suburban developments around metropolitan centers are creating new career opportunities. And, says the brochure, "numerous towns, cities, counties and metropolitan areas are providing many new career opportunities for trained administrators."

City Planning Fellowships. Ten two-year graduate fellowships have been granted and nine others renewed for their second year under

The Sears-Roebuck Foundation's City planning fellowship program for 1963.

Each fellowship includes a grant of up to $3,000 per year to the student plus an unrestricted grant of up to $1,000 per year to the school where the Foundation fellow studies.

Established in 1957 to increase the flow of trained personnel into city planning activities, the Sears Foundation fellowship program has, since its inception, made grants to more than forty-five men and women.

Serving on the Committee which selected the 1963 Sears Foundation fellows were: Dr. Edwin S. Burdell, consultant for the Cranbrook Institutions; Robert D. Calkins, president of the Brookings Institution; and Dennis O'Harrow, executive director of the American Society of Planning Officials.

The New York State Historical Association will hold its sixteenth annual Seminars on American Culture June 30–July 6, 1963 and July 7–13, 1963, at Cooperstown, New York.

This year's curriculum ranges from crime and the manner in which a society deals with it to folksong and some aspects of conservation.

A brochure about the Seminars calls them, "quite different from anything offered by University summer schools or graduate workshops." They are designed for the interested amateur as well as the spirited professional. The Seminars are held on the shores of Lake Otsego in the country made famous by James Fenimore Cooper.

42

Assateague Island Is Proposed As National Seashore

Assateague Island, off the Maryland and Virginia coast, was recently recommended by Secretary of the Interior Stewart L. Udall for development as a national seashore by public authority.

Secretary Udall rejected a plan for a combination of public and private development of the island.

The action is in keeping with a proposal of the American Planning and Civic Association, twenty-one years ago, that a public seashore be established in the area. The January, 1942, issue of *Planning and Civic Comment* said:

". . . There is no adequate public beach for Philadelphia. The Washington-Baltimore metropolitan community, because of poor and congested transportation facilities, is cut off from the seashore.

"Stretching from Rehoboth, Delaware, to Chincoteague, Virginia, is a sixty-five-mile barrier island strip of ocean beach that ought to be made accessible to the six million people around Chesapeake, for daily or week-end use.

"The most substantial portion of this beach, lying between Ocean City, Maryland, and Rehoboth, Delaware, is rapidly being covered by a hodge-podge of private beach houses and resorts. This is short-sighted national policy . . ."

Under Secretary Udall's proposal, the Federal Government would spend $12,300,000 to purchase private holdings and develop the island for public use.

IN MEMORIAM

Edgar P. Romilly, Administrative Assistant for the Cook County Forest Preserve District, Illinois, and a member of the National Conference on State Parks since 1947, died March 28, 1963, at the age of 75.

An active member of the American Institute of Park Executives, Mr. Romilly served as chairman of that organization's Education Committee for six years. In 1955, he was made an Honorary Fellow, the highest honor that can be bestowed a member of the Institute.

His appointment as Administrative Assistant to the General Superintendent of the Cook County Forest Preserve District came two years ago. He had previously served as director of in-service training, superintendent of maintenance and operations and assistant superintendent of recreation.

Surviving are his widow, Frances; a stepson, Roy V. Isaacs; two brothers; a sister; and two grandchildren.

43

PROJECTS IN REVIEW

(*Continued from p. 20*)

time a 180-mile segment of the Missouri to be known as the "Lewis and Clark National Wilderness Waterway."

A summary of the proposal from Howard W. Baker, Mid-west Regional Director of the National Park Service, characterizes the Missouri: Longest river in the United States, route of the Indian, fur trapper, explorer, the steamboat, gold rush, and settler. Of all its stories, the Lewis and Clark Expedition perhaps best caught the public's fancy and found a firm niche in history.

That portion of the Missouri between Fort Benton and Fort Peck Reservoir elicited glowing description by Lewis and Clark and was captured on canvas by the brush of Karl Bodmer. It probably contains the most striking scenery of the river's 2,500-mile course.

Geologically, it tells an outstanding story which includes the interesting epic of its disarranged drainage and the cutting of a new river course as a result of continental glaciation. Archeologically, the area possesses a number of sites representing the aboriginal culture of the Plains Indians.

Beyond all this, it is the only stretch of the Missouri to retain its primitive historic appearance. Most of it is essentially unchanged from the time Lewis and Clark first saw it.

Everyone having an interest in development of the Missouri River Basin is urged to read the brochure and discuss its contents with others. Say the officials, "Only through such discussion can public opinion become crystallized and your governmental representatives be made aware of how the public feels about the matter."

Specific recommendations will be made to the Congress following consideration of public views and those of interested agencies.

Northeastern Illinois Water Resources

How can local governments cooperate in the development and management of water resources?

The first attempt in a large metropolitan area to devise a strategy to make this achievement possible is reported in the 1962 Annual Report of the Northeastern Illinois Metropolitan Area Planning Commission.

The 18-month, $303,000 project got under way early in 1962 when three state agencies and the Metropolitan Area Planning Commission started work on the Northeastern Illinois Water Resources Study.

An especially important aspect of the study is its consideration of the relationship of future land use to future water needs. The cooperative study is undertaking:

1) Measurement of the metropolitan water resource;
2) Estimation of current and future demand for water;
3) A study of existing water management methods and possible alternatives and improvements;
4) And development of lines of action and recommendations for local governments.

DISPERSAL OF POPULATION, ETC.

(*Continued from p. 18*)

clearly as it should have. A bold scheme, visualising things in the future, would surely take all these errors into account.)

Assuming that the cost and facility of construction and maintenance for surface railway lines are more favourable than for tube railways, perhaps we should explore the possibility of having surface railway lines within the city even if that may mean some initial difficulty.

The primary point would be the feasibility of opening up a rail route from across the Ganges to the city. If the capacity of the existing Howrah Bridge is not adequate to carry electric trains instead of trams, or if the structure of the bridge itself, or its approaches, does not warrant the remodeling required by the laying of train track, then I think the *second bridge,* for which there is already some discussion at official levels, *should have provision for railway lines.* If, however, the only convenient place for it is somewhere between the present Howrah bridge and the Shalimar railway station, then the first objection—in absence of a provision to counter-act the same—would be, as already stated, that large ships would fail to utilise the Calcutta jetties.*

Proceeding on the assumption that construction of a tunnel is not feasible, I would suggest that if a

*If, judged by all considerations, tunnel proves to be a better choice than bridge, then, of course, the premises on which I am proceeding would have to be altered. (Here again we can perhaps think of having a "Skyway").

sufficiently high cantilever bridge, capable of carrying the load of buses, lorries and, other heavy vehicles, *as well as railway trains,* can be constructed somewhere opposite the maidan or near the Shalimar station** then it would not perhaps be much of a difficulty to run the line along the *Strand Road* and bring it to the nearest point of the *Eden Gardens.*

If the proposed line can, without detriment to the movement of Port Commissioner's railways, be placed by the side of that track, (or on the eastern side of the road) it may then be considered if the line can, with suitable modifications in the Howrah Bridge approach on the Calcutta side, be stretched further north and connected with the Chitpur Yard or with the main line near Dakshineswar, Baranagar or Dum Dum.

If, on the other hand, construction of a bridge to the south of the present one is not found to be feasible, or if the existing Howrah Bridge cannot be converted into a road-cum-rail bridge, then the other choice is perhaps to construct a bridge just to the north of the present one.

The rail line over the Willingdon Bridge would, in any case, have to be electrified and connected with

**Without disturbing the movement of ships. Here of course comes in the question of removing further south the Port, perhaps to Haldia; if this takes place mainly for the silting up of the river, then apart from such engineering difficulties discussed earlier, case for a second bridge somewhere in this region becomes stronger.

(*Continued on page 50*)

Planning and Civic Comment

STATE PARK NOTES
(*Continued from p. 32*)

Virginia. A proposal under which Virginia's tallest mountain, mile-high Mt. Rogers, would become the first new state park since 1950 has been made by the State Department of Conservation and Economic Development.

Valued chiefly for the view it affords of neighboring mountains and valleys, Mt. Rogers lies in a large undeveloped forest area on the border of Smith and Grayson counties in southwest Virginia.

New Hampshire. Major new recreational facilities totaling an estimated $1,400,000 are expected to be under construction in New Hampshire this spring as part of a nine-million dollar state park expansion program, according to the State Division of Parks.

In addition, studies for improvements to many existing state parks and historic sites are progressing. In accordance with a 1961 law, they will be presented, in stages, at public hearings and for final approval by the Governor and State Council.

New Hampshire packs a lot of public recreation into its compact 9,304 square miles, according to the New Hampshire Division of Parks.

Three fourths of the Granite State is forestland. But despite its size—it is 44th nationally in area— it ranks fifth among the states in revenue produced from the operation of its state park system.

Ohio. A day in the life of a typical park employee brings varied duties and some surprises. A stubbed toe may be bandaged, or a life saved on the swimming beach. The water supply may be tested for safety, a balky lawn mower fixed, a cabin window repaired or a lost youngster found.

"But more and more as park attendance increases, our people are answering the public's questions," says V. W. Flickinger, chief of the Ohio Division of Parks. "No matter what the person's primary responsibility, he is called on to offer advice and information. I watched a refuse collection crew working in the camping area at East Harbor last year; while they emptied 18 cans they answered seven questions."

The Ohio Division of Parks has just completed workshop sessions in each of the four districts in the state to help park managers train employes better to serve the public.

"The magnitude of the situation can best be seen by comparing the park picture of today with that of 1950 when the division was formed," stated Flickinger. "There were about three million park visits a year then, while we will have something over 20 million this year. We had about 500 picnic tables at that time; now our total is nearly 14,000. Thirteen years ago there were five or six lifeguards at a few beaches, but this year we are operating 39 beaches and will employ 120 lifeguards. The same story

(*Continued on page 50*)

"Keep America Beautiful"
Wins National Conservation Award

Keep America Beautiful, Inc., the national organization which is waging an aggressive campaign against litter on streets, highways and public lands, has been named to receive the American Motors Conservation Award.

A second award goes to the Texas Conservation Council of Houston for its successful drive to preserve unspoiled a national seashore on Padre Island.

The American Motors program was established in 1953 to recognize publicly outstanding achievements in the conservation of America's natural resources—wildlife, forests, wetlands, soil, and water.

Keep America Beautiful, with headquarters at 99 Park Ave., New York City, has used two slogans most effectively in its battle against thoughtlessly discarded rubbish: "Don't be a Litterbug" and "Every Litter Bit Hurts." It has devoted 10 years to public education and work with volunteer groups to prevent littering of cities, towns and the countryside. Programs are now operating in every state. The group's national advisory council includes four federal departments and more than 55 public interest organizations. The organization is supported by business and industry, labor unions and trade associations representing nearly every major industrial category.

PRAIRIE NATIONAL PARK—A PROPOSAL
(Continued from p. 30)

fascinating interrelationships of plants and animals, soil and climate. Impressive, there, would be the vast scope and many moods of the Prairie scene itself—its sweep, its ever-changing patterns of light and cloud, the rhythm of wind and grass, the spring flowers, the larks singing on the wing, the stand of native blue stem grass, shoulder high to grazing bison.

The importance of a Prairie National Park to grassland research would be enormous, while such a park would spread before every American "going West" an expression of nature that made America great.

47

Recent Publications

THE SCOPE AND FINANCING OF URBAN RENEWAL AND DEVELOPMENT: A Statement by the NPA Business Committee and A Report by Peter Wagner. Pamphlet 119 of the National Planning Association points out that urban renewal in the past has been primarily directed toward slum clearance and says, "In order to be truly successful, in the sense of re-creating our cities and suburbs as desirable places for future living and work, urban renewal must be approached from the broadest possible point of view. It is also necessary to integrate local initiative into a consistent regional pattern of urban renewal projects."

One chapter of Mr. Wagner's report on The Importance of A New Approach suggests that, beginning with transportation, genuine urban renewal has to include all aspects of everyday life and activity, including housing, places of work, and recreation activities. It points out that where urban renewal has been undertaken on a "total" basis, "it has captured the imagination and loyal participation of the public, indispensable ingredients for ultimate success." National Planning Association, 1606 New Hampshire Ave., N.W., Washington 9, D. C., 59 pp., $1.50.

SURVEYS FOR TOWN AND COUNTRY PLANNING. By John N. Jackson, Lecturer in Town and Country Planning at the University of Manchester. This book from England is written on the premise that land-use planning is a "new and emerging discipline with its own scientific and objective approach." It shows how surveys are essential to the greater understanding of land-use problems and in deciding planning policy. "The role of survey is to study the situation factually and objectively, to present clear and carefully reasoned reports, to provide the necessary understanding before decisions for development are made and to evaluate the effects of development."

Stressing that one function of the planning survey is to inspire action, the book considers the methods of investigation—the use of libraries and statistical sources, sampling techniques, interviewing, questionnaires and observation. It discusses types of surveys, including physical and land resource, land use and building, communication, traffic and parking, industrial, population and social surveys. Hillary House Publishers Ltd., 303 Park Ave. South, New York 10, N. Y. 192 pp. $2.50.

THE GOOD CITY. By Lawrence Haworth with a preface by August Heckscher. Architects, sociologists, and city planners have attacked the problem of the modern city from their various standpoints, but here a philosopher essays a unique and original approach. What, he asks simply, are we after? What human values do we wish to realize? How do we define the ideal city toward which we strive? This book is an attempt to formulate a systematic philosophy of the cit, connecting it at one end with ethical principles and at the other with the practical discipline of city planning, in the interest of providing criteria by which concrete programs may be judged. The author is a member of the Department of History, Government and Philosophy at Purdue University. His book grew out of research conducted in 1960 under a grant from the Rockefeller Foundation. Indiana University Press, 10th and Morton Sts., Bloomington, Indiana. $4.50.

RESOURCES IN AMERICA'S FUTURE. By Hans H. Landsberg, Leonard L. Fischman, and Joseph L. Fisher. All of America's natural resources—and needs for resources—are studied in this book from Resources for the Future, Inc. It presents the findings, in text, tables, charts and graphs, of a massive research project undertaken five years ago. It offers estimates of what America will need to grow on during the next forty years in the way of water, land, minerals, lumber, metals, chemicals, and other major resources and resource products. The Johns Hopkins Press, Baltimore 18, Md. $15.00.

RESOURCE CONSERVATION, revised edition. By S. V. Ciriacy-Wantrup, professor of Agricultural Economics at the University of California, Berkeley. Theoretical principles are illustrated with down-to-earth examples from diverse resources ranging from land and water to ores, oil, and nuclear energy. Agricultural Publications, 207 University Hall, University of California, Berkeley 4, California. $4.00.

(Continued on page 50)

American Planning and Civic Association
New Members January 1, 1963 to May 1, 1963

Canada
  Bibliotheque, Ecole des HEC, Montreal, P. Q.

District of Columbia
  Mrs. Henry H. Balch, Jr.
  Hon. Philip W. Bonsal
  Mr. Reuben Clark
  Mrs. Gerhard A. Gesell
  Mrs. Randall Hagner, Jr.
  Mrs. Middleton G. C. Train
  Mr. David N. Yerkes
  American University Library

Hawaii
  Oahu Development Conference, Honolulu

Indiana
  Elkhart County Plan Commission, Goshen

Japan
  Tokyo Shisei Chosakai, Tokyo

Maryland
  Mr. L. A. Gravelle, Bethesda
  Mrs. Charles Worth Sprunt, Chevy Chase
  Mrs. Francis D. Lethbridge, Chevy Chase

USSR
  Economitcheski Institute, Moscow

National Conference on State Parks
New Members, January 1, 1963 to May 1, 1963

Alabama
  Mr. James O. Evans, Fort Payne

California
  Mr. Lyle E. Watson, Elsinore

Colorado
  Mr. William R. Cheney, Denver

Michigan
  Mr. Edward Griglak, Caseville
  Mr. Frank Gilbert, Caseville
  Mr. Richard E. Hilligus, Mears
  Mr. Louis Witherspoon, Caseville

New Jersey
  Mr. Richard D. Goodenough, Titusville

New York
  Mr. Carl Crandall, Ithaca
  Mr. Morton Rosenberg, New York City
  Mr. Ralph D. Wallace, Watertown

Oklahoma
  Mr. Warren K. Jordan, Oklahoma City

Washington
  Mr. Len J. Berryman, Bridgeport

STRICTLY PERSONAL
(Continued from p. 36)

Floyd Cross, of Albuquerque, New Mexico, was recently named Superintendent of the new State Parks and Recreation Commission. He succeeds James Dillar who has been acting State Parks Superintendent since Eastburn Smith resigned about three months ago.

Mr. Cross has been in the insurance, real estate, and public accounting business since 1945. He was a member of the State House of Representatives from 1947 to 1949, served as chief clerk of the Senate during the 1963 session of the Legislature, and twice served as chief clerk of the House, holding that position in the 1956 and 1957 sessions.

Planning and Civic Comment

STATE PARK NOTES

(*Continued from p. 46*)

is seen in the areas of vacation cabins, camping and boating."

According to Mr. Flickinger, briefings will be held at Ohio state parks to acquaint new employees with the information needed to answer most questions from park goers. Many of these are seasonal or part time, but will be expected to offer help and advice to the public.

"We probably won't be able to answer them all," said the park chief, "for with 20 million visits you really get some dandies."

DISPERSAL OF POPULATION, ETC.

(*Continued from p. 45*)

the line that would enter into the city.

To sum up, if, side by side with other plans, a scheme for *planned dispersal of resident population* of Calcutta (with a *rigid control over land utilization* in the proposed radius) is made, and a net-work of railways (preferably surface railway if this proves to be less expensive to construct and to maintain as compared to underground railway) converges from different directions to the heart of the city, it is likely that while the unregulated encroachment on agricultural lands within the proposed radius would be stopped, planned townships all along the railway lines would relieve the city proper of its unhealthy congestion, and at the same time would enable the working population to move daily into and from Calcutta without having to waste unnecessarily much time and energy on the way.

RECENT PUBLICATIONS

(*Continued from p. 48*)

THE NEW BUREAU OF OUTDOOR RECREATION. United States Department of the Interior, Washington 25, D. C. This brochure on the Federal Government's newest conservation organization gives details on the "Birth of A Bureau," a statement of Bureau policy, and the seven main aspects of the Bureau's program.

SEARCH FOR THE CITTIE OF RALEGH. Latest booklet in the National Park Service's Archeological Research Series (No. 6). A detailed account of the historical and archeological investigations carried on in connection with the development of Fort Raleigh since its establishment as a National Historic Site in 1941. This report represents all that we now have learned through archeology of the ill-fated settlement on Roanoke Island and suggests directions that future work should take. The author, J. C. Harrington, has been associated with the development and growth of historic site archeology in this country almost since its inception.

METROPOLITICS: The Nashville Consolidation. By David A. Booth. Institute for Community Development and Services, Michigan State University, East Lansing, Michigan. 105 pp. $2.00.

THE CITIZEN'S GUIDE TO URBAN RENEWAL. By Alfred P. Van Huyck and Jack Hornung. Chandler-Davis Publishing Co., West Trenton, New Jersey

(*Continued on page 52*)

Watch Service Report

Following is the status of legislative measures as of May 15, 1963.

S. 20, Bureau of Outdoor Recreation, Organic Act. Sen. Anderson and others. Passed the Senate March 11, 1963 and then passed the House April 29, 1963, in lieu of H. R. 1762, after having been amended to contain the House-passed text. As we go to press, the Senate has disagreed with House amendments and has requested a conference to resolve differences.

H. R. 1762 and the House version of S. 20 authorize the Secretary of the Interior to formulate a comprehensive nationwide outdoor recreation plan. Specifically, he is authorized to: 1) Maintain an inventory of outdoor recreation needs and resources in the U. S. and prepare a system of classification; 2) prepare and revise a comprehensive nation-wide recreation plan, advising Federal and State officials; 3) furnish technical assistance to State and private organizations in outdoor recreation activities; 4) encourage regional and interstate cooperation in the field; 5) make studies and cooperate with educational institutions; 6) promote the coordination of plans of Federal agencies and provide them with technical assistance; and 7) accept donations.

During debate, the House adopted two amendments. One would require the Secretary of the Interior to file annual reports itemizing the source, value, purpose, and use of each donation. Another places a ceiling of $2,500,000 on annual expenses of the program. Rejected was a proposed amendment which would have created an independent body to be known as the U. S. Outdoor Recreation Agency in lieu of the Bureau of Outdoor Recreation in the Department of Interior.

S. 20 was recommended by the Outdoor Recreation Resources Review Commission.

S. 4, The "Wilderness Bill," establishing a National Wilderness Preservation System. Senator Anderson and others. Passed the Senate, April 9, 1963, by a roll call vote of 73 yeas to 12 nays—comparable to the 78 to 8 margin by which a similar bill was passed by the Senate in the 87th Congress. Referred to the House Committee on Interior and Insular Affairs. Several different versions of the Wilderness Bill have already been introduced in the House and referred to the Interior and Insular Affairs Committee.

Passage of S. 4 came in the Senate after debate centered upon several proposed amendments. The key vote came on Amendment No. 32, proposed by Senator Allott and 14 colleagues. It would have required positive action by the Congress on each new addition to the Wilderness System and was rejected by a vote of 35 yeas to 49 nays.

Also rejected were amendments: To authorize certain mineral leasing and mining; to provide procedures for inclusion of national forest primitive areas; to provide that authorizations for prospecting, mining, and facilities needed in the public interest shall be under jurisdiction of the appropriate cabinet officer rather than the President.

Adopted were amendments to eliminate certain restrictive language relating to livestock grazing; to allow continued use of aircraft and motorboats where well established; to authorize control measures against fire, insects and diseases; and to provide that where Congressional resolution of opposition to a Presidential recommendation respecting wilderness has been introduced, a motion to discharge the committee which has jurisdiction shall not be in order until the time for holding a hearing has elapsed.

S. 1, Youth Employment Act. Senator Humphrey and others. Passed the Senate April 10, 1963 by a vote of 50 yeas to 34 nays. Referred to the House where a similar bill, H. R. 5131 has been ordered reported favorably.

Senate action came after the Committee on Labor and Public Welfare filed a favorable report with amendments. Title I of the bill establishes a Youth Conservation Corps which would work on conservation and out-door recreational projects on Federal lands, principally forests, parks, and wildlife refuges. During the first year of operation, enrollment would be limited to 15,000 men between the ages of 16 and 21 years. The Senate cut the program back to $50,000,000 for the first year of operation. After the first year, enrollment would be determined by appropriations. Work by the Corps would be complemented by educational and vocational training.

All State and community participation in the program, including conservation projects, is under Title II of the bill, the "State and Community Youth Employment Program." This includes establishment by the States, if desired, of conservation camps

51

on State lands. Provision is made for a cost-sharing plan. The program would be limited to 60,000 full-time enrollees during the first year with an initial appropriation of $50,000,000. After the first year, the program would be controlled by appropriations.

S. 2, The Water Resources Research Act of 1963, passed, with amendments by the Senate April 23, 1963. Referred to the House Committee on Interior and Insular Affairs. The bill would establish water resources research centers at land grant colleges and state universities, and stimulate water research at other institutions. Annually, up to $100,000 would be granted an institution in each state, and a graduated scale of federal funds, up to $5,000,000 by 1968, would finance a dollar-for-dollar matching program. Also provided is a program, ultimately to reach $10,000,000 annually, for a second grant, matching and contract funds to help other institutions, private foundations, etc. with water research.

S. 792, Establishing the Sleeping Bear Dunes National Lakeshore in Michigan. Hearings held March 28 and 29, 1963 by Public Lands Sub-committee of Senate Committee on Interior and Insular Affairs.

Secretary of the Interior Stewart L. Udall testified in support of the bill, as amended. The national lakeshore proposed by the bill, and its suggested amendments, would include several islands in Lake Michigan.

The bill directs that in preserving the lakeshore and stabilizing its development "substantial reliance shall be placed on cooperation between Federal, State and local governments to apply sound principles of land use planning and zoning . . . and in developing the lakeshore, full recognition shall be given to protection of private properties for the enjoyment of the owners. . ."

H. R. 3846 and others to establish a Land and Water Conservation Fund. Proposals to implement many recommendations of the Outdoor Recreation Resources Review Commission. The Fund would be financed through user fees, the sale of surplus Federal land, and proceeds from the Federal tax on marine fuels. The monies then would be allocated to the States and Federal agencies for planning, acquisition, and development. Hearings scheduled for May 27 and 28, 1963, by the National Parks Subcommittee of the House Committee on Interior and Insular Affairs.

S. 1111, Water Resources Planning Act of 1963. Senator Anderson and others. This bill deals with river basin planning. In introducing it March 15, 1963, Senator Anderson pointed out that the original draft of the bill was sent to Congress by President Kennedy on July 13, 1961. Referred to the Committee on Interior and Insular Affairs.

RECENT PUBLICATIONS

(*Continued from p. 50*)

160 pp. $3.00. Ten or more copies, $2.50.

THE MUNICIPALITY'S ROLE IN THE NATIONAL ECONOMY. A selection of papers prepared for the Silver Jubilee Conference of the Canadian Federation of Mayors and Municipalities. Edited by George S. Mooney and Eric Beecroft. The Canadian Federation of Mayors and Municipalities, Sheraton Mount Royal Hotel, Montreal 2. 119 pages. $2.50.

1963 *oint Co   nce*

National Conference on State Parks
American Institute of Park Executives
American Association of
Zoological Parks and Aquariums

PLACE: WASHINGTON, D. C.

HEADQUARTERS: SHERATON-PARK HOTEL

DATE: SEPTEMBER 22-26, 1963

NATIONAL CONFERENCE ON

Every Member Get a New Member

Make Conference Reservations

Planning and Civic Comment

Official Organ of American Planning and Civic Association and
National Conference on State Parks

CONTENTS

Page

SEPTEMBER 1963

THIRD QUARTER—JULY—AUGUST—SEPTEMBER

PLANNING AND
CIVIC COMMENT

Published Quarterly

Successor to: City Planning, Civic Comment, State Recreation

Official Organ of: American Planning and Civic Association,
National Conference on State Parks

SCOPE: *National, State, Regional and City Planning, Land and Water Uses,
Conservation of National Resources, National, State and Local Parks,
Highways and Roadsides.*
AIM: *To create a better physical environment which will conserve and develop
the health, happiness and culture of the American people.*

EDITORIAL BOARD

HARLEAN JAMES   FLAVEL SHURTLEFF   CONRAD L. WIRTH

CONTRIBUTING EDITORS

HORACE M. ALBRIGHT   NEWTON B. DRURY
HARLAND BARTHOLOMEW   V. W. FLICKINGER
GEORGE L. COLLINS   JOHN NOLEN, JR.
KENNETH R. COUGILL   F. A. PITKIN
S. R. DeBOER   FRANK D. QUINN
CHARLES DeTURK   BEN H. THOMPSON

EDITOR

DONALD B. ALEXANDER

ASSISTANT EDITOR

ETHEL J. SWING

Second-class postage paid at Harrisburg, Pa., and at additional mailing office.
EDITORIAL AND PUBLICATION OFFICE, 901 Union Trust Building, Washington 5,
D. C.
Printed by the Mount Pleasant Press, The McFarland Company, Harrisburg, Pa.

Planning and Civic Comment

| Vol. 29 | September, 1963 | No. 3 |

Five Years of Metropolitan Planning:
A Special Report

By PAUL OPPERMANN, Executive Director of the Northeastern Illinois
Planning Commission

Reprinted through the courtesy of *Inland Architect* in which this article appeared
in April, 1963 with the exception that one section, "Planning To Prevent Flood Loss"
has been omitted in the present version. Mr. Oppermann, a past president of the
American Institute of Planners and one of the country's leading planning officials,
is a member of the Board of Trustees of the American Planning and Civic Association.
His candid account of planning activities in the Chicago area over half a decade is
of historic significance.

On a wintry morning a couple of
months ago, an important planning
decision was made in an office in
the middle of Chicago's loop. As
flash bulbs popped and cameras
ground, the presidents of forest
preserve districts of five counties
signed an agreement to work together in planning and acquiring
land for forest preserves, parks, and
similar "open space" purposes.

It was a rare event, this agreement by five or six counties in the
Nation's No. 2 metropolitan area to
plan for and acquire exactly that
kind of land which loses out first in
the intense, price-dominated competition for urban land. An important Federal official—William
Slayton, U. S. Commissioner of
Urban Renewal—was there to term
it "a milestone in coordination between public agencies to achieve a
common goal," and to point out
that only two other U. S. metropolitan areas (Denver and Washington) have put together similar
agreements.

The Commissioner's presence at
the ceremony was well in order. One
of the significant facts about Federal aid for various kinds of urban
improvement and development programs is its recent concern that
local governments receiving aid
shall work together and be guided
by large area plans and policies.
The Northeastern Illinois open space
agreement met exactly that kind of
stipulation in the Federal law of
1961 setting up a Federal program
of grants for acquiring outdoor
recreation facilities and other urban
open space. As a result, the participating counties became eligible
for 30 per cent grants for open space
acquisition, instead of 20 per cent
without the agreement.

There were other meanings in the
new agreement of at least equal
weight. For one thing, it represented a formal acknowledgment
of the fact that the Chicago metropolitan area of 1915, when the Cook
County Forest Preserve District
was established, is no longer the
Chicago metropolitan area. In 48
years since then the District has
done a grand job, has acquired
49,500 acres of green space and is

hard at work acquiring 5,300 acres more (with the help of the new agreement and the Federal Open Space Land Program).

But urbanization in the Chicago area has leaped far beyond the forests of Cook County, has reached into five additional counties in Illinois alone—to say nothing of the spread eastward into northwestern Indiana. The open space of the future will necessarily have to come from those other counties, just as the competitive land pressures of the future will be concentrating in those counties. In agreeing to work together in planning and acquiring open space land, the counties of Cook, DuPage, Kane, Lake, and Will were acknowledging that fact and undertaking to do something about it. Hopefully, the sixth county in the northeastern Illinois metropolitan area—McHenry—will take part also after it has established a forest preserve district.

There was yet another significance in the open space agreement—in the very special way in which it came to pass, through the "catalytic" services of a metropolitan agency of the special-purpose, advisory, "non-operating" kind. Months, and even years ago, the Northeastern Illinois Metropolitan Area Planning Commission had begun by studying the need for future outdoor recreation and other open space. Later it had formulated a metropolitan policy on open space preservation. Still later it had initiated the agreement, drafted it, argued for it before the county boards of five counties, and finally, signed it as the party of the first part with responsibility for co-ordinating the county planning efforts.

At the meeting last February, the president of the Planning Commission, Chester R. Davis, pointed out that this is the second such intercounty agreement initiated by the agency within the last two years. The earlier one brought six counties together with the U. S. Geological survey in a project for mapping the land subject to periodic flooding in the metropolitan area.

These seemingly disparate subjects are only part of it. The Commission also has responsibilities in the fields of transportation, water supply, sanitation, refuse disposal, land use in general, and capital improvements in general. In this it is not alone. There are more than 50 metropolitan planning commissions in America now, with more being added every month. And yet —so swiftly do events move—the Northeastern Illinois agency, which will complete its fifth year of operation about May 1, may very well be one of the oldest metropolitan planning agencies!

It may be worthwhile to review the activities of the Northeastern Illinois Planning Commission—many of which resemble only faintly the established image of the city planning department—to get an idea of what the metropolitan planning and coordinating function is likely to be, both here and elsewhere—and even more for the light it sheds on the true nature of the problem of bringing the great urban agglomerations most of us now live in into a state of order, efficient operation, and beauty somewhat nearer the heart's desire.

The Challenge of Metropolitan Growth

The creation of the Northeastern Illinois Planning Commission in 1957 by the Illinois legislature was, first of all, a response to the problem of growth—a vertical growth in numbers and population densities, and a horizontal growth in the amount of land used for urban purposes. The growth I am talking about here is national in scope, and most of us are more or less familiar with it—with the fact that in the 1950's, 84% of the nation's population growth took place in America's 212 metropolitan areas, and nearly all of it in the suburban fringes around the central cities; with the calculation, also, that by 1980, four out of five Americans will be living in those metropolitan areas, even as three out of five live in them today.

Most of us, also, have excellent chances to be aware of some of the effects of this growth—the continuing geographic expansion of urban America beyond city and village lines, the creation of scores of new communities, the increase in the number of neighboring and overlapping governments. By 1980 (another calculation), it is expected that close to 2,000,000 more people will be added to the population of metropolitan Chicago—the six counties of Northeastern Illinois. Also between 1960 and 1980, the "built up" parts of the metropolis are expected to increase by some 450 square miles—equivalent in area to two Cities of Chicago.

Yet again, we can easily sense that with this accelerating growth outward from one city into six counties there has arisen a new species of community problems, what we term *metropolitan area problems*. These are the problems, the causes and solutions of which reach beyond the jurisdictions of any one of the area's one thousand governments, and which concern such matters as shortsighted and disorderly land use and development, traffic congestion and inadequate transportation, flooding, water shortages, and water and air pollution problems.

It was in response to such needs that the Illinois legislature passed the Northeastern Illinois Metropolitan Area Planning Act in July, 1957, and that the agency it created began operations ten months later. Neither the act nor the commission can be understood except as a rather daring and—let us admit it—optimistic response to two seemingly incompatible claims: The need for large-area development solutions and policies, on the one hand, and the insistence on local governmental decision and discretion, on the other.

The key to this dilemma is, in two words, *guidance* and *coordination*—and guidance and coordination are the chief tasks assigned to the Northeastern Illinois Planning Commission: To achieve a better environment in the metropolitan area by devising and maintaining a procedure for cooperative development and by assisting the local governments in acting upon it.

True, the Commission is empowered to plan, and, in fact, the law becomes quite specific about it. We are to "prepare and recommend to units of government" generalized metropolitan plans and policies which "may include but need not

be limited to" plans for:
1. Land use, public and private.
2. Transportation facilities of all kinds.
3. Water supply and distribution.
4. Drainage, flood control, sewage disposal and pollution.
5. Schools, parks and recreation facilities.
6. Governmental services and facilities.
7. "Improvement in standards of urban esthetics and design."

This planning, and the research required for it, is quite an order in itself; but there is more, and what more there is is quite revealing. The Planning Commission, we are told, is to "review plans and projects of governmental units within the area and advise on their relationships to other plans and projects"; it is to "prepare and make available to local governments standards for zoning, building, and subdivision control ordinances and other planning regulations; it is empowered to "establish a program of public information in order to develop a general understanding of the function of comprehensive planning"; it is—especially—to give "primary attention" to correlating the various elements of metropolitan growth and development, including the plans and policies of the various governments. And, in general, it is to "cooperate with various units of government in comprehensive planning."

I have quoted so generously from an enabling act because—after five years' experience with it—I think it a very good act (except for a weakness with regard to financing), and because I think it reflects a

fundamentally cooperative approach to the solution of the problem of urban growth. Clearly, the Illinois legislature and the medley of interests which supported the establishment of a metropolitan planning agency in Northeastern Illinois had more than a plan in mind: They were thinking, rather, of a complex of planning services. They appear to have considered that the test of a metropolitan plan is its usefulness to local governments, and that the responsibility for action—and therefore the final responsibility for solving the urban growth problem—must rest with the local governments.

A critical difference becomes visible here between the conditions of city planning and metropolitan planning. In the city or village, the whole governs while the parts advise, petition, and seek to amend. At the metropolitan scale, the situation is reversed, and the parts govern while the viewpoint of the whole is, as the law I have been quoting says, "recommended to units of government." These governments, by the way, "may give due consideration" to metropolitan plans but are not required to act on them. The Northeastern Illinois Planning Commission is truly an advisory agency.

When you consider that municipalities alone number 250 in the 3,714-square-mile Northeastern Illinois area, and that there are about 750 other governments, my remark that the cooperative approach to metropolitan growth is a daring one may have some force. However difficult politically,
(Continued on page 51)

4

Action Programs for Community Development

From the Remarks of Fred D. Learey, President, General Telephone Company of Florida, Tampa, Florida, before the Community Development Luncheon, 51st Annual Meeting of the Chamber of Commerce of The United States, Washington, D. C., April 30, 1963.

All over this country—from 6,000-population Point Pleasant, West Virginia, to booming metropolitan areas like Tampa and San Antonio—citizen groups are rediscovering that the do-it-yourself technique in solving local problems really works. Works just as surely as the week-end hobbyist finds he can paint a house, build a bird house or assemble a cabin cruiser.

This new plan of action for community development is really not new. It's probably one of the most fundamental concepts handed to us by our founding fathers who faced the unmarked frontier with only their brains, courage and what few supplies could be carried in a covered wagon. Theirs was a case of conquer their basically unfriendly environment or die.

And, perhaps, this parallel is not so different today. Perhaps the comparison of the hazards of a frontier is not too inappropriate as we contemplate the unfriendly wilderness of blight, congestion, sprawl and all the other problems of urban America which each of us faces.

The plan—this do-it-yourself idea in community development—was conceived in the Construction and Civic Development Committee of the National Chamber of Commerce. It was tested in Erie, Pennsylvania, in September, 1960.

The first step was to focus attention on the need for a good, hard self-appraisal of the community by its leaders. The program was launched in Erie, as in each of the demonstration cities, with a city-wide meeting, to which every significant organization and group was invited. Civic clubs, garden clubs, women's groups, PTA's, labor unions and others sent representatives. Here the plan was outlined and agreement on the method was reached.

First named was an "Assumptions Committee" to project the growth, the need for municipal facilities, jobs and payrolls. Next followed a detailed examination of each community's problem areas. They ranged, literally, from athletic fields to zebra pens. Water resources, housing, power, public transportation, industrial development, parks, recreation, hospital facilities and hundreds more were listed. The number of study areas ranged from 32 in one case to 103 in another.

Next, the resource personnel of the community were assigned to the problem areas with which they were most closely associated and from which facts and figures could be most easily obtained. Cities of varying size required resource teams of varying numbers.

Amarillo, Texas, population 152,000, enlisted 361 persons who spent approximately 24 months on the job. Bloomington, Indiana, with 31,357 population, had 145

5

on their task forces for just about a year. Point Pleasant, West Virginia, with just under 6,000 population, developed full information on their problem areas in 20 months, using 55 local citizen experts.

Others in the pilot group included Hallandale, Florida; Jacksonville, Florida; Rapid City, South Dakota; and Tampa, Florida.

With facts in, a Priorities and Evaluation Committee was then appointed to analyze and synthesize the data. The solutions to some problems appeared immediately—other groups, public officials, already had solutions implemented and work under way. From the problem areas remaining, two courses of action were indicated:

1) If they were non-controversial, they were assigned a priority number in the list of jobs to be done. Each problem in this priority order eventually worked its way to the top of the list. At this point, public attention was concentrated on it so that every element of the community's leadership, fully informed on the facts, could join a mass frontal attack on the problem.

2) When the problem was controversial to the degree that no clear-cut consensus as to the best solution was evident, it was submitted to the citizen participation and public discussion phase of the program.

Many dramatic happenings have been reported by the demonstration cities during the past 18 to 20 months. Let me cite just a few.

First, in my own city of *Tampa*, never has anything captured the imagination and zeal of the average citizen with such force. Hundreds of volunteers put personal differences aside during the fact-finding phase.

When the Priorities Committee gave priority No. 1 to the construction immediately of a new $5,000,000 Convention Center in the Central Business District, public officials took up the cry. Within weeks, architects were given the go signal. The site clearing began, and the "psychology of success" was evident.

The Priorities Committee had stated in its report, "The Convention Center is not only a vitally needed economic and cultural asset, it is the key which will unblock the entire Central Business District revitalization stalemate."

These proved prophetic words, for today, just 18 months later, confidence in the future of Tampa's downtown has been restored and many firms, holding back, waiting and undecided for years, have decided to go ahead. And now, new buildings in excess of $33,000,000 are under construction.

Do I claim that Tampa's community development action program was solely responsible for our new look downtown? Of course not! Many factors were important. But the initial catalyst was, indeed, the report which said to our community: *This Is First—Let's Do It Now!*

In one community after another, success is being achieved.

Here's a part of the *Amarillo* story:

At the beginning of the community development program, which Amarillo gave the positive title, "Citizens' Action Program," two urgent requirements were

6

immediately established: 1) An expanded sewer system; and 2) a new building code. Here are a few specific results of the Amarillo program:

1) Recommendations by the Sewer and Drainage sub-committee have resulted in passage of a $5,000,000 sewage bond proposal, which, in turn, has allowed the city to proceed with the treatment plants recommended by the Citizens' Action group.

2) The city's building code is in process of being revised.

3) A land use study of parcels of city-owned land is scheduled for presentation to the Fine Arts Council for action.

From *Erie, Pennsylvania*, the pilot city: At the end of the first ninety days of the community development program a score card showed the progress made:

1) Water: New city reservoir approved.

2) Agriculture: One county reservoir projected.

3) Fisheries: Program near completion.

4) Highways: Erie-Pittsburgh freeway committed.

5) Resort Activities: Winter sports program launched.

6) Convention Promotion: Full-time convention bureau established.

7) Economic Base Study: Salt potential under study.

8) Wage Rates: Study being made.

9) Industrial Promotion: Program continuing.

10) Central Business District: New street lighting.

Hallandale, Florida, with a population of about 11,000, sent representatives to a four-state Demonstration Workshop staged in Tampa to show how the Community Development Program can provide the machinery for tackling these local problems. Then it took the bit in its teeth and in just six months reported:

1) The appointment of a professional firm to make new ad valorem tax assessment by the City. (No. 1 item on Priorities projects was to get the city on a sound fiscal basis.)

2) Decision of the city to borrow money for certain items which were high on the priorities list. The city has approved an outlay of $68,000 for the beautification and lighting of the two most important sections of throughways.

3) No. 3 item on the Priorities Committee recommendation was "Citizens' Participation Process." This included formation of Toastmasters International of Hallandale with the intent of producing in three months at least 20 skilled speakers who can lead discussions and speak before organizations on items which are given priorities in the Master Plan.

Jacksonville, too, got a late start but soon made up for lost time with a clear-cut demonstration of the effectiveness of the method. The local citizens know their needs better than the casual visitor and when teamed together with progress as their objective, solutions and action follow in rapid order.

Jacksonville reports: The listing of education as the No. 1 priority in the community development program. The second was public health, including acceleration of the coordinated sewer and drainage plan.

A total of $37,000 was budgeted for the Jacksonville Planning Board, the first adequate appropriation ever given the agency.

Under Port and Water Development, the No. 1 recommendation was a county-wide Port Authority. Legislation to accomplish this was projected for the 1963 session of the Florida Legislature. Under Traffic and Transportation, discussions were held for the solution of the airport problem, listed as No. 1. No. 2: A compromise between the county government and the Expressway Authority was effected.

The Housing and Urban Redevelopment Program has become the 1963 program of the Jacksonville Board of Realtors.

And *Point Pleasant, West Virginia,* has proved that even a relatively small city has, right at hand, the resources for getting the facts, facing the facts, and taking the action which the facts dictate. Here are just a few of Point Pleasant's accomplishments:

1) Recreation Facilities: The development of City Park is near completion.

2) Commercial Development: An old building has been removed. A movement is under way to secure two new tenants to occupy the old hotel building which will be rebuilt to suit the needs of two large retail operations. An architect is making a sketch of the proposed remodeling of the backs of the buildings in the three blocks.

3) Comprehensive Planning: A comprehensive plan for the growth and development of the city has been approved, and the Pilot Study Group will work toward its imple-mentation.

4) Zoning Regulations: New regulations have been prepared for the City Planning Commission. These have the approval of the Commission and the Pilot Study Group. The Pilot Group will aid in the public hearings and public educational work.

Rapid City, South Dakota, also gives a dynamic account of progress:

First, there was the inclusion of $25,000 in the city budget, earmarked for the purpose of providing studies and resources for the Planning Commission. This was the first time the Planning Commission had any funds to support their program. Other items on the priority list include: 1) The passing of a bond issue for a new armory and a new fire station for North Rapid.

2) Setting the date for a sewer bond issue and contemplation of a date for a school bond issue, probably for September, 1963. (These were joint undertakings.)

From every city, the reports are pouring in—and the percentage of problems successfully met and for which solutions are under way is far in excess of the failures.

But make no mistake. This is no easy task. Motivating several hundred busy civic and business leaders to invest from 50 to 100 man hours each in the program is, in itself, no small task.

But the enthusiasm of the leaders, once they get the feel of what can be done, is contagious and the importance of the work being done, in all but rare cases, sweeps opposition aside, or better still, enlists it in the program. Furthermore, the intimate

(Continued on page 50)

A Look At Historic Preservation

By LOUIS C. JONES, Director, New York State Historical Association

Reprinted through the courtesy of *Antiques* Magazine in which this article appeared in July, 1956 and of the National Trust for Historic Preservation which includes the article in its *Primer for Preservation*. A recent query to Mr. Jones indicates that he still stands by the things he says in the article, and we, too, are of the opinion that its message is appropriate today and, in fact, essentially timeless.

Does all this fuss and feathers about old buildings that are outdated and have served their original purpose really matter? Or is it just an outlet for neurotic antiquarians on the local committee who want to bask in the reflected glories of their pioneer ancestors?

In the world of shopping centers, high-speed thruways, and decentralized industries, of what earthly use is the old brick mansion, redolent of yesterday—which occupies the best possible site in town for a gas station? We can't stand in the way of progress, can we?

The answer, of course, is "no." There are times when the house should come down and the gas station should go up.

But progress goes from some place to some place. And if we would know where we are and where we are going, we must also keep a few points on the chart to indicate where we have been. Out of this knowledge should come a valuable kind of personal security such as a child is given in a loving home, or such as comes to those who find peace in one of the historic religions.

The past should have as many personal ties for each of us as possible. None should feel that he is floating in time, rootless, and unrelated to all that has happened to our fathers and to those who lived in our place before us.

To feel a part of the progression of mankind is to enter into full citizenship in the race of men. In the framework of the home, let there be hand-me-downs from yesterday—pictures and furniture, or a piece of lace from the old country, or the trunk that landed at Ellis Island. Things that have been in a family a long time have a magic of their own, asserting the values of life and its survival.

So it is with each village and city. They, too, need focal points of affection, of the historic community spirit. The variety of these places can and should be numberless, each suited to its own history and people. In a very real sense, these should be shrines where the spiritual values of our people are cherished and nourished.

In a land where few of us live in the town where we were born, there is an ever greater need to create a sense of identity and belonging for those who come from elsewhere. If we have to make this consciously rather than receive it as a birthright, well and good, let us do so as truthfully and skillfully as possible.

Given a historic house that has meaning for a specific town, what are we to do? Put back the original furniture, reproduce the wallpaper, train a guide in costume, and do a historically complete job of recreating life as it was once lived? Yes, if

9

we can do that well and also make the house into an active, functioning part of community life, constantly interpreting as many sides of the past as possible in terms the people of today can understand.

And if this is impossible, shall we do nothing? Shall we tear it down and build the gas station?

I'm for trying a lot of other possibilities first. Civic organizations or individuals can be encouraged to buy it, making what changes they must, but accurately preserving the exterior. There are values for a child on his way to school just in knowing that this house stood on this same site when his great-grandfather was a boy, even if that grandsire lived far across the sea.

Between the fully revitalized historic house, which is currently our ideal, and the preservation of the architectural shell, which is the least we can hope for, there are hundreds of possible compromises any one of which might be the solution for a specific community.

This raises the question of whether bad preservation is better than no preservation at all. Strongly as I believe in scholarly standards of research and veracity of presentation for historic houses—and I consider these of vital importance—yet I must admit that there are times when a holding operation is better than destruction; time itself may produce workable solutions.

I can think of a number of historic houses which, twenty years ago, were just being held together physically. A growing public interest and new concepts of historic preservation have made these into vital forces for the best kind of interpretation of community tradition.

Finally, what shall we save?

Frankly, I'm getting a little bored with the lengthening list of handsome residences of the "best people." We need to preserve buildings that speak directly to those of us whose families had callouses, as well as to those who had carriages.

It's a fine thing to exhibit the aesthetic best out of the past but it can be equally important to interpret the ways men and women worked and created and played. I want to see more gun shops, millineries, schoolhouses, covered bridges, taverns, foundries preserved for our people. Let's speak to Americans in terms that add meaning to their own everyday lives, that place their jobs, their responsibilities as citizens and parents, in historic context so that they see their present problems, not as exceptions, but as continuations of the challenges faced by their forefathers.

People need places out of their past which they can see and understand and ultimately love—that symbolize those who lived in these places before them, and struggled and suffered and built there. If those men and women could face and solve their problems, so can we.

We need such refuges all over the land, as we need churches and schools, that they may be seedbeds for the cultivation of a vigorous and informed love of country.

Aspects of the Program of the Housing and Home Finance Agency Related to Planning

From the Remarks of Robert C. Weaver, Administrator, Housing and Home Finance Agency, at a luncheon announcing a comprehensive transportation and land use planning program for Northeastern Ohio, Cleveland, Ohio, May 15, 1963.

Urbanization—the growth of urban areas—has been going on in this country for a long time. But for many years it was possible to ignore urban growth, or at least to take a *laissez faire* attitude toward it.

There was then very little realization that this growth represented the emergence in this country of a new frontier—a frontier of intensive development comparable in its challenges and opportunities to the old frontier of extensive development.

To the layman, city planning still seems to be a very esoteric study although city planners have been at work since the time of the ancient Romans, and probably before that.

The surveyors who laid out the streets of the frontier towns of this country were city planners—without benefit of theoretical knowledge, perhaps, but planners all the same. So are those who lay out the plans for the enormous subdivisions now being built on the outskirts of nearly every city in the country. They are exercising a powerful influence on our future.

The transportation and land use planning program for the seven-county area in northeastern Ohio, which you have made public today, is an impressive achievement. The very fact that seven counties, comprising a region where more than 2,000,000 persons live and 140 municipal and township governments exercise authority, can get together and come up with any plan at all is an achievement.

And it is an achievement that holds out a promise to dozens of similar regions throughout the country that they, too, can surmount their local rivalries and join in planning for their future.

Mayor Locher has told me that this study is the largest to be started under the new provisions of the Highway Act of 1962. The juxtaposition of highway construction and slum clearance has demolished great swaths through the centers of some of our cities. Very often, many of the hardships, caused by such massive dislocation of people and commerce, could have been avoided by more intelligent planning and coordination between construction activities.

At the President's direction, the Secretary of Commerce and I established a joint steering committee, bringing together representatives of the Urban Renewal Administration in the Housing and Home Finance Agency and the Bureau of Public Roads in the Department of Commerce. Regional committees were set up, and a beginning made in working out an effective system of coordination between State and local highway and housing officials.

The President has requested the Secretary of Commerce to make the

11

approval of highway planning funds in metropolitan planning studies contingent upon the establishment of a continuing and comprehensive planning process. This process, he says, should, to the maximum extent feasible, include all the inter-dependent parts of the metropolitan area, all agencies and jurisdictions involved, and all forms of transportation.

The President has recommended that the Federal-aid highway law be amended to provide that, effective in 1965, the Secretary of Commerce shall make a finding that highway projects in metropolitan areas are consistent with comprehensive development plans.

In his special message to Congress on Housing and Community Development, early in 1961, he said:

"The city and its suburbs are inter-dependent parts of a single community, bound together by the web of transportation and other public facilities and by common economic interests. Bold programs in individual jurisdictions are no longer enough. Increasingly, community development must be a cooperative venture toward the common goals of the metropolitan region as a whole."

The President called for the establishment of an effective and comprehensive planning process in each metropolitan area, embracing all major activities, both public and private, which shape the community.

And he emphasized that such a process" must be democratic—*for only when the citizens of a community have participated in selecting the goals which will shape their environment can they be expected to support the actions necessary to accomplish those goals.*

The Housing Act of 1961, signed by the President in June of that year, included a number of provisions strengthening Federal assistance to communities undertaking comprehensive planning.

That Act increased the Federal share of the cost of urban planning from one half to two thirds—to the same proportion as that for urban renewal assistance. It increased the total authorization for planning grants from $20,000,000 to $75,000,000. And it authorized the Housing and Home Finance Administrator to provide technical assistance to agencies undertaking planning.

For the first time, the Act made comprehensive planning for mass transportation expressly eligible. And—in a new program—it authorized $50,000,000 in loans to public bodies to finance the acquisition, construction, and improvement of transportation facilities and equipment where these were part of the development of a comprehensive transportation system.

The Housing Act of 1961 also established a new program to assist local public bodies in the acquisition of land to be used as permanent open space. This program authorizes grants of $50,000,000 for such aid. These grants can be for up to 20 per cent of the cost of acquiring such land. Or, if the grant is made to a public body with regional responsibilities, it can be for as much as 30 per cent. In either case, the land must be acquired in accordance with a comprehensive plan for the area.

(*Continued on page 45*)

Interpreting Our National Parks

By HOWARD R. STAGNER, Chief Naturalist, National Park Service

One leg of my desk is short. I have a small booklet, *Science and Human Values*, that just fills the gap. The desk is now level and stands solid. The book does the job well. A block of wood would do the same.

What a waste of a resource! To use the book to replace a block of wood denies mankind the benefit of the ideas it contains. The book is not physically damaged, but is this use good conservation?

Conservation means more than saving the physical entity of a resource. It means also, and more importantly, putting that resource to work in a way that capitalizes in highest measure upon its inherent values. To do less is waste, a loss as fruitless as if the resource were carelessly destroyed.

National Parks are a National resource. Preservation of their physical being has been an objective, intensively practiced, for many years. How about the other aspect of their conservation? Is our use of them designed to capitalize upon their true values? Are we getting the most from them? What are those values, and how may mankind benefit in highest degree from them?

National Parks are the scenic and scientific *treasures* of the Nation. Each park is distinctive and outstanding in the quality of its scenery, ecology, life community, or geology. The System, comprised of the great scenic and scientific National Parks, and America's most significant historic places, symbolizes America—

its history, its people, and its natural character. So considered, National Parks can be a source of National pride and unity, as well as places of personal enjoyment.

Congress in establishing the National Parks, laid down two rules: First, preserve these areas as nature made them; and second, use them for what they are, use them as they are. Travel through them, enjoy their beauty, hike over them, study them, but don't change them in the process. This boils down to preservation for a special use—educational, aesthetic, scientific. This is the concept embraced in the word *interpretation*.

A most fortunate circumstance today is the emphasis being given to outdoor recreation. The program will enlist the use of many kinds of lands, public and private, not as competitors or in duplicate effort, but as complementary elements of a mosaic—each, like the individual tiles of that mosaic, retaining its individual identity, but adding its color to the complete whole.

National Parks must select and concentrate on those elements of the recreation program which are appropriate to them—recreation which brings results commensurate with the high scenic, scientific and historic values of these properties, which contributes to the educational and inspirational purpose to which the National Parks were dedicated, which derives value from but does not impair the resource.

As enough outdoor areas are

developed to serve America's varied and growing needs for recreation, National Parks can emphasize, even more than in the past, the interpretive-inspirational part of the recreation spectrum.

To emphasize educational, interpretive and inspirational qualities of National Park use is not to deny the importance of physical types of recreation. The most satisfying and complete form of recreation is often one which combines physical effort, mental stimulation, and esthetic enjoyment at the same time. But the interpretive emphasis appears to set the truest course for National Park recreational use, one that best capitalizes upon the high quality of this resource.

Just before the first World War, an American citizen, Dr. C. M. Goethe of Sacramento, California, visiting Switzerland, was intrigued by something new to him: Groups of school children under adult leadership making excursions afield. These field trips were not primarily a recreational exercise but recreation with an educational content and a national purpose.

Switzerland, Dr. Goethe was told, included people of three national origins. Four different languages were spoken, and two basic religions prevailed. Even the geography of the country tended to divide rather than unify the people. In the face of growing nationalism and militarism in neighboring countries, some means of bringing these diverse population groups together—of developing among them a national consciousness, a sense of pride, of belonging—was sought. The Swiss found the means in the land itself.

Know your land, experience it recreationally, know its flora and fauna, its rivers, its geologic and geographic features. You take most pride in those things you know most about, are interested in, and take pleasure from. This was the secret of the Swiss program to unite a people.

This was something worth trying in America, and Dr. and Mrs. Goethe started a nature guiding program at a summer resort at Lake Tahoe, in California.

Stephen Mather, first Director of the National Park Service, happened to see this program in operation. Here was precisely what the National Parks needed, a program to fulfill the educational objective, interpreting and making meaningful the natural attributes of the National Parks. Together, Mr. Mather and the Goethes brought this program to Yosemite and personally financed it until appropriations were secured. This was the beginning.

The interpretive program expanded and other National Parks adopted it. An educational advisory committee appointed by the Secretary of the Interior in the late 1920's gave it new emphasis and clearer direction. The interpretive movement gained new strength through the MISSION 66 program, and today is a basic part of the National Park recreational experience.

From the modest beginning in 1921, the National Park interpretive program has had a gradual but continuous growth. Last year 1600 park naturalists, archeologists, and historians met over 40 million park

(Continued on page 57)

14

Planning for Hospitals
Developments in California

Here in America—where progress in combatting disease has already charted up astounding victories—we are still moving into new areas of development in hospital planning and construction.

Planning for hospitals and related health facilities on a regional basis received special impetus in 1946 when Congress passed the Hospital and Medical Facilities Survey and Construction Act, popularly known as the Hill-Burton Act.

Today, hospital construction is moulding an important feature of the American image. Yet the possibilities for citizen participation in this significant aspect of long-range planning have not always received consideration.

Certainly, this is not an area for namby-pamby experimentation nor for superficial participation. If there is to be citizen activity at all, the earnest efforts of those especially equipped to do the job, professionally and otherwise, would seem to be required in spite of what already may be excessive demands on their time and energies.

What is needed is the capacity to calculate, with a clear and certain eye, the health needs of the various segments of the Nation in the coming decades and to come boldly to grips with them by utilizing the best available talents in the medical, planning, construction and related fields.

Against this background, two reports which have recently come to the American Planning and Civic Association from the State of California are of particular interest.

Robert W. Murch, Consultant in Hospital Planning, says the need for beds and services in California was so great at the inception of the hospital planning program that planning did not have to be very definitive.

"However, since 1946," he continues, "hospital growth has been phenomenal . . . and has reached the point where it approximates the needs of the population and nearly all of the residents of California have some facilities and services available within reasonable driving time."

The State of California, for hospital planning purposes, is divided into 115 Hospital Service Areas. Each area is a planning entity unto itself. Mr. Murch points out that the Hospital Service Area combines "a compatible group of communities or related geography within which hospital facilities are, or should be, available to provide services to the population within one half hour's driving time of every resident." Driving time may be as much as one hour in rural areas where there is not sufficient population to support a facility within closer range.

Mr. Murch points out that state plan policies encourage master planning. "A facility built now," he says, "should foresee its growth needs five, ten or fifteen years from now." This means alloting adequate land for future development and creating ancillary areas originally over-sized so as not to have to be altered for later additions.

Now, how is citizen participation a factor in these important planning developments in California?

Says Norman Spuehler, Executive Director, Hospital Planning Association of Southern California, "I believe we can all agree that long-range planning for hospitals and related health facilities and services is a complex and specialized assignment. As such, it presents practical problems in the areas of evaluation and judgment for members of city and county planning commissions, boards of supervisors, and city councils."

Upon this bed-rock foundation, Mr. Spuehler relates how the Hospital Council of Southern California proposed organization of citizens groups within each of the local hospital planning areas—to be known as hospital planning committees and to be made up of *doctors of medicine, hospital administrators, and representatives of the lay public.*

The functions of each committee: 1) To learn the availability of community health services and to ascertain the anticipated increase; 2) to coordinate information prior to the development of a long-range plan for each local hospital planning area and for the region; 3) to evaluate all proposed health facility additions and deletions for the area against the best available planning information; and 4) to recommend approval, disapproval, or changes for all proposed health facility additions and deletions.

Each committee sits in an advisory capacity. Any committee recommendation is made in essentially the same manner as that of any other voluntary citizens' group in our free society. Furthermore, any recommendation which a committee may offer to such groups as planning commissions is not legally binding in any way.

Beyond all this, recommendations are made only after a committee has gathered the best available information pertaining to any specific matter before it. To this end, it is routine for a committee to hold open meetings as part of its fact-finding process and to invite a spokesman for a project under consideration to be present and offer the committee pertinent information.

In shouldering this sizable load of responsibilities, none of the members of any of the hospital planning committees is in any way financially compensated for his time or for expenses incurred in connection with the committee's activities.

Sources used by the committees in seeking pertinent information include the Bureau of Hospitals, health and welfare agencies, Blue Cross and other insurance plans in Southern California, independent surveys of existing health facilities, city and county planning departments and other local and regional governmental units.

The cooperative approach is stressed. Mr. Murch says:

"Our goal is to develop and implement good plans to meet the need for the best health care possible in the most efficient and effective manner. In attaining our goal, we must work cooperatively with other organizations, both private and official."

Zoning Round Table

Conducted by FLAVEL SHURTLEFF, Marshfield Hills, Mass.

COMPLAINTS AND VIOLATIONS

"Whenever a violation of this ordinance occurs, any person may file a written complaint with the zoning administrator," and from there the zoning administrator carries on, taking such action as the ordinance directs.

The quoted words, or words like them, are common in all zoning ordinances. They challenge the citizens to be alert if they want a well ordered community and the full protection of the ordinance.

Even with an adequate staff, the zoning administrator cannot be expected to discover "inside" types of violations, such as conversions to two-families to a house in a single family zone and many kinds of business operations conducted in homes in residential zones. Community consignment shops, although inside violations, are busy places, and can hardly escape detection, but it would be a bold administrator who would take action against a very popular community enterprise. This is the bargain mart of a considerable area.

More serious are the violations which are obvious. It may be a funeral parlor in a single family zone, permitted by the Board of Appeals as a variance either through a misconception, or in disregard of the stringent limitations on the granting of variance permits. Or it may be the many instances of spot zoning which are clearly in conflict with the comprehensive plan inherent in any sound zoning ordinance but which go unchallenged either by the citizens or the zoning administrator.

The evil lies not so much in the damage to the community, though this is cumulative and may be considerable, but, in the words of a recent Connecticut case, "in the creation of a situation which tends to weaken public confidence and to undermine the sense of security which every property owner must feel assured will always exist in the exercise of the zoning power."

When spot zoning runs wild, this lack of confidence may even become resentment and active opposition to the whole zoning program. Property owners, banded together to defeat a spot zoning threat and sharing the expense of court action, are naturally outraged by losing their case and their cash by what seems to them a legal technicality.

In a superior court case tried in Massachusetts last year, counsel for the applicants in cross-examination of a witness for the protesting property owners got into the record that, in the general area involved in the case, there were at least six or eight cases of changes of zones for parcels of land less than two acres in area.

As each instance was cited, the witness was asked, "Was this spot zoning?" and his answer started a long series of questions calculated to show the frequency of the practice of zone changes, even of small

17

parcels. The admission of this line of examination was questionable even in cross-examination, but the record stood and may have influenced the judge's decision.

In the case of Gricus *v.* Superintendent and Inspector of Buildings in Cambridge, which was a spot zoning case decided in April 1963*, the court said that the amendment of the zoning ordinance which permitted business uses in a multi-family residence zone was invalid under the circumstances, and the fact *that other parcels had been singled out for zoning change or spot zoned did not help the case of the applicant.* The decision should be a helpful precedent.

The procedure in violations calls for a special defender of the public interest with the characteristics of a fearless but tactful vigilance committee. The challenge to the citizens under the present procedure is too great. Either neighborhood acquaintance or the expense of court action too often prevents their initiation of complaints, and the zoning administrator cannot or will not commence something that will end in a legal battle and community expense.

Citizen organizations may be the answer. They can usually get enough legal advice without charge to be reasonably sure that the facts in the case will bring a favorable decision. Civic associations could add to their program the defense of zoning cases. In some Massachusetts communities, the League of Women Voters has had notable success.

*Advance Sheets of Massachusetts decisions, 1963.

The words of the Connecticut decision* quoted earlier in this comment, were used to describe a quite different situation, but they were equally appropriate for the evil of the unchallenged violation. In the Connecticut case, a member of the Planning and Zoning Commission of the town was president of an association which had contracted to sell a portion of its property to a broadcasting company, conditioned on the company's getting a permit to erect a broadcasting tower. The land was in a residence zone and an application for variance was denied by the Board of Appeals. Later the Planning and Zoning Commission initiated an amendment which permitted the tower, and passed it unanimously.

In the hearings on the variance and on the amendment, the member of the Planning and Zoning Commission appeared and urged favorable action. The court held that his participation in the hearings invalidated the amendment but was careful to specify that the evil was not improper exercise of influence but the weakening of the entire zoning program through lack of public confidence in its integrity.

*Daly *v.* Town Planning and Zoning Commission of Fairfield, Conn. 191 Atl. 2nd, 250.

Citizens' Committee in Detroit

Forty persons have united in the "Forum for Detroit Area Metropolitan Goals" to effect citizen guidance on problems of the six-county Detroit metropolitan area. A thirteen-member Executive Council has been established.

PROJECTS IN REVIEW

Proposed Buffalo National River—Two Reports

"A cool, free-flowing, clear-water stream which twists and turns through mountains and small valleys for a total course length of nearly 150 miles."

That is the Buffalo River in the Ozark Mountains of north-central Arkansas as described in an economic study recently prepared by the Bureau of Business and Economic Research and the Industrial Research and Extension Center of the University of Arkansas.

Located in one of the most scenic sections of the entire middle-west, and within an easy day's drive for over 20 million people, the Buffalo is a spring-fed stream, beautiful and "floatable"—and that, for a good part of the year.

The fishing? It's good. The Buffalo and its tributaries are said to constitute one of the richest areas in the nation in total number of fish species. The small mouth bass, the bluegill, perch, sunfish and unusual species like the studfish, chestnut lamprey, darter and many others abound.

Either the fisherman or the "floater" is quite likely to spot water fur-bearing animals like the beaver, otter, mink and muskrat, commonly seen along the Buffalo.

Or marvel at the "fernfalls"— cascades of ferns blanketing precipitous, treeless inclines which from a distance appear to be green-tinted waterfalls.

Or cheer the precarious progress of one crossing a swinging-foot bridge still in use across the Buffalo.

These bits of information and many more are contained in a second report of current interest in regard to the river—a field investigation report by the National Park Service which recommends "that the Buffalo River area be favorably considered for administration by the National Park Service as a National River."

The two reports are of special significance since possible construction of two dams on the Buffalo— the Lone Rock and Gilbert dams— is also under consideration. The U. S. Army Corps of Engineers has indicated that new studies of the Buffalo River Basin are probable.

The University of Arkansas report, which was prepared for the National Park Service, states that the Buffalo, together with nearby land areas, "merits preservation as a unique section of mid-America in its near-natural condition."

The report points out that five counties which would be most affected experienced a 17 per cent decrease in population and an estimated out-migration rate of over 32 per cent from 1950 to 1960. It suggests that conserving the Buffalo as a National River would be an "ideal complement to already existing tourist attractions throughout the Ozark Mountain region," and anticipates that tourist spending would reach an annual level of nearly $13,000,000 by 1970. This, and accompanying economic developments, it concludes, "would be most helpful in eliminating the tendency for significant numbers of the people to leave the study area in search of a better living."

The area under consideration is definitely Ozark Mountain territory in its characteristics and history as opposed to the southeast portion of Arkansas, which geographically, economically, and historically, belongs to the Mississippi River country and the deep south.

More than twenty archeological sites in the area of the river are known, and a time span dating back to perhaps before the year 500 is represented since some sites are of prepottery culture.

The Park Service proposal would keep part of the Buffalo River area definitely a wilderness type attraction. During the past 35 years, it says, the environment has reverted to a more suitable wildlife habitat.

White-tailed deer are numerous over the entire river basin, and the not-uncommon black bear is increasing in numbers. Bobcats are common as are coyotes and red wolves. Occasionally, the presence of a mountain lion has been authenticated.

Ornithologists have reported over 250 species of birds in the area, many of them common throughout the year. And the ruffed grouse, once extirpated, is now a common sight as is the bob-white quail, Arkansas' greatest game bird.

"In combination," says the Park Service report, "the scenic, scientific, and archeological values and the recreation potential of the area clearly indicate that consideration for preservation and administration at the national level is warranted."

ᴄꞁᴐ

City in a Garden

As late as 1948, a report characterized that part of the city, known as Lincoln Park, as "predominantly in a state of deterioration."

Rundown and shabby, with what might have been a sure seat on the downhill slide into urban blight, Lincoln Park was, of course, covered by the official seal of the City of Chicago, of which it is an integral part, and by its motto, "*Urbs in Horto*"—City In A Garden.

What might have happened to Lincoln Park is now anybody's guess because enterprising residents of the area set out to give Chicago's old motto new meaning.

In choosing "to retrieve, restore, and rescue," they have united in an inspiring story of neighborhood conservation. A pictorial glimpse of that story has been presented in a volume called "City In A Garden— Homes In The Lincoln Park Community."

Both the foreword to the publication by William A. Hutchison, M.D., President of the Lincoln Park Conservation Association, and the introduction by Paula Angle, Editor, suggest, in a few words, the leavening spirit which has made rejuvenation of the area a reality.

The pictures which make up the publication were selected from over a thousand photographs and slides supplied by home owners and tenants in the Conservation area.

"This", says Dr. Hutchison, "is typical of good neighborhood planning. It is not something done entirely by the city, nor by local

(*Continued on page 44*)

Commentaries

"Quote-Unquote:" When two leading figures in the conservation field get together for an interview on the subject of their special interest, the results are bound to be noted by a wide variety of people.

That's what happened recently when Edward J. Meeman, Editor Emeritus of the *Memphis Press-Scimitar*, interviewed Laurence S. Rockefeller, Chairman of the New York State Council of Parks, who is engaged in a number of conservation endeavors.

Mr. Meeman is a Vice-President of the American Planning and Civic Association and Chairman of the Board of the National Conference on State Parks. Mr. Rockefeller is a member of the Board of Trustees of the American Planning and Civic Association.

Mr. Rockefeller's philosophy, says Mr. Meeman in the *Memphis Press-Scimitar*, "includes the thought that private gifts need to be supplemented by large-scale investments of the people, themselves, in their outdoor resources."

To this end, he urged "public investment in recreation in two forms—user fees to be paid by the sportsmen, campers and scenery lovers who visit our parks, forests, lakes and beaches, and tax funds to provide proper development and maintenance of public outdoor areas."

In the same vein, Mr. Rockefeller said, "Land acquisition is not enough. You multiply an area's usefulness when you provide proper facilities for public enjoyment."

And, "We need to upgrade recreation, make it co-equal with education and health, consider it a necessity . . . Why? Because recreation in the out-of-doors is so important a part of our lives—so much a part that its benefits usually are taken for granted, left unspokenyand thus passed over at the legislative table."

According to Mr. Meeman, "Mr. Rockefeller believes it worth while to spell out that outdoor recreation satisfies every man's basic need for physical activity and a spiritual and mental lift." He quotes Mr. Rockefeller:

"The outdoors had much to do in the shaping of our national character and is essential to its continued vitality. That is a big reason why opportunities for it must be assured to all Americans, now and in the future."

❧

Water Re-use: It will be mandatory in Ohio in the opinion of C. V. Youngquist, veteran chief of the Division of Water, of the Ohio Department of Natural Resources, who points out that we must develop a new technology for removal of waste materials from water.

Mr. Youngquist's views on one State's aspects of a problem, which is of serious concern to the entire Nation, are ably expressed in an article by Robert W. Copelan in a recent issue of the Ohio Conservation Bulletin.

In explaining his position, Mr. Youngquist quotes a recent report prepared for the U. S. Public Health Service:

"Waste waters constitute this country's most immediately available, untapped water resource. They are available at every location at which water is used. They do not have to be pumped long distances over mountains, or from deep underground sources. When we learn how to renovate these waters efficiently and economically, a new dimension in water resources management will be opened."

Mr. Youngquist points out: "Almost any use of water degrades its quality. The highest degree of municipal and industrial waste treatment leaves undesirable organic and inorganic materials in solution which cannot be removed under present techniques. And yet in Ohio it is a necessity that we re-use water."

❧

Water Problem: "There is indeed a growing urgency for watershed understanding, for almost every part of the United States faces current or potential

21

the project. It would be constructed around the First Methodist Church which will remain intact on the site. Shops at the northern side will face State Street because the project has been conceived as but one part of the entire Central Business District.

John Graham AIA and James King & Son, Inc., have collaborated on several projects in the New Jersey area, including the Princeton Center for Industrial Research and the Dow-Jones Laboratory and Offices between Trenton and New Brunswick.

John Graham pioneered the development of the suburban shopping center when, in 1947, his firm designed the first planned regional center in the nation—Northgate in the suburbs of Seattle. Projects such as these have attracted millions of dollars in goods and services away from the old downtown central business districts.

The Graham firm now is working with business leaders and local civic groups in revitalizing old central business districts of a number of communities which are planning new or supplementary environments to attract investors, merchants, customers and business firms.

The Tocks Island Story

The Tocks Island dam and reservoir project, excluding the proposed National Recreation Area, was authorized by the United States Congress in 1962. In the 1964 Public Works Appropriations Bill, the Congress appropriated $250,000 to the Corps of Engineers to begin preliminary engineering and design work on the project.

The Delaware Basin Bulletin, a publication of the Water Resources Association of the Delaware River Basin, says the size and location of the Tocks Island project make it the keystone of the entire plan for developing and controlling the water resources of the Delaware River Basin.

According to the Bulletin: "It is, first, the only reservoir project in the Basin that will be large enough simultaneously to meet the rapidly expanding water supply needs of the Philadelphia metropolitan region and other metropolitan regions in North and Central New Jersey. Second, it is the one project that will afford substantial flood protection to such communities below the dam as Phillipsburg and Trenton, New Jersey, and Easton and New Hope, Pennsylvania. Third, it is the only project in the Comprehensive Plan for the Basin that will permit the development of hydroelectric power.

Inevitably, ramifications of the Tocks Island project are numerous. Not the least of them has to do with the developing economic impact on the three-state Tocks Island region and with how the lives of individuals within the area are being affected. Says the Bulletin:

"The unincorporated village of Bushkill faces a unique problem in that it is the only community that will be wholly inundated by the Tocks Island reservoir. At a meeting, April 16, the residents of Bushkill were given a fairly firm schedule of when their lands and homes would be acquired and the village inundated. More importantly, however, the residents were informed of the two alternative methods they could consider should they want to relocate to an entirely new Bushkill.

"These alternatives: 1) Coöperation with the Corps of Engineers under existing statutes to relocate Bushkill; 2) cooperation with a private developer, thus developing a new Bushkill wholly with private funds.

"Since land and homes in Bushkill probably won't be acquired before 1970, the residents of the area have considerable time in which to determine if they want to create a new Bushkill . . ."

At the April 16 meeting, it was emphasized that the Tocks Island project was not something that would happen overnight. Residents were told they would be given ample time in which to cope with the personal impact the project would have on their lives and livelihood and that the decision as to whether or not to create a new Bushkill rests with them alone. It is a decision only they can make.

New Homes—1963

The varying and complex factors which help to determine the construction of new dwelling units and, hence, to some extent the pattern of development in a crowded area, such as the New York Metropolitan Region, are clearly revealed in "New Homes, 1963," a recent publication of the Regional Plan Association.

Apartment building in the area dropped sharply in 1963. Calling attention to this, the publication says, "Ever since 1957, permits for apartment units have increased swiftly and steadily, from 28,000 to 90,000 in 1962, with a drop to 73,000 in 1963."

Between the end of World War II and the late 1950's, the housing industry in the Region concentrated on one-family housing. Between 1950 and 1960, two-thirds of the increase in housing units was in one-family houses and the number of one-family houses has since remained steady.

According to the publication, one of the strongest forces toward more apartment building during the past six years was probably the increase and anticipated further increase in families without school-age children, who frequently prefer apartment living. Not only have couples been living longer after their children move away, but the statistical bulge of young people between 18 and 30 (typically apartment years) has just begun.

The publication points out that the increased demand for apartments compared to one-family houses can be expected to continue into the 1970's when, again, there will be a striking rise in demand for one-family houses. By that time, babies of the post-depression and post-war periods will reach the age when they can afford to buy a house, and their children will reach the age when it seems easier to raise them in a one-family house.

Additional factors contributing to the increase in apartments in the New York Region over the past six years, according to Regional Plan are:

1) The dwindling of vacant land near the center of the Region while jobs remain concentrated near the center, putting a premium on the land close-in; 2) completion of a number of urban renewal projects in

23

Downtown Progress has recommended creation of a National Visitor and Student Center to help provide Washington's annual millions of visitors with "an enriching understanding of our American heritage."

It is proposed that the center be designed to receive 50,000 or more people a day, to impart the story of America by means of films and exhibits, provide places for visitors to meet with key representatives of the Congress and of executive agencies, direct visitors to places to see and things to do and provide activities for students in the evenings.

Basis for the action has been developed in comprehensive studies prepared for the **National Capital Downtown Committee, Inc.** by the Stanford Research Institute and by the Management Consultant firm of Booz, Allen and Hamilton, Inc. with participation by representatives of the National Park Service, the United States Civil Service Commission, the United States Travel Service, the National Capital Planning Commission and the Metropolitan Washington Board of Trade.

A brochure from the Downtown Committee on the proposed center says that more than 15,000,000 people visited the National Capital area in 1960. By 1970, visitors will be arriving at the rate of more than 24,000,000 a year, and by 1980, it is estimated that the visitor rate will exceed 35,000,000 a year, more than 13 per cent of the national population at that time.

The brochure points out, "The opportunity exists in Washington to convey to these visitors and students the inspiring story of the United States."

★ ★ ★

Knox Banner, Executive Director of the **National Capital Downtown Committee** and a member of the American Planning and Civic Association, emphasized that "Downtown, between the White House and the Capitol, is on the move," in a recent article in the *National Capital Area Realtor.*

"There has been more development action and development interest in Downtown east of 15th Street in the last three years than in any comparable period in this century," he said.

Pointing out, however, that mortgage financing, especially for residential construction east of 12th Street, is still difficult to obtain, Mr. Banner continued:

"Real progress cannot be made in Downtown until the area is designated for urban renewal action under a new concept that will encourage maximum development by private initiative with a minimum of public acquisition and in a minimum of time."

S. 628, a legislative measure, which would permit the use of urban renewal in Downtown Washington, was passed by the Senate on July 16, 1963. The bill is identical to one passed by the House of Representatives by unanimous consent in September, 1962, but which was not acted upon by the Senate during the closing hours of that session.

At present, says Mr. Banner, "Washington is the only one of the ten largest cities in the United

States which cannot make use of the urban renewal program in its Downtown area."

Charles A. Horsky, the President's adviser on National Capital Affairs, has urged residents of Capitol Hill to support proposed "long-term redevelopment" of their historic community.

Mr. Horsky spoke to the Capitol Hill Restoration Society and presented six awards to members of the group for civic contributions and outstanding restoration projects throughout the year.

The effort to prevent construction of high-rise apartments along the shores of the Potomac River was evident, again, in recent hearings regarding construction of the controversial high-rise Tantallon Apartments. The Prince Georges County Commissioners have since voted to approve construction of the apartments.

Whether or not, after construction, the apartments can be seen from the Potomac River or from Mount Vernon was one of the points in dispute.

Commissioner Gladys Spellman, who opposed re-zoning making the apartments possible, said the Commissioners "will certainly be besieged with requests for similar rezoning . . . and in only a few years the Maryland Shore line, as viewed from Mount Vernon, may well resemble that of New York City."

Bartholomew Resigns Maryland-National Capital Post

Harland Bartholomew, internationally respected planning adviser, has recently resigned as General Plan consultant to the **Maryland-National Capital Park and Planning Commission.**

Last year, he retired as head of the widely-known planning consultant firm, **Harland Bartholomew & Associates,** which he founded in St. Louis in 1919.

Both steps by Mr. Bartholomew, who is president of the American Planning and Civic Association and a former chairman of the National Capital Planning Commission, have been received with special regret throughout the Washington area where his contributions in the planning field are held in the highest esteem.

As consultant to the Maryland-National Capital Park and Planning Commission, Mr. Bartholomew has played an important role in drawing up the General Plan for the Year 2000, designed to guide the development of Montgomery and Prince Georges Counties in the Washington Metropolitan area. Adoption of the Plan, which was published last October, is expected this year. In resigning, Mr. Bartholomew noted that his work on the plan was completed.

A simple, but well conceived step in bringing order out of some of the confusion pervading current planning efforts has been made by the **Committee of 100 on the Federal City** in the publication of a mimeographed "Directory of Planning Agencies of the National Capital Region."

David Sanders Clark, in an editor's foreword to the publication, says, "Even citizens who are active participants in community affairs appear to be having difficulty keeping track of the multiplicity of governmental agencies which are now generating, passing upon, or implementing plans affecting the development of part or all of the National Capital Region."

Rear Admiral Neill Phillips, USN (ret.), Chairman of the Committee of 100 on the Federal City, and a member of the Board of Trustees of the American Planning and Civic Association, says, "It is believed that this Directory is the only one of its kind, and will be of great value due to the multiplicity of Agencies."

The Directory is intended to lend a note of clarity to a problem which Washington has in common with many other communities today. It lists forty separate, major planning and decision making agencies in the National Capital Region, including agencies in Baltimore and Richmond "which are engaged in activities that can and do affect the region's growth."

Fairfax County planners have proposed "suburban cluster" development as an alternative to "sprawl" in the western portion of the fast growing County in close proximity to the Nation's Capital.

Will the reorganized **Fine Arts Commission,** under the chairmanship of **William Walton,** make a slow, diplomatic, but nevertheless, certain break with the past?

The question is still being discussed in Washington as the new Commission prepares to take up its tasks in a period of rapid change in the Capital City.

According to the *Washington Evening Star*, "The reshuffled commission has been viewed as marking a change in emphasis of official control away from the traditional architecture of the past and towards more liberal acceptance of contemporary design for Federal buildings in Washington.

Says the *Washington Post*, "The appearance of the Capital in decades to come will greatly depend upon (the Commission's) taste, discretion and leadership."

But it has remained for the **Committee of 100 on the Federal City** to suggest a way to put more force into recommendations of the Commission which now has only advisory powers.

In a congratulatory letter to newly appointed Fine Arts Chairman Walton, the Committee of 100's **Chairman Neill Phillips** said:

"It seems logical that, at least, the Fine Arts Act should be amended to require that any Agency or official who chooses not to follow a Fine Arts recommendation must give his reasons therefor in writing to the President or his representative."

In Perspective

It was lost already—the place no one knew.

For how could it be anything but lost—unless it had meaning for *someone*? Deep meaning attuned to the very wonder and shivering awe of it!

This is the strange reality of Glen Canyon on the Colorado which has been brought belatedly, but masterfully, to reality for everyone by the unique genius of Eliot Porter, the physician-turned-photographer who has had exhibitions in many of America's foremost museums.

Mr. Porter has achieved this in a beautiful book called just that, "The Place No One Knew," published by the Sierra Club and edited by the Club's Executive Director, David Brower, who has written the publication's foreword.

Pulling no punches on one side of the highly controversial facts of Glen Canyon today, Mr. Brower says frankly, "The closing of Glen Canyon dam in our time was a major mistake to learn from."

He concedes that "there could be long and acrimonious debate over the accusation of mistake." And, indeed, there could be, and is. The subject has been argued and debated, has occupied the attention of some of the nation's foremost editorial writers, has found its way more than once into the *Congressional Record*.

To those who point to the benefits of hydro-electric power which the dam will bring and who insist that it will make feasible reclamation projects throughout the Upper Colorado River Basin, Mr. Brower says brusquely:

"Hoover, Parker, and Davis dams already exist and control the river adequately; they could probably continue to do so until Lake Mead is silted in completely, perhaps two hundred years from now."

Be that as it may, the fact is that "In The Place No One Knew," Mr. Porter has captured, for all time, some most breath-taking photographs—awesome pictures of majestically sculptured canyon walls, of Hidden Passages "streaked with organ pipes of black and rose and taupe," which just about defy description.

And, as if they, in themselves, were not enough, an appeal of many voices has been added—bits of text opposite each photograph from a number of eminent writers—a veritable chorus with a plea not only for the now lost Glen Canyon but for the preservation, and more especially, the realization of the eternal mysteries of the wilderness and of all creation.

From the text, come the words of August Fruge: "When your spirit cries for peace, come to a world of canyons deep in an old land; feel the exultation of high plateaus, the strength of moving waters, the simplicity of sand and grass, and the silence of growth."

Of J. Horace McFarland, first president of the American Planning and Civic Association, ". . . the glory of the United States must rest and has rested upon a firmer foundation than that of her purely material

27

Proposed Fire Island National Seashore. Although without roads, Fire Island shows evidence of the automobile everywhere. Deep ruts of beach buggies like these, in an undeveloped section of the eastern half of the Island, are believed to have contributed to the great erosion of the March, 1962, storm.

Courtesy National P- .

Proposed Fire Island National Seashore. A two-hundred-foot, white, fine-quartz sand beach stretches as far as the eye can see. This section is at Smith Point County Park. Beyond the boardwalk is a row of foredunes.

Courtesy National Park Service, U. S. Department of the Interior

Proposed Fire Island National Seashore. Behind the beach is a line of imposing dunes, some over 30 feet high, well stabilized by American beach grass on their lee slopes.

Courtesy National Park Service, U. S. Department of the Interior

Fire Island National Seashore—A Proposal

EDITOR'S NOTE:—This is the fourth in the series of articles on proposed National Park Service projects, prepared by the Park Service at our request.

At the very time when most park and recreation people are figuratively turning every stone in a desperate search for suitable park lands—"before it is too late"—it is perhaps ironic to find one of the best and relatively undeveloped stretches of seashore almost within the shadow of America's largest city. But this is exactly what the National Park Service found and reported eight years ago in *Our Vanishing Shoreline*, a study of this Nation's 3700-mile Atlantic and Gulf coast.

Off the southern shore of Long Island, at distances varying from a mile to ten miles, lies a great stretch of sand bar—part of that system of barrier beaches which stretch, although not continuously, along the Atlantic Coast from Massachusetts to Florida. In the middle of this barrier reef is the 32-mile, comparatively untouched Fire Island, currently being considered for inclusion in the National Park System as a National Seashore.

Fire Island is long and narrow, varying in width from a few hundred yards to half a mile. A two-hundred-foot white, fine-quartz sand beach, "as fine as table salt," stretches as far as the eye can see. It is clean and gently sloping.

The foreshore slopes gradually, insuring safe and enjoyable swimming; the Atlantic tempers the climate to a July average of 72°; an east-west axis makes it one of the few fortunate beach areas on the Atlantic which face the sun throughout the day.

Behind the beach are imposing dunes, some over 30 feet high, well stabilized by beach grass on their lee slopes. From their crest, the island slopes gradually back to the irregular shoreline of Great South Bay, where salt marshes occasionally border the water. Dune vegetation consists mostly of beach grass and low shrubs—bayberry, beach plum, bearberry, beach heath, winged sumac, and a few pitch pine trees.

On the western half of the island is one of the most important natural features of the area, and an outstanding example of its kind—the Sunken Forest. This virgin tract is dominated by American holly trees, some several hundred years old, accompanied by sassafras, shadbush, red cedar, pitch pine, red maple, birch, black gum and red oak. Below the trees is an understory of highbush blueberry, azalea, wild sarsaparilla, fern, and such vines as catbrier and Virginia creeper. In a few swampy places are sedges, common reed and marshmallow.

The western end of Fire Island is occupied, for four miles, by Fire Island State Park, now under development. By next summer a bridge will connect this area with the mainland, and the park will be opened for high density use to absorb the overflow from Jones Beach State Park (already exceeding a yearly mark of 10 million visitors), 15 miles to the west.

The six miles of island just east o f

Fire Island State Park contain several small but rather intensively developed communities reached by ferry from Long Island's Bay Shore. A half-mile east of Point O'Woods, the last of the fashionable summer colonies of the six-mile-strip, is the Sunken Forest area. Sixty-four acres of this unique biotic community have already been preserved, at a cost of $150,000 by public-spirited citizens, acting as The Sunken Forest Preserve, Inc.; the unprotected 50 acres to the east are worthy of preservation.

Between Point O'Woods and Moriches Inlet are five more summer colonies—connected with the mainland by ferries from Sayville and Patchogue, but, for the most part, not encouraging or catering to visitors—and four unconnected segments of superb beach, almost totally free from any type of development and totaling 18¼ miles. This area is well-suited for almost any desired type of seashore recreation and could well provide uncrowded beach activities for the huge metropolitan population nearby.

With the proposal of a bridge across Narrow Bay, the center of development in the Fire Island area shifted to Smith Point about eight years ago. A projected road, extending well to the east and west of the Suffolk County Park, aroused attention of real estate operators who acquired more than 13,000 feet of ocean frontage on both sides of the park with the idea of developing a modern ocean-front resort. When the bridge opened four years ago, the County developed a bay-to-ocean band 8,700 feet wide, but

the expected private interest developments did not materialize.

The west end of the Fire Island area is within 50 miles of the center of New York City; driving time *via* the State parkway system permits day-use for about 9,000,000 people. An additional 7,000,000 people in several states live within a 100-mile radius of Fire Island.

With the definitely established, country-wide pattern of heavier use each year of beach recreation areas, it can reasonably be anticipated that the six State Park areas on Long Island (including the newly developed Fire Island State Park) will ultimately be crowded and overtaxed. From Delaware to Massachusetts, there are 1,385 miles of recreational shoreline, according to the Outdoor Recreation Resources Review Commission. Of this 1,385 miles, only 70 miles, or 5 percent, is now publicly-owned and developed for recreation. The very paucity, then, of this resource for public use recommends Fire Island for preservation.

In March, 1962, a severe and unpredicted storm ravaged the Atlantic shoreline from North Carolina to Long Island. It was one of those great levelers that from time to time strikes the barrier beaches, flattens the foredune ridges and occasionally breaches the barriers to form new inlets. When erosion experts warned that another such storm would cause the ocean to crash through the barrier beach and endanger numerous communities on the south side of Long Island, interest in the preservation aspects of a National Seashore quickened.

(*Continued on page 40*)

State Park Notes

Minnesota. Governor Karl Rolvaag recently signed into Minnesota law a legislative bill providing for the start of a $50,000,000 long-range natural resources program.

He thus put the executive seal of agreement to action of the 1963 Minnesota State Legislature, which, with both Houses supporting, passed the most significant State Park legislation in Minnesota's history.

Under the bill, 14 new state parks will be created during the next two years, and extensive improvements will be made in about 20 other parks. Part of the funds will be used to improve state forests and fish and game management.

And a 14-member outdoor recreation resources commission will be set up to recommend what the state should do to provide adequate facilities by the year 2000.

Miscellaneous legislation enacted included authorization for the establishment of official canoe routes on the Minnesota, St. Croix, Big Fork and Little Fork Rivers.

Florida. A donor, who chooses to remain anonymous, recently presented Florida Governor Farris Bryant with a check for $2,350,000 for use by the Florida Park Service in purchasing additional land for the John Pennekamp Coral Reef State Park Headquarters site on Key Largo.

This is the second sizeable gift presented to the Park Service by the same donor, who specified that the current sum be used to purchase more than 2,100 acres of land on Key Largo, bordering on the Atlantic and Largo Sound.

The unique John Pennekamp Coral Reef State Park embraces some 75 square miles of protected living coral reef formations situated in the Atlantic off Key Largo. This unusual preserve was acquired by dedication of certain State of Florida lands and by Presidential Proclamation of United States lands.

The spawning grounds for numerous tropical fish, the area contains more than 40 species of living coral and is one of the last living coral formations in the Northern Hemisphere.

California. The California Legislature has approved the financing of a program to acquire and develop state and municipal beach, park, recreational, and historical facilities through the sale of $150,000,000 in bonds.

The proposed bond issue was called for by California's Governor

Brown in a special message to the Legislature and will be submitted to the voters in November, 1964.

The California press is already pointing up the significance of the coming election. Said a recent editorial in the *San Jose Mercury:*

"With California now the most populous state in the Union, it is none too soon to begin considering how—and where—these Californians, new and old, will spend their leisure hours. Next year's bond election for beaches and parks deserves the most careful consideration on the part of every citizen."

A sound trail program, involving all city, county, state, and federal agencies is needed in California in the opinion of Charles A. DeTurk, Director of Parks and Recreation.

News and Views, a publication of the Division of Beaches and Parks, recently stated that Mr. DeTurk "views with alarm the rapid loss of routes of travel historically available to the walker and equestrian due to the lack of a state-wide plan aimed at preserving existing trails and in providing additional facilities."

Mr. DeTurk has recommended that, wherever possible, with the approval of local government, trails be designed to take advantage of State, County and Federal parks and forests.

Ohio. State park visitors all across Ohio last summer were asked to answer thirteen questions intended to give a picture of park use.

A similar survey in 1958 revealed that less than 25 per cent of park attendance came from the county in which the park is located, that more than 50 per cent of Ohio park goers travel more than 100 miles during their visit, and that more than 50 per cent have an average yearly income exceeding $6,000.

Twenty-one miles of new hiking trails in Ohio have been opened to parkgoers at five state parks, according to V. W. Flickinger, chief of the Ohio Division of Parks. Fourteen new trails are now available in the state.

Connecticut. Governor Dempsey has signed into Connecticut law a legislative bill allowing a tax reduction for farm land used as open space. If the land is declared open space, its assessment will be based on its use as vacant land, without regard to the use of other land in the neighborhood.

New Hampshire. A natural science program was conducted in New Hampshire last summer for the third consecutive year, under the auspices of the Audubon Society of New Hampshire and the State Division of Parks.

Held at Bear Brook State Park in Allenstown, without charge to the public, the nine-weeks program was under the guidance of a full-time experienced naturalist and was designed to better acquaint children and adults with native plant and animal life.

The program has been recognized as an outstanding example of cooperation between state and private organizations. The Parks Division provided quarters for the center, including the main exhibition room, office, library and apartment for the naturalist, and materials for displays.

West Virginia. Some of the most beautiful scenic settings in this majestic mountain state became available for public enjoyment when the Scenic Railroad, at Cass, West Virginia, recently rolled again.

Visitors from 25 states—from Massachusetts to Washington and from Vermont to Florida—have already traversed the picturesque area in cars pulled by old Shay locomotives.

The eight-mile round trip on the line, long idle on its silent rails and steep mountainside, takes approximately two hours, according to Kermit McKeever, Chief of the Parks and Recreation Division of the State Department of Natural Resources.

Regular trips through mountains, which have traditionally signified the strength of West Virginia mountaineers as free men, are scheduled for the future.

Iowa. Let's face it.

If "outdoors" has come to mean traffic jams, shoulder-to-shoulder fishing, and generally cramped "roughing it", some of the problem may be that we are simply not seeking the spots where solitude abounds.

A recent issue of the *Iowa Conservationist* urges acquaintance with "little-known Iowa", saying numerous small areas in Iowa's State Park System beckon those seeking elbow room. To name a few:

Dolliver on the Des Moines River —where unique copperas beds, quiet glens, shady brooks and modern camping facilities combine in a blessing of solitude.

Pilot Knob, near Forest City, with its unusual sundew plants at Dead Man's Lake.

Or Wapsipinicon State Park, near Anamosa, with a list of features as long as its name—interesting cave formations, good fishing, good hiking, scenic beauty, and relatively light use.

Tennessee. "Stickball" and "Chunkey."

If these terms trigger a slight knitting of your brow, chances are you don't know the exciting story of Fuller State Park in Tennessee either.

Edward B. Smith, Associate Editor of the *Knoxville News-Sentinel,* says, "Those who have seen the Cherokees of today at play here in East Tennessee and Western North Carolina know about stickball. Chunkey is a game in which a flat-sided stone is rolled down a long alley while the players try to hit it with sticks or spears."

Both were games played by the Choctaw Indian tribe which lived in what is now Fuller State Park from about the year 1000 to 1600.

According to Mr. Smith, archeologists discovered remains of the ancient Indian village after the park was established. Called Chucalissa, which means "House Abandoned", the village is still being excavated. It ranges over about 30 acres around a central plaza which was the meeting place and playground for members of the tribe. The original poles, indicating the court where stickball was played are still there in the partly reconstructed village, according to Mr. Smith.

American Motors Corporation Announces Awards Program for 1963 in Appreciation of "A Nation's True Wealth"

American Motors Corporation has announced that nominations are now being accepted for its 1963 series of Conservation Awards.

The program is undertaken in the belief that "A nation's true wealth and the basis for its greatness and prosperity are in its natural resources."

"We bear the responsibility of maintaining our soil, forests, rivers and streams, and wildlife for the prosperity and enjoyment of future generations," says the Corporation.

Annually honored under the program is the work of 20 professional and non-professional conservationists and the conservation activities of two non-profit organizations.

Ten awards, each consisting of $500 and an engraved bronze plaque, are made to professional conservationists employed by non-profit organizations. Bronze plaques and citations are awarded to ten non-professionals whose conservation efforts are a voluntary expression of good citizenship. Awards of $500 each go to two non-profit organizations in recognition of outstanding achievements in special conservation projects.

In announcing the '63 Awards program, American Motors' president Roy Abernethy said that participation of concerned individuals and organizations is essential to the conservation of America's natural resources.

"*The total conservation need is too large and too diverse for federal and state supervision alone and there is a great opportunity for individual citizen accomplishment in the husbandry of our resources.*" he said.

"It is our hope that the American Motors Corporation Awards will stimulate increased public interest in good conservation practices by recognizing and honoring those who have made outstanding contributions."

Award winners are selected by a committee of prominent conservationists. They are: G. R. Gutermuth, vice-president of the Wildlife Management Institute; Carl W. Buchheister, president of the National Audubon Society; Arthur W. Carhart, authority on national parks and forests and consultant for the Conservation Library Center, Denver; Richard H. Pough, of Pelham, N. Y., director of Natural Area Council, Inc., and Harold Titus, conservation editor of *Field and Stream* Magazine.

Ed Zern, writer on outdoors sports and conservation, directs the awards program.

Objective of the Awards committee is to select winners whose conservation efforts have not received public recognition.

Nominations for awards should be submitted before November 15 by letter to: American Motors Conservation Awards Committee, Room 700, 555 Madison Avenue, New York 22, New York.

National Recreation Area Pilot Project Gets Underway with TVA as Administrator

A pioneer step in resource development was taken when President Kennedy recently announced that the Tennessee Valley Authority will develop a National Recreation Area in a section of land crossing the Kentucky-Tennessee boundary line, known as the "Between-the-Lakes" area.

Two thirds of the area lies in western Kentucky, the remainder in Tennessee, and it encompasses that land lying between TVA's Kentucky Reservoir on the Tennessee River and the U. S. Army Corps of Engineers' Barkley Reservoir just across the divide on the Cumberland River.

The project is intended to demonstrate how an area with limited timber, agricultural, and industrial resources can be converted into a recreation asset that will stimulate economic growth of the region. It is also intended to help establish and define guidelines for the acquisition, development, and operation of other outdoor recreation areas.

Nearly half the land is already in Federal ownership, under control of the Department of Interior, TVA and the Corps of Engineers.

In announcing the undertaking, the President noted that the Between-the-Lakes area is within 200 miles of nearly 10 million people living in the midwest. It thus meets the recommendation made by the Outdoor Recreation Resources Review Commission, and endorsed by the President in his Special Message to Congress last year, that recreation facilities for our more densely populated areas merit high priority.

TVA expects to start on the project at an early date. Lands administered by the Department of Interior will be turned over to TVA for the project, and other Federal lands will likewise be transferred.

It is expected that TVA will administer the area for the period required to complete the demonstration, estimated at about 10 years. At the end of that period, arrangements for permanent administration of the area for outdoor recreation will be determined.

Did You Know—

It was through the concerted public opinion focused by the American Civic Association, fifty-four years ago, that the international treaty between Canada and the United States recognized and preserved the beauty of Niagara Falls?

—As explained in American Civic Annual, 1929, edited by Harlean James, then Executive Secretary, American Civic Association and currently a member of the Board of Trustees, American Planning and Civic Association.

FIRE ISLAND NATIONAL SEASHORE—A PROPOSAL

(*Continued from p. 34*)

In the wake of the March storm, the 15-man Temporary State Commission on Protection and Preservation of the Atlantic Shorefront was appointed to study the erosion. Their *Final Report*, approved in July, 1962, recommended a four-lane "ocean boulevard" to connect Fire Island State Park and Smith Point Park and help hold the dunes in place. It would need a "strip of dunes approximately 300 feet wide" as a right of way, although the average width of the island is approximately 400 yards, including marsh areas, from bay shore to ocean beach.

Reaction to this proposal came fast and furious. To oppose the New York plan, a citizens' committee for the preservation of Fire Island was created. Aware of the National Park Service's interest in the island, the citizens' committee, backed by other interested people and organizations, requested that the Department of the Interior prepare an evaluation as to how Fire Island could best be preserved and used.

Following studies by the Bureau of Outdoor Recreation and the National Park Service, Secretary of the Interior Stewart L. Udall on June 11, 1963 in letters to the Chairmen of the House and Senate Interior Committees, urged approval of legislation to create a Fire Island National Seashore, 52 miles long and encompassing some 8,000 acres. The 20 miles of shoreline added to the project lies east of Moriches Inlet and includes Shinnecock Inlet, one of the 16 Atlantic and Gulf Coast areas classified by the *Our Vanishing Shoreline* study as having first importance for preservation.

The legislation recommended by the Department of the Interior (H.R. 6934, introduced by Congressman Leo W. O'Brien; H.R. 6393, introduced by Congressman William F. Ryan; H. R. 7107, introduced by Congressman Otis G. Pike) defines the proposed Seashore and sets forth the ground rules for its acquisition. After establishment, it would be administered in accordance with "the applicable provisions of the laws relating to the national park system."

All thinking, in terms of administration and development, has been, to date, tentative. But the direction this advance thinking is taking was reflected in a talk given by Ronald F. Lee, Northeast Regional Director of the Park Service at a symposium on *The Ecology of the Long Island Barrier Beach and Great South Bay Area* at Adelphia Suffolk College, Oakdale, New York, on June 17th:

"High density recreation in the form of intensive beach use would of course be a major and necessary factor. Intensive recreation use would be provided, however, only in designated locations, specifically Fire Island State Park and the Smith Point County Park which comprise the two bridge heads. The total amount of land necessary for this use would be kept in healthy proportion to natural areas and existing private development.

(*Continued on page 54*)

Assateague Island National Seashore Proposal Revived

EDITOR'S NOTE:—This article has been prepared by the National Park Service at our request.

Some 33 miles long, Assateague Island is the largest undeveloped seashore area between Cape Hatteras, North Carolina and Cape Cod, Massachusetts. The lower nine miles of the island are already in Federal ownership as the Chincoteague National Wildlife Refuge, and the State of Maryland is now in the process of acquiring 640 acres as a State Park. The remainder of the island—some 15 miles—is in private ownership.

As early as 1935, the National Park Service had surveyed the Atlantic coast to determine what areas might be worthy of Federal acquisition—to be set aside for public use and enjoyment. Assateague Island—a long barrier reef ranging from about one third to a little more than a mile in width—was one of 12 areas identified as suitable for National Seashore status. Inspired by the survey report, several bills were introduced in the Congress during the 1940's to establish a national seashore encompassing Assateague Island, but no action was taken.

A similar survey followed in 1955, but by that time a major portion of the Maryland Section of the Island had been purchased and subdivided by a private developer. The survey report concluded regretfully that "the advance stages of real estate development appear to preclude the possibility of this area being set aside for public recreational use."

Prospects for a national seashore were further dimmed when the Maryland Legislature in 1961 authorized the construction of a bridge to the island and followed this up the following year with an appropriation of $1,500,000—thus rekindling private interests in development of the subdivided area.

Then, on March 6 and 7, 1962, a storm of unusual proportions combined with high tides, lashed the shores of the Atlantic coast causing millions of dollars worth of damage to homes, summer cottages, shore installations, dunes and the shoreline itself. Most severe was the damage along the barrier beaches of six states: New York, New Jersey Delaware, Maryland, Virginia and North Carolina.

Secretary of the Interior Stewart L. Udall, Senator Clinton Anderson, Chairman of the Senate Committee on Interior and Insular Affairs, and National Park Service Director Conrad L. Wirth urged that immediate thought be given to the dedication of shoreline portions of the barrier beaches to public use. To determine the extent of storm damage, Secretary Udall organized a task force of Federal and State agencies to make an aerial and ground reconnaissance of the shorelines of the six States.

By March 26—in less than a week —the task force had completed its initial report. Of the northern portion of the area surveyed, the

41

general restrictions ought to be permitted."

The Court has frequently expressed its opposition to what may be a preference, and, in several late cases, has insisted that all three statutory requirements must be present before a variance can be allowed. If there is a *substantial* hardship peculiar to the property, it must also be established that there will be no substantial detriment to the public welfare and no derogation from the purpose of the law.

Helpful rulings which have been used as precedents are also found in decisions involving non-conforming use:

1) There must be *actual use.* Even where a building was completed before the adoption of a zoning ordinance but there was no evidence of its use, non-conformity was not established.

2) Increase in business volume is not a violation of a non-conforming use, especially where there is no enlargement of the building.

3) The character of the use cannot be changed by expansion. This is a well established rule although peculiar local zoning ordinance provisions result in apparently inconsistent decisions.

4) Loss of a non-conforming exemption by abandonment or cessation is primarily a question of intent, but long disuse may be shown as evidence of intent.

In many jurisdictions, rulings on specific uses are precedents which have been consistently followed:

1) Funeral homes are commercial uses which are properly excluded from residence zones.

2) A real estate broker is not practising a profession in spite of some professional aspects of his business.

3) The distinction between a farm and the commercial use of land for hog or poultry raising is clearly made in several states, and in Massachusetts, at least, a greyhound racing stable is neither an agricultural use nor a use accessory to a farm.*

The above citations do not exhaust the list of zoning categories where principles of interpretation have been established or rulings have been followed as precedents. This method of setting some bounds on the police power is to be preferred to fixing the bounds by statute, like the limit on living space requirements in a single family house fixed in Massachusetts at no greater than 768 square feet.

*Miodinszemski *vs.* Sangus, 337 Mass., 140 (1958).

Water Recreation In Arkansas

Arkansas contains 13 large, man-made reservoirs, numerous state, city and private lakes and six major rivers. Beaver Reservoir, the latest in a chain of White River lakes constructed in Arkansas by the Corps of Engineers, is filling rapidly. The system of waterways furnishes a varied source of water sports fun, including fishing, SCUBA diving, cruising and water skiing.

Seminars, Conferences and University Notes

Design. "Architects and city planners should recognize the fact that the automobile is a permanent part of the American environment, and should design the cityscape to accommodate the auto."

This was the position taken by Paul Rudolph, New Haven architect and chairman of the department of architecture at Yale University before the fourteenth annual International Design Conference held in June in Aspen, Colorado.

Mr. Rudolph was one of 23 internationally distinguished speakers from the fields of design, architecture, visual communication and related areas who discussed current design directions and dilemmas before the conference which was attended by approximately 650 design and business executives from 43 states and several foreign countries.

"The automobile is the greatest problem to American cities, but it also offers the greatest organizing element for the city of the future," said Mr. Rudolph. "The automobile should certainly be kept out of some areas of the city; and other areas should be redesigned so that they are consistent with the existence of the automobile. City planners still know very little about what to do about city streets, and how to use them to make cities more beautiful and more inhabitable."

Ivan Chermayeff, partner, Chermayeff & Geismar, New York, sought to rouse the conference to a recognition of the underlying difficulty in the broad field of design. Too many consumers, clients and designers today don't care very much about very much, he said. "The joy and pleasure of doing a good job for its own sake has not been discovered by enough people— consumers, clients and designers. This satisfaction factor has disappeared from this country and should be brought back."

And Robin Boyd, Australian architect, said that modern architecture is still threatening to make the whole world "a tired sort of world's fair." But conceded Mr. Boyd: Architecture "has come back at last from window dressing and ornamentation to the art of controlling space— not merely opening up space, or hiding a piece of it behind a space divider, or softening the break between indoors and outdoors, but a wholehearted control of levels, volumes, and the views within and beyond."

Cornell Conference. A course in Environmental Health Planning and one in Data Processing were included in the one-week 1964 Summer Institute in City and Regional Planning offered by Cornell University.

In 1963, a Training Program in Environmental Health Planning was established in the Department of City and Regional Planning at Cornell with the support of the U. S. Public Health Service. The 1964 summer course was offered in conjunction with that program.

It was offered in the belief that "professional city planners could play a vital role in alleviating the environmental health problems of our cities . . . As the country has

43

PROJECTS IN REVIEW

(*Continued from p. 20*)

associations, nor by individuals. It is something everybody does—together."

"Communities differ in their solutions of the many conservation problems," he continues. "Some excel in creating beautiful gardens and patios, others in restoring old and quaint architectural features."

But in improving their own neighborhoods, he points out, people have "indicated the validity of an established principle that 'the welfare of any neighborhood is dependent upon the welfare of all other neighborhoods and the city as a whole.'"

Miss Angle gives a miniscule history of Lincoln Park. The area, she says, was first settled in the 1850's by German truck gardeners. Most of the buildings were leveled during the Chicago fire of 1871, and it was during the next 25 years that most of the structures in the neighborhood went up.

The area became the home of De Paul University and McCormick Theological Seminary, numerous hospitals, churches, schools, and the Chicago Historical Society.

Of "City In A Garden", Dr. Hutchison says, "While much remains to be done, this volume attempts to show that the rebirth of the Lincoln Park area is no longer idle theory, and that the beauty and charm of Old Chicago are experiencing an exciting rebirth through the civic interest and pride of its citizens."

Wild Rivers

Sixty-four rivers or segments of rivers in thirty-five states have been selected for consideration as "Wild Rivers" by a five-man study team appointed jointly by the Secretaries of the Interior and Agriculture. In addition, a number of rivers, not included in the list, are being or have already been studied and will be considered in the final stages of the Wild Rivers program.

Purpose of the study is to identify those portions of streams and rivers which have the highest outdoor recreation potential, in order to dedicate them "to such use by appropriate legislative and executive action."

The study, the first ever made for this purpose on such a broad scale, grew out of recommendations by the Outdoor Recreation Resources Review Commission and the Senate Select Committee on National Water Resources.

The Senate Committee suggested that "certain streams be preserved in their free-flowing condition because their natural scenic, scientific, esthetic and recreational values outweigh their value for water development and control purposes now and in the future."

"Undeveloped rivers offer unique values to all Americans," the government study group has pointed out. "They are symbols of timelessness and continuity and of history."

The preliminary studies now under way will lead to more detailed investigation at a later stage of a limited number of the rivers. Six task groups have been formed from the two government departments to conduct field studies of the rivers which will extend through the fall.

The initial list of 64 rivers includes 11 in the Southeast, 11 in the Northeast, nine in the Lake Central States, 11 in the Mid-continent area, seven in the Pacific Southwest and 15 in the Pacific Northwest.

All were selected on the basis of their quality and variety as well as to realize broad geographical distribution. The advice and assistance of the Governors in the States where the rivers are located is being sought.

Specialized portions of the overall study are being handled by contract with the Battelle Memorial Institute of Columbus, Ohio, which is presently studying the Salmon and Clearwater Rivers in Idaho.

ASPECTS OF THE PROGRAM OF THE HOUSING AND HOME FINANCE AGENCY RELATED TO PLANNING

(*Continued from p. 12*)

Through the end of March, the grants made for urban planning under the Kennedy Administration have amounted to $32,100,000 for 697 projects. These included 78 grants to metropolitan or regional planning bodies and 36 grants involving transportation planning.

In the Housing and Home Finance Agency, we have given the strongest possible emphasis to the importance of comprehensive planning.

To coordinate the programs of HHFA related to planning and community development, I have established a new Office of Metropolitan Development. Assistant Administrator Victor Fischer, a man with extensive experience in this field, heads that office.

He works closely with John Kohl, Assistant Administrator who heads a new Office of Transportation

which is responsible for administering the program of loans and demonstration grants for mass transportation, authorized by the Housing Act of 1961. Both officials are in constant communication with the Urban Renewal Administration, a constituent of the Housing and Home Finance Agency, responsible for our major urban planning programs.

We believe strongly that planning for urban regions cannot be left exclusively to the technicians, be they city planners, highway engineers, economists or other specialists. The development of metropolitan areas must be guided by responsible local leaders, elected officials and others. At the same time, the technical planning needs to be tied closely to comprehensive planning carried out under local and regional auspices.

COMMENTARIES

(Continued from p. 22)

for redevelopment extend throughout the central business district. Thus the present central business district will be revitalized and the effect upon the areas adjacent to those rebuilt will be substantial.

What will downtown redevelopment mean to the Cincinnati area? "One of the important benefits," says Mr. Hartman, "is that it will enable Cincinnati to take its rightful place among the great cities of the world."

❧

Hospitals: "Growing demands for hospital facilities result from many factors including increases in the population, changes in its composition, advances in medical science and third party payment plans."

This was the statement of Dr. Daniel Howland, associate professor of industrial engineering, at Ohio State University, at the Third International Conference on Operational Research recently held in Columbus, Ohio.

Dr. Howland pointed out that the complexity of the hospital system planning problem is steadily increasing and said, "the planner must attempt to satisfy the medical, economic and educational requirements of physicians, nurses, patients and the public at large."

❧

Wild River: "Another unnecessary but alarming threat to one of America's precious remaining wild rivers—this time the Wolf River, Wisconsin—has apparently been defeated by the gathering forces of conservation, at least temporarily."

So reports a recent issue of the *SFA Bulletin*, a publication of the Sport Fishing Institute. The *Bulletin* states that the Wolf River Conservation Club campaigned to save the river by enlisting the aid of conservationists throughout the state and publishing a most informative and revealing booklet entitled, "A Real *Threat* To The Wolf

River."

Says the *Bulletin*, "In the process of impounding some 1,600 acres of three-foot-deep water, the uniquely beautiful white water wilderness trout stream that is the upper Wolf River would be obliterated through innundation with a shallow warm water lake."

❧

Plea for Promptness: From Sir Keith Joseph, Minister of Housing and Local Government, Whitehall, London, comes an ever-pertinent message on "the importance of not holding things up." Speaking before the annual meeting of the County Councils' Association, Sir Keith said:

"All of us concerned with planning need always to remember how much the public's willingness to accept the control of planning depends on the speed and intelligence with which applications are handled. . . . Planning in practice emerges in the handling of thousands and thousands of applications, the great majority small ones. And it is by this handling that planning is apt to be judged. None of us must ever forget this. . . .

"It is only too clear that our planning machinery is going to come under tremendous strain in the years ahead. We are going to have to turn right over to a positive approach to planning . . . while at the same time speeding up our handling of development proposals. I believe that none of the functions with which county councils deal is more challenging or provides more opportunity for shaping the future."

❧

Search: "Americans have a passion for ugliness."

The *Washington Post* terms this quote from H. L. Mencken "no longer so persuasive." "More and more," says the *Post*, "Americans have joined in the quest for beauty, whether in music, in painting or even in the unencumbered majesty of a national park."

46

Strictly Personal

Edward J. Meeman, editor emeritus of the Memphis (Tenn.) *Press-Scimitar* and conservation editor for the Scripps-Howard Newspaper Alliance, has been appointed a member of the Advisory Board on National Parks, Historic Sites, Buildings and Monuments by Secretary of the Interior Stewart L. Udall.

Mr. Meeman is chairman of the Board of the National Conference on State Parks and a vice-president of the American Planning and Civic Association.

A native of Evansville, Indiana, Mr. Meeman started his newspaper career in 1907 as a reporter on the *Evansville Press* and later served as the managing editor of the same paper. With the expansion of the Scripps-Howard Newspaper Alliance, he became editor of the Knoxville (Tenn.) *News-Sentinel.* In 1931, he moved to the *Press-Scimitar* and became its editor in 1933.

A leading proponent for preservation of wilderness areas in the United States, Mr. Meeman has most recently been instrumental in getting the entire *Scripps-Howard* chain to support the Wilderness Bill currently before the House Committee on Interior and Insular Affairs. His editorial comment is credited with being an early factor in bringing the need for such legislation to public attention.

As editor of the *Knoxville News-Sentinel,* he was instrumental in starting the movement to establish the Great Smoky Mountains National Park.

At one point in his career, during a tour of Europe, Mr. Meeman took note of the large state forests near large cities in Germany. "Why," he asked, "if poor cities can conserve such areas, cannot the United States set aside suitable recreation areas?" Upon his return, as editor of the *Press-Scimitar,* he took the lead in establishing the 12,500-acre Shelby State Park, just six miles from the city limits of Memphis.

The Board to which Mr. Meeman has been appointed, was created by the Historic Sites Act of 1935 and is composed of 11 non-salaried members appointed by the Secretary of the Interior.

———◇———

C. F. Jacobsen, former vice chairman emeritus of the Board of Directors of the American Security and Trust Co., Washington, D. C., has retired after 60 years service in the banking field.

Mr. Jacobsen, who started his career at 18 as a runner for the National Metropolitan Bank in Washington, became president of that institution in 1939. In May, 1958, when the bank merged with the American Security & Trust Co., he was named vice chairman and a member of the Board of Directors. He retired last year as an active director but remained as director emeritus and an officer of the bank.

Mr. Jacobsen is treasurer of the American Planning and Civic Association.

———◇———

Major General Ulysses S. Grant 3rd, has been given an honorary life membership in the Ohio Historical Society "for his distinguished service to the American people as soldier and educator."

General Grant is a member of the Board of Trustees of the American Planning and Civic Association.

———————◆———————

A recent issue of *Footlight,* published by the National Cultural Center, calls attention to the fact that *Conrad L. Wirth,* Director of the National Park Service, is a member of the Center's Board of Trustees.

It is well known to members of the National Conference on State Parks that Mr. Wirth, who has long been a member of this organization's Board of Directors, has been honored in many ways for his accomplishments in the field of park service and recreation.

In 1954, he received an honorary Fellowship in the American Institute of Park Executives. He is a Fellow of the American Society of Landscape Architects and a life member of the Board of Trustees of the National Geographic Society.

———————◆———————

Ethel Wilson Harris, who has managed the distinctive San Jose Mission State Park at San Antonio, Texas, for 21 years, is retiring from the State Parks Service.

Mrs. Harris is president of the Texas Historical Theater Foundation which presents the annual summer presentation of "The San Jose Story." She has devoted many years to studying costumes, markets and fiestas of Old Mexico and has exhibited Mexican Crafts at both the Chicago and New York World's Fairs. Mrs. Harris is a member of the Board of Directors of the National Conference on State Parks.

———————◆———————

Sidney S. Kennedy, former chief of the Division of Cooperative Services of the Bureau of Outdoor Recreation, Department of the Interior, has retired after 30 years of service with the Department, mostly with the National Park Service.

A native of Mount Pleasant, Michigan, Mr. Kennedy graduated in 1928, from the School of Design, Harvard University, with the degree of master of landscape architecture.

His work with the National Park Service has long involved providing cooperative assistance to Federal, State and local agencies on all aspects of park and recreation area programs, reservoir planning and management and park practice programs. His most recent responsibilities included providing technical assistance in outdoor recreation planning and operation to the States and their subdivisions.

At a farewell party honoring his retirement, Mr. Kennedy was presented with a bound folio of letters of appreciation from his many friends of present and past years.

———————◆———————

Edward A. Hummel has been named Regional Director of the National Park Service's Western Regional Office in San Francisco. He succeeds *Lawrence C. Merriam* who retired on July 5.

Seminars, Conferences and University Notes

Award. Seminars on city planning and urban affairs at the University of Cincinnati, held under sponsorship of the *Alfred Bettman Foundation*, have helped to earn for that Foundation the top award of the *Ohio Planning Conference*. Nationally known leaders have participated in the conferences.

The Foundation, which is devoted to "promoting the cause of city planning through research and education," has made over 20 grants-in-aid to planning students since its beginning in 1945.

Alfred Bettman, who fostered metropolitan planning in the Cincinnati area, also fathered Ohio's planning laws. His far-sightedness is said to have "laid a foundation by statute and court decision for solving planning problems cities had not dreamed of in his day."

Land Use. "The People's Stake In Land Use" will be the theme of the 54th annual Western Forestry Conference to be held in San Francisco, December 11 to 13, 1963, under the sponsorship of the *Western Forestry and Conservation Association*.

Owners and managers of at least half the forest land in the West will be included in the more than 500 persons expected to attend the Conference. Membership of the Association includes representatives of both the government and private forest land interests.

Sub-themes for the Conference include, "Land Use and Civilization," "The People's Stake in Private Land," "The People's Stake in Public Land" and "Outlook for Western Land Use."

N. B. Livermore, Jr., chairman of the 42-member program committee, says, "Increasing population pressures in the West have forced managers of both public and private lands to give more attention to multiple-use planning for the future. The conference will aid that objective by voicing opinions from all land users, including sportsmen, loggers, miners, stockmen and wilderness advocates."

Highways. The twenty-second short course on Roadside Development will be held October 7-11, 1963, at Columbus, Ohio under the joint sponsorship of the *Ohio State University* Department of Landscape Architecture and the *Ohio Department of Highways*.

Theme of the conference will be: The Complete Highway—Your State's Contribution, Operations, Development and Maintenance.

Campus Plan. Plans for the preservation and development of *The University of Michigan's Central Campus* were made known recently as University officials met with city, county and state officers and other representatives of the community to review a planning guide prepared by *Johnson, Johnson and Roy* of Ann Arbor, site planners and landscape architects.

The study is the third in a series which has included the North Campus Study of 1960 and the

Medical Center Planning Study of 1961.

In presenting the study, W. K. Pierpont, the University's Vice-President in charge of Business and Finance, said, "As has already been done with the North Campus and Medical Center plans, the University will work closely with the Ann Arbor City Planning Commission and the City Council in carrying out the ideas and concepts involved in this Central Campus plan."

Fellowships. Opening of the 1963–64 school year will initiate, or continue for a number of students, the pursuit of study in the planning, architectural and related fields, under fellowship awards made last spring.

Eight graduate fellowships in city planning, at six universities, have been announced by trustees of the *Loula D. Lasker Fellowship Trust.* Eleven additional fellowships awarded last year have been renewed.

The awards mark the second year of a projected ten-year program designed to help relieve the critical nation-wide shortage of professional city planners and persons trained in the fields of housing and urban renewal.

Elsewhere, seventeen graduating students of *Columbia University's School of Architecture* have been awarded *William Kinne Fellows Traveling Fellowships* for the 1963–64 school year.

ACTION PROGRAMS FOR COMMUNITY DEVELOPMENT
(Continued from p. 8)

knowledge of the real needs of the community on the part of the local people helps to develop solutions more quickly and at less cost. *The cash outlay is really very small in all these cities. In some cities, the work program for community development has been completed at a cost of less than $300. The highest cost yet reported is $1,644. The average is about $500. This is a far cry from the costs usually associated with government ventures.*

From my own experience in Tampa, may I say that the first and most important result of the Community Development Action Program was that it provided a vehicle which developed, for the first time

in recent years, an intimate knowledge of the city's problems on the part of a majority of the citizens and succeeded in getting literally hundreds of citizens talking about solutions. This, I feel, is as significant an achievement as any specific project which has been completed to date.

It is proof positive that when men and women of high purpose work together for the solution of their community problems, progress toward solutions will be made.

And, in the doing, we resurrect the initiative, the zeal, the enthusiasm for independence and self-determination which have been a hallmark of Free America from its birth to this very minute!

FIVE YEARS OF METROPOLITAN PLANNING

(*Continued from p. 4*)

metropolitan government is operationally the simpler approach, which no doubt explains its continuing hold on many people's imaginations. "Super government," however, is precisely what the cooperative approach attempts to obviate the need for. And in fact, a metropolitan government might very well not plan, anyhow, but simply operate (like many another government). In that case, the political problems would be aggravated and the problem of growth not really faced at all.

Can the cooperative approach to the urban growth dilemma work? Or, in other words, how has the Northeastern Illinois Planning Commission fared in its first five years and what is contemplated for the next five?

Toward a Comprehensive Plan

Last November, the 19-member Commission I serve adopted an expanded 1963 budget and work program aimed at the early completion of a comprehensive plan of land use, transportation and other public facilities, and natural resources development (and including, very importantly, a program for implementation by local governments). The stated goal was to complete the plan within five years, and the Planning Commission staff was directed to prepare, early this year, a detailed Comprehensive Plan Program, with costs included so that future one-year budgets can be based on it. (It was recognized that such a program—particularly

the preparation of a plan for all modes of transportation—would require appreciably more funds than are allowed for in the $150,000–$250,000 annual budgets we are accustomed to.)

Meanwhile, we have been working *toward* a comprehensive plan, and have done a good deal of work which will serve as the foundation for the completion of a plan. We have done the bulk of our most important basic research including a major economic study, *Employment in 1980 in Northeastern Illinois*, and a comprehensive population and housing study now being reviewed for publication. We have followed for some three years the preliminary goal of defining and working toward the solution of four specific functional problems: Flood control and drainage, water supply and waste disposal, the preservation of open space, and transportation.

In this preliminary program, we have issued *Open Space in Northeastern Illinois*, a technical report on future metropolitan open space needs and the ways and means of meeting them; we have acted on flood control; and we are engaged in a study of water needs and supplies from which we expect to be able, at the end of this year to propose a "strategy for intergovernmental cooperation" to satisfy our future water needs.

We are also about to issue a metropolitan report on *garbage* for which there is already a considerable appetite—for it is a local as well as a metropolitan report, with estimates of refuse disposal needs and capacities for each of 22 districts. Some of its findings are properly malodorous —such as the overall estimate that by 1980 our area will be faced with five million tons of garbage for which no facilities will exist under present plans (or lack of them).

Transportation, a vast apparatus of metropolitan problems in itself, we are only beginning to attack in depth. Much of the work in the comprehensive plan program concerns the preparation of such a plan.

Helping Local Governments Plan

The stress on practical utility in the planning work of the Northeastern Illinois Planning Commission will already be evident. Let me drive the point home with a statement on metropolitan planning strategy: A comprehensive plan is needed for Northeastern Illinois, but so also is a planning constituency needed—a body of local governments with active and effective planning programs which are in a position to make use of the recommendations contained in a metropolitan plan. Moreover, the problems of the local governments are pressing; they cannot wait for the unfolding of the process of research, policy development, consultation with local governments, and final preparation which is necessary in developing a metropolitan plan under our law.

These facts help explain the Northeastern Illinois Commission's early emphasis on critical functional problems like flooding and refuse disposal; they help explain, again, why the largest chapter in our technical report on open space

should be devoted to an elaborate "how to" analysis of "Methods of Preserving Open Space." And this same strategy also explains why local planning assistance, information and publications should have been important parts of our program for two years and more.

In 1962 alone, more than 100 governments received planning advice and guidance on a direct contact basis from the Northeastern Illinois Planning Commission, ranging from "how to set up a planning department" to "how to (and where to) establish a storm water detention basin." We have also arranged and taken part in dozens of local meetings, including several at which new flood hazard maps were discussed and presented to the counties and municipalities which will make use of them.

We have concentrated increasingly on assisting and helping to organize intercommunity planning councils, of which there are now 14 in the metropolitan area with 110 municipalities participating. Right now, we are seeking the financing for an expanded program of local planning assistance which will allow us to extend more help to these municipal councils and to their members in what we term "preparing for planning."

An important special project last year was a joint study by the staff of the Planning Commission and the Chicago Department of City Planning. The purpose: To review the policies on which the forthcoming general plan of Chicago is to be based, as they relate to metropolitan area planning policies. It is hard to overestimate the importance of a project of this kind since cooperation between city and suburbs is an essential element in any solution to the growth problems of Northeastern Illinois.

Education is another important function, as we see it, and the Planning Commission has initiated and participated in a number of planning courses and seminars and will continue to do so. Currently, we are co-sponsoring—with the University of Chicago and one of the aforementioned inter-community councils, the Regional Association of South Cook-Will County Municipalities—a basic training course on the principles, practices, and tools of municipal planning. The course is not for planners, but for village trustees, plan commission members, zoning board members, and other officials who make the big decisions on whether to plan and what to do with a plan after it has been prepared. The first of these "Municipal Planning Laboratories" is under way now in south Cook County, the response has been strong, and we hope that there will be successor courses throughout the metropolitan area.

Another instrument of mutual education is the Commission-sponsored Metropolitan Area Planning Conference, which for five years now has brought a steadily increasing number of citizens and public officials together to review metropolitan planning progress and to "workshop" specific local and metropolitan problems. Last year's conference—attended by a record 475 persons, including over 300 local government officials—is credited with providing much of the impetus for actions taken since last fall toward preserving open space land.

Finally, let me say that we have worked equally hard at passing the printed word, by means of a steady steam of technical reports, information bulletins, "Metropolitan Planning Papers," handbooks, manuals, newsletters, press releases, and other devices.

From Policy to Plan

At the beginning of this article, I told of a cooperative agreement on open space planning and spoke of a document the agreement was based on, a 15-point statement of "Open Space Policies for Northeastern Illinois" officially adopted by the Metropolitan Area Planning Commission on July 19, 1962.

That statement, among other things, recommended 31 large sites, aggregating 90,000 acres, for future parks, forest preserves, reservoir and conservation areas, etc.; it recommended that the State of Illinois increase its state park and other open space holdings in the metropolitan area by 65,000 acres by 1980 (as against today's 13,848 acres); it also recommended a 40,000–50,000-acre increase in county forest preserve holdings, and it included recommended standards (measured in acres per unit of population) for open space facilities. The statement also contained the following policy on the use of flood plains:

"The extensive flood plains in the metropolitan area are an important open space resource which are ideally suited to multiple purpose use and, where possible, should be developed for

passive recreation, flood water storage, and other appropriate uses."

The adoption of this policy statement by the metropolitan counties is an important step in metropolitan planning itself. From it will come, we hope, a group of coordinated county open space plans which may be regarded both as implementation of metropolitan planning by local governments and as an important contribution to the metropolitan plan itself.

Are policies sufficient, then, as a planning contribution by a metropolitan planning agency? Here, I would say no. For what is missing, and what the comprehensive metropolitan plan will provide, is or*der*—the placing of first things first and second things second, in time, in space and in cost—and *relationship*—the relating of needs and solutions so that (for example) proposed action on transportation sup-

ports, rather than frustrates, proposed action on open space preservation, and so that actions by one government support, rather than obstruct, actions of the neighboring government.

The comprehensive plan, then, can be seen as the culminating expression instrument of guidance to local governments and the occasion for coordinated action to solve the growth problems of Northeastern Illinois.

It should be clear by now, though, that plan and implementation are not going to follow in neat, rational procession. Instead, planning, local assistance, and coordinated action and implementation are being brought along together. For the need of the metropolitan area is not for one plan but hundreds of plans; and the metropolitan planning job is (paradoxical though it seems) to serve all of them.

FIRE ISLAND NATIONAL SEASHORE—A PROPOSAL
(*Continued from p. 40*)

Beyond the intensive use areas, careful attention would be given to the preservation of all those portions of Fire Island presently in a natural state. Use of these portions would be encouraged, but this use would be of a kind closely related to preservation of the natural scene. This implies extended areas where the hiker or beachcomber may walk freely along the beaches and dunes, unencumbered by the sights and sounds of automobiles and other man-made intrusions, where the sky, the sea and the sand are the primal elements for enjoyment. For the ecologist it would mean that in these areas and along the bayside

trails as well, the hiker could see the native plant and animal life made relevant and comprehensible in its own environment."

In transmitting the Department's recommendations, Secretary Udall noted that "of the proposed national seashore and lakeshore areas, Fire Island is under the greatest threat of loss to the people of the United States, both today and tomorrow."

"Nowhere else in the country," he said, "is there a greater need by so many people for additional outdoor recreational opportunities that can be supplied in abundance and variety."

IN MEMORIAM

FREDERICK BIGGER
1881-1963

Frederick Bigger was born in Pittsburgh, Pa., in 1881. He studied architecture at the University of Pennsylvania from which institution he received his graduate degree as an architect.

From 1908 to 1911, he was engaged in the practice of architecture in Seattle, Washington and from 1911 to 1913, he was similarly engaged in Philadelphia.

By 1913, Mr. Bigger returned to his home city of Pittsburgh to engage in a long professional career. The earliest years were devoted to architectural practice, but he soon became particularly interested in city planning, attended early national conferences, and, in 1917, became a charter member of the American City Planning Institute.

Through Mr. Bigger's efforts, there was organized the Citizens' Committee on the City Plan of Pittsburgh, a lay group of leaders in the business world, headed by Mr. Armstrong and Mr. Mellon. Under Mr. Bigger's direction, there was prepared the first city plan for Pittsburgh, one of the early comprehensive plans. Mr. Bigger then moved on to become a member of the official City Plan Commission in 1922, subsequently serving as Chairman from 1934 to 1954, and as consultant in later years.

Thus, for four decades, he was the guiding spirit in the planning and development of Pittsburgh. Many of the great improvements in that city are enduring monuments to his tireless self-effacing efforts.

Mr. Bigger was a skilled technician—in truth, a technician's technician. His ability became widely recognized and his services sought in several fields. During the depression years, he served as chief of the planning staff of the Resettlement Administration and was largely responsible for the pioneer effort of design of the Greenbelt towns: Greenbelt, Maryland; Greenhills, Ohio; and Greendale, Wisconsin.

He served as urban planning adviser to the Federal Housing Administration from 1940 to 1945, rendering unheralded but valuable services in the rapidly developing housing movement. It was during this period that, with Mr. Bigger as principal author, the Handbook on Urban Redevelopment was prepared and published. This was the precursor of Title I of the National Housing Act of 1949, the law which paved the way for federal cooperation with local communities undertaking urban renewal projects.

In 1948, Mr. Bigger was appointed by President Truman to membership on the National Capital Planning Commission, on which body he served with distinction for six years.

These long years of professional endeavor of a high order led to many honors. He was President of the American Institute of Planners, 1931–33, an honorary life member of the American Society of Planning Officials, a fellow of the American Institute of Architects, an honorary member of the American Society of Landscape Architects and a corresponding member of the *Deutsch Akademie fur Stadtban and Landes-planning.*

In 1953, he was the recipient of the Distinguished Service Award of the American Institute of Planners.

Mr. Bigger was a member of the Cosmos Club in Washington, the University Club in Pittsburgh, and the Sketch Club in Philadelphia. He was a long-time member of the American Planning and Civic Association.

His wise counsel, his penetrating sense of humor and his friendly manner will be sadly missed by his wide circle of friends in all of the design professions. H.B.

EDWARD CLIFFORD

Edward Clifford, former assistant secretary of the Treasury, died recently at the age of 89.

A native of Illinois, he was graduated from Washington University Law School and was admitted to the Illinois Bar in 1900. He first came to Washington during World War I as an adviser on war loans to Secretary of the Treasury William McAdoo.

He was later commissioned a Lieutenant Colonel in the Quartermaster Corps.

In 1923, he left the Treasury where he had served under Secretary Andrew W. Mellon and opened a law practice in the Capital City, continuing a distinguished career until his retirement in 1938.

Mr. Clifford was a member of the Augustus P. Gardner Post No. 18

of the American Legion, of the Chevy Chase and Army and Navy Clubs and of the Columbia Historical Society. He had been a member of the American Planning and Civic Association since 1926 and was an active member of the Committee of 100 on the Federal City.

Tribute comes in the heartfelt words of those who worked closely with him: "He, indeed, was a great citizen and we shall miss him very much."

MRS. EDWIN D. GRAVES

We record with deep regret the recent death of Mrs. Edwin D. Graves who had been a member of the American Planning and Civic Association since 1941. Her active and dynamic interest in the affairs of the Committee of 100 on the Federal City was unwavering and a source of strength to our organization. She will be greatly missed as a civic leader.

PAUL T. WINSLOW

Paul T. Winslow, one of the long-time outstanding leaders in the State Parks field, died August 13, 1963.

Mr. Winslow had retired December 31, 1962, after serving as general manager and treasurer of the Taconic State Park Commission in New York State for 36 years.

He had been a member of the National Conference on State Parks since 1947. Through his death, the organization has sustained a genuine loss and he will be greatly missed by his many friends in this field.

INTERPRETING OUR NATIONAL PARKS

(*Continued from p. 14*)

visitors at campfire programs, lectures, on guided trips, and in park museums, or extended their interpretive service through self guiding trails, roadside and trailside exhibits and publications.

Park interpretation does not try to make naturalists of park visitors, but to enhance the park visitors' enjoyment and appreciation of the natural scene around them. It seeks to lead people to an awareness of the natural world of which they are a part, and on which they depend, to stimulate interest, and provoke curiosity.

The National Park System, epitomizing our land and people, is an investment in something as simple yet as fundamental as good citizenship—Love of country, and appreciation of the natural and historic fabric of America.

National Parks are to be preserved in a state of highest ecological integrity. They are also to be used and enjoyed. The interpretive use capitalizes in highest measure on the superior, inherent values of National Parks, and justifies the high standards established for their preservation.

IN PERSPECTIVE

(*Continued from p. 28*)

construction of a dam or a hydroelectric plant or something else is already in the thinking stage?

Too, would it not be regrettable if "The Place No One Knew" should become the "book no one knew?" Its price, twenty-five dollars, in spite of the fact that it is worth it, is, nonetheless, somewhat prohibitive for the average person.

Yet, this is a book which might well be widely distributed in libraries, where every school boy can get some intimation of what a canyon really means. Conceivably, in hospitals, where a closer touch with the mystical wonders of Nature, even through the pages of a book, can work its healing power. At the hearthside, where, alone, a genuine appreciation for the natural marvels of America can come into being.

It is a book to be savored slowly again, and yet again—one to have and to keep and to peruse and to value.

If this were possible for the perceptive ones of every age throughout our land, then, the idea behind "The Place No One Knew" might come somewhat closer to fruition.

What is that idea?

"We shall seek a renewed stirring of love for the earth; we shall urge that what man is capable of doing to the earth is not always what he ought to do; and we shall plead that all Americans, here, now, determine that a wide, spacious, untrammeled freedom shall remain in the midst of the American earth as living testimony that this generation, our own, had love for the next."						E. J. S.

American Planning and Civic Association
New Members, June 1, 1963 to August 1, 1963

District of Columbia
Captain Peter Belin, USN (ret.)
Michigan
Oakland County Planning Commission, Pontiac

Ohio
Battelle Memorial Institute, Columbus

National Conference on State Parks
New Members, June 1, 1963 to August 1, 1963

Connecticut
Mr. Duryea Morton, Audubon Center, Greenwich
District of Columbia
Soil Conservation Service
Michigan
Mr. Murray W. Telsworth, Holly
Mr. Eugene T. Petersen, Lansing
Mr. Charles M. Leeson, Mason
New Jersey
Mr. Rodney Edward Mott, Woodbridge
New York
Division of Lands & Forests, Albany

Pennsylvania
Western Pennsylvania Conservancy, Pittsburgh
Tennessee
Mr. W. F. Moehlman, Knoxville
Texas
Mr. Joe W. Cariker, West Columbia
West Virginia
Mr. Robert V. Ellis, Charleston
Mr. S. C. Hill, Charleston

Recent Publications

OUTDOOR RECREATION PREFERENCES: A NATIONWIDE STUDY OF USER DESIRES by Leslie M. Reid, Assistant Professor, Park and Recreation Administration, Department of Resource Development, Michigan State University, East Lansing, Michigan. June, 1963. 288 pp. $6.50.

A paper-bound, multilithed report, derived from the author's doctoral dissertation which was undertaken in cooperation with the Outdoor Recreation Resources Review Commission. It explores a little-tapped area in the recreation field which is bound to be of increasing importance in the future. Its findings are based on a questionnaire survey of 10,982 visitor groups at 24 selected outdoor recreation areas, including four national parks, seven national forest areas, three federal reservoirs, nine state parks and one

metropolitan county forest area. The report's analysis focuses on visitor opinions, preferences and dissatisfactions.

CONSERVATION DIRECTORY, 1963 edition. National Wildlife Federation, 1412 16th St., N. W., Washington, D. C. 20036.

A complete and up-to-date listing of American and Canadian natural resource agencies and organizations, this year's Conservation Directory includes an alphabetical index to the thousands of key individual's names appearing between its covers. Many conservation groups are listed in the publication for the first time.

The Directory, which was published for 44 years by the U. S. Fish and Wildlife Service, is now part of the National Wildlife Federation's conservation education program.

Watch Service Report

H. R. 3846, Establishing A Land and Water Conservation Fund. Congressman Wayne N. Aspinall (Colorado) and others.

This bill, amended extensively, was ordered reported favorably by the Sub-committee on National Parks of the House Interior and Insular Affairs Committee on August 6, 1963. As we go to press, the full Committee is scheduled to consider it shortly.

The Citizens Committee for ORRRC says that a number of the Sub-Committee amendments—notably those concerning the proposed grant-in-aid program to the States—have strengthened the bill along policy lines recommended by the ORRRC Report.

As reported, the bill would authorize appropriation of $2,000,000,000 over the next 10 years for grants-in-aid to the States for outdoor recreation and for Federal recreational land acquisition.

Section 4 (a), though re-written, still provides that appropriations from the Fund would be available, 60 per cent for State purposes and 40 per cent for Federal purposes, with the President authorized to vary the allocations 15 per cent either way during the first five years in which appropriations are made.

Two fifths of the monies available for grants would be divided equally among the States. Three fifths would be apportioned on the basis of need by the Secretary of the Interior.

Revenues to the fund would come from three dedicated sources: Admission and other fees paid by recreation users of Federal land and water areas; receipts from sale of Federal surplus real property and related personal property; and receipts from the existing four cents per gallon Federal tax on gasoline used in motor boats.

An annual fee of not more than seven dollars would allow an auto driver admission to all Federal areas, with exceptions designated by the President. Fees for a single visit or series of visits to particular areas would be permitted. No fees would be charged on highways commonly used by the public as a means of travel between two places, both of which are outside the area.

Many endorsements of the Land and Water Conservation Fund proposals were expressed in public hearings conducted by the National Parks Sub-Committee. Secretary of the Interior Stewart L. Udall said: "If enacted substantially as recommended, I am firmly convinced that it will go down in history as one of the major pieces of conservation legislation of the 1960's."

S. 4, The "Wilderness Bill," Establishing A National Wilderness Preservation System. Senator Anderson and others.

At present, the Wilderness Bill is still before the House Committee on Interior and Insular Affairs to which it was referred last April when it passed the Senate by a roll call vote of 73 yeas to 12 nays.

Congressman John V. Lindsay (New York) recently introduced **H. R. 7877,** establishing a National Wilderness Preservation System. This is another of the several different versions of the Wilderness Bill which have already been introduced in the House and referred to the Interior and Insular Affairs Committee.

H. R. 6934 and H. R. 6936, Establishing Fire Island National Seashore, New York. Congressmen Leo W. O'Brien (N. Y.) and William Fitts Ryan (N. Y.), respectively. Referred to the House Committee on Interior and Insular Affairs.

These bills, as recommended by the Department of the Interior, differ somewhat from several other bills which have also been introduced to establish the seashore. Under them, boundaries of the national seashore would include some 52 miles of relatively undeveloped shoreline and 8,000 acres of seashore environment and would extend from Fire Island Inlet to the junction of Meadow Lane and Halsey Neck Lane in the village of Southampton.

Section 5 provides: "The Secretary shall permit hunting and fishing on lands and waters under his administrative jurisdiction within the Fire Island National Seashore in accordance with the laws of New York, except that the Secretary may designate zones where, and establish periods when, no hunting shall be permitted for reasons of public safety, administration, or public use and enjoyment.

"Any regulations of the Secretary under this section shall be issued after consultation with the Conservation Department of the State of New York."

S. 27, Establishing Canyonlands National Park, Utah. Senator Frank E. Moss. Passed the Senate August 2, 1963 and was referred to the House Committee on Interior and Insular Affairs.

One of the major objectives of the National Park Service in the 88th Congress, the bill was passed with amendments recommended by the Senate Committee on Interior and Insular Affairs which issued a favorable report.

S. 27 provides that the Canyonlands National Park would eucompass some 260,000 acres in southeastern Utah at the confluence of the Green and Colorado Rivers. Features would include mazes of canyons, gigantic standing rock formations, towering buttes, natural bridges and arches. Grazing and mining would continue under certain restrictions for 25 years. Areas with big game herds were excluded from the boundaries of the park as outlined in the bill.

H. R. 7935, Providing for Economic Development of the Appalachian Highlands. Representative Carlton R. Sickles (Maryland). Referred August 5, 1963 to the House Committee on Public Works.

This bill provides Congressional recognition of the need for a special program to accelerate development of the Appalachian Highlands.

H. R. 7234, Providing for Establishment of Water Resource Research Centers. Congressman Ed Edmondson (Oklahoma). Referred to the House Committee on Interior and Insular Affairs.

This bill is similar to S. 2, which passed the Senate April 23, 1963, and was also referred to the House Committee on Interior and Insular Affairs. It would establish water resources research centers at land-grant colleges and State universities, stimulate water research and promote a more adequate national program of water research.

Public Law 88-29, Organic Act for the Bureau of Outdoor Recreation. This was the first major piece of conservation legislation to be enacted by the 88th Congress and signed by the President. It authorizes the Secretary of the Interior to coordinate Federal and State programs for outdoor recreation.

Before enactment, conferees of the Senate and House decided against limiting an authorization for appropriation but agreed that the Secretary of the Interior should make a full explanation to the Committees on Interior and Insular Affairs, when necessary, to request more than the $3,000,000 annually for the outdoor recreation program provided for in the Act.

Said Secretary of the Interior Stewart L. Udall, "President Kennedy's signature of this law marks the beginning of a new era of government recognition of its responsibilities for coordinated, effective nationwide planning, acquisition, and development of outdoor recreational resources."

"Adequate outdoor recreational facilities
are among the basic requirements
of a sound national conservation
program . . . . The need for
an aggressive program of recreational
development is both real and immediate."

--President John F. Kennedy, Message on Conservation
to the Congress of the United States, March 1, 1962

Planning and Civic Comment

Official Organ of American Planning and Civic Association and
National Conference on State Parks

CONTENTS

DECEMBER 1963

Planning and Civic Comment

| Vol. 29 | December, 1963 | No. 4 |

The Conservation Challenge of the Sixties

By STEWART L. UDALL, Secretary of the Interior

The Horace M. Albright Conservation Lecture was delivered by Secretary of the Interior Udall before the University of California's School of Forestry on April 19, 1963. In view of its breadth of viewpoint and since it, in effect, charts a course for the future at a strategic hour in conservation history, it will be carried in this and the March issues of *Planning and Civic Comment*. The first part of the statement follows:

The Concept of Conservation

Horace Albright, among Americans who are alive today, has few equals in his awareness of the importance of conservation of natural resources and the conservation of our total environment. I hope my appearance here will be regarded as an act of personal homage to him.

A year ago President John F. Kennedy, in his March 1 special conservation message to Congress—the first presidential message of its kind in many years to be delivered to the Congress—undertook to do something that no other president has attempted; namely, to define the word "conservation." Conservation is difficult to define because it is a dynamic and constantly changing concept. But the President wrote in his message: "Conservation . . . can be defined as the wise use of our natural environment: it is, in the final analysis, the highest form of national thrift—the prevention of waste and despoilment while preserving, improving and renewing the quality and usefulness of all our resources."

A little more than fifty years ago our dictionaries did not contain the word "conservation." The word,

like the concept for which it stood, grew out of the ruminations of Gifford Pinchot and some of his friends. They applied it first to the idea of saving our forests and using them wisely. It was later applied to water and to minerals and it now, if we can see it properly, is a concept so broad in scope that it includes all of our dealings with natural resources and with our total environment as well.

If the forester and the reclamation engineer symbolized the conservation effort during Theodore Roosevelt's time, . . . the swift ascendancy of technology has made the scientist the symbol of the sixties: his ultimate instruments, the reactor and the rocket, have opened the door to an inexhaustible storehouse of energy and may yet reveal the secrets of the stars. I think an historical look at the subject of conservation would reveal an ebb and flow, with two high tides in conservation, one under Theodore Roosevelt and one under his cousin Franklin. Some of us would like to think, although this depends upon you and others like you, that we are on the verge of the third wave.

PLANNING AND CIVIC COMMENT
CEASES PUBLICATION

PLANNING AND CIVIC COMMENT ceases publication with this issue which has been purposively delayed in view of the major reorganization of the *American Planning and Civic Association* now in process.

The Association's entire publications program is being reconstituted and the new program is now being subject to review by the Board of Directors. As soon as recommendations are made final and approved they will be shared with the membership.

Reorganization of the Association has been made possible through a major grant from the Taconic Foundation of New York, and is designed to help the Association revitalize its activities, expand its program and extend its influence across the country.

—To all of you who have told us verbally and who have written us that you have found PLANNING AND CIVIC COMMENT a source of interest, help and inspiration—

—To our ever-increasing volunteer contributors who have, in a major way, helped attune PLANNING AND CIVIC COMMENT to vital needs across the country—needs which have been reflected in our continuous requests for re-prints—

—To, you, who, from the ever-increasing number who write us asking how to obtain our publication, have recently taken out subscription memberships—

—And, most especially, to all of you who have been our faithful readers and supporters—

We say thanks.

We have attempted to keep PLANNING AND CIVIC COMMENT informative in these swiftly changing days of our Nation's development. And we assure you that, as one of our guiding principles, we have attempted to keep faithfully in mind that an important goal of any publication is to strike a responsive chord in the minds and hearts of those who peruse its pages.

We wish you continued fruitful reading after the Association's new publications program is voted.

Preserving a Valley's Heritage and Beauty

By HOWARD J. GROSSMAN

**Assistant Director,
Montgomery County Planning Commission**

IN RECENT YEARS a trend toward joint participation among municipalities in comprehensive land use planning as well as providing other types of municipal services to residents has been noted. The area or regional approach to land-use planning in the United States is ever increasing. In Pennsylvania, there are several regional or area planning commissions currently in operation. Nowhere is area-wide planning, however, more in the spotlight than in Montgomery County, Pennsylvania.

The Upper Perkiomen Valley Area Planning Council is a pioneer effort in cooperative planning in Montgomery County, Pennsylvania. Formed under the General Cooperation Law of Pennsylvania, the Council consists of six townships and four boroughs (covering an area of 85 square miles and a population of 16,000) devoted to preparing an area-wide comprehensive plan and a detailed plan for each of the constituent municipalities. In 1962, the Council made application for Federal Urban Planning Assistance funds under Section 701 of the Housing Act of 1954, As Amended. The Council received funds for planning in 1963 and work officially began on September 18th of that year. The Montgomery County Planning Commission is acting as consultant to the Council in the preparation of plans. A planning program has been proposed to cover a span of four years. The first two years will produce a broad area-wide plan for the Valley. The second two years will see a plan

3

that it didn't matter how we dealt with them as husbandmen—has been supplanted by what we might call the Myth of Scientific Supremacy. Striding about as supermen, we tolerate great imbalances in resource uses, and shrug off the newer forms of erosion with a let-science-fix-it-tomorrow attitude.

This rationalization is potentially as destructive as the mischievous rain-follows-the-plow slogan of those who a few decades ago turned the land of the Great Plains into a Dust Bowl. Regrettably, the very men who are quickest to rely on the Myth of Scientific Supremacy are the same men who are usually opposed, on grounds of "economy," to the investment of public funds and the voting of public laws to do the conservation work of today.

Clearly, the task of wise resource management is now a joint venture among government, universities, and the managers of industry. Much of our success in conservation during this generation has resulted from the increasing commitment of American business to conservation research and conservation practices. By their very nature, however, governments must plan for the long haul and concentrate on long-term projects, but enlightened men of business have also learned that it is good business to look to the horizon. The creative competition of our industrial laboratories and the striving for more efficient use of raw materials has spurred constructive patterns of growth, while enabling us to use our resources with more insight.

But the front-line of what once was a rather simple movement, the conservation movement, now stretches from uranium to wildlife, from salmon to soils, from wilderness to water, and any conservation inventory must include a review of our total public and private effort. The work of the 1960's can be a stepping stone to a balanced future, and the creative leadership that President Kennedy has offered has seen new plans and programs presented to meet the challenge.

Let us examine some of these programs—and the "state of the union" as far as our resources are concerned.

New Sources of Energy

Our supreme conservation achievement this century has been the discovery of a self-renewing source of energy. So far as energy was concerned, the threat of shortage and eventually famine crippled our earlier thinking. The atomic scientists uncovered the edge of an infinite dynamo in Chicago in 1942, and the task for the future is to perfect techniques that will make it a versatile, safe source of power. We are consuming our fossil fuels at an alarming rate. Large reserves remain, but the fission of the atom has allayed our fears of fuel exhaustion.

In addition, the fine research teams of the petroleum industry have more than doubled oil-pool recoveries, and are now developing a process to transform the vast shale beds of the Colorado plateau into oil. In due course the self-refueling "breeder" reactors, and the development of controlled fusion, may make our fossil deposits

(*Continued on page 51*)

4

The Downtown Snarl—A Case for Sorting, Stacking, and Storing

Reprinted by permission from the October, 1963 issue of *Architectural Forum,* © 1963 Time Inc.

Resigned, dispirited, they stand waiting for the red light to halt the hurtling vehicles. They have learned that walking is not something to be done for pleasure; the narrow sidewalks are too crowded for that, the pace too fast, the sounds and smells of traffic too perilously near. It is not only the signal that forbids them to walk: It is the entire indiscriminate jumble of the modern city.

Some say that the people of the city have been sold out to the automobile. But alas, even the automobile is disadvantaged. Extravagantly swift (and designed to look even swifter), it is reduced to a plodding pace that a dray horse would disdain. It is thrown into a bitter struggle with darting taxis and huge trucks and buses simply to stay in motion. Endlessly stopping and starting, it stutters through the streets seeking a place of rest, only to find that parking lots and garages have been located not for its convenience, but solely according to the whims of the real estate market.

The city street has become the Great American Bottleneck: the clog, the snarl, the tangle. It is the point of convergence for the entire urban transportation network. It is also the point where the issues of transportation planning are fast becoming the issues of the city's survival.

A great deal of thought and money has gone into the network, but precious little has been done about handling the people—and the vehicles—that it brings into the city core. Emergency expedients have been tried: One-way streets, arcane sequencing of traffic lights, pedestrian scrambles, and even, where all else fails, law enforcement. But none have eased the congestion that swells inexorably.

There is a growing suspicion that a more basic remedy must be sought —that some way must be found to sort things out. It must be a way that preserves the concentration of activities that is the essence of the city, yet allows for freer movement of both people and their vehicles. It must be a way that takes into account both the pleasures of pedestrianism and the new mobility that the automobile has encouraged— lest people use this mobility to leave the city behind.

The principle of salvation by separation

The search for such a remedy has been going on for a good long time. Even Leonardo da Vinci tried his hand, proposing an ideal city in which there would be low roads and high roads. "The high-level roads," wrote Leonardo, "are not to be used by wagons or vehicles . . . but are solely for the convenience of the gentlefolk. All cars and loads for the service and convenience of the common people should be confined to the low-level roads."

Most present-day planners and architects would extend Leonardo's principle of separation. Any solution to the city's transportation problem, they would agree, must include four elements: Separation of people and vehicles; separation of autos and service vehicles; separation of through and intercity traffic, and a more rational relationship between traffic distribution and auto storage. They would also agree that the problem can only be solved by a total strategy of design which takes all four elements into account.

The development of these ideas in the United States is neatly illustrated by proposals for those rival Texas siblings, Fort Worth and Dallas. The first to reach wide public attention was the Victor Gruen design for Fort Worth, probably the most famous plan gathering dust in the files of any American city.

Gruen proposed that the square-mile core of downtown Fort Worth be surrounded by a ring road tied into the city's freeway system. From this road feeders would take autos into great parking garages penetrating the core, and trucks into an underground network of service alleys. Surface streets would be completely closed to traffic (except for slow-moving shuttle cars like the "elephant trains" at world's fairs) and would become pedestrian malls and walkways.

The Fort Worth plan dramatized the comprehensiveness of approach needed to reshuffle the mix of people and vehicles downtown. Gruen, however, did most of his shuffling on a single, horizontal plane. Six years later, when Dallas got *its* plan, a significant dimension had been added to the mix.

A giant vertical sandwich of six layers

The Dallas plan was the work of a team of Columbia University economists and graduate students of architecture and planning under then Dean Charles R. Colbert. It consisted of a detailed design for a 9¾-acre development called "Main Place" and a proposed application of its principles to the city's core (FORUM, *Projects*, May '62).

The Columbia team's plan proposed that densities be increased, varied uses blended, and through traffic siphoned off by a ring road. But its essence was the *vertical* sorting of people and vehicles. Main Place was to be a single giant construction with a six-layer base: the bottom layer for buses and trucks; the second for self-parking; the third for autos and shuttle buses on the city's existing grid of streets; the fourth and fifth for pedestrians, with shopping ringing a great open square, and the sixth for recreation. Above this sandwich would rise a group of major buildings, including an enormous H-shaped tower. And beneath—down to 600 feet beneath—would be pits for short-term parking, with cars carried in continuous vertical conveyors.

In the view of some urban theorists, however, even this scheme does not go far enough. Perhaps, they suggest, the new mobility has made the concept of a city core obsolete. Perhaps the focal points of city life —the stores and shops, the community buildings, the cultural

6

facilities—should be not only stacked vertically, but stretched out along the lengthening arteries of the transportation network.

One such theorist is Reginald Malcolmson of the Illinois Institute of Technology's department of architecture and city planning, who sees the future city as a ribbon of buildings with major transportation routes its "vertebrae."

Malcolmson calls his city "Metro-Linear." Its spine is a continuous, six-level building a quarter-mile wide, flanked by parallel one-way highways. The four stories above ground are used for parking, and the two below for railroads, subways, and trucks. Blocks of commercial buildings rise above the roof level of the spine at half-mile intervals, and radial apartments sprout from its sides. The long ribbon of the roof itself is given over entirely to the pedestrian, with civic and cultural buildings opening onto a vast series of plazas.

Reclaiming the wasted cubage of the core

Still, it is the vision behind the Dallas plan which is exerting great influence on present-day urban design: the vision of a compact city core in which people and vehicles move on many levels, instead of crowding onto a single one.

The vision has obvious advantages over reality. The single-level street was conceived in the days when feet, both human and animal, were the primary means of transportation; it survives on the brink of suicide by strangulation.

The conventional street, moreover, acts as a remarkably effective barrier. As Gordon Cullen has pointed out, it is as if great rushing rivers had been let loose between our buildings. (In Venice, which has real water to deal with, pedestrian bridges join the two sides of the canals; we use stop-lights instead to try to stem the flood of vehicles.) The street system is a relentless gridiron of chasms, carving urban land into isolated islands destructive of a sense of community.

The single-level street is also economically wasteful, as Colbert pointed out at a transportation symposium sponsored by the Automobile Manufacturers Association. "Real estate is more than a two-dimensional lot," he said. "It extends from the center of the earth outward to infinity; it is a volume, not a plane . . . We are only slowly coming to realize that air rights—the volume of spaces—are essential attributes of what we call property."

Consider now the vision, as expressed in the Dallas plan and, more recently, in Architect Paul Thiry's design for terracing much of downtown Seattle. It exploits this wasted cubage, making space out of air for plazas and promenades, digging space beneath the surface for unobtrusive storage of vehicles. It separates fast movement from slow (just as the early transit systems did by running their trains above or below the city's surface). And it allows existing street systems to be used with maximum efficiency.

History contains no record of Leonardo's ideal city ever being built. The Fort Worth city council approved the Victor Gruen plan, but the state legislature refused to pass the necessary enabling laws (prime opponents were the operators of private parking garages). The Dallas scheme is in abeyance, and there are no present plans for realization of anything quite like Mr. Malcolmson's Metro-Linear.

Such is often the fate of ideal cities when they bump up against some of the harsher realities of urban development —particularly, it must be said, in a political democracy and a free-enterprise economy. Colbert acknowledged this before the auto-makers: the multilevel principle, he said, "requires a re-evaluation of man and his customs, of procedures and practices now almost universally accepted."

Perhaps no such sweeping re-evaluation will take place until the oft-predicted day when everything finally grinds to a complete halt, and the city is choked with its own congestion. That day may well come, but meanwhile the concepts contained in the far-seeing plans outlined above are finding increasingly widespread application in some very real projects, both public and private:

In Philadelphia, Penn Center already offers the pedestrian what the Planning Commission brochure terms "fine broad open esplanades" above ground, and a concourse of his own below. Next step is completion of Market East, in which an eight-block spine between City Hall and Independence Mall will become a "transportation mechanism," in Planning Director Edmund Bacon's words, for Philadelphia's new core . . .

In Rochester, N. Y., the Midtown Plaza project (FORUM, June '62) is giving a convincing demonstration of how the Gruen planning principles can revitalize a city's core. A narrow congested street was transformed into an enclosed, three-story pedestrian mall lined with shops, exhibit spaces, and meeting rooms; a three-story parking garage, its ramps linked directly to a surrounding ring road, was built below ground; service vehicles were relegated to the basement level; two existing department stores were thoroughly remodeled; and new buildings of four and 18 stories were constructed . . . . . Midtown Plaza has been a resounding economic success, has spurred other new construction in downtown Rochester— and has brought an additional 25,000 persons a day, by Gruen's estimate, into the city center. Says Gruen, "Not even in our most optimistic moments could we have foreseen the extent to which the Plaza has become a focal point of civic, political, cultural and artistic life."

In Worcester, Mass., city officials and downtown businessmen have given an enthusiastic reception to a plan prepared by another Columbia team under Colbert. Its key elements: Closing streets to create a continuous web of walkways, construction of an elevated inner traffic loop with a two-level shopping mall beneath, moving-belt traffic conveyors (like those proposed for Dallas) placed above ground in vertical tubes. The Worcester plan is a kind of summary, showing how nearly all of the principles of separation can be applied to the heart of a medium-sized city.

Tomorrow's Annapolis:
Dichotomy or Synthesis?

By ROBERT J. KERR II, Vice-President, Corinthian Conservation Company, Inc., Annapolis, and formerly Executive Director of Historic Annapolis, Inc.

Reprinted by permission from the Fall, 1963 issue of *Architects' Report,* a publication of the Baltimore Chapter, American Institute of Architects.

For the first time in the city's long history, Annapolis is faced with the need to make a decision for or against the preservation of its architectural heritage.

For the first time, preservation of this heritage can be an active and dynamic facet of a conscious effort to renew the urban fabric, rather than a fortuitous consequence of a century and a half of a lack of pressure for growth and change.

After an early and dramatic growth as an 18th-century court town and seaport, 19th-century Annapolis was allowed to drowse peacefully in the dreams of its earlier glories. Bypassed by railroads and consequent industrial expansion, 19th century Annapolis had ceded commercial prominence as an international shipping port to Baltimore, closer to the market and producing areas of Western Maryland and Pennsylvania.

Left to the "Ancient City" were its roles as the seat of state and county government; as a market port for local fishing fleets; as a docking place for Chesapeake Bay packets and as the home of St. John's College. Even the advent of the Navy's Midshipman School in 1845 was accepted with little apparent change to life in Annapolis and even less effect on the old city plan.

As an historic document, the city plan ranks as a national historic trust, existing as the finest example of the application of 17th century baroque town planning principles in British North America. As the city's essential visual and functional framework, the plan presents a challenge to the planner and the architect to be met in no other American city.

If the patina of the past is to give vitality and dimension to the character of the modern city, planners and architects must hold a predisposition to preservation, just as they are predisposed to the solution of contemporary traffic and economic problems. The single most important problem facing the preservationist in Annapolis is the need to develop this predisposition in the architect and the planner, as well as in the minds of local citizens.

It is not impossible to conceive of the Old City area of Annapolis set aside as a special historic "precinct," protected by special codes and ordinances and by special functions. But in no way should this special consideration take the physical form of a museum village.

The Old City exists as the living and vital center of urban activity in the Greater Annapolis Area. *The integrity of its survival as a district must grow out of the manner in which it continues to serve as the city's functional and symbolic order.* Old buildings must be rehabilitated to continue their long tradition of service as homes, shops and places of public assembly. Inevitably, contemporary needs must be accommodated within the ancient character, and traditional uses must be made to provide solutions to contemporary problems.

If these historic assets are to serve the future as they have served the past, a positive program of conservation activity must be elected by the city government and the citizens of Annapolis. Such a program should begin with an official Design Study to determine the city's assets and liabilities, giving due attention to the impact which older forms have had on the development of Annapolis as a special and unique place.

Such a study will generate public and official support for a much needed architectural ordinance which will offer adequate protection to older buildings and areas and encourage the best type of design solutions for new construction and developing areas. The study should provide a stimulus for self-help rehabilitation activity in the Old City.

Beyond formal study, planning, legislative and project activity, one of the most desperately needed agencies in the city is one which will serve as a forum for the exchange of ideas and needs within the community. Due to the variety of governmental installations in Annapolis, it is particularly necessary that such an agency maintain adequate liaison with the Naval Academy, the state government, the Board of County Commissioners and the mayor and aldermen of the City of Annapolis.

So far, each agency of government has done its own planning with little or no regard for the needs of its fellows or of the civilian community. One of the greatest deficiences in the recently proposed Master Plan is the lack of any solid coordination or cooperation between the Navy's planners and the consultants who drafted the plan for the city.

No agency or aspect of life in Annapolis can exist independently of all other elements of the community. The preservationist must recognize the needs and the aspirations of the residential community; the residential community must understand the problems facing the city fathers and the city fathers must be sensitive to all needs and to the special qualities which make Annapolis a unique city

---

Site Planning

"Site planning has acquired new importance, but it is an old art which has been practiced with skill in other times and places.

"One thinks of such magnificent building groups as the Imperial Palace in Peking, the center of Pergamum, the Katsura Palace near Kyoto, the crescents of Bath, the Italian squares of the Renaissance, or many small New England settlements.

"Yet site design in this country today is monotonously conventional, careless, shallow, and ugly."

—Site Planning, by Kevin Lynch, published by The M. I. T. Press, Cambridge, Massachusetts, 1962, p. 5.

Panther Hollow—From Desolation to Development

From a report in the September, 1963 issue of *Internal Affairs*, published by the Department of Internal Affairs of the Commonwealth of Pennsylvania which says, "The City of Pittsburgh's famed urban renewal Renaissance has its second wind and is starting to roll again."

Ground will be broken next year for the first phase of a new $250,000,000 research park in the heart of Pittsburgh's Oakland district, an attractive residential community beyond the business and manufacturing districts.

The huge structure will be built entirely within the confines of an existing excavation made by nature eons ago—the Panther Hollow ravine, a wasteland which divides Carnegie Institute of Technology and Schenley Park from the University of Pittsburgh and the Oakland community.

This dramatic new research, residential and cultural complex is being developed under the aegis of the Oakland Corporation, a profit-oriented, tax-paying organization owned jointly by a group of Pittsburgh non-profit institutions.

"The research park project was conceived and developed for a high economic purpose," says Dr. Edward H. Litchfield, Chancellor of the University of Pittsburgh and board chairman of the Oakland Corporation. "This purpose is to lay the foundation for and to help build a new and urgently needed supplemental industrial complex in Pittsburgh and the surrounding region. Oakland, long the established cultural and educational center of Pittsburgh, two and a half miles from the Golden Triangle, is the most natural site for such a facility."

Until now, the very name "research park" implied a suburban if not rural location. But Pittsburgh's plan for a research park in the heart of the city gives both the term and the concept new dimension, new meaning and, according to the Oakland Corporation, immeasurably greater importance. It is unique in every respect, beginning with the name . . .

Panther Hollow is an entirely new concept in research parks. A Pittsburgh newspaper described it as an "upside-down research lab." In a sense, this is quite accurate. For one thing, the "park" part of the research park will be on top of the structure rather than around its base . . . while a railroad and crosstown highway will run beneath it. And this is quite an achievement in urban development: to create public parkland instead of obliterating it in a land-scarce city center.

But the most significant part of this new concept is the concrete realization that the men and women who engage in research and development activities are fundamentally and predominantly urban people who need the mental and spiritual sustenance found in greatest abundance in a vital, intellectually and culturally rich urban

an alert, aggressive, and understanding citizenry can muster. The people of Wisconsin have met challenges of similar magnitude and importance in the past. We are confident they will meet this one too."

The scenery of Wisconsin is a tremendously saleable asset to our tourist industry. It is said that the value of Wisconsin tourist business amounts to something more than six hundred million dollars annually. Further, it is a fact that more than fifty percent of the tourists visiting Wisconsin have indicated that the scenery of the countryside is the most important factor in their coming to Wisconsin.

Scenery—the charm and beauty of the countryside—then, is an asset, an important factor in the economy, the growth and the development of our state. It is something to be protected, preserved and further developed. If Wisconsin is to be more beautiful, then it will be because the citizens of this state, both men and women, are alert and vigilant in keeping what I call the *Seven Scourges of The Countryside* under control.

What are these Seven Scourges? Let me list them and tell you what can be done about them:

1) Automobile graveyards that line the highways.
2) Open, exposed garbage disposal dumps.
3) Abandoned buildings and unsightly farmsteads.
4) Homes built on the flood plains.
5) Commercial and industrial development intermingled with farm and residential land uses.

6) Bottles and cans and debris scattered along the highways.
7) Signs and billboards in all sizes, colors and in all stages of dilapidation.

What can we do about this situation?

First off, let's face it, we need to promote more interest in land use planning, including setback building lines, clear vision triangles at intersections of highways and railroads, off street parking and private loading docks for commerce and industry. We need to step up interest in carefully designed residential subdivisions, in building codes and in all the local ordinances and regulations that are needed in our communities. All of them should be designed to protect private property, to stabilize property values and to promote the orderly development of all our land and water resources for their highest use.

Second, we need more public participation in the development of local plans to improve the community whether this be for a county park, an auditorium, a new building on the fair grounds, or a community swimming pool. We need an enlightened and informed public on all of these important public programs. Our need parallels the national need for active informed citizens' planning committees are necessary today to help guide the development and the destiny of every community in the Nation.

This does not mean citizens' committees of men only. Last year Al Bennett, Editor of the *Atchison Globe* in Atchison, Kansas, was asked along with nine other editors to take a careful and critical look

12

at planning in the state of Kansas. In his report he said: "One other thing: *Use the women. If women became aroused, really aroused, they can accomplish anything. Women, by nature, think of the home, the playground, the traffic flow because they are thinking around the clock about their children and their children's future. Father, bless his heart, is pretty busy trying to make a living.*"

One of the important and inspiring things about our citizens' planning committees in Wisconsin is that we have women on many of them participating actively in the discussions and deliberations. We need more women taking an active, constructive part in all community planning activities *for the benefit of families—men and women and the children.*

Third, we need to continue to teach the basic elements in planning the use of the land, in the conservation of our soil, water, game and fish and wildlife, in the basic principles on which zoning is based, whether town, city, village or county zoning. We need to explain to high school civic classes about residential subdivisions, building codes and easements and about the need for public access to lakes and rivers.

Fourth, we need to register our preferences and our protests to elected officials on all questions of basic public policy involving land and water developments, many of which might involve the desecration of the countryside. This involves knowing what is going on in the community, what is proposed, what are the alternatives and finally,

would this be a good thing for the community's future?

Fifth, we need to look carefully at improving the roads_and highways leading to the entrances to our cities,. villages and towns. This again involves planning and zoning, setback building lines and building codes. It may involve a cleanup campaign, or several cleanup campaigns. It may involve the creation of new waysides and new park or parkway areas. It may involve some land leveling and some seeding. Whatever is involved, we can do much, and we need to do it to improve the gateways to our cities and villages.

In the July, 1960 issue of the *Readers Digest,* an article entitled "Cities in Bloom" tells of the work of one very effective and determined woman, Mrs. Mary Lasker of New York City. Mrs. Lasker, alone, pioneered the idea of creating new beauty by the careful use and selection of flowers in downtown New York City. It was difficult to get the idea started and she had to start small, but the idea spread to Birmingham, Alabama; Chicago; Norfolk, Virginia; Omaha, Nebraska; Philadelphia; Portland, Oregon; and many other cities throughout the United States. We have some nice new redwood boxes of flowers around the square in Madison, Wisconsin.

Businessmen in those cities with boxes of living flowers in the downtown area have discovered there is something very, very practical in beauty. Washington, D. C., for example, in 1960, drew more than 850,000 tourists just to see the famous cherry blossoms. In our own Door County, we have a million and

13

Planning and Civic Comment

Participation in Urban Renewal have reported a study of citizen participation in the metropolitan Boston area. Its conclusion: "Citizen participation is needed in urban renewal to educate both the city officials regarding the needs and wishes of the people, and the people regarding the facts that must be seriously considered and the opportunities that may be available through neighborhood improvement."

It behooves the Urban Renewal Administration to examine each community's projected program closely to determine whether the residents listed are truly involved. An examination of the minutes of meetings held by or for the citizens' advisory committee, in itself, may not be very revealing. Consideration should be given to the desirability of stipulating that the projected program must be reproduced, distributed to citizens, and discussed at a public forum.

Too often organizations and individuals with a special concern for the common good, such as community councils and clergymen, are by-passed when major decisions affecting the community are being made. They can contribute much to the success of urban improvement projects and help to ensure that special interests do not dominate the program.

Perhaps it is time we consider amending the Federal Housing Act to encourage local communities more generally to promote the formation of neighborhood improvement associations. The City Plan-

ning Department might have a role, not only in fostering such associations but in assisting them in drafting long-range plans for the improvement of their neighborhoods.

There are citizens in every neighborhood with interest and leadership potential in upgrading their neighborhoods.

Let's launch some training programs to develop the talents of these people. Sessions might meet one evening a week for six or eight weeks to consider subjects such as how to organize an improvement association, parliamentary procedure, publicity, sources of information and assistance, the functions of various public and private organizations concerned with general neighborhood conditions, methods of convincing residents of the need and desirability for improving conditions, tenants' rights and responsibilities, sources of funds and finally, outlining an activities program for the association. Material on the above subjects could be prepared, reproduced, and distributed at the sessions.

Neighborhood action is less costly than an urban renewal program and can function to conserve good areas where conditions do not warrant a federal project. The size and "glamour" of federal urban renewal projects may overshadow the positive accomplishments which can be achieved by neighborhood action. But one of the greatest benefits of neighborhood action is that it strengthens the existing community, whereas a clearance project breaks it up.

14

Commentaries

Cities Strike Back: "The Nation's older cities are launching a counter-attack against the efforts of suburban and rural towns to lure away their industries."

So reports Laurence G. O'Donnell in a recent issue of the *Wall Street Journal*.

"The reasons for the drive are obvious," says Mr. O'Donnell. "Since World War II such cities as Philadelphia, New Haven, Conn., and Providence, R. I., have suffered badly as companies abandoned old factories to build new plants on open suburban or country land."

Mr. O'Donnell points out that "the prospects for success in the cities' campaign are less obvious" but says that "many cities claim to be slowing down the flight, and a few, notably Philadelphia, say they have reversed it. A major reason: These cities have recognized that companies can't be kept in obsolete, cramped plants they have outgrown, but must be helped to find new land on which they can put up roomier and more modern buildings—even if these aren't one-story."

As to how the cities are going about it, Mr. O'Donnell reports that at the end of 1962, 201 cities had urban renewal projects earmarked for "predominantly industrial re-use," against 79 five years earlier.

Many cities also are assisting companies to finance new plants, in part by helping them get loans from local banks and businesses. Scranton, Pa., some years ago raised $2.9 million from its businessmen to set up Lackawanna Industrial Fund Enterprises (LIFE), a non-profit development company. Philadelphia claims even more success with a Philadelphia Industrial Development Corporation (PIDC), which primarily uses city resources. And the development corporation idea appears to be spreading.

℮ℛℴ

Altruism: American Brand: Puzzled by what residents of other lands sometimes take to be conflicting elements in the American make-up, James Fisher, a well-known British ornithologist and writer, has traced the origin of our National Park idea "to find out just how the wilderness-for-its-own-sake idea—the national park movement—started and who started it."

His conclusions were presented as a radio talk for the British Broadcasting Company and have been published as a "perceptive study" in the November-December, 1963 issue of *Audubon*.

"Near the heartland of the Yellowstone in those early days," says Mr. Fisher, "an idea was born which took the world—at least the Western world—at first by surprise, then swiftly by storm . . . It started for certain in the hidden sourceland of the Yellowstone River."

Mr. Fisher relates how Representative William M. Clagett's famous Park Bill "was passed after one of the most formidable and altruistic lobbying campaigns in United States history and was signed by President Ulysses S. Grant on March 1, 1872.

"Grant's enactment was an overt act of idealism," says Mr. Fisher, "and the thin end of a benign wedge of conservation acts and deeds that gradually spread the world over. . . .

"The Yellowstone pioneers could have staked claims and made a lot of money. They didn't: Because their spirit of private enterprise was leavened by a peculiarly American species of altruism which is, in my opinion, poorly appreciated and badly understood in the rest of the English speaking world.

"By the middle of the 19th century, a tremendous amount of enthusiasm for nature—mystical, realistic, earthy, elemental, transcendental, intellectual —the lot—had been aroused in the Western and English-speaking world. Nature's paradise was recognized— and what was recognized, too, was that it could be lost."

℮ℛℴ

15

Water Pollution: "Our knowledge of how to improve water quality and how to treat our sewage and wastes is not adequate for many situations now, and certainly not for the future.

"We are informed that despite the high degree of sewage treatment now effected by the Chicago Metropolitan Sanitary District, about 1,800 tons of dissolved organic materials and mineral impurities are added to the (Chicago) river water every day *after* passing through the District sewage treatment works—including twenty-five to thirty tons of nitrates and phosphates, thirty-five tons of detergents and so on. It is eminently clear that we must increase our knowledge and capabilities to deal with these and other pollution problems."

—From a statement by Hon. Robert E. Jones, Chairman, Natural Resources and Power Subcommittee of the House Committee on Government Operations, Chicago, Illinois Hearing, September 6, 1963.

❧

Change: "Shifting population trends, with some areas gaining and others losing population, are one indication of people's adjustment to technology," says William M. Carroll, Extension Specialist in Public Affairs at Pennsylvania State University, in a recent issue of *Internal Affairs.*

In Pennsylvania, he points out, "people from rural and urban areas share development ideas. Today, group after group is deciding that development efforts based merely on enthusiasm, promotion, and conviction fail, regardless of the sincerity of the developers. These groups are beginning to understand that efforts based on the application of scientific knowledge usually plead to satisfying results."

❧

Library Design: "A rather flamboyant design, with balanced elements and a faintly Aztec look," has filled the bill for a new library at Tufts University in Medford, Massachusetts, according to a recent issue of *Architectural Forum.*

Tufts faced a particular problem because, according to the *Forum,* "Perhaps the most attractive part of the University is its placement of major buildings along the ridge of a steep hill, leaving the long slopes green. When university officials decided Tufts needed a new central library, however, they found that the only open space they could use was right on this very hillside."

The new design, selected in a special type of closed competition, "keeps the feeling of the topography by stepping the building up the hill; it also preserves the natural landscaping by planting on the roof terraces." Yet it will not clash "with the older, more sedate buildings on the hill."

❧

The False and The True: From the ever-pertinent and penetrating observations of Ernest Swift in *Conservation News,* a publication of the National Wildlife Federation, comes a nostalgic review of "berry patch" days—and an earnest query as to just what we are putting in their place:

"Many a citizen of yesteryear learned his or her first outdoor lessons in the berry patch, where fathers and mothers pointed out wildflowers, herbs, trees, shrubs and birds. Simple facts were mixed with folklore, but most important, it created an interest which expanded with maturity."

Today, asks Mr. Swift: "How many children gather hazel nuts to put on a shed roof to dry, or gather hickory or butter nuts? How many know where their breakfast bacon comes from?

"Such thrift, such pleasures and such education would destroy the family status in the neighborhood. . . . But I am afraid we will keep on with our shallow illusions of conservation education and allow some of the most fruitful and endearing experiences of life to be bypassed by ignorance and false standards."

❧

Renewal: Drastic changes in New York's capital city of Albany are called

(Continued on page 26)

Zoning Round Table

Conducted by FLAVEL SHURTLEFF, Marshfield Hills, Mass.

SPECIAL EXCEPTIONS

During the ten years of the zoning round table, there has been occasional comment on the special exception, or as some zoning ordinances have it, the "special use permit"—notably, the confusion between special exceptions and variances which quite commonly exists. Even some state courts have made no distinction between them, treating both as exceptions to the regulations.

This error was briefly but clearly pointed out in a Connecticut case* in which the court said, "A variance is authority to use property in a manner forbidden by the zoning enactment; an exception allows a use only which the ordinance expressly permits."

The distinction is further illustrated in two cases reported early this year. In the Massachusetts case, the court was asked to review a decision of the lower court which upheld a finding of the board of appeals. The case involved a special exception which expressly permitted hotels, motels and tourist courts in single family zones. The board of appeals had approved an application to operate a hotel subject to several conditions. Among them was a stipulation that the water supply "must be settled to the satisfaction of all concerned" and that the road to the property must be opened and improved to a width of at least 20 feet. Since these two conditions required a further de-

*Fox et al vs. Board of Appeals, 147 Atl. 2nd 472.

cision of the board of appeals, the court ruled that the permit to operate the hotel was invalid, and that the board had no power to issue advisory opinions or make decisions which partially committed it to the issuance of a permit.**

In Summ vs. Zoning Commission*** the Connecticut Supreme Court approved a wide application of the special exception or special use permit. The ordinance allowed the use of land "for research and development in *any* zone" but provided that property so used must have an area of at least four acres, and that not more than 240 acres in the whole town could be used for this purpose. There were also extensive controls over the location of buildings, and over noise, smoke, dust and odors. The court interpreted an amendment to the zoning enabling act as giving to the local legislative body a very liberal discretion which should not be disturbed by judicial action.

Two other findings of the court are of interest in connection with a special use permit: First, that action under such a provision would not establish a "floating zone" since zoning boundaries were not changed; and second, that there would not be a violation of the comprehensive plan. "Comprehensiveness is fundamentally to prevent arbitrary, unreasonable and discriminatory exercise of the zoning power" and the

**Philip S. Weld et al vs. Board of Appeals Mass. Advance Sheets, Feb. 1963.

***186 Atlantic, 2nd 160.

17

court found ample evidence to the contrary in the case.

From the first zoning ordinance, there has been a wide difference, even in the same state, in the use of the special exception. It is not even mentioned in some of the early ordinances, and, in others, very few uses, one of which is usually the filling station, are compelled to apply for special exception permits. Some of these early ordinances are still working reasonably well without amendment in regard to this particular item.

The theory underlying the special permit was that some uses might be undesirable no matter in what zone they were permitted unless they were expressly limited in the ordinance and unless the application for the use was heard by the board of appeals at a public hearing.

The filling station is a proper retail business and it serves a public need, but the usual practice in zoning is to allow it in a business zone only as a special exception. Some of the incidents of the business may depress the value of neighboring retail establishments or may increase the fire hazard or even threaten public safety.

Excavation of earth materials is another use often found in the special exception category, and for some of the same reasons as those applying to the filling station.

There may be a trend in zoning practice toward a greater use of the special exception. A good case could be made out for such a change, particularly in areas where uses are many and complex. In any ordinance, the special exception can make for more flexible and more equitable regulation and an effective and continuing control over the operation of the use. But its desirable objectives can only be secured by the skill of the draftsman in fashioning the conditions under which the special exception is granted and the alertness of the administrators of the ordinance.

It is true that many ordinances by amendments, in the last ten years, have included more uses in the special exception category, have been more stringent in the limitations on these uses and more careful in restricting them to certain zones. Baltimore County, Maryland, in its revision of 1955, and Fairfax County, Virginia, in its code of 1962 are outstanding illustrations. The Fairfax County code shows ten groups in which the listed uses, fifty-three in all, are required to secure a special permit in some zones.

The courts have, on the whole, favored the special exception, even in states where there has been judicial disapproval of the variance.

If the Summ case above cited is followed and other uses are allowed as special exceptions in *any* zone, the Weld case also cited above is welcome evidence that restrictions are essential and will receive careful judicial attention.

Record

Carlsbad Caverns National Park, New Mexico, contains the largest under-ground chambers yet discovered. Each "room" is equivalent to the expanse of 14 football fields.

PROJECTS IN REVIEW

Metropolis of the Future

Let every man have his say. Hear him out.

The concept is simple, treasured and an integral part of the American way. But, as metropolitan living has become · immeasurably more complex, the challenge has come in finding a way to tune in on the individual voice which traditionally has played its part in shaping the common environment.

The Regional Plan Association, a 34-year old citizens' organization working for the coordinated development of the three-state metropolitan area surrounding the Port of New York, has accepted that challenge and right where it would seem to be most difficult to brace up to it—in the crowded New York metropolitan Region.

Under the Association's Goals for the Region Project, 5,600 residents of the area, embracing parts of New York, New Jersey and Connecticut, have voiced their opinions on five major issues facing the area if its population soars by six million over the next 20 to 25 years as experts predict.

In getting some indication of the New York Region people want, the Regional Plan Association has broken new ground for metropolitan growth. It has not done so superficially.

The Association, whose President is James S. Schoff and whose Executive Vice-President is C. McKim Norton, first projected the probable development if present trends con-

tinue. This it did through two basic studies.

First, a three-year study of the Region's economy and development forces, financed by the Rockefeller Brothers Fund, The Ford Foundation, the Merrill Foundation for the Advancement of Financial Knowledge and The Twentieth Century Fund, Inc., was conducted for the Association by a Harvard University research team.

A second study, financed by The Ford Foundation, Rockefeller Brothers Fund and the Taconic Foundation, projected the area's growth trends on the basis of the research findings of the first. Related research was supported by the Old Dominion and the Victoria Foundations.

Five major issues facing the metropolitan area emerged from the studies, and area residents, most of them active in civic or social organizations, were asked to comment on these:

1) How to get everyone to his job without traffic jams;

2) Whether to invest in vital central cities or let them deteriorate and lose population;

3) What pattern to set for the outer areas of the Region which probably will house almost all of the added population;

4) How much parkland to set aside for the public;

5) And how much effort to invest in making the Region beautiful.

Tackling the thorny transportation problem, Regional Plan pointed out that rush hour traffic could become seriously tangled as jobs increase and increasing numbers of employees have to drive to work. It suggested three possible approaches to the dilemma:

1) Locate new jobs in large enough industrial and commercial centers so that people can get to work by public transportation—and improve public transportation so that people will want to use it.

2) Make it possible for people to live nearer their jobs, cutting the number of miles travelled on highways.

3) Add highways as traffic begins to reach capacity.

Though a final compilation of the responses and interpretation of them will not be published by the Regional Plan Association until early in 1964, a preliminary report has been made by Dr. Allen Barton, Director of Columbia University's Bureau of Applied Social Research, which is analyzing the response. It shows that the majority of respondees favored trying all the above suggested approaches to transportation difficulties. However, reliance on public transportation was clearly the first choice, with almost no opposition. Nearly 99 percent of the participants favored improving public transportation; seven out of eight favored it "strongly."

Furthermore, though income groups included in the project, ranged from under $3,000 to $25,000 or more and though most participants have relatively high positions and income, most of them are willing to use public transportation themselves. About 40 percent of those employed already travel at least part of the way to work by bus or rail. And more than 40 percent of those using cars would switch to public transportation if conditions were right for it—for example, if public transportation were faster than car or if one conveyance would take them to within walking distance of work.

As to parks, Goal participants used those in the Region a good deal and wanted more of them—about 85 percent would support "large-scale public expenditures" to acquire more parks for the Region. Two thirds visited a large outdoor recreation area, other than a golf course, ten times or more during 1962. Seven out of eight used a large park at least once.

And, if Americans have sometimes been accused of laxness in seeking beauty in their surroundings, Goal participants in the densely built-up New York region proved that they, at least, are quite concerned with the way things look. Well over half strongly favored "some community control over the appearance of new buildings and renovations" in the cities. About half strongly favored "a large-scale effort to plant trees and shrubbery on city streets." And four out of five "strongly" favored "stronger" controls to preserve trees and natural landscape in new developments.

On the basis of the preliminary findings, the up-coming 1964 report on the remaining subjects covered in the survey—the choice of maintaining or abandoning the city's central core and on shaping the outer areas—promises to be of interest.

(Continued on page 40)

National Capital
Notes

IN THE STILLNESS OF WORLD TRAG- EDY, came a message to The City. It was *here* they came in homage to a martyred President—mute testimony from across the Nation and from all parts of the world that there is fundamental rightness in those democratic principles upon which our Nation rests.

And men and women, numbed with grief, could not know that a healing message, even then, was seeking to bridge the chasm of nothingness which sought to render the efforts of righteous men meaningless.

As the days unfold for those engaged in the trying effort to guide the physical development of the Capital City, the message may, perhaps, emerge most clearly in the form of a question:

Does the Nation's Capital—in a physical sense—speak eloquently of those bed-rock principles for which we stand? Even more, does it reflect the purposes of men everywhere who join in the quest for rightness and for good?

These are questions which cannot be ignored for, even to avoid them, is to answer in a way.

Man cannot escape the fact that, ultimately, he translates what he is into his surroundings and that he fashions his environment to his will.

This truth has inspired men and women of every age to join in civic undertakings and to pool their efforts in organizations such as the **American Planning and Civic Association** which, under the leadership of **Harland Bartholomew**, seeks the elevation of aesthetic standards for all American cities and a surer approach to their orderly development.

It has given hope to citizens' groups like the **Committee of 100 on the Federal City**, which seeks to give embodiment to the persistent plea of its **Chairman, Rear Admiral Neill Phillips, USN (Ret.)** that the Capital, cherished by all Americans, has special meaning as a symbolic city for the entire Nation— and that what we do here, now, is determining whether the City will develop physically to fulfill that destiny.

It urges the individual resident of a City—which, as the seat of the National Government, proclaims the greatest good for all as its primary goal—to evaluate in relation to the commonweal what seem to be his own privileges and rights in regard to real estate, transportation, highways, parks, or the Potomac River's banks.

And lastly, it calls all residents of the National Capital area to re-dedicate their efforts to make and keep the Capital beautiful—

In furtherance of the example set by a gracious **First Lady**, young in years, who, in a brief span of months, reached out with deft, sure strokes to make the White House reflect the National heritage that it might be an inspiration to all who came there—

And in tribute to the memory of a **President**, also young in years, whose courage was equated with his ideals, and whose vision for his country included a National Capital, fair in aspect, harmonious in arrangement, a visible reminder of the nourishing well-springs of freedom bequeathed us by our forefathers.

An inspiring statement called "Washington—The Living Dream" appeared in the November issue of *American Forests,* a publication of the **American Forestry Association.** Written by the magazine's editor, **James B. Craig,** a portion of the statement is re-printed here in the belief that it may be of special interest to those who would reflect, at this time, on the Capital City and its true meaning:

"Washington is our home. When we are away from it, we miss so many things. We miss the flash of color as a bearded African emperor sweeps past with siren-singing motorcycles; our knowledgeable people so proficient in so many different things;

"Our lively newspapers; urbane but always provocative lunches at the Cosmos Club; the Press Club on a day when a visiting head of state is to appear in a no-holds barred interview;

"The busy scientists who take time to lecture small groups in our primary and secondary schools; the rich good humor and laughter of our Negro citizens who bailed so many of us out of snowdrifts last Inaugural Eve and supplied coffee to those who were chilled even as was Abigail Adams;

"The church bells on Sunday; a Christmas service at the National Cathedral; the Potomac and Lincoln Memorial in moonlight; the Fourth of July fireworks display against the graceful symmetry of the Washington Monument;

"A boat trip to Mount Vernon with the five boys; a leisurely hike along the C. and O. Canal towpath;

"The never-ending interest in the still unexplored areas of our universe as exemplified by the great National Geographic Society;

"The delightful perverseness of our cherry trees in debating whether to bud or not to bud for the festival; the forsythia ablaze in the spring;

"The patience and friendliness of our Civil Service people in government who take time from their jobs to help us do ours; the myriad birds along the Potomac flyway; the Marine Band playing "Semper Fidelis" on the Capitol steps; the fun of a cookout under your own trees; Coolidge stories;

"The stabbing searchlights from Glen Echo Park; the State Department ablaze with lights in the small hours;

"The kindnesses of so many

A TRIBUTE TO
JOHN FITZGERALD KENNEDY
WHO VALUED OUR HERITAGE
AND IS NOW A PART OF IT

A Good Neighbor who never forgot Our City
Despite His Responsibilities to the Country and the World
A Man Looking to the Future with Confidence
Without Forgetting the Past
Who Believed that the City Could Grow and Still
Preserve its Natural Beauty and Architectural Treasures

John Fitzgerald Kennedy in his brief time as President gave a new focus to planning in the Nation's Capital. He wanted a better city for all its citizens to live in. Lafayette Square, the Cultural Center and Pennsylvania Avenue were his special concerns. He hoped to see the end of temporary buildings that mar the city's beauty. He supported the orderly development of the area through the Year 2000 Plan.

Only a few weeks ago President Kennedy said:

"I look forward to an America which will not be afraid of grace and beauty, which will protect the beauty of our natural environment, which will preserve the great old American houses and squares and parks of our national past and which will build handsome and balanced cities for our future."

We will miss his vitality, his inspiration and his concern.

—Resolution Passed By The National Capital Planning Commission, December 5, 1963

people to ourselves and our children; those fine Southerners, who give our town much of its rich flavor, helping us to integrate our elementary school even though they had serious reservations regarding its advisability;

"The hopefulness of rank and file people as the Senate debates the Treaty; the President's son meeting an astronaut; flying down the Potomac at dusk as your homecoming plane approaches National Airport.

"These things, and many others, are missed by Washingtonians when they are away—things that add up to an aliveness and an awareness that make our city unique.

"Each of us fortunate enough to live here, in a small way, is a part of this living dream in a city that is still in the process of becoming. So are you for this is your city too and you are inextricably a part of it whether you live in Kansas or Arizona, or Oregon or Alabama."

★ ★ ★

Planning and Civic Comment

According to the **National Capital Downtown Committee,** response to its proposal for a National Visitor and Student Center has been uniformly favorable from members of the Congress, other public officials and private citizens in Washington. Good reactions are also reported from other parts of the country. Legislation will be required to establish the Center, the avowed purpose of which would be to help provide Washington's annual millions of visitors with "an enriching understanding of our American heritage." The Downtown Committee states that descriptive brochures are available in reasonable quantities for distribution to individuals and to organizations.

As we go to press, the **House District Committee** has not yet taken positive action on S. 628, the Senate-passed bill to permit the use of urban renewal in Downtown Washington.

In an unequivocal note in the November issue of *Architectural Forum*, **Douglas Haskell**, Editor, offers some salient ideas about Art Commissions:

"Nobody is to be congratulated on being named to one. The most that can happen is that the city itself can be congratulated on those who are appointed to art commissions. Their job is thankless and in a sense always too late. Art commissions, if good, are composed of those who could have done better on most of what comes before them if they had designed it in the first

place, but they have not much chance to initiate. All they have a chance to do, usually, is to review and suggest improvements, if not to disapprove altogether."

Those sharing Mr. Haskell's misgivings are alert to practical suggestions for preventing efforts of such groups from becoming abortive. Already, a practical way by which the work of the National Capital's **Commission of Fine Arts** can become more meaningful has been proposed by the **Committee of 100 on the Federal City** and was reported in the September issue of *Planning and Civic Comment*. Now, from Mr. Haskell comes another practical suggestion for Art Commissions in general:

"The idea does occur that an alert art commission might well propose quite a few city beautification ideas and thereby gain the right to nominate the architects to make more specific proposals. Thus a commission unable to initiate designs itself could get good directions initiated."

The **Committee of 100 on the Federal City** recently expressed strong support for S. 1920, a bill authorizing construction of an Annex to the Library of Congress on a government-owned site just south of the present Library. In so doing, the Committee's **Chairman, Rear Admiral Neill Phillips, USN (Ret.),** urged that the "tendency to extravagant outlay for monolithic memorials" be checked and that something be done to bring "order and plan into Federal construction on Capitol Hill."

In Perspective

Uprooted from the mountains and the plains and scurrying from the villages, we—millions of us—are drawn, as if by magnet, to the greatest cities the world has ever known.

Once here, we boast of possessions literally beyond the dreams of kings of yesteryear. Yet, caught up in the vastness of the modern city, all too few of us sustain the compelling pressures of city life well enough to ask if *these* are the things we really want.

Why *are* we here?

What *do* we seek?

The chances of coping with the pressing mass problems of the American city today are intricately bound with these simple, basic questions—and, unless each of us, as individuals, answers them with a fair degree of certainty, the best of planners could well plan in vain.

Why are we here?

We, who were yesterday's miners, have watched the mines close down. Who once were farmers, with our hands deep in the good loam of the earth, know that the machine does well the work of the man formerly behind the plow. Whose fathers were foresters, have knowledge of the stepped-up yield of the power saw and the meaning of the diesel engine at the front of the log train.

Our motive for coming to the city? The most compelling in the world—to earn our daily bread—quite often in the city's expanding construction projects. It's a motive over-riding the deep-down desire of a man to live in any location he wishes—whether or not it be close to the earth.

Those, who aspire to plan for the future, need to take note of these men—for the stern hand of necessity has forced them to stake out claims in a *milieu* totally unfamiliar to them. Deeply uncertain, in many cases, they are still feeling for the groove of city life and finding it a little spongy.

These are the men who find the jar and tedium of traffic snarls even more irksome than others, who find the "fenced in" feel of city life constricting, who do not understand the green of a quiet, spacious park as an "amenity" but have literally been accustomed to something very much like it as a way of life. Though here, they have not, as yet, set down unyielding roots in the metropolitan community.

Others of us have come to the city willfully seeking the advantages and opportunities the city has traditionally offered. The atmosphere of our time has fostered it. The vast movements of our people, both in and out of the Armed Services during World War II and the Korean War—the most extensive mass movements in history—gave untold numbers of us a persistent taste for that exciting something just across the horizon. Anyone within earshot of G. I. Joe during the fiery days of trial remembers his sustaining dreams for the "future" which is now the present. In many cases, he, with numerous others, is here today—seeking.

Seeking economic opportunity,

certainly, but also cultural advantages—the drama, the music, the museums, the educational opportunities—which have always been the proud, unique offering of the city. Yes, and the great sports arenas, and the merciful aid of the world's most advanced medical facilities and the humbling awe of majestic cathedrals.

Seeking and finding that the price of these erst-while beckoning advantages is bucking the incredible traffic line and biding his time. No doubt, he is beginning to wonder if, once again, he has "hurried up to wait around." And, like many others, he is regretfully concluding that the advantages are here all right but latching on to them is another matter.

He, too, has a message for the planner. Essentially, he is not confused by basic desires. He knows what he's after. To all the builders of better cities, his is a plea not to flee the tempestuousness of the emerging pattern but to face it. To sort out the problems, define a strategy for attacking them, bring the burden which is ours *into clearer perspective*—but do it now!

Having been moulded in a hard crucible and one stamped with victory, he values well-laid plans and a decision to proceed carefully—so long as it is surely. But he distinguishes well between care and complacency.

To those who wait restlessly in the shadow of decision, the latter is at best a stumbling block. The former would seem to propose a little bit of keen, uncluttered, analytical thinking—a prerequisite never so easy to come by but, nevertheless, one essential to a clear-cut, workable plan of action—one tailored smartly to today's hard facts of city development.

E. J. S.

COMMENTARIES

(*Continued from page 16*)

for in a recently announced plan, according to *Architectural Forum*. The magazine calls Albany today "a grimy, badly planned commercial area moldering in the shadow of the hill-top State Capitol," and quotes Governor Nelson A. Rockefeller as predicting:

"Albany will be the most beautiful capital city in the nation."

✑

Townscape: "Good urban design is more than architecture alone."

So states *Urban Renewal Notes*, a recent publication of the Housing and Home Finance Agency, which quotes from *Townscape*, by the British writer, Gordon Cullen:

"One building standing alone in the country-side is experienced as a work of architecture, but bring half a dozen buildings together and an art other than architecture is made possible . . .

"In fact, there is an art of relationship just as there is an art of architecture. Its purpose is to take all the elements that go to create the environment: Buildings, trees, nature, water, traffic, advertisements, and so on, and weave them together in such a way that drama is released. For a city is a dramatic event in the environment. . . .

"If at the end of it all, the city appears dull, uninteresting and soulless,

(*Continued on page 40*)

26

Hartzog Succeeds Wirth As National Park Service Director

Change in command at the National Park Service will become effective in January as George B. Hartzog, Jr., Associate Director since February 1963, succeeds Conrad L. Wirth as Director.

In announcing the retirement of Mr. Wirth, who has served as Director since 1951, Secretary of the Interior Stewart L. Udall said, "Connie Wirth has won a place on the highest honor roll of those who have done the most to preserve a rich outdoor legacy for the American people."

Mr. Wirth joined the National Park Service in 1931 after a career in landscape architecture and three years of service with the National Capital Park and Planning Commission, the predecessor of the present National Capital Planning Commission. After entering the Park Service, he supervised Civilian Conservation Corps activities in various parts of the Nation and was also placed in charge of the Park Service's land-planning work. Following a series of advancements, Mr. Wirth became Associate Director of the Park Service in April, 1951, and Director in December of the same year.

Mr. Hartzog, an attorney, aged 43, began his career with the Park Service in Chicago in 1946 and brings a background of broad experience to his new post. He received a B.S. degree in business administration from the American University in Washington, D. C., and has done graduate work there.

From November, 1947 to August, 1948, he served as attorney at the Lake Texoma Recreation Area, Denison, Texas, now administered by the Army Corps of Engineers. He was an attorney-advisor in the Washington Office of the National Park Service until April, 1951, when he became assistant chief of concessions management in that office.

In August 1955, he was transferred to the position of assistant superintendent of Rocky Mountain National Park, Colorado, and served in that capacity until November 1957, when he was appointed assistant superintendent of Great Smoky Mountains National Park, Tennessee. In February, 1959, he was promoted to Superintendent of Jefferson National Expansion Memorial, St. Louis, Missouri.

In August, 1962, Mr. Hartzog left the National Park Service to become executive director of Downtown St. Louis, Inc., an organization of civic and business leaders devoted to the renewal and redevelopment of downtown St. Louis.

In administering the Jefferson National Expansion Memorial, a memorial to commemorate the westward expansion, Mr. Hartzog successfully negotiated for the construction of the Gateway Arch and Visitor Center, the largest single contract ever undertaken by the National Park Service.

In 1956, Mr. Hartzog received a Meritorious Award Certificate from the William A. Jump Memorial Foundation for exemplary achievement in public administration. The following year he was one of eight

Federal executives awarded scholarships by the American Management Association to attend a management course given by the Association in New York City. In 1962, he was awarded the Department's Distinguished Service Award.

Mr. Wirth, the retiring director, was a policy advisor with the United States Allied Council in Vienna, Austria, from September, 1945 to June, 1946. In 1946, he received the Pugsley Gold Medal "for long and valuable service in behalf of the national parks." In 1954, he received an honorary Fellowship in the American Institute of Park Executives and shortly afterward was awarded a citation from The Netherlands honoring him with the rank of Commander in the Order of Orange-Nassau. He was elected president of the American Institute of Park Executives in 1962.

Mr. Wirth received the Distinguished Service Award from the Department of the Interior in 1956. He holds the 1957 Conservation Award of the American Forestry Association, the Horace Marden Albright Science Preservation Medal, the George Robert White Medal of Honor of the Massachusetts Horticultural Society, the American Automobile Association Achievement Award for 1959, the Rockefeller Public Service Award for 1960–61 and the Distinguished Service Medal of the College of Forestry, Syracuse University. He has received honorary degrees from several universities.

He is a life member of the Board of Directors of the National Conference on State Parks, as well as a life member of the Board of Trustees of the National Geographic Society. He is also a member of the American Planning and Civic Association.

Mr. Hartzog has been a member of the National Conference on State Parks since 1956. He is also a member of the American Institute of Park Executives, the Press Club of Metropolitan St. Louis, the Missouri Park and Recreation Association and the Forestry Advisory Council, University of Missouri.

Regional Plan

George A. Roeder, Jr., executive vice-president of The Chase Manhattan Bank, New York, and *Paul Windels, Jr.,* of the law firm, Windels, Currie & Rice, have been elected to the Board of Directors of Regional Plan Association, a civic organization formed in 1929 to encourage coordinated development of the area surrounding the Port of New York.

Otto W. Manz, Jr., of Consolidated Edison, has been elected a vice-president of the Association.

New Board Members

Newly elected members of the Board of Directors of the National Conference on State Parks are Ira B. Lykes, Virginia, Chief, Park Practice, National Park Service, Washington, D. C.; Clair Greeley, Okanogan, Washington; Charles Harris, 2805 Lafayette Street, Lansing, Michigan; Francis Langdon, Tonkawa, Oklahoma; and L. L. Huttleston, Director of State Parks, Albany, New York.

Proposed Canyonlands National Park. Angel Arch in the Needles Country.
Courtesy National Park Service, U. S. Department of the Interior

Proposed Canyonlands National Park. View from Chesler Park, looking across Devil's Pocket, toward Island In The Sky.

Courtesy National Park Service, U. S. Department of the Interior

Canyonlands National Park—A Proposal

EDITOR'S NOTE:—This is the fifth in the series of articles on proposed National Park Service projects, prepared by the Park Service at our request.

In the southeast section of Utah just north of the Navajo Reservation is one of the largest expanses of little-known wonderland remaining in America.

This is a land of canyons, plateaus, and mountains, each equally enchanting, each possessing beauty and mystery beyond description. Two mighty rivers, the Colorado and the Green, join forces in the midst of all this grandeur and have scoured a canyon over a thousand feet deep. Wind and rain working together through the ages have carved arches, needles, and spires of all shapes, colors and sizes. In the heart of all this magnificence is the proposed Canyonlands National Park.

The unique scenery and geology of this area was recognized as early as 1859 when Dr. J. S. Newberry, geologist with the MacComb expedition, described the remarkable features. Later, members of the famous Powell expedition commented on the beauty of the scenery. In 1944, a recreation resource survey in the Colorado River Basin identified the Canyonlands area as a recreation area of great potential and led the way to further studies by the National Park Service.

In the summer of 1961, an official inspection trip to the Canyonlands by Interior Secretary Udall, Agriculture Secretary Freeman, and others generated publicity and called attention to the need for preservation of the area. The first proposal indentified a vast area of more than 1,500 square miles centering around the confluence of the Colorado and Green Rivers.

The first Canyonlands National Parks bill was introduced in Congress by Senator Frank E. Moss in August, 1961. Hearings were conducted in Washington, D. C., and Monticello, Moab, and Salt Lake City, Utah during March and April of 1962 in order to develop all the facts and views of interest bearing on the measure. Members of the Public Lands Subcommittee went into the park for a first-hand inspection in 1962 and made an air inspection of the area in July, 1963.

The bill did not pass the 87th Congress, but was again introduced in the 88th Congress. The amended bill, S. 27, passed by the Senate, August 2, 1963, provides for the establishment of a national park of 258,600 acres. The boundaries were altered to exclude possible mineral lands in the northeastern portion and hunting lands in the southern part. The present bill assures a continuation of mining operations in established mines beyond the 25-year period permitted for prospecting and patenting; however patents granted subsequent to establishment of the park are limited to minerals only and would not grant surface ownership of the land area involved. Further, the bill provides that the Secretary of the Interior may regulate and control mining activities in order to preserve the scenic, scientific and archeologic values of the area. Provisions are also made in the Canyonlands bill to permit limited grazing,

33

subject also to controls by the Secretary, for the lifetime of present holders of valid grazing permits.

The purpose of these provisions is gradually to eliminate all non-conforming commercial uses within the proposed park without creating a hardship on those currently using and expecting to use the land. The provisions recognize the high standards that apply to the use of national park land and provide for the ultimate achievements of these standards.

There are no private lands within the proposed park area, and with the exception of school sections and riverbeds, owned by the State of Utah, all the land involved is owned by the Federal Government. All of the proposed park is under grazing permit which has been the most intensive use of this region. However, since lack of water restricts grazing in the canyons considerably, it cannot be considered the most important use of the area.

There is presently no oil or gas production in the proposed park, although several wells have been drilled. Much of the area has been staked with uranium mining claims, most of which are now abandoned. Potash mining outside the proposed park has recently been developed and much of the land along the rivers is under permit for potash prospecting.

In general, the lands involved in the park proposal are not presently making significant economic contribution to the region. A study by the University of Utah indicates that, in the first five years, Government and tourist expenditures would total eleven million dollars as a result

of establishment of the park. This would result in wages and other income of nearly three million dollars. In the sixth year, it is estimated 250,000 visitors would enjoy the park, and would spend three and one-half million dollars, greatly bolstering the local economy.

The establishment of a national park would benefit the local economy without upsetting the existing land uses. Acquisition of the land would cost nothing since it is already in public ownership. The proposed boundaries have been drawn to exclude potential mineral lands while including the most significant scenic, geologic, inspirational and recreational features of the area.

The park would include the land between the Green and Colorado Rivers south of the Grand-San Juan County line near Deadhorse Point State Park, and extend south to a few miles above the tailwaters of Lake Powell created by Glen Canyon Dam. It would be approximately 20 miles wide at each end, narrowing to about 10 miles in the central portion. The major river canyons divide the proposed park into units connected visually and geologically, but accessible only from different directions.

The southeast portion, accessible from Monticello, Utah, includes the Needles country, Chesler and Virginia Parks, Druid and Angel Arch, and Horse and Salt Creek Canyons. In the Needles area, the sandstone is broken into blocks by close-set joints, and has eroded into a fantasy of rounded pillars, spires and balanced rocks. Close by, just to the west, the same sandstone is faulted into parallel grabens—sunken
(Continued on page 55)

34

State Park Notes

Ohio. As voters across the country approved a great majority of the state and local government bond spending proposals on the November ballots, park, conservation and recreation efforts received substantial support in some states. In Ohio, a $250,000,000 capital improvements bond issue approved by the voters included $25,000,000 for conservation and recreation, an amount which will be increased by about $15,000,000 in federal grants.

Florida. A State constitutional amendment authorizing the sale of revenue bonds to finance a long-range outdoor land acquisition program was approved by Florida voters at the November election. The bonds, to total $50,000,000, would be issued to acquire land for state parks, fishing spots, public beaches and hunting and camping areas.

To pay off the bonds, receipts from a new 5 per cent tax on most outdoor recreational equipment and from a special license tax on most pleasure boats will go into a special state land acquisition fund set up by the newly adopted constitutional amendment.

Meanwhile three sporting goods dealers have filed suit challenging the legality of the newly enacted 5 per cent tax, declaring that the act levying it did not contain a complete definition of fishing, hunting, camping, swimming and diving equipment.

The sporting goods dealers contend that the attempted classification of the persons and things to be taxed is unreasonable and arbitrary and have declared that the act is invalid "in that it amounts to an attempted expropriation of money from one group for the benefit of another and therefore does not constitute a lawful exercise of the taxing power."

Taxable items listed by the act include poles, rods, reels, lines, seines, nets, decoys, tents, sleeping bags, firearms, ammunition, diving tanks, water skis, tow ropes and many others. Excluded from the levy are commercial nets and seines, fuels, oils, lubricants, motor vehicles and parts, boats, engines, life saving gear and safety and first aid equipment.

Pennsylvania. In the November elections in the Quaker State, a $70,000,000 State bond issue providing for acquisition of park land and recreational areas, under a program known as "Project 70," won by 100,000 votes. Nineteen counties, mostly urban, accounted for the victory by outvoting 48 counties, mostly rural, which opposed the financing.

Of the bond sale, the total of which has been authorized by 1970, $40,000,000 will go for regional parks near urban areas; $20,000,000 for grants to local governments; and $10,000,000 for wildlife areas and hunting and fishing access.

New Hampshire. The first step toward removing the New Hampshire State Division of Parks from the merchandising business was recently taken by Governor King who acted under a reorganization act which went into effect in July, 1962.

Governor King asked private interests to submit bids on food and souvenir concessions which grossed $467,819 last year at three major State parks. He thus initiated action to lease similar sales operations at all stores in New Hampshire's State park system. Bids on a lease basis will be asked next spring for operation of all State park concessions selling trinkets and refreshments.

Sales of ski accessories this winter in ski shops at Cannon Mountain in Franconia and Mt. Sunapee in Newbury will be turned over to bidders able to meet the rigid qualifications imposed by the State. The Parks division will continue to offer rentals of equipment and repairs in both ski shops.

Operation of State park stores by private business has already been conducted experimentally on a small scale at some parks, and the projected leasing of all stores in New

Hampshire will end a system which began in 1950. Under the current plan, sales concessions at the three parks will be leased on five-year contracts to afford successful bidders the opportunity to continue their operations if they are successful. State law permits a maximum of five years for any state-operated concessions.

Mississippi. A unanimous decision handed down by the Mississippi Supreme Court has cleared the way for officers of the Pearl River Valley Water Supply District to condemn lands for public use which are on the perimeter of a 35,000-acre reservoir north of Jackson.

Although the opinion dealt with only 34.4 acres in the area, it clears the way for condemnation of any acreage needed for the development of the reservoir as a source of water supply, and its protection against pollution and for recreation purposes.

Written by Justice Robert Gillespie, the Court opinion held that there was no need for the official commission to give explanations or proof to landowners for every parcel of land sought for the reservoir area. It held that, in effect, the intent of the State legislature in creating the reservoir district was manifestly for development of the area for public uses outlined by the board of directors of the reservoir project.

When the reservoir is completed and filled, it is estimated that it will be visited by 2,630,000 persons a year with a daily average of 7,200 and 46,000 on peak days. And the number of visitors is expected nearly to triple in 10 years.

Planning and Civic Comment

Wisconsin. According to estimates in a report submitted to the State Conservation Commission by its comptroller, Elroy Baxter, Wisconsin's program of recreation land acquisition will take 21 years to complete at a cost of $150,000,000. Mr. Baxter said that the program cannot be carried out unless a 1-cent added cigarette tax voted by the 1961 State legislature for a 10-year program is continued for two decades.

Missouri. The Missouri State Park Board recently took the first step toward development of Watkins Mill State Park in Clay County by voting to retain a firm of specialists in historic restorations to prepare plans and specifications for repair of the four-story Watkins Mill building.

The firm, Coombs & Elgin of Kansas City and St. James, will indicate repairs needed immediately on the brick building which in 1861 housed Missouri's largest industry outside of St. Louis. The building contains intricate cotton and wool weaving machinery of the late 1880's, some of it being the only machinery of its type still existing in the United States.

The specialists will also develop a master plan for improving the area in the immediate vicinity of the mill building and the nearby antebellum home of the mill's founder, Waltus L. Watkins. Clay County residents last March approved a $184,000 bond issue to buy the land and buildings for donation to the State. The Watkins Mill Association, a private group formed to preserve the mill, are working with county officials to complete arrangements for the land purchases.

Besides being a historic shrine to early Missouri industry, it is intended that the Watkins Mill State Park, when completed, will also be a major recreation area for the Kansas City metropolitan area. Picnicking and over-night camping areas, nature trails and other park facilities are planned.

Louisiana. The first arboretum in the Southlands will be developed on a three-hundred-acre area in Louisiana Chicot State Park, according to the State Parks and Recreation Commission at Baton Rouge. Fencing of the area has begun under a 1963 special legislative appropriation of $40,000 which made development of the arboretum possible.

When completed, the project will be of great value for biological and botanical study, according to Dr. Sigmond Solymosy, Professor of Botany at the University of Southwestern Louisiana. A variety of native trees, including the largest beech tree in the State, now grows on the acreage.

Massachusetts. A new State Division of Conservation Services has been provided for by a bill recently signed into Massachusetts law by that State's Governor Peabody. Established within the State National Resources Department, the new division replaces the State Division of Soil Conservation which was removed from the State Agriculture Department.

"This legislation will improve our conservation program in two ways,"

Governor Peabody pointed out. "It will consolidate all land-use responsibilities in one agency, and it will bring together two important areas of local actions—the soil conservation districts and the city and town conservation commissions."

Arkansas. And from Lou Oberste, Arkansas Publicity and Parks Commission, comes an enticing description of "floating," a type of recreation in which Arkansas excels and which awaits those willing to venture away from the beaten path:

"Towering bluffs overshadow tumbling shoals and deep, quiet pools of crystal clear water. A sudden zephyr of cool air ripples the water, carrying with it the delicate aroma of some hidden blossom. The only sounds are of water bubbling over submerged boulders, the sudden harsh cry of a bird of prey as it dives on some unsuspecting victim, and the splash of a paddle as it is dipped into the depths to propel the canoe forward.

"This is the wonderful world of the wilderness camper who, ignoring the public camp sites, ventures forth on a float trip on one of Arkansas' many mountain bred streams.

"Floating, long a favorite pastime of the fisherman, is growing in popularity with the camping enthusiast who is looking for an unfenced, uncluttered, uncrowded, billboardless scenic wilderness in which to pitch his tent.

"Many streams in Arkansas lend themselves to the float-camping type of recreation. Notable are the famous White and Buffalo and the scenic James and Current, and the equally beautiful and challenging Spring, Strawberry, Mulberry, War Eagle, Eleven Point, Ouachita, Saline, Cache and Black, to name but a few.

"Take your pick and plan a trip among the unspoiled beauty to an isolated camp site inaccessible except by water. Enjoy vistas almost unchanged from those seen by the first human to explore the stream. Drink from springs so cool you wonder where nature's refrigeration lies.

"As night approaches, you pitch your camp on one of the many gravel bars along the river. The stillness of the day explodes into a chorus of sounds as the woods creatures sing the song of life. The persistent chirps of unnumbered insects are drowned out by the deep bass voice of the bull frog. Whippoorwills, and chuck-will's widows add their melodious voices to the virtuosity of the mockingbird and nightingale.

"You had better have a blanket or sleeping bag. Even in the summer, it gets cold on the river at night. As the campfire dies, the stars—more stars than ever existed in the city—spread a canopy over the scene as even nature settles down for the night.

"There will be a fog on the river in the morning, but as the sun tops the escarpments it will burn away the mist, new vistas will unfold, and you will know that the float-camping trip will long be remembered."

Historic Dodge House—Next Casualty?

The half-century old Walter Luther Dodge House on Kings Road, in the Los Angeles vicinity, is said by some experts to be one of the Nation's most "significant houses." Its fate as of this writing is uncertain as architectural groups and outstanding national and cultural leaders throughout the country rally to save it from demolition.

As might be suspected, its menace of the moment is a pending zone change which, by affecting the property on which it is located, would trigger its destruction and replacement by apartment units.

Dodge House was designed by Irving Gill. In a letter urging preservation of the House, Lewis Mumford says Gill "was beyond doubt one of the great leaders of American architecture, worthy to rank with Sullivan, Wright and Maybeck . . . The examples of his work are so few that their preservation should be a matter of national concern as well as local pride."

From other eminent sources, come words of praise for Dodge House: A letter from Brown University's art professor William Jordy, who is doing a book on 15 important United States buildings of which Dodge House is one, calls the structure one of the "most significant of American houses."

More than 400 persons recently visited the House to hear architect Lloyd Wright, son of Frank Lloyd Wright, appeal for support to save the historic building from the wrecker's hammer. Others joining in the battle to save the house include Dean Sam Hurst of the University of Southern California's School of Architecture and Architect Raymond Girvigian, chairman of the Historical Building Committee for the local chapter of the American Institute of Architects.

Where Did It All Begin?

In California, says a recent communicue from the California State Department of Parks and Recreation:

"In 1865, Abraham Lincoln approved purchase of the Yosemite Valley and the Mariposa Grove of Giant Sequoias by California as the first State Park in the nation.

"In 1890, Congress created a national park surrounding these state lands, and, in 1905, the State Legislature returned the Yosemite and the Giant Sequoias as an addition to Yosemite National Park."

PROJECTS IN REVIEW

(*Continued from page 20*)

And finally—have the volunteer participants given slap-dash opinions on the subjects under review? No, says Regional Plan. First, they watched five television programs and read five Background Booklets about the prospects for the area if present policies continue and what might be done instead. After each television program, they discussed the issues in small groups—then, as a final step, filled out the individual questionnaires.

Old Town

A detailed architectural and historical study of Old Town—which, with adjacent Fells Point, constituted the City of Baltimore for about 100 years—is being made by Baltimore Heritage Incorporated. The group plans to coordinate the work of members of the AIA and of historical organizations and preservation societies in Baltimore. Orin M. Bullock, in a recent issue of Architect's Report, the official publication of the Baltimore Chapter of the American Institute of Architects, says "many of the roots of Baltimore's greatness are traced to Old Town." A number of historic buildings remain, such as the restored Flag House and others which are still in salvable condition.

Pointing out that all of Baltimore will change radically in this decade, Mr. Bullock says that Old Town has been selected for study because of its potential in interpreting the city's architectural and historical heritage, its commercial potential as a tourist attraction and because it is destined for immediate and radical change. East–west and north–south expressways will connect within the area. Slum clearance and redevelopment projects are already under way and deterioration, over-crowding, incompatible land use and outmoded street patterns make additional projects inevitable.

COMMENTARIES

(*Continued from page 26*)

then it is not fulfilling itself. It has failed. The fire has been laid but nobody has put a match to it."

e/ю

Affluence: Also, from across the seas and from a high source comes a perceptive observation on what really makes life worth while:

The British publication, *Town and Country Planning*, quotes Prince Philip on TV:

"No one questions the need for man to keep alive, to make humanity free from hunger and suffering, but if a higher standard of living means anything at all, it means an opportunity for all men to enjoy a richer and a more rewarding life. It means a better chance to enjoy the rewards for his work or study, and enlightenment in the appreciation of the arts, and in the enjoyment of the wonders of the natural world."

The Role of Metropolitan Area Planning

By PAUL OPPERMANN, Executive Director of the Northeastern Illinois
Planning Commission

Millions of people and hundreds of governments joined in a loose but vital web of mutual needs and interconnected enterprises:

That is the metropolitan area, the urban setting where most Americans live today and where, it is estimated, four out of five will be living by 1980. During the 1950's, 84 per cent of the nation's population growth took place in 212 of these urban centers.

One of the world's largest and most complex metropolitan areas is Northeastern Illinois, the metropolitan area of Chicago. Its 3,714 square miles contain nearly 6,500,000 people, six counties, some 250 municipalities and nearly a thousand governments in all.

As with most metropolitan areas, the chief problem of Northeastern Illinois is growth—a vertical growth in numbers and population densities and a horizontal growth in the amount of land used for urban purposes.

Recent growth has tended to follow the automobile and the popular desire for more living space. The result has been a continuing geographic expansion that has carried Northeastern Illinois urban development across city and village lines, has created scores of new communities, and, between 1960 and 1980, is expected to increase the "built up" parts of the metropolitan area by some 450 square miles— equivalent in area to two Cities of Chicago. Also, by 1980, it is expected that close to 2,000,000 more people will be added to the metropolitan population.

With this expansion there has arisen a new species of community problems, termed *metropolitan area problems*. These are the problems, the causes and solutions of which reach beyond municipal and even county boundaries, and which concern such matters as short-sighted and disorderly land use and development, traffic congestion and inadequate transportation, flooding, water shortages, and water and air pollution problems.

To officials and citizens who grappled with these problems of area-wide growth in the 1950's, it became increasingly clear that they could only be solved at the metropolitan level. The need, it was realized, was for a body of metropolitan area policies and plans within which the hundreds of governments could cooperate to provide the variety of facilities—from expressways to sewer lines and forest preserves—which a metropolitan area must have if it is to prosper.

The need was not for a metropolitan "super government." Such a government might operate and still not plan, in which case the problems of government would be aggravated and the problems of growth not faced at all.

It was in response to such aspects of modern-day metropolitan life that the Northeastern Illinois Metropolitan Area Planning Commission was established by the Illinois Legislature in 1957, and the same facts of life have brought more than fifty other metropolitan planning agencies into being, with more being created almost monthly.

The critical question for the modern metropolitan area is how the dozens or hundreds of separate political units within its boundaries can solve large-scale problems while retaining their own powers and identities. Accordingly, guidance and coordination are the key roles of the Northeastern Illinois agency as of most other metropolitan planning agencies. Essentially, the aim is to achieve a better environment by establishing a procedure for cooperative development and helping local governments act upon it.

Conformance with the plans and policies of the Northeastern Illinois Planning Commission is voluntary. Its proposals are measured by their manifest value as instruments for meeting public needs, their economic feasibility and their acceptability to the people and governments of the metropolitan area.

For example, the Commission is now working toward early completion of a comprehensive plan of land use, transportation and natural resources development. To be completed in five years, it will bring together alternative solutions to critical metropolitan-wide problems *in relation to one another.*

Thus, the many competing needs for Northeastern Illinois' limited land resources should find a measure of alignment so that, for example, planning for additional open space facilities supports and is supported by proposals for transportation facilities, industrial land use, etc.— instead of competing with them.

Essentially, the elements of the proposed Comprehensive Plan include:

A land use and development plan;

A plan for all modes of transportation;

A plan for the use and management of water and air resources, including drainage, sanitation, and waste disposal;

A program for implementation by local governments.

The basic method of the Comprehensive Plan Program will be to work out a number of alternative proposals based on different sets of proposed policies for metropolitan area development. These will then be submitted to the local governments for review as to preferred development policies, after which a plan will be prepared based on their advice.

When completed, the metropolitan plan will not be *the* plan; rather, it will be a framework within which the governments of the metropolitan area can make their own plans and programs in terms of metropolitan as well as local needs.

Especially, it should be seen as a coordinating instrument in the light of which the governments of the metropolitan area can cooperate to meet the challenge of urban growth: To satisfy vast and diverse individual needs while still retaining— and enhancing—community order and beauty.

Developing Appalachia—The Hill Region Speaks

By
EARL KINNER

From an article appearing in the *Licking Valley Courier*, West Liberty, Kentucky, of which Mr. Kinner is the publisher, June 20, 1963.

What type program will bring Appalachia out of the doldrums and restore the region to its rightful status in America's growing economy?

We do not speak for all of Appalachia. But we do speak our piece for our own region—the foothills and mountains of east Kentucky, one of the most beautiful and picturesque regions in all America, a region that holds the last stronghold of pure Anglo-Saxon stock, a region of small farms, rushing mountain streams, forested hills, friendly people—a potential Switzerland of contented families and a vacationland unsurpassed in mid-America.

Already a mountain gardenspot, our east Kentucky could be the vacationland for mid-America and our native hill people could again enjoy a wholesome living standard, kept busy on small farms, in reforestation and timbering jobs, in wood product plants, and paper mills, in small craft centers, in catering to the thousands of tourists soon to flood the Appalachian area.

It could be all this—if . . . if our region were developed to its full potential.

But a depressed area cannot lift itself by its own bootstraps, particularly a mountain region that is already denuded of its virgin forests, shorn of most of its coal, ravaged periodically by rushing flash floods, short of connecting highways, and lacking many of the things that make for wholesome living, such as proper housing, proper educational facilities, libraries, hospitals, and colleges.

For such a potential gardenspot in a highland region the State and Federal Governments might well establish a regional authority like the Tennessee Valley Authority, the Great Plains Regional Authority, and others, and bring the region to its rightful fruition.

That is what we hope for. And we think this is what is envisioned. It will take long-term planning by a regional commission.

But in the meantime we should not grow lax in our plans to take advantage of short-term projects such as are now offered by the Area Redevelopment Administration, the Accelerated Public Works Act, the Kerr-Hill Act, the Soil Conservation Service, the State's reforestation program, highway program, parks and airfield programs, community college program, etc. These should all be pursued to the fullest, and immediately.

Then for the long pull, we suggest a regional program that would recognize these opportunities and develop them to the fullest:

Waterway improvement. Our

mountain streams offer great opportunity for recreation and as water supply for industrial purposes and people. But instead they now are sources of periodic danger due to flooding that devastates farmland and towns part of the year. They run sluggish and contaminated the rest of the year.

To correct this and realize their full potential, we need a threefold program geared especially to mountain terrain:

1. Clean out, deepen and straighten channels immediately.

2. Create a small watershed program that will benefit hill farmers like the same program now benefits farmers in flatland areas. But a special program will be needed. The present small watershed program, though liberalized recently, still is inadequate. To date, no watershed in east Kentucky has qualified under the liberalized cost-benefit ratio formula. Some watershed projects that straighten and deepen channels, build dams on tributaries for reservoir retention of floodwaters, and beautify banks and drain adjacent land—this program is sorely needed to protect hill farmers from periodic flash floods that have so devastated our scarce farming lands.

3. Build lakes for recreational purposes in areas that will do least damage to farmland and at the same time aid in flood control programs on our major waterways. . . .

Parks and tourism. Tourists spend an average of $7 to $11 per day. And the State parks service counted 610,000 visitors at five east Kentucky parks last year—Natural Bridge, Carter Caves, Greenbo Lake, Jenny Wiley, and Dewey Lake.

Tourism will bring in more new money with the least investment of any program—that is, if our mountain gardenland is developed to its fullest potential. The State already has established parks in some areas of this gardenland, and is building access roads. But more parks, more small lakes and motels and dining places are needed, and needed almost immediately.

Several of east Kentucky's most beautiful mountain areas now are inaccessible. Access roads need to be built so tourists can enjoy a vacation in our area to the fullest. Access roads particularly should be built to the ledges overlooking the Rough of Red River, a breathtaking beautiful expanse of mountain stream. Also access roads need to be built into other scenic and historic places, like Hells Half Acre in Magoffin County, the narrows of Licking in Menifee and Morgan, the Woodsbend area in Morgan, and many other such scenic areas.

But more than this, a program to preserve historic homes and public buildings in the hills, to mark historic sites, and prepare travel brochures and maps—this is needed to help keep the tourists an extra day. Too, a program to preserve our hill folksongs, folk dances and traditions, and make them available to visiting tourists—this needs attention. City people don't want to see city things when they come to the mountains— they want to see mountain things. For this reason mountain museums and libraries with mountain rooms need to be started.

44

Forward Atlanta

Adapted from an article by JAY JENKINS in *The Municipal South*, July, 1963

Wistful reminders of a courtly, romantic past linger on in Atlanta, but the Georgia capital is more concerned with the future—destined, her leaders feel, to become a city of vast global significance. The high shrine of the Old South has taken a new image.

But Atlanta's new role didn't "just happen."

Spawned by the Chamber of Commerce, "Forward Atlanta" is a promotional venture of considerable proportions. More than 90 per cent of the business and industry in Atlanta's five-county metropolitan area finance the undertaking through cash contributions. Hours, weeks, even months and years of painstaking effort preceded the "sudden" full blossoming of the economy.

The city's current jetspeed progress is a product of infinite planning. Research began in earnest two years ago, soon after it was evident "Forward Atlanta" monies would be forth-coming. Studies of the city's economy as well as that of the surrounding area were compiled. More than two dozen research reports have been published since the program began.

Atlanta—1,050 feet above sea level—is the highest metropolitan center east of Denver but a city which possesses few of the natural advantages. It isn't located on a navigable water way. There are no rich deposits of iron ore, coal or limestone nearby.

But it is strategically located, and it started out with a railroad.

First known as Terminus, the townsite was chosen by railroad surveyor Stephen Harriman Long in 1837. Long selected the place as a natural meeting point for transportation lines in the Southeast and staked the area out. With the arrival of rail workers, a community was established. Later called Marthaville, it was incorporated as Atlanta in 1847 and had grown to a bustling 10,000 by 1861. The Civil War brought its near-destruction when Sherman's army burned much of the town on his infamous march to the sea.

Today Atlanta moves ahead in all areas—business and industry, the arts and the sciences. With increasing frequency in past months, the story of its present-day development has been told in national magazines such as *Show* which featured Atlanta in its June issue and called it the "capital of Georgia and also the pace-and-taste setting capital of the entire Southeast."

A booklet titled "Facts and Figures About Growing Atlanta" points out that some 1,800 manufacturing concerns produce more than 3,400 commodities in Atlanta, including automobiles, aircraft, textiles, chemicals, furniture, food, iron and steel products.

The 1960 census placed the population at 1,017,188 in metropolitan Atlanta—a growth of 39 percent in one decade, moving the city into the circle of 24 American metropolitan areas with population of a million or more. Atlanta is the only city in that category in the Southeast.

Because of transportation advantages, the city is in position to collect raw and semi-finished materials from a wide area—textiles from the Carolinas, steel and coal from Alabama, pulp and paper from coastal mills, cement from local limestone, kaolin from mid-Georgia, and food, synthetic fibers, cotton, and tobacco from points throughout the Southeast.

The economy is represented by all major segments of manufacturing, trade and services.

But despite the enormous strides being made, the city leaders realize their town is still on its way.

Economic consultant Philip Hamner, first executive director of Atlanta Metropolitan Planning Commission, says available public and private services must be increased. He explains that the problem of governing a sprawling metropolitan area must be solved as well as a solution found to financing the new outer city.

"We must take a look at zoning regulations to allow for large-scale apartment developments in the suburbs, and we must vigorously tackle the problems of our 'gray' residential areas between downtown and the suburbs that are not being solved by urban renewal. We must do a better job of planning in Downtown Atlanta to replace obsolescence with modern efficiency and to open areas to expansion."

Mr. Hamner believes the city will become great, not just huge in population and size alone. He quotes the late Robert MacDougall: "There is only one way Atlanta can travel—first class."

Thus the storied old city is like a new, vivacious woman—sophisticated and exciting—suddenly become siren of the South, a gracious old girl turned ambitious, determined, designing.

But through the many magnificent changes Atlanta has retained her most priceless quality— above all, she remains a place of immense charm!

IN MEMORIAM

Chauncey J. Hamlin, founder and former president of the International Council of Museums, died September 23, 1963, at the age of 82. For 28 years, Mr. Hamlin, also a lawyer, politician and stockbroker, was president and director of the Buffalo Museum of Science. He was awarded the Chancellor Medal for distinguished service to the community by the University of Buffalo.

Mr. Hamlin was a candidate of the Progressive (Bull Moose) Republican party for New York lieutenant governor in 1914. He served as an officer in the field artillery on the Mexican border in 1916 and in France during World War I. From 1924–30, he was chairman of the National Conference on Outdoor Recreation. He was a former member of the Board of Trustees of the American Planning and Civic Association and was also a member of the National Conference on State Parks.

Strictly Personal

A. Clark Stratton, assistant director for design and construction at the National Park Service since 1961, has been named Associate Director to succeed George B. Hartzog, Jr., newly appointed Park Service Director.

Mr. Stratton, born in Aurora, Missouri, in 1913, joined the National Park Service in 1936, after serving as assistant director and business manager for the Federal Emergency Relief Administration at Fort Eustis, Virginia. His first assignment with the Park Service was to head an extensive dunes stabilization and beach erosion control project along North Carolina's famed Outer Banks, now part of the Cape Hatteras National Seashore.

From 1940 to 1943 he served as inspector and field supervisor for the Park Service in New York, New Jersey, Maryland, Virginia, and West Virginia. This assignment was followed by tours of duty as manager of the W. S. Sanders Co., of Norfolk, Virginia, a coastwide and West Indies transportation firm, and as vice-president of the Sanders Products Co., of Norfolk, a corporation operating a menhaden processing plant. In the latter post he was in charge of experimental work involving broadened use of fish products.

He returned to the National Park Service in 1951, to serve as project manager of the then Cape Hatteras National Seashore Recreational Area. While there he initiated an extensive program of land acquisition. In 1954, he transferred to the Service's regional office in Richmond, Virginia, as a soil conservationist and chief of operations. Subsequently, he was assigned to Washington, D. C., where from 1956 through 1960 he served as chief of concessions management and assistant chief of design and construction, respectively.

In 1955, in recognition of his noteworthy achievements at Cape Hatteras, Mr. Stratton received a Meritorious Service Award from the Department of Interior. The Department's highest honor, the Distinguished Service Award, was conferred on him in 1961 in recognition of his outstanding service in the field of concessions management and for his exceptional contributions to the public service.

In March of this year, he was honored by the American Institute of Park Executives for invaluable service to the profession.

———◆———

Hillory A. Tolson has retired as Assistant Director for Administration at the National Park Service.

In announcing his retirement, Park Service Director Conrad L. Wirth said, "His ability, dedication, initiative, insight and personality have made a 'Tolson Job' a synonym for outstanding work."

Mr. Tolson has been Assistant Director of the Park Service since August, 1943, and as such has been the principal officer in charge of many management and action programs—including finance, audit, personnel, management analysis, property and records management, safety, and incentive awards.

Early in his career, he compiled the Laws Relating to the National Park Service and initiated and developed the *National Park Service Administrative Manual.*

Mr. Tolson, a lawyer by profession and a veteran of the Marine Corps, entered the National Park Service in 1932, having previously been employed by the War Department, the Panama Canal and the Federal Bureau of Investigation.

In 1963, he received the Distinguished Service Award, the highest honor bestowed by the Department of Interior.

———————◆———————

Mrs. G. T. Smith, Jr. has been elected Chairman of *The Florida Board of Parks and Historic Memorials* for the coming year to succeed *Dr. James T. Cook* who has been named Vice Chairman.

Dr. Hale Smith, head of the Department of Anthropology and Archaeology, Florida State University, has been granted permission by the Florida Board to conduct archaeological field work at Fort Pickens State Park, near Pensacola.

Architecture

". . . The art of our century is architecture . . . it is the one art, among all arts, that our century has demanded without equivocation.

"Architecture is the one art in which old forms simply would not do, in which new forms invented themselves instead of being synthesized by theory.

"The skyscraper just grew. It is the symbol of our age—and it was self-created, carrying puzzled architects up with it as architecture suddenly shot skyward because it could no longer spread outward. Architecture is the one art in which technology and esthetics may be implacably independent of the designer and totally fused with one another. Yet, from these premises, architecture allows, at the same time, the grandest flights of imagination.

"Modern architecture is the art we have abused, misunderstood, held in check, and perverted—as opposed to our coddling of the other arts. Yet it is the one art that has flourished in spite of us."

—Excerpt from an address by John Canaday, Art Critic of the *New York Times,* published in the 91st Annual Report of the Fairmount Park Art Association, Philadelphia, Pa.

Seminars, Conferences and University Notes

Dedication. *Yale University's* new Art and Architecture building, a $4,000,000 structure that will house the Nation's oldest collegiate art school, was recently dedicated, with leading figures in the art and architecture world in attendance at the ceremonies.

Designed by *Paul Rudolph*, noted American architect who is Chairman of the Department of Architecture at Yale, the new building has already evoked wide comment from critics both here and abroad.

There are nominally nine stories in the capacious building—seven above ground and two below—but, such is the architectural achievement, there are actually 36 different floor levels in the building, effecting what Mr. Rudolph calls "a conquest of space." Designed to accommodate at least 375 persons, faculty and students, the building contains classrooms, offices, workrooms, the art and architecture library and a small auditorium for the School's teaching program in architecture, city planning, painting, sculpture, print-making and graphic design.

The building's rough-textured concrete and glass exterior is of interest. The concrete has a rippled surface produced by having the reinforced concrete poured in special forms to allow the aggregate to come to the surface. It was then exposed by having the workmen break off the leading edges with hammers.

Mr. Rudolph calls this rippled surface "exposed aggregate concrete," and wanted it for both aesthetic and practical reasons: The rippled surface catches the light in soft and attractive shadings, and, in the coming years, the uneven surface will weather better than a smooth, stark surface.

Mr. Rudolph, who has designed the art centers at Wellesley College and Colgate and the chapel at Tuskegee Institute, among other outstanding structures, considers the Yale building the most difficult assignment he has had in his career as an architect. He worked over a period of three years and drew up seven distinct schemes out of which came the final design.

The task was "formidable," according to Mr. Rudolph, because the new building will speak more impressively to his students during the coming years than anything he, himself, will be able to say.

That the architect has met the challenge is reflected in the words of Peter Blake, managing editor of *Architectural Forum:* "The tremendous importance of Yale's new Art and Architecture Building is that it will challenge, disturb, possibly inspire the students within it as few other schools of architecture anywhere have done in recent times. It is not really important to decide whether this is a good building or a bad one; the important thing is that it represents a clear commitment on the part of a strong artist. It will be a highly successful building, I am sure, for none in it can help but be moved by it—and it doesn't really matter which way. Education in America needs more shock-treatment, not less."

Dedication of the Art and Architecture building marks the culmination of the extensive building program started at Yale in the 13-year administration of the late *President A. Whitney Griswold*. Mr. Griswold's prevailing conviction that the leading architects of the times should design the new campus buildings is exemplified in the 26 new structures which have been commissioned during that period.

Appointment. Peter Stead of Yorkshire, England, has been appointed Visiting Professor in Architecture and Urban Design in the College of Fine Arts at the *Carnegie Institute of Technology*.

Prior to coming to Carnegie Tech, Mr. Stead was a consultant designer and planner and senior partner in the firm of Design Collaborative, England, with Professor David Neville Lewis, recently appointed Andrew Mellon Professor in Architecture and Urban Design at Carnegie Tech. Their work together includes the component house of aluminum, glass, steel and plastics which was chosen to represent Britain at the VI Congress of the International Union of Architects in London, 1961.

Fellowships. James T. Griffin, president of the *Sears-Roebuck Foundation*, has announced that applications for fellowships in the field of city planning are now being accepted for the 1964 Fall term. Twenty two-year graduate fellowships, including renewals, will be awarded for the 1964-65 academic year.

Prospective fellows must submit applications, available from schools of city planning and the Foundation, to the schools of their choice by February 1, 1964. Announcement of the winners will be made by the Foundation in March.

Designed to increase the flow of trained personnel into city planning, the Sears Foundation fellowship program is administered by the Foundation in cooperation with ACTION and the American Society of Planning Officials.

The committee which will select the 1964 Foundation fellows includes Robert D. Calkins, president of the Brookings Institution; Martin Meyerson, vice chairman of ACTION, and Dennis O'Harrow, executive director of the American Society of Planning Officials.

❧

Netherlands Planning Consultant

Dr. Cornelis de Cler, Chief, Town Planning Department, Ministry of Housing and Building, The Hague, Netherlands, arrived in this country on October 15, 1963, for a two months stay as a visiting consultant on planning for a healthful environment.

Dr. Cler came to the United States under the auspices of the Division of Environmental Engineering and Food Protection of the U. S. Public Health Service and under the technical assistance program of the World Health Organization which met expenses for his trip.

His itinerary took him across the entire country.

THE CONSERVATION CHALLENGE
OF THE SIXTIES

(Continued from page 4)

more valuable as raw materials than for combustion.

The federal effort is, as I see it at the present time, three-pronged. The first line is the Atomic Energy Commission's accelerating nuclear power development. Men in AEC laboratories are searching for the final secrets of fission and fusion. Second, the optimum development of the renewable waterpower of our rivers has been quickened, and a pioneering power plant to harness the continuous energy of the tides may be proposed soon at Passamaquoddy in Maine. Third, the integration of our electric power systems is being encouraged, and public and private region-to-region transmission lines carrying very high voltages will soon add to the efficiency of our over-all electric plant.

Products of the Land

Another sector of resources includes the products of our land.

Although a magnificent natural endowment of superlative soils has been the basis for our agricultural success, we have built solidly on that basis in the 20th century with conservation practices that have turned agriculture into a science. Men like Luther Burbank and Hugh Hammond Bennett, of soil conservation fame, and hundreds of anonymous researchers in agronomy, plant genetics and plant pathology have joined forces to make the land yield record harvests.

Fortunately, agri-science and the farm experimenters of the land-grant universities were favored by the Congress for many years, and, for decades, more than half of the federal appropriations for research went to agriculture. These wise investments now fill our granaries to overflowing, and make it possible for us to share our surplus—and our land wisdom—with people in all parts of the world.

Nor have our successes been confined to crops. Science-minded farmers and stockmen excel in raising animals, and the Pinchot gospel has taught our commercial tree farmers to respect the growth-cycles and growth potential of our woodlands.

Water Problems

Water, in some regions, is already on the edge of crisis, and the "mining" of groundwater supplies in some parts of the Pacific Southwest is so extensive that the desert is reclaiming parts of its old domain. But the greatest water problem throughout the Nation today is the senseless and extravagant waste that results from the pollution of our rivers and streams by the sewage of cities and industries—a practice as blind and destructive as that which led to the leveling of our finest forests. A pollution control program is getting underway, but most of our rivers today are a national disgrace and our water awakening is still in the future.

The quiet crisis in water is also magnified by the Myth of Scientific Supremacy—the mistaken notion that a quick trick of science will some day make the oceans potable, a program for which my department has responsibility. Such a myth could prevent us from facing the facts. Even if the cost of desalinization is sharply reduced, as it probably will be soon, transportation charges will make desalted sea water of use chiefly along the seacoasts. Water is the one imperative resource, and the growth of many areas will be stunted unless science and common-sense husbandry come to the rescue. We will not learn how to conserve water until we respect the geography of water.

Today our river-basin planning is in arrears, some states are making only a half-hearted effort to combat pollution, and our conservation practices are primitive or haphazard. Worse, our posture of preparedness is poor: our corps of water scientists is much too small, our investment in basic research is dangerously low, and we are only now taking a tardy look at what we could achieve through reclaiming and recycling available supplies of water.

The President's water prescription is a broad one, and if it stimulates an adequate level of effort by the States and by industry it can help solve many upcoming water problems. It includes:

1. The making of comprehensive plans for all major river basins—and the construction of multi-purpose reservoirs to provide adequate storage;

2. Larger investments in basic and interdisciplinary research on water resources, and the establishment of new water research centers in many of our land-grant universities;

3. Applied research that will enlarge our knowledge of rainmaking, the control of evaporation, and behavior of groundwater aquifers;

4. A sustained federal-state effort to cleanse our rivers;

5. The development of a low-cost process of desalting sea water.

We can have clean water—and have enough of it—if we become water savers and recognize in time the importance of the hydro-sciences.

Minerals and Marine Resources

The six per cent of the people who reside in the United States, and this is a very significant fact in relation to international politics, consume over 30 per cent of the world's raw material production, and we depend on imports for most of our supplies of more than a dozen major minerals.

In minerals, international interdependence is the trend: Nature's distribution is so capricious that we will approach a true common market of natural resources in this area more quickly than in any other. The mineral situation of tomorrow is indicated by the forceful fact that already foreign students outnumber American graduate students in the courses offered by the mining schools of the United States.

Our internal problem relates principally to waste, inadequate research, the depletion of some deposits, and the need for improvement of extraction and processing techniques. Industry carries the heaviest load in mineral conservation and research. The federal effort should be directed toward the most difficult exploration and extraction problems, basic geologic research, the conservation of helium, for example, and emphasis on salvage and re-use.

However, today minerals are not only found—they are "created": Many previously unusable substances—taconites, beryllium, aluminum, and molybdenum, for example—have been put to use through the alchemies of modern science.

The atmosphere and the oceans, save for the continental shelves and the littoral zones, are two resources that are owned in common by all of the people of the world. The oceans are, all agree, also an area of quiet crisis: Save for a few farsighted treaties, we have no common plan of management, and our inquiries into the biology of sea life and the nature of sea resources are superficial.

This unknown marine domain comprises the submerged 71 per cent of the earth's surface, and in its depths lies a vast storehouse of the resources of the future. Once a plan for processing is perfected, for example, enormous schools of what we now call "trash fish" can be converted into fish flour or protein concentrate that may alleviate much of the protein diet deficiency which afflicts two-thirds of the people of the world.

Because of ignorance and inadequate international planning, the resources of the sea are overexploited on the one hand and underdeveloped on the other. The law of the sea is as inchoate as its code of conservation, and the law of hunt-and-capture prevails—the law of the jungle as it were, reminiscent of the buffalo range in our own country. There will, one suspects, be much lamenting over vanishing sea species before necessity compels the nations to act. Oceanographic research has been nearly tripled and events will surely force the sea-oriented countries to plan the preservation of the renewable resources of the sea just as they have already successfully saved the fur seals and the salmon.

(The March issue will continue with a "State of the Union" discussion of "The Total Outdoor Environment.")

Young West Virginia Mountaineers Learn Conservation

Conservation education was taught to approximately 40,000 young people in an estimated 75 state camps in West Virginia last summer.

The State's Natural Resources Department personnel taught classes in game management, trapping, forestry, fish management, nature study, water conservation, youth conservation, care and use of firearms, fishing tackle, archery, Indian lore and fly tying. Classes in outdoor living were also taught at several of the camps.

The purpose underlying all of the camps was to acquaint West Virginia youth with the social and economic importance of natural resources, to train them for leadership in conservation, and to create within them a yearning and love "to serve and faithfully defend" these valuable renewable resources.

Planning and Civic Comment

PANTHER HOLLOW—FROM DESOLATION TO DEVELOPMENT

(*Continued from page 12*)

The interior structure will be terraced back from these spacious courts, seven all told. The courts will be landscaped and designed for recreational purposes. Parking and vehicular traffic will be limited to below-grade levels. Except for one existing bridge which crosses the structure, the roof gardens are designed exclusively for pedestrian use.

For nearly a mile, no cars will be seen or heard—yet the hundreds of cars parked below will be readily accessible. Approximately ten and one-half million square feet of laboratories, offices, shops, and instrumented areas will be created where previously only wasteland existed. It will be served by nearly eight million square feet of roads, parking areas, service facilities, utility distributing stations, a built-in railroad, bus station, theaters, recreation space and landscaping.

Potential subsequent development could multiply this area four or five times, since the ravine continues more than a mile beyond the area presently projected for development, making the center one of the largest in the world.

Architect Max Abramovitz, of the New York architectural firm of Harrison and Abramovitz, says Panther Hollow may well become the nucleus of the Nation's 21st century city, a city in which the individual can find rewarding employment, recreation, culture and higher education, all within walking distance of his home. He won't need his car for everyday living and automobile traffic will be out of sight and out of mind. "A person could live his whole life within a half-mile radius of this center—and an extraordinarily rewarding life it would be," Mr. Abramovitz said. He will have more landscaped open space at his disposal than most suburbanites. He will have more vital metropolitan advantages than most other city dwellers. And he can be as much a part of the academic community as though he were a full-time professor.

The Oakland Corporation and its founding institutions have high hope that the new concept will pay off in terms of a reversal of regional economic decline.

As most Pennsylvanians well know, the economy of the Upper Appalachian region is oriented toward heavy industry, metals and mining. There is a growing need for diversification and for the establishment of new types of industry if enough wealth is to be generated to provide prosperity.

Dr. Litchfield feels that research, with deliberately managed "spinoff" of laboratory developments into new and existing regional industrial activity, is close to the only solution to the problem. Thus, the Oakland Corporation, working with the cooperation of the best minds in Pittsburgh's institutions and industry, will place heavy emphasis on processes of translating new research findings into viable industries.

CANYONLANDS NATIONAL PARK—
A PROPOSAL

(*Continued from page 34*)

troughs in the earth's surface. Southeast, the highly colored sandstone has been cut by winding streams into a wilderness of alcoves, ridges, fins and arches. The placid Chesler and Virginia Parks, ringed by a forest of fantastic needles, are beautiful to behold. Elephant Canyon, offering new vistas at every turn, has towering Druid Arch as a climax at its head. Salt Creek and Horse Creek provide equally intriguing but different values including Indian ruins. In this section, also, is Cataract Canyon—the explorers' nightmare and river-runners' delight. At the Canyon's head, the Green and Colorado Rivers merge their silt-laden waters to form one of the wildest reaches of river on the continent.

A suggested development for this section includes a road through the Needles providing access by short spur roads to such features as Chesler Park, Devil's Pocket, Tower Ruin and the Confluence Overlook. Chesler Park would serve as a hub for trails fanning out to Druid Arch and Virginia Park. Squaw Flat would be the logical center for protection, interpretation and visitor accommodation facilities.

The northernmost unit includes the land between the rivers and is appropriately named the Island In the Sky. It is a great plateau surrounded by sheer cliffs and connected to the mainland mass by a narrow neck only forty feet wide. Grandview Point, the tip of the plateau, affords an incomparable vantage point from which to scan the canyonlands. Upheaval Dome, a unique geologic feature deserving recognition for itself alone, dominates the western portion of the Island. Between the plateau and the Green and Colorado Rivers, a resistant ledge, the White Rim, makes an esplanade from which to view the inner gorges, rivers, and basins, some of which enclose large and spectacular erosion remnants.

This section would be a primary public-use area, with roads, overlooks, interpretive devices including a visitor center and nature trails, a campground and food service. A road on the White Rim should circle the Island In the Sky and lead to Standing Rock Basin. On the river, a ranger station and campground would serve the public and protection needs.

Management and development should be carefully controlled under three main precepts: Administer the area so as to protect visitors and the significant values; make a total park experience available by suitable roads, trails and interpretive devices; and reserve appropriate portions of the park for proper wilderness use.

The historic, prehistoric, biologic, geologic, and, above all, scenic qualities make this proposed park of intense interest to people. Here they can stand on a promontory and catch the excitement of a great, varied vista of unspoiled canyons and then go down and see them from within. From the White Rim between the rivers, the land seems even bigger than when seen from above, for still

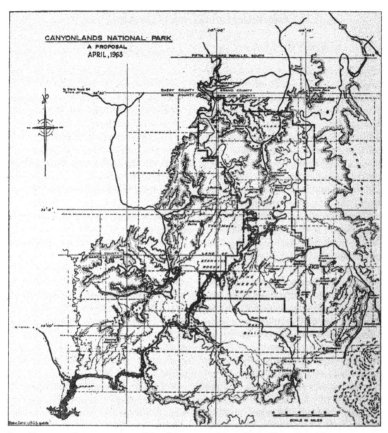

the distant views are possible, but now the Island In the Sky looms high above.

The drive into the Needles and further exploration on foot is a different experience. The rims are distant now, and the wildly-fashioned pinnacles and tortuous stream channels envelop the traveler. Here he will see and, with proper interpretation, understand the details of the physiography. This is country to camp in, to hike in, to see at sunset and at dawn. This is the land the

prehistoric Indians lived in. It touches the imagination as the traveler relates his experience to that of earlier people, and to forces that have formed the scene.

These canyons of Utah may well represent the Nation's last opportunity to establish a national park of the Yellowstone class—a vast area of scenic wonders and recreational opportunities unduplicated elsewhere in the world. They must be preserved for the enjoyment of all our people now and in the future.

Recent Publications

ACTION FOR OUTDOOR RECREA-
TION FOR AMERICA. Citizens Committee for the Outdoor Recreation Resources Review Commission Report,
1001 Connecticut Avenue, Washington,
D. C. 20036. 33 pp. Quantities of 10
or more, 10 cents each (including postage costs).

A digest of the report of ORRRC with
suggestions for citizen action, the booklet is intended to help citizens and
citizen organizations initiate outdoor
recreation programs and work responsibly with public officials to meet outdoor recreation needs in their communities and States. It offers suggestions for effective citizen action and
illustrates, with case histories, what can
be accomplished through local and
State action. Information contained in
the booklet can readily be used as source
material for speeches, panel discussions
and conference workshops.

THE PATIO HOUSE by William K.
Wittausch, Manager of Housing Re-
search, Stanford Research Institute,
edited by J. Ross McKeever, Associate
Director, Urban Land Institute. Urban
Land Institute, 1200 18th St., N.W.,
Washington 6, D. C. 1963. 37 pp. $5.00.

This most interesting presentation of
the L-shaped patio house, amply illustrated, will undoubtedly provide
welcome food for thought to those
facing the building of millions of additional housing units in metropolitan
areas in the coming decade.

What is the patio—or garden court
house? The report calls it "a brand
new idea, some 3,000 years old." Its
ancestry includes the Greek peristyle
and the Roman atrium. It is based on
lot line to lot line building of a house
on an urban plot with the family's
living being done around a garden
court.

The basic concept of the patio house,
presented by Mr. Wittausch, was the
winner in a German-sponsored architectural competition. It is an L-shaped,
single-family, single-story house designed by a young Swiss architect,
Armine Antes. Without basement,

attic, or stairs, it, nevertheless, is said
to provide maximum privacy in indoor
and outdoor living. Basically, the unit
is a square out of which one quarter is
cut for a wall-enclosed garden, leaving
the remaining "L" for the house.

The Urban Land Institute offers Mr.
Wittausch's design concept of the patio
house as a case study for a housing type
suitable to the needs of urban renewal
project planning. It commends the
study to the builder, developer, lender,
architect, planner, and public official for
their serious consideration.

It should also be of interest to those
who believe that the "row house"
leaves something to be desired.

Mr. Wittausch acknowledges contributions made by several people
toward the patio house concept as
presented in the bulletin. Among them
is Paul Oppermann, Executive Director, Northeastern Illinois Metropolitan
Area Planning Commission and a
member of the Board of Trustees of the
American Planning and Civic Association.

COMMUNITY DEVELOPMENT
SERIES: Seven pamphlets, each concerned with an important area of community concern, first published in 1960
but still of current interest. Construction and Civic Development Department, Chamber of Commerce of the
United States, 1615 H St., N.W., Washington 6, D. C. $3.00 per set; $.50 per
individual copy.

The pamphlets, each of which supplements the others, assume that existing
community organizations, with the right
kind of leadership and with improved
procedures, can find ways to develop
acceptable local solutions for even the
most difficult problems.

Subjects include: Balanced Community Development; Community Analysis;
Comprehensive Planning; Planning Urban Renewal Projects; Modernizing
Local Government; Financing Community Development; and Community
Leadership.

The initial pamphlet points out,
"The most successful community will be

the one which prevents problems from arising, not the one which produces the most adequate solutions for problems which have arisen."

Again, "No *standard* pattern of balanced community development can be created in a democratic country. Many different problem-solving devices must be employed to develop all the solutions which a complicated civilization must have."

The pamphlet on Planning states that comprehensive community planning can pay for itself many times if it prevents only a small percentage of possible mistakes in community development. It points out, however that no national or state pattern can be used without modification in a local planning program.

"In the formulation of a comprehensive planning program," says the pamphlet, "each locality is on its own. It has a particular geographic position and possesses natural resources different from those of any other place. There are different skills among its people. . . . It must try to formulate concrete objectives which take advantage of these unique attributes."

In calling Community Leadership, the "Key to Local Development," the final pamphlet in the series discusses the value of Community Development Teams as vitally important in citizen participation.

"Every community has an existing pattern of leadership," says the pamphlet. "But it is probably safe to say that every community has more resources for intelligent community leadership than have ever been mobilized and used to advantage."

Pointing out that, generally speaking, no one individual is in a position to solve community problems, the publication says that the individual's skills can be combined with those of other persons to help provide the answers. Mentioned as comprising the catalog of leadership, are engineers, architects, appraisers, bankers, lawyers, doctors, research workers, ministers, representatives of the press, radio and television and others.

And a largely over-looked reservoir of

talent is pointed out:

"In discussions of community leadership, the 'average' citizen is generally given little consideration. And yet, in a democracy, it is the great mass of people, to whom no one ordinarily looks for leadership, who possess the ultimate power. They must always be considered as a possible source of leadership."

A current check with the U. S. Chamber of Commerce indicates that this essentially readable series of pamphlets is still in large demand.

For those who have not already seen them, the pamphlets will undoubtedly be of interest—that is, if you believe the problems facing the American community today are such as to require nothing less than an open mind in the seeking of their solutions—and a receptiveness to all points of view.

PERTH AMBOY: BACKGROUND FOR PLANNING, by Herbert H. Smith Associates, Planning Consultants, 1241 Parkway Avenue, West Trenton, New Jersey. 65 pp. $4.50.

This is one of several planning reports on New Jersey municipalities, available from Herbert H. Smith Associates at prices ranging from $1.00 to $4.50.

A preface to the report states that it "identifies and comments on the problems of the City, none of which are peculiar to PerthyAmboy alone, but reflect the changing requirements of central cities."

Perth Amboy, which since the late 1600's has had a rich and colorful history, now stands at a turning point, it is pointed out.

Preparation of the document was financed, in part, through an Urban Planning Grant from the Housing and Home Finance Agency and, in part, by local funds and an appropriation of the State of New Jersey under the Expanded State and Regional Planning Program.

CONTROL OF HIGHWAY ACCESS by Ross D. Netherton. The University of Wisconsin Press, 114 North Murray Street, Madison 15, Wisconsin. 544 pp., 42 illus. $10.00.

(Continued on page 59)

58

American Planning and Civic Association
New Members, August 1, 1963 to November 1, 1963

District of Columbia
James G. Deane
Maryland
Francis T. Christy, Jr., Chevy Chase
Donald G. Shook, Silver Spring

Texas
Periodicals Department, Library, Texas
Tech. College, Lubbock

National Conference on State Parks
New Members, August 1, 1963 to November 1, 1963

District of Columbia
Walter S. Boardman
Michigan
Roman H. Koenings, Ann Arbor
Nevada
L. Dean Kastens, Carson City
New York
Joseph Verner Reed, Jr., New York City
Charles E. Rapp, Hartsdale
Ohio
W. E. Reinscheld, Hillsboro
Jack Steele, Pleasant Plain
Pennsylvania
John Sullivan, Rosemont
Peter W. Fletcher, State College
Tennessee
Edwin Dalstrom, Memphis
Kenneth H. Howard, Jr., Nashville
Donald M. McSween, Nashville

Texas
J. A. Ramsey, Bastrop
Doyle W. Clawson, Burnet
Jerome H. Tschauner, Canyon
Mrs. A. H. Zander, Denison
Doyle Taylor, Karnack
John C. Diggs, Pharr
Vermont
William J. Keogh, Burlington
Washington
Lt. Col. R. J. Reistroffer, Tacoma
Willis J. Hartman, Jr., Walla Walla
West Virginia
Mrs. Maxine Scarbro, Charleston
Canada
Henry J. Christian, Milliken, Ontario
H. C. McWilliams, Victoria, B. C.

RECENT PUBLICATIONS
(Continued from page 58)

In this book, the author analyzes the framework of statutes, cases and administrative law which has grown up around our policy of controlling highway access. Here, for the first time, the legal aspects of access control, as they relate to the principles and practices of planning, land acquisition, valuation and land-use regulation, are examined comprehensively.

A brochure, announcing the book's publication, calls it "an intensive study of legal issues which already have had a deep impact on the economic and social life of twentieth-century America and which must be resolved as we advance in the expressway era."

Watch Service Report

H. R. 9162 and Identical Bills H. R. 9163, H. R. 9164 and H. R. 9165, A New Version of the Wilderness Bill. Congressmen John D. Dingell (Mich.), Henry S. Reuss (Wisc.), Barrett O'Hara (Ill.), and Charles E. Bennett (Fla.), respectively. Referred to the House Committee on Interior and Insular Affairs.

Also, H. R. 9070, Another New Version of the Wilderness Bill. Congressman John P. Saylor (Pa.), ranking minority member of the House Committee on Interior and Insular Affairs. Referred to the House Committee on Interior and Insular Affairs.

The two new versions of the Wilderness Bill, both introduced in November, are similar and may provide the basis for breaking an apparent impasse over the establishment of a National Wilderness Preservation System.

One major difference relates to review of national forest areas presently classified as "primitive." H. R. 9162 would set up a ten-year period during which the primitive areas would be reviewed for possible reclassification as wilderness for inclusion in the National Wilderness Preservation System. H. R. 9070, in contrast, sets up a five-year period of review. However, both bills provide that these areas would be added to the wilderness system only when approved by Act of Congress. And both bills protect primitive areas in their present status during the period of review and until the Congress acts on classification.

Another major point of difference relates to the special provision on mining. Whereas H. R. 9070 allows for the gathering of information on mineral resources on national forest wilderness areas, H. R. 9162 maintains the status quo on mining for ten years but does not permit mining where not now allowed.

Both versions of the bill, in nearly identical provisions, would authorize the President to permit water developments, power projects, installation of transmission lines, and make other non-conforming uses of wilderness if in the best public interest. Grazing, where established, and hunting and fishing on areas now open are provided for in both proposals.

Purpose of the newly introduced versions is to break the deadlock on the Senate-passed S. 4 which has met with serious opposition in the House Interior and Insular Affairs Committee. The definition of wilderness in both the House versions is essentially the same as with S. 4 except that H. R. 9070 says an area of wilderness must be at least 5,000 acres in size.

All the bills include in the National Wilderness Preservation System those National Forest areas classified as "wilderness," "wild," and "canoe." Presently, there are 17 areas classified as "wilderness," including 6,409,284 acres; 32 "wild" areas, including 1,165,523 acres; and one "canoe" area, including 1,034,852 acres.

STATEMENT OF OWNERSHIP, MANAGEMENT, CIRCULATION, ETC. REQUIRED BY THE ACTS OF CONGRESS OF AUGUST 24, 1912, AND MARCH 3, 1933 OF PLANNING AND CIVIC COMMENT published quarterly, at Harrisburg, Pa. for October 1, 1963, Washington, D. C. as:

Before me, a Notary in and for the State and county aforesaid, personally appeared Donald B. Alexander, who, having duly sworn according to law, deposes and says that he is the Editor of PLANNING AND CIVIC COMMENT, and that the following is, to the best of his knowledge and belief, a true statement of the ownership, management, etc. of the aforesaid publication for the date shown in the above caption, required by the Act of August 24, 1912, as amended by the Act of March 3, 1933, embodied in section 537, Postal Laws and Regulations, printed on the reverse of this form, to wit:

1. That the names and addresses of the publisher, editor and business manager are: Publisher: American Planning and Civic Association and National Conference on State Parks, Inc., 901 Union Trust Building, Washington, D. C. 20005; Editor: Donald B. Alexander; Business Manager: None.

2. That the owner is: American Planning and Civic Association and National Conference on State Parks, Inc., 901 Union Trust Building, Washington, D. C. 20005.

3. That the known bondholders, mortgagees and other security holders owning or holding 1 percent or more of total amount of bonds, mortgages, or other securities: (If there are none, so state.) None.

Sworn to and subscribed before me this December 18, 1963.

Donald B. Alexander
(My commission expires Feb. 14, 1964)   Regina C. McGivern
Notary Public, Washington, D. C.

Planning and Civic Comment

Official Organ of American Planning and Civic Association and
National Conference on State Parks

*Selected Papers from the 43rd Annual
Meeting of the*

NATIONAL CONFERENCE ON STATE PARKS

HELD AS AN INTEGRAL PART OF THE FIRST JOINT
CONFERENCE OF
NATIONAL CONFERENCE ON STATE PARKS
AMERICAN INSTITUTE OF PARK EXECUTIVES
AMERICAN ASSOCIATION OF ZOOLOGICAL PARKS
AND AQUARIUMS

September 22-26, 1963

SHERATON PARK HOTEL
Washington, D. C.

National Conference on State Parks
901 Union Trust Building
Washington, D. C. 20005

DECEMBER, 1963

SUPPLEMENT—PART II

Planning and Civic Comment

Vol. 29   December, 1963   No. 4

43rd Annual Meeting of the National Conference on State Parks

The 43rd annual conference of the National Conference on State Parks, meeting jointly with the American Institute of Park Executives and the American Association of Zoological Parks and Aquariums, had as its theme, "State Parks, Their Past, Present and Future Role in Outdoor Recreation." Joint sessions of the participating organizations featured remarks by key government officials, Congressional leaders and some of the Nation's leading civic leaders. Among them were Vice-President Lyndon Johnson, Secretary of the Interior Stewart L. Udall and Secretary of Commerce Luther H. Hodges. Others were Robert C. Weaver, Administrator, Housing and Home Finance Agency; Rex M. Whitton, Federal Highway Administrator, Bureau of Public Roads; William L. Slayton, Commissioner, Urban Renewal Administration; Jennings Randolph, U. S. Senator from West Virginia; and Laurance S. Rockefeller, Chairman of the Outdoor Recreation Resources Review Commission, which submitted its highly regarded report to the President in January, 1962. Remarks of the principal speakers at the joint sessions were released to the press at the time of the Conference. The following selection of papers, arranged according to program sequence, has been limited to ones presented at those Conference sessions specifically designated for National Conference on State Park members. We regret that we are unable to include the excellent statement on "Natural Areas in State Parks" by Richard H. Pough, at the September 23 afternoon session, due to our inability to obtain a transcript of his remarks.

The same is true of Charles A. DeTurk, Director of the California State Department of Parks and Recreation, who was one of the principal speakers at the September 24 panel on "Growing Pains In State Parks" and of Thomas W. Morse, Regional Chief of the National Park Service Planning Service who moderated this interesting session.

Report and Message of the President

By
Earl P. Hanson

THE REPORT

Members and friends of The National Conference on State Parks: I welcome you to the 43rd annual conference of this organization being held jointly with the 65th annual conference of the American Institute of Park Executives and the American Association of Zoological Parks and Aquariums.

It is fitting that this "Parks and Recreation for America" conference, be held in the Nation's Capital, primarily because of the national scope of the recreation program and the needs of the Nation's citizens for adequate park and recreation planning. Being the seat of government, the Nation's Capital also permits us to meet with national leaders in the field. For this, we are both proud and thankful.

This is perhaps the greatest gathering of lay and executive park personnel ever to come together at one time and in one place, not only to enjoy a setting, which is the national Capital, but to coordinate our thinking in planning for the outdoor recreational needs of the multitudes of Americans who are seeking an experience in the out-of-doors which might otherwise be denied to them.

We can be proud of The National Conference in having one of our members, the Chairman of our Board of Directors, Mr. Edward J. Meeman, selected as a member of the National Parks Advisory Board by Secretary Udall of the Department of the Interior. We also take pride in the fact that one of our long-time members, for many years a Director of The Conference, Mr. Joseph Kaylor of Maryland, has been selected to fill a key post in the Bureau of Outdoor Recreation. Our own Charles A. DeTurk of California has been appointed to the Citizens' Committee for the Outdoor Recreation Resources Review Commission Report; Ray Mitchell of Iowa has advanced into the Corps of Engineers under our own Matt Huppuch. There are undoubtedly others, including Roman Koenings and Wilbur Rush of The Conference who have been allied with programs of national significance. We are proud to have them on our membership rolls.

Our able secretary, Mr. Donald Alexander, National Membership Secretary, has been dealing effectively with the business of The Conference under the adverse circumstances in which we find our finances and relationship with the American Planning and Civic Association. He will report to you on the details.

The Park Practice Committee, under Vic Flickinger, continues to do an able job and has greatly expanded its coverage under the executive direction of Ira Lykes, Chief of Park Practice. The Conference must give more nearly adequate financial support to the Park Practice in order to retain sponsorship of this fine program.

I especially wish to commend the Program Committee under the able chairmanship of Ben H. Bolen, who has successfully coordinated this Conference with that of the American Institute of Park Executives. His committee has been a hard-working one and, under Ben's leadership, has put together a well coordinated program that permits The National Conference to hold its own sessions concurrently with the joint sessions of both groups. I know also that Mr. Alexander has done a lot of hard work in connection with the arrangements and he has loaned us the services of Mrs. Alexander for coordinating the activities of the wives and other women attending the Conference.

I am grateful for the inspired leadership of Chairman Meeman who is making a particularly strong effort to lead a membership program that will create a greater interest in The Conference and to the effective financial support of it.

We are looking forward to the next annual meeting to be held in New Jersey, under the Program Chairmanship of Joseph Truncer. I am hereby appointing to serve with him, the following:

Joseph A. Blatt, Pennsylvania
Harold J. Dyer, New York
Peter Geldof, Delaware
Russell Myers, New Jersey
William Parr, Maryland
Ralph Wheatley, Ontario, Canada

EARL P. HANSON, President

THE MESSAGE

High on the arid, white mountains of California, gnarled, wind-twisted ghosts of the forest stretch their bony, wooden fingers to the sky. At the 12,000-ft. level, in the barren, rocky wilderness referred to as California's "Arctic" lies the home of the World's oldest living things, the bristle-cone pine trees.

The 4,000-year-old battered derelicts resembling living driftwood still possess a lifeline of bark-covered growing tissue, and have the ability to produce cones. The fact that there is so little tissue to nourish explains their longevity.

Blockaded by the snow-covered Sierra-Nevada range, the bristle-cone pines have continued to struggle for survival by clinging to the rocky cliffs. Actually, the desert-like white mountains were in existence long before the Sierra Nevada, which emerged later and now restricts the moist winds blowing from the west. The great forest which formerly covered the white mountains retreated to the uttermost peaks where the unusual stunted 50-ft. pine trees seem to barely survive. Yet, they have survived—some individual specimens for a period of 4,000 years or more—and there they are for Man to see.

(continued on page 32)

The Birth of State Parks

By S. HERBERT EVISON, former Executive Secretary,
National Conference on State Parks

When Ben Bohlen invited me to talk at this meeting, he asked me to discuss some such subject as "State Parks up to the Beginning of World War II." Recently, I found out my subject was "The Birth of State Parks." However much appearances may be against me, I hasten to assure you at the outset that I was not the attending physician at that birth. However, I was present at the organization meeting of this Conference and a member of its resolutions committee, of which Dr. Henry Chandler Cowles of the University of Chicago was chairman. I remember well a few things about that conference that are—I think —interesting enough to mention here today.

We were welcomed to Iowa by Governor Harding—no relation, so far as I know, of the other Harding who had just been elected President. I remember two points he made. One reflected somewhat the public attitude of that day—that people who got themselves all worked up about saving some of the native American landscape were a little "touched in the head." The Governor made some remark to the effect that he had been expecting a gathering of long-haired men and short-haired women, or vice versa; he seemed relieved that, in appearance anyway, the group to whom he was talking were just ordinary every-day Americans.

Also, the Governor flattered us all. "You are all experts on state parks," he told us. He then kindly defined an expert as "an ordinary man away from home;" and how truly he spoke of most of us then present!

All of you must know that the sparkplug of that first gathering was Stephen T. Mather who had then been director of the National Park Service for less than three years. It has often been said that he was interested in state parks primarily because they offered a means of easing pressures to get areas of less than national significance into the National Park System. However, I am certain that that was a secondary consideration. I knew Mr. Mather well; I know that he was profoundly concerned with seeing many good samples of the American landscape—desert, mountain, forest, lake, and stream—set aside and safeguarded and put to beneficial use. He gave time and effort and money and deep devotion to the state park movement.

Not long ago, Horace Albright—another survivor of the Des Moines meeting—reminded me that Oze Van Wyck, living in retirement in Puerto Rico, had been Mather's advance agent and arranger of the first national gathering of people interested in state parks.

Mr. Van Wyck kindly gave me a brief roundup of the part he played more than 43 years ago. His account began with his meeting Mr. Mather in Yellowstone in 1920, while he was serving there as a seasonal ranger— a 90-day wonder—and very successfully handling publicity for the park. (Van Wyck had worked for the Associated Press before and after World

War I.) Mather was impressed; later he had Van Wyck represent the National Park Service on a tour of the National Park-to-Park Highway. Then Mather asked him to come to Chicago. This was late in 1920. Mr. Van Wyck writes:

In Chicago, Mr. Mather arranged a meeting of key men, apparently old friends, who were active in civic undertakings. He thought the time had come to promote the creation of state parks, a statement he supported with the following argument:

National Parks, complemented by the smaller and less important national monuments, had been set aside to preserve many of the famous scenic and historical areas of the United States. It was his opinion that the truly great sites such as Yellowstone and Yosemite, Grand Canyon and Mount Rainier, had . . . . been taken over by the United States as public trusts. I think he stated outright that there were no sites in the East and South deserving of national park status . . . .

He said the country should create parks for rest and recreation in every state, to preserve some of the original wilderness for future generations and to provide outdoor places easily accessible to families who did not have time or money for an expensive trip to the Far West. It was his opinion that this was work for the States . . . . and he proposed that the conference to be held should effect an organization of such prestige that it would command attention from State officials and draw support from citizens who could afford to help in this movement . . . . .

Mr. Mather proposed Des Moines as the meeting place because of Iowa's fine record of establishing State parks. All of those at the meeting pledged money, not large sums but sufficient to start the work. I was employed by Mr. Mather who paid me $300 a month and my expenses. I left almost immediately for Des Moines.

In Des Moines, I met the Governor and he kindly gave me working space in the state historical building. The Curator, Dr. Harlan, a man of high intelligence, cultured and energetic, spared no effort to make the conference a success.

Organization of the conference was largely routine correspondence. We had to address all organizations and individuals from whom we wanted support. This involved compiling a list of mountaineering clubs, outdoor societies, and even the Garden Club of America . . . . whose individual members have a consciousness of the need of preserving wide open spaces for the public. We were also in contact with college professors who were advocating parks to keep species of flora and fauna from extinction. Fishing and hunting organizations were included for obvious reasons. Chambers of commerce were asked to send delegates from cities where tourist travel was desired. In short, no group was overlooked. Response was excellent. The prestige of Mr. Mather's name and position carried great weight. A formal invitation in the name of the governor of Iowa gave the proposed meeting official standing . . . . .

Woodrow Wilson had recently suffered a severe paralytic stroke and was believed to be transacting no business except to nod or shake his head when addressed. Nevertheless, we were able to get a letter on White House stationery endorsing the proposed conference and urging support of its work. It was signed "Woodrow Wilson" in perfect letter, but was evidently the best rubber stamp ever made.

Meetings were held at Hotel Fort Des Moines and the banquet took place there. I remember two members of the National Park Service who were there—Loy Miller who gave his famous recital of bird calls at the banquet, and H. S. Bryant, another naturalist . . . . Of course, Mr. Mather was one of the main attractions as he outlined the purposes of the conference.

Here ends Mr. Van Wyck's account. I spent an hour at Dr. Bryant's home in Orinda, California, last October, and I believe Dr. Loy Holmes Miller is also still living. I have a distinct remembrance of another still living person who was present; I have special reason to remember.

The morning of the last day of the meeting was unusual in that the program was moving ahead of itself. Realizing that there was going to be some time to spare, I slipped a note to Everett Millard, a Chicago attorney who was presiding, suggesting that he call on the representative of the Forest Service who was present. In due time he did so; and Arthur H. Carhart, then employed to plan recreational facilities in the national forests, gave a brief but good talk on the Forest Service's activities in this field. That was followed by the only real wrangle of the meeting. Mather, who had had his troubles with the Forest Service, rose to criticise its venture into providing recreational facilities; Dr. Frederick Bade, of the Pacific School of Religion, seconded his criticism. Dr. Cowles made a calm and excellent reply to the criticism and the temperature shortly returned to normal. A resolution passed by the conference strongly urged the use of public forests for recreation.

Certain personalities remain vividly in my memory at this distance. One was Peter Norbeck, just elected to the United States Senate after a term as governor of South Dakota, during which one of his proudest accomplishments was the establishment of Custer State Park. It was my good fortune to have many pleasant contacts with him in later years and up to his death. He was for many years a member of the Conference's board of directors.

Another was Mrs. Henry Frankel, whose memory I am sure is still bright—as is that of her husband—with many of you. I have a very vivid memory of Mrs. Frankel in action again in Des Moines, 14 years after the 1921 meeting; she was then chairman of the Iowa Conservation Commission. Friction between the Iowa state parks office and the National Park Service's district officer called for some frank discussion in Des Moines in which I represented Connie Wirth's ECW organization in Washington. The calm, intelligent way in which Mrs. Frankel handled the day's discussions occasioned a remark by somebody that she "was one of the best state park men in the business."

Mrs. Frankel was more responsible than anyone else, I am sure, for the fact that the 1931 Iowa legislature authorized a state park and recreation survey, on which Jacob L. Crane, assisted by George Wheeler Olcott, did a fine job.

That recalls that the first real state park survey seems to have been the one conducted in 1910 by John Nolen for the State of Wisconsin; that Albert M. Turner did an informal sort of survey job—but a very discerning one—for the State of Connecticut during his early days as field secretary of the Connecticut Forest and Park Commission; and that one of the most notable surveys in state park history was the one conducted in 1927 and 1928 by Frederick Law Olmsted. To me, Mr. Olmsted's report on this California survey, with its carefully worded criteria for selection of state parks and its perceptive appraisal of the areas recommended for state parkhood, is one of the classics of State park literature.

Of course, passage of the Park, Parkway, and Recreation Area Study Act in 1936 and the fortunate availability of CCC funds and personnel brought on state park and recreation area studies pretty much all over the United States. I think I am justified here in mentioning the 1935 report on "Recreational Use of Land in the United States," prepared by a committee of which George M. Wright was chairman; in putting it together he had the highly qualified assistance of L. H. Weir, of the National Recreation Association, and Roger W. Toll, then superintendent of Yellowstone. In somewhat the same category in pioneering overall treatment of park and recreation requirements is "A Study of the Park and Recreation Problem of the United States," prepared in 1941. Professor Jack Wagar of Colorado State University told me two or three years ago that this is still much used by his students in Forest Recreation.

In this year 1963, state parks are a pretty firmly established feature of American life. Before 1921 and for many years after 1921, this was certainly not so. Advocates of the establishment of state parks, of their proper development, and of competent, trained administration were in many places voices crying in a wilderness. Pleas to legislators for funds with which to buy park lands while they could still be bought at a reasonable price or while they were still worth buying more often than not fell on deaf ears. There were not many Governor-Al-Smith-and-Robert-Moses combinations able to persuade legislators and voters to approve bond issues of millions of dollars with which to make such purchases.

The early days of state park history are replete with stories of the difficulties faced by those who sought to save the Palisades of the Hudson; of the almost heart-breaking but ultimately successful campaign, in which Mrs. Juliet Strauss and Col. Richard Lieber were devoted and tireless workers and leaders, for the acquisition of land for Indiana's Turkey Run State Park; of the campaign that Lieber put on, mostly in Chicago, for money with which to buy Indiana Dunes State Park; of the bitter, almost violent, campaign to induce the state of Kentucky, by legislative action, to accept Senator Coleman DuPont's offer to give Cumberland Falls and its surroundings to the state. Those were days in which Governor Hartley of Washington could calmly permit the parks of that state to go through two years without a cent of appropriations.

After the 1929 meeting of the Conference at Clifty Falls, when the Cumberland Falls battle was at its height, I had the late Tom Wallace as my passenger, in the spavined and gaseous old Dodge coupe I was then driving, from Tom's home outside Louisville down to Cumberland Falls. We approached it from the west and had to be ferried across the river by rowboat a few hundred yards above the falls to get to the old Moonbow Inn where we spent the night. The Dodge was left overnight in the front yard of a mountain farm. Next day, when I got back across the river, I found scratched in its hard enamel finish with chalk the message, "To hell with the park, let's build the dam." Thanks more than anything else to the persistent campaign that Tom Wallace was permitted to wage through the columns of the *Louisville Times*, Cumberland Falls was one thing that the then well-nigh all-powerful Insull interests didn't get.

Notable in the history of state park planning is the fact that, early in his years as head of the Indiana Department of Conservation, Richard Lieber worked out a very basic principle of development which was truly a conservation principle, too. The core of the idea was this: Find a place where, without damaging any outstanding features of your park, you can put your picnic grounds and campgrounds—it took the Colonel a long time to realize that the two should be separate—your playfields, your hotels (if any), your service facilities of one kind or another, not unnecessarily spread out over the landscape but in proper relation to one another; bring your road to this service area and stop it there. People— especially Americans, perhaps—are gregarious; so most of the park visitors—I believe his figure was 85 percent of them—will never wander far beyond the service area. Thus, they will put no pressure, no wear and tear on the greater part of the park which will remain beautiful for the enjoyment of those willing to exert themselves a little to discover its beauties.

For the past 30 years, I have felt that it was fortunate that Connie Wirth, the man made responsible for directing State Park Emergency Conservation Work, had both training and experience in park planning; that he was sufficiently aware of the necessity of it that he found landscape architects and architects and engineers for the central offices and for the corps of inspectors who kept a check on work performance; and that he saw to it that central design offices were provided for those park agencies which had not established their own and which did not have the funds with which to do so.

Of course, the other side of the coin was that at that time there were many people in those three professions who were profoundly thankful for the opportunity thus offered to earn their bread and butter. As far as the landscape architects were concerned, it was probably the best thing that ever happened to the profession. The men in it were then largely accustomed to dealing with the estates of wealthy men or with the more formal aspects of city park work or with planning and directing the construction of golf courses, even with the planning of cemeteries. Certainly, the need of their kind of training in connection with developments laid upon the natural landscape and adjusted to the landscape rather than making it over, must have become apparent to many of them and have broadened their conception of the usefulness of their profession.

In his wonderful book on state parks, Freeman Tilden reminded his readers of the devotion and drive and imagination and generosity of many men and women who have helped make state park history. He has them on the record, and I don't propose to crib from Freeman. Rather I think this is perhaps a suitable occasion to mention some others who belong in the Hall of Fame. Included on my list are several women, of whom I have already named two—Mrs. Frankel and Mrs. Straus—with admiration. I want to add Mrs. Emma Guy Cromwell who, wholly new to state parks when appointed director of those in Kentucky, had the fine sense to look to experts for advice and to use them in connection with the conduct of Emergency Conservation Work; also Mrs. M. E. Judd of Dalton, Georgia, who put life into the movement for state parks in that state.

The advocates of scientific forestry got a head start on state park advocates in many states. As parks did get a start, they were often entrusted to state foresters. Fortunately, they were serious and competent men; I think of F. W. Besley of Maryland, C. P. Wilber of New Jersey, J. S. Holmes of North Carolina, H. A. Smith of South Carolina, Ed Secrest of Ohio, and, dating from way back when, C. L. Harrington of Wisconsin. Few people—even few Ohioans, I suspect—realize today that Ed Secrest was responsible for the acquisition of land for some of the finest of Ohio's state parks.

In the long-term history of state parks, it seems to me that the name of Percy J. (better known as Pete) Hoffmaster of Michigan, superintendent of state parks and later conservation director, will have an honored place. So, for different reasons, will Bob Burson, who managed to come up with six good state parks in Virginia in time to have the CCC start to work on them right from the start; so will Tom Cheek, who did much the same thing for the State of West Virginia.

On the New York rolls, belong, in my book, the names of Carl Crandall, who so long guided the destinies of the Finger Lakes state parks; of Robert H. Treman, chairman of the Finger Lakes Commission and donor of two of the loveliest of the parks in that region—Buttermilk Falls and Enfield Glen; and Jim Evans, who was director of state parks for so long most folks have forgotten that earlier he was in charge of the Central New York state parks. Mention of Jim reminds me that, in the early days of the CCC, we decided the Corps would not build golf courses. In the many categories of work on which reports were required were two called "Seeding and Sodding" and "Landscaping Undifferentiated." There was lots of this during the early days of the CCC from two of the Central New York parks. Ultimately it all added up to two golf courses.

In much of the midwest and southwest, there is solidity and fitness for the region and the surrounding landscape in scores of structures built in state parks during the CCC. Many architects produced the designs, yet on them the influence of Herbert Maier rests strongly, as it does on many national park buildings. One of the great beneficiaries of the Maier style of architecture was the State of Texas and the Texas State Parks Board when the CCC began. I remember that three camps of World War I veterans were assigned at the start to Texas' Palo Duro State Park; I remember, too, that after two or three periods of work there, Connie Wirth and I became aware of the fact that all of Palo Duro was subject to a tremendous mortgage, which just might be defaulted, with the distinct possibility that the mortgage holder might foreclose on land on which Uncle Sam had provided a couple of million dollars worth of development—whereupon we required Dave to get unencumbered deeds to all the land on which the work had been performed.

Many years ago, I went to Arkansas to look over a park lodge which bore the imprint of Herb Maier; that was at Petit Jean State Park, a truly first-class monument to the devotion of a country doctor, T. W. Hardison.

This is more of a roll call than I intended calling, but I cannot fail to mention the ebullient Sam Brewster of Tennessee and Harold Lathrop, who made a state park system of the Minnesota parks of which he had charge for so many years.

What a wonderful lot of people they have been—those I have named and such other diverse and devoted people as Sam Boardman, Major Welch, Newton Drury, Beatrice Ward Nelson, Harlean James, Ellwood Chapman, Will Carson, Madison Grant, Dr. John C. Merriam, Jay Downer, John D. Rockefeller, Jr., Capt. Charles G. Sauers, another survivor of that 1921 conference. Most of them I have known, many of them I have known well—and what a priceless privilege that has been. Probably my richest memories are of Richard Lieber.

And I am reminded of the time, early in the CCC, when I accompanied the Colonel down to the coast of Georgia where what were reputed to be the ruins of the Santo Domingo Mission had been deeded to the State to become a state park. We wanted Colonel Lieber's advice as to how to handle and protect what was left of the ancient structure. The Colonel, Doc. Gadsby (then a CCC inspector), Mrs. Judd and a young archeologist, named James Ford, and I were all week-end guests of the late Cator Woolford, donor of the property, at his fine home nearby.

We all duly inspected the ruined structure, and on Sunday morning in Mr. Woolford's living room, all of us solemnly offered our views as to how to protect it and display it. All of us, that is, but one; the young archeologist was silent until, after everybody else had had his or her say, he was asked for his opinion. (I should have mentioned that he had been on ground for some time before our arrival, examining the ruins and endeavoring to obtain historical data about it.) I can remember few more embarrassing moments than the one in which he announced his profound—and I might say well supported—conviction that our ancient mission was in fact a ruined, and much younger, sugar mill.

I am afraid it took some Georgians a longer time than it took us to accept the rather disconcerting truth. If there is any moral to this at all, it would seem to be, "Leave history to the historians and archeologists; it may save you embarrassment." And thank you for listening.

Growing Pains in State Parks

By THOMAS J. NELSON, Director of Planning, Kentucky State
Department of Parks

The discussion of the growing pains in state parks should make everyone who has been in park work from the period of 1946 to the present,
flinch in memory of their own individual growing pains. As one looks
back, a similarity is noted between the periods of growth in children and in
parks. Growth does not usually occur at a consistent rate but in spurts.
The first big spurt in state park growth was, of course, in the years of the
CCC. After this initial growth many of the southern and eastern states
did very little until after the end of World War II. The war years and the
lack of materials accounted for this, plus the fact that many of the southern States with which I am more familiar did not have the financial ability nor the inclination to develop and improve what they already had.
But, with the close of the war a great change occurred.

Probably never before had so many families moved hither and yon a-
cross the country, both in war work and in following husbands from camp
to camp. This opened their eyes to the wonders of this country and whet-
ted appetites for more leisurely travel when the war was over. On top of
this came the ever shorter work week, longer vacations and more money
for spending on things other than necessities. The shorter week made possible long week-end vacations to nearby parks where available.

Since the East and South had a larger proportion of this itchy footed
population, they were hard pressed to take care of it all at once. This accounted for the expanded state park growth during the period 1948 to
1952 in Tennessee, Kentucky and Oklahoma, followed by the phenomenal
growth in West Virginia.

In 1950 the South and East had 925 State Park Areas with an acreage
of 3,507,338. By 1960 this had grown to 1,221 areas totalling 3,882,090
acres. Areawise this growth compares favorably with a national acreage
of 4,657,155 in 1950 and 5,497,278 in 1960. However, let us not relax in
the effort to acquire additional lands while they are available and comparatively unspoiled.

There is a natural tendency in discussing this topic to relate a long
string of dates and events and stuff the audience with statistics. I hope I
have conquered this impulse since a repeat of history to those who have
gone through it is often boring. Most of you have either lived through
this period as Park Administrators or as interested friends and champions
of parks. You all know of the tremendous growth in recreation and the demands thus placed on state parks. While the primary purpose of state
parks remains the same—that is the preservation of outstanding state
areas—the greatest change is in the activity use by park visitors.

No longer do families vacation by sitting in rocking chairs on resort hotel verandas and leisurely playing croquet and bathing (not swimming)
in all-concealing suits both for men and women—but instead every member

of the family from the young to the grandmothers want active participation in numerous sorts of endeavors.

Several years ago I wrote an article for the magazine "Landscape Architecture" in which I described the apparent paradox of park visitors who would not walk more than 100 feet from a parking area to a cottage or picnic table, yet who would play 27 holes of golf and water ski all day with no thought of the energy expended. I did not mean to bring out in this article that I wholeheartedly approved of all the changes in park use and that I did not wholeheartedly uphold the basic concept for the preservation and enjoyment of true state park areas. I am sure I missed putting my ideas across to all, as Tom Wallace really castigated me with a fiery editorial, while at the same time and in the same paper, Grady Clay reprinted the article with a good review. In any event I still maintain that our parks growth should be influenced more by the change in the user participation than is often the case. But, please do not relax the need for a greater and greater acquisition of open spaces and the preservation of the natural scene as much as possible.

One hears and reads of the necessity for people to experience the out-of-doors, and with this I heartily agree. But—does this mean that this experience should be the same as that of the pioneers? Should our camp grounds not be equipped with modern, sanitary facilities? Just because Daniel Boone went unwashed for weeks at a time is no reason for me to do the same. The *Modus Operandi* of outdoor life changes and the evolution of our park development changes with it.

This experience is to me really the visual enjoyment of natural beauty, the sound of tumbling water and the ever changing sky. But I can just as easily enjoy this on a well designed golf course as I can hiking along a trail. However, I realize that there are some, and God bless them, who need the rugged wilderness or the wilderness areas adjacent to the developed areas of a park. I will paraphrase Voltaire in saying that although I may not wish to participate the same as they, I defend their desire to do so. It behooves all Park Administrators, planners and laymen alike to see that parks are maintained and developed and protected so that the legitimate desires of all park users can be attained.

Probably the most important impetus to recent park growth and one which caused several growing pains is the remarkable growth of the system of reservoirs all over the country. These brought large water areas to portions of this land which never had seen anything larger than a barnyard pond.

It made millions of persons water conscious and eager to engage in water sports. So—the corps of engineers and others who built such reservoirs were turned into recreation developers. Then they learned that states would readily accept areas along the water for parks. The increase in the total number of park areas from 1950 to the present is in great part due to the acceptance of such areas for state parks. And, may I say here, I am grateful that the corps has changed its acquisition policy to be broader in concept and allowing for purchase of better recreation space around these reservoirs. Large water areas certainly attract a larger number of park users than state parks without them.

The public is outdoor minded and increasing numbers flock to parks simply to get out of hum-drum city life. In order to protect parks of outstanding scenic value from over-use, many states have turned to the establishment of so-called State Recreation Areas located strategically about the state to take the load off of the true state parks. We cannot sacrifice irreplaceable scenery to serve the public's unthinking demands. The tempo of our life has so speeded up that sedentary recreation is soon boring. The public's appreciation of nature has not changed but merely his ability to take it in big doses without a more lively chaser.

Growing pains have also made themselves felt by a change in park facilities. I realize that some of you possibly do not agree with Kentucky's philosophy of park development, yet I believe that the yearly increase in visitation and the comments of not only the public but of many officials from other states will bear out our plan. Lodge and cottage design has changed from cramped, overly simple quarters to comfortable, modern and even luxurious facilities. This again goes back to what I said previously —our experiences are evolving and growing. I do not intend to get into a debate right now over this facet of growth except to say that it is a fact and one which I believe has had a great deal to do with increased park visitation and the pains that accompany it.

Colonel Lieber recognized the struggle going on—he knew there was a need for places for physical relaxation and activity. But, as Freeman Tilden so aptly pointed out, he did not want that to be the sole or even paramount requirement.

One of the reasons for some of our sharp growing pains has been the difficulty in defining the difference (if any) between park and recreation areas and the value to place on each one. This is a subject that I am sure could throw the entire panel into a heated discussion, but it is one that must be faced and somehow each state must make up its own mind on its own criteria.

My good friend "Cap" Sauers once remarked that neither State nor National Parks are in the tourist business, but that they are responsible for preserving the areas of a great cultural factor essential to our well being. I am sure that "Cap" as well as the rest of us realize that both systems are now in business and it is this influx of tourists that has really caused our growing pains.

In conclusion, I think that the most significant growing pains have been felt by those dedicated and determined park people who have recognized the shift in trends and have through hard work, readjustment of values and judicious and fair compromise, come up with the really fine park systems we are enjoying today.

The Challenge of the Future

By EDWARD J. MEEMAN, Chairman of the Board,
National Conference on State Parks

This is the 43rd year of the National Conference on State Parks.

It was in January, 1921 that about 200 conservationists met in Des Moines, Iowa, on the invitation of Gov. W. L. Harding and formed this organization. The instigator of the organization was Stephen Mather, creative director of the National Parks, who wanted to relieve the burgeoning national parks of the pressure brought by those who wanted their areas made into national parks; the new national parks were so popular that every state wanted a national park. Mr. Mather did not look at the situation only from the standpoint of the national parks; he was no less concerned for the states themselves. The nation could not, or at least would not, acquire even all the areas of admitted grandeur and national stature; the states in their own self-interest had better set aside with their own funds their scenic natural areas that did not become national parks.

We look back to a rewarding past of great accomplishment and forward to a challenging future, which demands greater accomplishment and the greater strength the bigger job calls for.

We are told by Freeman Tilden, author of that authoritative and fascinating book, "The State Parks, Their Meaning in American Life," that when Stephen Mather read the roster of state parks at that first conference at Des Moines there were 29 states that had no parks at all. California, the state of our president, a state which has been outstanding in its progress and now has 180 parks, at that time had only one!

Today there are about 2,800 state parks, and every state sees the need of adding to some of its parks and creating new ones.

Voltaire said that "If God did not exist, it would be necessary to invent him." Since the state parks have come to have such a large and important place in the life and government of the states, if this Conference did not exist, it would be necessary for the states to create a national organization of and for the state parks like this one.

So the only question before us is how do we meet the need that exists for our existence. How do we fulfill the destiny to which we were called back there in 1921 at Des Moines?

What are today's needs, what are the challenging demands of the future, which we must meet?

We face the pressures and demands of a rapidly growing population. It is estimated that the population of the United States, 180,000,000 in 1960, will have reached about 210,000,000 by 1970, an increase of 30,000,000, and that it will have more than doubled by the year 2000.

We must get more land, and get it now. I often quote, and this rich and homely wisdom can't be quoted too often, what was said by the grandfather of Jack Strain, our vice-president, who got a land grant from President Chester A. Arthur in 1884 and pushed west in a covered wagon. This is the advice he gave Jack when Jack was a little boy:

"Put your money in land, Boy, 'cause they ain't makin' that any more."

But I also like to quote Laurance Rockefeller, who declares that land acquisition is not enough, that sufficient funds for protection, maintenance and development of facilities should also be provided.

There are so many fruitless arguments as to which of two good things should be had. Most of them can be settled by saying not "either . . . or" but "both . . . and." Let us not spend too much time arguing whether the greater need is for more land acquisition or for maintenance and development. We need both, the need is present and immediate, and it will take a lot of money to meet both needs.

We can more profitably spend our time discussing: How do we get the money?

To get the money we need greater public support. To get greater public support we need more members in this Conference.

I suggest that the best way to get the members for our national organization is to have a state parks association functioning vigorously in every state.

The best way to build a state parks organization is to have a citizens' state parks committee working in every community that is close to a state park.

These citizens need to be informed as to what a state park is, how it should be used, and what its needs from government are.

But it is not only these organized supporters who should have this understanding—the whole public should have it.

These committees, and the state parks association which together they would form, can be of immense effectiveness in obtaining that public understanding.

In developing such organization, who knows what now unknown citizen conservationist we may not discover—what Theodore Roosevelt, what Ding Darling, what Tom Wallace, what Harlean James, what Horace Albright, what Laurance Rockefeller—you name your favorite citizen conservationist whom I have not named.

Tennessee has adopted one way. It may be the easiest and best way that citizens can be enlisted to form such park organizations. I have this letter from Donald McSween, Commissioner of Conservation:

Mr. Edward J. Meeman
Chairman of the Board,
National Conference on State Parks
Memphis Press Scimitar
Memphis, Tennessee

Dear Mr. Meeman:

We, in the Tennessee Department of Conservation, and particularly in our Division of State Parks, are becoming more and more aware of the value of citizens' organizations supporting these public facilities.

It has been my observation that, where a wide-awake, alert and aggressive group is organized for the purpose of promoting the best interest of a specific park, there we have a good park. It would be of untold value to us to have such an organization behind each of the twenty-one parks in the Tennessee system.

Toward this end, I am instructing our superintendents and the personnel under them in each of Tennessee's parks to make note of the names and addresses of visitors to their areas who express particular enthusiasm. These will be forwarded to me; and, from such lists, I hope we can obtain the nucleus for strong, local organizations dedicated to the development and expansion of our individual parks.

I shall also see that you and the National Conference on State Parks are furnished the names of these interested parties, so that you may invite them to join your organization and take part from that level in our mutual effort to promote these areas.

Sincerely,
Donald M. McSween

We need nature study not only in elementary schools but in secondary schools and colleges. We need adult education in nature. We need nature trails, both self-guided and naturalist guided, for these nature students to use and enjoy.

A school system might be persuaded to adopt this economical and effective way of conducting nature trips: Buy or lease a bus especially for the purpose. Put a teacher, preferably a science teacher, in charge as teacher-driver. This bus would be engaged by a certain class for a certain day. Soon its calendar for the school year would be full, and there might be a demand for a second bus with a second teacher-driver. In the bad weather the bus could take classes to plants to study industrial processes. Such a teacher-driver would learn so much, as well as teach, that his value to the school system would constantly increase and he would advance professionally.

Youngsters taken on such guided tours in their school days would learn the golden rule for visitors to natural areas, as it was stated by the sportsman-conservationist John Burnham:

"Take nothing out—leave nothing in."

We would be training recruits to be the future members of citizens' organizations to support conservationists.

We would be planting in some young minds and hearts the desire for a professional career in conservation, park or recreation work.

And how we need them!

Louis F. Twardzik, who teaches the course in Park and Recreation Administration which is offered by Michigan State University at Lansing, says that the demand for graduates has consistently been greater than the supply.

Can citizens alone do the job the National Conference on State Parks must do to meet the challenge of the future? No, indeed! It can be done only through the combined efforts of citizens, experts, officials, board members and park directors working together, in unison, working very closely, very intimately together.

The park directors! I salute them. They are the very heart of this Conference, this organization. Our very life depends on them.

We citizens, we laymen, can understand why the park directors want an organization of their own, and we are glad they now have one. They have problems and concerns peculiarly and intimately their own which they should discuss and act on by themselves. But I trust they will always meet at the same time and place as this Conference. No matter how well we may succeed in getting increased appropriations for the state parks, there will never be enough to buy all the additional land we need, to get the additional facilities we need, to get the additional personnel we need, to give the salary raises to present personnel which they have earned and should have—there will never be any money to waste. And so the states should not have to pay expenses of travelling across the country twice, once for an all-parks conference and once for a park directors meeting.

As Robert Goodloe Harper, who was, like the chairman of this session, a distinguished citizen of South Carolina, said in 1798, in defiance of revolutionary France, "Millions for defense, but not a cent for tribute," we say, millions for improvements in our parks and benefits to personnel, but not one cent for waste.

How should we finance this Conference, this organization?

I think that the basic financial support, sufficient to assure that it can always exist, can always function well enough to justify its existence, should come from the states, who should regard its existence and functioning as indispensable.

States are not equal in financial resources, and so it would not be right to assess all states equally. Some formula must be devised to make the assessment as nearly as possible in proportion to ability to pay. But it will never be possible to make the assessments absolutely and perfectly fair. I found, as an editorial executive, that it was not possible to keep salaries exactly in proportion to the abilities of the individual employees. Although I tried, I found that circumstances and conditions developed so that I could not prevent some persons from getting somewhat less than they deserved, others relatively more than they deserved. All I could do was do the best I could. I also observed that employees who tried to find out what others were making, and became disaffected when they thought someone else was getting too much, only made themselves unhappy, and hindered their professional progress. So let's do the best we can, work out the best formula we can, and then everybody accept it and be happy about it.

A proverb which is found in all languages says that "God helps them that help themselves." So also, foundations and individual philanthropists help organizations that accomplish their own basic financing themselves. If the states will furnish that minimum financing to this national organization of and for the states, I am convinced that the states will surely get rich returns in the additional financing that such a surely functioning and stable organization will attract. We will get many gifts which will permit us to enrich and expand our work. But first things first.

When an Iowa governor called the first meeting which led to the formation of this Conference, this organization, it was not the last time that the state of tall corn pioneered. A few years ago Iowa noted a new need, a challenge of the future, and met it brilliantly. The Iowa conservation and park officials saw that something needed to be done to relieve the pressure on the state parks, just as Stephen Mather saw, 43 years ago, that something was needed to relieve the pressure on the national parks. So they got a law passed which permitted a county, if the people so voted, to set up a County Conservation Board. "Permitted" is the key word. There was no compulsion, no appropriation, no salaries for county board members, only expenses. So it was easy to get the bill passed. But much resulted from the passage of this merely permissive bill. The people of nearly every county in Iowa, have voted, one by one, to set up county conservation boards. At the last information I received, these boards had acquired a total of 344 areas, totalling 17,200 acres. The boards cannot levy taxes of their own, so they are dependent on gifts of land they can obtain, and what money they can persuade the governing county authorities to let them have. But this limitation does not prevent great accomplishment.

Any state can do what Iowa has done. My state, Tennessee, has passed a law similar to Iowa's, and the people of two counties have voted to set up conservation boards. Shelby County, in which Memphis is situated, was the first, and Anderson County, in which the famous, progressive city of Oak Ridge, which was secretly built during World War II to make the atomic bomb, was the second. The Anderson board has received a number of gifts of land from TVA.

If you want to start this in your state, all you have to do, as the ad men say, is to write to the Conservation Commission, Des Moines,

Iowa, and ask for a copy of the Iowa law, and go from there. I also have copies of the Tennessee law for distribution and will be glad to send a copy on request.

We are, first and foremost, custodians of natural parks. Our first challenge is to preserve our wilderness areas. Our second challenge is to protect our natural areas. Our third is to restore worn-out areas to their natural character; it can be done. Visitors to Williamsburg see how painstaking architects have restored damaged buildings to their original character so that they look exactly as they did in colonial days. So our biologists, if we will give them the word and the means, could restore damaged land to the form and vegetation it had when only the Indians were in this country. We can not only preserve and protect our natural areas, we can create them anew.

Now we come to the last challenge of the future—the one that seems to me qualitatively, though not quantitatively, to rank first. That is to create a state park, or include an existing one, in the most ideal situation.

Urban renewal takes a run-down urban area, and through the power of eminent domain, gets possession of the entire area, and plans the future use of it. If rightly administered, the results are gratifying.

Why not employ the same principle to a rural area, which is suitable for development, where the problem is not to undo the planning and building of the past, but to assure that the planning and the building of the present is done in the best possible way, so as to assure the highest future value of property, and the highest future happiness is provided for people?

A federal law paralleling the urban renewal law could be passed, which would permit the setting up of a federal, state, county, or municipal Authority, which could acquire a large block of land to plan in perpetuity an ideal combined urban and rural community. It could be contiguous to a state park—for what could furnish a better background—or a state park could be planned contiguous to it. Such planning would make easy what is now very difficult in America—to get a greenbelt entirely around an urban area. For by the acquisition of a very large block of land, the Authority could acquire enough land to circle the urban community in perpetuity with a belt of farm and park land—mostly farm land. The farms, never to be sold, never to be devoted to any but agricultural purposes, would be leased by the Authority to farmers for terms of many years. What a fine balance this would give to landscape and to living! On a visit to Stevenage, one of the wholly planned British New Towns, I noticed how a tongue of farm land juts into the residence area, a bridge connecting the two residential areas. It is a pretty sight. So too is the University of Tennessee farm at Knoxville, now surrounded by the expanding urban area; may it be ever thus.

Such a planned community could be laid out with an ordinary city park. But a state park would be grander, and make it worth travelling to see.

A state park adjoining such an area would achieve its highest usefulness.

The Authority would get its money back after it had planned and zoned the whole thing, by selling off tracts as residential, industrial and commercial sites.

The wholly planned area would be an excellent source of tax revenue and industrial, commercial and tourist business prosperity.

Let's do it. If you are interested, let me know.

*   *   *

We need to expand and improve the merit system and the removal of political influence from the state parks. In this we should have the support of our political leaders who are wise, for such wise men know that "the best politics is no politics." The little influence that a few job holders can use to sway the votes of their friends and relatives is as nothing to the many votes of the hundreds of thousands of users of the state parks who will be alert to show their appreciation to the office-holders who give them an efficient administration. A political system cannot give the political leader such efficiency; a merit system can.

*   *   *

We need to get conservation organizations to working more closely together on the national level, the state level, and the local level. We do not need organic union, we might go so far toward federation as to have a permanent joint committee for action. By unity of spirit and continuous co-operation, joining forces for legislative and administrative victories, we can get results.

We can meet the challenges of the future.

The Nature Conservancy And The "Race for Open Space"

By WALTER S. BOARDMAN, Executive Director, The Nature Conservancy

The Nature Conservancy is a private corporation whose business is the preservation of natural areas by acquisition or by assistance to others seeking to preserve such land. In this discussion, a "natural area" is land that has either remained undisturbed by man or has returned to something of a natural balance of plant and animal life. It should also be pointed out that preservation, not ownership, is the objective. There is no desire to build a land empire. In fact, there is a real effort to find agencies or institutions that will take over and administer lands acquired, provided that there are adequate safeguards to make certain the property will be used for the purposes intended ,and not exploited in any way.

The Conservancy began as a committee of the Ecologist's Union back in 1917 and for 30 years remained a discussion group. In due course it became a separate organization and in 1951, incorporated under its present title. Progress in land acquisition remained slow until 1959, but since that time it has grown in an almost geometric progression. This has been partly because of increased funds and experience, but also because it has broadened its horizons and undertaken work in a great variety of new ways. It is recognized that whatever is saved will have to be done very soon and that if a territory is so located that it can be protected, and the past disturbance has not been too great, nature will step in quite rapidly to restore it. There has been increasing activity in the field of assistance to units of government, both State and Federal, in their efforts to acquire needed lands for park or other public service where protection of some part of the property as a nature preserve is anticipated.

Because what has been done in these cooperative efforts may be of particular interest today, I shall discuss this phase of our work first. Without mentioning names, here are a few examples. I am sure that these will have a familiar ring to a few who are here today.

A foundation wished to provide funds whereby a state might acquire a tract as part of its natural area system. It did not consider it appropriate to make a direct presentation to the state, so The Nature Conservancy was asked to acquire the property. Funds were made available for the purchase, negotiations were undertaken and title was given, the tract was turned over to the proper authority.

Somewhat more spectacular is the situation in which the State Conservation Department needed to acquire the property of an amusement center established on the doorstep of a state park. The property was for sale at public auction, but under the law, the state could not file a bid. A representative of The Nature Conservancy went to the auction and bid on the property, then sold it to the state when funds were available. In this case, land of little natural value was acquired, but the effectiveness of a park was preserved.

In another case, an important tract was desired for a state park system and the owners wished to negotiate the sale directly to the state—it might be added at a fraction of the actual value of the property. However, funds were not at the time available and the danger of death to one of the owners posed a very serious problem in delay. The Conservancy borrowed the money from a commercial bank, purchased the land and is now in the process of turning it over to the state. Thus the land was secured, the state avoided the risk of a much higher price, and the desires of the family fulfilled. The sellers have the added security of a reverter protection to insure that terms of the transfer would be respected in case a change in administration of Government were to endanger this.

In another instance, a loan to the owners of desired land was arranged so that they might hold the property until the state could make a direct purchase.

Basically, these are real estate finance transactions, but the interest of the people has been served and natural areas protected for the foreseeable future.

In a very different kind of situation, the Conservancy, on its own initiative, instituted a delaying action on a timberland sale in order to gain time for the state to marshall its forces and save a priceless virgin timber stand from being cut. There is no question but that here a truly great museum of primeval natural history was preserved to the benefit of the people both now and in the future. In another corner of the Nation, a Chapter Chairman using his legal experience, plus the weight of the organization, helped a land owner transfer property to the state to be kept as part of its park system.

Of a very different nature, was the acquisition of land by direct purchase by the Conservancy, the raising of funds to pay for it and then the presentation to the state as an addition to an already existing park. It might be added this cannot be done too often, the wear and tear on personnel in the fund raising for this kind of project is just too much.

The so called "Race for Open Space" needs no explanation to state park and conservation officials. At this hour, it is doubtful that there is such an agency represented that is not anxious to acquire at least one threatened area before it is too late. Many are in a position to find the money for purchase if given a little time. Some need only a third party to go in and handle the first steps of negotiations. Others know that it will be possible to make the purchase in one, two or three years, but cannot count on the owners waiting that long for payment. Conversely, it may even be a case where the owner wants to sell with payments distributed over from two to five years and state law does not permit the agency to operate that way.

The basic tool in all these operations has been what is called the MATCHING AND LOAN FUND. Actually, this is a revolving fund of three quarters of a million at the present time. When there is an area needed and a responsible group willing to undertake the purchase, money is loaned, sometimes for the full amount, but generally for only enough to constitute a down payment; when the money is raised locally or the unit of government is able to pay, it is turned back into the fund and can then be invested again to acquire other lands.

Right now, study is being given to a new method of finance where it may be possible to expand greatly the effective working capital. If this comes into being, it will be possible for the Conservancy to assist many more land acquisitions than is currently possible.

Another program that has been expanding very rapidly is the assistance to colleges in their efforts to acquire lands for studies in biology and ecology. In general, it would seem much easier to obtain funds for a new stadium or even a new science hall than a bog, woodland or prairie for outdoor laboratory use. Again, there are all kinds of variations in the approach to this problem, but it generally boils down to the college people's finding the land they want and obtaining an option. The Conservancy takes up the option, then works with the college to raise the necessary funds for payment. In some cases, the Conservancy has actually purchased the land and then when the funds were raised, given it to the college with suitable reverter clause. In one case, it has leased a unique swamp to a state university.

Perhaps here I should pause to explain what a "Reverter Clause" is:

In turning over property to a college, museum, scientific society or even a government agency, there is a responsibility to assure its continued use as a natural area, even though changes in the administration with different values or concepts of use may endanger preservation. For example, a college administration may today be natural science minded and eager to acquire a virgin forest for study. In a few years, others may see that, by sale of that forest, funds for a new stadium, or other facility could be readily obtained. A natural area is a fragile thing in a time of expediencies. To prevent this happening, deeds, when granted to other institutions, include a reverter clause worded as follows or with appropriate variations:

"This conveyance is made subject to the express condition and limitation that the premises herein conveyed shall forever be held as a nature preserve, for scientific, educational and esthetic purposes, and shall be kept entirely in their natural state, without any disturbance whatever of habitat or plant or animal populations, excepting the undertaking of scientific research and the maintenance of such fences and foot trails as may be appropriate to effectuate the foregoing purposes without impairing the essential natural character of the premises. Should the premises cease to be used solely as provided herein, then the estate hereby granted to the (NAME OF ORGANIZATION), its successors and assigns, shall cease and determine and shall revert to and vest in The Nature Conservancy, its successors and assigns, the said reversion and vesting to be automatic and not requiring any re-entry or other act or deed."

There is another phase of operations which is still in the development stage and which may be, on occasions, extremely difficult to enforce. It relates to a modified reverter clause, which a donor may have inserted in a direct gift to a park or conservation authority whereby title will revert to the Conservancy if the land is used for other than specified purposes. Many here have experienced situations in which individuals were somewhat hesitant to give land directly to a unit of government or to a college lest, with changing administration, someone might get the idea of sale or use in opposition to the desires of the donor. Your quick reaction may be one of resentment at this kind of restriction; however, it should rather be regarded as an assurance that your successors will be upheld in their desire to keep open spaces for public use. The park or conservation official is rare that would break faith, but policy is in the hands of elected officers and who knows when someone will see in the sale of these lands quick revenue, a reduction in taxes or means of gaining popular support. We all know there are those who are sitting up nights trying to figure how they can get in to exploit all public lands, and you know they are sometimes going to be successful.

It is believed that the support of a national organization holding a claim to title to the property, if the politicians came in, would be a tremendous benefit to hard-pressed park officials trying to protect their charges. They can simply say, "We cannot do what you suggest because of this clause in the deed." I wish I could see this as an easy responsibility in the years ahead, but all of us are aware of the population and what will happen if it mounts, especially if the current demand for outdoor recreation of the consumer type continues to grow. I am using here a term of my own "consumer type." By this I mean fishing until there are few fish to catch, picnicking until the natural character of the area is destroyed and people demand new places to spoil, hunting until species are eliminated or greatly reduced. These are problems I have faith we can solve, but they are certainly going to be with us in the years ahead.

In summary, any organization, whether a unit of government or a responsible citizens' group wishing to preserve some bit of our natural heritage may seek help from The Nature Conservancy. If, upon review the area seems worthy and plans are practical, resources will be marshalled to help.

In seeking help, it is necessary for the staff to know the following:
1. The location and description of the area.
2. The natural values that are to be preserved.
3. The estimated cost.
4. Ownership and problems in dealing with the owner.

5. What financial resources both immediately and in the future are anticipated.

If possible, it is best to arrange for Mr. Dowling, The Assistant Director for Natural Areas, to meet with the interested parties to discuss the project in detail.

With this information at hand, the "Project" is reviewed by a special committee of the Board of Governors which is followed by action by the Board itself. If the proposal is completely sound, this is not the long and cumbersome process that it might appear to be.

It is hoped that The Nature Conservancy may help many state park and conservation departments to meet the challenges for land preservation in the years immediately ahead.

Report of the Park Practice Policy Committee to the Board of Directors, National Conference on State Parks September, 1963

Many, in fact most, of those present here today were present at the Board of Directors Meeting held in Grand Teton National Park in the fall of 1955 when the Program we know as "Park Practice"was approved in its expanded form. Some here today may even remember the meetings in Des Moines, Iowa and in Texas when the original idea for the exchange of developmental plans was first conceived.

The Program today bears very little resemblance to the original concept which was to have been a plan exchange arrangement between state park authorities. Few people at the 1955 meeting could imagine, I am sure, the extent to which the then proposed Park Practice Program would reach or to what extent the Program would find acceptance in our work.

In July of this year, the Chief, Park Practice was asked by Director Wirth of the National Park Service to prepare a brief history of the Park Practice Program. It might be edifying if this history could be read by all assembled here today. This is not possible, but a portion of the opening paragraph should be quoted. "Few, if any, truly profound truths—or mechanisms—are conceived by a single mind at a single sitting. Rather, an idea is germinated, nurtured with reason, cultivated with purposeful design, and the fruits are then harvested. Just so with "Park Practice." This should afford some insight into the motivation behind the Program as we know it today and to qualify our efforts in sustaining it and extending it to its greatest degree of usefulness.

The seven years since 1956 are not a long time in a work such as ours, yet it has been long enough for this fledging Program to have gathered, prepared and issued thirteen volumes of useful information on subjects which concern each of us and our staffs, and to have earned for its two sponsoring bodies some degree of national and international recognition.

There have been, for example, 328 DESIGNS with 2-page index, 478 pages of GUIDELINE with 10-page index, 41 issues of GRIST with 6 indices, 4 issues of PLOWBACK, 18 issues of SUPPLEMENTS and 6 checklists; and whereas we had but 273 participants, including more than 200 national park areas participating in the Program in 1956, there are today over 1,500 participants in every state in the Union, every province in Canada and 14 foreign countries. While this may sound like healthy growth, these statistics become all the more amazing when we consider that there has never been any advertising of any kind to promote the Park Practice Program. Its growth has been almost entirely the result of personal contact or by letter, and the greatest part of this has been carried on by the Chief, Park Practice and his staff.

Unless some use is made of this information and these statistics, they remain purely academic. Your committee feels, however, that they clearly point a direction which should be followed. We cannot—indeed we should not—permit the Program to remain at its present membership level for sound economic reason. At the risk of launching a scare campaign, it must be stated in all honesty that the financial condition of the Park Practice, so far as the National Conference of State Parks is concerned, is a tenuous thing. The establishment of a sorely needed circulation office in Alexandria, Virginia this past Spring and the employment of a Circulation Manager has, and is, straining the resources of the Program. Coupled with this is the continual raising of publication, packaging and mailing costs. The Program, therefore, finds itself in the position of providing certain services to certain groups at a financial loss. Recommendation numbers 2, 3, and 4 hereafter look to the solution of this problem.

But in a larger sense, the Conference's participation in this Program can never be on a sound footing until the membership is widely expanded. Membership in the Program by state park organizations has long since reached the saturation point. Those three states not now participating in the full Park Practice Program and those states receiving only one copy each of DESIGN, GUIDELINE, and GRIST could not, if they were to participate to a fuller extent, appreciably change the financial picture.

The answer, therefore, seems to lie in that vast undertapped field of park authorities to be found in municipal governments, county governments and in the metropolitan and conservancy district organizations. But when we attempt to offer memberships to these organizations and agencies, we are met with the question: "What can state park agencies or what can the national parks offer me in solution to the problems at my level?" The question is often ill-advised for those asking it have not examined the wide range of material offered for all park and recreation areas where design and operating problems are indigenous. Yet the question persists.

For the Program to grow and provide a safe margin of financial return requires, under the present circumstances, a "personal contact" type of selling job. Still, it must be done for we do not advocate any form of advertisement. The direct mail contact by individual letter has proved effective in a large percentage of the cases, but the Program staff could not possibly cope with the magnitude of the potential.

Perhaps if the National Conference of State Parks expands its area of membership to include other park and recreation authorities, a vast new Park Practice membership potential will automatically open and the Program will enjoy a degree of financial security not likely under present circumstances.

Mr. James E. Yeo, Circulation Manager for Park Practice, has recently completed a cost estimate which points the way to certain modifications in the Program price structure. While the estimate is in considerable detail and available for the examination of the Board, it is sufficient to say here that the $30-professional membership actually costs the Program

$23.20 and returns $6.80 for reserve and expansion. From this figure, therefore, it is not too difficult to conclude that each student membership sold for $15 is costing the Program $8.20. The student renewal fee is $5 and the cost of materials furnished under the renewal is $3.59, returning the sum of $1.41 for reserve and expansion. Unfortunately, a very small percentage of students renew student memberships in the Program since most college courses in park subjects last but one academic year.

While one of the purposes to which the National Conference of State Parks has been dedicated is the development of qualified park personnel, we do not believe that such a Student plan should be conducted at a financial loss of this magnitude.

Another form of membership causing some loss in the initial year is the Extension Membership offered to employees of organizations already participating in the Program. The extension membership cost is presently $21, leaving a $2.20 loss for each one accepted.

The analysis further reveals that the Program is largely sustained by the fees derived from renewals at a cost of $10 per year. While the publication and distribution costs vary according to the quantity of material provided and depending upon whether additional GUIDELINE and DESIGN binders are needed, the reserve accruing from such renewals amounts to approximately $5 per year.

In light of the foregoing factors, the Park Practice Policy Committee recommends and requests Board approval as follows:

(1) That the renewal fee to Park Practice each year be retained at $10. To change this would break faith with those who have continued membership since its inception, and might tend to discourage new membership through increased annual rates.

(2) In an effort to establish a reasonable financial buffer, it is recommended that, as of January 1, the new professional rate be increased from $30 to $35. This will return $11.80 for reserve and expansion.

(3) That the student rate for schools and colleges participating for the first time be increased to at least $20 per student member. This will reduce the deficit to $2.30 per student member. The members of the committee will offer no objection to consideration of an increase of the student membership fee to $25 to completely eliminate the deficit and provide a surplus for reserve and expansion of $1.80 each student membership.

(4) It is recommended that Extension Memberships be increased to $25 each, beginning January 1, to provide a reserve and expansion return of $1.80 each.

(5) It is recommended that each state park authority now participating in the Park Practice Program be strongly urged to acquaint the various political subdivisions within their states with the advantages to membership in Park Practice in order that the Program can be made to serve their needs and to increase reserve and expansion income.

In concluding this report, I would again like to quote from the concluding paragraph of Mr. Lykes' *Brief History of Park Practice:*

"With the issuance of new items for each of its three divisions, Park Practice will continue to grow in size and scope. With a limited amount of distinctive promotion on the part of the National Conference on State Parks, the Program can be brought to the attention of a vast segment of the park and recreation movement, while at the same time bringing increased stature and prominence to its two sponsoring organizations, the National Park Service and the National Conference on State Parks."

V. W. Flickinger, Chairman
Park Practice Policy Committee

THE MESSAGE

(*Continued from page 4*)

"The civilized man needs the wilderness. What we call civilization and the highly developed industrial life of today is comparatively a new thing, limited to a period aproximating the age of the bristle-coned pine. Behind all of this lies an immeasurable background of time when Man was largely an outdoor animal. This background, this inheritance lies deep in the nature of us all. It affects our outlook on life, our physical and mental health and as modern Man has to preserve both, he must liberate now and then those tendencies in his being. He must go back to the great outdoors and there renew the Springs which nourished and sweetened his life."

The above philosophical quotation is from the introduction to the proceedings of the 2nd National Conference on State Parks held at Bear Mountain in Palisades Inter-state Park, New York, May 22–25, 1922. The National Conference was just then getting underway and the roster of delegates was a large one representing all walks of life in this early effort to establish State Park Systems in every State of the Nation.

The Conference is now closing in on a half-century of activity during which it has seen State Park Systems established in practically every State in the Union, a movement that is growing greater—to the extent that many States are now giving special attention to financing State Park and recreation programs through bond issues, car stickers and other financing arrangements.

The need of Man for open space in natural areas is just as great as it was 42 years ago when the first National Conference was held. In fact, it is greater, because highly urbanized forms of recreation have tended to displant the open space and wilderness concepts. It is now more important than ever that the Conference concentrate on the retention of the role of State Park Systems, as such.

It is even more important that groups and organizations vitally interested in retaining the basic elements of State Park Systems be alerted to the danger that these elements may well be lost if these valued outdoor recreation areas are not retained for the purpose for which they were acquired, i.e., providing outdoor experiences not otherwise available to the general public. Intrusion, such as freeways, reservoirs and other competing uses, must not be permitted to reduce the quality of outdoor living so that there will not be retained forever opportunities amid the outstanding landscapes for public recreation where people may go to relax and rest, rather than superimposing on such landscapes their urbanized pursuits at the expense of intrinsic values. Much needs to be done in the field of education and training, and in this, I believe the Conference should provide a commanding leadership.

There is need for the Conference to survive just as there is need for the 4,000-year-old bristle-cone pine to survive, not only as an enduring monument to the past, but as an element of life, giving hope to survival in the future.

I hope that if there are those among you who feel that The National Conference on State Parks has served its purpose, you will reconsider and contemplate the future for this organization, a future which requires that those things preserved must be held intact, must be properly managed by trained park administrators, must be fought for by interested lay persons and organizations and must be expanded to meet the great increasing outdoor recreational needs of the public.

Let us work together toward the survival and continuing leadership of The National Conference on State Parks.

Planning and Civic Comment

Official Organ of American Planning and Civic Association and
National Conference on State Parks

CONTENTS

MARCH 1964

PLANNING AND CIVIC COMMENT

Published Quarterly

SUCCESSOR to: City Planning, Civic Comment, State Recreation

Official Organ of: American Planning and Civic Association,
National Conference on State Parks

SCOPE: *National, State, Regional and City Planning, Land and Water Uses, Conservation of National Resources, National, State and Local Parks, Highways and Roadsides.*
AIM: *To create a better physical environment which will conserve and develop the health, happiness and culture of the American people.*

Second-class postage paid at Harrisburg, Pa., and at additional mailing office.

EDITORIAL AND PUBLICATION OFFICE, 901 Union Trust Building, Washington, D. C. 20005

Printed by the Mount Pleasant Press, the McFarland Company, Harrisburg, Pa.

The Conservation Challenge of the Sixties

By STEWART L. UDALL, Secretary of the Interior

Following is the concluding part of the Horace M. Albright Conservation Lecture, delivered by Secretary of the Interior Udall before the University of California's School of Forestry on April 19, 1963. The first part of this stimulating statement appeared in the December, 1963 issue of *Planning and Civic Comment*.

The Total Outdoor Environment

The quiet crisis in conservation in our country today is most acute when we consider our total outdoor environment. The assault on things natural has been massive during the past two decades. This has been perhaps the most significant conservation fact of the past generation. If it continues unimpeded, the face of the land and our relationship with it will be drastically and irrevocably altered. Our fascination with the dazzling things of an inventive era has seemingly diminished our love for the land. This trend has, of course, been quickened by the emphasis on urbanization and mobility, the seductions of spectatorship, the requirements of industrial growth, and the air-conditioned advantages that have made glassed-in living so appealing. It is understandable that, in hectic times, a sedentary and city-bound people would witness the erosion of outdoor resources without alarm.

But let us not mistake it. The deterioration of our environment has been the paramount conservation failure of the postwar years, and this is the sort of thing that would be disturbing above all to a sensitive man such as Horace Albright. Beset on every side by problems of growth and the pressures of progress, the American earth is fast losing its spaciousness and freshness and green splendor. We have grown too fast to grow wisely, and the inspiriting parts of our land will be irreparably mutilated unless we make environment planning and environment preservation urgent items of public business.

I speak tonight in the most populous state in the Union; a year ago I was in Vermont, a state that didn't grow at all during the past ten years. I happened to talk at that time to Senator George Aiken, who is somewhat of a philosopher. He wasn't disturbed about his state's lack of growth. Instead, he said to me: "Well, when we look around us at what's happening in other parts of the world—the type of growth that has taken place—we aren't too disturbed. We are going to wait a while and grow right." Not long before that my wife and I had spent a weekend visiting Robert Frost at his Vermont home and he told us how Vermont for many years had a brochure of the type that publicizes the state, a brochure that bore the legend "Come to unspoiled Vermont for your vacation." And he said he used to take it into restaurants and write on the bottom "And help us spoil it." So maybe we have grown too fast to grow wisely. But the center of the quiet crisis of the sixties lies here, today, where we are permanently fixing our pattern of land-use. The man-to-nature relationships of the future will largely be determined in our time, the period of time that you and I live. We forget sometimes that the outdoors, the world around us, has always had a special place in the American scheme of things—and is also our home.

Land conservation in the 1960's, is, like everything else, a complex business. It involves the appropriation of public funds, the enactment of laws, and of zoning ordinances, and a nationwide marshalling of public opinion. Organizations and individuals in your community or in others can win a last-ditch fight to save a marsh here or a strip of seashore there, but this is not enough. The days fifty years ago when large-scale preservation work could be done by the flourish of a President's pen, or through the use of emergency funds in the depths of a depression, are long past. We can do significant conservation work now only if Presidents and Governors and Legislatures and Congresses and Zoning Boards and City Councils really care about our continent and are really ready to act. A few national tasks perhaps deserve a higher priority, but conservation must take its place at the head

table at budget time or our best efforts will fall short. We have moved from a condition of land surplus in this country to one of land shortage, and our national policy has now come full circle. East of the Mississippi today, we face a situation where nearly all of our public lands were sold off in haste a century and a half ago. The improvidence of a policy of unlimited disposal is apparent on every hand. Choice lands that were virtually given away must now be purchased at almost prohibitive prices and returned to public ownership to fulfill the demand for outdoor recreation for the great urban populations. Scenic tracts, such as Cape Cod in Massachusetts, Fire Island on Long Island in the state of New York, which were available at a modest cost only a few years ago are today almost beyond the reach of the public purse.

The outdoor problem has been studied with thoroughness and with vision. The 1962 report of the Outdoor Recreation Resources Review Commission contained a comprehensive set of findings and guidelines. Do we have the will to implement this report? This is the issue we confront, for prime opportunities are lost each year as superb tracts most suitable for public use are preempted or despoiled. Each year the price of preservation spirals, and the inroads increase. If large areas are to be preserved it is no exaggeration to say that what this generation saves is all that will be saved.

To meet this quiet crisis President Kennedy has initiated programs that cover the whole spectrum of outdoor resources, has expanded old programs, and his proposals serve both to define our problems and to point the way toward some solutions. We can accomplish, in the 1960's, feats of conservation worthy of the two Roosevelts if we act in time, and act in concert.

The President's Program

The President's conservation-of-environment program today includes these things:

A Wilderness Bill (the proposal initiated more than a decade ago by the Wilderness Society) which would preserve roughly 2 per cent of the American land mass in its pristine condition, and fix the wilderness idea for all time as part of our national character. These remaining wild lands constitute an irreplaceable laboratory for the scientist, offer outdoor experience of the highest quality, and protect the headwaters of many of our major rivers. Wilderness legislation will, so some of us argue, give a wholesome dimension of depth to our land-use planning—indeed, it will be a pioneering act that may influence the conservation movement on other continents. Many nations no longer have a wilderness option; we must take ours up before it is too late.

We also have a last chance, in Alaska, to show the reverence for wilderness our forebears lacked. The wonders of the wilderness still abound in our next to newest state, and if we spoil them we cannot excuse ourselves with a plea of ignorance.

The second: *The Land and Water Conservation Fund* now pending as a proposal before the Congress will dedicate new federal user fees and other special revenues as a land-purchase fund to acquire prime land and water parklands for the future. This law reverses the policy that began in 1784, and conservation lands will now be added, by purchase, to the public estate. This special fund will, if Congress passes it this year:

Produce a broad-scale effort by all of the states in the preservation of the out-of-doors (a few states—notably California, New Jersey, New York and Wisconsin—already have such programs, but most do not);
Finance acquisition to save the best seashores for public use and provide public lands around federal reservoirs;
Underwrite new wildlife refuges for threatened species of wildlife;
Provide funds for new national parks, new national recreation areas, and those lands needed to develop the full outdoor recreation potential of the national forests.

Another program is the *Open Space Aid for Cities* program, authorized in 1961. This landmark program encourages urban areas to plan ahead and to preserve tomorrow's Central Parks and Golden Gate Parks today.

The Youth Conservation Corps already passed by the Senate (conceived as a permanent land maintenance force by President Franklin D. Roosevelt a generation ago) will let Congress help us rebuild parts of the land and heal its worst scars.

Also, *The Preservation of Selected Rivers* having superior recreational values (such as the Allagash of Maine, the Suwannee of Georgia and Florida, the Deschutes of Oregon, the Salmon River of Idaho, and the Ozark River of Missouri) will mark another new frontier of conservation.

A System of Scenic Roads and Parkways, a movement already afoot in this state, lags behind nationally, but is designed to give balance to our road-building program and open up the scenic hinterlands to unhurried drivers who prefer scenery to celerity.

The Wetlands Preservation Bill of 1961 is enabling us to acquire now the marshlands needed to sustain waterfowl populations—and we will let the duck hunters pay for them later.

A New Policy Toward Military Lands will treat these lands as a national reserve and enable us to identify tracts suitable for transfer to public agencies for conservation purposes.

And finally, *All Fresh Water Resources* created by federal funds will have their fish, wildlife and recreation potential fully developed.

But this is only part of the program. These are the forward thrusts of our policy that the America of the future should be beautiful and healthy, as well as industrially productive. In addition, we must curb increasing environmental contamination by means of:

An all-out attack on water pollution;
Research into air pollution control;
Regulating the kind of strip-mining that poisons rivers and uses up a nonrenewable resource while making a wasteland of some of the best outdoor recreation areas in the east;
Research directed against the unwise use of pesticides;
Action to combat the pollution of ocean estuaries and the littoral land.

However, assuming that most of the programs I have mentioned are successful (and some will not be supported adequately), other problems will increasingly complicate

the decisions of our resource planners. These will concern such things as population pressures, the order we give to our planning of that part of our environment we construct and remake ourselves, and the conflicting ideas of different resource-user groups.

Conflicting Uses

As our land base shrinks it is inevitable that incompatible plans involving factories and fish, dams and parks, highways and wildlife, will collide. Unless the alternatives are carefully evaluated many wrong choices will be made. Those who do the deciding must weigh the competing proposals with an eye on the computers, an ear to immediate needs, and with their thoughts on the future.

In this field it is easy to let our thinking become imprisoned by slogans. As appealing as it sounds, the popular concept of "multiple use" can be an invitation to confusion or a mask for exploitation unless it is properly defined. Some lands can survive what one might call maximum use, but any land use must respect ecological principles or serious mistakes will be made. Words must describe facts: both a reservoir behind a large dam and a new national park in one sense wholly pre-empt land, but each serves purposes as plural as multiple-use forests or grazing lands. Overuse in the short run may ruin land for higher uses in the long run. Crucial shortages will occasionally dictate one-sided decisions, but if we put our land to its highest and best use, the requirements of future

(Continued on page 51)

4

Our Outdoor Heritage—What We Are Doing to Preserve It

From the Remarks of LAURANCE S. ROCKEFELLER before the Theodore Roosevelt Association, October 27, 1963. Mr. Rockefeller is Chairman of the New York State Council of Parks, served as Chairman of the Outdoor Recreation Resources Review Commission, is currently Honorary Chairman of the Citizens Committee for that Report, and is a member of the Board of Trustees of the American Planning and Civic Association.

A fundamental problem of our society and one in which I perhaps am most deeply interested, is the task of making and keeping the outdoors a part of American life. As the first major national step to this end, in 1908, Theodore Roosevelt called what was known as the Governors' Conference. This was the first time that conservation and the problems of preserving our renewable resources got national interest and support.

And, with the exception of a relatively small study made under the Coolidge Administration, nothing in depth, nothing of great significance was done until our Outdoor Recreation Report.

We like to feel that this report exemplified two of President Theodore Roosevelt's outstanding qualities.

First, it was action-minded. Eight of our fifteen Commissioners were Congressmen, and this report was designed to get the facts and to project the policies and principles that would guide Congress. It was not written to be filed away. It was written to be a working document in Congress and throughout the country.

Secondly, it was people-oriented. It was concerned with the preservation of resources, but, in terms of their use and need for and by the people.

Congress initiated this Commission for various reasons. I think it was keenly aware of what we refer to as the "dynamics of demand," namely four factors—the growing population; increasing incomes; the ever-growing leisure time; and the increasing accessibility, due to roads, airplanes and automobiles, of all these recreational areas. These four factors, taken together, indicated a strong upward trend in demand.

Also obvious, of course, was overcrowding of existing parks, beaches and campgrounds, and the relentless action of our bulldozers, ever moving forward on houses and roads and airports. I think Congress was keenly aware of the impact of urbanization and industrialization on the lives of our people as well.

These two factors, taken together, present a very serious threat to the vitality and to the sense of purpose and meaning of our society. We are being removed progressively from nature in our daily experience, in our knowledge of it and in our recreation. And this factor, combined with the depersonalization, the urbanization, and the industrialization of our civilization, is bringing about serious adverse effects.

5

What can we do about it? This is the challenge.

A brilliant doctor, Viktor Frankl, has termed the effect of industrialization "an existential vacuum." And he sums up its impact this way:

"We must not draw the conclusion that the existential vacuum is predominantly an American disease, but rather that it is apparently a concomitant of industrialization. The existential vacuum seems to issue from man's twofold loss: the loss of that instinctual security which surrounds an animal's life, and the further, more recent loss of those traditions which governed man's life in former times. At present, instincts do not tell man what he has to do, nor do traditions direct him toward what he ought to do; soon he will not even know what he wants to do; he will be led by what other people want him to do, thus completely succumbing to conformism."

Now this may be an extreme presentation, but it is a very real problem in our lives today. I believe that the values of the outdoors can play an important role in filling this vacuum.

The ability to maintain contact with the natural environment is essential for our general health and welfare. It is also essential if we are to achieve that quality of American citizenship that Theodore Roosevelt longed for, as he put it, so that we might "become an inspiration and a beacon to mankind." If we're going to have that kind of citizenship in this country, we must have a renewal of vitality and a new sense of purpose and meaning. I believe

these are factors that we must not take lightly.

The ORRRC Report has accomplished a good deal. First, there is the impact of the Report itself—it is a store of knowledge and information available to the universities and governments throughout the country. The basic report is backed up by 27 research reports in depth. These have been widely read and accepted. We recommended three pieces of legislation that were vitally important. The first provided for the Bureau of Outdoor Recreation, which is already in action. The act creating the Bureau provides a means of coordinating the eighteen or twenty different government agencies at the Federal level in their recreational activities. The Bureau has the further responsibility of coordinating with the states and into the local community areas so that we can have a national planning agency.

Recently a second major bill recommended by ORRRC has come out of committee in the House and it's called the Land and Water Conservation Fund bill. This bill, if it goes through, will probably be the most useful, the most dramatic and far-reaching piece of conservation legislation that has ever been passed, because it will provide a vast sum of money annually—maybe 100 to 150 million dollars a year. Forty per cent of the money will be used at the Federal level, and sixty per cent will be for matching grants to the states for recreation planning, acquisition, and most importantly, for development.

We're all interested in and concerned about the Wilderness Bill.

6

This also was one of the recommendations of the Report. I am hopeful that this will get out of the stymie that it is now in and move forward.

Perhaps the most exciting and unexpected result of our Commission work was the action of New York State which didn't wait for the report. New York is an outstanding example of the fact that a large majority of the concentration of urban areas in this country is in the East whereas the major part of the recreational areas is in the West. Establishing a precedent, New York went ahead and initiated a 75-million dollar bond issue for land acquisition, a measure which was approved by a popular vote of 3 to 1. And just to make the story complete, there was a subsequent bond issue for an additional 25 million which went through by an even bigger majority. The interest and support of the people in protecting their future interests in outdoor recreation were fantastic.

Since then New Jersey, Wisconsin, and Connecticut have already acted on broad new programs, and Florida, Pennsylvania and California are in the process of doing likewise.

Of course a great deal is also going on in the municipal government area, and this is extremely important. There are various means of keeping open space open—tax abatements, easements, cluster housing developments. The last is a new thought of concentrating the buildings instead of making spread developments which give everybody a little yard but no real place to walk or move. In New England, particularly, they have initiated a series of Conservation Commissions which are working actively in communities, seeking opportunities to preserve and protect their recreational opportunities.

What remains to be done?

Much has been accomplished. But there are four basic areas in which work must go on really indefinitely into the future.

The first one, of course, is planning. The new Bureau of Outdoor Recreation is a centralized planning agency responsible for making a national plan. But there must be planning at every level of government, Federal, state, local, and in the private sector, because as most of us may not realize, over eighty per cent of the land in this country is privately owned. If we're concerned with maximum recreation-conservation opportunities, the private sector is mighty important. Add to that the fact that ninety-five per cent of our shoreline is also privately owned, and you have some very interesting and challenging problems.

In addition to planning, there is the matter of acquisition. This involves a great deal of question of priority and judgment, but I think that more and more it is becoming evident that the recreational opportunities must be accessible to people—in other words, where our cities are. Generally, they're on the ocean or they're on rivers or they're on lakes. Therefore, accessibility to the shorelines is one of the big problems of acquisition. And in addition, the question of more urban parks to bring a little green space to the cities is crucial.

Beyond acquisition, a third point is development. The use of any given area of land in terms of its recreational potential to a high degree is dependent on how much money has been spent in developing it. Thus, it generally costs two or three times as much to develop land in an urban area as it does to buy it. This is going to be a challenging problem because the sums are big, and this is where this Federal grant, this Land and Water Conservation Fund bill will be vital.

And finally, there is the question of education. The more you think of it, most of us have had unique outdoor opportunities during our childhood and throughout our entire lives. But today two thirds and, rapidly, three quarters or more of our people will grow up in the cities. If we don't educate them and train them to understand and appreciate the outdoors, they will not seek these opportunities or know how to appreciate and benefit by them. Therefore outdoor educational activity is needed. An example is the Nature Centers, which are really outdoor classrooms, where the children go from school, and the older people attend to enjoy firsthand outdoor experiences. This and many other devices are absolutely essential if we are going to have a balanced and continuing heritage of outdoor living.

In conclusion, clearly there is a tremendous job ahead. It is challenging now but consider how much more it will be so as our urban areas grow in size and in population. The best way to meet this future is to reaffirm the spirit of Theodore Roosevelt. He has left us a heritage: A concern for action and a concern for the outdoors not simply for itself but for the values it offers people in terms of enjoyment and well-being.

If his spirit can be re-vitalized, and if we, his heirs in tradition, have the will and the ability, the outdoors and its benefits can continue to provide physical and spiritual strength for our national character.

The Hill and The Plain

"Regional 'clutter' is, after all, a composite of local clutter, of local developments which have spread out over the land. We can bemoan the general loss of open space in California, but where has this occurred, except in our own neighborhoods?

"If there is a field where the meadowlarks used to sing, but where now a road, a parking lot, a subdivision, or a shopping center has needlessly replaced it, which community allowed the field to disappear?

"If a valley of orchards has been replaced by subdivisions, why did the county give up its agriculture and its beauty?

"If a park has been overrun by a power line or a freeway, or a potential park by a subdivision, how much of an effort did the people in that particular area make to prevent these occurrences?"

—From *The Phantom Cities Of California* by Samuel E. Wood and Alfred E. Heller, published by CALIFORNIA TOMORROW, 1963.

Fight for Our Cities: What The States Can Do!

By TERRY SANFORD, Governor of North Carolina

An address delivered before the 69th Annual National Conference on Government of the National Municipal League, Detroit, Michigan, November 19, 1963, and published in the January, 1964 *National Civic Review* under the title, "Action By States Needed." We are privileged to re-print it here through the courtesy of the *Review*.

The United States intends to lead the world today and to maintain and increase its influence tomorrow. To do this it will have to be strong at home. It must show visible proof that it can promote the welfare of its citizens and expand its economy.

A strong economy is the result of many forces. It is the result of decisions made by millions of people in private and public life. These forces come into play most strongly in our cities. The decisions are made there, and most of the people who make them live or work there. Our cities are the command posts and the communications centers of our technological society. Even the nerve ends of agriculture come together in the market place.

Cities are the heart, the eyes and ears of the great body-economic of the United States, and unless these vital organs are in good health the nation's life blood will not be pumped, and America will not then see and hear and think as clearly as it must to hold its position of leadership.

People create cities to serve the needs of their highly organized societies, and cities are for people. In the last analysis they *are* people. Not special people—not just city officials, not just real estate developers, not just merchants. Above all, cities are not masonry and pavement. Those are only the trappings.

Lewis Mumford puts it this way:

The city, as one finds it in history, is the point of maximum concentration for the power and culture of a community. It is the place where the diffused rays of many separate beams of life fall into focus, with gains in both social effectiveness and significance. The city is the form and symbol of an integrated social relationship; it is the seat of the temple, the market, the hall of justice, the academy of learning. Here in the city the goods of civilization are multiplied and manifolded; here is where human experience is transformed into viable signs, symbols, patterns of conduct, systems of order. Here is where the issues of civilization are focused: here, too, ritual passes on occasion into the active drama of a fully differentiated and self-conscious society.

Cities are man's greatest creation. They are not rivaled in complexity and wonder by any of his other works. As soon as he gave up nomadic life and entered into agriculture, the community became essential to man. Soon it was necessary to draw tighter for defense and for commerce, and the great cities of the world began to grow. Some were seats of learning, others the seats of government. Some were at the crossroads of commercial land routes while others sent ships to ply the world from their ports. Each city has its reason for existence. A few great ones dominate the world but every city dominates its hinterland, takes nourishment from it and in turn sustains it.

There were cities before there were states, even before the nation-states. It was from the cities that the power

9

to create nations was derived and organized. States therefore have an ancient allegiance to their urban ancestry.

In the early days of our still young nation, an inherited political and social system made it possible to have states before there were powerful cities on the continent. Here the situation was reversed and the states created cities, but the cities are no less important here and now than they were in the earlier days when they ruled the world. In fact, the metropolis today has power and productivity undreamed of by cities of old. But the power, the productivity, the vitality are threatened by urban cancer, by paralysis, and, though states and cities have so much to give to each other, contact between them has been lost. By long neglect the senior level of government helped contribute to the ills. It is only just beginning to realize it can, that it must, contribute to the cure.

In too many cases city leaders met with rebuff after rebuff at the hands of state governments. Too many times did the municipalities ask for legislation to cope with their problems only to have improperly apportioned legislatures turn them down. Too many times did city people ask for their share of state services and appropriations only to be told that they must settle for less. Little wonder it is that they went over the heads of the states to the federal government for help.

Legislative reapportionment is now coming. Cities will get a fair hearing in state government and should be able at least to get legislative power to help themselves.

There is ample evidence that the states have seen the need to lead their children out of their long exile in the slums and into the promised land of the city visualized by Mumford.

* * *

When we speak of the blight attacking our urban areas, the thing we must bring first to mind is the blight on the lives of *men*, not the blight on a decaying building or the scar tissue of slums beside the freeway carved through the neighborhood and the park.

We diminish *man* when we set him defenseless on foot amidst high-speed automobiles. We could separate them if we tried.

We defeat the spirit of *man* when we raise him in slums and return him to slums. We can rebuild the bricks and stones around him and we can rebuild his mind and spirit through education, so that he begets neither slum nor slum dweller.

It is the sensitivity of *man* we offend with glaring lights, junk yard and visual "barbed wire." We know how to design for beauty if only we will.

We pauperize the soul of *man* when we bypass the responsibility to provide libraries, recreation, trees, zoos and open space. We can find the money for them if we will admit their importance.

We frustrate *man* when we allow cities to grow together into an indefinable mass. He loses his identity as a citizen and he becomes depressed by the sameness of the urban scene. We could prevent overlapping growth.

We waste the life of *man* in traffic jams. We could have high-speed,

10

mass transportation if we would recognize the necessity.

We offend the nostrils of *man* by polluting the air he breathes, and we befoul his water with uncontrolled wastes.

Do we not know better? Of course we do! We can have the city beautiful, the city functional. We have the experience, the brains, the know-how to aspire to urban utopia if only we will—if the citizen will, if he will say "nay" to the slum landlord, "nay" to the inefficient official, "nay" to the money-hungry real estate speculator, if he will say, "I have a vision of greatness for my city and the good life for my family," the forces of greed and ugliness cannot prevail.

*   *   *

To be able to say these things man must be given a vision, and that is your job and my job.

I have a vision for my state and for its cities, and I can see a clear way for this vision to come true.

To realize my vision, North Carolina will have to do its share of rebuilding the mistakes of the past, but our industrialization has come late and so has our city growth. We are just beginning to experience the difficulties encountered by the older urban areas.

We have four hundred municipalities, and yet we're probably the least urban state in the union. Only 40 per cent of our citizens live in cities. Another third work in the city but live in nearby rural areas.

We have a metropolitan area, though an unusual one. Because of its location we call it the "Piedmont Crescent." It is a curving string of

cities two hundred miles long. The largest is 250,000 in population, and they are pleasant towns. As you leave one you drive through open countryside before the next appears. Any of them can be bypassed or you can drive downtown in a short time. The citizens live close to their work, and at one place or another in this area is to be found all of the cultural and business attributes of a metropolis of two million.

The crescent's growth is relatively late but it's mushrooming, and we've taken a look at the growth problems experienced elsewhere. We see no reason why our cities can't grow and yet be liveable, so we are determined that we will profit by the experience of others.

We mean to have downtowns with good shopping, pleasant and safe for pedestrians. We think that subdivision growth can be properly guided. We intend to look into the possibilities for satellite towns to hold some of the people.

We want to match water supply and quality with the location and needs of the population.

We will provide outdoor recreation for the family within a short drive of each city.

We intend to preserve open spaces between the cities, so that one will not become indistinguishable from another, and so that the vistas will include farms and forests as well as asphalt and bricks.

We will look at the possibilities for fast mass transportation between these cities, so that a dweller in one may go to an art gallery in another and return the same afternoon, so that a businessman may have a conference with his wholesaler in

11

another city and get back to the office for a day's work.

We think that with proper planning and strong state leadership we can build a crescent that will be workable, pleasant and exciting for its residents, and attractive to visitors and to industry. We can get the same results for all of our cities. Lewis Mumford said we could when he visited North Carolina. He also said it was up to us, and we agree with him. We're going to do something about it, and we have already initiated thinking about how to do a comprehensive planning job at the same time we are acting on some of the elements of the problem.

Whether the task is rebuilding cities, as it is in some states, or planning good growth in advance, as it is in North Carolina, the states must assume a great measure of responsibility. They must because they created municipalities.

They must because water supply and quality is a regional problem.

They must because parks for families' outdoor recreation will be shared by cities.

They must because growth crosses local government lines and cannot be controlled by any one local government.

They must because open-space preservation needs the attention and action of the state as well as the cities.

They must because intercity transportation can be planned and effected best by the state.

They must when industrial locations are outside of cities.

They must because germs and air pollution are no respecters of city limits.

Like it or not, the states are in the battle and they must win it because it is the battle for life itself.

What then must the states do when they have girded themselves and moved to the fore of the fight for great cities?

First, they can sound the trumpet to let the troops know they are on the attack and not in retreat, and they can offer battle plans and weapons.

Then they can establish communications. They can sit down with citizens and municipal officials and find out what is on their minds—what their problems are—what their hopes are. The next step would be to examine our state governments to see what resources we have to help—what new things we might appropriately do. I have a few suggestions.

Why not consider giving the cities power to help themselves, to make necessary governmental reforms, to plan, to build and to regulate, without the necessity for special grants of authority from the state?

Why should not every state, jointly with city officials, review its tax structure to insure that municipalities are getting the revenues which are appropriately theirs?

Let's review the possibilities for state financial aid to municipalities, both direct and indirect.

Let's see what can be done with intercity regional programs.

Let's look at the opportunities for joint planning and action programs in highways, transit, outdoor recreation, water supply, open space

(*Continued on page 53*)

12

Cities Are For Living In

By FRED SMITH, Vice-President, Prudential Insurance Company, Newark, New Jersey. Copyright 1963 by *Country Beautiful* Magazine. Reprinted by permission, Elm Grove, Wisconsin.

The city was never a deliberate thing. It never really happened by design; forever it has resulted from a convergence of necessities. In the earliest days the necessity was protection: You walled a city, fortified the wall and kept out invaders or robbers or barbarians. Then came the industrial revolution, and the city was a labor pool and a center of transportation facilities to bring in raw material and ship out finished goods. Circumstances, not the urge to create a place for living, spawned cities. Any planning that was done was mechanical —laying out symmetrical street patterns or designing buildings— often more to meet economic requirements than the needs and desires of human beings.

The danger these days is from atom bombs—and the city is the last place to seek refuge. Transportation is a matter of roads, and roads clutter cities so they become muscle-bound in urban areas, and the plants move out for access. Labor pools are no longer a fixed asset anywhere: They ebb and flow, they follow opportunity, their constitution changes like the patterns of oil on water—the machinist is on wheels, he goes where he wants; the punch press operator likes deep-sea fishing and finds a punch press where he needs it; the technologist is in short supply and can live where he wants and finds his work. Geography is no barrier. One no longer seeks a job, then adjusts to the locality; this has been turned upside down by automobiles, house trailers, highways and the dispersal of the industrial complex.

So what is the city now—an anachronism? Is it an impediment to highway construction? A site for badly conceived and shoddily built low and middle income housing units? Is it a staging area for minority groups and immigrants who must put in an apprenticeship as city dwellers before they can be certified for living in the suburbs? An arena for real estate operators and political manipulators?

If it is these things and nothing more, the city today may well be the Achilles' heel of Western civilization: A concentration of purposelessness, a creeping cancer which in the end will consume all the virtues that made us great and successful and prosperous.

The signs of degeneration are not hard to find. It takes only superficial looking. And superficial looking is so popular that any other kind engenders a sort of incredulity. Style and habit dictate that the citizen must tote up the liabilities, and view with despair. It happens in many places, but take, for example, one Eastern city in which the leading citizens were quoted in *Fortune* magazine (and many other places) expressing the deepest conviction that high taxes, unprincipled politicians, the pressures of minorities and all the other standard fallibilities of urban areas

13

had at last spelled the permanent doom of the city if not, in fact, of the state and perhaps of the whole section. "This city can never recover" was the verdict about six years ago, and one of the professional industrial developers, echoing the sentiment in an explosive statement to the press, threw in the sponge and retired to what he supposed were greener pastures. A leading local banker told a major industrial organization that was contemplating construction in the city: "People are moving out of this town, not into it." Deep, hopelessly deep, ran this conviction in many places. It was difficult not to believe.

However, there was another side to the story that those people were too close to see, but which now is becoming increasingly obvious. The city had assets—vast assets to attract the very people who could save it and infuse new life into it. It was an old city, with historic flavor, which some voluble city father had come to regard as evidence of retarded development. Instead it is a magnet that draws constructive-minded people. The narrow, crooked streets that delay traffic hold a charm that would be worth its weight in gold to the charmless industrial cities of the Midwest. Its network of educational and cultural and scientific institutions that contribute so little to the tax structure are in fact the foundation of a whole new generation of industrial and commercial activity that will replace lost mass employment factories and make the area all the better for the exchange.

And to pile irony upon irony, the politicians, power-hungry and devious as some may have been, had to be the ones who took the leadership in bringing about reforms (often in spite of the efforts of more respectable people) which have resulted in this city's forging ahead now at such a pace that the innate assets are sometimes in danger of being overrun, or at least overlaid, with almost incompatible structures of glass and steel and splash.

The moral in this story is simple and eloquent: Cities are like teenagers who go out of their way to create despair; and city fathers too often, like teenagers' parents, are filled with hopelessness at the sight of all the problems.

*   *   *

But cities, like teen-agers, may yet snap out of it. When and if they do, it will be because of inner resources that lie deep in the creature; it will not grow out of scolding or surface alterations.

There are hopeful signs.

In city after city, cultural centers are being built—in the face of television which (sparingly) provides culture to citizens while they sit in bedroom slippers with their feet up. Enough citizens, evidence indicates, will put their feet down, lace up their shoes, maneuver downtown traffic and enjoy culture in person by preference. Artur Rubinstein is in stereo, on film, on television—but a guaranteed sellout any time and anywhere he has a concert.

And in many cities, there is a healthy resistance—with increasing success—to the wanton ripping out of good neighborhoods because the architecture is less than modern, or because the location intrigues a developer whose analysis of a neighborhood is oriented exclusively toward economics. The delinquency and disorganization that so often follow on the heels of needless neighborhood disruption are beginning to be recognized—and avoided where possible.

A neighborhood with roots is worth preserving, because without roots there is no foundation for civic pride or personal obligation to neighbors or the community. There is no intrinsic virtue in the overfunctional glass and metal building, no lasting inspiration, even in good new architecture, which can compensate for the familiarity of the old and customary; thus, the wiser planners are thinking these days in terms of rehabilitation and reconstruction to improve appearances without eliminating flavor. In Philadelphia they are converting old town houses into new town houses but the newness does not shine through so sharply that the old surroundings are lost to sight—or feel.

The voices are small, even yet, and they lack a certain capacity to be heard or heeded because it is less profitable to augment and improve city living than simply to replace the old city with new structures. The financial minds find it difficult to figure the social and psychological imponderables, but the other way is easy: On one side of the ledger, land costs so much; construction, so much; taxes, so much. On the other side, there is depreciation, rental income, certain tax-avoiding measures and finally the possibility of sale after completion to realize capital gain advantages. Not that

we can walk away from economics. Money still makes the mare go. But in this, as in so much else, economics must be the tool, not the master.

The bookkeeping of urban redevelopment as it is practiced generally is understandable, but it becomes more complicated as the human factors creep in and begin to elbow out the statistics and rates of interest and depreciation calculations.

But these human factors must creep in. Cities are for living in. They are for people. Deep in their hearts, people recognize this, and will come back willingly and cheerfully when cities begin to adjust to the lives of their citizens with more thoroughness than is apparent anywhere at this writing. Small, halting steps, as have been indicated here, are being taken. What is needed now is a concerted effort to orient "redevelopment" toward people instead of toward economics —and if this is done, the economics, over the years, will take care of itself. It will take thinking, hoping, feeling and experimenting. It will not be easy. There will be opposition and impatience and disbelief. But it certainly will be done.

Cities will become more deliberate things. For the first time in all history, they will begin to shape themselves to spiritual and human requirements, and the architect and the contractor and the tax collector and the bookkeeper will learn to cut the cloth to fit the pattern. Impractical? A dream?

There is a whole vista of new inventions over the horizon that will make this possible. The raw material of economics is as real, as usable, as tractable as the raw material of mechanics. Edison made a lamp because he had the good sense to try everything that might work, knowing full well that it is the way elements are combined into a whole that brings eventual success. There are ways of combining the facts of economic life, too, into a practical pattern for preservation and rehabilitation—and these ways will be found. The Nation will be the stronger for it.

In the past ten years, there have been more inventions in real estate financing than during the century that went before—spawned chiefly by the more recent idiosyncrasies of the Federal tax structure, with ingenious tax lawyers as midwives; if any proof were needed of exciting possibilities, here it is. It is only the ultimate purpose that is different.

Another revolution in the making stems from the belated discovery that professional social planners may not know what is good for people after all. The people do. It may not be necessary to lay out recreation areas on a per capita basis, with facilities designed to improve the muscular flexibility or spiritual content of the human species; a plot of grass around an ugly building may not, by any stretch of the imagination, convince the prisoners within that they have freedom and an expanse of green for communing-with-nature purposes. It may only make matters worse. It may be that the youngsters who play in streets are better off playing in streets, and maybe something might better be done about automobiles than about herding youngsters into unresponsive playgrounds.

The deliberate city of the future is the one that starts at the neighborhood level and moves in all directions. It starts with the emotion of city living and builds the mechanics to suit. It starts with people. It ends with people. It is people.

ᕓᕗ

Twenty Forts in National Park System are Vivid Chapters of American History

Twenty historic frontier outposts and coastal fortresses—including America's oldest and the Western World's largest—are preserved in the National Park System to provide visitors and future generations with vivid chapters in the shaping of this country, according to a recent report from the National Park Service.

These imposing landmarks—extending from Fort Jefferson National Monument off the coast of Florida to Fort Vancouver National Historic Site on the Columbia River in Washington State—include scenes of tremendous battles, winter encampments of famous expeditions, headquarters of daring fur-trading companies, and immigrant landing depots.

Some of these units—such as Fort Union National Monument in New Mexico— are ruins which have been preserved as they are; others such as Fort Necessity in Pennsylvania, and Fort Raleigh in North Carolina, have been restored.

C. B. Colby, in his book, *Historic American Forts*, advises: "Visit them if you can, for to do so is to step back into history for a few moments, to a site where our early history was being forged. Perhaps you will feel as I did that from the . . . . . stone bastions of these great forts, America's future looks even brighter."

The Community Renewal Program As A Long Range Guide

Remarks of FREDERIC M. ROBINSON, Partner, Harland Bartholomew & Associates, Atlanta Office, before an Urban Renewal Workshop, Athens, Georgia.

My objective in discussing the Community Renewal Program is to broaden the concept of a very promising program in order to meet the requirements of the developing city. I am talking, therefore, of the Community Renewal Program or CRP as a long-range guide to the *total* development of the city, not just a part— even a very important part.

We may recognize that a city grows by four processes: By addition (of new property, population, resources); by transition (of land use, economic base, function); and even by attrition (by the failure of noble or ignoble schemes). The end product is the city—partly good, partly bad—partly the result of new construction, partly the result of reconstruction.

A tremendous force in shaping what is to be results from the less recognized importance of how well we use and maintain what already exists. If this is true, then the future aspect of our cities will be determined by the effectiveness of our urban renewal. By urban renewal I do not mean necessarily a specific government program, but rather a continual process of urban regeneration which unites the power of public and private effort—a process as unrelenting in its application as the forces of obsolescence which it opposes. Urban renewal in this sense includes, in addition to more widely accepted programs of clearance and rehabilitation,

the conservation of sound values and even the *guidance of future development*. This may sound a good deal like planning, but it bears a vital relation to the total renewal or regenerative process.

Unless the CRP is it, there is no vehicle to accomplish the comprehensive purpose of urban renewal. The city plan does much, but not all, of what is needed. Such a vehicle is desperately needed, and to make use of the CRP in this function we must beware of inhibiting its scope.

If the CRP lives up to its potential, it can become the most effective influence on urban development. If not, it is just another inventory— not without some value, but damned by what it needs to be . . . and isn't.

The inspiration of the CRP lies in the fact that it is truly comprehensive. This comprehensiveness filters into every aspect of city building and from this gains its value.

Scope

The CRP should include the entire urban area, all types of land use, all conditions of property and all planned development, all with full knowledge of economic potential. Although the CRP in itself is not a plan, it must include the plan and is inseparable from it. The CRP is based on the plan and must coordinate the expressed objectives of the plan with other efforts to build or improve

17

the city. A religious effort to separate the CRP from the planning function would be self defeating. A good CRP has as much power to influence the plan as the plan has power to influence the CRP.

Procedure

The method employed to produce a CRP has a determining effect on its ultimate usefulness. We know that a variety of procedures and direction are possible.

Although there are some who would debate the question, I am convinced that the most effective means of directing the preparation of a CRP is by use of a board similar to that used in the city of Richmond, Virginia. Here the heads of the more directly affected city departments or agencies—public works, planning, health, redevelopment and housing authority—were selected to meet as a control board for the direction and review of the work. In that city, the control board met faithfully, semi-monthly, and the corollary benefits of the broadened understanding which resulted are already being felt in other functions.

It had been suggested that it would be impossible to reach agreement, and that direction by this divided responsibility would be inefficient. Just the opposite has been true. The direction has been smooth and improved by the individual specialties of the members. If it is impossible to achieve agreement in the planning or programming phase, the prospects for actual building look dim indeed.

Personnel

Here again the degree of comprehensiveness is unique and should im-

prove with continued use of the program. The broader the base, in terms of people involved, the better. This includes public officials and employees, official boards and civic leaders, private investors and developers, and the individual citizen.

The actual preparation of the program should be done as much as possible by local staff drawn from the municipal departments (although use of a consultant is considered advisable). This helps to draw the departments together in their appreciation of the objective, utilizes the specialties of varying experience, and leaves a trained staff for the continuing annual review which is necessary.

Because the true CRP includes both private as well as public renewal action and individual as well as group effort, a wide-spread public understanding bred of actual participation is required.

In Richmond, the total information of the CRP was broken down into major geographical components to increase its appeal to the general public. The total urban story, what exists and what is needed, was presented for each one. It is unfortunate to note that the interest of many citizens is limited to their own specific areas of concern and not to the city as a whole.

Effect

The last area of comprehensiveness which I would like to note is that of results. This is the end of all planning, all programming, all building, and all urban renewal, regardless of definition. Here is the greatest opportunity of the CPR—to
(*Continued on page 44*)

18

Zoning Round Table

Conducted by FLAVEL SHURTLEFF, Marshfield Hills, Mass.

LARGE LOTS

From time to time in the Round Table the requirement of from one to five acres for residential lots has been reviewed and, in general, the conclusion reached from the decided cases that this restriction is within the grant of power to zone, but that the exercise of the power may be limited by the facts of the case. Aronson *vs.* Town of Sharon, decided by the Massachusetts Supreme Court January 6, 1964, is an excellent illustration in support of this conclusion.

The area involved consisted of a parcel of 70 acres which was zoned in 1957, when acquired by Aronson, for residential lots of 40,000 square feet in area and 150 feet in frontage. In 1961, as a result of a comprehensive planning study, a new rural residence district was established requiring lots of 100,000 square feet and frontages of 200 feet. The Aronson land was given that classification. Several lots originally part of the Aronson holdings had been sold and were occupied by homes. Town water was available on an accepted street which served these lots, but there was no sewer system in the town.

The comprehensive plan and the new residential zone were expressly based on a two-fold development program: a) to keep the land as open or at as low population density as the town would accept; and b) to initiate a program of land acquisition for town purposes.

The court cited with approval Simon *vs.* Town of Needham which is the leading case in Massachusetts on the subject of large lot restrictions, where the public welfare advantages from large lots were enumerated as:

a) More freedom from noise and traffic;
b) Less fire hazard;
c) More play space on the premises.

But the court noted that, in upholding an acre requirement for residential lots, the decision had these words: "We make no intimation that if lots were required to be larger than one acre, or if circumstances were even slightly different, the same result would be reached." The court concluded: a) that the law of diminishing returns was applicable, and all the advantages to public welfare cited in the Needham case could be attained without requiring lots of 100,000 square feet; b) granting the value of recreation to the community, the burden of providing it should not be borne by property owners unless they were compensated.

The case is notable as the first in Massachusetts to set definite limits on large lot requirements. However, it is not a ruling that 100,000-square-foot lot requirements are invalid as a general rule, but that special circumstances may make the requirement unreasonable.

An attempt by the Home Owners Association to replace the

uncertainty and expense of litigation by a legislative determination is now before the Massachusetts Legislature. A bill which provides a top restriction of 9,000 square feet for lots in areas which have town water and sewer available and 15,000 square feet otherwise was considered by a legislative committee during the week of January 26th at a largely attended and hotly contested hearing.

The proponents of the bill, of course, argued that the little man was shut out of some towns and might be confined to the cities, and that the large lot restriction was in fact an unreasonable expedient to control population growth and tax increase. Planning boards and other municipal agencies supported the right of the community to make its own determination and pointed out that the great differences in communities necessitated flexibility in restrictions.

We shall hope in the Round Table for June to record the progress of the bill.

SPOT ZONING

Schertzer *et al. vs.* City of Somerville *et al.*, cited in Advance Sheets of Massachusetts decisions 1963 at page 555, presents facts which make for a clear cut decision and better understanding of the troublesome subject of spot zoning.

The land involved was a corner lot which had been in a business zone since 1925 when the zoning ordinance was adopted. In 1955, this ordinance was reviewed in connection with a planning study, and the classification of the area was found to be in accord with a definite business growth. The owner of the adjoining lot carried on a used truck business and proposed to extend it to the corner lot. Owners of lots in the neighborhood secured the adoption of an amending ordinance which made the corner lot residential. The court had no trouble with these facts in ruling that the amendment was arbitrary and unreasonable and said: "If not spot zoning, it is analogous to it and violative of the principle of uniformity." There may be a helpful suggestion in the decision. Spots or islands of preference are not the essentials in a proof of invalidity in this type of zoning case. Any arbitrary or discriminatory action which, in the words of the Schertzer case, is "violative of uniformity" may be sufficient to bring a ruling of invalidity.

VARIANCE VS. CHANGE OF ZONE

In Burchard *et al. vs.* Ramos *et al.,** decided in November, 1963, the hardship relied upon for a variance was the lack of demand for new dwellings in the area involved. Although there might be proved a heavy economic loss, this was not the kind of hardship which would support a variance, since it was not peculiar to the lot. There were other lots in the same area which had the same economic situation. The fact that a property cannot be put to an economic use is, in the words of the court, "a hazard that often accompanies the ownership of property along or near zone boundaries."

*Adv. Sheets 1963, p. 1071.

(Continued on page 44)

20

Commentaries

Landscape Survey: Word comes to us from *Landscape Architecture Quarterly* that one of the most comprehensive landscape surveys ever undertaken in the Nation has been completed by the State of Wisconsin, as part of its effort to promote tourism. The whole state, its scenic, natural, and historical resources, has been intensively mapped and studied.

In an article, "Quality Corridors for Wisconsin," appearing in the January issue of the *Quarterly*, Philip H. Lewis, Jr., landscape architect and consultant to the Wisconsin Department of Resource Development, tells how it's being done.

Chief worry to Wisconsin's planners is that uncontrolled and strip development along highways, lakes, and scenic ridges will spoil the state's charm for sportsmen, vacationers and tourists. The whole state has been mapped with an eye to preserving, unspoiled, the thousands of square miles of still undamaged countryside.

"Environmental Corridors," the name given to the state's natural resource and landscape patterns, have been inventoried over the state; 61 separate areas of distinctive character have been identified. Ultimately, many of these will be connected by a proposed perimeter highway system.

Says Mr. Lewis in the *Quarterly*, "Enjoyment of our natural and cultural heritage means something to the present generation; but only through careful planning, and sound environmental design will it continue to be enjoyed by future generations. The task is mounumental . . . the time for action is now!"

＠

Helicopters: While the problem of city traffic congestion becomes more acute daily, a budding new worry from the helicopter may be just beyond the horizon.

The Journal of the American Institute of Planners, February, 1964, calls attention to the fact that continued growth in the use of the helicopter and the development of other means of aerial travel could create a whole new set of city planning problems.

"Urban Planning And The New Mobility," an article in the *Journal* by Melville C. Branch, Lecturer in Engineering at the University of California and a member of the Los Angeles City Planning Commission, points out: "We are witnessing a rapid increase in the use of helicopters. In the last dozen years, the number of helicopters produced annually has grown from very few to over a thousand and commercial helicopter miles available and flown have skyrocketed literally and figuratively."

In fact, continues Mr. Branch, "Commercial helicopter operations have already created new problems of transportation and city planning. In Los Angeles, locational control of heliports is achieved through permitted use in industrial zones and conditional use elsewhere." Requests have already been received by the Los Angeles City Planning Department for the approval of home sites

21

for private and personal helicopter use.

"Although few people can afford the private purchase of these craft today," Mr. Branch points out, "we cannot conclude this will not change. Small-size prototypes have been under test for some time. With significant advances in performance per unit weight, greater inherent flight stability, simple operation, lower initial operating costs, noise suppression, and safety provisions—particularly against air collision—a family or individual helicopter may not be too many years away."

* celo*

Water: "There was a day when you could stick a well down anywhere and not bother anybody. Now each year, there are new problems of competition for particular underground water resources—and no law to guide us."

Thus does *County Planner*, a publication of the Montgomery County Planning Commission, Dayton, Ohio, sum up local aspects of a problem which is receiving increasing national attention.

"Demand for water in Ohio is huge," continues the *County Planner*. "It takes 60,000 gallons to make a ton of paper, 65,000 gallons for a ton of steel. About nine-tenths of our water use is industrial—11 billion gallons a day."

Pointing out that space is increasingly in demand—space for cities, for highways, for factories, for parking lots, for golf courses, the publication continues: "And space for water. We don't seem to realize that water requires space until a river leaps its normal banks and demands the rest of its historic channel—the part we call its 'flood plain.' It takes space to contruct emergency water-storage areas—known as 'flood control reservoirs'. It takes space to have enough water surface area for recreation."

celo

Sanctuary: "Wilderness experience as a deliberately planned adventure in search of solitude and quietude in an atmosphere of reverence and in a setting of great natural beauty is, indeed, a practical reality to many people. There is much to be said of the wilderness as a sanctuary. Prayer is a natural state of mind for some in such circumstances, not a special effort to rise above adverse conditions. Appreciation of supreme natural beauty is a concomitant of this kind of prayer. To many people there can be no higher reward in life than to be successful in adventure of this kind."

—From "Transfiguration In Wilderness," by C. Edward Graves in The Living Wilderness, Winter-Spring, 1962-63.

celo

Paradox: "Are we running out of outdoors?" The February-March issue of *National Wildlife*, a colorful bi-monthly magazine of the National Wildlife Federation, spotlights this question.

In the opening article, Thomas L. Kimball, Executive Director of the Federation, emphasizes that America is still short of recreation space, despite some 283,000,000 acres of land already designated as public recreation areas. Pointing out that most of this open land and the

(Continued on page 48)

22

PROJECTS IN REVIEW

Senior Citizens Activity Centers

Community planning for those we have come to speak of as our "senior citizens" is moving close to center-stage in public thinking at this time. While the gathering effort is still primarily in the "comment" area, earnest consideration—preferably, more of it from the "seniors", themselves—may do much to groove the somewhat diffuse beginnings into a channel of purposiveness.

To explore this general area, a Northern California Regional Conference on "Recreation's Responsibility To Senior Programs" was held last year at Sacramento State College under the sponsorship of the California State Department of Parks and Recreation and the Citizens Advisory Committee of the State Health and Welfare Agency.

A report of the proceedings carries excerpts from an address by William D. Bechill, Executive Secretary, Citizen's Advisory Committee on Aging. Suggestive of the fact that we must find a way to tap that reservoir of wisdom and insight which time and experience have bequeathed to certain favored ones of us, he says:

"Many senior programs often provide concrete ways by which retired people are enabled to make *very real contributions* to community life and directly strengthen their own individual capacities and interests. Such voluntary or paid community service efforts need to become an integrated part of all leisure time programs. We believe that there is a tremendous range of possibilities here if we are

bold and imaginative and not afraid of a few failures."

The idea that the elderly have a special and genuine contribution to make to the community has not always been highlighted in current thinking in this general area. It will, perhaps, come more to the fore as debate is held on proposed legislation such as S. 1357, the Senior Citizens Community Planning and Services Act which has, among its major provisions, grants to States and local communities for community planning and services for senior citizens and also a matching grant program for the construction of recreational activity centers for seniors.

Says Mr. Bechill, "It is clear that we have to apply a very different interpretation to the purposes and meaning of recreation to retired people than that which is customarily thought of for children or youth."

Pointing out that "California is far ahead of the rest of the Nation, both in terms of the number of programs, their scope and their quality," he continues, "but in all honesty, I believe that we have merely scraped the surface in arriving at the types of programs and activities which are desired by seniors today."

Significantly enough, some of the most practical suggestions during the California conference, came from individual evaluations in problem areas such as transportation. "How about school buses during off hours for the use of senior groups?" the participants asked. "What about a used car dealer who would supply station-wagons, covered by insurance for use by senior club members?"

And even, "Why not the purchase of transportation vehicles by local service organizations?"

The questions were probing, if random, but they do suggest that if, where, and how senior citizen activity centers are to be incorporated in community planning and construction programs for the future, then a sharper definition of their aims and purposes might seem to be subjects for consideration now.

Park Land in Medina

Just about everybody's talking about the need to preserve open space, but the conversation sometimes has a way of easing into broad generalities, spirited enough to fire enthusiasm, not always specific enough to stimulate action.

Now from Medina, Washington, a city encompassing an area of 906 acres, comes a refreshing report that it has come down to cases.

Medina's aim: When maximum density of the city is reached, to provide one acre of park land for each sixty families. Every Medina family, if present plans materialize, will, in time, be within three quarters, of a mile of a large park area.

Medina presently owns 11.5 acres of park lands. It proposes the addition of another 18 acres which result in a ratio of one acre of park land to 30 acres of residential property, including streets. Medina residential property is zoned for an average of two families per acre.

To purchase the additional park land, the Medina City Council has authorized an eighty thousand dollar bond issue to be placed on the March election ballot. The parks would consist primarily of two large natural wooded areas.

Says Gregory C. Cullins, Medina's City Manager: "We believe that Medina, in acquiring open-space lands for the benefit of existing and future Medina families, is setting an excellent example."

Metropolitan Water Study

The 1964 study of water has been given Number One priority by the Inter-County Regional Planning Commission, Denver, Colorado.

The Commission states that it recognizes the tremendous importance of this service to the growth and well-being of the Denver metropolitan area and that it is aware that the water problem is at the heart of many other metropolitan problems and that a solution to it can lead the way to other solutions.

The study will include a survey, inventory, and analysis of the present and future water resources and water supply capacity of the total metropolitan area and an investigation of the administrative structure required for more effective operation of the water supply service.

❦

Water Quality Committees

All Ohio cities through which streams discharge into Lake Erie will be urged to sponsor the formation of local water quality advisory committees if the recommendation of the Ohio Commission of the Great Lakes Commission is carried out. The group has urged the Ohio Water Pollution Control Board to lend its support to such action.

National Capital
Notes

President Lyndon B. Johnson spoke the following words at a recent Presidential Prayer Breakfast, held at the Mayflower Hotel in Washington, D. C.:

"This Federal City of Washington, in which we live and work, is much more than a place of residence. For the 190,000,000 people that we serve and for many millions in other lands, Washington is the symbol and the showcase of a great Nation and a greater cause of human liberty on earth.

"In this Capital City today, we have monuments to Lincoln, and to Jefferson, and to Washington, and to many statesmen and many soldiers. But at this seat of government, there must be a fitting memorial to the God who made us all. Our Government cannot and should not sponsor the erection of such a memorial with public funds, but such a living memorial should be here. It should be a center of prayer, open to all men of all faiths at all times . . .

"The world is given many statistics about the per capita vices of Washington, but the world knows all too little about the per capita virtues of those who live and labor here.

"I believe . . . that the true image of Washington is not that of power or pomp or plenty. It is rather that of a prayerful Capital of good and God-fearing people."

★   ★   ★

Will the arts, including the performing arts, assume a more prominent position in the future life of the Nation's Capital?

That's the root-question behind a rising volume of public query and comment concerning the size, requirements, cost and location of the proposed John F. Kennedy Center for the Performing Arts, now assured the support of the American people through act of their Congress and, under current plans, to be built in Washington, D. C. on the banks of the Potomac.

With public interest increasing, lively discussion on the location of the Center took place at the

February meeting of the **Committee of 100 on the Federal City** which has long been alert to the need for an appropriate Cultural Center in Washington and which, in the past, has placed emphasis on *feasibility* of size and design.

In the belief that the Potomac site now selected for the Center will "fail to give the desired contribution to the city's life," the Committee, following consideration of able arguments pro and con, adopted a resolution supporting recently introduced legislation, providing for a study of a cultural center site in downtown Washington.

The resolution, as adopted, stated that the Potomac site "presents great difficulties in transportation and parking." Argument for the resolution, as summarized by the Committee's **Chairman, Rear Admiral Neill Phillips, USN (Ret.)**, held that the huge underground parking facilities proposed for the Potomac site will be fabulously costly to build and entirely uneconomic to maintain since they will be largely vacant during periods when no performances are being given at the Center.

Argument against the resolution, as summarized by the Chairman, held that no in-town site is available for such a large construction project and that the riverfront location will generate its own dynamism and contribute to the vitality of the city.

Meanwhile, **Robert J. Lewis,** writing on "Cities and People," in the *Washington Sunday Star*, pointed out that Congress has acted promptly in authorizing support for the Center and asserted that "there never has been a clear public statement by the architects or sponsors that gives the full dimensions of this project."

Citing facts and figures, Mr. Lewis said, "If the present design is to be used as the final one for the building, it is evident that what is proposed here is one of the largest structures in Washington."

In a plea for understanding about the Center and a suggestion that the facts be faced squarely, Mr. Lewis continued: "We do not refer here to the dimensions of this project to harm it but to help it—and to prevent further misunderstanding in the future."

"Now is the time," said Mr. Lewis, "for all the facts about the current design to be made public by the architects and sponsors in a form everyone can understand. If Congress fully understands what is being proposed, it can then make informed decisions on lands and funds that will minimize the prospect of later recrimination."

Secretary of the Interior Stewart L. Udall has suggested that citizen groups mass behind the drive to collect scenic easements along the Potomac Palisades in an effort to prevent construction of high-rise apartments along the Potomac.

In an address before the annual awards dinner of the Fairfax County Federation of Citizens Association, Mr. Udall spoke as a neighbor to neighbors who live in the area. He said that if Fairfax County, with its abundant natural beauty and historical endowments, succumbs to "uglification," there is not much hope for the rest of suburbia.

He described the scenic easement idea as "one of the most exciting new conservation concepts" of the decade and suggested that it may catch on in all parts of the country.

Work will begin this year on remodeling the historic Old Patent Office at 8th and F Streets, N. W., Washington, D. C., into a National Portrait Gallery and a museum for the National Collection of Fine Arts under the supervision of the Smithsonian Institution.

This is the word from **Downtown Progress** which, in its most recent Report, says that plans have been completed and funds appropriated for the reconstruction work.

The Report also indicates that two Demonstration Blocks on F Street, between 12th and 14th Streets will be constructed "where new pavement, street trees, streets lights, canopies, and benches will establish a high standard of public elegance to stimulate the renovation and development of adjacent private properties in the heart of the shopping area."

Downtown Progress began operations on April 1, 1960, on the recommendation of a Joint Policy Committee of the Federal City Council and the National Capital Planning Commission. It functions under the auspices of the **National Capital Downtown Committee, Inc.**, a non-profit corporation formed and financed by Washington business and civic leaders to prepare and help carry out plans for the revitalization of Downtown Washington, east of 15th Street, between the White House and the Capitol.

Its recent Report expresses appreciation to a number of public and private organizations, of which the **Committee of 100 on the Federal City** is one, "whose representatives contributed valuable suggestions and advice at hundreds of meetings and conferences held since the Fall of 1960 to consider studies and proposals leading to the development of the *Action Plan* for Downtown."

A history of the Pension Building on Judiciary Square in Washington, D. C. has been published by the **General Services Administration** of the U. S. Government.

Describing the building as a memorial to the soldiers and sailors of the Civil War, the history is a prototype for others to be issued on significant buildings and areas in the Nation's Capital. It has been prepared as a cooperative effort with the **National Capital Planning Commission** program for preservation of landmarks in Washington, D.C.

Included among those buildings for which booklets are to be prepared are: Agriculture Administration Building, Old Post Office, National Archives Building, Tariff Commission Building, Old Patent Office, Old City Hall, Treasury Building, Executive Office Building and the Winder Building. Area studies of the Federal Triangle and Lafayette Square will also be covered by booklets.

Foundation Makes Grant to APCA for Field Survey

The Taconic Foundation recently made a grant to the American Planning and Civic Association to provide for a field survey to help crystallize the Association's future work program.

Mr. Henry Fagin, Professor of Planning at the University of Wisconsin, has been employed to undertake the survey.

In carrying out his assignment, Mr. Fagin will visit a number of cities to appraise the nature of the most urgent present day community development problems.

The APCA Executive Committee considers the survey of special significance at this time in shaping the future work program of the Association.

★   ★   ★

The Need for Voluntary Associations

"For the effective discharge of physical planning, two quite separate kinds of bodies appear to be required in addition to those invested with statutory responsibilities.

"One main need is for voluntary pressure groups of all kinds to 'till the ground' of public opinion . . . Practical experience shows that legislation is only a part of the battle, and that as long as planning has to be practised as a broadly coercive activity with which most people are out of sympathy, then the results tend to be limited in value.

"If there were wider understanding of the reasons why land use has to be controlled, and if there were a higher standard of public taste in civic design and architecture . . . then the task of planning would be much easier. In many respects, the United States, where the legislation is embryonic compared with our own, seems now to be producing better results largely through an incredible fructification of voluntary associations which are steadily influencing public opinion into a more receptive mood."

—Professor Colin Buchanan, 1963 Presidential Address, Journal of the Town Planning Institute, December, 1963, p. 338, 18 Ashley Place, Victoria, London S.W.1.

TOCKS ISLAND, *Upstream View. On the right is Kittatinny Ridge.*
On the left, the cultivated flood plain of the Delaware River.
Courtesy National Park Service, U. S. Department of the Interior.

DELAWARE WATER GAP, *Pennfield, New Jersey. Part of the proposed Tocks Island National Recreation Area.*

Courtesy National Park Service, U. S. Department of the Interior.

SUNFISH POND, WORTHINGTON STATE FOREST, New Jersey. *Area under consideration for inclusion in the proposed Tocks Island National Recreation Area.*

Courtesy National Park Service, U. S. Department of the Interior.

RAYMONDSKILL FALLS, *scenic feature being considered for inclusion in the proposed Tocks Island National Recreation Area.*

Courtesy National Park Service, U. S. Department of the Interior.

Tocks Island National Recreation Area —A Proposal

EDITOR'S NOTE: This is the sixth in the series of articles on proposed National Park Service projects, prepared by the Park Service at our request.

A comprehensive plan has been prepared for the development of the Delaware River Basin. Disastrous floods in the Basin in August, 1955 caused the Congress to authorize the Corps of Engineers to make a comprehensive survey of the water resources of the Basin. As a result, residents of the area have an opportunity to benefit from potential public park and recreation facilities to be provided in conjunction with proposals for flood control, water supply and electric power.

This comprehensive plan for the development and use of the water resources of the Basin identifies and evaluates the recreational resources of the Delaware River Basin and the recreational needs of the people living in or near the area. The plan dramatically reveals the outstanding recreational potential of the proposed 12,350-acre Tocks Island impoundment and the land surrounding it.

A dam at Tocks Island would create a beautiful lake surrounded by steep to rolling wooded hills and valleys. The lake would extend from a few miles above Delaware Water Gap to Port Jervis, a distance of almost 33 miles, would have an average width of one-half mile, and a maximum width of one and one half miles. It would be located on the Delaware River where an excellent supply and quality of recreation water is assured. It would be on the western edge of Megalopolis,

that great new regional city the geographers have identified along the eastern seaboard, and between the long established recreation regions of northwestern New Jersey and eastern Pennsylvania's Pocono Mountains. There are 20 million people living within 75 miles of the site and 30 million within 100 miles. Recreational planners estimate that the resources of the area would produce almost 7,000,000 visits a year if adequate adjacent lands are acquired to accommodate facilities and to preserve and restore the attractiveness of the natural environment.

The study by the Corps compared and evaluated all resource factors. It concluded that the Tocks Island project should be proposed for multiple-purpose development to provide for the storage and use of water, flood control, production of hydroelectric power, and recreation.

The recreation aspects were proposed for development and administration by the Federal Government. This was recommended because of the magnitude and significance of the proposed project for non-urban recreation, the enhancement of the adjoining lands for recreation, the broad regional significance of the project, the large population to be served, the interstate character of the project area, the critical need for a recreation area of this size, and the fact that such an undertaking would exceed the

33

normal capabilities of the States most directly concerned.

For these reasons, augmented by a study and review of the natural, historical and scenic resources of the project, it was determined that the project would warrant development and management by the National Park Service as a National Recreation Area.

The inherent and potential qualities of the Tocks Island project seem to have been created to fit the specifications of a National Recreation Area established by the Presidential Cabinet-level Recreation Advisory Council. Accordingly, it is not surprising that Phase I of the Comprehensive Plan, adopted March 28, 1962, by the Delaware River Basin Commission recognizes that a National Recreation Area is the most logical and effective means of assuring the full and appropriate use of this outstanding recreation resource.

In general, the suggested boundaries include the famous Delaware Water Gap and sufficient space through the valley and upstream upland area to protect its natural and scenic qualities. This will permit a wide variety of recreational facilities, both along the water's edge and on the high ground.

In places, the eastern escarpment of Kittatinny Mountain is followed as the most logical natural boundary. In other places, existing roads and heights of land are followed. The territory embraced in the study boundary includes the Worthington Tract, owned by the State of New Jersey. It may also include Childs State Park, Pennsylvania, and encompassed state game lands. Trans-

fer of any of these to the Federal Government for the recreation area will be the decision of the states.

The reservoir, of course, would form the central feature of the recreation area. It is planned to have the reservoir pool stabilized during the recreation season (May to November) to provide 12,350 acres of water surface, with about 100 miles of attractive shoreline.

Additional features included in the recreation area on both sides of the Water Gap would include Mount Tammany; six miles of free-flowing river below the Tocks Island Dam; approximately 10 miles of the Kittatinny Mountain ridge, averaging about 1,800 feet in elevation; and rolling plateau country on the Pennsylvania side, scored with a number of scenic streams flowing through hemlock gorges, a score of small fresh-water ponds, both natural and artificial, and at least two notable waterfalls. About 75 percent of the area is woodland.

Bills to establish this area as a National Recreation Area have been introduced in both Houses of the 88th Congress. To date, no conclusive action has been taken on them. Under the proposed legislation, the Secretary of the Army would acquire the needed lands and the Secretary of the Interior would be authorized to establish and administer the Tocks Island National Recreation Area as a part of the Tocks Island Reservoir project.

The legislation would instruct the Secretary of the Interior to adopt and implement a land and water use management plan which would

(Continued on page 54)

34

State Park Notes

Forward—Without Forgetting the Past

It is hardly possible these days to discuss State Park and conservation matters intelligently without discovering, upon analysis, that much of the conversation has a familiar ring, that one has heard or read it before.

Since coming back to this work a year and a half ago, I have been re-reading much of the material published twenty and thirty years ago when I was first in this field.

In an address delivered at the Ohio Valley Regional Conference for State Parks in Indiana in 1925, the late Dean Stanley Coulter of Indiana said:

"But we are fallen upon strenuous times. We live in a swiftly moving age, fiercely driven by the machines which we have invented . . . Little wonder, then, that men . . . collapsed at their desks, that sudden shock or unexpected strain took such fearful toll of human life."

He goes on: "Happy is the citizen of a Commonwealth who can find a refuge such as this park affords, and, in its silences, find the recreation which he must have or die."

Remember, he spoke these words in 1925.

Thirty-seven years later in May, 1962, Congressman John Saylor of Pennsylvania, speaking at the White House Conference on Conservation, uttered the exact same sentiments in language of striking similarity.

However, we are also hearing comments regarding State Park planning and development which are somehow disturbing. At a recent meeting of State Park Directors, there was a

35

rather spirited discussion of development policy, some of which gave me the uneasy feeling that some of the principles implicit in the early philosophy of State Parks are giving way under the present day pressures for more income production, evident in the activities of some of the States, toward more intensive recreational development at the expense of the natural area concept.

To preserve natural values and meet the active recreational demands of our ever-increasing population is no sinecure, but this dual responsibility must be recognized as the greatest challenge of the day as well as a prime opportunity for enlightened public service in this field.

Basically, this goes straight to the question of classification of areas and a stricter adherence to the appropriate planning and development of each, according to accepted criteria.

While it is agreed that there are many obstacles to such an accomplishment, geographical, financial and political, as much positive leadership as possible should be exerted to maintain the integrity of our well established and long held principles.

DONALD B. ALEXANDER.

★　　　★　　　★

New York. Governor Nelson Rockefeller recently released a detailed progress report on the first three years' operation of New York's $100,000,000 program for land acquisition for parks and recreation.

Prepared at the Governor's request by Laurance S. Rockefeller, Chairman of the State Council of Parks, and Conservation Commissioner Harold G. Wilm, the 16-page study outlines the purchase of more than 292,000 acres of recreation land acquired since 1961.

Highlights of accomplishments in park land acquisition in New York are shown in a number of plates and tables in the report. Seventeen

new State Parks have been acquired along with significant additions to half of the previously existing 87 parks. Over a quarter of a million acres have been added to the reforestation, preserve, game and multiple purpose areas of the State.

The report pays tribute to the local governments which have made use of the grant provisions of the park land program under which the State defrays 75 per cent of the cost of approved local park land acquisitions. Using this phase of the program, nearly 15,000 acres of local park land have been approved for acquisition at a cost of nearly $50,000,000 of which over

$35,000,000 will be reimbursed by the State.

Said Mr. Rockefeller and Mr. Wilm in a joint foreword to the Report: "The role of the people of New York State was vital. Their enthusiasm and support set an encouraging new precedent and put policy makers across the Nation on notice that people are willing to support and pay for outdoor recreation opportunities."

Virginia. A bill establishing a commission to study the need for outdoor recreational facilities in the Old Dominion State has been favorably reported to the State Senate by its general laws committee.

Under the measure, the 25-member commission would study the need for outdoor recreational facilities and determine the responsibility of the federal, state and local governments in meeting that need. It would submit recommendations outlining how the State would meet its responsibilities and how it might help localities meet local needs.

Washington. A long-range plan for establishment of under-water parks to protect marine life and provide recreation for skin-divers has been announced by Charles H. Odegaard, Director of Washington State Parks.

Mr. Odegaard pointed out that there are salt water areas and possibly fresh water lakes, developed by volcanic eruption, which could be set aside as underwater parks in the State. He indicated a desire to prevent the "wanton misuse" of underwater fish and plant life which

---

BOR REPORT

"State Outdoor Recreation Statistics for 1962," a summary of information received from 213 agencies in 50 States, has just been released by the Bureau of Outdoor Recreation of the Department of the Interior.

The data presented were obtained from a questionnaire, "1962 Records On State Outdoor Recreation Areas," which went to 290 State forest, park, reservoir, highway, and fish and game agencies concerned with outdoor recreation. Returns were received from 213 of the agencies.

Included in the report, at the request of the National Conference on State Parks, is a separate comparative statistical tabulation on State parks and related recreation areas.

It is expected that statistical data for future reports will be obtained in different form from that for the present Summary. As an aid to the States, The Bureau of Outdoor Recreation is currently preparing manuals offering guidelines for statistical presentation.

---

has occurred in some parts of the country.

Ohio. A new era has dawned in Ohio. Today's strip mine areas are becoming tomorrow's playgrounds in the Buckeye State.

Governor James A. Rhodes has called for mine operators and landowners to create recreational facilities on reclaimed lands from "Youngstown to Portsmouth." In so doing, he commented that a 38-million-dollar outdoor recreational program he recently authorized "will meet less than half of the demands of Ohio's outdoorsmen."

Since 1948, coal operators in Ohio have reclaimed 89.6 per cent of lands stripped, according to I. I. Dickman, chief, of the Ohio Division of Reclamation. A total of 77,891 acres has been planted in trees, 45,932 acres in forage and the balance of nearly 9,000 acres converted to water impoundments. Under Ohio law, reclamation must be completed within two years after coal has been removed.

Idaho. Plans for major expansion of three Idaho State Parks this year have been announced by State Parks Division Director Jon Soderbloom.

In addition to opening up new areas, added and improved sanitary facilities and additional trailer facilities will be provided. Also planned, in cooperation with the State Highway Department, is a highway sign program intended to make public use of the parks easier.

In commenting on the stepped-up program, Mr. Soderbloom stated that Idaho park use was up considerably in 1963 and that another rise can be expected this year.

Arkansas. Because the pioneer spirit of years ago has been displayed by the people of Poinsett County, Arkansas, Lake Poinsett State Park was recently dedicated by Governor Faubus of that State.

At the dedication ceremonies, Horace Smith, banker and a prime mover in the park development, told a thousand enthusiastic people of the history of the lake and park development, going back to a little more than a year ago when the first meeting of the Poinsett County Development Council was held and the idea of a State Park was discussed.

A committee, representing all of the larger towns of the county contacted State Senators and Representatives and was instrumental in having a bill introduced in the 1963 Legislature for the creation of Lake Poinsett State Park. Next, the Committee presented to the State a deed to 80 acres of land adjacent to a 600-acre lake built by the Arkansas State Game and Fish Commission.

In his dedicatory talk, Governor Faubus pointed to the growth of the park system in Arkansas and called attention to the fact that only seven parks were operating in 1936 when Lake Catherine became a part of the park system. After that, the establishment of parks in Arkansas waned until 1955. Since that date, fifteen additional parks, museums and historical monuments have been placed under the jurisdiction of the Arkansas Publicity and Parks Commission—a growth in eight years far exceeding the past thirty.

Rhode Island. A special State Commission has been established to study the feasibility of creating a Rhode Island Recreation Authority. Of special concern in the Commission's study will be the question of state recreational development financed by user fees.

Billboard Jungles—Efforts to Control Them!

By HOWARD W. BAKER, Assistant Director for Operations, National Park Service

At the time the following article was prepared, Mr. Baker was Regional Director of the National Park Service Midwest Region, with headquarters in Omaha, Nebraska.

Uncontrolled roadside advertising is becoming more irritating each year to the many millions who travel our major highways for business and pleasure. Increasingly, individuals and organizations who hold that the traveler has the right to see and enjoy roadside scenery are losing patience with those who think only of attracting attention to their places of business.

Public officials having responsibilities for or appreciating the need for protecting segments of scenic America have done much to stimulate campaigns and programs to control billboards. Conrad L. Wirth, former Director of the National Park Service, in a *U. S. News and World Report* interview in 1962, said: "Drive along and look for scenery along the highways. In a good many places you can't see past the billboards." A State park official commented: "Advertising signs are sprouting like dandelions along completed but unprotected sections of our roads."

Editors have noted that much discussion has been provoked, but tangible gains appear to be few. One newspaper has suggested that teeth must be put into existing laws if "highway slums" are to be eliminated. Another asserts that laws are not necessary if each business community is willing to clean up and police its own back yard.

South Dakota, a land of infinite beauty and variety, like many another section of our country, has had some claim also to fitting into the "billboard jungle" category. Regretfully, this has been especially true in the unique, attractive Black Hills area. One of the worst sections is the 25-mile stretch south from Rapid City to the boundary of Mount Rushmore National Memorial. A second stretch equally obnoxious, existed until the past year, along the seven miles of U. S. 16A between the town of Wall and the Pinnacles in Badlands National Monument.

Pressure for legal measures to eliminate roadside signs and billboards was suddenly brought against the 1963 session of the South Dakota Legislature. Three anti-sign bills were introduced, highly recommended by the Garden Clubs of South Dakota. New legislation to cure the obnoxious situation seemed to be the final answer. However, at a State Senate Committee hearing on the bills, a dozen or more local associations opposed such legislation. One potent argument advanced by opponents was that voluntary control could be made to work with the help of reputable businessmen and association members.

A high point in the controversy was reached at a Legislative Subcommittee meeting on billboards, held in Pierre in July, with officers from some six associations opposing the anti-sign bills. There the Subcommittee was told about the highly successful control program that had been undertaken and carried out between Wall, South Dakota, and Badlands National Monument on a voluntary basis by the businessmen of Wall, including Ted Hustead, owner of the well-known Wall Drug Store.

Encouraged by the National Park Service and sparked by local businessmen facing the prospect of unwanted legislation, the motel operators, service station operators, cafe operators, owners of Wall Drug Store and other business interests formed the "Wall Cooperative Sign Association" in the spring of 1963. The purpose of this Association was to lease the sign rights on U. S. 16A between Wall and Badlands, and to get all of the merchants in Wall to cooperate on just three highway signs. The 10 motel operators got together on one sign, the four cafes on another, and the rest of the business places—20 in all—on a third. Ninety percent of the businessmen in Wall agreed to go along with the cooperative sign program,

and the Wall Drug Store lent its cooperative efforts to all.

In the early spring of 1963, 84 signs between the town of Wall and Badlands National Monument smothered the highway. Through the new voluntary program, about 90 percent of these signs were removed and the three large cooperative signs erected in their place. Two of the signs are 10 by 20 feet in size, and the third is 10 by 32 feet. All three are electrically lighted and the lights come on automatically when it gets dark. They are turned off by a clock three or four hours later.

Many States have laws on their books which are adequate to control signs if properly policed and enforced. Voluntary community action such as the program undertaken by the businessmen of Wall is by far the best solution, for this becomes a local project stimulated by a sincere sense of pride and community spirit. It clearly demonstrates that advertising can be provided but in a manner which is not objectionable to the traveler and most certainly removes the "billboard jungle" tag.

HERITAGE

"Williamsburg's spirit, and not merely its return to colonial appearance seized my father's interest and imagination and rewarded him with the greatest satisfaction. His regard for Williamsburg, and that of his friend, Dr. Goodwin, came from their appreciation of Williamsburg as a symbol of the principles of democratic government, and of the human freedoms cherished and won by courageous sacrifices of our forefathers. All who understand Williamsburg today know that these principles and these freedoms, to be retained, must be earned by each succeeding generation."

—Winthrop Rockefeller, Chairman of the Board of Colonial Williamsburg.

Seminars, Conferences and University Notes

Watershed Congress. Watershed development in the United States during the next ten years will be the theme of the *Eleventh National Watershed Congress* to be held in Little Rock, Arkansas, April 26-29, 1964.

Discussions will focus on pollution control, water quality, recreation and wildlife in watershed development, river basin planning, water rights, and the magnitude of watershed development in the future.

An annual event of growing importance in the conservation field, the National Watershed Congress is sponsored by more than 20 of the Country's leading agricultural, conservation and business organizations of which the *American Planning and Civic Association* is one.

The Watershed Congress provides a forum for the discussion of ways and means of expediting and broadening local watershed programs. It affords an over-all review and discussion of watershed programs, problems, and progress.

This year's Congress, like those of the past decade, will be centered on forum discussions of watershed topics and field trips to nearby water projects—many of which were launched under the National Watershed Protection and Flood Prevention Act of 1954.

The program will include, in addition to various committee reports, a review of the "First Ten Years of Progress In Developing The Nation's Watersheds" by Hollis R. Williams, Assistant Administrator for Watersheds of the Soil Conservation Service, and a final committee report and discussion covering the "Magnitude of Watersheds In The Future" —an appraisal of the program in the coming decade.

Plans are being made for a total registration of about 500 participants at the April meeting. Members of the American Planning and Civic Association desiring to attend the Congress should contact the National Watershed Congress Steering Committee, 1424 K Street, N. W., Washington 5, D. C.

Award. *Walter DeS. Harris, Jr.,* Associate Professor of City Planning at *Yale University,* has been decorated by the government of Peru, for his long work in assisting South American nations in urban and regional housing and planning.

Mr. Harris, at recent ceremonies in Lima, Peru, received a Distinguished Service Award from *Fernando Belaunde Terry, Peruvian President,* who conferred on the Yale professor the rank of Comendador of the Order of Merit. The presentation took place at ceremonies marking the first graduation exercises of the Inter-American Program at the Peruvian National Engineering University.

The award of the high Peruvian honor to Mr. Harris came as a complete surprise. In a speech accompanying presentation of the Order of Merit medal, President Belaunde praised Mr. Harris not only for his work as Consultant to the Organization of American States (OAS), but for his pioneering efforts in establishing the big housing-planning center in Lima, which has taken its place as one of the largest graduate planning schools in the world.

41

In 1959, Mr. Harris served as Chief of the Joint U. N. -OAS Technical Mission in Lima, and late that year he was granted a leave of absence by Yale, where he has been on the faculty of the Department of City Planning for several years, to become Director of the Inter-American Housing Center in Bogota. This institution, known as CINVA, has been called the most complete housing and training research center in the world. It is attached to the National University of Colombia.

In 1961, Mr. Harris' many efforts in his field came to fruition in an inter-American agreement signed at Yale to launch a large-scale program to assist educational institutions in Latin America in dealing with the rapidly developing pressures for housing, urban and regional development.

The pact signed jointly by representatives of the 21-nation OAS and Yale, not only set up machinery to furnish the OAS with technical and policy guidance in housing and planning, but created in Yale's city planning department a research and training center for Latin American architects and planners.

In the last two years nearly 25 men have been brought to Yale, either for depth research, or to study for Yale's Master of City Planning degree.

Mr. Harris has remained the Principal Advisor, under the OAS-Yale pact, to both large centers at Lima and Bogota, and makes frequent trips to them each year.

His decoration by the Peruvian government for distinguished service to the nation, is his second honor in that country. In 1960, he and Dean Gibson A. Danes, of the Yale School of Art and Architecture, were awarded honorary professorships at the National Engineering University, Dean Danes in architecture and Mr. Harris in city planning.

Community Development. The Office of Community Development at *Ohio State University* has been reorganized to provide a central office through which the University can assist Ohio communities with problems of growth, change and development.

Operating within the School of Architecture and Landscape Architecture under the College of Engineering, the reorganized office will direct inquiries from communities to the proper University sources for advice or service. The office formerly was administered by the Engineering Experiment Station.

Cooperating with the office will be the College of Commerce and Administration, which has established a center to perform research in community and regional analysis under the direction of Dr. Bryon E. Munson, professor of sociology and anthropology.

Also assisting in the program are the College of Agriculture and Home Economics, which has designated the Cooperative Extension Service to provide community development services, and the College of Education, which will participate in community development programs through the Bureau of Educational Research and Service.

The various departments and Colleges of the University will be available to assist communities having problems in such areas as transportation, land-use and zoning, water and other natural resources, community organization, economic development, social services, schools, recreation and housing.

Israel Stollman, professor of city and regional planning in the School of Architecture, has been named coordinator of the Office of Community Development.

Assisting Professor Stollman will be Dr. W. Raymond Mills, who recently joined the architecture faculty as assistant professor of regional planning. He formerly was research officer for the Northeastern Illinois Metropolitan Area Planning Commission in Chicago.

The new Office of Community Development will continue to sponsor the Community Development Conference which has been held on the campus annually for the past five years.

Travel Course On History of Art In Europe. *The University of Rhode Island Summer Session* has announced a new program of study and travel in Europe in the summer of 1964 under the personal management and direction of William M. Kane, M. A., Instructor of the History of Art at the University of Rhode Island, Kingston, Rhode Island.

Sojourns of from three to ten days will be made in such cities as London, Amsterdam, Paris, Munich, Venice, Florence, Rome and Madrid. In addition to a detailed exploration of painting, sculpture, and architecture in the European countries, the nine-week course will include an investigation of aspects of urban European civilization from antiquity to the present.

The group will travel within Europe by plane for longer distances and by tour-bus for shorter trips.

Award. *Dr. Robert Branner,* associate professor of Art History at Columbia University, has been awarded the Alice Davis Hitchcock Award for the most distinguished book on architectural history by an American author published in 1963.

Professor Branner received the award for his *La cathedrale de Bourges,* an architectural history of the famous Gothic cathedral in Bourges, France.

The award, an inscribed plaque, is made annually by the Society of Architectural Historians for the most distinguished book on architectural history by an American or on an American subject.

Studio Design. *Stanley Tigerman,* partner in the Chicago architectural firm of Tigerman and Koglin, has been named to direct the studio design course offered under the Graduate Program in Urban Design at Washington University, St. Louis, Missouri.

The graduate program, one of a few of its kind in the United States, leads to a master's degree in architecture and urban design.

Chairman of the planning committee of the Chicago Chapter of the American Institute of Architects, Mr. Tigerman received his master's degree in architecture from Yale University. He has served as a lecturer at the University of Illinois and as visiting critic at Cornell University.

THE COMMUNITY RENEWAL PROGRAM AS A LONG RANGE GUIDE

(*Continued from page 18*)

coordinate all of the building and re-building efforts of the city—public and private—to stop wasted effort.

The public will never be able to understand why plans for one urban function operate to the detriment of another. With a coordinated approach, this can be avoided. The dislocation caused by highway construction can be compensated for in advance perhaps by slum clearance with a minimum loss to the city. The spectre of an area of recent redevelopment required for a highway, public building, or other major use will be eliminated.

Perhaps I expect too much from the CRP. If so, we need a program that will do these things. What we need is an all-inclusive procedure of cooperating toward an agreed objective. I believe the CRP to be it.

In a one sentence summary— the value of the Community Renewal Program, as a long-range guide, lies in its ability to provide a coordinated all-inclusive program for urban development. If it is drafted with that objective, it can serve that tremendous purpose.

To quote the Housing and Home Finance Agency, "The governing criterion is that all activities aid in . . . scheduling renewal actions for correcting blight and *preventing its spread.*"

The job is too big for correction. The greater part will result from prevention. The CRP must be a program for both.

ZONING ROUND TABLE

(*Continued from page 20*)

The case emphasizes an important difference in the zoning process. The evidence that was presented would support a finding:

a) No demand for residential development in the area;

b) Many light manufacturing and mercantile establishments in the neighborhood;

c) A business zone and an industrial zone not far away;

d) No recent construction in the vicinity;

e) A pronounced trend to mercantile and manufacturing establishments.

The above facts could support a change of zone to business by amendment, but amendment is exclusively in the jurisdiction of the legislative agency and the Board of Appeals, by its power to grant variances, should never be allowed to encroach on the legislative right.

Strictly Personal

Laurance S. Rockefeller has received the 1963 Distinguished Service Award conferred by The American Forestry Association "in recognition of outstanding service in the conservation of American resources of soil, water and forests."

The citation, presented by Edward P. Stamm, President of the American Forestry Association, read in part:

"A businessman can be an artist just as surely as a composer who writes a symphony or a painter who transforms a bare wall into a beautiful mural. All three are creators.

"The businessman-philanthropist selected for The American Forestry Association's Distinguished Service Award is an enlighted exponent of creative business in our twentieth century. He has combined a lifelong interest in aviation with the more recent challenge of space. He has backed both ventures with capital investment, particularly in young companies founded on new and exciting ideas. He has used the dividends of his many successful enterprises to make our Nation a more enjoyable, healthy and worthwhile place in which to live.

"His generous gifts to conservation in many of our states include the Jackson Hole Preserve in Wyoming and the Virgin Islands National Park. His helpful influence was a factor in the launching of a $100,000,000 parks and recreation program in New York State. He became even better known to most of us in his role as Chairman of the Outdoor Recreation Resources Review Commission. In 1962, his commission delivered to the President a proposed action program for meeting the Nation's recreation needs in the next four decades. Like so many things he has done or had a hand in, the ORRRC Report is regarded as something new in American creativity."

In accepting the award, Mr. Rockefeller said he wished to acknowledge a "tremendous debt to others—my father, Sam Dana, Horace Albright and Fairfield Osborne, just to name a few." Mr. Rockefeller paid a special tribute "to my friend and associate, Carl Gustafson, who will be remembered as a true conservationist."

———◇———

Paul Oppermann has resigned as executive director of the Northeastern Illinois Metropolitan Area Planning Commission after nearly six years of service with the public agency. Mr. Oppermann, who became the Commission's first staff member after nine years as Director of Planning for San Francisco, resigned to join the faculty of Massachusetts Institute of Technology as a lecturer in metropolitan planning and to become a partner in Adams, Howard & Oppermann, planning consultant firm headquartered in Cambridge, Massachusetts.

The Planning Commission accepted Mr. Oppermann's resignation with regrets and with "deep appreciation for his major contribution in helping the Planning Commission to establish itself as an essential service to local governments."

Mr. Oppermann is a member of the Board of Trustees of the American Planning and Civic Association.

———◆———

Matthew L. Rockwell, deputy director of the Northeastern Illinois Metropolitan Area Planning Commission since last April, has succeeded Paul Oppermann as executive director of that organization.

Nationally known as a planner and a specialist in urban design, Mr. Rockwell is a licensed architect and engineer. From 1945 to 1961 he was a partner and co-founder of Stanton & Rockwell, Chicago-based firm of architects and planners, where he served as planning consultant to a number of Northeastern Illinois communities, including Chicago Heights, Highland Park, Glenview, Deerfield, Wilmette, Northfield and Villa Park.

———◆———

Victor W. Flickinger became chief of the National Park Service's newly created Division of Federal Agency and State Assistance in January. He will direct that division's participation with the Department's Bureau of Outdoor Recreation in recreation site planning for Federal, State and local agencies.

For the past 14 years, Mr. Flickinger has served as chief of the Ohio Division of Parks and Recreation. He served as president of the National Conference on State Parks from 1952 through 1954 and holds the Cornelius A. Pugsley Silver Medal for "outstanding service in park practice and management." He is a graduate landscape architect of Iowa State University.

———◆———

Ernest J. Gebbart, 1414 Mulford Road, Columbus, Ohio, has been named chief of the Ohio Division of Parks and Recreation, replacing V. W. Flickinger. The 49-year-old Gebhart, a 17-year department veteran, transferred to the former Ohio Division of Parks in February, 1962, as assistant chief. Prior to that time he had been with the Division of Forestry as a ranger and later as staff forester in charge of reforestation.

Mr. Gebhart served in the Army Air Force from 1941 to 1945 as a fighter pilot. A native of Marietta, Ohio, he was graduated from the University of Minnesota with a B.S. degree in Forestry in 1946 and joined the Forestry division the following year.

———◆———

Malcolm H. Dill, for the past 16 years Director of Planning for Baltimore County, Maryland, retired from that position in February. Mr. Dill will continue in a consultant capacity with the County at the same time that he will undertake general planning consulting activities. Formerly a member of the Board of Trustees of the American Planning and Civic Association, he has been a member of the organization since 1936.

———◆———

Lawrence F. Cook, whose career with the National Park Service spans 40 years, has been appointed to the newly created post of field assistant to the Director. Moving up from the division of ranger services, where he has been chief since 1959, Mr. Cook's new assignment calls for him to assist the Director of the National Park Service by carrying out a series of studies and duties related to the Agency's program. He will also undertake special functions in connection with Park Service relationships with other Federal agencies concerning outdoor recreation facilities and open spaces.

◆

C. D. Harris, formerly Chief of Field Operations of the Parks and Recreation Division, Michigan State Department of Conservation, has been named a Regional Manager of the Department. In this capacity, he will assume responsibility for all field activities pertaining to fish, forestry, game, law enforcement, education and information within an assigned area of the State. His new responsibilities will entail a transfer from the State Parks and Recreation Division.

◆

Governor John Connally, of Texas, has named the following to a three-man commission, responsible for guiding the new Texas State Parks and Wildlife Department which came into existence in late August, 1963, with the merging of the Game and Fish Commission and the State Park Board:

Will E. Odom, Chairman of the Parks and Wildlife Commission, Austin, Texas.

A. W. Moursund, Johnson City, Texas, director of the American State Bank of San Antonio and Citizens State Bank of Johnson City.

James M. Dellinger, Corpus Christi, Texas, president of J. M. Dellinger, Inc., a heavy construction firm.

J. Weldon Watson, assistant commissioner for the Texas State Department of Public Welfare since 1955,

and a lifetime career state administrator, was named Executive Director of the Parks and Wildlife Department by the newly appointed three-man commission.

In speaking of Mr. Watson's appointment, Mr. Odom commented: "Watson is a career public service official who is widely acknowledged to be one of the Nation's foremost administrators."

◆

Conrad L. Wirth was honored recently when it was announced that the new administration building at the National Park Service's Stephen T. Mather Interpretive Training and Research Center, Harpers Ferry, West Virginia, will be known as the Conrad L. Wirth Hall.

The honor was conferred at the suggestion of *U. S. Senator Jennings Randolph* of West Virginia and *Bradley D. Nash*, former Under Secretary of Commerce. In a letter to Secretary of the Interior Udall, proposing the designation, Mr. Nash said:

"In view of the very central part played by Director, Wirth in the establishment of the Mather Center, and in recognition of his 30 years of service in the cause of conservation in the Park Service, it is suggested that the new administration building be known as Conrad L. Wirth Hall."

◆

Lemuel A. (Lon) Garrison, formerly Superintendent of Yellowstone National Park, has been named Regional Director of the National Park Service's regional office in Omaha, Nebraska.

Mr. Garrison will be replaced at Yellowstone by *John S. McLaughlin*

(*Continued on page 48*)

COMMENTARIES

(Continued from page 22)

people who would use it are thousands of miles apart, Mr. Kimball suggests America's recreational paradox: "Where there's space, there are few people; where there are people, there isn't enough space."

e⁄ɔ

Mr. National Park Service: "To many, Conrad Wirth today is 'Mr. National Park Service.' He is a staunch defender of national park ethics and practice. His enlightened research and development programs for the National Park System have been convenient blueprints for many States in the planning of their own parks and recreation sites. He insisted upon a high degree of coordination between all agencies, national and local . . .

"Connie Wirth's character as Director is best reflected by the esprit de corps that characterizes park personnel. The park ranger in uniform has become a living symbol of public service . . . The spirit of service has been praised in high and low places, by royalty, the learned, scientists, farmers, and laborers, from within the boundaries of our Nation and from without . . .

"One of Connie's great contributions has been to the popularity and usefulness of park interpretive services. Through interpretation park visitors can make their trip a significant, memorable experience. Many international visitors express the opinion that this experience, has been a significant reward of their visit to the United States. The na-tional parks have been described as the world's greatest outdoor laboratories as well as the greatest facility for meaningful out-door education."

—From the remarks of U. S. Senator Harry Flood Byrd of Virginia, upon the retirement of Conrad Louis Wirth as Director of the National Park Service.

e⁄ɔ

Change: "We have seen the face of the land alter year by year, and it is clear that striking changes lie a-head. . . All of these developments call for policy decisions about land use. The critical question is how well these decisions take into account both the interests of the individual and the welfare of the community. Planning and zoning are both essential. To do one without the other is to do only half the job."

—Statement by J. L. Stauber, Marsh-field, Wisconsin before the Northern Great Lakes Regional Conference, September, 1963.

e⁄ɔ

STRICTLY PERSONAL

(Continued from page 47)

who is transferring from the superintendency at Grand Canyon National Park, Arizona. And the top job at Grand Canyon will be filled by *Howard B. Stricklin* who has been serving in Washington as chairman of a task force planning ways to meet national park system needs in future years.

The Need for Three-Dimensional Planning and Regulation

By MICHAEL M. BERNARD, General Plan and Research Division, Chicago Department of City Planning.

Space—specifically, airspace—is a limited resource.- It is limited with respect to its dimension, and it is limited with respect to its content. It is the place in which man survives and it contains the substance that is most essential to his survival.

It seems that urban planning has not yet fully recognized the true nature of its subject matter in this regard. It has dealt with so-called *land* problems and somehow also tried to bring its efforts to bear upon air pollution problems and upon the many problems resulting from increasing air traffic of all types.

The Need for A 3-Dimensional Plan

The 2-dimensional approach to planning is, in fact, quite archaic, and it is doubtful whether a preoccupation with the land surface was ever really the most meaningful definition of the subject matter for planning. Even more, the aesthetic, or urban design effort would have had to reject, and has rejected, the flat surface as its primary medium. It must be admitted that the Master Plan in map form is a hopelessly boring aesthetic product.

The Development of a Concept of Social Space

There can be seen arising, rather, a concept of space in multi-dimensional terms that is well-suited and relatable to the needs of good physical design, to the knowledge of social dynamics, and to the technical

and scientific understanding of our environment. A sense of what is developing has persisted, and can be found in all the worthwhile resource conservation endeavors of the past: That we should be attempting to reconcile man with his greater environment, and more important, man with man within this greater environment. Therefore, the matter at issue really relates to the broadening of our understanding of environment as the subject matter of our endeavors.

The Future Subject Matter for Planning

What is man's environment? Right now, it might be described as a double shell with a thickness several miles above, and, perhaps, a few hundred feet below the land surface. In the outer shell, the airspace, literally billions of passenger-miles are now traversed and billions of ton-miles of freight are hauled per year. The volumes also appear to be going up considerably every year.

Although the sub-surface area exhibits no great activity as yet, interest in it is constantly increasing as are efforts to rearrange the levels of the land and water surfaces, themselves, for various purposes.

Solving 3-Dimensional Planning Problems

In attempting to relate complex utility and transportation systems both below and above the surface of the earth, in "blocking" altitudes for

49

the assignment of flight traffic, and in developing criteria for ground obstructions to aircraft, it has become abundantly evident that man needs not only to plan but to regulate his environment according to some broader geometry.

In the upper and lower portions of the environment, attempt will have to be made to solve air and water pollution problems of serious proportions created by the disposal of more and more tons of man's debris every year. In dealing with these problems, future planning and regulatory efforts will need to employ the use of 3-dimensional techniques to reconcile conflicting needs and uses. The scientist, the architect and the engineer have already gone a long way toward preferring the use of 3-dimensional devices in lieu of 2-dimensional drawings as the basic tools for communicating about and solving the problems of the physical environment.

In using a broader concept of space, we may also find new ways for assuring that the various needs of recreation, air travel and building construction are met in some related and harmonious way. More important, it seems possible that this approach may at last provide the means for creating a common language for technical, aesthetic and social considerations.

For one thing, there will need to be greater use of working models with transparency to show the relationship of various uses and activities along multiple levels of space. This will help to provide a truer picture of all the economic location choices that are available in our environment: That is to say, we must finally

be made to realize that we can go up and down in various ways as well as just move along the "flat" earth.

It would also seem that space allocation will ultimately have to depend upon some meaningful system of economic and social priority. This system will be needed to answer questions such as: How much of the airspace directly above the surface of the earth should be preempted by aircraft use? What surface uses should best be assigned to the hazardous flight areas (which can cover hundreds of square miles)? How can helicopter traffic be best accomodated within the city? Should parking lots be required to go underground or be covered over with another (say, recreation) use on top? What should be done with the airspace above railroads, highways and other "surface only" uses? Specifically, what should be done about future proposals such as New York City's Grand Central Station-Park Avenue-Pan American development? Is there a meaningful basis for controlling building height? (Note the beginnings made in this direction by Harrison, Ballard and Allen, *Plan for Rezoning the City of New York*.) Should a mile-high building be permitted, if proposed? Should a shopping center be allowed half-way up a tall building? (Recall Le Corbusier's Unité d' Habitation.) These are but a few of those questions that are already upon us.

In conclusion, along the lines that have been mentioned, the effort in urban planning may more closely fulfill its implied promise to produce satisfying cultural solutions to the problems posed in our physical

(Continued on page 56)

THE CONSERVATION CHALLENGE
OF THE SIXTIES

(Continued from page 4)

generations will always loom large in our deliberations.

A final challenge concerns the choices we make in organizing and creating the man-made part of our environment: the buildings, the homes, the highways, and all of these things. Once we accept the idea that open space, clean air, green acres and attractive surroundings are not amenities, but necessities of a society that aspires to greatness, we will bring the artists and artisans to the forefront of our social planning.

Too many conservationists are wont to wash their hands of the man-made world by indicting the agents of progress. The enormous projects which will shape a part of the world of tomorrow—the freeways, the urban renewal projects, the airports, the industrial parks, and the new subdivisions—need not be ugly or inhuman if enough people are ready to fight for harmony, order and beauty, ready to demand creative land-use planning by creative people. We can have more man-made masterpieces and more man-managed landscapes that please the eye if, as the great architect Walter Gropius said recently, we "can find the right balance and coordination between the artist, the scientist and the businessman." Science has given us a wide assortment of tools: we can build for beauty, or build expediently with no regard for elementary esthetics. Science has given us the orchestral instruments, if I may use the figure

of speech—the instruments we need to play a heroic symphony of our own. We can waste this gift on discordant solos, or, if we are wise enough to let the architects and artistically gifted wield the baton, we can do a noble and enriching work in the re-creation of our land.

And what about population pressures—those pressures that compound all of our problems? Current government planners operate in a sort of bureaucratic trance, it seems to me from my seat in Washington, on the actuarial assumption that the population of the United States will double by the year 2000. A corollary assumption of these people is that the good, the true and the beautiful will somehow be enhanced if the Nation is more populous, and I suspect that this is an assumption that operates in your state as well.

Needed: New Questions

We have growth room in this country, but it may be that the time has come for thoughtful men to ask questions about such assumptions.

What is the ideal "ecology of man"—the ideal relation of human population to environment? Is it not time to ask whether man is subject to the laws of nature that govern other species—the laws which hold that for every species in any environment there is an optimum population? What is the carrying capacity as far as the human species is concerned? What is the proper man-land ratio for a

51

particular continent? How much living space do human beings need in order to function with maximum efficiency—and to enjoy maximum happiness?

If we are to discharge our high duty as custodians of the future must we not at least ask such questions? If the fulfillment of the individual is our ultimate goal, and the highest concepts of morality inform our thinking, surely we can explore this terrain without untoward controversy. If we are to reach the golden avenue that Robert Frost called "a new Augustan age," assuredly individual excellence will be more important than the accomplishments of the mass, and quality will be more important than quantity.

Geography must of necessity be a global science, and our outlook must be increasingly global if the optimum use of resources is to be achieved. Nature is still the master architect, and all parts of the natural world, from minerals and marine life to the gulf streams of the oceans and the jet streams of the upper atmosphere, obey a single set of laws.

Resource Interdependence

It would be foolhardy in the 1960's for us to forget that the people of the United States, who constitute a mere 6 per cent of the world's population, use nearly 40 per cent of the raw materials produced in the free world. From the viewpoint of resources and economics our fate is increasingly linked with that of other peoples, and the events of each year operate to increase interdependence. We

can welcome the fact that the second phase of our misnamed "foreign aid" program largely involves the export of conservation know-how, and let us try our best to understand what this is all about. We must be generous enough and practical enough to share our resource insights with the farmer of Pakistan, the Peruvian fisherman, and the manager of wildlife in east Africa—gladly accepting the land lessons they can teach us, and the fact that they have something to teach us. The region or the river valley was the proper setting for resource planning a generation ago, but the new technology now makes *the world* the appropriate arena for conservation planning.

In the long run resource interdependence will encourage world stability, and will play a large role in creating amicable forums where the conservationists of all countries may meet as they are meeting today. In the years ahead we can compete ruthlessly in a world context of scarcity, or we can cooperate for abundance. For example, the common management of the vast resources of the sea (a task that rational men must surely undertake soon) can do much to forge new links of unity; and the scientists themselves, with their commitment to conservation and their overriding emphasis on the hope of the human enterprise, may, if we can yank them out of their specialization, turn out to be bold pioneers of a peaceful world.

Only foolish men, and feckless societies, need contend with want in the future. The nations that
(*Continued on page 53*)

FIGHT FOR OUR CITIES: WHAT THE STATES CAN DO!

(*Continued from page 12*)

acquisition, and in health, welfare and education.

Why not examine closely all the federal programs- which aid cities and all the federal policies which affect cities? Then let's see how they can better meet our needs and further our goals. •

Let's tell Washington where we think improvements can be made, and put it to them as strongly as we can that we must have a chance to advise on all programs touching cities and on the projects. I think we can make a case that review by cities and states will improve coordination and make their programs more effective.

So that we can keep open the channels for discussion between cities and states and with the federal government, let's provide a permanent point of contact in state government. Why not set up a state agency which can give technical assistance in city planning, city administration and finance, and which can be the advocate of cities

with other state agencies and with Washington?

Most of all let's talk about the people of the cities, about how they can make the most of their opportunities in life. As we are attempting to do with our North Carolina Fund, let's see how we can "break the cycle of poverty" in the slums through special programs in education, health, and welfare and housing. Let's see what we can do to keep the children of the disadvantaged from becoming the parents of the disadvantaged.

While we're sitting at the table together let's cover the concerns of the present, the things we can do now. But let us not stop at that. Let us build a vision of our cities on the promise that they can be our greatest creation. Let us then bend our best efforts toward fulfilling our dream.

I am convinced there is no nobler enterprise on which the states can embark. It will not only create great cities. It will in the end create stronger states.

THE CONSERVATION CHALLENGE OF THE SIXTIES

(*Continued from page 52*)

practice conservation, and stabilize population growth in time, will surely prosper. It is also certain that the most influential countries in the decades ahead will be those that bring water to arid lands, and electricity and resource wisdom to emerging societies.

In the years ahead our decisions on resource policy must always

reflect, I hope, our highest aspirations. If we plan the use of our land and the development of our resources so that material progress and the creation of a life-giving environment will go hand-in-hand, we will not only ensure our own prosperity but will, as well, leave a rich legacy for those who follow.

TOCKS ISLAND NATIONAL RECREATION AREA
—A PROPOSAL

(*Continued from page 34*)

include specific provisions, in order of priority, as follows:

1) public outdoor recreation benefits;
2) preservation of scenic, scientific, and historic features contributing to public enjoyment;
3) such utilization of natural resources as in the judgment of the Secretary of the Interior is consistent with and does not significantly impair public recreation and protection of scenic, scientific, and historic features contributing to public enjoyment.

The National Park Service would have the responsibility of formulating and carrying out the land and water use management plan.

All National Recreation Areas to date have been established in the more remote regions of the West, where their main purpose is to preserve scenic and natural recreation values and to provide enjoyment to those visitors who are attracted to them. Tocks Island would serve a large and concentrated population in the East.

The task will be to plan, develop and manage these lands and waters to accommodate the greatest possible number of recreationally beneficial and meaningful uses without damaging the capacity of the area to provide such benefits in the future.

Careful and thorough coordination of recreational uses with other concurrent uses of the impoundment and associated lands must be considered and a mutual agreement will be required with the Delaware River Basin Commission, the Corps of Engineers, and state and local governmental agencies.

If the proposed dam and flooding of the impoundment are completed, perhaps between 1970 and 1975, there will be an almost instantaneous public need for access and for facilities for boating, swimming, and sightseeing. The optimum visitor capacity of the area probably will be reached quickly.

The area would be developed for recreational activities associated with a natural outdoors environment oriented to water, woods and hills. Facilities would be provided for visitors ranging from the pleasure driver who does not leave his car during his visit to the camper who may spend his vacation in a family or group camp. Most visits would have a major concern with the impoundment in one or more aspects. Visitors would be able to tour substantial portions of the area on both sides of the river.

Constant care and skill would be exercised to assure proper scale and balance between improvements and nature. Historical sites and structures would be inventoried, evaluated and preserved.

Exceptional ingenuity and skill must be exercised to achieve the subtle weaving of the natural and historic values into the recreational experiences of many visitors who have had little or no acquaintance with these highly rewarding aspects of our natural and cultural heritage.

A Kentucky Town Pulls Itself Up

From the *New York Times*, December 8, 1963

Lost Creek, a community in the northeastern hills, Kentucky, has found itself. It is being called an example for other communities, including some in the Appalachain region where a Presidential Commission is studying needs.

The story of Lost Creek is told by the University of Kentucky Extension Service as follows:

"In finding itself, this Greenup County community also has made a name for itself in the Ashland area's 10-county Northeastern Kentucky Area Community Development Association. . . ."

"It's a 'name' for having gotten under way and done things without appreciable outside help," says L. C. White, Jr., the Service's area agent.

"And if other communities in the area take hold the same way Paul Stephens and his Lost Creek neighbors have, development of Eastern Kentucky may fan itself into a bright blaze."

Lost Creek, 10 miles from the town of Greenup on the Ohio River had only a gravel road, no telephone system and was "bogged down in the status quo."

In January, 1959, Mr. Stephens and some neighbors met in a small store to see what they could do. Agencies connected with rural development, such as the Extension Service, the Soil Conservation Service and Vocational Agriculture, outlined a program. Lost Creek adopted it.

Ten persons signed personal notes of $50 each to raise working funds.

Their first project was a community building. It took a lot of free working time and loads of material.

Today Lost Creek has as nice and useful a community center as any in Kentucky. It means something to the people.

"I've got a stake in this place," Mr. Stephens says. "I got hung up in a snowdrift across the creek there, hauling out a load of pulpwood. But I got the logs out."

The program went on. Leaders organized turkey shoots and raffles for hams, quilts and ponies. They kept the organization going.

What emerged was a blacktop road running nine miles into the area; a new telephone system that will soon be in operation; a woodworking class that taught youngsters enough about the craft to furnish the community center; and possibilities for a smokehouse where Kentucky hams could be cured and sold.

Other improvements were made. Melvin Hester, president of the area group, and Don Wade, secretary, are pleased with the project. They say:

"The people have done this themselves, without any charity donations. We think it will be a while before their work will be felt income wise, but you'll notice that everything they have done in community improvement eventually may have some effect on local income."

County Agent Z. L. Newsome feels the same way.

"These people really took hold
(Continued on page 57)

55

A Point of View

"Seeing the world from our strictly human point of view, we tend to exaggerate our presence in it.

"People live in clots, look at one another's faces all day, and worry that the earth is crowded and over-crowded with cities, with the works of man. Similarly, bees must feel that the earth is covered with beehives.

"Yet, there are very few places in the world from which, in an hour, in a car, you cannot find wilderness—and there are the vast land areas where people have never lived permanently at all.

"The earth exists very much as it always has—a broad, continuous inert surface, folded and undulating, crumbled into rocks and stones and sand into which the twisting roots of living things push down so that they may stand up and feel the air upon them. These are the simple basic facts of the living and the dead which underlie the fantastic, the marvelous, the unbelievable variety of expression in shape and color and consistency surrounding us, so that each handspan of land is unique and yet an integral part of the whole."

—From "The Ecological City," by Architects Mort and Eleanor Karp, in *Landscape*, Autumn, 1963, Santa Fe, New Mexico, J. B. Jackson, Editor.

THE NEED FOR THREE DIMENSIONAL PLANNING AND REGULATION

(*Continued from page 50*)

environment. The press for "performance standards" and "planned developments" in our present forms of land regulation can only be explained as an indication of the growing need for reconciling human demands upon space in terms of a far broader rationale than that previously employed. Such a rationale, however it may ultimately develop to meet our complex needs, must above all take into account the full dimension of the human environment, and man's growing activity within it.

While our values may still need to be communicated and related in a number of different ways, they must ultimately be translated into terms of height, depth and breadth in their application to the physical world. Determining what and how, why and how much space is to be occupied is certainly the future task with which we will all have to deal using both our highest professional competence and our fullest creative understanding.

56

State Park Lore—California's Castle Crags

(Adapted from an article by William Kaiser, Supervisor of Castle Crags State Park, in a recent issue of *News and Views,* published by the California State Division of Beaches and Parks.)

Towering, jagged ridges of granitic upthrust—these are the Castle Crags which rear their bristling spires some four thousand feet above California's Sacramento River. They are the dominant feature of Castle Crags State Park, located in the Klamath Range of mountains on both sides of the Sacramento River Canyon, which includes 3,496 acres of State-owned property with an additional 1,835 acres of U. S. Forest Service land under special use permit.

The crag formation is not uncommon in the High Sierras. Several other masses are to be found. There are the Cathedral Spires in Yosemite and the Minarets of the High Sierras.

But Castle Crags State Park is a favorite of many fishermen because of excellent fishing in the Sacramento River and five clear fishable streams. For the hiker, there are old logging roads through the Park, a 2.7-mile trail into the Crags and a 2-mile trail along the east bank of the Sacramento River.

Of interest to visitors for its animal and bird life, Castle Crags State Park also boasts a great variety of shrubs, trees and flowers. There are the Valley Oak of the upper Sonoran Life Zone and the Red Fir and Jeffrey Pine of the Canadian Life Zone. Along the river are the Western Yew, Park Orford and Incense Cedar, the Sugar and Ponderosa Pine, and various firs and oaks. The comparatively rare Weeping Spruce, along with the Pinemat Manzanita and many flowers found only at high altitudes, appear farther up the 2.7-mile trail to the Crags.

Fall is picturesque with the striking color of the Dogwood, Vine and Broadleaf Maples and oaks in display against the gray background of the Crags.

Columbian Black-Tail deer frequent the Park, particularly in the spring and fall. California black bears are often seen during the summer and frequently help themselves to the campers' food. Upper elevations of the Crags where man seldom travels provide a refuge for the mountain lion, bobcat, fox and coyote. There are squirrels, chipmunks, porcupines, opossums, racoons and skunks. And bird life is plentiful.

A KENTUCKY TOWN PULLS ITSELF UP

(*Continued from page 55*)

themselves, and with only a moderate amount of direction from us, started the ball rolling," he says.

"This is what we want all communities to do—get advice, then take off on their own. It means so much more when communities do it themselves."

Recent Publications

STATE PARK SYSTEM IN ILLINOIS by John E. Trotter. Department of Geography Research Paper No. 74, University of Chicago, Chicago 37, Illinois. 1962. 152 pp. $4.00.

An interesting report in the January, 1964 *Illinois Wildland* states that this study analyzes the factors which have affected the location of Illinois State Parks. It summarizes Professor Trotter's observations and conclusions, in part, as follows:

"Present Illinois State Parks should be reclassified into state scenic parks, state historical parks and state recreational parks. (In addition, the present categories of memorials, parkways, and conservation areas would be continued.)

"Retaining the term 'state park' in each of the new categories should allay the objections of those who wish their local park to have the prestige of State Park status. Such a classification would contribute to public understanding of the nature and purposes of State Parks. Comparisons between parks of unlike kind and purpose could be eliminated. It would also enable park administrators to maintain clear distinctions in acquisition, development, and management policies for the various types of parks.

"Each of the three types should receive due attention. Scenic and historic sites of good quality can still be acquired and it is not necessary for all new parks to be of the recreation type. Outstanding scenic and historic parks attract more visitors from greater distances than do recreational parks."

"In presenting this study," says the *Wildland*, "the author has brought a degree of sophistication to the analysis of State Park problems that has been lacking in the past. He has provided a new evaluation of Illinois parks and opened the way to better park selection in the future. Present conditions and historical influences are doubtless sufficiently similar elsewhere so that many other States may likewise profit from the study."

A PLACE TO LIVE, 1963 Yearbook of Agriculture, U. S. Department of Agriculture, Washington, D. C. Superintendent of Documents, U. S. Government Printing Office, Washington, D. C. 20402. 608 pp. $3.00.

Of interest in view of its far-ranging examination of the effects of urbanization on many aspects of American life. Included among other topics are urban and suburban sprawl into farmlands, parks and open spaces, the growing demand for outdoor recreation, and the management of water and air pollution.

The 79 chapters have been written in nontechnical, informative style by 92 men and women, among them officials of State and Federal governments, college professors, garden club leaders, planning officials, sociologists, and economists.

Orville L. Freeman, Secretary of Agriculture, in a foreword, writes: "This is a time and this is a book that call for discussion, cooperation, and vision to channel great forces of change in directions that ensure that America will always be a good place

(Continued on page 59)

58

American Planning and Civic Association
New Members, November 1, 1963 to March 1, 1964

Illinois
General Library, Southern Illinois University, Carbondale
Mr. Marion J. Smith, Executive Director, Chicago Chapter, American Institute of Architects

Oklahoma
Mr. Philip B. Hawes, Norman

Tennessee
Tennessee Federation of Garden Clubs, Chattanooga
Mr. Paul L. Russell, Paris

Washington, D. C.
Mr. Wolf Von Eckardt
Mr. Gerald G. Schulsinger

Canada
Library, Saskatchewan Technical Institute, Saskatoon, Saskatchewan

National Conference on State Parks
New Members, November 1, 1963 to March 1, 1964

California
Mr. Thomas A. Crandall, Big Basin

Massachusetts
Mr. Marcel F. Crudele, Springfield

New York
Mr. James Gragg, Saratoga Springs
Mr. George E. Heggen, Saratoga Springs
Mr. Roland A. Block, Staatsburg

Pennsylvania
Dr. M. Graham Netting, Pittsburgh
Mrs. J. Lewis Scott, Pittsburgh

Virginia
Superintendent, Blue Ridge Parkway, Roanoke

RECENT PUBLICATIONS

(Continued from page 58)

to live . . . We have an opportunity to bring closer together all parts of our population, our economy, and our geography and so to help us realize that the prosperity of city people is tied closely to the well-being of rural people, that many traditional distinctions between city and country no longer are true, and that the United States is one Nation, indivisible."

Watch Service Report

H. R. 3846, Establishing A Land and Water Conservation Fund. Congressman Wayne N. Aspinall (Colorado) and others.

As we go to press, the bill, which has been reported in previous issues of PLANNING AND CIVIC COMMENT and which would authorize appropriation for grants-in-aid to the States for outdoor recreation and for Federal recreational land acquistion, is still awaiting action by the House Rules Committee. The bill has been reported favorably by the House Interior and Insular Affairs Committee, and an affirmative vote from the Rules Committee would move the bill to the House floor for debate and vote.

Though, as yet, the Committee has given no indication when it might take up the bill, Secretary of the Interior Udall has termed chances for enactment of the Land and Water Conservation Fund bill in the current session of Congress "very good."

It is reported that citizens across the country are writing to their Congressmen urging passage of the bill.

H. R. 9070, H. R. 9162 and Other Versions of the Wilderness Bill. Congressman John P. Saylor (Pa.), Congressman John D. Dingell (Mich.) and others.

The House Committee on Interior and Insular Affairs has completed western field hearings on various versions of the Wilderness Bill and Secretary of the Interior Stewart L. Udall has gone on the record with a note of optimism: "With a little statesmanship and give and take, I believe we can have a Wilderness Bill by July."

S. 2, Water Resources Research Act of 1964. A bill to establish water resources research centers at land-grant colleges and State Universities, stimulate water research at other institutions of higher learning and promote a more adequate national program of water research.

The bill, which was reported favorably, with amendments, February 11, 1964 by the House Committee on Interior and Insular Affairs, may have been killed when the House Committee on Rules denied a rule on the bill. A motion for reconsideration or a swell of interest by House members will be necessary if the Senate-passed proposal is to reach the House floor.

H. R. 1803, Establishing The Ozark National Scenic Riverways In Missouri. The House Committee on Interior and Insular Affairs ordered a favorable report on this bill February 26, 1964.

The bill sets aside portions of two outstanding Missouri streams, the Current and Jacks Fork Rivers, in their natural, free-flowing conditions. It is of unusual significance in that it establishes a new classification, scenic riverways, for administration by the National Park Service under the same principles as those of a recreation area in which hunting is permitted.

The bill says that the Secretary of the Interior "shall permit hunting and fishing on lands and waters under his jurisdiction within the Ozark National Scenic Riverways area in accordance with applicable Federal and State laws. The Secretary may designate zones where, and establish periods when, no hunting shall be permitted, for reasons of public safety, administration, or public use and enjoyment and shall issue regulations after consultation with the Conservation Commission of the State of Missouri."

★　　★　　★

'The Pivotal Role'

"The States should play the pivotal role in providing outdoor recreation opportunities for their citizens.

"Since other responsibilities that affect outdoor recreation opportunities such as highway construction and the management of forest, wildlife and water resources, are also generally focused at this level, the State governments can make sure that these programs are in harmony with recreation objectives.

"They can be particularly effective in stimulating counties and municipalities to take separate and joint action.

"Finally, they are the most effective avenue through which Federal aid can be channeled to meet varying needs."

—The ORRRC Report

Planning and Civic Comment

Official Organ of American Planning and Civic Association and
National Conference on State Parks

ANSAS CITY MO
PUBLIC LIBRARY

♦

CONTENTS

JUL

JUNE 1964

PLANNING AND CIVIC COMMENT

Published Quarterly

SUCCESSOR to: City Planning, Civic Comment, State Recreation

Official Organ of: American Planning and Civic Association,
National Conference on State Parks

SCOPE: *National, State, Regional and City Planning, Land and Water Uses,
Conservation of National Resources, National, State and Local Parks,
Highways and Roadsides.*
AIM: *To create a better physical environment which will conserve and develop
the health, happiness and culture of the American people.*

Second-class postage paid at Harrisburg, Pa., and at additional mailing office.

EDITORIAL AND PUBLICATION OFFICE, 901 Union Trust Building, Washington,
D. C. 20005

Printed by the Mount Pleasant Press, the McFarland Company, Harrisburg, Pa.

Planning and Civic Comment

Vol. 30　　　　　　　June, 1964　　　　　　　No. 2

American Planning and Civic Association
1904—1964
Have We Completed a Cycle?

By HARLAND BARTHOLOMEW, President, American Planning
and Civic Association

In 1904 the American Civic Association was formed in response to a growing popular demand for improving the character and appearance of American Cities.

Now some sixty years later there is a new and growing demand to do something about the drab, disorganized, and depressing character of so much of our American cities. "Urban Design" is the new term used to describe the projected effort to produce a more satisfactory city—a new Urban Environment.

Why this new demand? Have we merely completed a cycle? Is the American City today less satisfactory than the 1904 model? Will a new effort have greater chance for success? What do we really mean by "Urban Design" or by "Improved Urban Environment?"

A very brief review of some of the more important planning endeavors during these past sixty years may aid in gaining perspective—and in projecting our thinking of the city of the future.

Wide public interest in improving the character and appearance of American cities was first aroused by three quite unrelated events that took place near the turn of the present century. These were: A) the World's Fair (Columbian Exposition) held in Chicago in 1893; B) an English publication, "Garden Cities of Tomorrow" by Ebenezer Howard in 1898; and C) the Report of the Committee on Congestion of Population in New York City in 1900.

A) The unusually pleasing composition of buildings so well arranged in an attractive setting at the Columbian Exposition was a revelation to the American public. Up to this time American cities had been so busy growing that there had been little or no time or money with which to create attractive plazas, parks, and boulevards such as were to be seen in European cities. Here in the "White City" on the lakefront in Chicago, whether or not one may agree with its neo-classic design, there was demonstrated for the first time the possibility that American cities could also be made attractive.

B) "Garden Cities of Tomorrow" was the outgrowth of a proposal to re-house low income families from the slums of London into complete self-contained suburban communities where working and living conditions in an attractive environment could be enjoyed by families of modest means heretofore compelled to live in slum areas. These small cities were to be carefully designed and limited to approximately 30,000 total population. They were to be built 25 miles or so from London with a wide belt of surrounding open space to preserve their individuality and their character. This was a new and revolutionary concept that attracted great interest in this country by all those concerned with improved urban environment and social welfare.

C) The report of the New York Committee on Congestion of Population was the result of a study with supporting statistical data showing that an abnormally large percentage of persons from the over-crowded Lower East Side were coming under supervision of the welfare agencies, the hospitals, the courts and correctional institutions of New York City. The report demonstrated for the first time that there was an unusually high degree of disease and crime in an area of high population density and bad housing. Among other things this report caused prompt revision of New York's Tenement House Laws.

The economic, the social and the aesthetic significance of proper community planning and development of American cities, so dramatically demonstrated by these three events, produced widespread public concern and an urge for action to improve the American City. They launched

the City Beautification movement which for several years gained great momentum. Its early manifestation took the form of creating civic centers in cities such as Cleveland, Denver, San Francisco and the Parkway in Philadelphia. In Washington, President Theodore Roosevelt appointed a Commission to revive and up-date the L'Enfant Plan. The latter resulted in the magnificent Mall connecting the Capitol, the Washington Monument and the (subsequent) Lincoln Memorial as well as in the new Union Station and Plaza, and an expansion of the Park System.

Daniel Burnham, architect of the Chicago World's Fair and Consultant on the revised plan for Washington, produced bold Comprehensive City Plans for Manila, for San Francisco and for Chicago. Charles Mulford Robinson gave lectures throughout the country and wrote a book, "The Improvement of Towns and Cities," that did so much to stimulate many small cities to plant street trees, create parks, eliminate poles and wires on city streets, regulate signs and billboards, and such.

The American Civic Association, formed in 1904, was conceived as a strictly citizens' organization and clearing house to further public interest and action in improved community design and appearance. Subsequently, the Association's interest was extended to include conservation of natural resources on the national scale.

Gradually "city beautification" as such, lost force. It failed to satisfy the deeper demand for more orderly control of the whole process of city design and construction. Lack of open spaces, buildings too closely built together, the initial appearance of the skyscraper, growing problems of traffic congestion on streets, and the invasion of residential areas by commercial structures, all pointed to the need for a stronger form of control over city growth and development. Thus was born the city planning movement as a replacement of "city beautification," presumably without abandoning the original concept of improved appearance of the city.

In 1909, the National Conference on City Planning was formed. It was composed of engineers, architects, landscape architects, sociologists and others concerned with the ever expanding economic, social as well as aesthetic problems and needs of the American city. At about this same time, official recognition was given to planning by the appointment of City Plan Commissions in several cities.

Numerous "city plans" were prepared during the succeeding twenty years before the great economic depression of the 1930's set in. Many of these early city plans such as those for Pittsburgh, Memphis and Cincinnati were comprehensive in nature in their attempt to anticipate all then forseeable needs for 25 years or so ahead. These city plans included studies of population growth and expansion and of land use as well as detailed plans for major traffic streets, for transportation and terminals, zoning, for parks, schools and recreational facilities and for housing and civic art. Not all of the cities succeeded in carrying out all of these broad comprehensive

plans. Many of them were soon limited in scope, particularly to the more pressing problems of zoning and of new and improved street plans for meeting traffic demand. Zoning, which soon became embroiled in legal proceedings over the question of its legality, was a most important new tool for controlling wasteful practices and abuses. Questions of its constitutionality were raised by lawsuits in several states. It was not until 1926 that this question was resolved by the U. S. Supreme Court in the notable Euclid Village decision.

By 1917, city planning was recognized as a profession when the American Planning Institute, subsequently reorganized as the American Institute of Planners, was formed. Private citizen interest continued along with official and professional interest. To strengthen and consolidate *citizen* interest and effort, the National Conference on City Planning and the American Civic Association were merged in 1934 to form the present American Planning and Civic Association. The latter has continued to the present time as a strictly citizens' organization and clearing house, independent of but cooperating with both the professional and the official organizations and agencies in the broad field of community improvement. The published proceedings of the early annual meetings of these two parent organizations afford valuable enlightenment even today to all concerned with problems of community development.

The early comprehensive city plans such as those published in San Francisco in 1904, in St. Louis (by the St. Louis Civic League in 1907 and by the City Plan commission in 1918), in Chicago (by the Commercial Club in 1909), and in numerous other cities, were without official sanction and status. They were lacking in ways and means for effective implementation. To meet this need, a special committee was appointed by Secretary of Commerce Herbert Hoover in 1923 as part of his broad program for the prevention of waste. It produced the Standard Zoning Enabling Act and the Standard City Planning Enabling Act, which Acts, through subsequent adoption by legislatures in most of the states, gave new impetus to planning and encouraged the adoption of many city plans as the official guide for future growth and development.

The great economic depression which started with the stock market crash in late 1929 and lasted through all the early 1930's had a tremendous impact upon all citizens, upon the cities and upon the city planning movement generally. For the first time in their history, American cities not only merely ceased to grow but some actually experienced a loss in total population. This had the effect of discouraging the further preparation of comprehensive city plans, especially, since there was little or no more growth in prospect. An even greater impact was the discovery that growth, *per se*, was not an unmixed blessing.

It was found that new growth on the city's fringes had been designed primarily for higher income groups, while the older central city areas had been neglected, thus forming large areas of blighted property and even

some substantial areas of slums. A research study by the St. Louis City Plan Commission in 1935, "Urban Land Policy," disclosed interesting factual evidence that these older neglected areas paid substantially less taxes than the cost of public services in them. The huge deficits had to be subsidized by the taxpayers of other parts of the city that were still in good condition. It disclosed also that blight was progressive in nature.

A revolutionary new form of attack on city development was initiated by the Federal Government. Its object was essentially social in character, *i. e.* to eliminate slums by replacement with publicly subsidized housing for families of low income who were otherwise incapable of finding satisfactory living accommodations in a decent environment. This objective was set forth in detail in the first Public Housing Act passed by the Congress in 1937. This Act was buttressed by large appropriations of federal funds to assist the cities in building substantial public housing projects to replace slum areas.

The early concept of bold city plans to give direction and control to the whole process of city building, and of thus producing more attractive and desirable cities, became submerged in this new approach to urban ills. It has not since been resurrected, as will be discussed later.

After some ten years of effort and despite the expenditure of several hundred million dollars in the federal aid program, under which many thousands of new low cost living accommodations were constructed in

(*Continued on page 51*)

4

The Community Nature Center—A New Concept in Urban Planning and Growth

By JOSEPH J. SHOMON, Director, the Nature Centers Division, National Audubon Society, New York City

Several new towns and communities, and many revitalized old cities, are planning and developing so-called community centers of "land for learning." These new centers, better known as *community nature centers*, are a new concept in urban planning and conservation education in America.

Coming at a time when cities and urbanized counties are finding it increasingly more difficult to hold on to park land and open space, the nature center idea fills an important void in community action. By putting idle, undeveloped lands—park lands, natural or semi-wild areas—to immediate good educational use, a sensible, practical method has been found to forestall encroachment upon open space, and provide the community with a much-needed educational-cultural facility. Moreover, the nature center itself can help build within the community the permanent awareness which is essential if park lands are to have lasting integrity in the future.

Today city and urbanized county parks are under severe attrition. They are being nibbled away parcel by parcel by those who seek development of one form or another. Any open space within a city or close to a city which does not show demonstrable worthy public use or at least use in the public interest is a prime target for development—schools, sewage treatment plants, highways, subdivisions or commercial development.

Now, no intelligent planner or planning group or well-meaning citizen is opposed to growth and development of our cities and suburbs. Space must be provided for houses, stores, roads and factories. We must have new schools and churches and thruways. However, the question we must ask ourselves is this: Must we sacrifice *all* open space, *all* undeveloped and natural land, for these other uses? Is it not just as vital that we save some areas for breathing space, for beauty, refreshment, enjoyment, inspiration . . . and learning?

This is what the nature center concept attempts to provide in the average American community—to keep some land in permanent open space for learning and enjoyment.

What A Nature and Conservation Center Is and Does

In good planning the ideal community nature center will embrace three vital elements. *First*, it will encompass at least 50 acres of land in one, single, undeveloped area. *Second*, it will include an interpretive building and other educational facilities for the benefit of the visiting public. *Third*, it will have a small but highly competent staff to run the center and to do the teaching.

A nature and conservation center is, in a very broad sense, an institutional device which brings land and people together on intimate terms. It is a special outdoor area where the

5

young people as well as the old—
under the inspiration and guidance
of trained interpreters—are taught
to see, hear and feel something of
the natural world about them. It is
a place where people can develop the
kind of personal values and conscience they need in order to live as
better citizens.

A nature and conservation center,
as envisioned by the Nature Centers
Division, National Audubon Society, is really a concept in what might
be termed "ecological conservation."
The philosophy embraced here is
that man is a product of the land and
a partner of nature and a steward of
the land. The physical earth, fauna
and flora, after all, were here before
man. When man entered the picture
he emerged as part of the biotic
world complex. The world was not
created just for man alone. He himself is part of nature. Thus, man
cannot morally usurp all natural resources entirely unto himself—at
least not without dire consequences.
Only by being a part of and working
with nature, by thinking of and planning for the future, can man hope to
realize his great potential on this
planet.

The development of proper attitudes and, eventually, that of an
ecological conservation philosophy,
then, is perhaps the greatest value
of a community nature and conservation center. Unless people have
the right understanding and appreciation of nature and conservation,
the *will* to *protect* and to *conserve*
will have little meaning. As a result, the people concerned will lose
the very assets and values they hope
to preserve. In other words, unless
proper attitudes are built in the

minds and hearts of people, there
exists the continued likelihood that
we will have continued resource
abuses, short-sighted planning and
eventual deterioration of our whole
natural environment.

It is an established fact that people will not safeguard what they
don't know, let alone what they
don't understand. They will not
protect and treat kindly what they
don't appreciate. A nature and conservation center, then, is designed
to help them understand, to help
them learn, see, and to be good stew-
ards of our land.

What is a typical nature center
like? At the typical nature center
one finds an educational building
which serves as a focal point of outdoor education activity. A system
of trails allows the visitor to journey
into different habitats. Expert
teachers take school classes and
other groups out on organized study
trips. Each trip is designed to tell
an ecological and conservation story.
Many visitors learn by "doing," by
direct experience. For those who
prefer to learn alone, there are self-
guided trails. For those wishing to
develop outdoor skills, there are
practical projects involving work experiences.

Cities and urbanized areas which
are plagued with crime, juvenile delinquency, vandalism, school drop-
outs and a lack of things for young
people to do should seriously consider an investment in a nature center. New towns and new communities just forming should, in their
planning, very definitely provide for
a nature education center. Park and
recreation departments and planning

(*Continued on page 50*)

6

Urban Renewal À La Mode—
Education the Key

By CHARLES E. PETERSON, F. A. I. A., Architectural Historian,
Restorationist, and Planner

Reprinted through the courtesy of *Antiques* Magazine in which this article appeared in October, 1963, as part of a "symposium-on-paper" addressed to the question— Preservation and Urban Renewal: Is Coexistence Possible?

Urban renewal and historic preservation can coexist but the struggle in many places seems almost hopeless. There are just enough exceptions, however, to make the situation interesting. I have visited a good many project areas from New Hampshire to Hawaii and have seen enough to believe that there is a sporting chance in most communities to get things done right— when it is not too late.

The difficulties generally arise on the one hand from the fact that the agency administrators and their staffs do not understand—or are indifferent to—the problems of old buildings. The informed people in this field are usually self-trained private enthusiasts who are not available for hiring or, once employed, are not skillful or persistent enough to put their ideas across. There is no "how-to" literature and there are almost no executed projects worth emulating.

Ignorance—not greed for the quick buck—is the greatest obstacle to progress. The rebuilding of our cities now has plenty of money and legal powers to draw on. But few Americans have either the education or the experience to plan historical work successfully. I refer particularly to the trained aptitude for recognizing historical values, for keeping buildings protected during the ordeal of area redevelopment, and the technical knowledge for designing restorations. The official procedures—legal, administrative, and fiscal—of redevelopment in typical city areas are complicated enough to challenge the patience of the best minds in the business. Historical questions added to the others may seem frivolous to many men in authority.

Education is the key to successful renewal but education is hard to get and may not come in time. The dramatic article "Doomed" (*Life* Magazine, July 5, 1963) is excellent. But can it save the splendid Pennsylvania Station and other New York treasures which some are finding profitable to destroy? What is being done about the country as a whole?

The worthy pamphlet *Preservation of Historic Districts* prepared by John Codman of the Beacon Hill Civic Association, Boston, and published by the American Society of Planning Officials in 1956 has probably reached the attention of few urban renewal officials or planners—even though a special printing was distributed by the National Trust for Historic Preservation. Incidentally, it is to be hoped that the latter organization will take a more positive stand in the future regarding the "land clearance" threat. I believe that for preservationists the lack of established techniques of planning urban renewal is the great misfortune of our time.

Two other national organizations —the American Institute of Architects and the Society of Architectural Historians—often take an anguished view of local situations but have no national executive staffs ready to create and maintain pressure on the large and growing community of renewal administrators and the even faster-growing coterie of planners and consultants whom they commission for advice.

A 212-page generously illustrated volume which gave great hope to preservationists was issued in 1959. Describing the interesting and promising project for near-downtown Providence, it is entitled *College Hill, A Demonstration Study of Historic Area Renewal.* This attractive book, which includes an architectural-historical section of basic local information (for which Antionette Downing was largely responsible), went out of print almost immediately. For some mysterious reason it isn't being reprinted. Placed in the hands of planners and architects, it would wake up many to the problems involved.

The Urban Renewal Administration, under fire for much destruction wrought across the land, has slowly come around to admitting that there may be something in the idea. Their booklet *Historic Preservation through Urban Renewal*—prepared by Margaret Carroll—in press for many months and finally out in May 1963, should be a very useful tool to citizens trying to convince their local authorities that something should and can be done. It is hardly adequate, though, to guide urban renewal staffs—the personnel that give orders and make decisions at national, regional, and local levels. The URA has been petitioned again and again—without apparent effect—for some positive precepts to be set forth in their *Manual* that would stimulate timid, puzzled, or lazy administrators to take positive and appropriate action when the fate of historic buildings is in balance.

The August 1962 issue of *The Journal of Housing,* devoted to historic preservation, is one of the few publications that have come through professional channels. It fails, however, to mention a subject that is uppermost in all minds: MONEY. If the fabulous write-down in the cost of land for the promising twelve-acre Strawbery Banke project at Portsmouth, New Hampshire, were better known, it would start a national movement. (See *Urban Renewal in Portsmouth, New Hampshire,* prepared by the Portsmouth Housing Authority in 1961, p. 24.)

We soon become aware of the backgrounds of the people with whom we have to deal. Just how planners come to be is a relevant question. City planning has been taught in a number of respectable professional schools and a graduate from one of them is certainly qualified to become an apprentice planner. Architects, engineers, and landscape architects are, through their experience with site planning, entitled to serious consideration.

(Continued on page 16)

Seward, Alaska Begins Anew

By ETHEL J. SWING

With a population of just 1,900, it was the smallest of all this year's winners—Seward, Alaska—one of eleven All-America Cities selected by a jury of distinguished civic leaders as communities that exhibited outstanding examples of "citizen action" in 1963.

On Good Friday, a warm and beautiful day with more than a promise of spring in the air, Seward's Mayor Perry Stockton, with his wife and local officials, had gone to Anchorage, Alaska, to arrange a big celebration for April 4–5. For Seward was preparing to observe the honor conferred on it in the annual All-America City contest cosponsored by the National Municipal League and *Look* Magazine.

Then, in a moment, the little community in all its glory was crushed and burning and dropping into Resurrection Bay.

As citizens throughout America listened in shocked silence to radio and television reports of the earthquake which had struck Alaska, many became acquainted with Seward for the first time.

Some were familiar with Seward as a name, but it simply hadn't registered with them as a living, striving community with a unique mission to perform. Thus, it was on the ninety-seventh anniversary of the purchase of Alaska by William Seward that a partially detailed picture of the town which had been named for him emerged from the reports of devastation which literally was wiping it away.

With the earth's great heave and the subsequent seismic waves, fuel storage tanks ruptured and, with an immense roar, burst into flames, spreading burning oil over Seward's entire waterfront. Only a short distance away from the center of the quake, a 5,000-foot chunk of the waterfront slipped into the bay, taking a cannery, docks, warehouses and offices with it. Rail facilities were obliterated. Fifty freight cars of the Alaska Railroad were swept away from the tracks and scattered like a child's toys. One train, loaded with $2,000,000 worth of freight was lost. A huge 60-ton diesel engine was overturned and carried over 100 yards by a seismic wave. The only highway to Seward was hacked apart and bridges were swept away without a trace. All communications were destroyed. Homes were lost.

The submarine landslides and the huge waves had done their worst. Seward was in shambles. Edward McDermott, Director of President Johnson's Office of Emergency Planning, summed it all up: "awful, awful."

Sixty miles south of Anchorage and key supply center for Alaska, Seward had been a seaward terminus and one of two all-weather termini of the 420-mile-long Alaska Railroad which maintained two excellent docks there, each with the latest equipment. Over the years, this had become the chief reason for the town's existence.

Now, a dazed inventory by red-eyed men with sharply drawn faces could have suggested that the living, pulsing purpose of the town was gone. But out of the blackened remains of a dozen oil storage tanks came an intimation that Seward's task was not yet done. As Governor William A. Egan warned Alaskans they must "take a good hard look at the future," they vowed, with indomitable courage, to rebuild everything bigger and better than ever.

Thirty-six hours after the quake, with most people not having paused for sleep, crews were working everywhere to repair the roads and clean up the debris so that Seward could start rebuilding. A community kitchen had been established and food and bedding had been commandeered and placed in a central location.

"This town isn't going to fold up," came the word from James W. Harrison, Seward's City Manager, "though we couldn't float a bond issue on peanut butter right now."

The promise, hopefully taking form amid the obliteration, was indicative of a spirit which had already become embedded in the little town's essence. For before the catastrophe, Seward had come of age. It had learned what many communities hundreds of times its size never learn—that constructive accomplishments ensue when people resolve their differences, set their goals and work together to achieve them. And that the power unleashed from a spirit of flourishing civic cooperation is great enough to put things on the upward course of progress when nothing else will turn the trick.

Like many another town, Seward's greatest problem before it got on the track that led to national recognition had been inability to pull together.

"An unfortunate political storm centered around the firing of the city manager," said *National Civic Review* in announcing this year's All-America Cities. "It divided the community right down the middle and resulted in a successful recall movement against four members of the city council. Actually, the wrangling finally culminated in the realization of the dispute's folly and out of it came a determination to work together."

What were the positive results of the new-found community spirit? An aggressive street improvement program, the construction of a new library and fire house, a wave of new private building construction, the expansion of several industrial firms, the start up the road to a sound and vital economy.

At one point, two large fish processing plants had moved from the small, remote community, leaving it a legacy of unemployment. But such had been the upward pace in Seward that its newspaper of March 26 not only announced the All-America award but also carried a story of extensive new wharfage and docking facilities to be installed.

Small wonder, then, that as the eyes of all turned to Seward, public spirit was aroused.

Within hours after the tragedy, the National Municipal League and *Look* Magazine, co-sponsors of the All-America Cities contest, began to receive telegrams from current and former winners of the All-America award asking how they could aid Seward.

At the suggestion of Allentown,

Pennsylvania, an SOS fund, standing for "Save Our Seward," was established to solicit and collect financial aid. A nine-man trusteeship committee was named to administer the funds.

Sympathetic residents of Allentown donated $20,000 through the Red Cross to the hard-pressed people of Seward. And a huge Mack truck loaded with furniture, dishes and other household goods—all donated by merchants in Allentown—took off on the 4,700-mile trip to Alaska and the aid of the Seward disaster victims. Use of the truck, its fuel and the necessary relays of drivers were all contributed.

In Alexandria, Virginia, which led the list of this year's All-America winners, the Mayor's wife, Mrs. Frank E. Mann, sought local contributions as chairman of the Seward Relief Committee, and quickly collected some two thousand dollars as an emergency fund.

Of immediate concern was the plight of some 94 householders, dock workers some of whose homes were already mortgaged and who now faced the fact that their mortgages were secured by disordered piles of lumber.

Relief funds came quickly from other All-America Cities, those which were winners in this year's competition and those honored in former years. Among them: Neosho, Missouri; San Diego, California; Louisville, Kentucky; Roseville, California; and Woodstock, Illinois.

As citizen aid helped ease the immediate crisis, the question on everyone's lips was whether the Alaska Railroad, which is under the direction of the U. S. Department of the Interior, would rebuild the docks and the railroad into Seward and how soon. If it could get construction under way, men, now without jobs and with no hope of a pay-day, could do construction work until they could re-establish themselves as longshoremen. Without the Railroad, all of Alaska would be imperiled economically and, also, prompt, affirmative action by the Government would encourage private industry to rebuild in Seward as well as in other Alaskan municipalities.

The last week in April, Senator Clinton P. Anderson of New Mexico, appointed by the President as Chairman of the Federal Reconstruction and Development Planning Commission for Alaska, gave the assurance of the President that the railroad will be rebuilt to Seward and that such facilities as are necessary will also be constructed although it is now apparent that rebuilding the docks just as they were at the time of the disaster is not feasible. A preliminary evaluation by the U. S. Geological Survey warns that "the newly formed shoreline at Seward is unstable for it is steep— and the ground behind it contains many tension cracks; the possibility that future large submarine landslides may occur there cannot be dismissed lightly."

According to Edwin N. Fitch, Assistant to the General Manager of the Alaska Railroad, the debris has been cleared up and the Railroad, with continuous emergency repairs and the aid of thousands of tons of gravel, is now operating to the point of Whittier. From Col. William Penly, Acting Executive Director of the Alaska Reconstruction

Commission, comes the word that work is under way on the railroad branch from Portage to Seward. Geologists are working with the Railroad to suggest ways of repairing the major damage to the lines.

But, heartening though this may be, it does not replace private property, and nearly seven million dollars worth of public property in Seward also must be replaced—schools, roads, sewers, waterlines. In addition to collapsed bridges, numerous snow avalanches, triggered by the violent ground motion during the quake, crossed the Seward highway. To help meet such contingencies throughout Alaska, President Johnson on March 27, signed into effect legislation amending the Alaska Omnibus Act and authorizing an additional grant of $23,500,000 to Alaska for earthquake recovery purposes.

The next day, Alaska's Senator E. L. Bartlett and others introduced S. 2881, a bill which, if enacted into law, would further amend the Alaska Omnibus Act to allow up to $15,000,000 for reconstruction and repair of highways and grants for urban renewal projects up to $25,000,000. It also provides for adjustments in federal loans.

Alaska's Congressman Ralph J. Rivers has introduced identical legislation in the House of Representatives.

Helping to keep spirits high in Seward, as in all Alaska, as the rugged and courageous citizens now tackle their man-sized problems are the miraculous facts that so many survived the ordeal of March 27, that the seismic waves struck at low rather than high tide, and that

the schools had been closed in observance of Good Friday, tending to keep families together during the supreme trial which lay just a few hours away.

In near-by Anchorage, itself an All-America award winner in 1956 and also hard-hit by the quake, nine-year-old Johnny Higgins has told how he handled the situation when he, his mother and little sister ran from the front door of their home to find the earth churning and crumbling and sinking away beneath their feet.

"I prayed," he testifies simply. "It worked too."

Probably he speaks for most of those who now begin to build anew in the face of an uncertain future—knowing that somehow amid the crushing ruins, their prayers have, indeed, already been answered and that the fullfillment of those answered prayers will, in due course, come.

Ancient Roads and Renewal

According to the May, 1964 issue of *Better Roads*, two historic old roads in Syria will soon be getting a modern paved surface to facilitate vehicular traffic through one of the oldest inhabited regions of the world.

The roads, extending from Damascus to Aleppo and from Aleppo to Raqqah, were used during the Crusades and have seen centuries of camel caravans. They now serve agricultural regions, refineries and food-processing plants.

Community Planning—Seven Steps to Make It Effective

By R. E. HARBAUGH, City Manager, Oshkosh, Wisconsin

Reprinted from the March, 1964 issue of *The Municipality*, a publication of the League of Wisconsin Municipalities

I would suppose that while being in contact with certain problems over the years, one becomes consciously or subconsciously opinionated. I am no exception to that premise.

One of my pet prejudices formulated during my 13 years of administration is that I feel that a huge amount of talent, energy and taxpayers' dollars are wasted when comprehensive plans are prepared and then lie on the shelves collecting dust.

I have formed definite opinions on a procedure that should prevent this from happening. I would hastily grant that this procedure is not infallible . . . but I offer it in the hope that it may stimulate discussion.

Step No. 1. The need for a comprehensive plan must be established, understood, and accepted to a point where people are asking . . . what are we waiting for . . . we should have had such a plan years ago . . . let's get going. People look to their elected representatives to initiate the machinery. The need for planning can, and, perhaps preferably, should be established by study groups, civic organizations, chambers of commerce, taxpayers' associations, union committees as compared to the local governing body.

Extreme care and discretion must be exercised at this point in avoiding a witchhunt on personalities, namely, former elected representatives. It must be recognized that elected representatives generally reflect the goals and wishes of the people. Perhaps these goals were to keep the tax rate down, show a large surplus and save by not spending, regardless of future savings. Therefore, it is necessary not only to permit but to encourage these former elected representatives to participate from the very inception. Planning should be introduced and sold on the basis of the realization that the many parts of the urban area are interrelated and interdependent and that a planned land usage will result in a more economical and healthy environment.

Step No. 2. Formulate goals. This may sound somewhat elementary for most communities will have the same goals such as:

Job opportunities for anticipated population.

Adequate educational facilities to prepare for job opportunities.

Adequate park and recreational areas.

Provide livable conditions and protect property values.

Permit movement of people and goods with the least amount of irritation.

Provide adequate city services for anticipated population.

Improve the city's appearance.

It is my contention that the preparation of a comprehensive plan must be structured within the framework of accepted goals. If this is not done at the outset, one can find himself lost in the maze of subject matter and studies presented. He will also find it difficult to explain why certain tools are necessary such as extra territorial zoning, official map, minimum standard housing, etc. Without the overall goal perspective many people regard additional restrictive legislation as abrogating their basic freedoms.

Step No. 3. Establish criteria or standards. Today the numerous professional associations have established minimum standards for effecting a good environment. These standards should be explored, chewed, and accepted or revised. In order not to confuse standards with goals, I am referring to standards such as these:

An elementary school within $\frac{1}{2}$ mile of every home.

A junior high school within a mile of every home.

A neighborhood playground within $\frac{1}{2}$ mile of every home.

Pavement widths to carry certain volumes of traffic.

School capacity on the basis of 30/classroom.

One nine-hole golf course for each 27,000 persons.

One tennis court for each 2,000.

One softball diamond for each 3,000—

plus many other standards based on engineering studies and experience. Once the standards are set, then we are ready for the next step.

Step No. 4. The next step is to take an inventory as to how well the city compares with the standards today. For example, how many present elementary schools have a site of five acres plus one acre for each additional 100 students? Are the neighborhood playgrounds (4–7 acres) properly located in that the children are within $\frac{1}{2}$ mile walking distance? Is it possible to define neighborhoods by major streets or is the city completely on a grid system with traffic running through each residential neighborhood? Is there a fire station within $\frac{3}{4}$ mile radius of high value areas?

Step No. 5. The next step is to perform an economic base study. Project the population growth at least 25 years, indicate on a map present land usage, and then propose a land use map based on the needs of an anticipated population and projected population distribution densities in conformance with goals and standards adopted. Other basic studies might include projection of school population, origin and destination survey to determine layout of future streets and other engineering studies to satisfy extension of services.

Step No. 6. The final step in the formulation of the preparation of the comprehensive plan is the definite proposals necessary to achieve each of the goals. Although vision and imagination are required here the recommendations must be real and realistically attainable. In other words, the ideal solution may have to be supplanted by an alternate solution that is attainable.

Step No. 7. Effecting the plan. Certain tools are necessary to place this adopted plan into effect. One of the most important tools is the capital improvements program which

(Continued on page 56)

14

Colonial Town Uses Soil Survey in Planning for Today's Growth

By BERNHARD A. ROTH, Field Information Specialist, Soil Conservation Service, U.S. Department of Agriculture

Reprinted from the January, 1964 issue of SOIL CONSERVATION

What does a skilled consultant think of the usefulness of a soil survey in community planning? The question has been answered favorably and emphatically by Mrs. Charles R. Thomas, member of a firm that has just prepared a master plan for the fast-growing seacoast town of Hanover, Massachusetts.

The Town of Hanover, approximately 20 miles southeast of Boston, was one of the first to be settled in the country. Use of the land has undergone several transitional periods since the town was settled in colonial times. The most recent transition has led the town to become increasingly residential. . . .

While helping Hanover blueprint its future, Mrs. Thomas worked closely with Soil Conservation Service soil scientists, learned the complexities of their mapping techniques, and referred to their findings.

"We've relied heavily on precise soils information whenever we could get it in planning other towns," Mrs. Thomas said. "At Hanover, we found it tailored exactly to our needs."

As a result of her experience, the Massachusetts consultant has written a guide to use of soils interpretation for community planning. Mrs. Thomas said accurate soil maps removed much of the "educated, intuitive guessing" from her type of work, and that the onsite survey lent authority to decisions affecting properties involved in land-use regulation.

The Hanover plan and Mrs. Thomas' soil science evaluation have been published for wide distribution by the Massachusetts Department of Commerce Planning Division. The two documents will serve as case studies for hundreds of other Bay State communities grappling with the problems of rapid expansion. Offered as models are nine color-rendered maps delineating soil areas in relation to sewage effluent disposal, homesites, athletic fields, wetlands for wild waterfowl, sources of sand and gravel, roads, woodland, surface runoff, and agriculture.

Success of the Hanover project has spurred requests for additional soil survey assistance in towns throughout the 15 soil conservation districts which blanket Massachusetts from Cape Cod to the Berkshire Hills. In response, the Soil Conservation Service has agreed to supply soil survey information on a cost-share basis to the community. Cooperative agreements have been signed with 39 towns embracing 640,000 acres. Fifteen other towns are considering similar action.

Kinds of maps furnished vary from general soil groupings for overall planning to detailed maps outlining smaller parcels, for use by subdividers and municipal developers.

Since interest began to quicken, the SCS has continually added refinements to soil maps prepared for community interests.

As an example, symbols recently have been added to make understanding of the soil maps easier for urban planners coping with soil areas having severe or very severe limitations for use. The revised symbols indicate the precise nature of limiting factors such as shallow depth to bedrock, high water table, or very stony condition. This information tells the consultant, town officials, or developers the specific difficulty that needs to be overcome or planned around.

In concluding her evaluation report, Mrs. Thomas said:

"If planning boards had made use of such information in the past, they would have more clearly complied with their purposes in regard to health and general welfare and could have avoided many costly errors. In the case of Hanover, serious errors could have been avoided."

URBAN RENEWAL À LA MODE

(*Continued from page 8*)

There are also sociologists, lawyers, real-estate operators, and others who have been received into official agencies as bona fide "planners."

What do all these kinds of people know about historic American buildings—either singly or as grouped together in cities? The question is almost too embarrassing to ask.

Among the few institutions where architectural history and the appreciation of early American buildings have been taught are our architectural schools. But most of these in recent years have become so preoccupied with the kind of architectural design which spurns the past and lusts after novelties that the students of the younger generation don't take history seriously. Some of the older practicing architects are genuinely interested but very few are really experienced in solving historical problems. And very few raise their voices in protest when the lives of old buildings are at stake.

The whole subject deserves close scrutiny and plain talking at the highest level in Washington. In the meantime debate on this subject is impeded by semantic troubles. Friends of preservation often argue among themselves in trying to draft guiding principles. After much cut-and-try, I have come to recommend this simple precept: *Don't let them pull anything down unless they are committed to put up something better!*

NOTE: For the past ten years ANTIQUES has reported on preservation projects which have saved hundreds of buildings and old neighborhoods. In the "symposium" in which the above article appeared, the editors asked distinguished preservationists some leading questions: How can the decision be made as to what is or is not worth preserving? Who should have the final say? Who should organize the necessary architectural and historical research? How can thorough architectural and historical research be assured as a part of every master plan? What should be the relationship of federal, state, and private funds in such a project?

Zoning Round Table

Conducted by FLAVEL SHURTLEFF, Marshfield Hills, Mass.

WHAT ZONING ORDINANCE?

The Massachusetts subdivisions control law permits the submittal of a preliminary plan before getting into the greater expense of a definitive plan. The requirements in the preparation of a preliminary plan are purposely made less exacting to induce a general acceptance by developers of this first step in the subdivision process. But the two plans raise a question in zoning administration. What zoning ordinance controls—the one in effect when the preliminary plan is submitted, or a later one which may be in effect when the definitive plan is submitted? The legislature answered this question in the text of the law, and the rule is that the date of the first submitted plan establishes what zoning ordinance controls, providing the first plan, if preliminary, is followed by a definitive plan submittal within seven months.

In the very recent case of Lavoie Construction Co. vs. Building Inspector of Ludlow the issue was whether a preliminary plan submitted only to the planning board satisfied the statutory requirements, since the subdivision law provided that such a plan may be submitted "to the planning board and to the board of health."

The Court ruled that the zoning law contained no mention of the board of health in the section involved and consequently the preliminary plan* was proper and fixed the controlling old subdivisions.

*Advance Sheets, 1963, P. 895, Zoning regulations.

In Toothaker et al vs. Planning Board*, the plaintiff owned 1,200 lots in a subdivision recorded in 1914. In 1951, when subdivision control was adopted in the town, 649 lots had been sold and at least 20 houses had been built and were occupied. Following closely the rule in a pertinent section of the subdivision control law, the court ruled that the lots were sold and the ways appurtenant to them were not governed by the law, but that the rest of the land in the subdivision must comply. In any widening of ways appurtenant to the sold lots, compensation must be paid for any land which had to be acquired.

PROCEDURE

Three Massachusetts cases involving jurisdictional questions in zoning and subdivision control may well be useful precedents in other states.

In Kalodny et al vs. Board of Appeal,** the plaintiffs appealed from a refusal in writing by the building inspector to revoke a building permit. The court ruled that this refusal was not a "decision" which could be appealed. It was merely an affirmation of his decision to issue the permit. To allow an appeal in such a case would in effect modify the statutory provisions.

The Board of Appeals*** attempted to review the issuance of a liquor license by the Selectmen because of

*Advance Sheets, 1963, P. 895.

**Advance Sheets, 1963, P. 899.

***Bradshaw vs. Board of Appeals, Adv. Sheets, 1963, P. 1235.

17

an alleged violation of the zoning regulations, but the court said that there were adequate means of enforcing the regulations without recourse to a power for which there was no statutory authority.

In Rounds et al *vs.* Board of Water and Sewer Commissioners,* the planning board endorsed its approval of a subdivision plan subject to a covenant by the plaintiffs that construction of a way and installation of utilities would be completed in accordance with the regulations. Later the defendant board refused to supply water to three lots in the approved subdivision until the plaintiffs replaced a two-inch main by a six-inch main.

The court ruled in favor of the water board. The planning board could not bind another municipal agency which had responsibility for municipal services. The plaintiffs should have appealed from the planning board's decision. Otherwise their action constitutes acquiescence.

LARGE LOTS

In this year's March Quarterly, the attempt of the Home Owners Association to have the Massachusetts zoning law amended by establishing maximum lot sizes of 15,000 square feet in residential dis-

*Advance Sheets, 1964, P. 277.

tricts was cited. We hoped in this issue to report the decisions of the committee which heard the bill, and possibly the action of the legislature, but the bill is still in committee, and a compromise bill is being prepared by the Home Owners which may more nearly meet the objections of the planners to the present proposal.

Any compromise would be a further surrender of treasured local rights. The zoning law is a wide grant of power from the state to its cities and towns. Already several amendments have put restrictions on its exercise, notably by exempting from any regulation the use of land for religious and educational use, and by prohibiting a requirement of more than 768 square feet for the living space area of a single family residence.

The present proposal is even more drastic. It strikes at what may be a strong desire of the great majority in many towns to preserve the openness or rural character of the town. Lots limited to a maximum area of 15,000 square feet in any considerable subdivision would introduce suburban conditions.

The Home Owners Association and the planners are apparently far apart. They have widely differing objectives. It will be interesting to see if there can be a successful compromise.

John Muir Wilderness Area

The recently created High Sierra Wilderness has been renamed for John Muir, a man who spent most of his life exploring that high country and imbuing in others the need for conservation of its natural resources.

Mr. Muir, a Scotsman by birth, who came to this country as a boy in 1849, was a naturalist, philosopher, and writer. He introduced President Theodore Roosevelt to the Sierra Nevada. His influence on the thinking of the conservation-minded President is said to have been instrumental in decisions leading to establishment of many national forests and national parks.

18

Commentaries

Excellence: "While the attention and industry of our public policy have been focused through these postwar years on crises in Berlin, in Cuba and the Far East, America almost behind our backs has been more and more taking on the physical appearance and the cultural atmosphere of a honky-tonk of continental proportions.

"This is not to suggest that intellectual, artistic and scientific excellence has been abandoned in our country. On the contrary, it is being pursued by more people with more energy and more striking results than at any time in our history.

"But the pursuit of excellence and creativity remain the occupation of an elite segment of our society.

"I do not think we can avoid the conclusion that, despite a broadening interest in the arts, the level of popular taste in America remains far below what it can be, and ought to be."

—Senator J. W. Fulbright, of Arkansas, in an address at the University of North Carolina at Chapel Hill, as quoted in the *Wall Street Journal*, May 7, 1964.

Unquiet Crisis: "It is up to the public to meet the deadline for Grand Canyon, and this is no quiet crisis."

So says David Brower, executive director of the Sierra Club, in a recent issue of the *Sierra Club Bulletin*.

In an article titled, "The New Threat To Grand Canyon: Action Needed," Mr. Brower asks:

"Shall we keep for the future all we can of what is still natural there? Shall we insist that the alternatives to this destruction, alternatives which exist but which have hardly been considered yet, be sought out?"

"After all," he points out, "neither Marble nor Bridge Canyon dams put a drop of water in the river. . . . There are other ways to pay for pumping water than to destroy the living river that gives Grand Canyon its shape and its meaning."

Building: "Construction is the oldest science on earth and the nation's largest industry, but it has made the least progress."

So says Lev Zetlin, professorial lecturer of civil engineering at Pratt Institute in New York City and principal of a consultant firm which has supplied structural engineering advice for the buildings of nine major exhibitors at the New York World's Fair.

Reasons given by Mr. Zetlin in a lecture sponsored by Cornell University's College of Architecture are:

Lack of understanding by each member of the construction team as to what the other person's contribution to the joint effort can be.

And, a failure to appreciate the importance of "creative engineering" in building design.

He points out that "in many sectors of the construction field, we are still using today the same techniques, the same materials, and the same structural systems as we used a century ago."

19

Why the lag in the construction industry which actually had its beginnings when man first began to build shelters and long before he worried about transportation, chemistry or other present-day sciences?

Mr. Zetlin blames building codes, calling them "strait-jackets," and the timidity and lack of inner drive "to utilize more advanced engineering principles within the limits of the building codes."

He maintains that progress can be made through "the ability to create economically structural systems most suited to the functional and architectural purpose of a building."

As an example, he notes, if a 30-foot span is actually required to help a building to fulfill its purpose best, it is false economy to use a 15-foot span. Real economy, he points out, would come through creative development of a 30-foot span costing no more than one of 15-foot size.

❧

Leisure Lost? In the May issue of *Conservation News*, Ernest Swift sounds a long over-due note of warning about the hazards besetting us in the use of substantial, if hard-won leisure hours, now a reality to most of us:

"Great evils can be spawned unless an understanding is developed between leisure and idleness. Between the niceties of these two philosophies, there is no slide-rule definition that can be taught or applied as yet to thousands of recreationists.

"Leisure is for re-creating oneself *after* a period of *intense work* involving productivity or creativeness. If this is not the threshold for utiliza-

tion of leisure, then leisure and recreation become meaningless. . .

"No nation has yet been able to cope with too much leisure; it can so easily erode the aggressiveness and purpose which are the all-important elements of survival. Can the United States become an exception?"

❧

Duality: In a recent statement on the conflicts between outdoor users of differing tastes, Fred E. Morr, Director of the Ohio Department of Natural Resources, depicts two essentially different types of people whose needs are and irrevocably will remain unblendable.

"It boils down to how you find your pleasure," says Mr. Morr in the May issue of *The Ohio Conservation Bulletin*. "Do you always enjoy being with a group with constant talk and laughter? Or do you prefer the eloquent silence of space and unbroken time?"

He continues with some observations which not only cut to the heart of the land use problem but which appear to be pertinent to a variety of areas of our national life today: "We have developed a mass ethic, based originally on utilitarianism, which is now destructive of those who are not endowed with great social urge.

"Most modern virtues have a social base and the lone person is suspect. Yet, our greatest contributions arise from lonely situations where, as individuals, we face and solve problems. In groups we tend to lean on the mass conscience which is not always good or right."

❧

20

PROJECTS IN REVIEW

Anchorage, Alaska

Merchants and officials of quake-rocked Anchorage are starting to replace their old trade center with an even greater one.

The City Council has approved a preliminary fifty-million-dollar urban renewal plan for a reconstructed 350-acre central district, submitted by Candeub, Fleissig and Associates, Community Planning and Urban Renewal Consultants.

The plan was prepared within one week when a nine-man team, gathered from six of the firm's 14 offices throughout the country and under the personal direction of the firm's president, Isadore Candeub, flew into Anchorage to prepare it. It was then submitted to the Alaska State Housing Authority and Anchorage City Council which voted approval on April 16. A target date of 1970 has been set for completion of all phases of reconstruction, and it is expected that by that time a new, more vital Anchorage business area will have replaced the old one.

Anchorage, a valley port leading to Cook Inlet and surrounded by snow-capped mountains, is Alaska's largest city and most important trade center. The 200,000-megaton shock wrecked 20 years of its economic growth.

The heart of the 100,000-population trade area was the long, narrow downtown Anchorage business section which, apart from its scenic background, looks like any other "Main Street, U. S. A." And now that much of the rubble has been cleared away, fissures filled, waterlines laid and "business as usual" signs are out again, the preliminary plan would convert the long, narrow business strip into a modern, compact shopping center. New office structures and apartment buildings would be developed in a fringe around the rehabilitated business section.

Attesting to the trade at Anchorage's disposal, one area, soil-shifted by the quake and considered unsuited for structures of substance, may provide facilities for 2,000 cars. Covered promenades would permit winter-time Alaskan shoppers to walk from their parked cars into newly designed stores without exposing themselves to the elements.

Another area similarly affected by the quake would be converted into a frontier tourist center of relocated log cabins, a museum, and other attractions designed to cause the passing traveler, seeking Alaska's famous game or fish, to tarry in Anchorage awhile.

Explaining why his planning team was able to meet the tightest urban renewal timetable on record, Mr. Candeub said, "Our firm's experience with disaster such as towns ravaged by floods or mine cave-ins, is that in a crisis people respond fast—and we had plenty of cooperation." Officials of the Federal Urban Renewal Administration, not waiting for normal paperwork and communications, flew into Anchorage, going over plans and making recommendations as his staff drafted them, he said.

Better Community Contest

The Pennsylvania Better Community Contest, sponsored for the tenth year by the State Chamber of Commerce to stimulate beneficial community-wide planning and improvement, this year becomes a two-year competition. Every Pennsylvania community is eligible to compete in the contest which offers prizes totalling $27,500.

The West Penn Power Company will make matching cash awards to communities winning prizes in the service area of the company.

New Stadium for Philadelphia?

Citizens' Council on City Planning has urged that citizens and organizations interested in community improvement support a current proposal to erect a new stadium in the Quaker City.

In so doing, it pointed out: "Professional teams in baseball, football and other major sports are an essential element in the recreational activity of a major city. In addition to providing spectator attractions for city and area residents, these activities generate economic activity which support many business enterprises in the community. . . . Professional sports are fast-growing enterprises, which are highly desired by public officials of cities which are not now 'major league.' "

At the same time, the Council cautioned: "The proposal to use federal urban renewal grants to pay part of the cost of this project raises issues which could delay or possibly prevent construction of the stadium. Citizens' Council suggests that the city investigate the possibility of financing this project with private and city funds alone rather than under the cumbersome and slow federal urban renewal procedures."

A Broader View

"Historically, what conservationists have sought is *non*-development and for them the developer and his bulldozers have seemed the natural foe. There are many good reasons for this attitude, certainly, and those who have been working to save our open spaces would not have accomplished much if they had not had this fighting spirit.

"The time has come, however, for conservationists to take a much more positive interest in development—not just for the threat that it poses, but for the potentials that it holds. It is going to take place; and on a larger scale than ever before. But what will be its character? The answer to this question is critical to the whole problem of preserving the influence of the outdoors in American life."

—Laurance S. Rockfeller in the Foreword to *Cluster Development* by William H. Whyte, published by the American Conservation Association.

Centennial Year to Observe Preservation of Yosemite Valley as State Park

Celebration of a centennial year, beginning June 30, 1964 and ending June 30, 1965, will be held to commemorate the signing of a significant act bearing on State Park history by President Abraham Lincoln.

It was on June 30, 1864, that President Lincoln signed an Act of the Thirty-Eighth Congress of the United States of America granting "to the State of California the Yo-Semite Valley," and the land embracing the "Mariposa Big Tree Grove."

The National Conference on State Parks has recognized this Act "as the significant legislation which created the first State Park in the Nation and led eventually to the establishment of the National Park concept."

In 1890, Congress created a national park surrounding these state lands, and, in 1905, the State Legislature returned the Yosemite and the Giant Sequoias as an addition to Yosemite National Park.

Historians have been prone to accept the fact that the national park idea was born at a campfire in Yellowstone in 1879. Sponsors of the Yosemite Valley centennial year hope that its celebration will bring the evolution of the national park idea into focus in that they believe Yosemite is the point of departure from which the new idea began to gain momentum.

To a limited degree there had been public parks in this country since the beginning of colonization. When Penn laid out the original plan of Philadelphia, he assigned for public use a number of squares, the largest of which had measured ten acres. And there were "commons" such as those in England in most of the New England settlements.

Grants to states were made frequently in the middle nineteenth century and national public opinion was, by no means, aroused by the federal action in making the Yosemite grant to the State of California. However, what was really new about the grant was that it served a strictly non-utilitarian purpose. The grant was given "upon the express conditions that the premises shall be held for public use, resort and recreation, shall be held inalienable for all time."

In 1856, the *Country Gentleman* republished an article by the *California Christian Advocate* which declared the "Yo-hem-i-ty" valley to be "the most striking natural wonder on the Pacific" and predicted that it would ultimately become a place of great resort.

Delegates to the organizational meeting for the Yosemite Valley Centennial Year included representatives from the staff of Yosemite National Park, the National Park Service Regional Office, the State of California, the Mariposa County Board of Supervisors, the Mariposa County Historical Society and the Yosemite Park and Curry Co.

American Motors Corporation Announces 1963 Conservation Award Winners

Ben H. Thompson, assistant director for resources studies at the National Park Service and treasurer of the National Conference on State Parks, was one of twenty-two winners of the American Motors Conservation Awards for 1963.

The awards, inaugurated by American Motors a decade ago to highlight the need for conserving water resources, soil, forests and wildlife in the United States, are presented annually to individuals and groups for outstanding efforts in various areas of conservation.

Nine men and two women were named as winners of professional awards and nine men and one woman were selected for non-professional awards. Professional winners are career conservationists, while non-professionals are individuals whose contributions to conservation are apart from their occupations.

Mr. Thompson, one of the winners in the professional category, is recognized as an authority in the selection and establishment of national parks, monuments, historic sites and recreation areas. A native of Ohio, he has specialized in the areas of planning, policy and other work associated with the establishment of nationally-controlled conservation locations such as parks, monuments and sites. He has been with the National Park Service for 33 years.

Included in the non-professional category of winners were three physicians, two of whose activities are of special interest to members of the National Conference on State Parks.

Dr. S. Slidden Baldwin, a physician in Danville, Illinois, launched a campaign to alert the people in the Kickapoo State Park area that a strip coal mining bill had been introduced and passed which would permit mining in the park. Seeking to save the park in existing form, he enlisted the aid of the Vermilion County Audubon Society and arranged public discussion meetings and newspaper interviews. As a result of his campaign, the governor of Illinois vetoed the bill.

Dr. Neil Compton of Bentonville, Arkansas spearheaded a campaign to prevent construction of a dam on the Buffalo River, one of the few remaining free-flowing mountain streams in the Ozark Mountains. In his campaign to "Save the Buffalo", Dr. Compton addressed conservation groups, schools, service clubs and other organizations throughout the area.

In announcing the 1963 winners, Roy Abernethy, president of American Motors, pointed out that "much of the fundamental strength of a nation lies in the manner in which its people manage its natural resources today and plan soundly for their use tomorrow."

Each Award winner received an engraved bronze plaque designed by Robert Weinman, noted sculptor, and, in addition, an honorarium of $500 was also given to each winner in the professional category and to group winners.

National Capital *Notes*

FOUR CLEARLY DEFINED OBJEC-TIVES, which could well set a pattern for guidance to civic groups across the Nation, were recently ascribed to the **Committee of 100 on the Federal City** by its **Chairman, Rear Admiral Neill Phillips USN (ret.).**

They were incorporated in an incisive report on the Committee's activities made by the Chairman at a meeting of the Board of Trustees, **American Planning and Civic Association,** January 18, 1963, in Washington, D. C.

Admiral Phillips detailed fifteen endeavors in which the Committee has participated during the past year, ranging from efforts to bring the Capital City's strangling traffic situation into adjustment, to efforts to increase protection of the Potomac shoreline across from Mt. Vernon and to protect Glover Archbold Park —perhaps the finest natural forest area within any city in the world— from highway encroachment and from erosion due to mis-managed right-of-way clearing.

In pursuit of its goals, the Committee of 100 holds monthly meetings at which policies are originated, supported or opposed which are likely to have, and, in the past, have had

a profound effect on the appearance and development of the National Capital. The Committee's Chairman carries out policies as directed by vote of the membership and the work of the Committee is carried on by various sub-committees under the direction of the Chairman.

An affiliate of the American Planning and Civic Association, the Committee is an autonomous group composed of individuals from various walks of life, individually independent in their views and deeply desirous of preserving the sacred heritage of independent citizen thinking, but united in the goal so often expressed by their Chairman: "To make Washington a great nation's capital and a fine place to live."

The four objectives which chart the course of the Committee's embracing activities, as outlined by the Chairman, are:

1) To create in the Washington metropolitan area the finest attainable urban and suburban environment.

2) To make Washington a capital city symbolic of the best in our culture and our system of government.

3) To preserve and use effectively our natural environment, and our

architectural, historical, and cultural heritage.

4) To preserve and enhance the individuality and essential character of our city.

★   ★   ★

Revitalization of down-town Washington became a subject for increased discussion when the House District Committee, on March 17, 1964, approved S. 628 with a series of amendments. House action on the bill is expected later this summer.

Basic purpose of the measure, which was passed by the Senate, July 16, 1963, is to authorize the District to use Federal urban renewal powers in predominantly commercial areas.

At present, in the District, urban renewal support for a commercial area is available only if it is within a larger neighborhood that is predominantly residential. Of the ten largest cities in the United States, Washington's down-town area, alone, cannot participate in the urban renewal program.

Downtown Progress, a business-sponsored group organized to spearhead downtown modernization, recently announced that it supports passage of S. 628 *without* amendments. The group recently received the commendation of the President:

"It is encouraging that Downtown Progress, representing the business community of Washington, is continuing to work for the improvement of the vital area between the White House and the Capitol, so that it may become an asset to the Nation as well as a good place in which to work, shop and live."

★   ★   ★

Those interested in the preservation of open spaces will find a recent article called "Let's Save the Farms" from the **Northern Virginia Regional Planning and Economic Development Commission,** of interest.

"There are distinct advantages to keeping farmers in areas such as Northern Virginia—where about 150 new houses or apartment units a week go up and 2,500 new people a month move into the area," says the Commission.

"Here is what happens today: Developers put up new houses, apartments and shopping centers in areas which have been farm land. For one reason or another, a few near-by farms escape development. Newcomers, who move into the new houses, of course, want increased county services—more schools, sewers, and better streets. County taxes go up to pay for these new services and these costs are passed on to the owners of the new houses and businesses.

"But the poor farmer, living and working nearby, finds that he, too, must pay for these increased services which he usually neither wants nor needs. He then pays the same land tax rate on his 300 acres as a new home-owner pays on his one-quarter or one-half acre lot. Frequently the farmer simply cannot do it, and he is forced to sell for still more subdivision development."

The result: "The community loses forever the beauty and conservation assets of a near-by operating farm. The farmer, whose only skill often is farming, is forced off the land. City folks living nearby can no longer buy farm-fresh eggs and vegetables.

Dairies must go farther out to buy milk for the city's children to drink. The open farmland disappears forever."

★   ★   ★

More than a million riders attest to the popularity of a sturdy little bus with a candy-striped top, called the Minibus, which recently made its debut on Washington's crowded streets.

Introduced under the auspices of **Downtown Progress, and others** the Minibus, with its ring-around-seat won quick acclaim from shoppers who were enabled to enjoy the full and exciting view of department store display windows as they moved about downtown.

Offering a ready ride, if a slightly rough one, the Minibus makes its appearance every two and one-half minutes. It furthermore holds forth a compelling attraction in that, while few things can be had in the Nation's Capital today for an old-fashioned nickel, it can.

Hence, it is not surprising that others besides shop-hounds have been quick to see the advantages the spunky little bus offers.

Hence, also, it is not surprising to see a whole fleet of minibuses incorporated in a proposal made by Metropolitan Washington's four transit companies for a commuter bus system intended to help solve Washington's throbbing transportation headache.

Requiring a public investment of twenty-five million dollars, the proposed commuter bus system would serve either as an interim operation until a rail rapid transit network is built or possibly as a full substitute.

Of the twenty-five million dollars, half would be for terminals and fringe parking lots. From one proposed terminal near the Bureau of Engraving, a fleet of minibuses would transport passengers to and from downtown destinations.

★   ★   ★

A hundred thousand tulips, and more, came resolutely through the late spring snow and brought a blaze of color to Washington's parks this year.

Bringing pronounced cheer to the exodus of a long, hard winter and heralding the perennial beauty of the National Capital in spring-time, the abundant blooms inspired **Rear Admiral Neill Phillips, Chairman of the Committee of 100 on the Federal City,** to write a congratulatory letter to **T. Sutton Jett, Regional Director of the National Park Service,** under whose direction the floral beautification program was started last year.

On behalf of the Committee, and with an ever-watchful eye on the appearance of the Nation's Capital, Admiral Phillips said:

"The upkeep and care which the National Park Service gives to its parks is always of a high standard, but the 1964 spring flowers, particularly the tulips, are more glorious than I have ever seen in my many years of living in Washington. . . .

"Not only is this a joy to us who live here, but also this civic beauty must be a very important factor in drawing out-of-town visitors, and promoting the vital tourist trade."

Notable among the varied floral displays were a new carmine red tulip called Halcro Cottage which

(Continued on page 28)

27

View of the proposed Sleeping Bear National Lakeshore.

Courtesy National Park Service, U. S. Department of the Interior.

View of the proposed Sleeping Bear National Lakeshore.

Courtesy National Park Service, U. S. Department of the Interior.

Sleeping Bear National Lakeshore
—A Proposal

This is the seventh in the series of articles on proposed National Park Service projects, prepared by the Park Service at our request.

The proposed Sleeping Bear National Lakeshore lies along the east shore of Lake Michigan—some 294 miles from Chicago, 239 miles from Detroit, and 125 miles from •the Mackinac Bridge.

A survey of the entire Great Lakes shoreline, conducted by the National Park Service in 1957-58 to determine what remaining areas could be set aside for public pleasuring grounds or preserved for their scenic qualities and scientific values, identified Sleeping Bear as one of the most outstanding of over 60 areas it recommended for public use and enjoyment. Detailed studies following the preliminary survey revealed an area of even greater natural values and recreation potential than had been initially anticipated.

Four scientific phenomena are evident to an unusual degree in the Sleeping Bear Lakeshore proposal: the effects of continental glaciation, the postglacial processes of shoreline adjustment of Lake Michigan, the work of the wind in the formulation of a great variety of dunes, and finally, the processes of plant succession. The slow but meticulous hand of nature used three great geologic tools, ice, water and wind, to shape the Sleeping Bear landscape.

These scientific processes so vividly portrayed in the Sleeping Bear region are also responsible for its unexcelled scenery. Vistas, intimate and expansive, are everywhere to be seen. The long sweeping crescent-shaped beaches anchored on their extreme ends by bold, high bluffs of lake-eroded moraines, give it a special character.

Within the embayed lowlands are numerous lakes, once part of ancestral Lake Michigan and now sealed off by sandy beach ridges. The lowlands are surrounded by high morainal hills from which one may appreciate best the beauty of these lakes.

In Sprague's *History of Grand Traverse and Leelanau Counties, Michigan,* published in 1903, it is interesting to note a description of one of these vistas, so complete and detailed and so like the scene today that anyone familiar with the area will be amazed. Part of it is quoted here:

"From an eminence about four hundred feet high, two or three miles inland from Glen Arbor, on the northeast side of Glen Lake, can be seen one of the most varied and beautiful landscapes to be witnessed in any country, and one which is well worth the pencil of an artist.

" . . . On the left is a portion of Glen Lake, its nearer shore concealed by the forest and the remote one exposing a white, pebbly margin from which the verdant hills beyond rise hundreds of feet above the watery mirror in which their forms are so clearly fashioned. In front of us the green hills separate Glen Lake from Lake Michigan and conceal from view the desert sand fields of

33

Sleeping Bear. Not completely, however, for the naked and glistening flanks of the northern slope stretch beyond the forest-covered ridge and embrace the placid harbor, which struggles through the intercepting foliage and blends with the boundless expanse of the great lake, still beyond. Farther off, in the midst of water, rises the green outline of South Manitou Island. . . . Still farther to the north rises the form of North Manitou, which seems to be trying to hide itself behind the towering bluff of North Unity, that guards the entrance to the harbor from the north. Two little lakes nestle in rich woodland that spreads its verdure between us and the harbor . . . It is doubtful whether a scene superior to this one exists in any country . . ."

Dune formation creates a diversity of scenic forms unusually well displayed within the Sleeping Bear proposal. Dunes of the lowlands, rich in their variety of plant environments, dunes perched atop receding headlands, dunes actively moving across the landscapes, all these types in varied stages of ecological plant succession are represented.

In addition to the diversity of land forms, it contains a great variety of plant environments ranging from the first plant life associated with dune stabilization to pure stands of white birch and cedar bogs. On old beach ridges, lines of red pine give an open, parklike effect to the landscape. An outstanding spruce bog of several thousand acres is located east of the Platte Lakes, while on South Manitou in a tract of virgin timber there exist other rare plants and the largest known northern white cedar in the United States.

In 1961 Senators Philip Hart and Pat McNamara introduced legislation calling for preservation of a Sleeping Bear area, with boundaries corresponding to those recommended by the National Park Service in its detailed study reports.

This proposal included 77,000 acres, 45.5 miles of Lake Michigan shoreline—13 of these surrounding South Manitou Island—and 11,500 acres of inland lakes. The embayments associated with Glen Lake and the Platte Lakes were also included, as well as the morainal ridges overlooking the basins. It provided for a scenic and scientific entity within which a glacial story is told, vividly tracing the advancing and receding ice masses and the subsequent changes in land forms. The inland highlands provide many of the most spectacular vista points within the entire area, overlooking inland lakes and embayed sections.

Although strong support in favor of the proposal prevailed throughout the state generally, local opposition existed and was especially vociferous and organized in the vicinity of Glen Lake and Platte Lakes.

By 1963 the two Senators had introduced their third bill, S. 792, encompassing the same 77,000 acres, but modified in other respects to resolve differences that had been encountered when the proposal was first put in legislative form. One of these modifications, intended to meet objections in the inland lakes areas, was the inclusion of inland lakes residential areas. Some 3,500

(Continued on page 47)

State Park Notes

Tidal Wave Does Some Damage to Oregon Coast State Parks

The following report is from Harold Schick, Oregon State Parks Superintendent, who points out: "The word 'tidal wave' is actually a misnomer since the wave is not caused by a tide but as a result of the under-water disturbance due to the earthquake. It could more accurately be called a 'storm wave.' The water has a rapid rising action rather than one of a rolling wave crashing onto the shore."

The aftermath of the Alaska earthquake brought considerable damage to only four of Oregon's State Parks—all of them "seasonal parks" along the central Oregon coast. And, though over-all damage to the 58 parks and waysides along the entire coast was minor, logs, driftwood and debris were thrown upon the beach all along the shore line, bringing with it a major clean-up problem. Thousands of fish were thrown onto the beaches and lived several days in the pools of water left by the receding "tidal" wave.

Fortunately, when the wave caused by the earthquake struck the coastline during the night of March 27, 1964, very few Oregon parks were open and in use since only five parks are open to campers during the winter season.

Only one of the five, Beverly Beach, had any report of casualties, and there tragedy occurred *outside* the park area. A family, camping on the beach beyond the park limits, had not registered at the camp-ground and park employees had no knowledge that it was parked on the beach. When the wave hit the beach, three of the children were swept out to sea.

Considerable damage was done to Sunset Bay and Ona Beach State Parks, with a small amount to Beachside and Devil's Elbow, bringing the estimated cost of the destruction to the four to $11,000.

The most damage, an estimated $5,000, occurred at Sunset Bay State Park where two footbridges were washed up into the picnic area and permanent tables were ripped up and destroyed. Water stood four feet deep in the kitchen shelter area and sand was deposited in the stoves. A wing was torn from one of the rest station buildings.

At Ona State Park, the tidal wave surged over the entire park area, tearing up shrubbery, up-rooting trees, tearing up black-top trails and littering the park with logs and debris. Footbridges were tossed about with picnic tables and garbage

35

cans, and many picnic tables were ripped apart and destroyed. Logs and debris were deposited and stoves and tables were damaged at Beachside and Devil's Elbow State Parks.

The 85 costal parks and waysides were used by about half of the 13,000,000 people who visited Oregon's State Parks during 1963 and by more than half of the campers.

Michigan. With three years of history, Michigan's State Park Bond program is sound.

This is the conclusion of H. C. MacSwain, Assistant Chief of the State Parks and Recreation Division, in a recent report on the program.

"The bonds are a sound investment for the bondholders," says Mr. MacSwain, "with ample revenue to cover bond debt service, with ample reserves and with surplus revenue used to improve park facilities. The bond funds have made it possible to expedite the State Park Land Acquisition and Improvement Program and have made facilities available to provide for the enjoyment of many more people at a time when it is needed."

"The only drawback to this program," he concludes, "is its limitation of $10,000,000, as this is only one fifteenth of what is required to keep pace with the needs."

Florida. A warning that South Florida faces a serious water shortage in the next two decades has been sounded by Florida Secretary of State Tom Adams.

Mr. Adams has urged that the State's fifty-million-dollar recreation bond issue should be spent to spur both recreation and water conservation.

"The demands of a growing public are outstripping our efforts to provide a continuing water supply adequately," Mr. Adams said. "Unless something is done soon to preserve and conserve South Florida's existing water resources . . . our great metropolitan areas will find themselves without sufficient water adequately to sustain their people, their industry, their agriculture and their recreational requirements."

Mr. Adams pointed out that the constitutional amendment authorizing the issuance of bonds to buy recreation land recognized the concept of multiple use and gave priority to lands that would fulfill several public needs.

Georgia. The first phase of a major recreation development program to build up Georgia's mountain region got under way this spring.

The North Georgia Mountain Commission, created by the 1964 State Legislature to plan development of projects to rehabilitate the region, has awarded a $2,241,000 contract to Clarence Mobley Construction Co. of Augusta to build Ponderosa Lodge.

Scheduled for completion in 1965, the lodge will serve a mountain resort including nearly 900 acres on the northeast side of Brasstown Bald, the State's highest mountain, with access to unlimited acres of surrounding lands of Chattahoochee National Forest. It will provide every kind of living quarters from campsites to luxury apartments.

Colorado. Rapidly changing travel habits are prompting the Colorado Highway Department to "take another look" at roadside parks, according to Chief Engineer Charles E. Shumate.

He says the department plans to ask the State Game, Fish and Parks Department to submit from 10 to 15 sites which would adapt to development as roadside rest areas. The proposed sites would then be studied by highway engineers and parks department personnel for safety, availability of water and other factors. Principal emphasis on roadside parks will be placed on those highways which will feel the impact of the interstate system.

Vermont. Vermont starts the 1964 summer season with a six-fold increase in the number of campsites compared to 1958.

The highlight of the expansion program financed by $3,200,000 in general obligation bonds since 1957, will be an island campground in Lake Champlain.

Burton Island, a 300-acre state park opposite St. Albans Bay, was acquired in 1962 and the initial phases of construction began in the Fall of 1963. The 1964 season will initiate use of 30 tentsites and a new marina. Access to the island will be from St. Albans Bay State Park.

Woodford State Park campground on Route 9 near Bennington will also open for the first time this spring. This area, surrounding a beautiful mountain pond, promises to be one of the most popular spots in the southern part of the state.

Early indications based on requests and reservations point toward a heavy camping use in 1964 and according to Robert B. Williams, Deputy Commissioner, the 15 per cent increase in number of available sites may well prove to be a conservative expansion.

Maryland. The 1962 Annual Report of the Maryland Board of Natural Resources indicates that almost six times as many visitors used Maryland State Parks in that year as twelve years ago.

Greatest increase has been in tent and camp trailer camping, a park use taxing facilities to the utmost and making provision of additional campsites mandatory in the near future. The report states that camping pressure increased from approximately 15,000 campers twelve years ago to approximately 182,000 in 1962. And, in many areas, campers had to be turned away because existing campsites were filled. In others, overflow areas were used to accommodate and meet the demand.

Wisconsin. Administrative changes separating forestry and recreation activities within the Wisconsin Conservation Department have been made recently. Two divisions, the Forest Management Division and the State Parks and Recreation Division, will henceforth carry out appropriate responsibilities, and primary use of an area, whether it be for fish, game, forestry or recreation, will determine which field division administers it.

Arkansas. "Something awakened me in the pearl gray light of dawn. I became aware of a slight rocking motion of the whole room and a bumping noise against the side of the cabin. . . A freshening breeze again set our houseboat to rocking slightly and the fishing boat tied alongside banged against the hull; a slight chill crept through the compact cabin in the early November morning."

Thus does Lou Oberste, of the Arkansas Publicity and Parks Commission, describe his first experience at houseboating—an avocation that is attracting a growing number of enthusiasts each year. He reports that he has seen expanding colonies of these leisure time party craft on almost every major lake and river in Arkansas.

Houseboating offers distinct benefits as a form of recreation, according to Mr. Oberste:

"The houseboater can enjoy community life with his neighbors in the buoyant village at dockside; he can weigh anchor and cruise at will, following the sun, or the fish; he can seek out new neighbors, or a quiet anchorage in some remote cove if solitude is his desire. Houseboating also appeals to the romantic soul of a man, making him captain of his own ship; or the debonair host on his own yacht."

Tennessee. Why do people visit the parks? C. M. Gorman, Jr., State Park Planner, addresses himself to this question in the April issue of the Tennessee Parks and Recreation Newsletter.

"People visit the parks," says Mr. Gorman, "to see snow on the trees, the flash of light from a trout, to catch a glimpse of a deer. People like to be a little frightened by a black snake, to be awed by a view of cliffs, waterfalls or a great fallen tree. People like to dare to cross a swinging bridge. People like to watch a wood fire, and to cook bacon in the open air. People like to hear wind in the leaves, rain on a tent, the silent fall of snow. People like the smell of a park and the feel of rough-cut timber."

"But when we try to state the answer in so many words," he concludes, "we lose the joy of the experience we know is there."

Nineteen Archeological Units Afford Vivid Reflection on America's Past

Nineteen units of the National Park System offer visitors as well as archeologists a vivid portrait of the important role played by prehistoric Indian cultures in our country's history.

These areas—extending from Ocmulgee National Monument in central Georgia to Montezuma Castle National Monument in Arizona—contain earth mounds, cliff ruins, and other village sites, and have been established by the Federal Government specifically to preserve the dwelling places of these ancient people.

Not all these areas are open to the public on a regular basis, since, in many cases, access roads to the ruins are rough or almost nonexistent.

Strictly Personal

William R. Ewald, Jr., development consultant of Washington, D. C,. has been named by the U. S. Department of Commerce to direct a technical assistance project designed to promote establishment of an Appalachian Institute. Purpose of the Institute would be to strengthen and improve research, training and technical assistance activities of the universities, colleges, research institutes, and other public and private organizations in the Appalachian region.

The President's Appalachian Regional Commission, a State-Federal organization concerned with the economic development of Appalachia, recommended the project which will be carried out by Mr. Ewald working with a 9-State Appalachian Institute Committee.

Mr. Ewald, Jr., who heads his own firm in Washington, D. C., was formerly Chief of Development of the Arkansas Industrial Development Commission, consultant to the Commonwealth of Puerto Rico, Assistant Commissioner of the Urban Renewal Administration, and Senior Vice-President of Doxiadis Associates, Inc. He has recently been a member of the Board of Trustees of the American Planning and Civic Association.

———————◆———————

A brief sketch on *Nicholas Roosevelt*, member of the California Recreation Commission, was carried recently by the California Division of Recreation's *Highlights*, which also announced that Neal Phillips, former Mayor of Alturas, had been reappointed to the Commission.

Mr. Roosevelt's interest in conservation and recreation, says *Highlights*, dates back to early association with his cousin, President Theodore Roosevelt, and has remained lively throughout a career as journalist, diplomat and author.

He was closely associated with Horace M. Albright, Madison Grant, Newton B. Drury and the late Stephen T. Mather in the movement to expand national parks.

Mr. Roosevelt has been a Councilor of the Save-the-Redwoods League for many years and for 15 years has been Chairman of the Big Sur Advisory Committee of the County Planning Commission. Together with Mr. and Mrs. Nathaniel A. Owings, he was active in formulating the Monterey County Coast Master Plan.

He is a member of the steering committee of Californians for Beaches and Parks, an association of citizens allied in support of Proposition One, The State Beach, Park, Recreational and Historical Facilities Bond Act of 1964.

———————◆———————

Robert G. Baylor, Superintendent, Fort Pickens State Park, Pensacola Beach, Florida, has been awarded the Florida Park Service Certificate of Merit by N. E. Miller, Jr., Director. Only three other persons have received the award since it was established two years ago.

Mr. Baylor has been cited for his recent manual for state park use regarding the correct procedure for cleaning public buildings and for rodent and insect control. Savings of up to 75% in some supplies are being realized where procedures outlined in the manual are being followed, and efficiency of sanitizing and cleaning are not sacrificed by the suggested method. "After following the instructions in the manual," says Mr. Baylor, "your buildings will be hospital clean."

Requests for the manual have been received from more than a half dozen recreational systems in the Southeast.

———————◊———————

Harry R. Woodward, director of the Colorado Game, Fish and Parks Department, has been named to the nation-wide Cooperative Forestry Research Advisory Committee. The committee was formed recently under legislation permitting the U. S. Department of Agriculture to assist the states in carrying on a program of forestry research.

———————◊———————

Donald J. Mackie has been appointed Superintendent of the new State Parks and Recreation Division of the Wisconsin Conservation Department. He replaces Roman H. Koenings who recently resigned to accept a position with the Bureau of Outdoor Recreation.

Mr. Mackie, who has worked for the Department for 25 years, moves to this position from Superintendent of the Research and Planning Division. A graduate in forestry from the University of Michigan, he was formerly located at Northern Highland State Forest and later served as Forestry Research Coordinator and as Executive Secretary to the Forestry Advisory Committee.

The new State Parks and Recrea-

tion Division, headed by Mr. Mackie, will be responsible for planning and establishing standards for all recreational developments on Department properties.

———————◊———————

C. West Jacocks has retired as South Carolina State Park Director after 18 years with the South Carolina State Commission of Forestry. E. R. Vreeland, Assistant State Park Director since 1949 has been promoted to replace Mr. Jacocks.

Mr. Jacocks' long career of public service includes 13 years with the U. S. Fish and Wildlife Service. He joined the South Carolina Forestry Commission in 1946 as Head of Recreation in the Division of State Parks and was promoted to State Park Director in 1948.

Mr. Vreeland was appointed Superintendent of Kings Mountain State Park in 1947. In 1948, he became Chief of State Park Operations and Assistant State Park Director the following year.

———————◊———————

A seventh generation central Ohio farmer is the first chairman of the Recreation and Resources Commission of the Ohio Department of Natural Resources. He is *John H. Dunlap, Jr.*, Williamsport, who manages 31 farms with 12,000 acres. Benjamin R. Drayer, Columbus, treasurer of the League of Ohio Sportsmen, is the Commission's vice-chairman and Dr. Myron T. Sturgeon, Athens, chairman of the Department of Geography and Geology, Ohio University, is secretary.

(Continued on page 58)

40

Seminars, Conferences and University Notes

Water Resources Center. A Water Resources Center has been organized at the *Georgia Institute of Technology* to serve as the focal point of Georgia Tech's public image as a regional center for water resources education and research.

The Center will work with the several Schools and Departments concerned to facilitate and stimulate the development of a broad-based, interdisciplinary program in water resources education and research. It will aim to bring to bear on the water resources problem competence in such related fields as hydrology, hydraulics, water-control structures, soil mechanics, sanitary engineering, water chemistry and biology. Additionally, systems analysis and computer technology, geology, social science, resource economics, city planning, industrial engineering and industrial management, as well as physics, chemistry and mathematics.

Carl E. Kindsvater has been named Director of the Water Resources Center. Professor Kindsvater has devoted the major portion of his time for the past three years to an analysis and evaluation of current trends in water resources technology and education. He is widely recognized as eminent in the field of water resources engineering.

Mr. Willard M. Snyder has also been named to the water resources engineering staff. Mr. Snyder is an eminent hydrologist with a background of education in civil engineering, mathematics, and meteorology and an outstanding reputation in simulative (or synthetic) hydrology, statistics, and automatic data processing.

In announcing the organization of the Water Resources Center, *J. W. Mason,* Dean of Engineering of Georgia Institute of Technology said:

"Numerous developments within recent years have dramatically brought to the attention of all Americans the critical importance of the wise utilization and control of our water resources. The creation of the Water Resources Center is evidence that we recognize the need to adjust our educational and research programs to the increasing gravity of associated sociological as well as technological problems.

Seminars on American Culture. Each July the *New York State Historical Association* welcomes some 350 Americana enthusiasts of all ages and occupations from all over the United States and Canada to Cooperstown, New York, for its annual two-week Seminars on American Culture.

The 1964 Seminars, seventeenth in the series, to be held July 5-11 and July 12-18, will include twelve courses which seem especially well chosen to give a sense of a living past. Ranging from baseball to lighting in America, cooking to museum security, religious history to historic preservation and city planning, they also include a course on architecture worth saving.

A brochure about the Seminars presents some attractive details on the courses. For example:

Saving The Past: Historic Preser-

vation and City Planning: There are ways of fighting for the significant remains of our past and this course was devised to give practical advice about, as well as significant developments in, historic preservation and city planning. Prof. Stuart W. Stein, Prof. Barclay G. Jones, and Prof. Stephen W. Jacobs, all of the faculty of the College of Architecture, Cornell University, will present the materials, in addition to citing many case studies.

Architecture Worth Saving: Harley J. McKee, Professor of Architecture, Syracuse University, in this course will use central New York State as a typical cross-section of American architectural patterns, stressing the importance of local historic buildings, architects, builders, and craftsmen . . . Professor McKee knows that failure in preservation efforts throughout the nation has often been the fault of those who are foggy about criteria and what to save. In this course, he will seek to dispel the fog.

Folklore in Baseball History: The game of baseball, known for more than a century as America's national pastime, is a treasure trove of curious lore. . . In presenting this course in Cooperstown, the traditional birthplace of baseball, Lee Allen, historian of the National Baseball Hall of Fame and Museum and author of six books on baseball, will emphasize, not the statistics, but the anecdotes that explain the game and its people.

The Seminars are designed for the interested amateur as well as for the spirited professional and they are held on the shores of Lake Otsego in one of America's loveliest villages in the country made famous by James Fenimore Cooper.

Correspondence in regard to the Seminars should be addressed to *Frederick L. Rath, Jr.,* Vice-Director, New York State Historical Association, Cooperstown, New York.

M. I. T. The twenty-sixth in a series of annual two-week Special Summer Programs in City and Regional Planning was scheduled by the *Massachusetts Institute of Technology* to be held this year in Cambridge, Massachusetts, from June 22 through July 3.

As in former years, the Program was arranged to include a comprehensive review of the principles of city and metropolitan planning and of the administration of planning programs. Special emphasis on the relationship between comprehensive planning and urban design was afforded through a series of seminars on the visual aspects of city and metropolitan development.

City Planning Fellowships. *James T. Griffin,* president of the Sears-Roebuck Foundation, has announced that ten two-year graduate fellowships have been granted and nine others renewed for their second year under the Foundation's city planning fellowship program for 1964.

Each fellowship includes a grant of up to $3,000 per year to the student plus an unrestricted grant of up to $1,000 per year to the school where the Foundation fellow studies.

Established in 1957 to increase flow of trained personnel into city planning activities, the Sears Foundation

(Continued on page 49)

Planning for Camper Tourist Areas

By REA AGNEW and RUDOLPH F. JASS

This past year over 15,000,000 vacationists took to the highways for camping vacations. Some went to camp in the mountains, along the lakes and seashore, and enjoyed a variety of outdoor sports. Others took tours, visited scenic areas, historical monuments, saw the sights of our major cities and attended festivals and other events.

For camping equipment they used tents, tent trailers and the small travel trailers. Those who take tours, the so-called travel or tourist campers, make up a good proportion of the total number of campers. While there are many campgrounds in forest and rural areas, few are to be found to serve the tourist camper. Such camping areas are needed along major highways, at or near large cities, and convenient to tourist resorts.

The most notable example of a transient campground in the United States was that at the Potomac Park Motor Court in East Potomac Park in the District of Columbia. Situated on an island in the Potomac River with ready access to the 14th Street Bridge, the campground was only minutes away from the heart of Washington. It was an admirable location for tourists wanting to see the sights of the Capital. An area for tent camping and another for travel trailers were provided. All campers used the large central washroom with flush toilets and showers. The campground was under the supervision of the National Park Service through the National Capital Region. It was run by a concessionnaire and during the summer months was well filled. This campground was permanently closed in 1962 due to sewer construction through the property.

Tourist campgrounds may be operated by: 1) a private entrepreneur; 2) an agency of a municipality, state or the Federal Government; or 3) a private concessionnaire on government land. There are many opportunities for private parties to provide facilities for tourist campers. Camping is a desirable economic use for land. There is a good demand for camping space. Providing such space will not only serve campers who are touring and need overnight accommodation, but it will benefit the communities where the campgrounds are placed. Campers spend money locally for many goods and services, and this money will flow into the pockets of the local merchants. Two recent surveys, in the states of Maine and Washington, reported that a camping family on vacation spent an average of $20 to $25 per day for all wants.

Campgrounds furnishing flush toilets and other washroom facilities may charge two dollars per campsite per night and up, depending on location and facilities offered. Campgrounds recently started up in the New York area to serve World's Fair traffic are charging up to four dollars per site per night. The main tourist season is the ten-week period from late June through Labor Day when a campground might expect to be pretty well filled. For other weeks in the spring and fall, a lower

43

rate of occupancy is to be expected. In some southern regions, campgrounds could remain open for the entire year where traffic warrants this.

Characteristics of a campground will determine where it should be appropriately placed in the community. These are:

1) Certain numbers of people will be served. Access to a street with adequate capacity is necessary. This traffic must not bother residential districts.

2) Campers live in the outdoors much of the time. The camping area ideally should have screening from neighboring land and streets for the benefit of the campers as well as for those in adjacent areas.

3) The campground needs to be placed near the large arterial highways although it need not border on them.

4) A campground should have some shrubbery, shade trees and landscaping to render it attractive. However, the chief function is overnight accommodation, and woodsy surroundings are not mandatory. Open, flat land is perfectly suitable.

5) Campers need goods and services. A location within a reasonable distance of a shopping center is desirable.

Camping tourist areas hold a place in the community different from that of trailer courts which admit the large mobile home. Residents of trailer courts can become relatively permanent and the courts thereby become a basically residential use. Consequently, the residents expect the same amenities and services as those of single family homes, *i.e.*, parks, schools, etc. Some communities object to trailer courts because the children of families residing in them go to school, thus adding to the school costs while, at the same time, relatively low tax assessments for the area prevail. This situation, of course, does not apply to campgrounds which accommodate only transients. The camper tourist primarily seeks an inexpensive stopping-off place as he travels and visits various attractions.

Most communities have areas suitable for campgrounds although the zoning classification may have many different designations, depending on the size of the town or municipality and area of the country in which located.

Many points must be considered in order to arrive at the optimum design for a particular piece of land. Size, topography, and access are the three principal features which determine the use of the land. In addition, functional aspects of development such as utilities, have their influence upon a particular use.

Campgrounds can be permitted by specific reference in the local zoning ordinance. In addition to the local health, sanitary and building code in effect, other minimum standards could be specifically set forth such as the following:

1) Not more than 20 camp sites per acre of land.

2) No camp site should be less than 1,600 square feet in size.

3) Access roads should be not less than 18 feet wide. One-way roads should be not less than 12 feet wide.

4) No camp site should be located less than 50 feet from any street.

5) Side yard requirements or
(*Continued on page 48*)

IN MEMORIAM

HE LEFT US HIS CAUSE, HIS TORCH, HIS SWORD

By EDWARD J. MEEMAN, Chairman of the Board, National
Conference on State Parks

Howard Zahniser has left us.

The heart trouble which, in his waking hours, he never allowed to inhibit him from constantly fighting and working for the preservation of America's wilderness, or from enjoying that which he dedicated his life to save for all of us, took him in his sleep at the age of 58, on May 5, 1964. It was only last year that he rode into the Bob Marshall Wilderness in Montana, named for a man who, like "Zahnie," roused us to keep forever that, which, once lost, we can never replace.

It was Bob Marshall whom Howard Zahniser quoted in his great statement of our cause, in an editorial in The Living Wilderness in 1957, entitled "Forever Wild."

Zahniser quoted Bob Marshall's description of the enemy we are fighting as "the tyrannical ambition of civilization to conquer every niche on the whole earth."

In this fight, Zahniser would brook no defeatism. He wrote:

"We who are striving for wilderness preservation are not engaged in a rear-guard action. There are those who tell us that we are, and they include some of our most earnest champions. . . . They say that we cannot hope to see areas of wilderness last forever, that the best we can do is to slow down the progress of mechanization, road building and development, and pre-

serve as long as possible the benefits of an inevitably disappearing resource. . . . We believe they are wrong, for we see before us a farther vision, a hope for the preservation of wilderness in perpetuity. . . .

"American conservationists today are the vanguard of what must surely become a program in perpetuity. The tenseness of our responsibility and opportunity is in our necessity to fashion wisely a program that will successfully keep the wilderness forever wild. . . .

"It may seem presumptuous for men and women who live for only 40, 50, 60, 70 or 80 years to dare to undertake a program for perpetuity, but that surely is our challenge.

"The wilderness that has come to us from the eternity of the past we have the boldness to project into the eternity of the future.

"As champions of this forward movement we should realize that we are indeed working to fashion the kind of policy and program that will insure now—before it is too late—the preservation of wilderness forever wild."

This is the challenge Howard Zahniser leaves with us.

As editor he leaves us his torch.

As fighter for legislation he leaves us his sword—this gentle but formidable knight, "without fear and without reproach."

In his spirit we can, we must, win!

45

Planning and Civic Comment

EDMUND RANDOLPH PURVES
1897-1964

We record, with deep regret, the recent death of Edmund Randolph Purves, an outstanding architect who had been an active and distinguished member of the Committee of 100 on the Federal City for a long time.

Major Purves served as executive director of the American Institute of Architects from 1949 to 1961. He was named an A.I.A. Fellow in 1944.

He served with the American Field Service in 1917, with the A. E. F. from 1917 to 1919 and as a major with the 7th Air Force, U. S. Army from 1942 to 1946. His decorations included the Victory Medal with four clasps, the Pacific-Asia Ribbon with bronze star, the Croix de Guerre with silver star, and the Verdun Medal. He was the recipient of the Kemper award, A. I. A., in 1958.

A tireless champion of the architectural profession, Major Purves lent the benefit of his authoritative judgment to the deliberations of the Committee of 100. He has been characterized by appreciative colleagues as an unassuming man who could always be counted upon to contribute the appropriate and helpful comment at just the right time. He will be greatly missed.

Plans for North American Conservation Hall of Fame Gain Momentum

Representatives of the states and provinces and delegates from the major conservation organizations of the United States, Canada and Mexico will assemble during the summer of 1964 to elect the first members into the newly formed North American Conservation Hall of Fame, according to a statement by Wayne H. Olson, Commissioner of Conservation, Saint Paul, Minnesota.

Proposal for establishment of the Hall of Fame was made by Minnesota's Governor Karl F. Rolvagg to the International Association of Game, Fish and Conservation Commissioners and the American Fisheries Society in September, 1963. Following unanimous endorsement by both organizations, numerous expressions of good will, congratulation and endorsement have been received by Minnesota officials from throughout the country.

In proposing establishment of the Hall of Fame, Governor Rolvagg said that conservation—"the wise use of our God-given heritage for the benefit of all the people for all time" represents one of the major facets of the endeavor to activate the noble principles enumerated in the great goals of Democracy.

Commissioner Olson has announced that nominations to the Hall of Fame are already legion, and it is expected that the first selections will be posthumous. Names proposed include Gifford Pinchot, Henry David Thoreau, Theodore Roosevelt, Aldo Leopold, Ding Darling, Hugh H. Bennett, John Muir, Luther Burbank, as well as many others.

SLEEPING BEAR NATIONAL LAKESHORE —A PROPOSAL

(Continued from page 34)

acres could be affected by this zone in which lands could not be condemned if approved zoning regulations are adhered to; where new homes could be constructed; and where no public use facilities could be developed for 25 years regardless of how lands came into public ownership.

In January of 1963, Congressman Robert Griffin, in whose district the Sleeping Bear proposal lies, introduced H. R. 2400 calling for 37,000 acres, including 19,330 acres in South and North Manitou Islands, with 19 miles of mainland Lake Michigan shoreline and 35 miles attributed to the two islands. Also in 1963, Mr. Neil Staebler, Michigan Congressman-at-large, introduced H. R. 4201, a companion bill to S. 792. To date, no hearings have been held in the House of Representatives.

The Senate passed S. 792 with revisions, on December 21, 1963. Senate Act S. 792, authorizing a Sleeping Bear Dunes National Lakeshore, reduces the total land and water area to 47,600 acres, but retains to an astonishing degree the purpose and features of the 77,000-acre proposal, including approximately the same Lake Michigan shore.

The reduction in acreage includes the large inland lakes and their attendant residential areas, as well as some of the high morainal ridges surrounding them. It is on these high promontories that some of the finest scenic overlooks are possible. The Act authorizes the construction of parkways to take advantage of, and provide for, such scenic overlooks along the east side of Glen Lake and also south of Platte Lake to capture the scenic values there. A definite improvement is the authority to construct a connecting parkway between the southern (Benzie County) portion and the northern (Leelanau County) portion, thus making possible a continuing parklike road throughout.

The general policy, first developed in the Cape Cod Seashore Act, is followed in exempting from condemnation private residential property where local zoning ordinances are in effect and construction was begun prior to December 31, 1962. Senate Act 792 goes one step further in protecting the individual in the event local zoning is not enacted, or at some future time repealed. An individual may continue to enjoy exemption from condemnation by filing a simple declaration of intent to use his property in accordance with the minimum zoning standards contained in the bill.

Many individuals and organizations have given generously of their time and energies in the hope that Congress will preserve the unused combination of superb scenic, scientific and recreational values of the Sleeping Bear Dunes area by making it a national lakeshore.

⸱⸱⸱

PLANNING FOR CAMPER TOURIST AREAS

(*Continued from page 44*)

setbacks from all property lines should be at least equal to that required by the closest residential zone or district as established by the community.

6) Size, type and location of advertising or identification signs should be specified.

If these types of standards are established beforehand, then the developer has the flexibility to design his specific camping area to maintain the tree cover and to fit the physical limitations of the site as he desires, and the community has the protection of the local zoning regulations.

If camping tourist areas are allowed as "special permit" or "special exception" uses, additional conditions or controls can be added applicable to a specific site, to further protect the community and the integrity of the regulations, and this type of procedure usually requires a public hearing where the applicant can make a presentation and opponents can be heard. The burden of proof is on the applicant that the proposed use will not cause any problems to the community, and the reviewing authority is required to make a positive finding of fact on a set of specific regulations regarding traffic, effect on neighborhood, etc. The reviewing authority might require a screening or fencing along boundary lines to protect adjacent properties, or because of a dangerous traffic situation, designate points of access to the campground from adjoining streets.

Naturally the camping area must be placed in a location in the community where it will harmonize with neighboring land uses. As the primary concern of the camper tourist is convenience, locations of campgrounds close to major highways are important. Essentially, the operation of a campground is a commercial operation similar to a motel. Highway service districts would be an appropriate zone for a campground. In rural parts of the country certain agricultural or forest zones might be used. In areas known for tourist attractions, *i. e.*, near National Parks, recreational or open space zones would be appropriate. A location within or near a large city's commercial or industrial zone could be utilized. Some communities use the technique of "temporary" or "holding" type zones until a proper designation can be decided upon. Since few permanent improvements would be necessary to establish a camper tourist area, this type of use could be properly allowed in such an area until a decision is reached.

In addition to private campgrounds permitted within communities, municipalities can also provide camper tourist facilities using the same principles and standards of design stated previously. Whereas private campgrounds provide a return on an investment in land to the owner, the community realizes increased property assessments and tax revenues without adding

(*Continued on page 55*)

(*Continued from page 42*)

fellowship program has, since its inception, made grants to fifty-five men and women.

Students Plan Restoration. Plans to restore and maintain the historic Old Town area of Benicia, California, were recently assigned to 13 *Stanford University* architecture students as a class project. *Prof. Thomas T. Williamson's* class in Architecture 101, elementary design, accepted an invitation from the Benicia City Council earlier this year to study the city's growth problems and make recommendations and plans for its future.

The class was divided into three groups to study the city's general plan, the Old Town proper, and the development of the scenic waterfront. It got under way immediately with a contour map of the areas involved, large map-type drawings, and models which indicate suggested remodeling of older buildings and the installation of new.

Professor Williamson reports that all of Benicia's 6,500 inhabitants are agog over the program, with opinion more or less evenly divided between "status quo" and progressive elements.

Field Study. An unusual opportunity to take a combined course of biology and earth science is being offered to students and teachers of biology, earth science, conservation or general science this summer.

Sponsored by *Colorado State University* the eight-week course will be held at the University's high-altitude, field research and training center at Pingree Park, northwest of Fort Collins. Biology and geology will be taught in the field, with the courses ecologically oriented and taught as a single unit. One week will be spent in each of the ecological life zones, interpreting the interrelations of plants and animals with each other and with their physical environment.

In-camp seminars and special lectures by outstanding authorities in the fields of biology, ecology and geology are additional features.

The course is open to those who are at least juniors in college, majoring in biological science, conservation, earth science, general science, or a closely related field.

Park Administration. *The University of Massachusetts* has announced a newly accredited undergraduate curriculum in Park Administration, bringing to five the number of colleges in the United States offering such courses for a major.

The program is offered by the Landscape Architecture Department and is designed to give the student a broad education in land use, emphasizing physical organization, development and administration of parks.

According to Earle D. Whitney, an instructor for the newly announced program, the curriculum has been arranged in recognition of the demand for better management of public and private park areas.

THE COMMUNITY NATURE CENTER—A NEW CONCEPT IN URBAN PLANNING AND GROWTH

(Continued from page 6)

commissions or groups should seriously investigate the possibilities for a nature center on unused park land or open space. Architects and professional planners should know something about nature centers, what they are and what they do, and incorporate one or more good center plans into any master plan for a city or region.

Nature Centers Spreading

Today there are some 200 nature centers under way in America. Some are being developed by government agencies, some by private organizations, and some by the joint efforts of public agencies and private groups. Some 40 of these centers are now fully operational. Others are in various stages of planning or development.

New nature centers are now being planned at Kalamazoo, Michigan; Mahwah, New Jersey; Harrisburg, Pennsylvania; Denver, Colorado; Philadelphia, Pennsylvania; Mamaroneck, New York; Wilmington, Delaware; Richmond, Virginia; and Salisbury, North Carolina, to mention a few. The new community of Reston, in Fairfax County, Virginia, is developing a modern nature center. Los Angeles County now has four nature centers; eight more are planned. Chicago has several nature centers. A unique and remarkable nature center plan has been prepared for Prince Gallitzin State Park near Altoona, Pennsylvania, a depressed area.

The Nature Centers Division, National Audubon Society, which functions as a nationwide, private planning and counseling service, is spearheading the nature centers movement in America. In less than three years it has cooperated with some 200 separate community groups or agencies in America. These organizations have in turn saved or set aside over 40,000 acres of land for education, all in areas of increasing urbanization. The division's goal is 2,000 nature centers in America by the year 2000.

The most far-reaching influence that the community nature centers will have will be in the area of balancing growth and development with the preservation of some aspects of our "whole" environment. Unless America also plans for the preservation of its *country beautiful* and *land for loveliness* and naturalistic identity, we stand to lose much. We may even end up a tattered, torn, disheveled world with nature only a haunting memory.

This cannot happen to our beloved land. It will not happen if we plan *now.*

MORE PEOPLE—MORE HOUSING

A significant milestone in the development of the City of Los Angeles was passed recently as the number of residential dwelling units forged across the one million mark.

AMERICAN PLANNING AND CIVIC ASSOCIATION
1904—1964

(Continued from page 4) .

numerous cities, it was found that slums and blight continued to grow. In 1949, the Public Housing Act was amended to provide for a new broadened program known as Urban Renewal, the object of which was to prevent the spread of blight and slums by providing substantial federal funds to assist cities not only in rebuilding slum areas with various types of redevelopment, not just public housing, but also to initiate a vigorous new program of rehabilitation of blighted areas and thus to attack the basic problem at its source. This program has been slow in implementation because of its complexity and the requirement for strong local regulations and enforcement which have not always been forthcoming. Substantial progress in redevelopment has been made in several cities, however, notably in Norfolk, Philadelphia and Washington.

About 1937, through the generosity of the Laura Spellman Rockefeller Fund, a central clearing house for public administration in the field of municipal government was formed at Chicago University, *i. e.* the Public Administration Institute. A special building was constructed to house this agency which has done much to improve the science of municipal government. National organizations in all fields of municipal government were centered in this building, including two new organizations, the American Society of Planning Officials and the National Association of Housing Officials. Over the years these two agencies have rendered most valuable services in improving municipal administrative practices in fields particularly related to and integral with city planning.

Because of the protracted economic depression of the 1930's many families were unable to meet mortgage payments and thus lost their homes. To prevent recurrence of this situation, a government program under the auspices of a Home Owners Loan Administration was created. Another agency, the Federal Housing Administration, established in 1934, provided federal insurance for long term mortgages at reasonable rates of interest. This was a powerful stimulant to home building, particularly during the post-war period. It has been responsible for vast construction that has since taken place in suburban fringe areas.

While cities had ceased to grow during depression years, the subsequent advent of war, and the sudden upsurge in the birth rate, brought about a phenomenal change in population trends. So great has been the increase in population in postwar years that all forecasts have been exceeded. The "population explosion" has produced unprecedented urban expansion. Of special significance is the fact that most of the new population has been attracted to the larger cities because of greater employment opportunities

51

and a wider range of cultural activities.

The cities were so slow to appreciate the magnitude of growth, both numerically and area-wise, and they were so restricted legally in their ability to expand their corporate boundaries, that there are now virtually no remaining self-contained cities. The modern urban community has become a vast urban complex consisting of central city, numerous incorporated suburban governments, and a vast sprawling unincorporated area under the jurisdiction of rural oriented county governments. The early unified cities now have become sprawling metropolitan areas. The U. S. Bureau of the Census has now delineated some 220 such standard metropolitan areas.

Another event of significance in the field of community development was the report of the Interregional Highway Committee appointed by President Franklin D. Roosevelt to study traffic and highway problems in cities and throughout the nation. Up to that time all Federal aid highway funds, with matching state gasoline tax funds, had been spent for highway construction in the rural, non-urban areas.

The Committee emphasized the magnitude of the growing traffic congestion problem in cities and recommended the creation of a 40,000-mile special system of highways to connect all large cities. The National Highway Act was amended accordingly in 1944, with provision for 25% of total funds to be expended for extensions into and through city areas. Subsequently, the Congress authorized large appropriations for completion by 1970 of the city extensions, federal aid funds being provided on a 90-10 matching basis. This program is now in progress. Its impact on urban development will be enormous, the full effects of which can scarcely be appraised as yet.

This brief review of some of the more important milestones in the process of planning of American cities omits mention of all too many significant actions and events by federal, state, local and citizen agencies, i. e. the Regional Plan of New York sponsored by the Russell Sage Foundation and the effective Regional Plan Association which grew out of this effort and is now celebrating its 35th anniversary. It has been set forth merely as a prelude to a brief consideration of present trends of urban growth, probable future trends, a consideration of the direction our planning should take, and this, of course, in light of our Association as a citizens' organization and clearing house whereby we may be of assistance in helping form policy and stimulate action for more effective planning and for improved livability within our new metropolitan communities.

As we look back and compare the American City of 1900 with today's new metropolitan community, it is apparent that city planning has been of immeasurable aid to cities during this past half century. In many respects our communities are indeed much more satisfactory than in 1900. Vast public monies have been spent to build innumerable public improvements. We have more complete and improved utility systems, more orderly development through zoning (despite too many ill-advised "re-zonings"), new and greatly improved street and highway systems, several fine metropolitan park systems, better housing facilities for medium and low income families, numerous civic centers, more and better schools and playgrounds.

Why, then, is there concern today about the need for a new program of Urban Design? What is meant by this new term of Urban Design? Is it really intended to mean removal of the most blatant abuses—the clutter of billboards, the rash of hot dog stands and honky-tonks along heavily travelled highways? If so, it is basically a revival of the early "city beautiful" movement.

On the other hand, if Urban Design signifies a deeper concern for a completely orderly, wholesome and attractive city, it necessarily must embrace the full planned control of the entire city building process—a rational distribution and density of population, a genuinely sound land use pattern, orderly arrangement of public buildings, an effective and stable zoning plan as well as an adequate system of open spaces, a full complement of utility services, rapid transit in the large metropolitan areas to relieve excessive traffic congestion, grade level separation of pedestrians and vehicles at centers of large commercial concentration, as well as progressive elimination of ugliness through large and small scale architectural design.

The drab and depressing appearance of so much of the cityscape today is the inevitable result not only of inadequate and incomplete planning control but lack of good urban design. Since the 1930's specialized planning has for the most part replaced comprehensive planning. In the great housing projects, in express highway design and construction, in the huge shopping centers, our technology is second to none. But in the provision of adequate open spaces and in the control of sheer ugliness and in giving our urban design talent a chance to assert itself, we are astonishingly weak. No truly satisfactory and attractive city will ever be built unless and until there is first, a full command of overall planning, and secondly, a full coordination of specialized planning of all component parts of the entire city building process. Our difficulty is that we lack effective overall comprehensive planning for the new metropolitan city area. Without this, chaos and confusion are inevitable.

Specialization, technically and design-wise, is an inevitable characteristic of our modern age. It is an essential attribute of modern urban growth. However, where specialized design of individual components of the city building process is undertaken with inadequate regard for the over-all pattern of population distribution and density, for a rational pattern of land use, and for each and all of the other components, and of the economic and social consequences involved, confusion is compounded.

Basically, each component must be conceived and designed as an integral part of the over-all comprehensive plan, *i. e.* the total urban complex. Specialization should not develop independently but should have its *origin* within the framework of the over-all plan and design of the urban structure. The significance of such over-all plan and design is today sorely in need of re-assertion and re-invigoration.

At this point must be mentioned the very obvious fact that we have been lacking particularly in effective specialization in control of civic appearance. This is just as much a part of good living conditions, of good Urban Design, as the seemingly more urgent segments of the total comprehensive plan. Much of the ugliness is but a cheap, parasitical commercialization which, like a fungus or a barnacle, generates from carelessness or neglect.

Preparation of the highly necessary new comprehensive Metropolitan Area Plan must be a concert of specializations and of specialists. In today's dynamic and changing era many skills will be required. All of the specialized skills should be fully used and coordinated. While the task is complicated, it is nevertheless imperative if only a minimum desirable result is to be achieved. Only by such coordination can there be a *unified* comprehensive structural Urban Design that is economically sound, socially desirable and aesthetically attractive. To enumerate all of the specializations, or skills, is not the purpose of this article. Some, such as the highway engineer, the housing architect and the architectural designer, have been mentioned. The city planner, whose specialty is the pattern of land use and population distribution, will be a most important member of the team, if not the leader. The economist and the social scientist must also be participants. Certain other specialists having less current popular status, such as the landscape architect and the

large scale new town planner, must likewise be part of the multi-skill design team.

Public dissatisfaction with today's city is widespread. It is due to the fact that in the past 60 years so little has been done about those processes of city building that make for attractiveness and desirability. What about the American city 50 or 60 years from now? Will it be desirable and attractive? That depends almost entirely upon the decisions we make today, particularly in the field of Urban Design. Desirability and attractiveness cannot be achieved by reliance upon controls and regulations which are too rigid in nature.

Certainly times have changed enormously since 1900. Even within the past 30 years the rapidity and degree of change in the American city has been greater than during the entire previous life history of these cities. There will be vast change in the years ahead. It has been estimated that the new urban development in the next forty years will equal the sum total of all urban development in the recorded history of man.

One of our greatest deficiencies has been that our plans have not been sufficiently dynamic. We have not anticipated the full impact of total population growth. The second great deficiency is that our plans have not envisioned present or probably future technological changes and needs. As one result we have urban sprawl, or scatteration, with little or no firm control over the growth that now characterizes the expansion of most metropolitan cities.

What should be the structural form of the modern metropolitan community 25 or 50 years from now? We should now face up to this question. We should have comprehensive metropolitan plans as bold and as dynamic as the city's new change in character, in form, and in scale, for example the Year 2000 Plan for the Washington, D. C. area and the proposal of the Regional Plan Association of New York for a second New York Regional Plan. Failing this, planning will have but minor significance.

True, we lack a metropolitan agency of government by which to adopt and implement a comprehensive plan for today's metropolitan city. However, if we wait until any such new agency of government has been created, it is certain that no comprehensive metropolitan area plans will ever be prepared in time to be effective. The time to prepare such bold, dynamic plans is now—today, before additional growth takes place. Such plans, once drawn, will furnish citizens and citizens' or-ganizations the inspiration to devise and to bring about the creation of the necessary agencies of government by which such comprehensive plans may be realized. This is not a question of what comes first. First there must be the plan.

In a democracy such as ours, the citizen leadership must see to it that a proper plan is drawn and also that political action is taken whereby the plan can be transformed into reality. We know now, after sixty years of experience, that a fully desirable city can be built only as a result of three forces, *i. e.* citizen leadership and action, enlightened political administrative endeavor for plan implementation, and skilled technical over-all planning, utilizing the specialized planning talent for each of the components of the urban structure. Failing this, the new metropolitan city now in process of formation can only become more of a hodge-podge, more wasteful, far less satisfactory, and infinitely less attractive than anything we have yet seen.

PLANNING FOR CAMPER TOURIST AREAS

(Continued from page 48)

additional residents to the community. A municipality might provide a campground as a public service for tourists attending special events such as a fair, festival or rodeo. By so doing, the municipality may help to increase the attendance at such an event and at the same time hope to generate additional business for the local merchants and property owners.

Private developers wishing to establish campgrounds may obtain assistance from civil engineers for design and lay-out. Tent campers and travel trailers may be admitted to the same campground and occupants of travel trailers may use the central washroom facilities. However, some campgrounds may wish to install water, electric and sewer connections for travel trailers, charging higher fees for these. For some areas the county agricultural agent and technicians of the Soil Conservation Service will render assistance.

(*Continued from page 14*)

will result in a capital budget. How fast should we go? A formula should be devised in the community to determine the pace. This formula is extremely important to the plan. For otherwise, the community will operate in spurts, doing nothing for years and then have to do everything at once which operates a hardship on the then taxpayers. Other tools include the zoning ordinance, official street map, minimum standard housing code, urban renewal, extra-territorial zoning, uniform traffic ordinance, building, electrical, plumbing and fire prevention codes, and other ordinances pertaining to the appearance of the city. I mention these at this point because oftentimes these tools become ends in themselves with little thought to the comprehensive plan. . . .

One might wonder at this point if all this is done how a plan could be "shelved." It can happen and does oftentimes. To prevent this from happening, I recommend the following measures:

1. That one person be designed as planner, full time or part time. If part time, that a consultant firm be retained on an advisory basis.
2. That the plates showing the plan be visible in the council chamber at all times to keep the councilmen aware of the comprehensive plan.
3. That each year, perhaps in January or February, the council hold a capital budget meeting to review the plan and set forth projects for the coming year revising the five year capital budget. Administrative personnel, planning commission members and the council should be parties to this conference.
4. That each request for a change in zoning be viewed carefully in light of the comprehensive plan. . . .
5. That the concept be introduced that the plan is subject to change each year, that it is dynamic and responsive.
6. That citizens' groups be used extensively in participating in revisions and effecting the plan.
7. That publicity be sought continuously on the comprehensive plan.

In conclusion, I believe that every community regardless of size should have a comprehensive plan for development. In order for a plan to remain alive, it must have the participation of as many people in the community as possible and have their general acceptance. This involves a sales program of no mean proportion but is absolutely necessary if we are to give our best to our constituents.

A recently issued report of the Bureau of the Census, dealing with the mobility of the population of the United States, April 1961 to April 1962, indicated that 35.2 million persons, or 19.6 per cent of the population, moved at least once in the 12-month period. This was somewhat less than for prior years since 1953.

Recent Publications

CLUSTER DEVELOPMENT by William H. Whyte with a Foreword by Laurance S. Rockefeller. American Conservation Association, 30 Rockefeller Plaza, New York 10020. April, 1964. 130 pp. $3.00.

Now and then a revealing study on a major trend in environmental development appears in time to help blaze the trail and so forestall some rough journey on the course ahead.

Such a one would seem to be this report on Cluster Development which Laurance Rockefeller characterizes in the publication's foreword as "a major new trend in housing."

"Rather than a definitive study after the fact," says Mr. Rockefeller, "the aim was a firsthand report in time to help people shape the movement."

"Cluster is on the verge of becoming the dominant pattern of new residential development, and probably for many years to come," is the provocative first statement of the Report's introduction.

Cluster goes under many different names—density zoning, planned unit development, environmental planning. But what the cluster idea calls for, essentially, is grouping the houses more tightly together and using the land thus saved for common greens and squares.

Sometimes the open spaces are ceded outright to the community; sometimes they come under the province of a homeowners' association. But, in any case, it is the homeowners who pay for the common land. And it is this key fact which, no doubt, has helped to make cluster development, if one of today's most promising trends, also one of the most controversial.

And it is precisely for this reason that this publication, at this time, is of significance. It is an effort to bring together what has been learned so far; to see which approaches are working out well, and which are not—now, while the cluster movement is still highly malleable.

The great promise of cluster, according to the publication, is in the exciting opportunities there are for linking the various open spaces within a community together so that, in some cases, continuous acres of green may emerge. Philadelphia, for example, has demonstrated that this can be done.

But the lasting value of Mr. Whyte's work may not prove to be in outlining the unparalleled advantages of cluster development, interesting as these are. The enthusiasm with which building developers are hopping on to the cluster idea will likely assure that this part of the message gets across.

Of perhaps more especial interest is the frank appraisal of the conceivable problems harbored in the cluster approach.

"Cluster could be frozen into a format as stereotyped as the conventional layout it is replacing," he says. "Imitation has a way of missing the quality of the prototype, and as the copies go up the uniformity could be appalling."

Again, "Cluster should not be used
(Continued on page 58)

57

American Planning and Civic Association
New Members, March 1, 1964 to
May 1, 1964

California
Mr. Carl Mooers, Canoga Park
Illinois
Mr. Franklyn H. Moreno, Murphysboro
Maryland
Mrs. Warren J. Vinton, Chevy Chase
Michigan
Dr. Paul A. Herbert, East Lansing

New York
Dr. Joseph J. Shomon, New York City
North Carolina
Mr. I. John Tinga, Wilmington
District of Columbia
Mrs. Thelma N. Dawson, Washington

RECENT PUBLICATIONS
(*Continued from page 57*)

as a device to achieve unreasonable densities. Standardization would be bad enough; worse yet would be both standardization and compression. What appeals most to many developers, let us remember, is the cluster, not the open space: the doughnut and not the hole."

In pointing out that people like to live in cluster developments, Mr. Whyte makes the interesting observation that "people have to know how to use open space to appreciate it."

"Where the people have come from the central city," he continues, "the kind of open spaces—such as streams, valleys and woods, for example—so familiar to country people, can seem a downright menace, and mothers forbid their children to go near them. It will be interesting to see how the new generations respond."

In any case, Mr. Whyte has capably set forth here, with examples and illustrations, a balanced view of the assets as well as the hazards incorporated in the cluster development idea. As such, he has performed a real service and his work merits consideration by all those interested in the general trends and problems of community development today.

STRICTLY PERSONAL
(*Continued from page 40*)

Charles D. Harris has been named deputy director of the Michigan State Conservation Department in charge of staff operations to fill the post left vacant when Dr. Ralph A. MacMullan recently became head of the Department.

Mr. Harris had been regional manager, stationed in Lansing, Michigan, since February and prior to that had served as chief of field operations for the Parks and Recreation section.

Watch Service Report

H. R. 3846, Establishing A Land and Water Conservation Fund. Congressman Wayne N. Aspinall (Colorado) and others.

The Land and Water Conservation Fund Bill cleared another important hurdle May 27, 1964, when the House Committee on Rules granted a rule for four hours of debate on the House floor and final consideration by the House.

As we go to press, no date has been scheduled by the House leadership for consideration of the bill but, according to the office of House Majority Leader Carl Albert (D-Okla.), it probably will be scheduled for debate and vote some time in June.

In taking its action, the Rules Committee granted an open-and-closed rule. All portions of the bill are open to amendment except Title II, relating to the motorboat fuel tax provisions. Two hours of debate will be allowed each side on the controversial bill.

Many members of the House report they already are receiving quantities of mail on the bill and this volume is expected to build up as the voting time nears.

Meanwhile, in anticipation of favorable House action, the Senate Committee on Interior and Insular Affairs scheduled an open hearing on the bill for June 2, 1964 to be restricted to testimony from the Secretaries of Interior, Agriculture and the Army. The Committee held hearings on S. 859, an earlier version of the proposal, last year.

As reported in previous issues of PLANNING AND CIVIC COMMENT, a special fund with revenues estimated at $150 million to $200 million a year would be set up by H. R. 3846. The fund would be financed by nominal user fees paid by visitors to national parks and other Federal recreation areas, by the Federal tax now paid on motorboat fuel, and by receipts from the sale of surplus Federal land.

About 60 per cent of the Fund would go to state and local governments as 50–50 matching grants to help them plan, acquire, and develop outdoor recreation areas. The Fund also would be used to buy recreation lands for the national park system, national forests, and wildlife refuges, as authorized by Congress and for recreation developments at Federal reservoirs.

H. R. 9162 and Other Versions of the Wilderness Bill. Congressman John D. Dingell (Michigan) and others.

On June 1–2, 1964, the Public Lands Subcommittee of the House Committee on Interior and Insular Affairs began executive session mark up consideration on H. R. 9162 and other bills proposing the establishment of a National Wilderness Preservation System. On May 1, 1964, the Subcommittee concluded hearings on the bill held in Washington, D. C., encompassing portions of five days of testimony. Field hearings on the bills were held earlier in the year at three points in the West.

In the course of the hearings, it appeared that much of the opposition to the bills had been allayed. Some user groups which had opposed previous proposals now endorse H. R. 9162, with suggested amendments.

At the Washington, D. C. hearings, several members of the Congress joined the Department of Agriculture, conservation groups and others in supporting the wilderness proposals. A representative of the Federal Power Commission asked for an adequate "savings clause" to safeguard the public interest in the development of water resources on U. S. lands through licenses issued by that agency.

The late Dr. Howard Zahniser, representing the Wilderness Society, presented a detailed report on the various proposals, complete with maps. Under questioning, he pointed out that "wilderness preservation is an application of the multiple use concept." He pointed to the watershed protection and water production values of wildernesses which can be added to public educational and recreational benefits.

Planning and Civic Comment

H. R. 2441, H. R. 2632, and H. R. 8696, Bills Establishing the Tocks Island National Recreation Area along the Delaware River in Pennsylvania and New Jersey.
The National Parks Subcommittee, House Committee on Interior and Insular Affairs, scheduled public hearings on these bills June 8–9, 1964 in Washington, D. C.

According to the proposals, the Recreation Area to be administered by the National Park Service would be located along 32 miles of the River. Hunting and fishing would be permitted under laws of the States involved. Over 20,000,000 persons, including residents of New York City and Philadelphia, live within 75 miles of the proposed Recreation Area.

H. R. 11117, Providing for Establishment of Assateague Island National Seashore off the coast of Maryland. Congressman D. B. Morton (Maryland). Introduced May 4, 1964 and referred to the House Committee on Interior and Insular Affairs. Other bills to establish the Seashore on Assateague Island, a narrow island extending for 32 miles and located off-shore from the Maryland-Virginia mainland, have also been introduced.

A later version of a proposal introduced earlier by Mr. Morton, H. R. 11117 provides for 600 acres of land adjacent to a State Park to be developed by concessionnaires for public accommodations.

Senator Alan Bible (Nevada), chairman of the Public Lands Subcommittee of the Senate Committee on Interior and Insular Affairs, has stated that he has been swamped with requests of interested parties to present their views to the Committee on both Assateague Island and Tocks Island.

S. 502, Preserving The Jurisdiction of Congress Over Colorado River Projects. Reported favorably, with an amendment, May 14, 1964, by the Senate Committee on Interior and Insular Affairs.

The bill would preserve the jurisdiction of the Congress over construction of hydroelectric projects on the Colorado River below Glen Canyon dam. It would prevent the Federal Power Commission from issuing licenses or permits for the construction of power facilities on the Colorado River between Lake Mead and Glen Canyon until December 31, 1965.

S. 2792, A Bill To Close Loopholes in Existing Pesticide Control Laws. Senator Abraham A. Ribicoff (Connecticut). Referred to the Committee on Agriculture and Forestry.

Introduced April 30, 1964, following findings that massive fish kills in the Mississippi River may have been caused by pesticides.

On May 12, 1964, the Senate Committee on Commerce ordered a favorable report on S. 1251 to prevent or minimize injury to fish and wildlife from the use of insecticides and pesticides.

S. 2862, Facilitating Management of Appalachian Trail. Senators Gaylord Nelson (Wisconsin) and Harrison A. Williams, Jr. (New Jersey). Referred May 20, 1964 to the Senate Committee on Interior and Insular Affairs.

The bill provides for establishment of the Appalachian Trailway with the Secretary of the Interior issuing necessary regulations for its management, administration and protection. Its purpose: To facilitate the management, use and public benefits from the Appalachian Trail, a scenic trail designed primarily for foot travel through natural primitive areas, extending from Maine to Georgia.

NATIONAL CONFERENCE ON STATE PARKS

44th Annual Meeting

PLACE: MORRISTOWN, NEW JERSEY

HEADQUARTERS: GOVERNOR MORRIS HOTEL

DATE: SEPTEMBER 20–25, 1964

Make Conference Reservations Promptly

Planning and Civic Comment

Official Organ of American•Planning and Civic Association and
National Conference on State Parks

CONTENTS

SEPTEMBER 1964

PLANNING AND CIVIC COMMENT

Published Quarterly

SUCCESSOR to: City Planning, Civic Comment, State Recreation

Official Organ of: American Planning and Civic Association,
National Conference on State Parks

SCOPE: *National, State, Regional and City Planning, Land and Water Uses,
Conservation of National Resources, National, State and Local Parks,
Highways and Roadsides.*
AIM: *To create a better physical environment which will conserve and develop
the health, happiness and culture of the American people.*

Second-class postage paid at Harrisburg, Pa., and at additional mailing office.
EDITORIAL AND PUBLICATION OFFICE, 901 Union Trust Building, Washington,
D. C. 20005

Printed by the Mount Pleasant Press, the McFarland Company, Harrisburg, Pa.

Planning and Civic Comment

| Vol. 30 | September, 1964 | No. 3 |

The Maricopa Story—A Study in Scientific Park Planning

By ROGER P. HANSEN, member of the Colorado Bar and Associate with Sam L. Huddleston & Associates, Denver planners and landscape architects

Foresight, imagination and unique scientific planning are combining to make the Maricopa County (Phoenix), Arizona Regional Park System one of the finest approaches to superior metropolitan recreation in the nation.

Nearly 100,000 acres of natural, open space are being both preserved and developed to give crowded city dwellers a chance to "get away from it all"—in a few minutes. Future generations of Maricopans will be able to walk a lonely trail, sit around a wilderness campfire or study desert flora and fauna within a half hour of home. But it wasn't always so.

As late as 1952, the Maricopa County park system—supposedly devised to serve 370,000 people—was almost a joke and a mockery of recreation planning. It consisted of eight underdeveloped "neighborhood" parks with facilities generally no more extensive than a bare spot in the desert for weiner roasts. Outdoor lovers picnicked, hiked and rode horseback where subdivisions, highways and shopping centers now checkerboard the desert. Of course, the City of Phoenix, with a parks and recreation system of long standing, did much to fill the gap.

The "catch as catch can" method was an almost acceptable substitute for planned recreation until the Goliath in Maricopa began to grow— 100% to 664,000 people in 1960. It became obvious even earlier that the area's insatiable appetite for more and more land would soon present Maricopa with the plight of other metro-regions whose citizens escape from their jungles of concrete and steel only during once-a-year vacation periods—if they're lucky.

Spurred on by a reform County government in 1953, the Maricopa County Parks and Recreation Commission (an eleven-man citizens' advisory group appointed by the County Supervisors), the City of Phoenix, a community citizens' council, and the National Recreation Association had, by 1957, joined forces to produce a comprehensive survey of park and recreation needs.

This early work became the touchstone for future professional master planning. It dramatized one tremendous and compelling need: the need to acquire more park land in huge quantities—and fast. Within 30 days after the survey was completed (a remarkable feat in public administration), the Maricopa County Board of Supervisors filed applications with the Bureau of Land Management to lease nearly 68,000 acres. It was Secretary of the Interior Stewart Udall who finally made it possible for the county to lease 73,000 acres in 1961 at 25 cents an acre per year. Subsequent acquisitions and applications comprise the county's system of 10 parks—four regional, four semi-regional and two special use areas. In all, they total nearly 93,000 acres.

The system master plan, created by the Maricopa Parks and Recreation Department, Kenneth J. Smithee, Director, and Sam L. Huddleston & Associates of Denver, Colorado, consultants, considered uses for the entire system—regional and semi-regional alike. However, the Master Plan concentrated on these four regional parks: 14,382-acre Lake Pleasant, the only water oriented regional park, 35 miles northwest of Phoenix; 16,779-acre Estrella Mountain, 6 miles southwest; 20,368-acre McDowell Mountain, 15 miles northwest of Scottsdale; and 28,554-acre White Tank Mountain, 15 miles west.

The very establishment of these four great parks spotlights a new concept in recreation—the regional park. To be sure, there are almost as many opinions as to what constitutes a "regional park" as there are definitions of "open space." Nevertheless, cities contemplating large, natural recreational preserves should examine some of Maricopa's guidelines.

In the Maricopa concept, a regional park is a large, natural, unspoiled preserve removed from the urban area. Ideally, it is protected from urban encroachment by a "buffer zone" of undeveloped land.

Outdoor activities are generally "passive" in character, *e.g.*, hiking, walking, horseback riding, picnicking, camping and nature study. Open spaces are kept open, vegetation is protected in its natural state, "development" is minimized and what there is made to conform to natural surroundings. Use areas such as picnic tables, campsites, etc, are designed at a low density—far enough apart to avoid congestion even on peak weekends.

Within this framework — laid down by the county supervisors in February, 1963—urban or neighborhood parks are to regional parks what a drive-in hamburger joint is to a quality supper club. The whole idea of a regional park is to give people in an urbanized, mechanized, over-organized culture a chance to retreat, to escape, to seek some quiet, peace and solitude. And this includes an escape from highly developed recreational facilities with busy ball diamonds, teeter totters, swimming pools and tennis courts.

Once an over-all policy was established, the next problem was that of translating such a policy into a master plan for the system. A time-honored method of park planning is to acquire a given acreage and then determine how many facilities will fit into it. This often occurs regardless of whether the public to be served needs, wants or will use such facilities in the first place.

Besides, there are two (and more) fundamentally opposing modern viewpoints in park planning. One might be called the "economic" approach. This method follows from a purely *quantitative* analysis of recreation needs: how *many* people will

2

Planning and Civic Comment

use how *many* facilities of what kind? It also champions the old acres-to-people ratios, *e.g.*, if population projections show that *x* people will be living in an area in 1980, then *x* acres of recreation will be needed. The logical next step, then, is to get the land and fill it with picnic tables, campsites, boat launchers, volley ball nets and garbage cans. The public has been served, or has it?

The obvious difficulty with this tendency to become obsessed by a god of numbers—how *many* boating, how *many* hiking, how *many* spending money—is that *quality recreation* is literally and figuratively trampled to death in the rush. This is gross error because the sociological value of the recreational experience is really determined by multiplying the *number* who participate times the *quality* of their participation. Nobody should argue that a picnic on a wooded, grassy knoll overlooking a beautiful lake is a vastly different recreational experience from a Fourth of July reunion amid dozens of squalling children, obnoxious beer guzzlers and fly-infested watermelon rinds.

Quality recreation does not necessarily decrease in direct proportion to increases in quantity. But there is a point at which quality loss proceeds from quantity gain. The approach should be something like this: if 12 picnic tables are added here, if 15 more campsites are established there, if a boat launching facility is constructed at this location, will the resulting increase in public service decrease the *qualitative* value of what the public wanted in the first place?

In order to understand how this philosophy of quality recreation is applied in the Maricopa County Regional Park System, it is necessary to review some of the unique planning procedure. One of the most unusual aspects of the Maricopa Story was the exhaustive scientific research program that preceded or accompanied the actual planning. Maricopa officials were determined that all physical, historical and biological characteristics of the parks would be fully examined before *any* construction of facilities took place. They wanted to preserve the beauty of the desert and the treasures of the past—artifacts left by Indian, explorer and pioneer. For the most part, the Regional Park System was a vast wilderness, previously uncharted with any degree of scientific accuracy. Its history and natural attributes were part fancy, part fact. Ordinary incidents of the past had become preposterous legends, until the line between reality and pure romanticism had grown indefinable.

To overcome this deficiency, "supplemental studies" were conducted by qualified experts and institutions, such as the University of Arizona and Arizona State University. These studies explored in great detail these aspects of each park: climate, hydrology, history, archeology, geology, botany and zoology. The result is that each individual park master plan can be created more intelligently with precise information on water resources, flora and fauna, geological formations, Indian petroglyphs, etc. It will not be likely that a bulldozer will scrape away an ancient Indian village or that part of the Butterfield stage route will

3

be widened into a highway. Every bird and bug, rodent and serpent, cactus and sagebrush, archeological sherd and village ruin has now been "tagged" for protection. Generally, this type of study is not conducted until years after a park is constructed—if ever.

But these studies only laid a foundation for the actual planning. The Maricopa County Regional Park System Master Plan, created by the Huddleston firm, is probably the first park plan in the nation to make extensive use of research findings of the Outdoor Recreation Resources Review Commission. In fact, ORRRC's figures on effects of certain socio-economic characteristics of population on participation in certain activities were used as part of the "input" of a computer mathematical model. Therefore, the Maricopa "projections" concern many factors other than mere numbers of people; they are also concerned with climate, water supply, transportation and the age, education, occupation and income of various segments of the population.

The only way this complex approach can be understood at all is by examining a simplified summary of planning procedures. They are as follows:

1) Population distribution maps were made for 1960 and 1980 to determine growth patterns of the Phoenix Urban Area and the county as well as population projections based on figures of several research agencies, including the Advance Planning Task Force of Phoenix and Maricopa County.

2) Points equi-distant in both

time and *distance* between the proposed regional parks were located on a map of Maricopa and adjoining counties. "Time-distance" lines were then plotted at 15-minute intervals from each park outward to one hour's driving time. The geographic area thus defined and used throughout the study was called the "region of use."

3) Population socio-economic characteristics were then correlated with population densities. The characteristics of median age, median family income, median years of education and "occupational index" were graphically plotted on maps of the Phoenix Urban Area to determine average characteristics of three density groups: low (0-4.9 per acre); medium (5-19.9 per acre); and high (20 up per acre). A definite correlation between certain socio-economic characteristics and certain population densities was established.

4) The projected 1980 population 12 years of age and over was then computed, according to the three density groups, for each of the regional park regions of use.

5) The effect of the socio-economic characteristics of each density group on participation rates in 12 major outdoor activities was then derived from the studies of the Outdoor Recreation Resources Review Commission. This was accomplished by a complicated mathematical model run on a
(Continued on page 53)

4

Planning, Patching and Progress

By EUGENE VAN CLEEF, Professor Emeritus, Department of Geography, The Ohio State University

Whoever views comprehensive city planning as an act of futility is likely to be rated as out of his mind. Has not city planning proved its value? Is there anyone bold enough to say that the planning of Washington, D. C. has not paid off? Or that Chicago, New Haven or Hartford, Connecticut, or Boston and still other centers have not demonstrated beyond question the validity of sound urban planning?

The fact is that, except in the case of a new land development under central control, a comprehensive plan cannot be realized in total. A plan for the future of any established city can come into approximate being only one step at a time, that is by the patching process. This procedure means the original plan is not likely to be consummated.

Those, whose responsibility it is to execute plans, generally meet with some opposition. This can arise for one or more reasons; but primarily because proposals for rearranging the layout of a city generally focus upon one part of a community while, for the moment at least, other districts remain undisturbed. Many citizens object to being inconvenienced unless everyone is placed in the same boat at the same time. It is probable that this dissatisfaction would not arise if the public were fully informed concerning the total program. People must be shown what benefits will accrue to them and given the reasons for the imminent sequence of events.

No matter how well conceived a plan may be, the public must be made to realize that no magic can bring a plan into being instantaneously. Those in charge of executing a plan must make it clear to all the citizens that carrying out a plan is time-consuming; that it is impracticable to attempt to rebuild all parts of a city simultaneously; that only the patching procedure is feasible.

As is well known, the Urban Renewal Administration will not approve a neighborhood renewal project unless a comprehensive plan has been drawn up showing how the renewal will fit into the general scheme. All too often, in its zeal to obtain funds, a local commission will prepare an overall plan of sorts merely to meet the legal requirements. The results may not be the best, but good or bad, the area to be renewed will become a patch in the urban landscape, with the likelihood that the final comprehensive plan for an indefinite future, will incorporate numerous departures from current proposals.

A plan for the development of vacant land located either well within the political limits of a city or on its periphery, can be made to harmonize with adjacent lands or to clash. More than likely the pattern will be expressive of ideas not even conceived of when the adjacent areas were originally developed. If this be the case, the resultant new layout is certain to assume patch-like characteristics.

5

Planning and Civic Comment

These comments are not meant to be disparaging. Surely, progress is much more likely with a plan than without one. Consider the comprehensive Burnham plan for Chicago, produced over a half century ago. When the businessmen of Chicago commissioned Daniel Burnham, noted landscape architect of his day, to draw a plan for the future of their city, no limitations were placed upon him. So impressive were his suggestions that his drawings were exhibited in other parts of this country and in foreign lands as well. As stimulating as the plans were, only a very small part of them has been realized. Even so, it is amazing that so much has been brought to pass. But as remarkable as the rebuilding of various parts of Chicago has been, the fact remains that the Burnham revisions are patches in the complex fabric of the city as a whole.

Cities are dynamic, some more so than others. This means continual change. No one other than a sooth-sayer can hope to predict the status of a city a score or more years ahead. Who, for example, could have predicted in 1945 that in New York City roughly 200 massive office buildings would be erected by the year 1964? In most cities transfor-mations, even without planning, have occurred in the past few dec-ades and many of those in progress now could scarcely have been fore-seen.

The population "explosion," in itself, complicates the future. The current net rate of increase an-nounced by our government as equalling one person every twelve seconds can be frightening. It sug-gests seemingly insuperable urba problems involving land occupanc public utilities, cultural facilitie and many other elements of concer to every community. New inven tions, not dreamed of today, ma have far-reaching influences upo cities of a coming future day. In th light of these circumstances, plan-ning will prove increasingly com-plex, so much so that some day planning may be classified among the "hazardous occupations." Faced with this situation, planners are likely to become increasingly con-servative, wary of the many possible pitfalls, and thus tend more and more to feel their way by resorting on an ever grander scale to patching procedures.

Much patching is under way throughout the nation but in pro-portion to the number of urban cen-ters it does not loom large. Malls of various types seem at the moment to attract considerable favor, but even their numbers are so few they can be listed in a brief space. They have not always been successful. Toledo and Middletown, both in Ohio, have experimented with them, but subsequently abandoned them. On the other hand, Kalamazoo, Michigan, after trying out a small mall, liked it so well the original lay-out has been extended. In Philadel-phia, a re-created residential area has been replaced and seemingly has met with approval. Civic centers in Cleveland, Ohio, Springfield, Massa-chusetts, Columbus, Ohio, Kansas City, Missouri, and elsewhere have been viewed with considerable en-thusiasm by the local inhabitants. All of these phenomena are patches,

(Continued on page 47)

6

Wisconsin Counties Advance in Planning

By WALTER A. ROWLANDS, Specialist in Land Planning, Department of
Agricultural Economics, University of Wisconsin

Adapted from the Circular, "A Citizens' Development Plan For Every County"
by Mr. Rowlands, published May, 1963, by the University of Wisconsin
Extension Service

When county government was first established, state legislatures laid out specific responsibilities.

The county's job was essentially to provide for a system of county roads, keep land records, levy and collect taxes and provide protection to citizens through a system of county courts, the district attorney and the county sheriff.

Land owners controlled what happened on the land—what it was used for, how it was used. This was a free country. We were in a hurry to develop it—and sometimes we exploited it. We built farms and homes, roads and railroads, and introduced business and industry throughout the land.

Open space abounded. So did jobs. There was no need to stabilize employment or to balance the development of existing communities. We were busy selling and settling undeveloped land, and we had plenty of it to work with.

Today this situation has changed. Many cities and villages have outgrown their original boundaries. In Milwaukee county, Wisconsin, town government is gone. In Waukesha county and other southeastern Wisconsin counties, scores of new residential areas have taken over large areas of once-productive farmland.

People are moving into once quiet farming towns and using expressways or the interstate highways to drive to work in cities some 20, 30, or 40 miles away. These new non-farm country people require roads, police and fire protection, and school facilities. Sewage disposal and safe water supply problems complicate a situation, already crucial. Furthermore, these needs usually are urgent before the community starts to take in the tax money to finance new construction.

Today, in many counties, we've begun planning our beauty spots, our recreation centers, our parks and our neighborhood playgrounds. Many communities are applying careful thought and care to the design of new residential and recreation areas, school systems, industrial parks, and transportation and communications systems.

Now, every community has individuals with special planning talent. They may be private citizens working on their own, club leaders representing their groups, or local officials acting in their job capacities. All can help in the basic educational job of acquainting local people with the problems and opportunities of new resource development.

For example, a northern Wisconsin county, looking for expert leadership on a hospital campaign, was surprised to find exactly the specialized experience and organizing skill it needed among its own people. Other counties have had and can have similar experiences.

7

In Wisconsin, many counties have enlisted the cooperative support of from 50 to 200 citizens in Citizens' Planning Committees. Town boards, sometimes assisted by county committees, select these special groups of citizens who are often exceptionally well qualified to help, perhaps experts in their own specialized fields.

In some counties, citizens' groups and county staff work directly with professional planners in making comprehensive plans for the community inasmuch as some counties hire professional planners. In others, local technicians from schools, highways, industry, agriculture, forestry and recreation work side by side with local citizens and town and county officers. Frequently, the planning group works under the direction of a special steering committee of the county board, with the county extension agent serving as secretary.

In any case, the Citizens' Planning Committee's ability to recommend measures to improve the community is limited only by the imagination and ingenuity of its members. Every individual must recognize his responsibility in county planning since everyone sees civic problems and accepts proposed solutions differently. The variety of backgrounds of its citizens makes the typical American community an exciting place to live. Citizen knowledge, interest and action provide the life blood of our democratic society.

Just so, Wisconsin counties differ widely in their problems and their opportunities for development, as well as in the direction and emphasis they place on local planning. For instance, some counties have created new wealth by developing and protecting new recreational and residential development around existing lakes and newly-created flowage lakes.

Other counties concentrate on promoting a better land use balance through industrial development that will stabilize employment throughout the year.

Still other counties are making basic 10 to 15-year recommendations on over-all county development—agriculture, schools, libraries, roads, residential development, commercial and industrial development, parks and wetland and conservation areas.

This broad approach will involve considerable time and effort by many people. And, just as many cities and villages throughout America could improve their appearance, so every Citizens' Planning Committee should look carefully and critically at the Wisconsin community from the viewpoint of the vacationing motorist. We've cluttered our main highways with automobile graveyards, garbage disposal dumps, and signs in all stages of dilapidation.

We need to do in a public way what every good family does when company comes—clean up the premises. The nation needs a collective housecleaning.

We will need wise plans to insure the full development of every county in Wisconsin, as in all America.

Such citizens' plans may become the most valuable and the most important community documents the counties will ever possess.

Three California Beach Cities with Two Choices

By VICTOR GRUEN, F.A.I.A., Victor Gruen Associates

An address delivered by Mr. Gruen before the South Bay Board of Realtors, Redondo Beach, California, June 18, 1964, with representatives from Redondo Beach, Hermosa Beach and Manhattan Beach in attendance

Nothing, of course, is more welcome to me than an opportunity to convince large groups of people that master planning is important and needed. After all, our organization is engaged in this activity and we make a living from it. But I must confess to you in all honesty that the activity of master planning, with the exception of creating some employment for planners, makes little sense if there is not, first of all, clarification of a distinct aim as to what planning procedure should achieve.

If I am correctly informed, there are greatly differing sentiments in this respect existing in the three communities which are represented here, and there are also great differences of opinion in each one of them as to what would be the desirable goals of planning. I am sure there are even some people who feel strongly that no planning at all would be the most desirable activity.

If my information is correct that there is, in fact, disunity on the aims of planning and the necessity of planning, it would actually not be very surprising. The three communities which you represent are actually in a very unusual situation. Though each of them has established boundaries and its own municipal governmental structure, which supposedly can determine, on the basis of the will of the people, the future characteristics of each one of the three communities, the realities of life make you actually all dependent on the impact of outside forces over which you have little control.

The very fact that your communities are located in a most desirable position along the beaches of the Pacific Ocean and that you enjoy better than average climatic conditions is at the root of your problems. The natural desire of those who have settled in this potentially beautiful and pleasant stretch of land would, of course, be to be left in peace and to be allowed to enjoy, unmolested by others, the views of the Pacific, the pleasantness of the beaches, and all the recreational activities which can be derived from the opportunities existing here. There was a time when this was possible to a high degree. In addition, it was even feasible to make some income from hotel, restaurant and harbor facilities by attracting inlanders coming from far away Los Angeles by means of the Pacific Electric Railroad. There were not too many of them truly to disturb the peacefulness of your area, and they came usually only on weekends. But all this has radically changed with the explosive population growth of the greater Los Angeles area and, most of all, with the advent of the automobile as a means of mass transportation.

The position in which your three

9

cities find themselves reminds me of the experiences which an uncle of mine, who was a rich man, had to go through. He built himself a beautiful house on a lake, with swimming pool and tennis courts and other paraphernalia, in the hope of getting rest and enjoyment. Unfortunately, he had a large family, none of them economically as fortunate as he was, who invaded the place in swarms; and inasmuch as he was a kind man with great family sense, he did not have the heart to throw them out. There was neither rest nor enjoyment left for him, however, and so he packed up and went on a nice quiet trip around the world.

You people in the three beach cities are blessed with about 6,000,000 poor relatives who all want to come to visit you. You can't keep them out because there are no legal means by which to do so, so you have only two choices. You can discourage the visitors by making things as unpleasant as possible —and this can be easily achieved by poor access, poor street systems, a lack of parking space near the beaches, and many other means. If you choose to do this, you will reduce the visitor stream somewhat, but you will also create disorderly conditions under which you will have to suffer just as much as the visitors.

Or, you will have to make up your minds to become professional hosts, making things as pleasant and enjoyable as possible, taking advantage of the visitor stream financially, through income (and the resulting tax benefits for the cities) from good marinas, hotels, stores, cultural activities, etc. You will then be able to utilize the funds which will flow in to make life for your own residents as pleasant as possible by arranging traffic patterns in such manner that your residential areas are free from any through traffic and from beach users' parking, and by giving your own populace the benefits of better public services, better schools, etc.

I said you have a choice and I believe you do—but not in the long range view. It may very well be possible that poor traffic conditions and parking conditions and difficult access may keep out the metropolitan visitors, or at least reduce their numbers for some time. But the community which acts so will probably soon find that the nuisances created by the reduced number will still be sufficiently large to make the entire environment for the residents less enjoyable, and financial difficulties for the municipality because of insufficient income from taxes will probably force action at a later time.

Once you have made up your minds to become professional host cities to a potential of 6,000,000 metropolites, then the undertaking of a master plan starts to make sense. It would, of course, be wise to coordinate master planning of each individual community with that of the neighboring ones, with the County and with the State, because there are certain problems which do not respect city boundary lines and which can be resolved only jointly with others. This refers to shoreline improvements, freeway and highway patterns, water pollution problems, air pollution problems, etc. Beyond these problems, (*Continued on page 52*)

10

Historic Preservation Without Federal Aid in Georgetown, D. C.

By DOROTHEA DE SCHWEINITZ, Archivist, Historic Georgetown, Inc. and Chairman, Fine Arts and Historic Buildings Committee, Georgetown Citizens' Association

Abstract of a speech given at the 17th annual meeting of the National Trust for Historic Preservation, Washington, D. C., and reprinted through the courtesy of *Historic Preservation* in which this statement appeared in the 1964 Volume 16, Number 1 issue

Historic preservation begins *as soon as a new building is completed and put to use. The owners may not realize it but the best form of preservation is continued use for appropriate purposes. Other forms of preservation are restoration for residence by new owners, restoration and adaptation for museum use by historical societies, and remodeling and restoration for commercial use by civic groups or by business men.

All of these forms of preservation may be accomplished without the aid of government money, although city ordinances and other legislation may aid in the program.

Georgetown provides demonstrations of these four methods of preservation. The outstanding example of continued use is Tudor Place, which has been occupied continuously for more than 160 years by descendants of Martha Custis Washington. Other communities, such as Bethlehem, Pa., and Salem, N. C., have maintained to this day their buildings of the mid-eighteenth century because the Moravian settlers built them to last as homes, churches, schools, colleges and other community services. In many New England towns one finds the early eighteenth-century clapboard houses continued as residences perhaps by a succession of families and now reclaimed

and improved, often by descendants of the original settlers who return to enjoy the village green and elm trees which shaded their ancestors.

The Georgetown movement toward preservation and restoration of residences began to stir primarily in the 1920's and more energetically in the 1950's. Following the two World Wars there was evidence of a recognition of the fine architecture of the early years of our country and a revulsion against the wholesale construction of ginger-bread and uninspired houses of the late nineteenth and early twentieth centuries.

One by one, persons began to purchase, remodel and restore the original beauty of the Georgetown homes constructed in the 1790's and the first decades of the nineteenth century. This has been going on for more than forty years without benefit of taxpayers' money.

Just after 1800, some of the best construction in Georgetown occurred when the national capital was moved from Philadelphia to Washington. At that time, because Georgetown already existed, government officials and government clerks of all ranks made their homes in Georgetown as they do today. It became especially desirable during the first half of the nineteenth

11

century. In fact, a correspondent of the London *Times*, William Howard Russell, in his *My Diary*, published in 1863, wrote: "It (Georgetown) is a much more respectable and old-world looking place than its vulgar, empty, overgrown, mushroom neighbor, Washington."

By 1920, certain parts of Georgetown had become slums and the preservationists of that period were considered hardy and courageous. They braved rats, roaches, and noisy neighbors, all because the fine architecture remained and beckoned for restoration and also because Georgetown was so near the center of Washington, convenient to offices and shops and still possessed of open space and gardens.

Property values soon became so high that occupants of slum dwellings, whether owners or tenants, moved out after sales at the new prices. Simple four-room houses have been prettied up with brass knockers, carriage lamps and iron railings making them attractive to young people—writers, artists, government employees—not only to affluent political leaders as the public press would have us believe. Little federal aid has been sought in the resurgence of Georgetown. The bulk of the improvements have come about because someone saw a house, liked it, bought it and fixed it up.

Preservation for museum purposes has also developed. Dumbarton Oaks, which was remodeled in 1920 and used as a residence by Mr. and Mrs. Robert Woods Bliss, is now a museum, given by the Blisses to Harvard University. Dumbarton House, the headquarters of the Colonial Dames of America, is also a museum financed without federal funds. Built possibly in 1750, it changed hands many times until it was purchased by the Colonial Dames in 1928. The purchase price, renovation and furnishings were provided by the 40 state societies and the one in the District of Columbia. Quotas were set and the ladies organized benefits and sales and all the other schemes women devise when they are out for money. Dumbarton House is maintained by a head tax of the members.

While mentioning museums, it must be admitted that the Old Stone House in Georgetown was financed through federal monies. It is one of the few pre-revolutionary structures in the area and demonstrates the simple living of a middle-class craftsman, with his shop on the first floor. In 1950, at the same time that the Old Georgetown Act was wending its way through Congress, a bill was introduced and passed authorizing the National Park Service to purchase, restore and maintain the property as an educational feature for the public. This was necessary because the owners refused to sell and the property had to be secured by eminent domain.

Government can aid without the expenditure of money. State legislation, zoning regulations and city ordinances further the cause of preservation and restoration. Individual effort at preserving a house is defeated if the character of the area is not maintained or reclaimed. In 1924, a Homeowners Committee of the Georgetown Citizens' Association aroused sufficient interest to amend the zoning legislation of 1920 to restrict building height to 40 feet,' to prohibit the construction of apartment houses in certain areas and reduce the areas which could be used for commercial purposes. In 1948, these restricted areas were extended.

In 1950, the two citizens' associations in Georgetown stimulated the Congress to enact the law which designated Georgetown an historic district, and called for the recommendations of the Fine Arts Commission on building permits for construction or demolition.

Passing a law is only the beginning of the job. Citizens must support the recommendations of the Architectural Review Boards and help find solutions for the problems created by the owners, primarily of commercial property, who appeal from recommendations on the grounds that they must be allowed to use their land or buildings to the full extent of their value. No sooner had the Old Georgetown Act been passed than it was learned that four buildings at 30th and M Streets, one pre-revolutionary, might be demolished to form a parking lot.

A few citizens banded together, raised contributions of $600 for a preliminary survey in the spring of 1951, to see whether the buildings could be bought, remodeled and rented as a business venture. It was estimated that the investment might bring a return of three percent. Ten men were sought to invest $10,000 each. But ten good men could not be found in Georgetown, that is, good to the extent of risking $10,000. Two such subscribers materialized and some other substantial pledges were forthcoming.

The preliminary committee incorporated as Historic Georgetown, Inc., and the sales contract for $75,000 was signed in November, 1951. By the time settlement was made, after a long title search, $60,000 had been obtained. The down payment was $20,000 and the estate which owned the buildings agreed to a $55,000 mortgage.

With approximately $40,000 available, it was decided to reconstruct the basements and the three shops on the first floors. Apartments were planned for the upper stories. Additional funds were obtained by the sale of one of the houses facing Thirtieth Street to a purchaser who promised to restore it appropriately. This sale, together with some land behind the buildings sold to neighbors, brought in $23,000.

By December 1953, the first-floor shops were ready for occupancy and tenants were obtained immediately. Because the full capital was not raised at the outset, the rentals had to be used to complete the remodeling instead of providing income for the shareholders, ultimately over a hundred in number. Plans changed from six apartments on the two upper floors to the establishment of France's restaurant on the second floor, with storage and offices in the space originally alloted to two apartments on the third floor. The restaurant opened in 1956. One duplex apartment was prepared for occupancy in 1959, thus completing the basic task.

Two hazards were experienced in the period of soliciting investment in Historic Georgetown, Inc. Prospects assumed the attitude that they were making a contribution—hence not subscribing the amounts sorely needed. On the other hand, some

13

enthusiastic inquirers knowing of the appreciation of property in Georgetown wished to subscribe, but needed continuing income from their capital. They had to be advised not to purchase shares unless they could afford temporarily the loss of income involved. The would-be contributors, in a number of cases, gave their shares to the National Trust for Historic Preservation, thus taking an income tax deduction and causing the National Trust to become the largest shareholder. It is hoped that, in the not-distant-future, the Trust will benefit from these gifts.

Historic Georgetown is now in the black, has a substantial reserve fund and has reduced its mortgage to $45,000. It has paid some of the dividends on the cumulative preferred stock and the present prospects indicate a resumption of payment of dividends. The preferred stock amounts to $30,000 and the common stock adds up to $86,000.

The remodeling and restoration of these three Historic Georgetown houses on a business street, in 1952-53, demonstrated what could be done with the many fine structures on Georgetown's two business streets, Wisconsin Avenue and M Street. In addition, a stimulus was provided by a program of the Progressive Citizens' Association. Every year an award of merit is given to the owner and the architect for the best facade that has appeared on a commercial building during the previous twelve months. The attitude of the merchants has changed from one of wonder or scorn to an interest in the history of structures throughout the area. Preservation and res-

toration by the business community have taken place without federal funds.

In 1959, the Georgetown Redevelopment Corporation was created to purchase properties in danger of destruction or inappropriate use. During the two years of its existence, three structures on business M Street were purchased for re-sale to persons who would remodel and restore them properly. One was purchased from the Corporation by the founders of a newly formed club called the City Tavern in recognition of the building's use in the 1790's. The purchase and restoration of the Club building was financed through debentures bought by the founders and charter members and through the initiation fees of some 900 members. The inevitable mortgage will be paid off from the operating income of the Club.

The Georgetown Redevelopment Corporation had eight members and no one invested more than $5,000. The principal purpose of the body was to preserve buildings, not to make money. However, no money has been lost and, because the sales were made at a slight increase over the prices paid, there was a modest financial reward. A new corporation has been formed recently for similar purposes. . . . . .

These private efforts have renewed a business section without federal funds. As indicated above, the residential section presented fewer problems but all areas of Georgetown have benefited from preservation legislation which in the case of Georgetown is federal aid but not money.

℮↝

Ohio's Flint Ridge State Memorial

Reprinted from Echoes, Vol. 3, No. 7, July, 1964, a publication of the
Ohio Historical Society

Centuries ago Indian trails from villages and camp sites throughout the Midwest converged upon an irregular range of hills about ten miles in length located between the present cities of Newark and Zanesville, Ohio. Along the trails through tangled forest growth and on nearby river waterways prehistoric Indians on foot or in dug-out canoes made their way to these hills for material they sorely needed—flint.

In the Permian Period, approximately 200 million years ago, a stratum of the hard flint deposit began to be elevated, part of which was later exposed by erosion. In a five- or six-square-mile area outcroppings of the colorful rock caught the eye of roving Indians. Nowhere in what is now the Midwest had better flint been found. Inevitably, quarrying operations were begun to extract the highly-prized flint, to process it into useful and easily

(Continued on page 16)

AMERICAN LANDMARKS CELEBRATION

The American Landmarks Celebration, which is being observed in this country from August 1 to November 30, 1964, has been planned to include a special American Landmarks Week from September 28 to October 4, 1964. Officially opened by Mrs. Lyndon B. Johnson at Woodrow Wilson House in Washington, D. C., on July 30, 1964, the Celebration represents United States participation in UNESCO's International Campaign for Historical Monuments.

Purpose of the American celebration is to draw the attention of state and local authorities, as well as individual Americans, to the urgent need to preserve the richness and diversity of the historical, architectural and natural heritage of America. Mr. Earl P. Hanson, President, National Conference on State Parks, has served as a member of the Steering Committee for the American Landmarks Celebration.

In the words of President and Mrs. Lyndon B. Johnson, in a message to Mr. Rene Maheu, Director General of UNESCO:

"Among the most cherished of a nation's treasures are the monuments of its past. Scenes of triumph or disaster, memorials to great men or great thoughts, supreme technical or artistic achievements, simple reflections of an earlier culture are all significant. Each contributes to the historic texture of society."

As an interesting example of a "reflection of an earlier culture," in this great land of ours, we reprint the above story on Flint Ridge, which appeared in the July, 1964 issue of Echoes, a publication of the Ohio Historical Society.

transported form, and to carry it across the land to villages where finely executed tools, implements, and weapons could be fashioned when needed. Specimens from Flint Ridge have been discovered on the Atlantic seaboard, in Louisiana, and as far west as Kansas City.

The first quarry workers at Flint Ridge soon discovered that the flint which had been exposed to the elements was useless. Fine cracks and checks caused pieces to fall apart when worked. But below the surface a layer of good quality flint from one to ten feet in thickness lay waiting to be extracted.

Great physical force was needed to quarry the flint. Large hammerstones or mauls, granite or quartzite boulders worn smooth by glacial action and weighing up to twenty-five pounds, were found in the vicinity and were used to drive wooden or bone wedges into natural cracks in the flint stratum. With great labor, rectangular chunks of the raw mineral were extracted. As the quarrying continued over the centuries, deep pits were formed, and piles of broken pieces and chips accumulated.

Workshops were operated near the quarry. Indians skilled with small hammerstones and other tools "blocked-out" rough pieces of flint from three to twelve inches long and two to five inches wide using pressure and percussion techniques. The resulting blade-shaped pieces were characterized by rounded or square bases.

The blades were then either transported to villages for further refinement or were finished at workshops near the Flint Ridge quarries.

Experienced Indians performed the meticulous work of forming arrow and spear points, drills, knives, and scrapers from the blades as each tool was needed.

Cores were also shaped at Flint Ridge. Special workshops fashioned blocks of flint from which knives were flaked at nearby workshops or occasionally at the villages. Some of these cores from Flint Ridge have been found at prehistoric village sites and in mounds throughout Ohio.

When the first pioneers of the Old Northwest rediscovered Flint Ridge, they too learned of the superior qualities of the translucent and varicolored mineral. Many a flintlock rifle, musket, or pistol was equipped with Flint Ridge flint; many a pioneer fire was kindled in tinder boxes fired with this same rock.

A lower grade of flint from the western portion of the ridge possessed a structure containing minute cells which early settlers found ideally suited for making buhrstones. Millers in central Ohio paid from $350 to $500 a pair for these stones for grinding at their water-powered mills. Small buhrstones were finished for home grinding purposes.

Engineers building the National Road through Muskingum and Licking counties spied the heaps of broken flint discarded by the prehistoric Indians and hauled the pieces to form the roadbed.

Today the significance of Flint Ridge is historical rather than economic. In 1933, The Ohio Historical Society established the Flint Ridge State Memorial to preserve this unusual site.

16

Commentaries

.City **Planning.** In a stimulating editorial titled "City Planning," *The Dallas Morning News*, on August 16, 1964, paid high tribute to the article by Harland Bartholomew, President, American Planning and Civic Association, in the June, 1964 issue of *Planning and Civic Comment.*

Though the article is titled "American Planning and Civic Association, 1904–1964, Have We Completed A Cycle?" the editorial rightly has sensed its broader interpretation and has termed it a "remarkable review of efforts by American cities since 1904 to better their character and appearance."

The editorial terms the "most significant thought" in the article, "a prediction that urban planning henceforth must be on a metropolitan basis if we are to cope with the expansion in the vast urban complexes of today and tomorrow."

Saying that Dallas has a special interest in the author's findings because it owes much of its cumulative planning as a city to him, the editorial emphasizes that "the burden of initiating such plans · falls on citizens acting outside of formal governmental bodies."

Mr. Bartholomew drew up the Dallas master plan of 1944 on which much of the postwar growth of the city has unfolded. Born in 1889, he has, as the *Dallas News* editorial points out, "lived through the whole cycle to date of the movement to instill better design and appearance in our mushrooming cities."

Wilderness: Still another appreciative and interpretative item on wilderness preservation has come from Edward J. Meeman, Chairman of the Board of the National Conference on State Parks and Editor Emeritus of the *Memphis Press-Scimitar.* With the passage of the Wilderness Bill, Mr. Meeman, who has given generously of his own time and energies as a long-time advocate of wilderness preservation and who has been equally generous in his praise of others who have worked to make preservation a reality, has written the following editorial which has appeared in The Scripps-Howard Newspapers throughout the country:

"Congress has acted to make America's heritage of wilderness secure.

"The Senate and House have reconciled their differences and sent the Wilderness Bill to President Johnson, sure that he would promptly approve it, for he had asked them to pass this legislation.

"If it is not a perfect bill, certainly it is far better than conservationists had reason to hope for at the beginning of the session and they proudly regard it as a landmark achievement in conservation history.

"It means that nine million acres administered by the U. S. Forest Service and now classified as 'wilderness, wild, and canoe' areas must remain such unless some future Congress should change their status, and that is not likely to happen. Until this wilderness act was passed, there was nothing to prevent some

Secretary of Agriculture from giving away 'with the stroke of a pen' the people's irreplaceable resources of unspoiled nature. It was the purpose of this legislation to make that impossible.

"This is just the start of our wilderness preservation system. The law provides that, within the next 10 years, on recommendation of the Secretary of Agriculture and the President, Congress can add to it, tract by tract, national forest lands now classed as 'primitive,' up to a total of more than five million acres.

"Similarly, many millions of wilderness acres in the national parks and monuments and wild life refuges can be given permanence in the system on recommendation of the Secretary of the Interior and the President. Gifts of land from private sources also may be accepted.

"When the system is completed we will be assured that 2 per cent of the lands of the United States will remain as all of it was when the Indians roamed its vast spaces—a land of green forests, clear streams, blue lakes and pure air—

"Where plants and animals can reproduce themselves unfailingly and no species will be lost.

"Unmarred by automobile roads and the litter that cars bring, but open to all to explore by foot trail and horseback.

"For hunters of big and small game, for those who would fish in fast water or calm lake, for birders, for the myriads who shoot only with cameras.

"As the outdoor laboratories for scientists who must have primitive nature to study if they are to find out how we must live in civilization.

"For those who want to 'get away from it all,' from the neon, the smell of gas and chemicals, the noise and odors of cities, and hear only the sound of the wind, the songs of birds and the cries of animals, smell only the fragrance of pine and cedar, and be alone with nature, and, as most would add, with nature's God.

"The wilderness preserved means much to the stay-at-homes, just to know that it is there, and to see its refreshing scenes in pictures in newspapers and magazines, and in movies and on TV, both in travelog and the background of stirring or romantic drama.

"To Senator Clinton Anderson and Representative John Saylor, the authors of the bill, and to all, in and out of Congress who had a part in this great conservation victory, our thanks and congratulations.

"Like Moses, Howard Zahniser, executive director of the Wilderness Society, who died fighting for the cause, was not here to enter the promised land of wilderness preserved. We wish he could have seen how we have answered his plea that we project the wild 'that has come to us from the eternity of the past into the eternity of the future.' "

A Question of Density. Acknowledging that "hammers, nails and poured concrete will continue to characterize Northern Virginia for almost 40 years," *Housing 'Sights' Newsletter'*, a publication of the Northern Virginia Regional Planning and Development Commission, points out: "Growth here has been fantastic in the past. The supply of housing has increased four-fold since 1940. Half of the houses and apartments we saw in 1960 did not even exist in 1950. During this ten-year period, the housing increase ranged from 25 per cent in Loudoun County to 160 per cent in Fairfax County. Housing in Fairfax has increased 620 per cent in the twenty years between 1940 and 1960.

Pointing out that seventy per cent of the region's dwellings are now single-family homes, the publication cites the possibility of greater demand for apartment rental units in the future.

"Since Northern Virginia does have vast quantities of unused land, there are good arguments for both kinds of development. A piece of earth for every man in the form of single-family houses is an argument with merit. Home owners care more about their community, it is said. A single-family community is more stable, less transient. So we can find good reasons for keeping densities at today's levels.

"There are equally good arguments for putting 50 per cent of the population into apartments. Eventual rapid transit becomes more feasible when there are compact population centers. Families can live closer to Washington if we avoid sprawl. They can live within walking distance to shopping areas— thus we remove some cars from ever more crowded highways."

 ✐

Water—Key To Life. "Water, one of the keys to South Dakota's booming recreation industry, is the key to life itself. Take it away or defile it sufficiently and life, as we know it, will fade away."

This is the position of "Conservation Highlights," a report of the South Dakota Department of Game, Fish and Parks, which continues: "This could not honestly be written without sounding a warning that we are rapidly losing the most valuable of all outdoor resources. We must have water in one form or another. Without it, we face a dead future."

Pointing out that man, in all his knowledge, has been unable to conquer drought, a whim of nature, the report says: "Rainfall still provides an uncertain water supply, with one section of the countryside getting too much moisture while another gasps for even a brief shower. . . .

"Lack of rainfall is too often compounded by man-made drainage of available water supplies.

"Draglines, which destroy the holding potential of a marsh or pothole, destroy an equal portion of the under-ground water table. Sixty per cent of all pothole drainage goes directly into streams, adding to flood threats. Straightening of a river channel to hurry water downstream does the same thing.

"The fact that valuable wildlife habitat is also being destroyed, is actually a minor matter when compared to the long-range view of what it will eventually do to human survival.

"Hurrying of water from the land is conservation in reverse."

Turning to the increasing menace of pollution, the report says water quality and quantity is rapidly being reduced in South Dakota by pollution.

"Water, polluted by siltation, is

almost any part of the United States. It is hardly possible to realize or comprehend the loss of naturally created beauty, on the east coast, the west coast, and around every large city and metropolitan area across the country. Moreover, the speed at which we are losing the natural beauty of our land is being accelerated."

ℰ𝒓𝒐

Parkways. Edward J. Meeman, recently re-elected Vice-President of the *American Planning and Civic Association,* had some interesting comments after an inspection trip with the Advisory Board on National Parks down the 469-mile length of the Blue Ridge Parkway.

A parkway at its best, he says, "is more than a highway where the view is unmarred by billboards and neon signs." In the definition quoted by landscape architect Stanley Abbott, "a parkway is an elongated park with a road in it."

"It may be even more than that," says Mr. Meeman. It may be what the Blue Ridge is—a chain of parks. Your stopping to linger in each one of these 'parks,' to savor the distinctive delights which each one of them offers, means as much as the pleasant drive through unfolding vistas from one to the other. Not only is there a great national park at each end of the Blue Ridge Parkway—Shenandoah at the north and Great Smoky Mountains at the south—but there are 11 recreation areas along the way, more than one of which might proudly be called a national park if it stood alone."

Mr. Meeman, who made the trip "when the crimson, purple and yellow of the hardwoods glowed in a golden October sun against the contrasting evergreens," kept an observant eye on the man-made innovations in the area—the "wide places in the road."

"There are the Peaks of Otter," he says, "where you find a recently built inn, fresh and original in design but so timeless in spirit that it shames the shoddy, merely 'contemporary' that you so often see elsewhere. Those of us who got up at dawn saw bull elk fighting on the front 'lawn.'

"As you stand on one peak and see the blue-misty mountains stretch range on range, the heavens are very close and you think Heaven itself could offer no more pleasing prospect.

"You understand why the National Park Service asks more parkways, with the enthusiastic backing of Interior Secretary Udall.

"When a parkway is planned with a right-of-way broad enough that it meets the definition of 'an elongated park with a road in it,' and enough 'wide places in the road' that it becomes a chain of parks, such a project will deserve universal support."

ℰ𝒓𝒐

Libraries. According to the September, 1964 issue of *The Municipal South,* people from all over the southeast have visited the new public library in Gadsden, Alabama.

Gadsden's Mayor Les Gilliland points out that a library is considered to be a yardstick of measurement for the community.

National Capital

Notes

A CITY IS SO MANY LITTLE THINGS. And what *you* are will help determine what it will become—a backdrop for living with zest and meaning or for an existence without savour.

Within the past months, a contagious feeling that an indeterminate ingredient is lacking in the Washington area, the fastest growing urban center in the country, has seized some of the city's key leaders. And the seizure seems to be taking hold of city officials, spokesmen for the Federal government, civic leaders and the National Capital's press.

"When we come to Washington," says the *Washington Evening Star*, ". . . aside from some parks, a few sidewalk cafes and some flower carts, there seems to be a dearth of the pleasant minutiae that give a city a charm of its own."

The concentration on "minutiae" came full bloom, if it didn't actually bud when **District Commissioner Walter N. Tobriner** returned last fall from a European vacation with a strong urge to dress up Washington with more charm and a warmer atmosphere.

What emerged in the ensuing criss-cross of responses were suggestions for streetside kiosks operated by natty little merchants, benches where the foot-sore and just plain weary can rest, eye-appeal protection for the thousands who battle the elements to board homeward-bound buses and a dozen other little amenities ranging from flower boxes to guide maps mounted in glass-faced containers.

Out of the host of suggestions, two, especially, were buoyed up for exhaustive consideration and possible action. The one would transform the stately, but some would say somewhat sterile, beauty of the Mall from the Lincoln Memorial to Capital Hill into a setting for more leisurely enjoyment by the millions who go there. The other, simpler in concept, but with equally imaginative appeal and actually part and parcel of the other, would put ice skaters on the Reflecting Pool through the installation of freezing and pumping equipment and the construction of a concrete bottom.

Members of the **Committee of 100 on the Federal City** are playing prominent roles in the consideration of both proposals. A special committee composed of outstanding citizens, including ample representation from the Committee of

the project. It would be constructed around the First Methodist Church which will remain intact on the site. Shops at the northern side will face State Street because the project has been conceived as but one part of the entire Central Business District.

John Graham AIA and James King & Son, Inc., have collaborated on several projects in the New Jersey area, including the Princeton Center for Industrial Research and the Dow-Jones Laboratory and Offices between Trenton and New Brunswick.

John Graham pioneered the development of the suburban shopping center when, in 1947, his firm designed the first planned regional center in the nation—Northgate in the suburbs of Seattle. Projects such as these have attracted millions of dollars in goods and services away from the old downtown central business districts.

The Graham firm now is working with business leaders and local civic groups in revitalizing old central business districts of a number of communities which are planning new or supplementary environments to attract investors, merchants, customers and business firms.

The Tocks Island Story

The Tocks Island dam and reservoir project, excluding the proposed National Recreation Area, was authorized by the United States Congress in 1962. In the 1964 Public Works Appropriations Bill, the Congress appropriated $250,000 to the Corps of Engineers to begin preliminary engineering and design work on the project.

The Delaware Basin Bulletin, a publication of the Water Resources Association of the Delaware River Basin, says the size and location of the Tocks Island project make it the keystone of the entire plan for developing and controlling the water resources of the Delaware River Basin.

According to the Bulletin: "It is, first, the only reservoir project in the Basin that will be large enough simultaneously to meet the rapidly expanding water supply needs of the Philadelphia metropolitan region and other metropolitan regions in North and Central New Jersey. Second, it is the one project that will afford substantial flood protection to such communities below the dam as Phillipsburg and Trenton, New Jersey, and Easton and New Hope, Pennsylvania. Third, it is the only project in the Comprehensive Plan for the Basin that will permit the development of hydroelectric power.

Inevitably, ramifications of the Tocks Island project are numerous. Not the least of them has to do with the developing economic impact on the three-state Tocks Island region and with how the lives of individuals within the area are being affected.

Says the Bulletin:

"The unincorporated village of Bushkill faces a unique problem in that it is the only community that will be wholly inundated by the Tocks Island reservoir. At a meeting, April 16, the residents of Bushkill were given a fairly firm schedule of when their lands and homes would be acquired and the village inundated. More importantly, however, the residents were informed of the two alternative methods they could consider should they want to relocate to an entirely new Bushkill.

"These alternatives: 1) Cooperation with the Corps of Engineers under existing statutes to relocate Bushkill; 2) cooperation with a private developer, thus developing a new Bushkill wholly with private funds.

"Since land and homes in Bushkill probably won't be acquired before 1970, the residents of the area have considerable time in which to determine if they want to create a new Bushkill . . . "

At the April 16 meeting, it was emphasized that the Tocks Island project was not something that would happen overnight. Residents were told they would be given ample time in which to cope with the personal impact the project would have on their lives and livelihood and that the decision as to whether or not to create a new Bushkill rests with them alone. It is a decision only they can make.

New Homes—1963

The varying and complex factors which help to determine the construction of new dwelling units and, hence, to some extent the pattern of development in a crowded area, such as the New York Metropolitan Region, are clearly revealed in "New Homes, 1963," a recent publication of the Regional Plan Association.

Apartment building in the area dropped sharply in 1963. Calling attention to this, the publication says, "Ever since 1957, permits for apartment units have increased swiftly and steadily, from 28,000 to 90,000 in 1962, with a drop to 73,000 in 1963."

Between the end of World War II and the late 1950's, the housing industry in the Region concentrated on one-family housing. Between 1950 and 1960, two-thirds of the increase in housing units was in one-family houses and the number of one-family houses has since remained steady.

According to the publication, one of the strongest forces toward more apartment building during the past six years was probably the increase and anticipated further increase in families without school-age children, who frequently prefer apartment living. Not only have couples been living longer after their children move away, but the statistical bulge of young people between 18 and 30 (typically apartment years) has just begun.

The publication points out that the increased demand for apartments compared to one-family houses can be expected to continue into the 1970's when, again, there will be a striking rise in demand for one-family houses. By that time, babies of the post-depression and post-war periods will reach the age when they can afford to buy a house, and their children will reach the age when it seems easier to raise them in a one-family house.

Additional factors contributing to the increase in apartments in the New York Region over the past six years, according to Regional Plan are:

1) The dwindling of vacant land near the center of the Region while jobs remain concentrated near the center, putting a premium on the land close-in; 2) completion of a number of urban renewal projects in

23

New York City and in other older cities and villages; 3) a return to the luxury apartment market after thirty years; and 4) the desire of builders to begin construction before the standards were raised by New York City's new zoning ordinance. The new rules raise building standards by allowing less floor space for the same area of land which results in an increase in the cost per square foot of apartment.

High Density Communities

The conversion of an existing Cook County, Illinois country club into a high density residential community with an adjoining golf course provides an ideal pattern for economic and aesthetic use of any large tract, according to Zalman Y. Alper, of Alper and Alper, Architects, Chicago, Illinois, writing in *Urban Land,* official publication of Urban Land Institute. ULI of Washington, D. C. is an independent research organization specializing in urban planning and development.

The Chicago architect's study for the development of Old Orchard Country Club in Cook County is described in a five-page illustrated article that deals broadly with the problem of how to preserve fast disappearing open space where the population is steadily increasing and land values are high. According to Mr. Alper, "The retention of open space is an absolute necessity if we are to retain any vital contact with nature." He defines open space as the space left for recreation, parks, playgrounds, forest, lakes, and land in its natural state. It is also space needed for flood plains, drainage, water-sheds, conservation areas and wild life preserves.

"The only way in which open space can be retained and the need for housing met at the same time is to create a relatively high density on part of a site and leave the balance either as natural open land or as man-made open space," Mr. Alper states. He points out that the alternative is monotonous rows of single family dwellings with the probability of cities stretching hundreds of miles.

It was decided at the beginning of the Old Orchard study that the golf course would be retained as a recreational facility. Plans for the remaining land involve a creatively designed development that will have two sites for multi-story apartment buildings, one for a service type commercial use, one for a nursing home, one for a small office building, one for ten groups of atrium town houses, and one site for a lodge and meeting facility.

The plan calls for the apartment buildings to be so arranged that each will have a view of the golf course. Pedestrian paths will make it possible to circulate within the course. The roofs of partly underground parking garages will be used for tennis courts, ice skating rinks, and general outdoor facilities for tenants.

In suggesting the Old Orchard plan as a concept for other developers, Mr. Alper stresses that it combines the private interests of the owners for the highest and best economic use of the land with the public's interest in the preservation of open space.

℮ℛℴ

National Capital
Notes

IT'S THE "AVENUE OF THE PRESI-
DENTS" known to millions
throughout the world. It's the link
between two great structures, symbolic of American democracy: The
national Capitol—seat of law-makers
"of, by and for the people," and the
White House—official residence of
the President, elected by the people
as their Chief Executive.

Between the two—and equally
familiar to the millions who participate in the periodic pageantry of
inaugural and innumerable ceremonial parades up and down Pennsylvania Avenue—is an extended
facade of tired buildings which, obviously, have long since done their
bit in the passing parade and which
now emit nothing so much as a de-
spairing suggestion that their time
is ripe for tumbling down.

Just how to go about abetting
this and remaking Pennsylvania
Avenue into the "grand axis of the
Nation" has occupied the attention
of the nation's experts since 1962.
In June of that year, **President
John F. Kennedy** appointed a
**President's Council for Penn-
sylvania Avenue** consisting of ten
of the country's respected architects,
planners, landscape architects and
others. Its commission: To arrive at

a redevelopment plan for Pennsylvania Avenue which will complete
L'Enfant's dream of a grand national boulevard through the Federal City.

In May of this year, the President's Council released the plan.
Its features are said by **Douglas
Haskell,** editor of *Architectural
Forum,* to attempt to return the
original concept of L'Enfant, revised to fit the auto age. They include among others: A great National Square, a large reflecting pool
to mirror the Capitol on the east,
giant pedestrian platforms and overlooks, courts, tunnels, underground
parking, grandstand sidewalks for
parades, appropriate use of trees
and, in general, the provision of new
and pleasurable urban vistas.

Charles A. Horsky, White House
advisor on National Capital affairs,
has asked 18 agencies to report their
views on the plan by September 1.

Downtown Progress, a group of
businessmen striving to revitalize
downtown Washington, has ap-
plauded the plan for the way in
which it has included and provided
for business needs.

And as early as June 17, the
**Committee of 100 on the Federal
City** endorsed the Plan and

commended the Council for Pennsylvania Avenue for its skill in drawing it up.

The Committee's action came after **Cloethiel Smith,** a member of the Pennsylvania Avenue Council, outlined the goals of the Council and its hopes for the plan to the Committee.

She said that the plan aimed at creating a broad avenue—not just for ceremonial functions every four years on inauguration day—"but for every day." She characterized it as a design which would make Pennsylvania Avenue "a truly living comprehensive part of the city."

On June 24, 1964, on behalf of the Committee of 100 and in keeping with a resolution which it had adopted, **Rear Admiral Neill Phillips,** USN (ret.), the Committee's Chairman, wrote **President Johnson** with a concrete proposal for action:

"It is our understanding," said Admiral Phillips, "that the Council on Pennsylvania Avenue is not a continuing body; that, having finished its assignment of producing a plan, it now has become inactive. It, therefore, is essential that a Commission be appointed to take up where the Council has left off. We believe that this is a task of such magnitude as to warrant a full time Commission devoted solely to this assignment, though close liaison should be maintained with the National Capital Planning Commission and the Fine Arts Commission.

"We now urgently recommend that the President at the earliest practicable date appoint a Commission or executive body with the necessary force and authority to implement the Plan, to get it started, and to follow it through to completion."

As thirty years of planning, debating, and honest-sweat construction reached its climax this August, Washington participated hopefully in what has been promised as some amelioration of its frustrating traffic situation.

The completed Capital Beltway, reflecting the traditional proposals by highway engineers for bypasses around crowded American cities, became a reality on August 17, 1964, when the Washington area cut the ribbon on the last 25-mile section of the largest single public works project in its history.

The $189-million 65-mile-long highway now sweeps around major suburban cities and counties of the Washington area and encircles the District of Columbia.

Designed to move long-distance traffic around the Capital City and ease the plight of commuters, it has been calculated that the four and six-lane super-highway will save the average commuter about 10 minutes per trip—and untold wear and tear on already jangled nerves.

C. W. Puffenbarger, a staff writer for the *Washington Evening Star,* reports that it saves him both and "has virtually eliminated the nuisance of the more than three-dozen stop lights the old route included."

A high speed highway built for a high speed age, the Beltway has 38 major exits, four of which will not be open for periods ranging from several months to several years.

The exits are the vital points on the Beltway. It is in their vicinity that suburban developers are already locating huge industrial parks and that shopping centers are being developed. Regional planners say that in years to come suburban development will center more and more around the Beltway's 38 major exits.

Hailed as a triumph in planning and engineering, the highway makes Washington, along with Boston and Baltimore, the only cities the Bureau of Public Roads lists as true beltway cities.

The concept of the beltway was introduced to Washington in a one-sentence reference in the 1950 "Comprehensive Plan" for Washington, drawn up by the **National Capital Park and Planning Commission.** The nationally known planning firm of **Harland Bartholomew & Associates** participated in drawing up this plan.

It is reported that one of the most helpful things to highway officials during the years that the Beltway moved forward to completion was the way that official planners, both in Maryland and Virginia, kept subdivision development away from the right-of-way.

At this stage, planners are turning a critical eye on the profound effect the Beltway is having on the business and industrial development of the Washington area. While admittedly a spur to the development of outer suburbia, the question is whether it can also become a noose to strangle down-town Washington. There is a growing conviction that this need not be if a way can be found to build a better central city

with improved transportation facilities to and within it.

Meanwhile, the Maryland State Roads Commission is starting to study changes in land use and property values in areas near the Beltway and is conducting interviews in shopping centers to determine changed traffic patterns. A similar study, to be made by the University of Virginia over the next several years, will evaluate the change in property values, shifts in population density, and changes in land use from residential to commercial near the Beltway.

What effect the Beltway will have on the recreational activities of Washington area residents has yet to be determined, but for the many who have questioned whether a trip to the beach was worth the frustration and exasperation of getting in and out of Washington, the Beltway will likely be a boon. Some areas have already developed extensive recreation facilities in expectation of the beltway's completion and numerous sight-seeing attractions will be more readily available.

And just the prospect that the invigorating benefits of sea and mountain air will become more readily available to residents of the National Capital area has afforded millions an uncustomary lift in sweltering summer days this year.

The National Park Service has asked Congress for $540,000 to acquire additional land opposite Mount Vernon as a step toward preserving the Washington shrine's scenic overlook. The item was embodied in a supplemental appropriations request by the Departmentof the Interior.

★　　★　　★

The Agriculture Administration Building is the subject of Historical Study No. 2 in the series now being published by the **General Services Administration.**

According to **Bernard L. Boutin,** Administrator of General Services, who has written the publication's Foreword, "The recognized need for preserving Federal buildings that enrich the Nation's heritage requires knowledge and understanding of their roles in the corridors of history. These studies are an essential step in this direction."

The Agriculture Administration Building is located between 12th and 14th Streets at Independence Avenue, S.W., on the Mall. According to the publication, it was constructed between 1904 and 1930 at a cost of $3,369,083.

Most residents of the Washington area are familiar with the twin memorial archways connecting the Administration Building with the South Building which the publication characterizes as "one of the outstanding engineering aspects."

The historical study points out that the strong Greek influence evident in the Mall facade identifies the building with the Classic trend so pronounced in the architecture of the Federal Triangle.

The building materials are marble, brick, concrete and steel. The framing of the wings is reinforced concrete—one of the first examples of its use for Government buildings. White Georgia marble is the facing on all exteriors of the newer section and the principal exteriors of the wings, especially those visible from the Mall, are faced with Vermont marble.

★　　★　　★

The long-needed administration and research building at the 415-acre National Arboretum was dedicated last spring in a service attended by some 300 horticulturally oriented guests from throughout the United States and from several foreign lands.

The $1,300,000 Arboretum headquarters, located at 28th and M Streets, N.E., Washington, D. C., is built in a contemporary style in accordance with the restrained design of **Deigert & Yerkes Associates.** Its two-story rear wing houses the Arboretum's famous 400,000-specimen herbarium reference collections which are used in plant research studies.

★　　★　　★

Heritage

"The ice-covered earth, the rain forests, the small areas of fruitful soil, the hardy men whose women came with them into untold hardships because there was love between them!

"All they had was character. All they did was work. All they wanted was self-respect. The sum of these three traits became America.

"They built their own churches, their own town halls, their own schools with their own hands."

—Frances Bolton, U. S. Congresswoman from Ohio, at opening ceremonies of the Hall of Historic Americans, Smithsonian Institution, 1964.

28

Proposed Cape Lookout National Seashore. The Cape's present Lighthouse beamed its first light two years before the Civil War broke out.

Photo by Bob Simpson

Courtesy, National Park Service, U. S. Department of the Interior

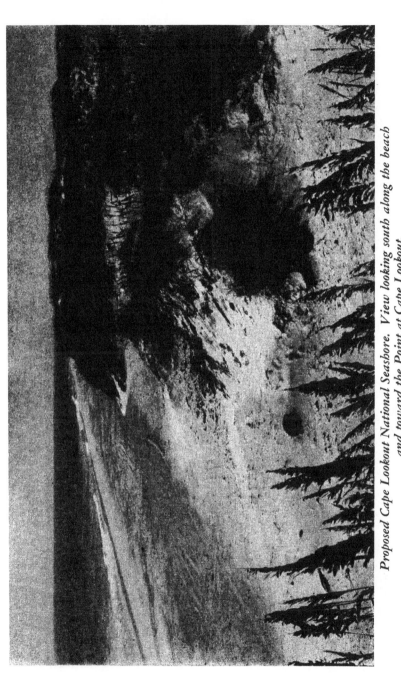

Proposed Cape Lookout National Seashore. View looking south along the beach and toward the Point at Cape Lookout.

Photo by Bob Simpson

Courtesy, National Park Service, U. S. Department of the Interior

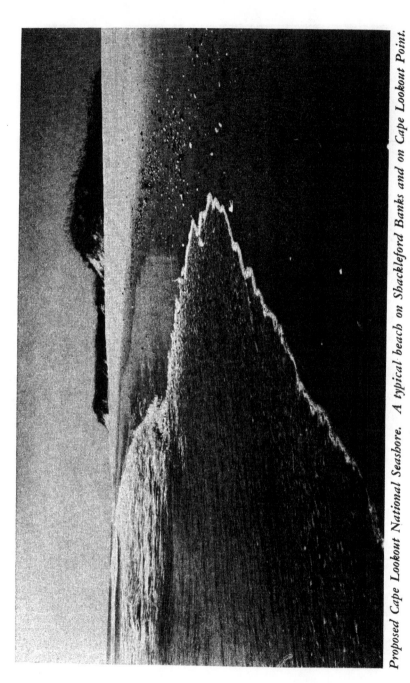

Proposed Cape Lookout National Seashore. A typical beach on Shackleford Banks and on Cape Lookout Point.

Photo by Bob Simpson

Courtesy, National Park Service, U. S. Department of the Interior

Cape Lookout National Seashore
—A Proposal

This is the eighth in the series of articles on proposed National Park Service projects, prepared by the Park Service at our request.

Some day Cape Lookout may be as well-known a place name on North Carolina's Outer Banks as Cape Hatteras is today. It appears that the State of North Carolina—the State in the nation with longest experience in such matters—believes National Seashores are a good thing. Having given the American people their first—Cape Hatteras—North Carolina is well on its way toward presenting us with a second—Cape Lookout National Seashore.

If, through our duly elected representatives in Washington, the people accept this second gift, the new National Seashore ". . . shall comprise the lands and adjoining marshlands and waters on the outer banks of Carteret County, North Carolina, between Ocracoke Inlet and Beaufort Inlet . . ." So reads H.R. 8855, the bill that Congressman David N. Henderson has introduced in the House of Representatives. Jointly, Senators Sam Ervin, Jr. and B. Everett Jordan have introduced an identical Senate bill.

Similar in some ways to the existing string of offshore islands that comprise Cape Hatteras National Seashore, the island group that would make up this new unit of the National Park System differs in several ways. Perhaps the most obvious difference is that these southerly "outer banks" are not quite as far out as their counterparts to the north, and therefore offer less protection to the mainland. While the Cape Hatteras group lies offshore about 20 miles on the average, Core and Shackleford Banks are only about two or three miles from the mainland.

Increasingly vulnerable to the battering of mountainous waves and hurricane winds, the Outer Banks for years have been losing their protective powers, primarily because man has interfered with the balance of nature. If the vegetational cover had not been disturbed by man's influences, the urgent need for stabilization would not be so critical today. For at least 150 years, tree cutting on Shackleford Banks and grazing livestock on the Core strand have altered the natural conditions. A gradual decrease in the amount of vegetative cover has made the long strand of sand islands more vulnerable to the assault of wind and wave; each storm leaves the barrier a little less resistant to the next.

For years the State studied the problems of restoring and preserving the outer banks of Carteret County, but found it difficult to work out an effective program with private property owners. Governor Terry Sanford, therefore, recommended that the State acquire all of the outer banks from Ocracoke Inlet to Cape Lookout and as much of Shackleford Banks as necessary to stabilize Barden Inlet. Also recommended was a long-range plan to restore and preserve the area. North Carolina's General Assembly in 1959 appropriated $600,000 to carry out these recommendations—$400,000 for land and $200,000 for surveys, studies, and a detailed restoration and preservation plan.

The disastrous Ash Wednesday storm of 1962 focused nationwide attention on the inestimable loss of the country's already limited seashore recreation resource. This led to discussions on a plan to preserve the North Carolina seacoast, which were participated in by Governor Sanford, Secretary of the Interior Stewart L. Udall, Conrad L. Wirth, then Director of the National Park Service, his National Park Service staff, and civic leaders in the State. Studies by the State and by the U.S. Corps of Engineers, already underway, revealed that rehabilitation, development, protection, and administration of the area as a public seashore was a project of such magnitude as to be beyond the State's ability to undertake.

By the time it was decided to propose a new National Seashore, the State had purchased 80% of the needed land. This alone increased the likelihood of the bill's approval and, perhaps, makes the proffered gift of this publicly owned playground more acceptable than would be the case if the entire 15,800 acres had to be bought with Federal funds. Most of the land as the bill prescribes, ". . . may be acquired by the Secretary of the Interior only through donation . . ." The Secretary, however, ". . . may purchase lands and marshes of Shackleford Banks—about 2,000 acres."

There you have the background and a brief account of the cost of giving. Now we shall examine the gift itself and have a quick look at the proposed Cape Lookout Na-

tional Seashore—to help decide the cost of accepting.

Use trends and traffic patterns of the proposed Cape Lookout National Seashore are expected to differ from those of Cape Hatteras. These are offshore, or "sea islands." This fact of somewhat complicated accessibility, coupled with the distance from Cape Hatteras to the north, is among the reasons for the proposal to make Cape Lookout a separately managed unit of the National Park System. Eventually a bridge may connect the mainland with Shackleford Banks. But unlike Cape Hatteras, no highway will span the length of the Core Banks islands and no bridges will connect them to the mainland.

The only automobiles that can "navigate" these sand stretches are jeeps with four-wheel drive, called "beach buggies." For them, special "buggy" routes and use areas will be planned, in order to preserve, as much as possible, Core Banks' wilderness qualities. Since no bridges are planned, these little vehicles, usually owned by surf fishermen, will come and go between Core Banks and the mainland via ferry boat.

In fact, all but the Shackleford Banks visitors must come by boat, and since the mainland is closer, visitors will likely be coming across Core Sound *via* all the adjacent mainland communities—Morehead City, Beaufort, Harkers Islands, Marshallberg, Otway, Davis, Stacy, Sealevel, and Atlantic. Such a pattern, of course, would spread visitor use more evenly.

If statistics for Cape Hatteras are a dependable gauge, a steady increase

34

in the number of visits to the new Seashore can be expected. In 1955, the count for Hatteras was 264,000. Eight years later, in 1963, the National Seashore counted 873,300 visits. The number may exceed the million mark in 1964.

A ferry line operated by the State of North Carolina would take visitors from the historic old town of Beaufort to the western end of Shackleford Banks. Enroute to their vacation in the sun at Cape Lookout, visitors would enjoy the old buildings of Beaufort. This beautiful old (1709) town is proud of its claim to some of North Carolina's most important historic architecture.

Once on the island, tourists would be encouraged to go first to a Visitor Center for orientation and general information on the National Seashore. This, the Service's main interpretive center, is where visitors would learn something of the history and natural values of the region. Here, too, the visitor would get information about a multitude of seashore recreation opportunities that await him.

From Cape Lookout, itself—the southernmost tip of the proposed new National Seashore — to the northernmost land area of Portsmouth Island, 12 developed centers are included as part of the Service's tentative plans to accommodate a variety of recreational pursuits— swimming, boating, camping, picnicking, hiking, waterfowl hunting, beachcombing, birdwatching and other nature study activities. Six major centers of activity are envisioned for Shackleford Banks. These include two picnic areas; a

causeway and visitor center at the ferry landing; two swimming beaches—one on the sound side, the other on the ocean; and two campgrounds. Core Banks will have 4 campgrounds, 3 camping and fishing stores, 2 picnic areas, 2 swimming beaches, 2 interpretive centers, 2 marinas and 3 tie-up docks and boat landing areas.

By the time the first facilities are ready for visitors to Shackleford Banks, the National Park Service very likely will have started its program of restoration for the whole area. Being one of the few long stretches of undeveloped ocean beaches left in the entire Eastern Seaboard of the United States, its restoration, protection, and preservation is given top priority by the Service.

While the first visitors are enjoying the new facilities on Shackleford Banks, large dredges may have begun their enormous task of erosion control on Core Banks to the north. National Park Service officials say they will concentrate first efforts on dune construction, beach restoration, and planting.

The backbone of the National Park Service restoration plan is to build dunes by using materials from a boat channel to be dredged through the shallow marshlands on the Sound side of the islands from Barden Inlet to Portsmouth. This plan has a three-fold purpose. It provides: 1) vitally needed materials for dune construction; 2) the boat channel (a recreation bonus); and 3) and most important of all, well planted and protected dunes which will reverse the trend of the outer banks' mounting vulnerability to total destruction by storm.

Such loss would be extremely detrimental to the Carolina mainland. If there were no barrier islands, the mainland would have to withstand the full brunt of raging storms. "Without these banks," one North Carolinian said, "we might be surf fishing in Wilson." Destruction of the outer banks themselves, of course, would be a tremendous loss of vital concern both to the State and to the Nation. A seashore of outstanding intrinsic beauty and high recreation potential so badly needed by America's exploding population would be lost.

Though not especially significant nationally, the area's history is nonetheless colorful. Before this island string was settled, Coree Indians hunted on the long barrier strip and gave Core Banks its name. Traces of their past are now all but gone from the shifting sands.

"Blackbeard," the pirate, operated in these waters and for a long time prevented colonists from moving onto the islands. But after 1718 the island chain opened to settlement. That was the year Lt. Robert Maynard's Expeditionary force slew the famous bearded pirate aboard his own ship, *Adventure*.

Among the first settlers to come were whalers who camped along the beaches, lived in huts, and fished for mullet during the off-season. Local fishermen sometimes were joined by New England whalers who used Lookout Bight as a seasonal base for their operations.

Portsmouth, established by order of the North Carolina Assembly as a "Maratime Town," was created especially to protect the lower banks from Spanish privateers. This was the first and, for many years, the largest town on the Outer Banks. As long as heavy draught cargo vessels moved through Ocracoke Inlet, the town thrived. But when two new inlets—Hatteras and Oregon—opened to the north, most of the people left, and, by the turn of the century, Portsmouth residents were either piloting the few remaining ships that passed through their inlet, or milling corn for a living. "Bankers" traded salted mullets for corn to be ground in their windmills. John Gray Blount and John Wallace in the 1790's built what was probably the first corn mill at Portsmouth.

The Cape's first light house was finished in 1812 and replaced in 1859 by the one now standing. This 150-foot-high structure beamed its first light two years before the Civil War broke out and Confederate raiders damaged it during the war. Today the lighthouse still sends a beacon out across the Atlantic.

Toward the end of the 19th century, two small communities, Wades Hammock and Diamond City, sprouted and died on Shackleford Banks; their residents were driven off by the tremendous hurricane of 1899. Now there's no trace of Diamond City. Only old graveyards still remain. Across Barden Inlet, Cape Lookout Lighthouse, painted in huge black and white diamonds, stands virtually alone.

Today, Shackleford and Core Banks are used primarily for sports fishing, waterfowl hunting, and vacationing; summer vacationists concentrate on Shackleford Banks and around Lookout Bight.

(Continued on page 56)

36

State Park Notes

Pennsylvania. Governor Scranton has signed into Pennsylvania law enabling legislation for carrying out the state's $70-million recreation and conservation program, known as "Project 70."

The new legislation implements a state constitutional amendment authorizing a $70-million bond issue for acquisition of land for parks and recreation.

Of the total authorized, $40 million has been earmarked for the purchase of state park lands; $20 million as matching grants for the development of local parks; and $10 million for new hunting and fishing areas. Land acquisition under the program is scheduled to be completed in 1970.

Indiana. *"Outdoor Indiana,"* an attractive publication of the Indiana Department of Conservation, reflects the spirit which has made the Hoosier State eighth in the Nation in camper day use in the park system.

In the May, 1964 issue, Donald E. Foltz, Director of the Conservation Department, says that the number of campsites has increased from 920 in 1961 to 1,911 in 1963. The number of campground users has increased from 452,577 to 622,376 in the same period.

Director Foltz reports a steady increase of trailers in camp use with an increase of seven percent in 1963 over the previous year. "There has not been a single year that tent camping has not increased," says Mr. Foltz, "but trailer camping is increasing more rapidly and I think calendar year 1964 will show more trailers than tent campers in Indiana State Parks."

Indiana is fortunate in that its park system is one of the very early ones in the country, and the state has been able "to acquire some of the choice natural areas before their primitive beauty was destroyed by too many man-made improvements."

For the lucky residents of the state, "a vacation does not have to lie a thousand miles down some interstate highway," says *Outdoor Indiana*, "since practically every Hoosier lives within about an hour's drive of a state park."

Iowa. As Iowa added up the score for 1963 and concluded that park attendance was up one million over the previous year, Jack Kirstein, writing in a recent issue of the *Iowa Conservationist* observed:

"You can be a happier hiker this year in Iowa's state parks because of a comprehensive program of building new foot-trails and re-working

37

existing ones. The State Conservation Commission has added a number of new bridges, many miles of new trails, and countless loads of gravel, steps and handrails to the facilities of the individual parks."

For example, the strange, mysterious beauty of a walk through Wild-Cat Den State Park has been made available to even the most inexperienced hiker by the addition of new steps and bridges.

At Pikes Peak, a new trail is now being added to make it easier to travel from Bridal Falls to the area up around the Indian Mounds. A trail along the Mississippi river with high overlooks provides breath-taking views of this mighty waterway.

Two County Conservation Boards in Iowa have assumed ownership of former State Parks. Silver Lake State Park, long popular for picnicking and fishing, has become the responsibility of the Delaware County Conservation Board and the Palo Alto County Conservation Board is the new owner of Lost Island State Park, famous for its bullhead fishing.

South Carolina. The nationwide interest in family camping is reflected in South Carolina state parks, according to a recent report from the State Commission of Forestry.

Family camping at South Carolina state parks has shown an increase of more than 400 percent in the past six years. Sixteen state parks and one wayside park have designated areas for family camping with developed facilities such as water and electric connections, tables, latrines and garbage collection.

Since inauguration of South Carolina's system of state parks, back in 1934, family cabins have also been popular with vacationing South Carolinians. Nine of the state parks have family cabins, all equipped with electric lights, electric stoves, electric refrigerators, and bathrooms with running water.

West Virginia. Over three million people visited West Virginia State Parks, Monuments and Forests from July 1, 1963 to June 30, 1964, according to Warden M. Lane, State Director of Natural Resources. Attendance, which has shown a steady increase over the past 10 years, was up 320,162 over the previous year. But, says Kermit McKeever, Parks and Recreation Chief, the Mountain State can accommodate even more visitors.

Kansas. Plans for development of seven new state parks and for new facilities at 12 parks are being processed by the Kansas Park and Resources Authority.

Land for the new parks will be secured from either the State Forestry, Fish and Game Commission, the U. S. Bureau of Reclamation or the U. S. Army Corps of Engineers.

According to Kansas Park and Resources Authority Chairman, C. V. Bargeman, the seven new parks would materially move Kansas ahead of its park program. The Authority plans to build mushroom picnic shelters at all the parks plus shower-latrine buildings, campsites, trailer parks, boat ramps, swimming beaches and bathhouses.

Texas. The accent is on accessibility for the more than fifty State Parks in Texas which values its wealth of history among its greatest heritages.

One could drive over 5,000 miles from state park to state park in Texas and still not see them all, according to a recent brochure from the Parks and Wildlife Department. But to facilitate the venture, more than 1,000 roadside parks have been constructed between the state parks by the Texas Highway Department. These clean rest-stops, offer the traveler a pleasant place to pull over and rest awhile.

Preserved through the Texas State Parks system are such historical events as the Siege of the Alamo, the Battle of San Jacinto, the Signing of the Texas Declaration of Independence from Mexico and the long era of Spanish mission activity.

Nevada. A park at Lake Tahoe? Ever since it was first observed by John C. Fremont in 1844, men have talked about preserving this scenic jewel. Mark Twain called it "the fairest picture the whole earth affords." Thirty years ago a few Nevada people proposed such a park and recent action of the Nevada Legislature seems to bring the prospect very near to certainty.

A statute enacted by the 1964 special session of the Nevada Legislature authorizes the state to acquire lands by exchange, lease, gift, grant or purchase within the park boundaries set forth.

For, says the Nevada Division of State Parks, "Tahoe is the largest of all the lovely high lakes caught in the Sierra Nevada range. This was the lake that startled and amazed the explorers after months spent crossing the American desert. For them it lay unbelievably high, clear and beautiful in that last, upthrust barrier of the transcontinental journey."

Much of the lake basin is already developed with hotels, resorts, and homes. Clusters of population lie near, both in California and Nevada. But on the northeast shore there still exists a forested area perhaps as natural as it was when Fremont first looked.

"Here the deer, the mountain beaver and bobcat follow their mountain trails; the grosbeak, tanager and water ouzel nest and feed; and the streams are lairs for trout. Here grow undisturbed the pines and cedars, the manzanita and the squaw-carpet."

Favorably located near the California-Nevada boundary in the High Sierra, the park, it is believed, would fill a recreational need for California's increasing millions and for Americans coming from throughout the country.

Lands within the described park boundary exceed 13,500 acres, The 1963 general session of the Nevada Legislature authorized the purchase of 5,120 acres. The remaining private lands to be acquired total 8,245 acres, including 7½ miles of shoreline. Of nine individual ownerships, seven parcels vary from 2½ to 200 acres in size. The largest land owners have indicated willingness to sell to the state for park purposes and several of the smaller land owners have likewise concurred.

To finance the land acquisition, a state park and outdoor recreation acquisition and development fund has been established. A sum of $1,500,000 to be expended for the acquisition of lands has been appropriated to the fund by the Legislature.

Monies placed in the fund may also be gifts and grants from individuals, corporations, foundations, associations or trusts, and financial assistance from the federal government.

According to Nevada's Governor Grant Sawyer, "The hope is that private funds will be made available to augment appropriated money, so that the entire area can be purchased."

Tennessee. Self-guided nature trails, nature walks and talks, and the guidance of full-time ranger naturalists for each park—these are the ingredients of an interesting nature interpretation program in Tennessee State Parks.

Mack S. Prichard, one of the Parks Naturalists, interprets the unique contribution of the naturalist to richer park enjoyment:

"The dual responsibility to Nature and man forces the Naturalist to see things from a different perspective than most of us. He knows variety is Nature's strength and best defense against parasitism. He bridges our specialized society by re-lating us to the balance and wholeness of the wilderness world.

"He values our past heritage as the only position from which we may comprehend the future. Often, he must slow us down and show us the fine points, those little things which we have been passing by. "He must remember the lines:

Looking upward, looking downward,
Looking all around;
Seeing something, seeing nothing,
What is to be found?

There is something in that nothing
That you will not see
Lest your eyes are used to looking,
Lest your mind is trained to see . . .

and keep training the minds of park visitors to really see with understanding.

"The nature interpreter would say that dead and fallen trees have a special loveliness as they rot back into Mother Earth and nourish chipmunks, insects, mushrooms and new seedlings. And that man cannot fight for long against Nature but only with Nature.

"Finally, the naturalist's interpretation must affirm that Nature's way is God's manifestation here on earth and that any deepening in nature wisdom strikes the spiritual fiber in all of us."

Under certain conditions, Blue Mountain in Stone County, Arkansas, roars. When the weather turns cold suddenly, the mountain makes noises like the singing of hundreds of telephone wires in a stiff breeze in cold weather.

Zoning Round Table

Conducted by FLAVEL SHURTLEFF, Marshfield Hills, Mass.

PRINCIPLES AND PRECEDENTS IN ZONING CASES

The statement is often made in planning reports and in briefs of lawyers that, in the determination of the rights of parties in zoning cases, there are few helpful principles of interpretation because the nature of the police power defies fixed boundaries. Consequently, each zoning case must be decided on its own facts.

This statement is sound enough, but must be accepted with some limitations. It is well illustrated by the decisions which involve discrimination or spot zoning. Claims of spot zoning are usual in cases where a change in zoning boundaries is in issue, whether that change covers an area as small as a lot or as large as a city block. Trial court judges with all the arguments on each side before them have as often been overruled as supported by the upper court on appeal. Lawyers have been heard to say, "Does any one know what spot zoning is?" An area of several acres in Manchester, Connecticut, which had been changed from residence to business was declared a spot zone because it "invaded" an area zoned for residence,* but on very similar facts the Rhode Island Supreme Court could find "no island" of discrimination and upheld a change from residence to business.**

*Miller vs. Town Planning Commission, 142 Conn. 265.
**Hadley et al vs. Harold Realty Co. et al, decided March '64 and not yet reported.

Although it is difficult to reconcile decisions in spot zoning cases or even to find conformance to a pattern, the courts in several jurisdictions have made rulings which may not amount to principles of interpretation, but, nevertheless, have value as guides to local legislative agencies and to boards of appeal which are called on often to decide close cases. There is, for instance, a presumption of validity in the adoption of a change in zoning boundaries, but a clearly arbitrary and preferential change will be struck down. Schertzer vs. City of Somerville*, a recently decided Massachusetts case, has an excellent discussion of this well established ruling. Where the changed area 1) adjoins an existing area of the same zoning classification or 2) is separated only by a cross street therefrom, or 3) is the third or fourth corner at an intersection containing at least two corners zoned like the changed area, courts will probably support the change on the theory that the legislative action is at least debatable, and cannot be ruled arbitrary or preferential.

The Massachusetts Supreme Court has gone even further toward establishing a legal precedent in its rulings on variances. In one of the earliest zoning decisions (1926), the Court said: "The power of authorizing variation is designed to be sparingly exercised. It is only in rare instances and under exceptional circumstances that relaxations of the

*Mass. Adv. Sheets 1963 P. 555.

41

general restrictions ought to be permitted."

The Court has frequently expressed its opposition to what may be a preference, and, in several late cases, has insisted that all three statutory requirements must be present before a variance can be allowed. If there is a *substantial* hardship peculiar to the property, it must also be established that there will be no substantial detriment to the public welfare and no derogation from the purpose of the law.

Helpful rulings which have been used as precedents are also found in decisions involving non-conforming use:

1) There must be *actual use*. Even where a building was completed before the adoption of a zoning ordinance but there was no evidence of its use, non-conformity was not established.

2) Increase in business volume is not a violation of a non-conforming use, especially where there is no enlargement of the building.

3) The character of the use cannot be changed by expansion. This is a well established rule although peculiar local zoning ordinance provisions result in apparently inconsistent decisions.

4) Loss of a non-conforming exemption by abandonment or cessation is primarily a question of intent, but long disuse may be shown as evidence of intent.

In many jurisdictions, rulings on specific uses are precedents which have been consistently followed:

1) Funeral homes are commercial uses which are properly excluded from residence zones.

2) A real estate broker is not practising a profession in spite of some professional aspects of his business.

3) The distinction between a farm and the commercial use of land for hog or poultry raising is clearly made in several states, and in Massachusetts, at least, a greyhound racing stable is neither an agricultural use nor a use accessory to a farm.*

The above citations do not exhaust the list of zoning categories where principles of interpretation have been established or rulings have been followed as precedents. This method of setting some bounds on the police power is to be preferred to fixing the bounds by statute, like the limit on living space requirements in a single family house fixed in Massachusetts at no greater than 768 square feet.

*Miodinszemski *vs.* Sangus, 337 Mass., 140 (1958).

Water Recreation
In Arkansas

Arkansas contains 13 large, man-made reservoirs, numerous state, city and private lakes and six major rivers. Beaver Reservoir, the latest in a chain of White River lakes constructed in Arkansas by the Corps of Engineers, is filling rapidly. The system of waterways furnishes a varied source of water sports fun, including fishing, SCUBA diving, cruising and water skiing.

Seminars, Conferences and University Notes

Design. "Architects and city planners should recognize the fact that the automobile is a permanent part of the American environment, and should design the cityscape to accommodate the auto."

This was the position taken by Paul Rudolph, New Haven architect and chairman of the department of architecture at Yale University before the fourteenth annual International Design Conference held in June in Aspen, Colorado.

Mr. Rudolph was one of 23 internationally distinguished speakers from the fields of design, architecture, visual communication and related areas who discussed current design directions and dilemmas before the conference which was attended by approximately 650 design and business executives from 43 states and several foreign countries.

"The automobile is the greatest problem to American cities, but it also offers the greatest organizing element for the city of the future," said Mr. Rudolph. "The automobile should certainly be kept out of some areas of the city; and other areas should be redesigned so that they are consistent with the existence of the automobile. City planners still know very little about what to do about city streets, and how to use them to make cities more beautiful and more inhabitable."

Ivan Chermayeff, partner, Chermayeff & Geismar, New York, sought to rouse the conference to a recognition of the underlying difficulty in the broad field of design. Too many consumers, clients and designers today don't care very much about very much, he said. "The joy and pleasure of doing a good job for its own sake has not been discovered by enough people— consumers, clients and designers. This satisfaction factor has disappeared from this country and should be brought back."

And Robin Boyd, Australian architect, said that modern architecture is still threatening to make the whole world "a tired sort of world's fair." But conceded Mr. Boyd: Architecture "has come back at last from window dressing and ornamentation to the art of controlling space— not merely opening up space, or hiding a piece of it behind a space divider, or softening the break between indoors and outdoors, but a wholehearted control of levels, volumes, and the views within and beyond."

Cornell Conference. A course in Environmental Health Planning and one in Data Processing were included in the one-week 1964 Summer Institute in City and Regional Planning offered by Cornell University.

In 1963, a Training Program in Environmental Health Planning was established in the Department of City and Regional Planning at Cornell with the support of the U. S. Public Health Service. The 1964 summer course was offered in conjunction with that program.

It was offered in the belief that "professional city planners could play a vital role in alleviating the environmental health problems of our cities . . . As the country has become more urbanized and industrialized, a new environment characterized by a new set of health problems has emerged as the normal habitation of most of our population. At present, with almost 80 percent of the population living in or near urban centers concentrated on a small percentage of our land, the health problems of the urban environment become a matter of major concern."

Arctic Study. An Ohio State University professor of architecture who specializes in urban planning went off on a fact-finding trip this summer to one of the least-urbanized areas in the world—arctic and sub-arctic Canada.

Professor Laurence Gerckens mapped out plans to visit two isolated Canadian pioneer communities in July to study life and the physical environment there.

The 30-year-old New York-born architect planned to study conditions in Yellowknife, on the Great Slave Lake, and to spend a week in the tiny community of Inuvik, 150 miles north of the Arctic Circle, which was constructed by the Canadian government as an experiment in creating communities in the arctic wasteland.

Canadian government workers and their wives, plus a post of the Northwest Mounted Police, live clustered together in the hostile climate of Inuvik where the mean temperature hovers around 16 degrees above zero.

On the basis of his recorded data, Mr. Gerckens hopes to determine if so-called "frigid-region settlements" are simply extensions and modifica-

tions of communities in moderate temperature zones, or are built with severe weather conditions taken into account and effectively dealt with.

The research was undertaken in the belief that it may take a page from the book of the Eskimo way of life, perhaps pointing to the desirability of domed structures to minimize the amount of heat-emitting surface area per cubic foot of enclosed space and complete community mobility instead of conventional western housing.

Other towns under study in the project are the sub-arctic Canadian communities of Thompson, Manitoba, and Uranium City, Saskatchewan; and Barrow, Alaska. Ranging in population from 500 to 3,500, most of these communities were constructed around mines and are based on mine production.

Water Resources Research. U. S. Congressman Olin E. Teague, of Texas, has paid tribute to Texas A. & M. University, located at College Station, Texas, as a leader in water research and conservation.

The Water Research and Information Center at Texas A. & M. has recently been re-named the Water Resources Institute and the organization will place greater emphasis on research and education in water resources on a multi-disciplinary basis.

A water advisory council was first organized at Texas A. & M. in 1952 and eight water-for-Texas conferences have been held on the campus with published proceedings available the country over. A water and hydrology collection, which includes many publications not available elsewhere in the country, is housed in the Texas Professional Engineers Library located on the Texas A. & M. University campus.

At present, over 100 Texas Agricultural Experiment Station research projects deal either directly or indirectly with water and, in the past four years, over 100 graduate theses having some bearing on hydrology have been completed at Texas A. & M. University.

Mellon Fellowships. Fellowships in city planning and urban renewal are to be established in graduate schools of ten universities in the United States through a $1,000,000 grant of the Richard King Mellon Charitable Trusts.

Each school will receive $100,000, payable over a five-year period in annual installments of $20,000. Half of this amount is to be granted by the school as fellowship aid to one or more Mellon Fellows in city planning or urban renewal. The other half will be allocated to the schools for faculty salaries to support the fellowship programs.

The fellowships are designed to improve the professional capabilities of men and women now involved in city planning, urban renewal, or closely related fields and to encourage a greater number of talented persons to achieve excellence in urban development.

In announcing its action, the Board of Trustees of the Richard King Mellon Charitable Trusts stated: "It is apparent that the relatively new but highly important professions of city planning and urban renewal are being neglected in comparison with other graduate fields. Many business organizations offer graduate fellowships in the areas of their interest, but there are relatively few sources of funds for scholarships and teaching posts in urban planning.

"As a result, it is difficult for graduate schools concerned with urban planning and urban affairs to attract exceptional students and to hold able, full-time faculty members."

The Trustees pointed out that the demand for men and women trained for these complex urban tasks is so great that the schools cannot begin to meet the need in an age when every progressive U. S. city must have a comprehensive development and renewal program.

"It is estimated, for example, that in the one field of city planning fewer than 250 men and women are graduated annually, and that these are fewer than one-half the number of top-flight openings. In urban renewal education, the number of graduates is but a trickle in relation to the annual requirements."

The ten universities, selected on the basis of need, demonstrated excellence, and geographical distribution, to receive the fellowship grants, are University of California, Berkeley, California; Georgia Institute of Technology, Atlanta, Georgia; Harvard University, Cambridge, Massachusetts; University of Illinois, Urbana, Illinois; Massachusetts Institute of Technology, Cambridge, Massachusetts; University of North Carolina, Chapel Hill, North Carolina; University of Pennsylvania, Philadelphia, Pennsylvania; University of Pittsburgh, Pittsburgh, Pennsylvania; Syracuse University, Syracuse, New York; and

45

University of Wisconsin, Madison, Wisconsin.

Richard King Mellon, donor of the Charitable Trusts, is Governor and President of T. Mellon & Sons, Pittsburgh, investment management firm. He has been active in Pittsburgh's post-war urban renewal and redevelopment program and continues as one of the original directors of ACTION, Inc., a national public service organization concerned with the physical environment of cities.

William Kinne Fellowships. Because a young architect was ever grateful for a traveling fellowship he received nearly 70 years ago, 36 Columbia University architecture students and graduates studied abroad last summer.

That is the largest number of William Kinne Fellows Memorial Fellowships and Scholarships awarded in one year since they were established eleven years ago by Mr. Fellows' widow. A total of $66,000 was awarded to the 36 graduate architects, planners and students, who studied in more than 30 countries on grants ranging from $1,500 to $2,700.

The awards were opened to foreign students and fourth-year students this year for the first time.

One young architect from Yonkers went to Europe to study the relationship between medieval towns and modern town planning. A young man from Durham, England, in turn, studied urban problems in the United States.

William Kinne Fellows was graduated from Columbia in 1894 and subsequently won the University's only traveling fellowship available then to graduates in architecture. He used the $1,200 grant to study in Europe and felt ever after that the experience had been invaluable to his growth as an architect. He died in 1948 after a distinguished career as head of his own architectural firm in Chicago and later as a partner in the Chicago firm of Hamilton, Fellows & Nedved.

His widow, the late Elizabeth Steele Fellows, established the traveling fellowships in his name at Columbia in 1953 with an endowment gift of $560,000. Later gifts by other members of the family have brought the total endowment to nearly $1,000,000.

Planning

"It has been said that planning 'is the orderly drawing together of all threads making the shape, color, and texture of a community.' It this be true, the far-flung activities of the Planning Office are among the brightest, strongest threads in the community fabric . . . Commitment to so many diverse problems—open spaces, industrial development, future highways, and regional planning—reveals the size and scope of planning in Baltimore County, and accentuates its twin roles of co-ordinator and catalyst for County growth and development."

—Progress & Program, Baltimore County Planning, Office of Planning and Zoning, Towson, Maryland, 1963.

(Continued from page 6)

some of them conceived without a comprehensive plan. They have none-the-less contributed, respectively, to the livability of each of the urban areas.

City planning is a humanistic matter. This in itself makes it hazardous. The human is one of the most variable and unpredictable components of the earth. Add to these characteristics such complicating elements as a vast variety of vested interests which must be served and a diversity of viewpoints which must be satisfied. The outlook for successful planning sometimes becomes discouraging. Nevertheless, it would seem we have a choice to make between hoping to come up with a perfect plan, essentially an impossibility, or patching as we go, taking chances on committing errors. Somehow a judgment must be reached representing at least an average of the best thinking of planners and of the citizenry.

Drawing plans takes so much time that local economic and social conditions may have changed in important ways by the time they are completed after several years of investigations, surveys, and discussions. If, at this time, planners must begin all over to meet the new changes, obviously, putting a plan into work becomes an impossibility. The sequence of events, namely, planning, revising, planning again and revising, *ad infinitum*, can lead only to frustration.

Planning commissions need to take the public into their confidence more than they do. The occasional report to the public is not enough. The public should be urged to attend meetings. Neighborhood committees ought to be encouraged to give consideration to local problems and to make recommendations to the commission. Commissions themselves should initiate conferences with neighborhood representatives and, on more than a single occasion, hold general meetings to which all the residents of a neighborhood are invited.

The objective is not only the education of the "man on the street" with respect to planning in general but to provide understanding as to why the patching procedure is unavoidable and perhaps the only practicable procedure. Sight must not be lost of the fact that the average person, well educated or not, is not informed in the field of urbanistics. Not until he is enlightened in this field can he judge wisely in matters associated with planning.

Planning Commissions must reveal to the public their concern for the interests of all parts of the community even though they concentrate their attention momentarily upon only one neighborhood. They should act so carefully and with such discretion that they will win strong public support. Commissions, as matters stand now, have little more then advisory powers. But they can develop such public confidence that city Councils will hardly dare reject their recommendations.

To make certain our point of view is clear, we state once again that we stand for comprehensive

47

planning. Nevertheless, we emphasize the impracticability of putting all of a plan into work at once. The job can be done only on a piecemeal basis over a rather extended period of time. This fact demands flexibility in the comprehensive plan and also flexibility in the thinking of those who are charged with implementing it down through the years.

The end result, if there ever be an "end" to the carrying out of a plan. will of necessity, represent a sumtotal of patches, but hopefully, of patches that will harmonize, even if they do not always match, and will bring to the community a physical and functional environment in which living will be found to be eminently worthwhile.

Preserving The Past in Ocean Springs, Mississippi

The story of America today is not all told in the millions who have come to the great metropolitan centers. There are those who are building on the past in small towns across the country—and their record is vital and vibrant.

Such a record is being written in Ocean Springs, Mississippi—where D'Iberville in 1699 established the first permanent settlement in the entire Mississippi Valley.

As reported in the March-April issue of *Down South*, "Woody" Blossman, ex-marine of World War II and a graduate engineer turned businessman, landed at Ocean Springs in 1950 and saw in it a good place to live and build a business. He promptly took over a small butane gas company.

"That business," says *Down South*, grew and today Blossman Gas, Inc. numbers 250 employees with offices in Mississippi, Alabama, Georgia and North Carolina.

Recently, the historic half century old Gottsche grocery store, long empty and neglected on tree-lined Washington Avenue, was remodeled and reopened as the headquarters of the growing Blossman enterprises. The sturdy exterior walls, roof and floor of the building were carefully restored. Through the talents and efforts of a number of people, including Mr. and Mrs. Blossman, the Company's art consultant and distinguished American painter William Steene, and the architects Slaughter and Smith, an entirely "new" building emerged, retaining a touch of Ocean Springs' early French heritage and deftly combining with it the facilities of a strictly modern business office and corporation headquarters.

A large mural "Landing of D'Iberville" has been painted by artist William Steene expressly for this historic building.

Strictly Personal

William H. Whyte, nationally prominent author and conservationist, has been retained by the Connecticut Development Commission as an open space and recreation planning consultant.

Mr. Whyte will analyze changing public attitudes toward land conservation, analyze the structure and function of open space planning and define general responsibilities for open space acquisition and activity by various levels of government.

He is expected not only to provide general consultation on open spaces and recreational programs but to do original research in these fields as well.

◆

Secretary of the Interior Stewart L. Udall has announced the appointment of *Dr. Joe B. Frantz and Dr. Emil W. Haury* as members of the Advisory Board on National Parks, Historic Sites, Buildings and Monuments.

Dr. Frantz, Chairman of the Department of History at the University of Texas, is the author of a number of books and articles. He received the 1951 Texas Institute of Letters Award for his book, "Gail Borden, Dairyman To A Nation."

Dr. Haury, head of the Department of Anthropology, at the University of Arizona, has served as director of the Arizona State Museum at the University of Arizona since 1938, was a Guggenheim fellow in 1949-50 and has been chairman of the Division of Anthropology and Psychology, National Research Council, since 1960. In 1950, he was awarded the Viking Fund Medal for anthropology.

The Advisory Board, created by the Historic Sites Act of 1935, is composed of 11 non-salaried members appointed by the Secretary of the Interior for a six-year term. The two new appointees will fill vacancies created by the expired terms of Harold P. Fabian, Salt Lake City, Utah, and Dr. Edward B. Danson, Jr., Flaggstaff, Arizona.

Other members of the Board are: Dr. Stanley A. Cain, Chairman, on leave of absence from the Department of Conservation, University of Michigan, to Resources for the Future, Inc., Washington, D. C.; Vice Chairman, Dr. Wallace E. Stegner, Los Altos Hills, Calif.; Secretary, Mrs. Marian S. Dryfoos, Director of Special Activities, *The New York Times;* Dr. Melville B. Grosvenor, President, National Geographic Society, Washington, D. C.; Edward J. Meeman, Editor Emeritus, *Memphis Press-Scimitar,* Memphis, Tenn.; Sigurd F. Olson, Ely, Minn.; Paul L. Phillips, President, United Papermakers and Paperworkers, Albany, N. Y.; and Dr. Robert G. Sproul, President Emeritus, University of California, Berkeley.

◆

Dr. George Sprugel has been named chief scientist of the newly established division of natural science studies, headquartered in the National Park Service's Washington office.

Dr. Sprugel, who has been director of the environmental biology program at the National Science

Foundation since 1954, will be responsible for the overall formulation and staff direction of a Service-wide natural history study program.

Establishment of the new division which Dr. Sprugel will head, according to Park Service Director George B. Hartzog, Jr., is in line with the recommendations of the Leopold Wildlife Management Committee and the National Academy of Sciences.

These organizations have stressed in reports to Secretary of the Interior Stewart L. Udall that, if America is to retain what it has inherited in the National Park System, it can no longer merely "protect," it must effectively "manage" these areas, to offset the effects inflicted on them by man.

———————◇———————

Charles Goodwin Sauers, general superintendent of the Forest Preserve District of Cook County, Illinois, since May 15, 1929, has retired.

"Cap" Sauers, during his 35-year tenure as chief administrator of the District, piloted its growth and development until it comprises 50,000 acres within a county of more than five million people and has become world famous.

Prior to his association with the Cook County Preserve, "Cap" Sauers had served as assistant director of the department of conservation in Indiana where he planned several of its famous state parks.

Known from coast to coast, he enjoys universal respect for his integrity, courage and ability.

———————◇———————

Conrad L. Wirth, former director of the National Park Service and a member of the Board of Directors of the National Conference on State Parks, has been named by the 1964 Lilac Time Committee of Monroe County, New York, to receive its first National Award for Parks Service.

The award, an engraved silver tray provided by the *Rochester Democrat & Chronicle* and the *Rochester Times Union,* was presented by the *Honorable Frank Horton,* U. S. Representative to Congress from the 36th Congressional District of New York.

It is planned that the National Award for Parks Service will become a feature of the annual Lilac Time festivities in New York. The award will go, annually, to an individual who has made noteworthy contributions to the citizenry of America through efforts in the parks and recreation field.

———————◇———————

Granville B. Liles has been appointed superintendent of Rocky Mountain National Park, Colorado.

Mr. Liles, formerly assistant superintendent at Yosemite National Park, California, replaces *Allyn Hanks,* who is retiring after 36 years with the National Park Service.

———————◇———————

Donald Krouskop has been named manager of Indian Lake State Park, Logan County, Ohio, to fill the vacancy created when *Bob Hammond* recently moved up from that position to assistant chief of the Division of Parks and Recreation.

———————◇———————

50

Mrs. Rudd Brown has been appointed Chief of the Division of Recreation of the California Department of Parks and Recreation to succeed *Elmer Aldrich* who has resigned.

Mrs. Brown, wife of Cal Tech geochemist and author, Harrison Brown, has served on the California State Recreation Commission since 1960 and has resigned from that post to become Chief of the Recreation Division.

———◆———

Chairman George A. Garratt of the Connecticut State Park and Forest Commission has announced the appointment of *William F. Miller* of New Britain, Connecticut, as Superintendent of State Parks. Mr. Miller served as District Park Supervisor prior to his present appointment. He succeeds Elliot P. Bronson, of Winchester, who retired in June of this year after 40 years of state service.

———◆———

Karl T. Gilbert has been appointed superintendent of three National Park System units, located on North Carolina's famed outer banks: Cape Hatteras National Seashore, Wright Brothers National Memorial, and Fort Raleigh National Historic Site. He will be headquartered at Hatteras.

Mr. Gilbert, moves up from assistant superintendent of the Natchez Trace Parkway, replacing *James B. Meyers*, who was recently transferred to the National Park Service's regional office in San Francisco.

IN MEMORIAM

Frederick C. Sutro, former president of the New Jersey Parks and Recreation Association and a pioneer in the Green Acres development project in New Jersey, died recently at the age of 86 in Elizabeth, New Jersey.

Mr. Sutro's interest in the development of New Jersey parks and recreation facilities dated from 1912 when he was appointed a commissioner of the Palisades Interstate Park Commission by then Governor Woodrow Wilson.

In 1958, he was cited by the National Recreation Association for "outstanding service." One of his last efforts as "watchdog" for New Jersey's park development was his work on the successful Green Acres bond issue, an impressive undertaking providing state funds for the purchase of open land for parks.

Mr. Sutro was, for many years, a member of the National Conference on State Parks.

ℯℐ☺

THREE CALIFORNIA BEACH CITIES WITH TWO CHOICES

(Continued from page 10)

however, individuality in approach from each of your communities would be highly desirable. If each of your communities would have a "personality" of its own, each one would serve visitors who desire differing types of recreation and enjoyment and those who wish to have changing experiences from one visit to the other.

In developing and implementing revitalization efforts, it would be well to recognize that those which are undertaken by close cooperation between government and private enterprise have proven to be the most successful ones. There are certain things which only government can do, and they concern mostly public improvements and, in some cases, the assembly of land where this can be accomplished by the right of eminent domain.

There are other things which private enterprise can do better than government because, through their coordinated activities, a more interesting pattern of variety and versatility can be created.

The aim of the master plans for your cities should be to receive visitors with open arms but to channel the visitor stream through your cities in such manner as not to interfere with the privacy and restfulness of your own residences. A secondary aim should be to bring income to your citizens and to your municipalities. And a third aim should be to enrich the life of the visitors but also, to a very high degree, the life of your own residents, by the provision of better beaches, better parks and cultural and recreational facilities which can be financed because of the availability of the visitor stream, but which will be available to all citizens of your communities at all times.

I believe that, through a good master plan, which should not be imposed on you from above but which should be the result of joint efforts of citizens' groups and government, you can achieve the highly desirable goal of having your cake and eating it too.

You can create the income which is potentially possible because of the outstanding features which your cities possess, and you can utilize this income to improve magnificently your communities and their environmental qualities.

Our National Forests

There is at least one national forest within a day's drive of practically any point in the United States. . . . It would take a full lifetime of year 'round camping—more than 75 years—to visit all of the national forests and spend just a few days in each campground.

—From the remarks of Secretary of Agriculture Orville L. Freeman at the Food and Home Fair, Jefferson Auditorium, U. S. Department of Agriculture, Washington, D. C., April 15, 1964.

THE MARICOPA STORY: A STUDY IN SCIENTIFIC PARK PLANNING

(*Continued from page 4*)

Burroughs 205 computer at the University of Denver. The result was in the form of "percent participating" figures for all three density groups in 12 activities.

6) These "percent participating" figures were then multiplied times the population of each Region of Use to arrive at the total number of participants for any activity in any region in 1980.

7) Once the number of participants was determined, it was multiplied by the number of user days per participant for a three-month "peak" period of use. This resulted in a total number of "user days" for a three-month peak for all 12 activities. This in turn was reduced, by a rather complicated procedure, to the *number of persons participating in any one of 12 activities on a peak weekend day.*

8) These participants were then converted to "units" of campers, units of picnickers, units of horseback riders, etc. since many activities are engaged in groups rather than individuals.

9) At this point, the total amount of area, trail, road, water surface or whatever was computed, based on definite "design standards." The standards were created long *before* the actual need was determined—created to provide *quality* recreation rather than merely make the facilities exactly equal the need. Thus, for example, a region of use might *need* 5,000 picnic sites while the design standards would provide only 3,000 sites. In such a situation, the answer is *more land* and not the jamming in of more picnic units.

Fortunately, due to Maricopa County's farsightedness, the 93,000 acres of regional park will accommodate *most* of the facility needs while following design standards to the letter. The Parks and Recreation Commission is determined not to compromise this policy to any great degree.

Actual recreational facilities in the park system are divided into two categories: 1) "Standard Facilities" such as picnic areas, campgrounds, hiking-riding trails, roads, etc.; and 2) "Special Facilities" such as restoration of an old fort, excavating unusual archeological sites, and other attractions or recreational features unique to each park. Design standards are described for both types.

Perhaps one of the most unique features of the Maricopa County Regional Park System is the plan for a whole system of resident Audubon-type nature centers. Under such a system, closely coordinated with school authorities, every sixth grader in Maricopa County would have the opportunity *during the school year* to spend a week at one of four nature centers where he could learn of the outdoors in a great living laboratory. Part of the facility of such centers would be "multiple use" in that it would also serve as a nature interpretive center for the general public. However, the school youth portion would remain isolated and for students only. During such a week, students would attend lectures by professional naturalists, visit game enclosures, dissect plants or animals, study stars, etc. The result in many cases would be to stimulate an interest in nature that could well last a lifetime. The National Audubon Society has had success with similar programs on a less ambitious scale in other parts of the country.

While the Semi-Regional Parks (which function partly as regional parks and partly as urban parks) are considered in the master plan, there is not space to discuss them in detail. These parks comprise 10,752 acres and are a vital part of the overall Maricopa recreation picture.

The Maricopa County Regional Park System as proposed undoubtedly has some faults and flaws. Nevertheless, more and more cities are bound to look to the Southwest when they begin to feel the crushing weight of recreation demand by their own citizens. It can be stated without exaggeration that Maricopa has become a pace setter in modern, scientific recreational planning.

Scripps-Howard Foundation Establishes Edward J. Meeman Conservation Awards

The Scripps-Howard Foundation has announced that prizes totaling $2,000 will be awarded to newspapermen or women in recognition of outstanding work in the cause of conservation published during 1964.

To be called the Edward J. Meeman awards, they are named for the editor emeritus of the *Memphis Press-Scimitar* and conservation editor of Scripps-Howard Newspapers. Mr. Meeman is Vice-President of the American Planning and Civic Association and Chairman of the Board of the National Conference on State Parks.

The awards will consist of a $1,000 first prize; a second prize of $500; and five additional prizes of $100 each.

The work of any newspaperman or woman in the United States is eligible. Material may be submitted from news stories, editorials, cartoons, sports or women's page articles and photographs. A headline or slogan could prove prizeworthy.

Only work published from January 1 through December 31, 1964 will be eligible and must be postmarked not later than February 15, 1965.

Recreation for Rural America—The County Can Help Meet The Growing Need

From THE COUNTY LETTER, a publication of the National Association of Counties.

Recreation—the creative use of one's free time—is of great importance today in all areas of our nation. But nowhere is there a greater need for bold and prompt action than in rural America.

Twenty-two million young people live in rural sections of the United States. Whether they stay in the rural areas or move to metropolitan areas, they will have to solve their recreation problems as well as the many other problems of a changing environment.

Recreation programs are most fully developed in urban areas. This very fact creates problems for rural youth moving to the cities as they are not prepared to participate in such programs. Hunting, fishing and hiking, easily available to the farm youth, do not prepare a rural youngster for the vastly different activities of urban people.

And, for the adolescent that stays in the rural environment, his recreation wants and needs are not the same as before, thanks to radio, TV, national magazines and frequent trips to nearby towns and cities, and he's not finding the recreation opportunities he seeks.

Counties can and should help fill this growing need of youth, and in many instances they are taking action. The National Recreation Association recently looked into this problem and found that more and more counties are studying how they can best satisfy recreational needs.

County programs number close to 300 today, varying widely in size and scope. But there appears to be one basic reason why counties are such an important factor in rural recreation—money. Often, the county is the only unit with sufficient resources to do the job.

Luckily, counties in most states have statutory powers to purchase parks and, in many cases, to finance broad recreation programs. The first step for any county is to be aware of its powers. Then it can launch into any of a variety of recreation programs, such as:

Kern County, California . . . population 292,000, area 8,170 square miles . . . has a Recreation Department that administers 42 "area" parks . . . designed to meet the specific needs of local "area" people . . . and 12 "general" parks throughout the county providing everything from camping facilities, ski lifts, golf and fishing to a zoo and midget race track.

Wayne County, North Carolina . . . population 82,059, area 555 square miles . . . built the Wayne County Memorial Community Building to honor the memory of those who died in World War I. Facilities include dormitories for servicemen, gymnasiums, swimming pool, reading and writing rooms. It serves as headquarters for the American Red Cross, the Boy Scouts, and the Community Chest . . . admin-

(Continued on page 58)

CAPE LOOKOUT NATIONAL SEASHORE
—A PROPOSAL

(Continued from page 36)

Operating on the optimistic side, the National Park Service submitted a thorough study to the Department of the Interior recommending that the seashore recreation area be established. The Bureau of Outdoor Recreation reviewed the proposal and reported that it meets the criteria for a national recreation area.

Toward the end of April of this year, Secretary Udall endorsed the Service's report and his Department supports the legislation that would authorize establishment of the seashore area as a national park.

Here are some summary statements from the National Park Service study along with the conclusions and recommendation as they were submitted to Secretary Udall:

The area studied and reported on here presents an unusual opportunity to make available the recreation resources of a nationally significant stretch of seashore for use and enjoyment of the people of the United States.

Concern over loss of seashore for public use was highlighted by the National Park Service in its reports on the seashore recreation area survey of the Atlantic and Gulf coasts, published in 1955. Made possible through the generosity of anonymous donors, the survey was assigned the task "to identify the major remaining opportunities for conservation of natural seashores or coastal areas for recreational or other public purposes."

The seashore is a limited and diminishing resource of scenic and scientific interest, of first rank importance in the natural heritage of the nation. Much of the seashore has been pre-empted by commercial and private developments.

In the 1955 seashore recreation area survey, the following analysis was made: "If Core Banks could be restored by an adequate sand fixation program, they would possess first rate potentialities as public beaches." Of Shackleford Banks

the report read: "This is a potentially valuable public beach of a type that might well render greatest service if acquired for that purpose and kept in natural condition."

These statements, true in 1955, are also true today. The study area remains relatively undeveloped. Most of it is available through donation by the State of North Carolina. The establishment of this public use area has local and State support.

The combination of Portsmouth Island and Core and Shackleford Banks encompasses some 15,800 acres and about 58 miles of ocean shore.

The boundaries proposed encompass a definite geographic unit which can be effectively preserved, administered, developed, maintained and operated for public use.

More than five million people live within 250 airline miles of the area.

Present development consists of a few houses at Portsmouth, three hunting and fishing camps and one rod and gun club between Portsmouth and Cape Lookout, a number of vacation cottages on Lookout Bight, Coast Guard and lighthouse installations at Cape Lookout, and ten weekend or vacation cottages on Shackleford Banks.

Present use consists of sport fishing, waterfowl hunting and vacationing. Commercial fisheries harvest shell and finfish from the adjacent waters.

The study area forms a comprehensive unit embracing the territory required for effective preservation, administration, and development for visitor use. It is also a geographic entity.

Restoration and preservation of the land area and marshes always must be first order of business. The aim should be to restore and preserve the beaches in as nearly their natural condition as possible. These efforts will include dune construction, planting, and other beach restoration and erosion control work.

Development for and actual visitor use cannot be unlimited. To prevent loss of the natural scenic and recreation values, the optimum carrying capacity of the area must not be exceeded.

The suggested Cape Lookout National Seashore offers a nationally significant opportunity for recreational use of natural

(Continued on page 57)

56

American Planning and Civic Association
New Members, May 1, 1964 to August 1, 1964

California
Miss Elisabeth C. Cunkle, Chico
District of Columbia
Mr. Frederick H. Bunting
Mr. C. M. Fesler
Oregon
Mr. J. Michael McCloskey, Eugene

Virginia
Mr. Stewart B. Knower, Arlington
Mrs. John A. Bross, McLean
West Virginia
West Virginia University Library, Morgantown

National Conference on State Parks
New Members, May 1, 1964 to August 1, 1964

California
Mr. Edward F. Dolder, Sacramento

Michigan
Mr. H. B. Guillaume, East Lansing

Washington
Mr. Howard Martin, Camas
Mr. James Whittaker, Redmond
Mr. Ted McTighe, Spokane
Mrs. Eleanor Berger, Tacoma
Mr. Joe Hamel, Sedro Woolley
Mr. James Hovis, Yakima

CAPE LOOKOUT NATIONAL SEASHORE
—A PROPOSAL

(Continued from page 56)

resources and preservation of an outstanding scenic seashore.

The area possesses significance in both historical and natural science.

Within the area are many sites suitable for development of recreation facilities to meet immediate needs. Additional development sites will become available as beach restoration work progresses.

Establishment of the Cape Lookout National Seashore is officially supported by the State of North Carolina and the County of Carteret. In addition, it has widespread citizen support.

The State of North Carolina will donate most of the required land. The United States will need to acquire less than 2,000 acres.

Cape Lookout National Seashore would be an economic asset to the area in which it is located.

It is recommended that the Carteret County, North Carolina Outer Banks from Ocracoke Inlet to Beaufort Inlet be favorably considered for addition to the National Park System as Cape Lookout National Seashore.

As man begins the task of correcting his own abuses of the past 150 years, forbearance and patience will be required. In the beginning, visitor use will have to be controlled. This is not to say that Cape Lookout National Seashore will be less accessible or more difficult to enjoy than in the past. Actually, it will become far more accessible for public use. But great care must be exercised to prevent over-use and over-development from defeating the very purpose for saving it: To protect and strengthen these outer banks of North Carolina so that they can provide an even greater recreational opportunity for future generations.

57

Recent Publications

The Economic Implications of the Regional Park System in Maricopa County. Prepared under the direction of Kenneth E. Daane. Bureau of Business Research and Services, College of Business Administration, Arizona State University, Tempe, Arizona. $1.75.

This study was prepared for the Maricopa County Board of Supervisors to assist in planning the development and utilization of over 85,000 acres of land recently acquired by the county for recreational purposes.

Ralph C. Hook, Jr., director of the Bureau of Business Research and Service of the Arizona State University College of Business Administration, points out that original research into the economic effects of parks and recreation is not readily available and declares that "while this study deals specifically with the regional park system in Maricopa County (Phoenix, Arizona, area), its applications are of a much broader scope.

"In view of the continually pressing need for advance planning and development of parks and recreational facilities by all levels of government in all parts of the United States, we believe the methodology as well as the findings of Dr. Daane's study will be of value to other agencies and departments dealing with parks and recreation throughout the country."

The report estimates that the economic benefits of all types from development of the Maricopa County recreational land will equal approximately $30 million and $75 million for the years 1976 and 2000, respectively.

(For an interesting account of the trail-blazing activity surrounding the development of the Regional Park System in Maricopa County, Arizona, see page 1 of this issue of PLANNING AND CIVIC COMMENT.)

RECREATION FOR RURAL AMERICA—THE COUNTY CAN HELP MEET THE GROWING NEED
(*Continued from page 55*)

istered and financed by the County.

Cobb County, Georgia . . . population 114,174, area 348 square miles . . . affords a good example of county, city and Federal governments joining forces on a recreation program—County gave 46 acres and $36,000, Uncle Sam contributed $126,000, and the City of Marietta gave $40,000. Now the county and city jointly operate the recreation building and the 46 acre county-city park . . . and share the salary of a recreation staff.

Successful county programs are those that have assessed all factors . . . along with recreation needs of young and old alike . . . and have designed organizations and programs to meet or resolve all problems. What is your county doing in this field?

Watch Service Report

The "make or break" hour for what has been generally described as major "landmark" conservation legislation has come and gone—with some legislative measures of the greatest conservation import having already been signed into law. As we go to press, others, having passed both Houses of Congress, are awaiting Presidential signature. The long-contested legislation received bi-partisan support from both houses of the U. S. Congress.

Public Law 88-577, Establishing A National Wilderness Preservation System.

Culminating a decade of effort to effect establishment of a National Wilderness Preservation System, S. 4, The Wilderness Bill, was signed by President Lyndon B. Johnson, in a ceremony at the White House Rose Garden on September 3, 1964.

On August 17, 1964, Senate and House conferees agreed to a compromise version of S. 4, establishing a National Wilderness Preservation System. The House adopted the conference report on August 20 and the Senate followed suit the same day, thus clearing the bill for signature by the President.

H. R. 9070, the House version of the wilderness measure, was passed July 30, 1964 by an overwhelming margin of 373 to 1, thus moving the bill along to the conference committee which worked out the differences between it and S. 4, the Senate version which had been adopted by the Senate in April, 1963, with the support of 85 percent of its members.

As reported by the conference committee, S. 4 brings more than nine million acres of National Forest wilderness, wild and canoe areas into the wilderness system at the outset. It provides that the Secretary of Agriculture and the Secretary of the Interior may review and recommend to the President, and the President to the Congress, the creation of further wilderness areas out of another 50 million acres in forests, parks, monuments, and fish and wildlife refuges and ranges.

More than five million acres of the National Forest primitive areas will be reviewed over a ten-year period and any Presidential recommendations for inclusion in the Wilderness system from this area will be subject to approval by Act of Congress. Areas classified as "primitive" will continue to be administered as such until the Congress has determined otherwise.

Roadless areas in units of the National Park System and National Wildlife Refuge System also will be reviewed over a ten-year period and areas recommended for incorporation into the Wilderness System from this area must also be approved by Congress.

Provision for such action by the Congress was a key House Interior Committee requirement for passage of the Wilderness Bill.

A major area of difference between the House and Senate versions of the bill concerned mining. The Senate version permitted prospecting in a manner not incompatible with the wilderness environment but not mining unless the President so authorized. The House version allowed mining on National Forest areas for 25 years. The compromise version, agreed upon by the conference committee, provided for a 19-year period during which National Forest areas will be open to prospecting and mining under certain conditions.

The conference committee considered use of the San Gorgonio Wild Area for a skiing development site, but decided to place it in the Wilderness System. The House report, however, has this comment: "Nonetheless, it is noted that the matter is not considered as closed; and, if the people of California continue to desire a restudy of the area, they should make their views known to their Representative in Congress and be in a position to have legislation introduced at the start of the next Congress. This will permit consideration at hearings devoted solely to this matter."

59

Described during debate on the House floor as "landmark legislation . . . that will stand out through the years as one of the most significant conservation measures enacted by the Congress in this century," the wilderness measure was strongly supported by the bipartisan conservation leadership of both the House and the Senate.

Public Law 88-578, Establishing A Land and Water Conservation Fund. This major conservation legislation was signed by the President on September 3, 1964, after having cleared both houses of Congress.

Representatives of the House and Senate agreed, on August 19, 1964, to reconcile differences between versions of the Land and Water Conservation Fund Act of 1964 as passed earlier by both houses.

By the overwhelming margin of 92 to 1, the Senate on August 12, 1964 joined the House in approving H. R. 3846 but with some features that resulted in the seeking of a conference.

The House of Representatives passed the Bill on July 23, 1964. Passage by a voice vote, following two days of debate and voting on proposed amendments, sent the bill along to the Senate. Several attempts to amend the bill were beaten back before final passage by the House and several perfecting or clarifying amendments were adopted.

None of the bill's provisions for the Federal grant-in-aid program for outdoor recreation were at issue in the Conference Committee.

The major point of controversy related to the use of the Federal portion of the Fund. The Senate version would have authorized appropriations from the Fund to the Federal agencies for the construction and development of recreational facilities as well as for land acquisition. Conferees agreed to limit use of the Federal funds to acquisition, particularly since 85 per cent of the Forest Service purchases would be in the East. Money for recreational development will be sought from regular appropriations and the states are also expected to develop some recreational areas with their share of the funds.

Another significant Conference agreement provided that appropriations from the Fund to the Forest Service may be used to purchase private inholdings within boundaries of existing and future national forest wilderness areas.

The conferees deleted a Senate provision prohibiting fees *for access* to waters of Federal reservoirs and other Federal recreation areas. The Senate had adopted language which said that no fee shall be charged for the "use of any waters or access thereto." The Conference Committee removed the reference to "access."

A right for the governors of states to demand hearings on proposed fees, as proposed by the Senate, was removed.

H. R. 3846, which will undoubtedly have far-reaching effects in recreation development throughout the country, has been reported in detail in previous issues of PLANNING AND CIVIC COMMENT. In brief, through establishment of a Land and Water Conservation Fund, it authorizes a new program of Federal matching grants-in-aid for state and local outdoor recreation planning, land acquisition and development projects. It also provides a means of financing the acquisition of recreation lands by the National Park Service, the U. S. Forest Service and the U. S. Fish and Wildlife Service.

S. 1305, Establishing A Fire Island National Seashore, New York. This bill was cleared for the signature of the President on August 21, 1964 when the Senate concurred with House amendments. The House version, H. R. 7107, was passed by a voice vote on August 20, 1964.

Favorable, but differing reports had been filed in both houses of the Congress on bills to establish the Fire Island National Seashore, the proposal for which was reported in full in the September, 1963 issue of PLANNING AND CIVIC COMMENT.

Fire Island is a natural barrier reef lying just off the south shore of Long Island.

"HIGHWAYS can be planned to blend with forested and scenic areas. Very often an historic building can become a central feature of a new development rather than a casualty. And the only remedy for indifference is our own conscience —that of the individual and of the nation."

—Circular announcing The American Landmarks Celebration

Planning and Civic Comment

Vol. 30   March, 1965   No. 4

STEPHEN R. CURRIER IS ELECTED
New APCA President

Expresses Hope That Association Will Play Vital Role
in Building More Beautiful Communities—
New Board of Trustees is Elected

STEPHEN R. CURRIER of New York was elected president of the
American Planning and Civic Association, and Harland Bartholomew, former president for many years, was elected chairman of the
board, at the annual meeting of the Association's board of trustees in
Washington, D. C., December 18.

Other officers elected were: C. McKim Norton, Vice-President;
Edward J. Meeman, Vice-President; Donald B. Alexander, Execu-
tive Director; Alfred S. Mills, Treasurer; William B. Mehler, Jr.,
Assistant Treasurer; Clyde Bergen, Assistant Treasurer; Walter F.
Leinhardt, Secretary.

Mr. Bartholomew told the meeting that within the coming months,
the Association would map a bold, new program and hailed the election of Mr. Currier, who was co-chairman of the Committee for a
Park at Breezy Point in New York. The Committee was credited
with saving the Breezy Point part of New York from being transformed into a mammoth housing development and being preserved
instead as a future great oceanfront park and beach.

In a brief acceptance speech, Mr. Currier said it was his hope that
APCA, when its new program is developed, would play a leading and
vital role in helping build more beautiful communities.

PLANNING AND CIVIC COMMENT
CEASES PUBLICATION

PLANNING AND CIVIC COMMENT ceases publication with this issue which has been purposively delayed in view of the major reorganization of the *American Planning and Civic Association* now in process.

The Association's entire publications program is being reconstituted and the new program is now being subject to review by the Board of Directors. As soon as recommendations are made final and approved they will be shared with the membership.

Reorganization of the Association has been made possible through a major grant from the Taconic Foundation of New York, and is designed to help the Association revitalize its activities, expand its program and extend its influence across the country.

—To all of you who have told us verbally and who have written us that you have found PLANNING AND CIVIC COMMENT a source of interest, help and inspiration—

—To our ever-increasing volunteer contributors who have, in a major way, helped attune PLANNING AND CIVIC COMMENT to vital needs across the country—needs which have been reflected in our continuous requests for re-prints—

—To, you, who, from the ever-increasing number who write us asking how to obtain our publication, have recently taken out subscription memberships—

—And, most especially, to all of you who have been our faithful readers and supporters—

We say thanks.

We have attempted to keep PLANNING AND CIVIC COMMENT informative in these swiftly changing days of our Nation's development. And we assure you that, as one of our guiding principles, we have attempted to keep faithfully in mind that an important goal of any publication is to strike a responsive chord in the minds and hearts of those who peruse its pages.

We wish you continued fruitful reading after the Association's new publications program is voted.

Preserving a Valley's Heritage and Beauty

By HOWARD J. GROSSMAN

**Assistant Director,
Montgomery County Planning Commission**

IN RECENT YEARS a trend toward joint participation among municipalities in comprehensive land use planning as well as providing other types of municipal services to residents has been noted. The area or regional approach to land-use planning in the United States is ever increasing. In Pennsylvania, there are several regional or area planning commissions currently in operation. Nowhere is area-wide planning, however, more in the spotlight than in Montgomery County, Pennsylvania.

The Upper Perkiomen Valley Area Planning Council is a pioneer effort in cooperative planning in Montgomery County, Pennsylvania. Formed under the General Cooperation Law of Pennsylvania, the Council consists of six townships and four boroughs (covering an area of 85 square miles and a population of 16,000) devoted to preparing an area-wide comprehensive plan and a detailed plan for each of the constituent municipalities. In 1962, the Council made application for Federal Urban Planning Assistance funds under Section 701 of the Housing Act of 1954, As Amended. The Council received funds for planning in 1963 and work officially began on September 18th of that year. The Montgomery County Planning Commission is acting as consultant to the Council in the preparation of plans. A planning program has been proposed to cover a span of four years. The first two years will produce a broad area-wide plan for the Valley. The second two years will see a plan drawn for the ten participating municipalities.

The Council was the first organized legally-constituted cooperative planning venture in the County. Since its inception, a second Council has been formed. Eleven townships and boroughs have joined together in the County, in what is called the North Penn Area, to develop and implement a four-year planning program. This study is now under way. There are, also other efforts being made to develop cooperative planning within the County in other areas.

In developing an approach to comprehensive planning in the Valley, the two staff planners assigned to the program have suggested, and the Council has approved the following reports to be published during the first two years of the study:

1. *The Past and Present Settlement of the Upper Perkiomen Valley.* This report will cover the history, regional setting, population, economy, governmental organization and school-age forecasts for the ten Valley municipalities and the Area as a whole.

2. *An Analysis of the Community Questionnaire: A Look At Ourselves.* This report will be a summation of a questionnaire distributed to all Valley families. Here, the citizen effort is foremost whereby civic groups and service organizations, as well as the municipal planning commissions, distribute and pick up the questionnaires.

3. *Natural and Man-made Features of Upper Perkiomen Valley.* Here, intensive effort is given to the landscaped features of the Valley, including soils, slope, geology and other natural features, as well as existing

land use, public utilities and community facilities. It is in this report where open space and natural amenities will be identified for latter inclusion in the Valley Plan.

4. *Transportation in the Upper Perkiomen Valley.* This report will contain a traffic and circulation plan for the Valley and relate the plan to traffic conditions in Montgomery County and surrounding areas.

5. *A Comprehensive Plan for the Upper Perkiomen Valley.* This report will contain a comprehensive land use plan for the Valley, identifying recommended areas for industrial, commerical, residential, recreation and other types of land use.

6. *Implementing the Comprehensive Plan—A Program for Action.* Here, recommendations will be made for implementing the plans through zoning, subdivision regulations and the other legal and non-legal tools at the disposal of the ten municipalities and the Council.

One important factor which makes this cooperative venture unique is that this area is the most rural sector of the County. The County is essentially suburban and lies directly adjacent to the City of Philadelphia. The County's population as of 1960 was 516,682, which was a 46 per cent increase over 1950. It is estimated that a population of 883,000 will reside in Montgomery County by 1985.

Through the efforts of the Council and the Montgomery County Planning Commission, a massive effort is being made to preserve large areas of open space in the Valley. The opportunity for creating a permanent landscape of open space is of major and paramount concern to many of the officials and leaders in the Valley. The Valley offers the last large open space reservoir in Montgomery County.

Several publications have already been produced on population, economy, governmental organization and other facets of Valley growth which constitute *The Past and Present Settlement of the Upper Perkiomen Valley*. The ten townships and boroughs form a diverse picture and the problems of the boroughs, in many respects, differ from those of the townships; however, they are inexorably tied together in terms of transportation, water supply and other planning related matters.

A massive citizen effort is being made to create what will be called Perkiomen Valley Watershed Association. The Perkiomen Creek flows through the Valley and an abundant opportunity is available for making the Creek Valley one of the beauty spots of the County and the Philadelphia Metropolitan Area. The Council has emphasized the relationship of a watershed association to an expanded industrial base whereby the preservation of a water supply is a key to creating industrial growth.

Another unique step taken in this area was the publication of a news bulletin, entitled "The Valley Planner" which discussed planning activities as they relate to the ten townships and boroughs. The Valley Planner is intended to be a periodic review of planning and community development activities for mass distribution and has received wide attention in the Valley.

One important note is the lack of any full-time municipal employee among the ten townships and bor-

oughs in the Valley. This has created a real hardship in running municipal government for the municipalities, and in turn, has created a vacuum, so that emphasizing joint participation for municipal services becomes somewhat easier. The municipalities are beginning to recognize the need for joint cooperation and partnership in solving Area problems including the question of open space.

The Upper Perkiomen Valley Area Planning Council has been stimulated toward open space preservation; also, by the Federal Open Space Program, the State Grant-in-Aid Program, the latter being the only known County Aid Program for open space in the Nation. One of the participating boroughs has been motivated enough to acquire about 28 acres of land for a recreation area, using County funds and, hopefully, receiving State funds.

The Council will continue to meet and discuss various problems affecting the growth and development of the Valley. Perhaps the largest and most critical problem facing the Valley is the retention of its agricultural interests, while planning for an increased population. This question is receiving the greatest amount of attention among planners and officials of Montgomery County.

While the Valley is the leading agricultural area within Montgomery County, its long-range future probably does not lie in this field. It would seem to offer a potential for a rapidly growing tourist industry which takes advantage of the abundant open space and naturalistic features throughout the Area. The role of agriculture is one which must

5

be met, and efforts are being made to explore this question in depth. For example, contact was made with officials from Pennsylvania State University to try and develop a research study on the future of agriculture in the Valley. At the time this investigation was made, Penn State could not undertake such a venture but continued efforts in this vein are being made.

The newly enacted federal legislation entitled the Land and Water Conservation Act of 1964 may have a real impact on the Valley. Together with the aforementioned federal, state and county aid programs, this Act would make it almost foolhardy for municipalities not to acquire lands for open space now, and at least to set them aside for future use.

Within the Valley are many large areas for open space use and preservation. The largest County park, approximating 555 acres and one of the most beautiful in the State, is located here. The Philadelphia Suburban Water Company, which serves a large sector of the Philadelphia Metropolitan Area, has a 2000-acre reservoir and associated facilities, some of which are open to the public within the Valley. A major effort will be made to open for additional public use the facilities of the Water Company. There is a large scout camp of about 700 acres located within one of the municipalities in the Valley. These three examples provide some idea as to the recreation and open space found in the Upper Perkiomen Valley. Studies have been made also on the economy generated by these open spaces. The parks and camps of the Valley pour

thousands of dollars in the local economy through payrolls and purchases from local merchants and farmers. Much of the open space within the Valley lies in land unsuitable for development through poor soil conditions and other factors. Thus, the economy of the Area is and will continue to be oriented towards using open space not only as a basic amenity but as a tourist and economic factor. We may look at this field from the following viewpoint. Open space preserves natural beauty, and in a sense is a commodity, and in many respects it is a commodity that municipalities throughout the Nation are paying for dearly. The opportunity for preserving what already exists within the Valley is one which is not being overlooked.

The first reports published by the Council with the assistance of staff members of the County Planning Commission have already explored some ways to strengthen the Area's economy and cultural as well as historic heritage. One of the reports pretty well sums up the attitude and thinking of planners and officials along the following lines:

"The Upper Perkiomen Valley would do well to keep its age-old character of beautiful, open fields and farms, surrounded by woodlands. Through land use planning, zoning, and open space programs, much of the Valley's beauty can be preserved. The type, amount, and timing of residential, commercial and industrial uses can be programmed through planning and zoning techniques along with the retention of the Valley's beauty.

"A study of the Valley's history and restoration of various historical sites throughout the area would do much to heighten community awareness. Moreover, history of the Germanic settlers in the Valley is interesting and colorful. It is recommended that an historical society be formed by those

(Continued on page 16)

6

Planning Techniques of Tomorrow

By John Graham

EVERYONE IS FAMILIAR, in a general way, with what has been happening to our cities since the war. The fire of the exploding metropolis flamed by easy credit, an economy geared to mass production, an unlimited highway program supplemented by unprecedented automobile sales, have set in motion a force that is threatening to roll over our cities.

Even before the war, the country's industrialization had encouraged a movement of the population from rural into the metropolitan areas. Now, within the large cities, major dislocations have developed, due to the internal shifting of industry and population. Industry, seeking low cost operations through modern, single-level plants, is relocating in the suburbs, where it finds cheap

Excerpts from an address, "The Architect's Contribution to Urban Planning," delivered by John Graham, A.I.A., John Graham & Co., Architects, Seattle, Washington, before the Canadian Institute of Realtors in Banff, Alberta, Canada, May 7' 1964.

land and a ready source of employees who have already preceded it—stimulated by mass housing, financed through easy F. H. A. credit. Then follow the retail centers and the single purpose office buildings, banks, societies, insurance companies and medical services. In the end, all of the facilities normally found in the city center have moved, in part, to the suburbs.

Today, cities are divided into many complexes, but basically the competition is downtown against the outskirts, or urban against suburban. This battle is still in its infancy. It will continue with ever increasing fierceness.

In spite of the overall population growth, I think it is safe to say, the central business districts have been losing their competitive position to the suburban developments. There is hardly a city in North America which has not become aware of this.

The leaders of business and government have joined forces and are working diligently, and in many cases most effectively, to reestablish the central business district as the heart of the metropolis.

Until recently, the planning of the metropolitan area, itself, was aimed principally at taking care of the immediate problems caused by the tremendous increase in vehicular traffic. This constituted the widening of arterials and construction of freeways to by-pass congested areas.

Too, some of the major metropolitan areas have already made great strides in the overall planning for the future of their central districts; others have hardly started. But in any event, now is the time for all cities to consider and determine their future image. If the city does not plan into the future, then how can its component businesses intelligently plan for *their* future?

One hears a great deal about planning the new town. Most of such planning is concentrated in England, but the basic planning requirements are the same here as there, and so we can logically take advantage of their experience. One would think that planners, starting from scratch, and controlled *only* by the terrain, would create new concepts which would revolutionize city plans so as to make obsolete old cities. I cannot see where this has been done. The challenge still remains.

Our great concern, however, is not with new towns, but with the old ones. What is to happen to them when the population has doubled and the traffic congestion is so great that commerce practically grinds to a halt? The answer is, that we must provide against this, and that requires planning now—for the future.

During the past few years, a number of extensive and interesting planning concepts have been applied to some of our major cities. A few, like Washington, D. C., have been on a comprehensive scale, but most have been aimed specifically at a small segment of the city. Of course, there have also been a great many theoretical planning proposals set forth without any specific application.

From all this, and from the work which has already taken place in some of our major cities, such as Baltimore, I have a feeling that a new planning concept, which will obsolete many of the current planning theories, is on the verge of development. The planners and planning techniques of tomorrow will be radically different from those we know today. The dramatic comeback of some of our major central business districts, during the past few years, is only a beginning—and a light to point the way—to the future possibilities.

The new concepts will be reasonable and flexible. They will deal with the people as individuals, rather than people as masses. They will conform to the requirements of good living, rather than attempt to reconform society into a predetermined image.

How often do we hear, "The city will explode"—"the city will choke to death?" How often do we hear planners say, "We must limit the automobile"—"we cannot allow the automobile into our cities"—"we must make plans that leave the cars on the doorsteps, along with the wooden shoes?"

Assuming that the population continues to increase at its present pace into the indefinite future, the demand for automobile ownership

8

will continue until it reaches a saturation point. Everyone who wants a car will have one until other means of transportation have been developed. The bus, train, monorail and helicopter all offer means of transportation aimed at supplementing the automobile, and, in my opinion, they will never—and can never—replace it.

It is important to remember that as long as we have a democracy, controlled by the voting populace, the government will be determined by car owners; hence, governments will have to respect the desires of the auto-minded electorate.

Judging from experience gained in New York City, people will continue to use their cars in spite of congestion and cost. It will not be practical, or perhaps even possible, to legislate the use of automobiles. There can be no solution to the city's long range planning problems, without giving full consideration to the automobile. The concept of controlling traffic by limiting the parking spaces, in my opinion, is doomed to failure. It just won't work. Without doubt, the automobile, or vehicular traffic, is the number one problem—so let's start with it.

Planning should be based on the fact that the number of cars, like population, will continue to increase. This will require an ever-increasing number of highways, expressways, ring roads, collector streets, and then, at the end of the road, adequate parking. When parking lots become inadequate, we will deck them over and develop garages. This is not to say that there should not be a vigorous expansion of public transportation in all of its forms, even at the expense of governmental subsidies. After all, it is the people who are demanding the services, and it is their taxes which will have to pay for it.

As the requirements for future use of real estate become greater, real estate values increase, and so it follows that new and larger buildings will replace old, outmoded buildings. This is the historic growth pattern of cities. In the same way, as highways become inadequate, they will need to be widened. When they cannot be widened, then they will need to be double-decked.

In some respects, the city of the future that I visualize is not very different from some of our better existing ones. Obviously, we must plan for the tremendous traffic requirements of the future. At the same time, if the central business district is to compete with suburban business districts, on a financially economic basis, there must be strong, compelling factors that will influence business to locate in the downtown area. Also, quite obviously, the most significant factor, for a merchant at least, will be whether his volume is so much greater that operating profit will justify the substantially higher occupancy costs. Each individual business will have its own particular requirements, but, in the end, the determining factor is resolved by the bottom line net profit and long range security.

I visualize a city of the future, where the central business district is designed into a series of "*environmental complexes*" such as the financial district, the retail district, the amusement district, the governmental center, and the industrial park, in such a manner that each will be a compact, efficient unit with ample opportunity for flexible expansion. The interiors of these complexes will be planned for pedestrian circulation whereas the exterior streets and roadways will be planned for serving vehicular traffic. Parking and service will be provided for under the buildings, supplemented by adjacent garages connected to large, well-planned ring roads or a network of arterials and streets.

Public transportation will be provided for in several ways. First, on the surface along exterior streets and ring roads; second, through monorails above ground, or subways, underground. These transportation facilities will connect each "environmental unit" with the other. Throughout the central business district, there will be landscaped park areas, plazas, malls or pedestrian ways, so arranged as to eliminate the pedestrian conflict with vehicular traffic.

Due to a set of different requirements and circumstances, each environmental complex will take a different planning concept; that is, the requirements for an efficient retail center will produce a plan quite dissimilar from the one required for the financial center or the governmental center.

The planning need not be restricted by any rigid controls. There should be a complete freedom for private enterprise. Historically, it has been proved that similar businesses prefer a close association with their competitors—that "like attracts like."

Even so, the plan need not be so rigid as to prohibit a mixing of facilities within the various areas, such, as office buildings in the retail center, hotels in the government or financial districts, etc. The principal advantage of breaking the city down into environmental complexes is that it becomes a much more efficient unit, and that the people who visit each area are there for a specific reason. This does two or three things: for example, the merchant is confronted only with traffic that is interested in shopping. This applies not only to the pedestrians on the walkways but to cars in the garages and to traffic on the streets. This eliminates a very sizable part of the congestion problem caused by a mixture of people going to and from, without specific purpose, in the areas they find themselves.

In the end, then, the retail district would cater to shoppers like a suburban regional shopping center, while the financial business district would cater to people interested in commerce, and the governmental center would cater to people concerned with matters of government.

This is the era of specialization. I see no reason why central business districts should not specialize. I believe this planning concept is capable of being superimposed on top of most any of our existing cities. It requires a long range plan, and possibly some governmental help in certain areas of land assemblage, but, on the whole, it should be done by free enterprise with the minimum of governmental controls and interference.

The planning of successful regional suburban centers has borrowed from the established

(*Continued on page 49*)

Condensation of an address delivered by Mr. Rowlands, Specialist in Land Planning, Department of Agricultural Economics, University of Wisconsin, before the Wisconsin Homemaker Conference at the University of Wisconsin, Madison, Wisconsin, June, 1964.

Keeping Wisconsin Beautiful

By Walter A. Rowlands

L ET'S TALK about housekeeping. Not the kind of housekeeping you are normally engaged in every day of the year—but a new kind of housekeeping, involving the total order and beauty of our Wisconsin countryside.

Years ago, it was unnecessary to talk about this kind of housekeeping. America was so big, her mines, her forests and potential farm land so extensive, so abundant and so productive that it seemed all men had to do was to exploit these resources which, it was thought, would go on forever and ever.

Today, all this is changed. The Interstate highway system, new shopping centers, new airports, recreation projects, new industrial park areas, new residential subdivisions, the new suburbs, the consolidated school districts—all make it so. We are becoming as a people, as a Nation, increasingly concerned about the tremendous growth and development of our population, our cities, our suburbs, our countryside—and *with it the unwise and unnecessary waste and despoilation of natural resources and natural surroundings.*

Henry Ahlgren, Associate Director of the Cooperative Extension Service, University of Wisconsin, once said: "Wisconsin with its green mantled hills and valleys—its diversified agriculture—its neat farmsteads—its clear waters with their timbered shore lines—its ever changing scenery—is a constant inspiration to all who travel its highways and byways."

"To keep our Wisconsin countryside clean and green, to safeguard its beauty while at the same time making provision for new homes, new businesses, and new industry is a task that will fully challenge all the energy and initiative that only

11

an alert, aggressive, and understanding citizenry can muster. The people of Wisconsin have met challenges of similar magnitude and importance in the past. We are confident they will meet this one too."

The scenery of Wisconsin is a tremendously saleable asset to our tourist industry. It is said that the value of Wisconsin tourist business amounts to something more than six hundred million dollars annually. Further, it is a fact that more than fifty percent of the tourists visiting Wisconsin have indicated that the scenery of the countryside is the most important factor in their coming to Wisconsin.

Scenery—the charm and beauty of the countryside—then, is an asset, an important factor in the economy, the growth and the development of our state. It is something to be protected, preserved and further developed. If Wisconsin is to be more beautiful, then it will be because the citizens of this state, both men and women, are alert and vigilant in keeping what I call the *Seven Scourges of The Countryside* under control.

What are these Seven Scourges? Let me list them and tell you what can be done about them:

1) Automobile graveyards that line the highways.
2) Open, exposed garbage disposal dumps.
3) Abandoned buildings and unsightly farmsteads.
4) Homes built on the flood plains.
5) Commercial and industrial development intermingled with farm and residential land uses.
6) Bottles and cans and debris scattered along the highways.
7) Signs and billboards in all sizes, colors and in all stages of dilapidation.

What can we do about this situation?

First off, let's face it, we need to promote more interest in land use planning, including setback building lines, clear vision triangles at intersections of highways and railroads, off street parking and private loading docks for commerce and industry. We need to step up interest in carefully designed residential subdivisions, in building codes and in all the local ordinances and regulations that are needed in our communities. All of them should be designed to protect private property, to stabilize property values and to promote the orderly development of all our land and water resources for their highest use.

Second, we need more public participation in the development of local plans to improve the community whether this be for a county park, an auditorium, a new building on the fair grounds, or a community swimming pool. We need an enlightened and informed public on all of these important public programs. Our need parallels the national need for active informed citizens' planning committees are necessary today to help guide the development and the destiny of every community in the Nation.

This does not mean citizens' committees of men only. Last year Al Bennett, Editor of the *Atchison Globe* in Atchison, Kansas, was asked along with nine other editors to take a careful and critical look

12

at planning in the state of Kansas. In his report he said: "One other thing: *Use the women. If women became aroused, really aroused, they can accomplish anything. Women, by nature, think of the home, the playground, the traffic flow because they are thinking around the clock about their children and their children's future. Father, bless his heart, is pretty busy trying to make a living.*"

One of the important and inspiring things about our citizens' planning committees in Wisconsin is that we have women on many of them participating actively in the discussions and deliberations. We need more women taking an active, constructive part in all community planning activities *for the benefit of families—men and women and the children.*

Third, we need to continue to teach the basic elements in planning the use of the land, in the conservation of our soil, water, game and fish and wildlife, in the basic principles on which zoning is based, whether town, city, village or county zoning. We need to explain to high school civic classes about residential subdivisions, building codes and easements and about the need for public access to lakes and rivers.

Fourth, we need to register our preferences and our protests to elected officials on all questions of basic public policy involving land and water developments, many of which might involve the desecration of the countryside. This involves knowing what is going on in the community, what is proposed, what are the alternatives and finally, would this be a good thing for the community's future?

Fifth, we need to look carefully at improving the roads and highways leading to the entrances to our cities, villages and towns. This again involves planning and zoning, setback building lines and building codes. It may involve a cleanup campaign, or several cleanup campaigns. It may involve the creation of new waysides and new park or parkway areas. It may involve some land leveling and some seeding. Whatever is involved, we can do much, and we need to do it to improve the gateways to our cities and villages.

In the July, 1960 issue of the *Readers Digest*, an article entitled "Cities in Bloom" tells of the work of one very effective and determined woman, Mrs. Mary Lasker of New York City. Mrs. Lasker, alone, pioneered the idea of creating new beauty by the careful use and selection of flowers in downtown New York City. It was difficult to get the idea started and she had to start small, but the idea spread to Birmingham, Alabama; Chicago; Norfolk, Virginia; Omaha, Nebraska; Philadelphia; Portland, Oregon; and many other cities throughout the United States. We have some nice new redwood boxes of flowers around the square in Madison, Wisconsin.

Businessmen in those cities with boxes of living flowers in the downtown area have discovered there is something very, very practical in beauty. Washington, D. C., for example, in 1960, drew more than 850,000 tourists just to see the famous cherry blossoms. In our own Door County, we have a million and

13

more cherry trees and this beautiful sight draws many tourists every spring to the county.

Sixth, we need to regulate auto graveyards in every county in Wisconsin, and, incidentally, this is a need that extends to every county in America. *These graveyards depress property values in the vicinity and help create rural slum areas.* They should not be permitted to locate on land that ought to be used for higher purposes.

In the new county zoning ordinance enacted in 1961 by Columbia County Board of Supervisors, Wisconsin, there is a special provision covering automobile graveyards. In the future, all auto graveyards in the county must be located in the industrial use district. They cannot be located in any other use district. Further, the exact location must be approved by the county zoning adjustment board after a public hearing is held and in advance of development. If such an auto graveyard is approved, the owner must completely screen the area by a solid wall or fence at least six feet high except for one entrance or exit not more than twelve feet wide and not directly facing a public street or road.

Seventh, we need to regulate and control the signs and billboards on our highways. Perhaps we should consider having a special use district under zoning for billboards or limiting them strictly to commercial districts with some exceptions for the farmer and real estate operator.

Since scenery means so much to Wisconsin's economic future, let's borrow an idea followed by all good families when company comes. What do they do? They clean up the premises, cut the grass, clean the windows, dispose of the rubbish, put out the good linen and china and entertain their guests. So let's get rid of *these seven scourges* of the countryside. Let's provide a proper place for them and then let's keep these things in their place.

If we wish it and work for it, we can become a great recreational state. We must continue to build and improve our setting for the tourist industry, and, in doing this, we will need all the initiative, the imagination and ingenuity we can muster. We have few historic battlefields and fewer national monuments to draw tourists. We have no Gettysburg, no Valley Forge, no Plymouth Rock—but we do have clean, clear crystal lakes and rivers with sand beaches, timbered shore lines and the charm and beauty of hills, valleys and rock formations.

And finally—if the State Homemaker Club members and other women's organizations through their local and state organizations in Wisconsin *will speak up on their need for:*

1) Long range and continuous planning in community and county affairs—
2) Orderly development of all our outdoor resources—
3) Citizen participation in all phases of local planning and development—
4) The protection and preservation of the beauty and charm of our Wisconsin countryside—

Then—they will have done something for this state that will long be worthy to be remembered.

☙

Colonial "Strawbery Banke" Is Restored

CITIZEN ACTION BRINGS RESULTS IN PORTSMOUTH, NEW HAMPSHIRE

Reprinted from *History News*

MORE THAN 300 years ago, in 1630, settlers found a carpet of wild strawberries on a hillside and established a colony there, naming it "Strawbery Banke." That colony later became Portsmouth, New Hampshire. The original settlement grew into the business district of colonial Portsmouth, while prosperous residents built their homes near the colony's waterfront.

Many of the colonial residences were still standing on a nine-acre site near the waterfront when the

This article first appeared in the October, 1963 issue of **History News,** *a publication of the American Association for State and Local History, 132 Ninth Avenue North, Nashville, Tennessee, under the title, "Urban Renewal Area In Portsmouth, N. H. To Become Colonial "Strawbery Banke."*

Portsmouth Housing Authority designated the area for urban renewal. The area had deteriorated through the years, and the Housing Authority, backed by federal funds and a $200,000 local bond issue, planned to buy up all the buildings, destroy them, and use the site for low-cost apartment houses. The plan failed in 1957 when federal authorities refused to insure the project on the basis of too-high rent and inadequate demand for apartments.

At this time, several interested individuals came forward with another plan, one which would turn the area into a historic site and provide a home for Portsmouth's rapidly disappearing colonial dwellings. The Portsmouth Housing Authority liked the plan, and on November 12, 1958, "Strawbery Banke" became a corporation.

Strawbery Banke, Inc., had to face an immediate obstacle. A New

15

Hampshire law required that all buildings in a renewal project be demolished, regardless of value. Wanting to preserve, rather than destroy, the new corporation set about to change the law. That goal was accomplished in 1959. In 1960, the federal government gave official approval to the project, naming Strawbery Banke as the redeveloper.

Carl A. Johnson, a retired Navy officer, was chosen to become the full-time director of the project, with the title of executive vice-president. Miss Dorothy M. Vaughan, a Portsmouth librarian whose talk before the city's Rotary Club several years ago, led to the first steps toward the area's preservation, was elected president of the corporation.

Acquisition of the parcels of land and structures within the area, a responsibility of the Portsmouth Housing Authority, formed the first phase of activity at Strawbery Banke.

Only two buildings were moved to the large rectangle on the city's waterfront; 25 are already in the area and will be restored there. The buildings brought in from elsewhere in Portsmouth will be separated from those already there by "Old Puddle Dock," where ships formerly came to discharge cargoes and be fitted out for voyages.

The two buildings moved to the site are the Daniel Webster House, which served as his home and law office from 1813 to 1817, and the Governor Goodwin Mansion, a home built in 1812 and occupied by New Hampshire's first Civil War governor. The two buildings, plus the restored Old New Hampshire State House, originally built in 1758, will form the State House Group in the southwest corner of Strawbery Banke.

When the entire project is completed, houses, craft shops, wharves, a 1770 tavern, a "Liberty Pole" and Liberty Bridge, and appropriate landscaping will contribute to the recreation of Strawbery Banke as it was during the Revolutionary period.

Support has come from all sides: the state appropriated $134,000 to move the Goodwin Mansion; a New York resident gave $100,000 for the Chase House restoration as a memorial to a Portsmouth physician; the public is buying Strawbery Banke bonds at $10 each.

Others are sharing the vision, and because of it, another part of the American heritage is coming alive.

PRESERVING A VALLEY'S HERITAGE AND BEAUTY

(Continued from page 6)

persons and groups interested in historical preservation.

"It is also recommended that future land use planning and zoning include provision for open space zones. Much of the land in the townships is not developable, for reasons of excessive slope, land that is not suitable for "on-site" sewerage facilities, or land situated in areas subject to periodic flooding. The above mentioned open space zone will put this undevelopable land to good use as hiking trails, fishing sites—land uses that future generations, as well as our generation, will find priceless."

Commentaries

Rural Commuters. *The Wall Street Journal* has called attention to a little noticed trend in farm life which is developing into an interesting facet of the pattern of American life today.

"When night falls," says James P. Gannon, Staff Reporter for the Journal, "more and more farmers are leaving the land they till for homes in nearby towns. Their reasons for doing so vary, but most of them are seeking fuller and easier lives for themselves and their families."

According to the U. S. Department of Agriculture, roughly 300,000 or about 10 per cent of today's full-time farmers live off their farms and commute to work. Only 7.6 per cent of all farmers were commuters in 1959 when the last official agriculture census was taken.

Why do they do it? For one thing, says Mr. Gannon, the trend reflects the farmer's increased desire to share in what seems to him to be the better things towns have to offer, notably bigger schools and more social and cultural activities.

Desire for modern housing also is drawing farmers into town. Although equally modern homes can be built on the farm, some farmers prefer to build in town because mortgage financing is easier to obtain and town homes generally are easier to resell.

Other factors: Husband and wife move to town when, though still working, they are beginning to plan for retirement or because the wife wishes to hold down a job of her own in town.

But the over-riding factor is the basic changes in American agriculture which have been taking place over the years and which have been making commuting more practical for farmers. Increased mechanization of farm work—ranging from bigger, faster tractors to automatic live-stock feeding systems—has reduced the number of hours a farmer must spend on his land.

The old fashioned farm—needing constant care with its patchwork of different crops, a few milk cows and a flock of laying hens—has largely given way to more specialized, one or two crop operations. Such specialization has made it easier for the farmer to move off his farm. Commuting farmers have bought automatic equipment to tend the animals while they are at home in town. Others hire a full-time hand who lives in the farmhouse the owner left behind when he moved to town.

ॐ

Past and Present. Whereas the suburbs have a problem of making little parcels of land out of big ones, the problem in our downtown areas is assembling little parcels of another era into the big parcels needed for today, states Max S. Wehrly in an article in *Urban Land*.

Mr. Wehrly is executive director of Urban Land Institute, an independent research organization located in Washington, D. C. and specializing in urban planning and development.

To be successful, downtown must be compact in terms of land coverage and building heights and this compactness can be achieved only through unified action on the part of merchants, building and land owners, and the city fathers, Mr. Wehrly contends. These elements must work together as a team in order to cope with eighteenth or nineteenth century patterns of land subdivision which created 20- and 50-foot lots in downtown areas. Without concerted action, new buildings will appear, but obsolete lot lines will remain.

Mr. Wehrly holds that downtown areas have the capabilities for regeneration without subsidy inasmuch as private financial resources are usually present and new urban redevelopment concepts, utilizing the powers of condemnation, can be used against holdout owners of unimproved or obsolete property as well as in cases of clouded titles. "What the business community must do," he states, "is combine its efforts and financial resources rather than continue on the divisive paths of the past."

He points out that downtown's function as a focal point for all the activities of the whole metropolitan area can never be fulfilled by the regional shopping center. Downtown takes in central or main offices of local firms and corporations, branch offices of national institutions, the surgeon, the patent attorney, the newspaper, city hall, the financial district, and the people who man and patronize these activities.

☙

Monuments. With every square foot of the good earth being forced more and more to run the gauntlet of appropriate use, the proper area to be allotted to man-made monuments in the man-made scheme for space, is an ever-present question.

A new report from the New York City Department of Parks, called "30 Years of Progress, 1934-1964," presents some hard facts that could help lift the subject out of the realm of pure emotionalism.

"In 1934," says the report, "the newly consolidated Park Department became responsible for the care of some 500 monuments and memorials, ranging from imposing edifices to miniature bronze tablets.

"Regardless of esthetic or sentimental consideration, most of them have been out-and-out troublemakers. Because they were either poorly constructed, designed with utter disregard for practicality, vulnerable to incessant vandalism, or made of materials unable to withstand our climatic changes, almost all must be restored over and over again.

"Whether a monument 'speaks' in the booming voice of a brave equestrian, the eloquence of a majestic arch, or the small voice of a tiny tablet—all are the responsibility of the Park Department and must be maintained. Should we let them fall into disrepair, criticisms come quickly, usually from those who have little comprehension of the scope of the problems involved.

"The number of monuments increases each year. In 1959, there were 649. Today we are responsible for over 700. To insure the City against unnecessary additional maintenance, we have attempted to establish and adhere to new principles and standards. We now work with sculptors, architects, and other designers of monuments and memorials from the drawing board stage to dedication.

"Monument maintenance and rehabilitation is highly specialized work requiring many skills difficult to find in today's labor market. A plan is now under way to establish a program "for on the job training" of monument craftsmen.

"For the past twenty-nine years, the same small devoted group of artisans has struggled with the problem. Despite the lack of adequate professional personnel and insufficiency of funds, we have completed 643 restorations, relocations, rehabilitations, and reconstructions since 1934. In addition, 165 new monuments and memorials have been dedicated. During the past two years, 70 restorations or rehabilitations have been completed, and 38 new monuments have been acquired."

෴

Recollection. Ben H. Thompson, young enough to have known the haunting beauty of the Arizona desert, yet old enough to have witnessed its man-made transformation, made poignant reference to both at the 1964 annual meeting of the Nature Conservancy.

Recalling that he first went to southern Arizona as a youngster, Mr. Thompson, formerly Assistant Director of the National Park Service and also Treasurer of the National Conference on State Parks, continued:

"The desert, broken only by scattered ranches, reached away in all directions to the mountains and beyond. It seemed limitless. The air was clear and you could see blue mountains with sharp clear outlines for a hundred miles . . . There is almost infinite variety in the natural grouping of desert plants and rocks that presents natural gardens of exquisite beauty wherever you might look.

"I remember going swimming in the Gila River, second only to the Colorado River as they both flow through Arizona. The Gila was a sparkling clear, clean stream flowing at the base of desert mountains . . .

"But if you go there today . . . you will see that there is no Gila River. Its waters have been entirely impounded many miles upstream for irrigation. The bed of the once clear stream is now lost in brush and weeds, for over two hundred miles. The desert that reached limitlessly to the mountains has vanished into cotton fields and mile after mile of houses. The sandy desert road that was such fun to walk in barefoot, is a four-lane concrete highway over which tractor-trailers, trucks, and cars roar ceaselessly night and day."

Said Mr. Thompson: "I mention the southern Arizona desert because in doing so I can state from firsthand experience what all of us have seen happen in our lifetimes in almost any part of the United States. It is hardly possible to realize or comprehend the loss of naturally created beauty, on the east coast, the west coast, and around every large city and metropolitan area across the country. Moreover, the speed at which we are losing the natural beauty of our land is being accelerated."

೧৩

Parkways. Edward J. Meeman, recently re-elected Vice-President of the *American Planning and Civic Association,* had some interesting comments after an inspection trip with the Advisory Board on National Parks down the 469-mile length of the Blue Ridge Parkway.

A parkway at its best, he says, "is more than a highway where the view is unmarred by billboards and neon signs." In the definition quoted by landscape architect Stanley Abbott, "a parkway is an elongated park with a road in it."

"It may be even more than that," says Mr. Meeman. It may be what the Blue Ridge is—a chain of parks. Your stopping to linger in each one of these 'parks,' to savor the distinctive delights which each one of them offers, means as much as the pleasant drive through unfolding vistas from one to the other. Not only is there a great national park at each end of the Blue Ridge Parkway—Shenandoah at the north and Great Smoky Mountains at the south—but there are 11 recreation areas along the way, more than one of which might proudly be called a national park if it stood alone."

Mr. Meeman, who made the trip "when the crimson, purple and yellow of the hardwoods glowed in a golden October sun against the contrasting evergreens," kept an observant eye on the man-made innovations in the area—the "wide places in the road."

"There are the Peaks of Otter," he says, "where you find a recently built inn, fresh and original in design but so timeless in spirit that it shames the shoddy, merely 'contemporary' that you so often see elsewhere. Those of us who got up at dawn saw bull elk fighting on the front 'lawn.'

"As you stand on one peak and see the blue-misty mountains stretch range on range, the heavens are very close and you think Heaven itself could offer no more pleasing prospect.

"You understand why the National Park Service asks more parkways, with the enthusiastic backing of Interior Secretary Udall.

"When a parkway is planned with a right-of-way broad enough that it meets the definition of 'an elongated park with a road in it,' and enough 'wide places in the road' that it becomes a chain of parks, such a project will deserve universal support."

೧৩

Libraries. According to the September, 1964 issue of *The Municipal South,* people from all over the southeast have visited the new public library in Gadsden, Alabama.

Gadsden's Mayor Les Gilliland points out that a library is considered to be a yardstick of measurement for the community.

20

National Capital
Notes

A CITY IS SO MANY LITTLE THINGS. And what *you* are will help determine what it will become—a backdrop for living with zest and meaning or for an existence without savour.

Within the past months, a contagious feeling that an indeterminate ingredient is lacking in the Washington area, the fastest growing urban center in the country, has seized some of the city's key leaders. And the seizure seems to be taking hold of city officials, spokesmen for the Federal government, civic leaders and the National Capital's press.

"When we come to Washington," says the *Washington Evening Star*, ". . . aside from some parks, a few sidewalk cafes and some flower carts, there seems to be a dearth of the pleasant minutiae that give a city a charm of its own."

The concentration on "minutiae" came full bloom, if it didn't actually bud when **District Commissioner Walter N. Tobriner** returned last fall from a European vacation with a strong urge to dress up Washington with more charm and a warmer atmosphere.

What emerged in the ensuing criss-cross of responses were suggestions for streetside kiosks operated by natty little merchants, benches where the foot-sore and just plain weary can rest, eye-appeal protection for the thousands who battle the elements to board homeward-bound buses and a dozen other little amenities ranging from flower boxes to guide maps mounted in glass-faced containers.

Out of the host of suggestions, two, especially, were buoyed up for exhaustive consideration and possible action. The one would transform the stately, but some would say somewhat sterile, beauty of the Mall from the Lincoln Memorial to Capital Hill into a setting for more leisurely enjoyment by the millions who go there. The other, simpler in concept, but with equally imaginative appeal and actually part and parcel of the other, would put ice skaters on the Reflecting Pool through the installation of freezing and pumping equipment and the construction of a concrete bottom.

Members of the **Committee of 100 on the Federal City** are playing prominent roles in the consideration of both proposals. A special committee composed of outstanding citizens, including ample representation from the Committee of

100, has been appointed by **Secretary of the Interior Stewart Udall** to weigh the possibilities of the Reflecting Pool skating project. The **National Park Service** has estimated that it will cost more than two and one half million dollars to convert the Reflecting Pool into the biggest ice-skating rink in the world.

As to the Mall, Interior Secretary Stewart Udall has given enthusiastic endorsement to a proposal of New York landscape architect **Richard Webel** which would convert the Mall into an enticing congregating area with kiosks, flower stalls and a promenade. **Mrs. James H. Rowe, Jr.**, chairman of the **National Capital Planning Commission**, has also expressed approval of the proposal.

The Webel plan would move all the streets crossing the Mall underground and eliminate 15th Street on the Mall. It calls for intense development in the museum areas of the Mall and the Washington Monument grounds and for more subdued development at the Lincoln Memorial and the Capitol.

Some four to six parks are envisioned with small pools, fountains, flower beds, kiosks and roaming vendors and, perhaps, even outdoor restaurants.

But the Webel plan, according to Mr. Udall, may take 10 to 15 years or more to implement and its implementation will require appropriations from Congress. Meanwhile, funds for enlivening the Mall are already included in the Interior Department's budget and the immediate question is: What can be done now?

"The Park Service can begin right now," says the *Washington Evening Star*, "to install benches and build walkways under the four rows of lovely old trees which border the open Mall. And it should do so right now—in time for use by the thousands of tourists who will throng to the Capital next spring. This obvious and necessary first step would not be expensive. It would not disturb a single tree, or impair any other single value of the park."

Mr. Udall, on the other hand, is believed to favor beginning with one section to demonstrate what might be done rather than merely "strewing benches all over" the green expanse between the Capitol and the Lincoln Memorial.

In any case, as officials and civic leaders grapple with this aspect of what the city is and ought to be, numerous pervasive questions are arising.

Has "a veritable kioskomania," as **Wolf Von Eckardt**, *Washington Post* Staff Writer, puts it, taken hold of the city?

Would a vendor, American brand and roaming on the Mall, lend the same comforting note as his European counter-part who seemingly emanates from his background and somehow avoids the appearance of having been superimposed upon it? How many, or how few, vendors and kiosks would be needed to provide refreshment for the twenty-four million visitors, who, it is estimated, will be arriving in the Nation's Capital annually by 1970?

And if the passive beauty of the Mall gives way to a more active and enlivened atmosphere, even though an attractive one, has a bit of daily refreshment been diminished for the thousands who now partake fleetingly of its unadorned serenity on the way home after a crowded city day? For that matter, will a frozen Reflecting Pool offer the same restoration to harried souls as does still water?

Nobody exactly has the answers.

Nevertheless, the gropings arise from and are nourished by a desire to make Washington, not only more attractive, but also more livable. As such, they are welcomed by all those who seek to make the National Capital a symbol of graciousness to all who come here and their ultimate outcome, and, hopefully, benefits, are awaited with interest.

Meanwhile, the long, homeward-bound lines stand, still without protection from the elements, awaiting buses on the city's crowded streets.

"We hope to make the Potomac a model of beauty and recreation for the entire country," **President Johnson** told Congress in his message on the State of the Union.

The President spoke after a Presidential task force had considered various aspects of the matter, and his position is already being felt in the day-to-day decisions which bear on proposed development along the river's banks.

Recently, the **National Park Service,** while citing the President's proposal, asked Alexandria officials to delay decisions affecting future development of the city's Potomac waterfront and asked for information about re-zoning applications to permit "high rise apartment dwell-

ings and other structures" on the river. Interior **Secretary Stewart L. Udall** asked the Montgomery County Council to reconsider its approval of high-density apartment houses along the river at Cabin John.

Meanwhile, the technique of scenic easement is being used increasingly to assure the preservation of various sections of the riverfront. The easement leaves title to the land in the owner's hands but commits him to restrict its use according to Government regulations which usually restrict development to low-density residential uses.

Probably the best known example is that of the 47-acre Merrywood estate in Fairfax County wherein the Government will pay owners of the land $744,500 for the scenic rights.

The Accokeek Foundation, an organization headed by **Congressman Frances Bolton,** of Ohio, has negotiated scenic easements on 78 parcels of land totaling about 460 acres behind the shoreline facing Mount Vernon. The Foundation's goal is to obtain easements on more than 2,000 acres.

Rear Admiral Neill Phillips, USN (ret.), Chairman of the **Committee of 100 on the Federal City,** was among the twenty individuals invited by **Mrs. Lyndon B. Johnson** to meet with her and **Interior Secretary Stewart Udall** at the White House recently to discuss the formation of a Committee for a More Beautiful Capital.

"As a Nation," wrote the First Lady, "we are more and more interested in enhancing the beauty of our land.

23

"There are many ways in which this can be done through private initiative and through government example. The planting of roadsides, the better design of public buildings, and the encouragement of open space in city and country are illustrative.

"For the citizen who wants to help in such endeavors, there is no better place to begin than the place where one lives. It is in our own communities that we can best participate in creating an environment which has beauty, joyousness and liveliness, as well as dignity."

Mrs. Johnson sees her concentration on beautifying the Nation's Capital as a logical follow-up to the efforts of her immediate predecessor, Mrs. Jacqueline Kennedy, to make the White House reflect the national heritage, and she regards the project as her particular contribution to her husband's program to beautify America.

If you've had doubts about the flamboyant building flanking the White House and now known as the Executive Office Building, the third in the series of **General Services Administration** Historical Studies will afford you the comfort of knowing you're not alone.

"The Executive Office Building is an esthetic issue which has been constantly debated for more than 90 years," says the Study. "The first attack was leveled at its architecture as early as 1874 soon after the south wing began to display the intricate detail of its French renaissance style."

On the other hand, if you're an ardent advocate of the symbolic quality of the building, you'll find that you, too, are in articulate company.

"They've been trying to tear this down for 20 years," the *Washington Star* of April 4, 1958, quoted President Truman, "but I don't want it torn down (with a chuckle). I think it's the greatest monstrosity in America."

"Throughout its life," says the Historical Study, "the building has been able to evoke tart, humorous, and exaggerated comment, favorable and unfavorable—testimonials to the building's vitality . . . Criticism over the years forms a study in architectural counterpoint with one or another of the rival sets of opinions as the dominant theme."

The ruffled course of the building's destiny, which began to emerge soon after President Washington's proclamation of the boundaries of the newly formed District of Columbia on January 24, 1791, is unfolded in the 100-page study. This is the third in a series which has been undertaken by the General Services Administration in the belief that the collection of authentic historical data will help to assure that buildings of true worth in the National Capital will be preserved.

One of the most extensive historical restorations ever undertaken by the **National Park Service** in the Nation's Capital was initiated on November 29 when Ford's Theatre building was closed for restoration to its appearance at the

(*Continued on page 28*)

24

PROJECTS IN REVIEW

Baltimore's Charles Center

In the short span of five years, Charles Center has become famous for the ingenuity of its design and plan.

But the story of Charles Center is far more than what a segment of Baltimore's Downtown will look like, or even be tomorrow—striking and exhilarating as that story is.

In addition, it is a stirring tale of the initiative, drive and cooperation which have permeated the project from its genesis—when men began to react to the bad news that O'Neill's department store had orders to close two days after Christmas in 1954. It is a story of mounting enthusiasm against tremendous odds as reaction gave way to the generation of an idea, as an idea evolved into a plan, a plan became a project and a project was translated into a Downtown Center in one of America's great cities such as to arouse the admiration of men far beyond the city's gates.

That Charles Center will go down in the annals of modern city development in this way seems assured by a recently issued report called "Baltimore's Charles Center—A Case Study of Downtown Renewal" which has recently been issued by the Urban Land Institute in Washington, D. C., an independent research organization specializing in urban planning and development.

The report, edited by Martin Millspaugh, covers one of the well-known Panel Studies in which ULI's Central City Council specializes and is a condensation of 15 papers which were delivered in a two-day symposium by the men "who personally conceived the aims and produced the results" as they reconstructed the story of Charles Center for the Urban Land Institute.

Ten years ago, there was a sense of impending disaster for Downtown Baltimore. Downtown employment in the city hadn't grown in 20 years. Between 1952 and 1957, assessments in the central business district declined 10 percent and downtown department store sales declined 12 percent. Property was sometimes selling below its assessed value, and the vacancy rate was as high as 25 percent in some blocks.

But in the view of David A. Wallace, Former Director, The Planning Council of the Greater Baltimore Committee, Inc., the negative conditions were probably necessary to the success Charles Center has enjoyed. Mr. Wallace believes the sense of impending disaster made it possible to raise the kind of money necessary and to put into effect the sort of planning operation that took place. "The reaction to the realization of disaster," he says, "was a faith in the future, and a willingness to move ahead on the basis of that faith."

How far that faith had to stretch can be measured by the fact that the project had to be "do-able," *within the capacity of the City of Baltimore and its citizens.* In 1957, projects did not qualify for Federal

25

subsidy if they did not involve housing either before or after redevelopment.

Also, as Mr. Wallace points out, "in Baltimore at that time, the municipal planners couldn't give the necessary kind of concentrated attention to the downtown situation. In effect, the city government encouraged the business community to do it themselves."

Hence practicality, feasibility and workability became governing features of the project, determining site and boundary selection. "First of all," says Mr. Wallace, "it had to be adequate in size: big enough and dramatic enough to do the job. It also had to be small enough to be feasible without Federal aid."

Hence, came one of the distinguishing features of Charles Center: Most of the development will be privately financed inasmuch as the essential feature of the project is that Charles Center represents a sound basis for encouraging private investment.

Charles Center did, in fact, become eligible for Federal aid when the Housing Act of 1959 was enacted, and in February of 1960, machinery was set in motion to have Charles Center approved for the three-quarter Federal grant formula under which Baltimore operates. But the basic consideration of feasibility has not changed. All Center buildings have stood the stern test of whether or not they are workable within the over-all plan.

Mr. Wallace points out: "In analyzing the buildings that were within these boundaries, we used an approach somewhat different from the usual redevelopment approach

at that time—perhaps because no Federal subsidy was available, and the project had to be self-supporting. We started with the question: what could we save (rather than: what could we get rid of)? Our analysis was based not on what was eligible for Federal aid, but on how little could be torn down and still create the necessary opportunity."

And from this premise has come a second distinguishing feature of Charles Center: Unlike most downtown renewal projects, it leaves standing some sound old structures, providing links of continuity with the rest of the central business district.

Mr. Millspaugh says: "Instead of the sterile, wide open spaces which are typical of many mall-type projects, Charles Center relies on a concentration of high densities, which are expected to produce a redoubled daytime population and a quickening of human activity day and night."

However, on the other side of the coin, sacrifice, sometimes on the part of those who were prime instigators of the development, was called for and made without whimpering. For building after building was cancelled out—"not necessarily because they were all obsolete, but sometimes because they would simply destroy the eventual implementation of any really consistent plan." Included in this category were Hamburger's apparel store and the Gas and Electric Company Building, both of which have been re-placed by new buildings within the scope of the plan.

As to the design of Charles Center, George E. Kostritsky, former

Project Director, The Planning Council of the Greater Baltimore Committee, Inc., says, "the basic design theme for Charles Center became the space between buildings. Other themes, some of them based on local tradition, were: Monuments, water, light, trees and sculpture.

Trees, which have been banned in some downtown city areas, are being planted in downtown areas of Baltimore now. In fact, the landscape plan for Charles Center calls for trees on all the streets with special treatment in the parks, themselves. There are three public squares: one at the north, one in the middle and one at the southern end of the project.

Not forgotten were the church spires, landmarks in the old historic city and spires for the spirit in the harried hustle bustle of crowded downtown today. To preserve the view of St. Alphonsus Church, the towers of two new buildings were deliberately placed so that the Church could be seen through the gap between them, looking from the space created by one of the parks. The upper or northern park was left open on the east side in order to let St. Paul's Church have some breathing room.

The well-known pedestrian platforms and walkways in the Charles Center Plan were conceived as "covered pedestrian promenades and pedestrian walkways above the streets."

"They may not work completely right away," says Mr. Kostritsky, "but I think we have to sow the seeds today and begin to develop them. We can't get rid of the auto-mobile, for instance; we will only get rid of it to a certain extent; so these pedestrian walkways will become extremely important in the cities of the future.

"To minimize the presence of the automobile, we visualized garages buried under the ground . . . not just small structures, but on a large scale."

So today Charles Center stands at the half-way point of its 10-year development period, with one-half, or $50,000,000 of its goal of $100,000,000 in new development, either completed or under construction. Men of all types have had a hand in bringing it to this point—planners, real estate experts, retailers, bankers, developers, politicians, civil servants.

And one cannot peruse the story of its development as told in the Urban Land Institute's Technical Bulletin 51, without being struck by the appropriateness of the observation of the Report's Editor, Mr. Millspaugh:

"It was quickly established that Charles Center has been successful not only because the plan was created by an elite team of designers and executed by one of the most efficient local renewal organizations, but also *because the right man has always seemed to appear at the right time, to push the project along the way toward reality.*"

Perhaps it may also be said that the right report on the 10-year program has now appeared at just the right time, with the right note of objectivity, to help lend a guiding hand to other cities embarking on programs to save their downtown areas.

To Keep New York City Clean

An intensive year-round Clean-Up program, reaching into every borough and segment of the City of New York, has been reported by the November, 1964 issue of the *Communicator*, a publication of the National Clean-Up, Paint-Up, Fix-Up Bureau, located in Washington, D. C.

Included among the projects undertaken throughout the year by the Citizens Committee To Keep New York City Clean, according to the *Communicator*, is the Miracle Garden program which dates back to 1956 and which is being extended to include window boxes.

The Miracle Garden program involves the conversion of city-owned vacant lots into gardens planted and maintained by neighborhood school children. Last year, as the beginning of a five-year plan to beautify Brooklyn, the program was extended to include window boxes. A pilot project was tested in the Park Slope section of the borough with 100 window boxes complete with flowers and potting soil having been furnished to 40 residents. It is hoped, in subsequent years, to spread the use of window boxes to all Brooklyn neighborhoods.

National Capital Notes

(*Continued from page 24*)

time of President Lincoln's assassination.

A contract of $1,390,000 for the restoration of the theatre's interior, to be completed within 540 days, has been awarded to **Coe Construction Inc.**, of Washington, D. C. The 88th Congress authorized the expenditure of $2,073,600 for restoration of the Theatre which is now a national memorial administered by the Capital Region of the National Park Service and which, since 1932, has housed on its ground floor the Lincoln Museum. Restoration plans call for a new museum in the basement of the building.

Ford's Theatre, built in 1863, was closed immediately after President Lincoln's assassination on April 14, 1865 and since that time has had a varied history. In June, 1865, the building was returned to its owner who planned to reopen it as a theatre. But public opinion was aroused and the Federal Government again took charge of it and that same year began to remodel it into a fireproof building for Government records. All woodwork was removed and the building was divided into three stories with the second and third floors supported by cast-iron columns and wrought-iron girders and beams.

A second tragedy occurred in the building on June 9, 1893, when the three floors collapsed, killing 22 clerks and injuring 68 others. The building was restored the following year. In 1931, it was renovated and made ready for the Oldroyd Collection of Lincolniana, the museum items which will be protected in storage during the present restoration project.

Proposed Guadalupe Mountains National Park, Texas. El Capitan, the landmark at the southern tip of the Guadalupe range, visible for over 50 miles.

Courtesy, National Park Service, U. S. Department of the Interior

Proposed Guadalupe Mountains National Park, Texas. Scene in South McKittrick Canyon

Courtesy, National Park Service, U. S. Department of the Interior

Guadalupe Mountains National Park—A Proposal

Ninth in a series on proposed projects, prepared by the National Park Service

THE GUADALUPE MOUNTAINS form the southern terminus of the exposed part of the Capitan reef—a vast formation of Permian marine limestones that is recognized as the most extensive and significant fossil reef in the world. It features a highland area that rises from an elevation of 3,100 feet in the Pecos Valley near Carlsbad, New Mexico, to 8,751 feet in Texas —the highest point in that State— 60 miles to the southwest. This highland comprises the northeast arm of the Guadalupe Mountains range which resembles a huge "V," with the point of the "V" in Culberson County, Texas, and the two arms extending northwestward and northeastward into New Mexico. The latter contains Carlsbad Caverns National Park.

At the south end of the Guadalupes, 4,000 feet of Permian rocks are magnificently exposed. The headland, El Capitan, with its sheer, thousand-foot cliff, is visible for 50 miles or more. Deep canyons, principally McKittrick Canyon and its forks, incised in the highland by running water, contain a unique assemblage of plants and animals that is, at least in part, a relict association of the Pleistocene epoch. The Texas portion of this rugged scenic and biologic resource, containing the point of the "V" of the range, is the proposed Guadalupe Mountains National Park.

The special qualities of this area and its potential for National Park status have been recognized for some time. In October, 1938, a report entitled *Some Geological Observations on the Guadalupe Mountains* was submitted by Junior Geologist Ross Maxwell of the National Park Service, and a companion report prepared for the Texas State Parks Board entitled *Narrative Report on McKittrick Canyon* was submitted by Assistant Landscape Architect Obert. The first report summarized the general geology of the area, and the second commended the area to the State for the finest state park in Texas. More recently, three specific investigations—in April, 1958, May, 1961, and June, 1963—were made by the Service to evaluate the scenic and scientific resources of the Guadalupes for National Park purposes.

In the meantime, acceptance by the Federal Government of Mr. Wallace Pratt's generous donation of 5,632 acres in the superb North McKittrick Canyon area of the Guadalupe Mountains in Texas was completed in 1961. At that time it was proposed that the donated tract would be established eventually as a detached section of Carlsbad Caverns National Park, but it is now included as part of the larger proposal for a separate Guadalupe Mountains National Park of some 77,800 acres. This latter area, besides rounding out a unique physiographic unit of significant geologic and ecologic values, would provide the additional terrain for the administrative and public-use developments and recreational use that could not be accommodated in the restricted bottom lands of McKittrick Canyon without severe impairment of its fragile nature and environment.

The additional land in the Guadalupes proposal is now available, for Mr. J. C. Hunter, Jr., of Abilene, Texas, who owns some 71,790 acres of ranchland adjoining the Pratt donation and comprising most of the rest of the Guadalupe Mountains in Texas, wishes to sell the ranch. Mr. Hunter would prefer that it be preserved for public use. This is the basis of the current proposal, in which the Federal Government would acquire the Hunter lands and, combined with the North McKittrick Canyon area that is already owned, establish them as a National Park. The proposed park can be visualized as having two components—a scientific reserve in the McKittrick Canyon area and a high, cool region suitable for more intensive use in the high Guadalupes.

The National Park Service completed a study of the Guadalupe area in September, 1963, and recommended it for a national park. Upon reviewing this study and visiting the area, the Secretary's Advisory Board on National Parks, Historic Sites, Buildings and Monuments, at its November, 1963 meeting, unanimously recommended that National Park status would provide the most effective means of preserving and interpreting the unique values of this area. Almost immediately after this action, both Senator Yarborough and Congressman Pool introduced similar bills to provide for the establishment of the Guadalupe Mountains National Park in the State of Texas. The bills provided for the establishment of the National Park, consisting of the land already donated by Wallace Pratt and most of the J. C. Hunter ranch, plus about 4,780 acres in other private ownership. Most of this park area lies in Culberson County, and the balance in Hudspeth County, Texas.

The present economic use of the J. C. Hunter Guadalupe Mountain Ranch is for mohair wool production with a herd of about 4,000 angora goats. Other economic resources of the area are meager. Some building stone, road material, and salt have been produced. No oil or gas has been found, and it is believed there is only a slight chance that any will be discovered. Minerals in the proposed park area are mostly state-owned. Ground water is a valuable resource, where found, and several springs issue from the base of the mountains.

The wildlife resources of the Guadalupes have been supplemented by transplants of species which have prospered under the commendable conservation practices of the land-owners. The Merriam elk that once ranged here is now extinct, but the related wapiti, or American elk, was introduced in the mid-1920's and there are an estimated 500 animals in the herd now, perhaps half of them spread across the state line into New Mexico. Very few elk or the native mule deer are harvested on the Hunter ranch, where hunting control is discretionary with the owner under State permit. The native Merriam turkey disappeared from the Guadalupes years ago but was reintroduced in 1954, and there are now about 200 birds in the range. There have been mountain sheep (Texas bighorn) in the Guadalupes, but the last sighting was in 1956. Bluegill and rainbow trout, both exotic, have been twice planted in South McKittrick Canyon, and now reproduce naturally in the only stream in Texas which can claim this distinction for trout. In addition to a very few mountain lions and black bear in the rougher canyon areas, the wildlife of the proposed park area includes such carnivores as bobcats, gray fox, coyotes, raccoons, and skunks.

To describe adequately the complex botany of the region, it is necessary to analyze the varied ecological factors that prevail in it. Biotic associations range from Lower Sonoran in the typical Chihuahuan Desert environment at the base of the western escarpment to Transition and some Canadian zone elements in the highlands, and the zones are intricately modified by localized slope, exposure, and moisture conditions. South McKittrick Canyon, itself, offers an ever-changing botanical picture—a mixture of forest and desert vegetation. The dryer slopes and stream channels of the lower reaches are clothed with such species as ponderosa pine, alligator-bark juniper, Texas madrone, Texas walnut, netleaf hackberry, and gray oak. The presence of a permanent stream here further influences a varied growth including sotol, chokecherry, chinquapin oak, and an occasional Douglas fir. As the canyon walls narrow and become higher upstream, these trees and shrubs are joined by century-plant, limber pine, bigtooth maple, hop-tree, and yucca. In the highlands is a strongly contrasting botanical province, dominated by a forest of ponderosa and pines interspersed with Douglas fir and a few quaking aspen and Gambel oak.

Of the many attributes that contribute to the significance of the area, however, the geology must be given highest rank. The Guadalupe Mountains, a great wedge-shaped upland bounded on its southeastern edge by a steeply dipping escarpment and on the western side by a tremendous fault scarp, present a spectacular exposure of the famous Capitan barrier reef and its contemporaneous fore-reef and back-reef marine deposits. The controlling factor in the deposition of these rocks was the presence, in a large part of what is now Texas and New Mexico, of a vast marine basin throughout the Permian period. Lime-secreting algae were chiefly responsible for the growth of this barrier, and other organisms contributed their remains to the structure and aided in trapping and holding limey sand in the growing deposit. The fine display of the several facies of Permian sediments makes the Guadalupes area of outstanding interest to the world's stratigraphers and paleontologists, and, with but little interpretation, they are understandable to the layman. The world's best-known fossil reefs are found within this region, and the Capitan, the greatest of them, has been described as the most extensive fossil organic reef on record.

Even the activities of man, from the long-term occupancy of the area by cave-dwellers beginning 6,000 years ago, and later by Mescalero Apaches, and finally the white man, have left their mark on the area and contribute to its significance. The highlight of this human chapter came with the establishment of the Butterfield Stage Trail through the area in 1858, when the old Pinery stage station was built at the mouth of Pine Spring Canyon in the shadow of Guadalupe Peak. Remnants of this station, used for less than a year until the trail was re-routed far to the south, are still visible and are marked by a bronze plaque. Approximately half of the ruins are located on the property of Mr. J. C. Hunter, Jr., the remainder being in other private ownership.

Add to the range's highly significant geology the unique ecological assemblage in the branches of McKittrick Canyon, as well as the highest and possibly the most rugged and scenic portions of Texas with their geographic proximity to centers of growing population, and the park and recreation potential of the Guadalupes is evident. A sense of healing relaxation results from contact with the primitive character of the Guadalupe Mountains country, the cool forested uplands of which offer terrain for camping, picnicking, hiking, and nature study, as well as delightfully scenic drives. Incidental to these benefits but important in its own right is the certainty that the establishment of a National Park in the Guadalupes would generate benefits to the local economy through tourism, without appreciable offsetting loss caused by displacement of existing land uses.

The suggested theme of management and development in the Guadalupe Mountains National Park would be twofold: To preserve, with a minimum of development and by provision for foot access only, the fragile and unique biotic environment of the canyons; and to provide for heavier public use in the uplands where adequate space is available.

The latter objective would require construction of a scenic road leaving U.S. 62-180 in the vicinity of the Pinery Stage Station and ascending the north wall of Pine Spring Canyon, topping out somewhere near Bush Mountain. From there one fork would follow the ridge eastward and terminate at the Bowl where the park's major camping facilities would be located.

ероь

State Park Notes

California. By a margin of three to two, recreation-conscious voters in California last November approved a $150,000,000 bond issue—the largest state outdoor recreation bonding measure yet proposed—to provide funds for state beaches, parks and recreational and historical facilities.

They thus joined the ranks of a growing number of states approving bonding measures for financing outdoor recreation. Two additional states, Rhode Island and Washington, also took such action at the November elections. And five states, New York, New Jersey, Pennsylvania, Ohio and Florida, have taken similar action since 1960.

The California measure had been proposed by Governor Edmund G. Brown in a special message to the California Legislature and was later approved by that body. Governor Brown and former Governor Goodwin J. Knight served as honorary co-chairmen of Citizens for Beaches and Parks, a bi-partisan committee which led the campaign for the bond issue.

Of the total amount approved, $85,000,000 will be used to acquire additional state parks and beaches; $20,000,000 has been earmarked for minimum development of these new state areas; $5,000,000 will go for new hunting and fishing areas and public access rights; and the remaining $40,000,000 has been approved for state incentive grants to cities and counties.

Washington. Two significant financial measures, promoted by Citizens For Outdoor Recreation, a bi-partisan group in the state of Washington, were approved by the voters at the November elections. A $10,000,000-bond issue, to help buy and develop additional state parks and other types of recreation areas, was approved, seven to five.

A second ballot proposal—to earmark $1,500,000 in state motorboat fuel taxes for shoreline acquisition and development and to set up a focal point within the state government to coordinate outdoor recreation planning—was approved five to three. The fuel tax measure was placed on the ballot by Citizens For Outdoor Recreation by petition through the initiative process after the Legislature failed to act. Both incumbent Gov. Albert D. Rosellini and his successful challenger, former State Representative Dan J. Evans, supported both proposals.

37

Rhode Island. Rhode Island's $5,000,000-"Green Acres" bond issue carried two to one at the November elections.

The Rhode Island plan for "Green Acres" projects includes purchase of land for seven new state parks, beach development and woodland and marsh preservation. Cities and towns will be eligible for one third of the money for local projects.

The plan presupposes that, under the new federal land and water conservation act, equal matching funds will be obtained for the state projects. And the $1,700,000 of bond revenue earmarked for local communities could be quadrupled since the "Green Acres" act provides that bond money will be put up to match amounts appropriated by cities and towns. The combined community and state funds could then be matched equally by federal money for a total of $6,800,000.

Utah. A survey to determine Utah's outdoor recreational needs, as well as its individual citizen wants, will be conducted this year by several of the state's agencies, according to Dr. Reed C. Richardson, economics professor at the University of Utah.

A detailed questionnaire to ascertain what residents, in all walks of life, do with their leisure time will be mailed to heads of 2,500 families living in all areas of the state.

Results of the survey, combined with further studies of choices of out-of-state visitors for Utah outdoor recreational facilities, are intended to provide direction in the development and expansion of recreational facilities in the state.

The questionnaires will correlate age brackets and income groups and will ask specific questions regarding amounts of leisure time, length of annual vacations, recreational budgets and amounts invested in boats, skis, summer cabins, camping paraphernalia, and other out-door recreation equipment.

A similar national survey has recently been completed by the University of Michigan.

Arizona. The Arizona State Parks Board has received title to 60 acres of federal land following its purchase at $2.50 per acre.

The total $150 cost of the area is in accordance with provisions of the Recreation and Public Purposes Act and a pricing schedule set by Secretary of the Interior Stewart L. Udall, whereby state, county and city governments, plus other qualified agencies may purchase public land at the nominal price of $2.50 per acre or lease it for 25 cents per acre annually.

The land purchased by Arizona adjoins Lyman Lake in Apache County and will become a part of Lyman Lake State Recreation area which features a 1,500-acre maximum fishing and boating reservoir.

Under terms of the patent, the State is to establish and maintain a public park with construction of facilities to begin within two years. Improvements and park construction already are well under way at Lyman Lake, including a campground, picnic areas, boat launching and rental service and other recreational facilities.

The Federal government reserves all mineral rights to the land and the Bureau of Land Management will manage all other values of the land consistent with the recreational objectives.

Approximately 638 acres of additional park land for Tucson Mountain Park have been presented to Pima County, Arizona, by the U. S. Bureau of Land Management.

The area was obtained in keeping with an over-all plan to preserve and protect the natural vegetation within the 11,500-acre park, including an extensive "forest" of giant saguaro cacti.

The land was acquired under the Recreation and Public Purposes Act which, as indicated above, provides that county, municipal and other governmental agencies may purchase land for certain public uses at $2.50 per acre or by leasing it for 25 cents per acre each year.

Illinois. The first Illinois state nature preserve was dedicated last October by the state Department of Conservation.

Area included in the preserve consists of the south portion of Illinois Beach State Park—a tract which has been informally designated as a nature area since the park was first established and which has been protected from encroachments by the efforts of the Illinois Dunesland Preservation Society. The area includes examples of sand prairie, low dunes and marshland. It harbors unusual plant specimens including the Waukegan juniper,

prickly pear cactus, blazing star, gentian, and bearberry.

Iowa. "The Iowa Conservation Commission is as far advanced in recreational planning as any other state in the midwest region."

This is the summation of Carol Buckmann who, in a recent issue of the *Iowa Conservationist*, has written a comprehensive report on completed portions of the planning program now being carried out by the Planning and Coordination Division of the Conservation Commission under the direction of Glen G. Powers.

In a review of the physical features and natural resources of Iowa, transportation, history, archeology, geology and climate were inventoried.

One major problem facing Iowa is lack of land space inasmuch as the Iowa Conservation Commission owns less than one precent of the total Iowa area. Percentagewise, according to Mr. Powers, this is the smallest area set aside for outdoor recreation in any state of the Union.

The studies of the Planning Division show that one way Iowa is coping with the problem is by private development of outdoor recreational areas. Many of the private developments relate to programs of various federal agencies which have provided assistance to private industry in outdoor developments.

A second area of emphasis is the County Conservation Boards which are "close to the pulse of the people and can maintain and develop the area accordingly." The Commission is continuing its study regarding the possibility of transferring some small parks to local county conservation boards. It is intended that transfers will be made where areas have more local than statewide significance and where county boards have proven that they have the ability to manipulate and manage recreation areas.

It is the hope of the Commission that every county will soon have a county conservation board.

Florida. In the wilds of Myakka River State Park, miles away from civilization, a 30-foot high lookout tower is providing wildlife lovers and bird watchers with an opportunity to observe first-hand one of the largest bird rookeries in Florida.

The tower enables visitors to view the rookery, which contains from 500,000 to 1,000,000 water fowl, without disturbing the birds. Its viewing platform, partially shielded from the rookery by trees and high bushes, is 30 feet above ground and can accommodate 24 people at one time.

Myakka River State Park, situated 17 miles east of Sarasota, embraces nearly 29,000 acres and is considered one of the most interesting in the Florida state parks system. It is nationally noted for the variety and quantity of aquatic and other birds and its several large rookeries.

State park and Audubon officials had been anxious for the lookout tower to be built since the rookery was discovered nearly three years ago. Since the rookery is approximately seven miles from the main entrance to the park, a small school bus has been scheduled to make four tours weekly to and from the rookery site.

Louisiana. A new state park in East Baton Rouge Parish, Louisiana, became a reality recently under a resolution approved in the State Senate and by virtue of a private donation.

The resolution authorized the Wildlife and Fisheries Commission and the Forestry Commission to turn over a 236-acre tract to the Louisiana State Parks and Recreation Commission for development as a state park. The land had previously been donated to the two state agencies by the late Frank H. Waddill and the late Camilla deBat Waddill.

Colorado. Just as fainter hearts were beginning to wonder wearily if conservation is one thing and transportation another and the twain can never meet, Colorado came up with the hearty announcement that they can very well meet in Colorado—and, in fact, do.

Charles Shumate, chief engineer of the State Highway Department, and Harry Woodward, director of the Game, Fish and Parks Department, have jointly pointed out that cooperation between the two state agencies, each acting in an advisory capacity to the other, can reduce threatened destruction of wildlife resources by highway construction to a bare minimum in Colorado.

How? Mr. Shumate says that when his department plans road construction that might threaten a fishing stream, the construction plan is first studied with the Game, Fish and Parks Department.

Reprinted from the 1964 Summer Edition of The Conservation Volunteer, a publication of the Minnesota State Department of Conservation.

Archeologic Values in Minnesota State Parks

By Creighton T. Shay

MINNESOTA has been the home of Indian tribes for at least 10,000 years. Past and current archeological research by the University of Minnesota and other institutions is gradually unfolding the history of these prehistoric inhabitants.

Unfortunately, these materials are scattered throughout the state, preserved in settlements and burial mounds, and *they are in danger of being obliterated completely by the march of modern civilization.* New highways and housing projects are destroying the record at an ever-increasing rate, not to mention the depredations of thoughtless relic-hunters. Although a number of sites have been salvaged before they were destroyed by construction activities, countless others have been lost.

It is fortunate that many areas in our state have been *set aside for parks and historic monuments. Almost*

every one of the present and projected state parks contains one or more important archeological sites. Thus these sites can be preserved until they are excavated by trained archeologists. More importantly, however, our state parks have museums and outdoor displays which can help to educate the public about our prehistoric Indians. Several museums already exist and more are being planned.

Although far from complete, the story of Minnesota prehistory is a fascinating one of cultural development and adaptation to our native Minnesota plant and wildlife resources. Our story begins about 12,-000 years ago when nearly the entire state was covered by massive glaciers that had entered Minnesota from the north and extended as far south as Iowa. As the climate became warmer, water from these melting ice sheets became blocked behind moraine ridges, producing a number of large glacial lakes.

One of these lakes was the massive Lake Agassiz in the present Red River Valley, the *largest glacial lake* in North America. Others included Lake Granstburg north of the Twin Cities, and Lakes Aitkin and Upham in northern Minnesota. Lake Superior, or glacial Lake Duluth, was much larger than it is today, its shores extending 600 feet higher than present levels.

Not long after the ice retreated from an area, plants and animals began to colonize the bare soil. Soon spruce trees were able to grow, as well as larch and aspen and other hardy northern hardwoods. Some of the animals that inhabited our state at the close of the ice age are still here today, while others have become extinct. Mammoth and mastodon, a large species of bison, musk ox, giant beaver and other smaller mammals were present soon after the retreat of the ice.

With such an assortment of large game, it is easy to understand why man was attracted to our area. We don't know exactly when these first hunters moved in, but a reasonable estimate is about 10,000 years ago—nearly a thousand years after the glaciers had completely retreated from Minnesota. These people were descendants of the first migrants who had crossed the Bering Straits from Asia and entered North America some five to ten thousand years earlier. Because they preyed mainly on the larger herd animals, their way of life demanded mobility. Camps were small and shelters were probably quickly-erected skin tents.

These are the groups whose r mains archeologists call *Paleo-Ind an.* Although their tool kit wa simple, consisting of flint spea points and scrapers, probably a fe bone and wood tools and skin con tainers, they appear to have bee efficient hunters. Unfortunatel most of what they made was perisl able, so that we know only of thei excellent flint work. Finely-flake lanceolate-shaped spear points wer fashioned from quartzite and flint and these have turned up as iso lated finds in several parts of ou state. A buffalo kill-site that ma date from the end of the Paleo-Indian period is *currently being investigated in Itasca State Park.* This site consists of the remains of butchered buffalo of an extinct species along with other animal, fish and shell remains and flint butchering tools.

We have little knowledge of how these people cared for their dead. One burial belonging to this period was found at *Browns Valley* in western Minnesota in a gravel pit. The burial had been placed in a pit lined with red ochre (powdered hematite) along with several parallel-flaked lanceolate spear points of the Paleo-Indian type. Another skeleton, not a burial, which might belong to this period or the following period was found near Pelican Rapids. This find has been labeled "*Minnesota Man*" but was *actually a young girl*, presumably drowned in a lake and subsequently covered with sand and silt. An elk dagger and a perforated Gulf Coast conch shell were found with the skeleton.

This early hunting pattern survived for perhaps several thousand years, and archeologists believe it ended with the extinction of the mammoth and mastodon and the replacement of the large bison by the modern species. At that time the climate had warmed enough to approximate our modern conditions. The majority of our present plants and animals had entered the state and developed the characteristic associations seen today in our coniferous and deciduous forests and prairies. The limits of these various vegetation zones, however, have fluctuated throughout the ensuing millennia. The disappearance of the large animals may have been due in part to climate, as well as to man's hunting activities. Whatever the reason, by about 7,000 to 8,000 years ago a new pattern of adjustment to the Minnesota wilderness had begun to emerge.

This new way of life, termed the *Archaic*, was adapted to a modern fauna and required less mobility than the preceding Paleo-Indian pattern. Now deer, elk and other forest animals were hunted and more attention was devoted to native plant foods such as nuts, berries and roots. Fish were caught in streams and lakes with bone fishhooks and shells were collected from beaches. Since food and game were plentiful, forest groups living in central Minnesota were able to settle for longer periods of time. Their camps were probably not large and may have consisted of a number of bark or skin-covered huts. In the southeastern limestone country, caves and rockshelters were used as habitations. In the west, prairies had appeared and hunting groups there continued to subsist largely on buffalo.

Not only were more natural resources used during the Archaic, but new types of tools were introduced as well. A greater variety of spear points was made, the spearthrower or atlatl came into use, and ground stone tools gradually gained prominence. These latter were made by hammering, pecking and polishing igneous rocks to make axes, adzes, mauls and foodgrinding implements.

During this period a new raw material for tools and ornaments was also introduced. This new material was copper, obtained as chunks in glacial drift in eastern Minnesota and mined in the Lake Superior basin. Socketed and tanged spear points, knives, axes and other woodworking tools, as well as fishhooks, were formed by cold-hammering. This native copper industry continued into the historic period when early explorers referred to its use by the Sioux and Ojibwa tribes.

The Archaic way of life persisted with gradual changes until about three thousand years ago, or 1000 B.C. The *Woodland* period began then, ushered in by the introduction of pottery making. Pottery means many things—a new kind of storage and cooking container as well as a medium for artistic expression. The earliest vessels that have been found are thick-walled, simple in form and decoration and apparently not very sturdy. During the succeeding centuries a variety of shapes and sizes was developed and decoration became increasingly elaborate; surface finish and designs were executed with sharpened and carved sticks and cord-wrapped wooden paddles.

Many other changes were taking place during this period. It is apparent that in late Archaic times more attention had been devoted to care of the dead; early burial mounds without pottery are scattered throughout the western part of the state. Burials were in long low mounds in sand and gravel ridges. The bones had been covered with red ochre, and various stone, shell and copper objects accompanied the dead. Later mounds built by pottery-making peoples were larger and grave offerings were more elaborate. One of the largest of these mounds, the Grand Mound in Itasca County, measures 117 feet in length and 45 feet in height; its preservation in a state park is being planned.

Hunting and gathering was still practiced in the Woodland period, as agriculture had not yet been introduced. It was sometime in this period that the inhabitants of northern and central Minnesota learned to gather wild rice and collect maple syrup. The rice was probably gathered in dugouts or birchbark canoes and then processed either by parching in a pottery vessel over a small fire or by sun-drying, thrashing, and then winnowing. Rice was probably as much of a delicacy then as it is today and may have been traded to tribes outside of our area. Excavations have uncovered clay-lined pits used for storing the wild rice. Maple sap was collected in containers placed under a gash cut into the tree trunk, then boiled to make syrup.

The settlements of the Woodland period were larger and more permanent than those of earlier periods,

as evidenced by thick deposits of habitation debris at favorable locations near lakes and streams. Recent excavations in Itasca State Park have uncovered a late Woodland site at Hill Point on Lake Itasca which is some five hundred years old. There is also an extensive settlement and burial mound complex at *Mille Lacs in Katbio State Park* that will be surveyed and mapped in the future. This pattern of more stable hunting and gathering societies continued in the central and northern parts of Minnesota to the time of white settlement.

About 12-1300 A.D., several hundred years before the first Europeans entered the area, another important cultural development occurred in Minnesota. Maize, which had been domesticated far to the south in Mexico, spread into the southern part of the state.

It is hoped that more steps will be taken in the future to preserve this rich Indian heritage. The job lies with the public as well as with state agencies. Landowners should be encouraged to leave burial mounds and settlements on their property intact whenever possible and prevent unauthorized excavation. Surface finds of artifacts should be reported to a professional archeologist and collectors urged to document their collections so that sites can be located and excavated. Archeological sites, unlike forests, cannot be regenerated; we must take steps now to preserve our prehistory for the future—and in our State Parks are archeological treasures which are perpetuated because of the vision of many Minnesota citizens.

Seminars, Conferences, and University Notes

Award. Alvar Aalto, Finnish architect and one of the great founders of contemporary architecture, was recently awarded an honorary degree by Columbia University, adding one more to the many honors which have been conferred upon him.

Dr. Aalto, born in Kuortane, Finland, in 1899, came to the United States for the first time in 1938 following completion of a number of major works which had brought him prominence outside his native land. Included were such buildings as the Viipuri Library, the Tuberculosis Sanitorium in Paimio, his own house in Munkkiniemi, Helsinki, and the Finnish pavilions for the Paris Exposition in 1937. He gave a series of lectures at Yale University. Returning to this country in 1939, he erected the Finnish Pavilion at the New York World's Fair, an undertaking which drew such wide attention that he was invited to teach at the Massachusetts Institute of Technology for which he designed a famous dormitory with undulating walls in 1947.

Fundamental to Dr. Aalto's work is a love of nature. He handles wood masterfully, plans around ledges and rocks and uses them to bring indoors some of the rough, untouched quality of his country— a practice which, perhaps, in part, influenced Frank Lloyd Wright to call him a genius.

In 1938, the Museum of Modern Art in New York organized an exhibition of Dr. Aalto's works which was subsequently circulated to a dozen other cities. He was awarded an honorary degree of Doctor of Fine Arts from Princeton University in 1947 and the Gold Medal of the American Institute of Architects in 1963.

Included on the schedule for Dr. Aalto's current visit to the United States was attendance at the dedication of a floor which he had designed for the new building of the Institute of International Education at 809 United Nations Plaza, New York.

Science Center Appointment. Dr. Jean Paul Mather has been appointed executive vice-president of the University City Science Center, Philadelphia, Pennsylvania.

The University City Science Center is a non-profit institution incorporated last winter to plan, monitor and participate in the development of research facilities, including land sites and laboratories for sale or lease to private industry.

Its stockholders are: University of Pennsylvania, Drexel Institute of Technology, Pennsylvania Hospital, Temple University, Philadelphia College of Pharmacy and Science, Jefferson Medical College, Bryn Mawr College, The Presbyterian Hospital in Philadelphia, The Children's Hospital of Philadelphia, and Lehigh University.

In its initial stages, development of the Center will involve a site of approximately 26 acres on both sides of Market Street between 34th and 40th Streets at the heart of one of the Nation's great educational and medical complexes and adjacent to Philadelphia's business and transportation centers. The plan has been approved by the City Planning Commission and the Philadelphia Redevelopment Authority which will assist in making the property available through the urban renewal process. Under present estimates, construction of the complete Center facilities will cost from $40,000,000 to $50,000,000.

According to Paul J. Cupp, president of the Center, the institution, as it develops, will prove to be a magnetizing force drawing to the Philadelphia area large research-oriented industries from throughout the Nation. "The Center should stimulate scientific research and development throughout the Middle Atlantic area and will focus attention upon the significance of this activity for the economic growth and health of Delware Valley," he said.

Dr. Mather, under whose guidance, the Science Center will be brought into tangible reality, re-signed as vice-president and general manager of the Purdue Research Foundation to assume his new duties on November 15, 1964. He served as president of the University of Massachusetts from 1954 to 1960, having been named provost of that institution in 1953.

He previously had served as a staff associate of the American Council on Education and as lecturer at Woodrow Wilson School of Public and International Affairs at Princeton University.

A native of Colorado, he holds a bachelor's degree from the University of Denver and master's degrees from that institution and Princeton University. Seven colleges, including Amherst and the University of Hokkaido, Japan, have awarded him honorary doctoral degrees.

Students Plan Vallejo Development. Thirteen advanced architecture students at Stanford University have been summoned by Vallejo, California to survey the city's needs, including industrial areas, downtown development, the waterfront - reclamation - recreation complex, and cultural and transportation problems.

The students, participants in Professor Tom Williamson's Community Development Laboratory, are the same group which last year developed plans to restore and maintain the historic Old Town area of Benicia, California. Benicia has since adopted many of the student recommendations for preserving the "old town" and improving the new and is moving forward with the student plan which includes a

46

unique offshore water fountain shooting a powerful spray into the air—a landmark like none other this side of Lake Geneva, Switzerland.

"Vallejo," according to Professor Williamson, "was once considered for the state capital back in the middle of the last century. The students want to see if they can come up with a plan that will link Vallejo's past with the Bay Area's future. It seems to be a matter of discovering and clarifying the city's image more than anything else."

Costs of the Stanford survey are to be borne by several of Vallejo's service clubs and the Chamber of Commerce.

Conference. The Georgia Institute of Technology, in Atlanta, has announced the 14th Annual Georgia Highway Conference and two short courses in traffic engineering and urban transportation planning and analysis to be held in 1965.

Theme of the conference will be "Responsibility of the Highway Industry." The program is offered annually to provide information on the latest developments in state and county highway construction and maintenance and to promote understanding in cooperation among the various groups concerned with highway building and maintenance in Georgia and the Southeast.

The course in urban transportation planning and analysis is designed to familiarize qualified persons with the basic problems and techniques required for urban transportation planning.

The short course in traffic engineering will be offered May 17–21, 1965.

Park Administration Course. A three-week course of study for park directors from other countries will be offered May 10–29, 1965 by the Department of the Interior in cooperation with the School of Natural Resources, University of Michigan. The Department of Agriculture and the International Union for the Conservation of Nature and Natural Resources will assist with the project.

Purpose of the course is to review legislation, policy, planning, and new developments in national parks, with emphasis on the preservation and wise use of these resources. It will be open to those responsible for the administration of national parks and equivalent reserves whether or not they actually bear the title of park director.

A week of intensive study on the Michigan campus will be followed by a two-week period of field study and demonstrations in selected park, forest, and recreation areas in the United States.

A staff selected from the faculty of the School of Natural Resources, University of Michigan, and cooperating agencies will supervise the on-campus studies, utilizing the talents of outside speakers internationally known in special fields. The field studies will be under the supervision of such cooperating agencies as Interior's National Park

Service and the Department of Agriculture's Forest Service.

Subjects expected to be discussed on the tour will be design, construction, and maintenance of facilities; educational programs; and park, parkway, and forest administration.

Inquiries and correspondence regarding attendance and other matters concerning the short course should be addressed to the Director, National Park Service, Department of the Interior, Washington, D. C. 20240.

Fellowships. Trustees of the Loula D. Lasker Fellowship Trust have announced the fourth consecutive year of the Trust's fellowship grant program for graduate study in housing, city planning, and urban renewal.

Though the standards are subject to modification, in general it may be said that the fellowships for the 1965–66 academic year will be awarded for study in accredited educational institutions which offer a graduate degree in the fields noted above, which have the equivalent of at least two full-time faculty members in these or closely-related subjects and which have graduated at least one class and at least ten students.

Maximum stipends will be $2,500 per year for single students and $3,000 per year for married students and the exact amount of each award will depend upon the financial need of the recipient and his or her ability to contribute to the cost of education. It is anticipated that ten or more grants will be awarded this year, including renewals and grants made to advanced students.

During the current 1964–65 academic year, seventeen Loula D. Lasker Fellows are studying for advanced degrees in the Universities of North Carolina, Pennsylvania, California, Pittsburgh, and Wisconsin; at Harvard, Cornell, and Brandeis Universities; and at Massachusetts Institute of Technology and Georgia Institute of Technology. Of these, three are Master's candidates in their first year of graduate study, five are Master's candidates currently in their second year of study, and nine are Ph. D. candidates.

Conservation Film. "Camping —A Key To Conservation," a 23-minute film stressing the importance of preserving the beauty of our campsites through good camping practices, has been produced by the Audio-Visual Center of Indiana University in cooperation with the American Camping Association.

It is the story of Jerry, a thirteen-year-old boy who narrates the film, describing his camping experiences and telling of his overnight trip with five other boys and two counselors. It is intended for use in intermediate and junior high grades, for conservation units, school and summer camp programs and camp leadership training programs.

Information on film rental and purchase may be obtained from the Audio-Visual Center, Indiana University, Bloomington, Indiana 47405.

PLANNING TECHNIQUES OF TOMORROW

(*Continued from page 10*)

downtown business districts, and so in turn, as the downtown business district is reconstituted, it will borrow ideas from the successful suburban centers. The relationship of one building to another is becoming the most important single architectural problem.

As to the automobile, traffic congestion occurs in cities when drivers have no place to park after arriving at their destination and drive around aimlessly searching for a resting place. Congestion is also caused by traffic, destined to a distant location, being shunted through the feeder streets required to serve the immediate needs of adjoining properties.

With an adequate ring road connecting major arteries and freeways, the driver is able to proceed directly to the exit serving the area of his destination. At that point, there remains only the problem of having adequate parking which will efficiently remove the cars from the streets. Once the car is parked, the balance of the journey is made as a pedestrian, but with proper planning, the distances are short and should be pleasant. When an individual travels from one business section to another, it is done as a pedestrian, or by mass transportation, rather than the re-use of the automobile. Actually, when a shopper goes to a department store, he expects to leave his car at the door. In the same manner, there is no need for cars within a compact business district, except for those which are parked underground.

Thus, by eliminating these two major automobile movements, the congestion caused by this increased traffic is subject to a reasonable engineering solution.

This planning concept may appear at first to be similar to the Ft. Worth plan, but I think, on closer examination, the differences will become apparent. By breaking down the central business district into smaller, component environmental units, people, for the most part, will be able to drive directly to the building of their destination, park, and proceed on in quite a normal fashion. Actually, there will probably be established a secondary system of ring roads, which will surround each component business unit. In this way, the great volume of traffic will be spread over many smaller feeder streets, some of which may be congested for short periods of time. But because their distances are so short they will not become a serious burden.

This proposed plan would provide for a much closer and more intimate relationship for the people and their city. Parking would be within or adjacent to the building the individual desired to reach. The buildings, in turn, would be planned so as to be integrated with landscaped, pedestrian malls, enclosed or otherwise, and connected with open areas of parks and plazas.

In the case of the retail center, the stores would be located along a shopping mall, in the manner of the current regional center. Stores would continue to enjoy the relationship they have had in the past with the hotels, office buildings, and service facilities, usually found in the heart of a city. In fact, with the removal of congestion caused by automobiles, there would be a much closer relationship between the various business functions of the city.

In some cities, there are already forces pointing towards an ultimate planning solution, similar to the one set forth.

We are familiar with tremendous developments with regard to highways and roads, and they are, in most cases, pointed toward the heart of the city. Around most cities, there are already circumferential roadways under construction or at least being planned. A basic network of roads and streets leads to the city center. It remains, then, for an additional ring road to be built closely around the central business district, with required service to each of the environmental units.

Already, private enterprises are building what we now term "super blocks" in the hearts of cities. These super blocks form the first stages of environmental units, and, with the establishment of several super blocks, create a business unit.

A super block, as its name indicates, is a large project usually involving more than one city block, therefore, requiring street closures or relocation. These complexes are pre-planned with an integration of the facilities, giving particular consideration to the pedestrian and the garaging of his car. There may be a department store with satellite shops, hotels or motels, office buildings, theatres, doctors' offices, and,

of course, parking and provision for public transportation.

The super block is planned so that the pedestrian is separated from the traffic and is able to move within the project with ease and comfort and without concern for the weather.

The Master Plan of Seattle, for instance, can easily be developed further into an environmental unit plan. The retail complex is presently well-established and would lend itself easily to separating the pedestrian from the vehicular traffic. A retail core plan could be established for Seattle, which not only would take care of all of the present day requirements but also would allow amply for future expansion in a manner hertofore described.

There presently exists a well-defined financial district and a well-defined governmental district. Both of these sections are adjacent to each other, and somewhat removed from the retail section.

The elimination of traffic on the retail streets, headed toward the financial districts, or conversely, traffic on the financial streets, headed for the retail district, would go a long way in reducing traffic congestion.

Then, too, in Seattle, there is another area, sort of an "uptown" office building area, that contains the majority of hotels and amusement facilities. Here again, it would be quite practical to combine this section into a single, planned unit. This leaves a comparatively large area, sort of a no man's land, lying in between each of these compactly planned areas. This land is available for expansion for each of these units.

(Continued on page 56)

50

Strictly Personal

Maurice D. Arnold has been named to head a new Division of Grants-in-Aid in the Department of the Interior's Bureau of Outdoor Recreation.

The new division, established under the recently enacted Land and Water Conservation Fund Act, will be concerned with the Federal grants-in-aid, now available to the States on a matching basis for planning, acquisition and development of recreation areas.

Mr. Arnold was formerly Chief of the Operations Branch, Grants and Training, at the National Cancer Institute, Department of Health, Education and Welfare in Washington, D. C. A native of Arkansas, he holds a master's degree in public administration from Syracuse University's Maxwell School of Citizenship and Public Affairs.

Dr. John M. Corbett has been named chief of the National Park Service's division of archeology studies, one of two newly established divisions stemming from the mounting importance of archeological and historical research in park conservation.

Robert M. Utley will head a second division, that of history studies, which has been created to replace the former division of history and archeology studies.

Since 1958, Dr. Corbett, aged 50, has headed the Service's branch of archeology which is now replaced by the new division of archeology studies.

Before entering park work, Dr. Corbett served as field supervisor on archeological projects in Peru, Ecuador, Guatemala, Mexico and in various parts of the United States. His education was obtained at Princeton University, the University of Southern California, and Columbia University, where he received his doctorate. He has written a number of articles dealing with archeological programs.

Mr. Utley, aged 34, has been historian at the National Park Service Southwest Regional Office in Santa Fe, New Mexico, since 1958. Prior to that time, he had assisted with the compilation of a political-military history for the Joint Chiefs of Staff at the Pentagon, Washington, D. C.

In 1964, he received the Bison Award of the New York City chapter of The Westerners for his book, *Last Days of the Sioux Nation.* He is also the author of *Custer and the Great Controversy: Origin and Development of A Legend.*

A native of Arkansas, Mr. Utley is a graduate of Purdue University and holds an M. A. degree from Indiana University.

Ben H. Thompson, Assistant Director for Resource Studies at the National Park Service, retired on December 30, 1964, after approximately 35 years of service with that government agency.

Mr. Thompson, a recognized authority in the selection and establishment of national parks, monuments, historic sites and recreation areas, has played a major role in the Service's programs for park planning for nearly two decades. In October, 1961, he was promoted to Assistant Director, Resource Planning, and was named Assistant Director in charge of Resource Studies in December, 1963. He continued to lay important groundwork for establishing new additions to the National Park System until his retirement.

In recognition of his outstanding accomplishments, Mr. Thompson has been awarded the Pugsley Gold Medal by the American Scenic and Historic Preservation Society, the Distinguished Service Award by the Department of the Interior, and the American Motors Conservation Award in the professional category.

Upon retirement, Mr. Thompson was presented a port-folio of letters from some of the many friends whose loyalty he has inspired to an unusual degree. He has recently been re-elected Treasurer of the National Conference on State Parks.

———◆———

Robert T. Nahas, nationally known land developer of Oakland, California, has been elected president of the Urban Land Institute, a non-profit research organization located in Washington, D. C. and devoted to improving standards of urban planning and development.

Mr. Nahas has developed a number of shopping centers, apartments, and industrial properties in the northern California area. As president of Coliseum, Inc., he paved the way for Oakland's new thirty-million-dollar stadium and arena complex currently under construction.

A leader in civic endeavor, Mr. Nahas formed the committee which has been instrumental in efforts to revitalize downtown Oakland.

———◆———

Harold Schick has resigned as Superintendent of State Parks and Recreation for the Oregon State Highway Department to become Superintendent of the Fairmount Park Commission, Philadelphia, Pennsylvania.

Mr. Schick's new duties will include supervision of 7,700 park acres in Philadelphia, including art centers, museums, zoos, and historic mansions. The Philadelphia program operates under an $11,000,000 annual budget and the Fairmount Commission supervises all city parks.

Mr. Schick, who has been with the Oregon Highway Department since 1962, was previously a Regional Director of Parks in Oregon. He was also formerly with the Resources Development Department of Michigan State University from which institution he received both his Bachelor's and Master's degrees in parks management.

Since Mr. Schick became Oregon State Parks Superintendent in 1962, the Highway Department has added eight new state parks to the system, bringing the total to almost 200 parks and waysides.

———◆———

Lawrence M. Orton, a charter member of the New York City
(Continued on page 57)

IN MEMORIAM

CATHERINE BAUER WURSTER

Catherine Bauer Wurster, nationally known associate dean of the University of California School of Architecture and a member of the Board of Trustees of the *American Planning and Civic Association*, died in November, 1964.

Death came while she was on a hike up 2604-foot Mt. Tamalpais in Marin County, California, north of San Francisco's Golden Gate. Her body was found by a search force on November 23 after she had been missing over two days and as rain and freezing temperatures blanketed the rugged, heavily wooded mountain area in which Mrs. Wurster, an avid hiker and outdoor enthusiast, was accustomed to hike.

Mrs. Wurster had been a Professor of City Planning at the University of California since 1950 and had previously taught at Harvard University.

She served as an advisor on housing to the Administrations of Presidents Roosevelt, Eisenhower, Kennedy and Johnson, and, through her published works, is credited with having been influential in development of the 1937 Housing Act.

Her many writings included *Modern Housing* (1934), *A Housing Program For Now And Later* (1948), and a Chapter in *Goals for America* (1960), the report of the Presidential Commission on National Goals.

She is survived by her husband, William, recently retired dean of the University's School of Architecture.

❧

LEONARD L. HUTTLESTON

Leonard L. Huttleston, formerly Director of State Parks in New York and also a member of the Board of Directors of the National'Conference on State Parks, died December 8, 1964 after a brief illness.

Mr. Huttleston first became associated with the park system in 1933 as Chief Engineer of the CCC camp program for the Central New York state Parks Commission with headquarters in Binghamton. In 1938, he succeeded Mr. James Evans as General Manager of that park region and continued in that post until 1951 when he was made Assistant Director of State Parks at Albany. On January 1, 1961, he again succeeded Mr. Evans, this time on his retirement as Director of State Parks.

Mr. Huttleston served in World War II as a Seabee company and battalion commander in the Navy in the Aleutian and Mid-Pacific theatres, being discharged as a Lieutenant Commander in 1945. He attended public schools in Cortland, New York and graduated from the College of Civil Engineering of Cornell University in 1926.

In addition to the National Conference on State Parks, he was also a member of the American Society of Civil Engineers and the American Institute of Park Executives.

He is survived by his wife, Mary, and two daughters, Martha and Nancy.

ℰℐ∂

FRANCES D. BARTHOLOMEW

Frances D. Bartholomew, wife of Harland Bartholomew, former chairman of the National Capital Planning Commission and Board Chairman of the American Planning and Civic Association, died January 8, 1965 at Union Memorial Hospital in Baltimore.

A native of Terre Haute, Indiana, Mrs. Bartholomew was a member of the New York Avenue Presbyterian Church and the Friday Morning Music Club in Washington, D. C.

Memorial services were held for her on January 11 in Washington, D. C. and on January 12 at Muncie, Indiana.

ℰℐ∂

JOHN E. DOERR

John E. Doerr, Superintendent of Olympic National Park at Port Angeles, Washington, died in December, 1964. Formerly with the National Park Service in Washington, D. C., Mr. Doerr had been a member of the American Planning and Civic Association since 1948.

ℰℐ∂

HARRY K. FISHER

Harry K. Fisher, a member of the American Planning and Civic Association and of the Committee of 100 on the Federal City since 1961, died on October 25, 1964.

Recent Publications

Conserving American Resources, 2nd Edition, by Ruben L. Parson. Prentice-Hall, Inc., EnglewoodCliffs, New Jersey. 1964. 521 pp. $8.95.

This new, second edition of Mr. Parson's successful book emphasizes the interrelationship among all resources. New, in this edition, is the Chapter on "Mineral Fuels and major Metals" and latest statistics.

The author has aimed here at a book rigorous enough for the professional conservationist, yet not too technical for the intelligent reader who wants to learn how he may help conserve this Nation's bountiful resources.

Public Relations In Natural Resources Management by Douglas L. Gilbert, B.S., M.S., Ph.D., Associate Professor of Wildlife Management, Colorado State University, Fort Collins, Colorado. Burgess Publishing Company, 426 South 6th Street, Minneapolis, Minnesota 55415. 1964. 227 pp. $4.50.

One of the few, if any, books designed and written on the important public relations field specifically for professional conservationists. ℐ

Zoning Round Table

Conducted by FLAVEL SHURTLEFF, Marshfield Hills, Mass.

PRINCIPLES AND PRECE-DENTS (CONTINUED)

Two recent Massachusetts cases illustrate the use of principles in the decision of zoning cases. In Smith *et al vs* Zoning Board of Appeals *et al**, the Smiths were owners of a large parcel of land abutting on a lot owned by the Mayers, and the Mayers had a 50-foot right-of-way over the Smith lands. Before the Mayers built on their lot, the Smiths presented a subdivision plan showing the Mayers' right-of-way as part of a 50-foot street. This plan was duly approved by the proper authority. Thereafter, the Mayers started the building of a house and garage, the latter being 15 feet distant from the approved street. This was a violation of the local zoning ordinance which required a 30-foot distance from the street for any building. The violation was called to the attention of the enforcing officer who ordered the removal of the garage. The Mayers refused and applied for a variance, claiming a peculiar situation and a substantial financial hardship. The Board of Appeals granted the variance.

At the time of the complaint, the Mayers could have complied with the requirement for less than $500, but at the time the variance was issued, the cost would have been $5,000.

The court reversed the Board of Appeals on the ground that there was no substantial hardship since:

*Adv. Sheets of 1964 (July), p. 1115.

1) The added cost could not be relied on. The hardship was due to an initial violation.

2) The lesser cost of $500 for fill and "other items" is too speculative to support a finding of *substantial* hardship.

Since there is considerable uniformity in the provisions of state zoning laws covering the issue in this case, the two principles controlling the decision can be useful precedents.

In New York Central Railroad Co. *vs* Department of Public Utilities *et al***, the Department refused an exemption from the terms of the local ordinance on the ground that the activities for which the exemption was sought were not in the public interest. The railroad wanted to use ten acres of land for parking automobiles unloaded from railroad cars prior to local distribution. The land involved was in a residence zone.

The court had discussed the question in only one zoning case in which the facts were quite different, but from analogy to cases other than zoning in which the right of a public utility to exemption was discussed, the court found that its only concern in such cases was whether the state department's decision was supported by substantial evidence and whether the correct principles of law were applied to the facts found.

In sending back the case to the department for a fuller record, the **Adv. Sheets, 1964, p. 921.

court announced a principle that cases like this demand the presentation of evidence on a broad basis because of the many aspects of the public interest.

Here again, is a ruling which can be cited as a precedent since public utilities are uniformly treated in state zoning codes.

Space. Citation of zoning cases from other states may not be helpful. The first state zoning laws followed the standard zoning law drafted by the advisory committee on zoning of the Federal Department of Commerce, but experience of 40 years brought many changes in these laws so that in important particulars there are differences from state to state. Generally, the scope of the law, for instance, may vary. Some state laws include more purposes for which local ordinances may be drafted.

Specifically, in Georgia and possibly other states, variances can be granted only for hardship rising out of area restrictions. A variance for *use* of land or buildings which is prohibited by a local zoning ordinance will be struck down as invalid. In Massachusetts, no regulation of floor area for living space of a single family residence greater than 768 square feet will be valid, and a recess commission is now considering a proposal to set a statutory limit to the regulation of the size of lot areas for residences.

In the same state, local zoning ordinances may have vastly different regulations, and this may affect the pertinence of a citation.

The administration of a zoning law and the local ordinance thereunder may be so different from community to community that two cases involving almost exactly the same facts may be differently decided by the Board of Appeals and may result in decisions by the court of last resort in apparent conflict because the court has applied the established principle of law that where a decision is debatable, it will be allowed to stand. A very liberal board may have granted a variance. Either because no appeal is taken or because the board's decision is allowed to stand, a precedent is established and the town may get many variances, some of which are clearly rank violations of the local zoning code.

Planning Techniques
(*Continued from page 50*)

as well as for the providing of the necessary parking.

Seattle has already established the first phase of a monorail system. This could be extended, so as to loop the business district, and provide for intra-city transportation. A well established transit system would provide the surface service.

Surrounding the central core would be a wide band of secondary buildings, including highrise apartments for downtown living, and a further extension of the garage facilities.

Probably the greatest hope for downtown Seattle's future, as well as for your own cities, is large-scale private redevelopment. This calls for creative selling of the highest order by the real estate profession in collaboration with enlightened investors, experienced architects, and local planning agencies.

Strictly Personal

(Continued from page 52)

Planning Commission, has been reappointed to his fourth eight-year term by Mayor Robert Wagner.

Mr. Orton was first appointed to the City Planning Commission in 1938 by Mayor LaGuardia and was subsequently reappointed to eight-year terms by Mayor LaGuardia in 1941, Mayor O'Dwyer in 1949 and Mayor Wagner in 1957.

He has served as planning consultant to a number of municipalities in this country, Puerto Rico and Canada and began his career in 1923 as an economic investigator with the Committee on the Regional Plan.

Donald P. Van Riper has been named principal landscape architect for the California Division of Highways, Department of Public Works.

For the past 17 years, Mr. Van Riper has been in charge of landscape architectural activities for the California State Office of Architecture and Construction. In assuming the newly-created position, he will not only assume responsibility for the State's 30-year-old roadside planting program, which now involves more than $4,000,000 in new projects annually, but will also work with all units of the Division involved in the scenic highway and roadside rest program, and will act as consultant to other state agencies and groups, notably the Governor's Advisory Committee on Scenic Highways.

Mr. Van Riper was graduated from the University of California in 1929 in landscape architecture and was a naval officer in World War II. His previous experience includes work with the National Park Service and as assistant superintendent of parks for the city of Sacramento.

Robert W. Copelan, aged 70, retired as chief of the Information and Education Section of the Ohio Department of Natural Resources on December 31, 1964.

Mr. Copelan started his newspaper career as a reporter for the *Cincinnati Enquirer* in 1941 and went to the *Cincinnati Times-Star* in 1924, eventually becoming managing editor of that paper. He served in both World Wars, attaining the rank of colonel of infantry in World War II, during which he was engaged in military intelligence activities.

Erwin C. Zepp, recently retired as director of the Ohio Historical Society, a seventy-nine year-old organization which administers fifty-eight State Memorials.

A native of Cleveland, Mr. Zepp became affiliated with the society in 1933 after having graduated from Ohio State University and serving on its faculty. He served the society as assistant curator of State Memorials, curator of State Memorials,

(Continued on page 58)

American Planning and Civic Association
New Members, August 1, 1964 to
December 1, 1964

California
: Mr. Robert J. Sully, Los Angeles

District of Columbia
Mr. Alan D. Hutchison
Mr. Nicholas Satterlee

Hawaii
Hawaii Natural History Assn., Hawaii Volcanoes National Park

Maryland
Mrs. John G. Scharf, Bethesda

New York
Prof. Betty van der Smissen, Brooklyn
Mr. Laurence Alexander, New York
Mrs. Katrina McCormick Barnes, New York
Mr. Julian H. Whittlesey, New York

Pennsylvania
Mr. Clinton B. Mullen, Philadelphia

South Dakota
Mr. Fred Courey, Lennox

Virginia
Mr. Leslie Logan, Arlington
Mr. G. Alan Morledge, Williamsburg

National Conference on State Parks
New Members, August 1, 1964 to
December 1, 1964

California
Mr. Claude H. Mondor, San Jose
Mr. Robert L. Perkins, Santa Cruz
Mr. Cliff M. Bisbee, Sonoma

Delaware
Mr. William J. Hopkins, Lewes

District of Columbia
Mr. William L. Duddleson
Mr. Theodor R. Swem

Illinois
Mr. J. L. Donoghue, Park Ridge

Massachusetts
Norfolk Co. Agricultural School, Walpole

New Jersey
Mr. Douglas F. G. Eliot, Englewood

Ohio
Mr. Robert Hammond, Degraff
Mr. H. Roger Hamilton, Newbury

Pennsylvania
Mr. Frank E. Masland, Jr., Carlisle

Tennessee
Mr. Mack S. Prichard, Nashville

Virginia
Mr. Ben H. Bolen

STRICTLY PERSONAL

(*Continued from page 57*)

and as vice director before being elected director in 1947.

———◆———

Chester W. Martin has been named to fill the newly created post of Assistant to the Director of the Connecticut State Park and Forest Commission.

Mr. Martin, in the capacity of Forest Land Purchaser for the Commission prior to his present appointment, successfully negotiated the purchase of many acres of park and forest land. He will continue to be active in the area of land acquisition and will represent Donald C. Mathews, Director of the State Park and Forest Commission, in many negotiations with public and private conservation groups.

———◆———

Watch Service Report

The forward sweep of an Inaugural year is not particularly conducive to a backward glance at the record of a preceding Congress. Yet, before the 88th Congress adjourned **sine die**, October 3, 1964, it had, through bi-partisan effort, compiled such a singular conservation record that the details will continue to be recorded and interpreted for some time.

The September issue of PLANNING AND CIVIC COMMENT reported on three of the most significant of the newly adopted legislative measures. Following is a statement on additional measures considered by the Congress.

Public Law 88-590, Establishing the Canyonlands National Park in Utah.
S. 27, establishing Canyonlands as our newest and thirty-second national park, was signed by President Johnson, September 12, 1964.

A Senate-House conference committee, on September 2, 1964, had issued a favorable report resolving differences between versions of S. 27, establishing the Canyonlands National Park in Utah and had agreed upon a park containing 257,640 acres already in Federal or state owership. Thus, no land acquistion cost was involved, but long range development could require up to $17,000,000.

The House, on August 19, 1964, had passed S. 27 under the unanimous consent procedure after amending it to substitute the text of H. R. 6925. The bill was then returned to the Senate.

A full discussion of this major picturesque area was included in the December, 1963 issue of PLANNING AND CIVIC COMMENT. It is a "land of canyons, plateaus, and mountains, each equally enchanting, each possessing beauty and mystery beyond description—one of the largest expanses of little-known wonderland remaining in America."

Public Law 88-492, Establishing the Ozark National Scenic Riverways In Missouri.
A new concept of outdoor recreation became a reality on August 27, 1964 when President Johnson signed S. 16, a bill establishing the Ozark National Scenic Riverways in Missouri.

The Senate had concurred in the House-passed version of S. 16 on August 14, 1964, clearing this significant bill for final action by the President.

By a voice vote, the House, on August 11,1964, had passed H. R. 1803, establishing the Ozark National Riverways in Missouri, after adopting a committee amendment that supplied a new text. This passage then was vacated and S. 16, a similar bill, was passed in lieu after being amended to contain the House-passed language.

The bill sets aside portions of two outstanding spring-fed natural Missouri streams, the Current and Jacks Fork Rivers, in their natural, free-flowing conditions. It authorizes up to $7,000,000 for land acquistion for an area not to exceed 65,000 acres in size. Development costs are estimated at $2,100,000.

The bill, which was reported in the *Watch Service Report* for March, 1964, is of unusual significance in that it establishes a new classification, scenic riverways, for administration by the National Park Service under the same principles as those of a recreation area in which hunting is permitted. Under the new law, hunting and fishing will be allowed under provisions of state law.

Public Law 88-639, Establishing the Lake Mead National Recreation Area.
Lake Mead became the first site to be designated a national recreation area by statute on October 8, 1964, when the President put his signature to S. 653, which had been introduced originally by Senators Howard Cannon and Alan Bible of Nevada.

S. 653, establishing the Area, was cleared for Presidential signature on September 28, 1964, when the Senate agreed to a House amendment to the bill.

Lake Mead has already been administered as a national recreation area by executive order and was visited by 3,049,600 persons in 1963. Under the new law, hunting and fishing on the area will be permitted in accordance with State and Federal laws.

Planning and Civic Comment

Public Law 655, Establishing the Ice Age National Scientific Reserve in Wisconsin. Signed by the President, October 13, 1964.

H. R. 1096, authorizing the Secretary of the Interior to cooperate with the State of Wisconsin in the designation and administration of the Ice Age National Scientific Reserve, came out a winner late in the Congressional session when the Senate passed the bill October 1, 1964, thus clearing it for Presidential signature.

The bill, sponsored by Congressmen Lester R. Johnson (Wisc.) and Henry S. Reuss (Wisc.) had gotten off to a slow start earlier in the session when the House, by a record vote of 164 yeas to 154 nays, on August 3, 1964, refused to suspend the rules and pass it. After gaining clearance by the House Rules Committee, however, the bill was passed September 23, 1964 by the House on a record vote of 180 yeas to 118 nays.

The legislation provides for establishment of the Reserve to protect unusual educational features left behind by retreating glaciers. The Federal Government will contribute $50,000 to help the State of Wisconsin draft a comprehensive plan for development and interpretation of the Reserve. The Federal Government will also contribute $750,000 as part of Wisconsin's allotment from the Land and Water Conservation Fund as matching funds for the purchase of 12,000 acres of land, costing about $1,500,000. This area for the Reserve will be acquired to go with 30,000 acres already under State ownership.

Public Law 88-630, Establishing the Lewis and Clark Trail Commission. Signed by the President, October 6, 1964.

H. R. 12289, establishing a commision to coordinate plans for identifying and marking the famous Lewis and Clark Trail, was another bill which came out favorably in late Congressional action. The bill, introduced by Congressman Ben F. Jensen (Iowa), was cleared for Presidential signature when it was passed by the Senate, without amendment, September 24, 1964 in lieu of S. 3116.

The new law provides for establishment of a 27-member Commission to further objectives set forth in H. Con. Res. 61, passed earlier by the Congress. The Commission will coordinate efforts to identify and mark the route traversed by Captains Meriwether Lewis and William Clark on their famous expedition of 1804-06 from St. Louis to the Pacific Northwest.

STATEMENT OF OWNERSHIP, MANAGEMENT, CIRCULATION, ETC. REQUIRED BY THE ACTS OF CONGRESS OF AUGUST 24, 1912, AND MARCH 3, 1933 OF PLANNING AND CIVIC COMMENT published quarterly, at Harrisburg, Pa, for October 1, 1964, Washington, D. C. as:

Before me, a Notary in and for the District of Columbia, personally appeared Donald B. Alexander, who, having duly sworn according to law, deposes and says that he is the Editor of PLANNING AND CIVIC COMMENT, and that the following is, to the best of his knowledge and belief a true statement of the ownership, management, etc. of the aforesaid publication for the date shown in the above caption, required by the Act of August 24, 1912, as amended by the Act of March 3, 1933, embodied in section 537, Postal Laws and Regulations, printed on the reverse of this form, to wit:

1. That the names and addresses of the publisher, editor and business manager are: Publisher: American Planning and Civic Association and National Conference on State Parks, Inc., 901 Union Trust Building, Washington, D. C. 20005. Editor: Donald B. Alexander. Business Manager: None.

2. That the owner is: American Planning and Civic Association and National Conference on State Parks, Inc., 901 Union Trust Building, Washington, D. C. 20005.

3. That the known bondholders, mortgagees and other security holders owning or holding 1 percent or more of total amount of bonds, mortgages, or other securities: (If there are none, so state.) None.
Sworn to and subscribed before me this 14th day of December, 1964.

(My commission expires Feb. 28, 1969)

Donald B. Alexander
Regina C. McGivern
Notary Public, Washington, D. C.

Planning and Civic Comment

Official Organ of American Planning and Civic Association and
National Conference on State Parks

*Selected Papers from the 44th Annual
Meeting of the*

NATIONAL CONFERENCE ON
STATE PARKS

September 20-25, 1964

GOVERNOR MORRIS HOTEL
Morristown, New Jersey

National Conference on State Parks
901 Union Trust Building
Washington, D. C. 20005

MARCH, 1965

These victories are not the conclusion of a crusade, but only the launching.

We have been given new and powerful tools, but with these tools come a heavy load and a mighty challenge.

In short, gentlemen, we are on the spot. We've won our point. The money and the authority which we have been seeking for years have in large measure been provided. Now we are going to have to deliver the public benefits we've promised in return.

And let it be noted that there are those who question whether park, recreation and conservation people can do the job. They say we are bureaucratic and inefficient. We've been described as cold to new ideas, as narrow and parochial. And we've been charged as being more interested in preserving resources than with serving people.

THERE may be some truth in these charges, even though exaggerated. But the fact that there is doubt in our capability is a reality—and we must overcome that doubt.

And let me say at this point that I speak to you not as a critic but as a fellow working park executive—as the Chairman of the New York State Council of Parks.

I think we are going to do the job. If we do not do it superbly, we will never get a chance like this again.

If we do not, the public will become dissatisfied, political support will wane, and this great chance will slip from our hands. We will have failed, but much more importantly, this chance to shape America's future growth will be lost.

I would like, therefore, to offer for your consideration and for the consideration of others, a program of action for park people, for recreation people and for conservation people.

Since this is the season for it, I'll call it a platform, if you will. And I might add, it is open to amendment.

As a first and fundamental plank, let us affirm that we are concerned with the full range of both natural and man-made beauty in America.

We who share this concern have diverse responsibilities and interests—for city and county parks and playgrounds, for state and national parks, for forests, for fish and wildlife.

But let it be made clear that the total effect of our effort is a concern for the environment. Our job is to see that this country will be a better and healthier place to live and labor and enjoy the fruits of labor.

WE MUST provide good parks and good playgrounds, but we also must provide a public conscience for the land and the water. We must be the advocate in the public forum for health and beauty wherever they are an issue.

And they are at issue in how we plan our cities, how we build our roads, how we use our streams and rivers, how we use our air. Indeed, they are at issue in almost the full range of human activity.

I do not suggest that we stubbornly oppose building and growth. I do suggest that we constructively propose tasteful and well-done building and growth.

The ultimate net effect of our diverse concerns should be a more beautiful, a more pleasant, a better America.

Second, this concern for the kind of country we are building must have a greater voice in the councils of the federal government.

The Bureau of Outdoor Recreation is charged with coordinating the score of federal agencies involved in recreation, but perhaps that is not enough.

Certainly, the implicit responsibility of the Bureau for the full range of environment should be made explicit. Perhaps its name should be changed to reflect more than outdoor recreation. And it may be that its status within the Department of the Interior is not the most forceful place for it.

The Recreation Advisory Council of cabinet officers with some responsibility for outdoor recreation provides a degree of government-wide supervision. It could do more. Perhaps it could become that one place in government where conservation, recreation and natural beauty are considered across the full range of federal activity. The BOR might serve directly as a secretariat to the Council.

Another move which would help is the appointment of an Advisory Committee to the Recreation Council. I suggest that this committee might be made up of members of Congress and informed citizens representing a diversity of interests. It should, of course, be bi-partisan.

This Congressional, citizen, bi-partisan approach follows the ORRRC pattern. I suggest that it is a most appropriate and effective one.

Third, we should affirm that the states must play a key role in this effort.

They are ideally situated for it. They are close enough to the scene to take account of sectional differences, and they are strong enough to carry forward effective programs.

THE states must play the pivotal role of bringing together the efforts of the federal government on the one hand and the local units of government on the other.

Unlike some federal grant-in-aid programs, the Land and Water Act provides that grants be made through the states. If the cities and counties want federal money, they must go to their state capital to get it.

This means that the states must work well with the federal government and that they must work well with local governments.

We must cooperate closely with the Bureau of Outdoor Recreation. Its mission of coordinating the various federal programs and those of the various levels of government and the private sector is vital. From it a cooperative nationwide effort must evolve.

I know that there may be some old antagonisms and some old prejudices lying around. I know that some new ones may have developed.

I know also that as a new bureau starting from scratch, BOR has had its problems, and these problems can be irritating to people who have been around a long time. But I have confidence in the Bureau, and I urge you to help it succeed in our mutual self interest and in the interest of the country.

The other half of the state job is the relationship with the local units of government. In too many cases state programs are administered as if local governments didn't exist.

They do exist, and they must be very much a part of these programs. Counties, for instance, are becoming increasingly active and important.

The local governments have to be part of the statewide planning effort.

And I suggest that they be encouraged to become full partners. States must be more than a pipeline for federal money. They should offer planning and technical and, in many cases, financial assistance to local governments.

Fourth, we must put our state administrative machinery in order to do the job. In many states, the park, recreation, forest, fish and game, highway and other agencies are competing with each other. Or even worse, they are ignoring each other. There is no agency concerned with the big picture.

One of the strongest recommendations of the Outdoor Recreation Resources Review Commission urged each state to establish a government focal point for outdoor recreation. This is even more crucial if we are to undertake a concern for the entire environment.

The Land and Water Conservation Fund Act gives special urgency and incentive to comprehensive coordinated planning.

The Act requires a comprehensive statewide plan. I hope we will see this requirement not as red tape—not as a barrier between ourselves and some attractive federal money—but as the finest opportunity we have ever had to build well for the long haul.

Fifth, I suggest that we must evolve an entirely new and very much more comprehensive concept of access to outdoor opportunities.

What is involved here is more than roads and traffic control, although physical access is important. But we must think of access in an even broader term.

We should make it our responsibility to see that every segment of our society—whether they be black or white, rich or poor—has an opportunity to use public facilities. We share a continuing responsibility to encourage appreciation of quality—quality in the environment and in the uses we make of it. For millions who have no tradition of outdoor experience, there is need for basic programs to teach the skills and convey the love of the land which combine to make outdoor recreation meaningful.

In many cases this boils down to provision for those who do not own an automobile. Our park systems tend to be predicated upon automobile ownership—and even in this affluent society there are many who do not have one available to them.

Access also means actively encouraging people to use all parts of our outdoor areas. It is sometimes easiest to control people in tight perimeters. But we must encourage them to seek the remote and the more inspiring areas away from the parking lots and snack bars.

This means imaginative use of educational devices and trail markers. It means good personnel contact with the public. It means good maintenance.

Most of all, it means a concern with people. It means that they be treated as welcome guests who are to be encouraged to benefit from the outdoors.

Sixth we must strive for a balance of outdoor opportunities for the public.

This balance consists of a mixture of opportunities of all kinds —from high density urban areas to the remote wilderness.

For too long conservationists have been squabbling about doctrine—where roads should be allowed and where they should not; where hunters can come in and where they can't, and so on. These battles have been fought to the point of tedium at a thousand meetings and conferences across the land.

I suggest that the time has come to stop quibbling. Let's agree that we must make provision for all kinds of use—and create a planned balance.

An important part of this issue is development. As pressures increase on outdoor areas, there will be need for more development, for development increases capacity to serve people. Where and how this development takes place should be part of a well-thought-out balance of opportunities.

The obvious tool for doing this is the statewide recreation plan required under the Land and Water grants. If these plans are well drawn, provision can be made for all uses.

The forum for debate can be the planning agency—not the hotel lobbies and the fish and game columns in the daily press.

I realize that this is very much easier said than accomplished, that tough decisions must be made.

But this is very much part of our challenge—to make some tough decisions that will stick. And the Land and Water grants offer us the opportunity to make them under the pressure of necessity.

Seventh, we must give far greater emphasis to conservation in our cities and suburbs.

TODAY this is the crucial arena for conservation and recreation. Here is where the people are. At least two-thirds of the population live in urban surroundings now and an even greater percentage will do so in the future.

Our park work—particularly at the state and national level has had a rural orientation in the past. We must reapportion our efforts to provide outdoor opportunities for city people.

Part of this can be done by greater cooperation with local government for traditional park programs.

But we must also try to build conservation and recreation into the environment as we create roads and houses. The cluster concept which calls for tighter development patterns and dedication of the land thus saved to open space is a promising new idea which is catching on. And the idea of tying open space together with stream networks and pathways can provide a whole new look to our suburbs.

Certainly, federal loan regulations and local zoning ordinances should encourage well-planned developments of this kind.

A review of the relationship between the open space program of the Urban Renewal Administration and the new Land and Water Act will provide opportunities for more help for the urban areas.

Eighth, let us not be afraid to use new devices or imaginative old ones.   •   ,

Outright acquisition of land may not always be the only answer. Indeed, in some cases, it may not be the best one.

Scenic easements, purchase of rights-of-way, tax abatement programs, hunting and fishing rights, and sale lease-back arrangements offer an array of tools we should use. Sometimes bureaucratic inertia has blinded us to these opportunities because they seemed like too much trouble or simply because they had never been used before.

But these less-than-fee acquisitions can often achieve the public goal at less cost and with less disruption to other uses than traditional acquisition.

Ninth, we must strengthen the private conservation and recreation organizations.

There are over a thousand of them. But there is duplication, overlapping and inefficiency. Too much time is spent in jockeying for position or mailing each other literature.

Diverse groups dedicated to single purposes have a value, but I think we have overdone it to a point of weakness.

I would hope that in the near future we would see a trend toward consolidation of some of these groups with similar purposes.

IN ADDITION, we must look to others with whom we have not been well enough acquainted in the past. The women's organizations and the civic organizations are our natural allies. We must enroll them in the ranks.

Consolidation and greater cooperative efforts by private organizations could and should provide a strong source of continuing support for the goals we seek.

Tenth, and finally in all of this, I urge that we maintain a bipartisan approach. Conservation has traditionally been above partisanship. We have had and do have great leaders and friends in both parties. Let's keep it that way.

I do not mean to imply that we should consider ourselves above politics. Almost every goal we seek requires government action, and we must be a part of the political process to get that action.

But we must maintain our roots in both great political parties and work to strengthen them where we and they are weak. We will lose much of our vast reservoir of public good will if we should ever be so foolish as to identify ourselves with only one party.

This platform I have outlined is an ambitious one. It is a big job. It will require great effort, great patience and considerable wisdom. It will not be completed in a year or a decade, but it must be a continuing responsibility.

The Congress, the President and the people of this country have said that what we are doing is important. They have said it must be done. They have given us a vote of confidence, but we must perform.

To us is given the task of helping to mold the growth of the country; to us is given the task of seeing that growth brings not only a bigger but a better America; to us is given the task of insuring that leisure is a blessing, not a curse of idleness.

So let us rededicate ourselves to our work. Let us so perform that future generations will look back and say of us—These men saw the vision not only of a strong America, not only of a prosperous America, but of a beautiful America as well!

I thank you.

Statement of Conrad L. Wirth, September 23, 1964, on becoming Chairman of the Board of the National Conference on State Parks

I FEEL it is a great honor to be chosen by this Board to be its Chairman. I am well aware of the history of the National Conference on State Parks and the fact that one of its founding members was Stephen T. Mather, the founder of the National Park Service. To follow in the footsteps of such greats as my immediate predecessor, Ed Meeman, and others like Tom Wallace, Steve Mather, Horace Albright, and Richard Lieber fires my desire to do all in my power to try to equal their record.

We are, at the present time, entering into a new era of park development—not only on the State level, but at all levels of government. The Land and Water Bill has been passed, the new Bureau of Outdoor Recreation has been established, and the States will take on a new key role in the development of a national system of park and recreation areas. I understand that you will hear tonight a talk by Mr. Laurance S. Rockefeller which will emphasize the position of the States. Other statements by a person in a very high position in government will be read to you tonight at the banquet, further emphasizing the States' future role.

YOU, the State Park organization, will be the main cog in the planning and carrying out of the great expansion of park and recreation developments that this country must undertake to satisfy the needs and requirements of its people. I know that we are going to live up to the trust placed in us, because we are all dedicated to this principle of serving the people through the preservation of our great scenic and historic heritage and providing them with other necessary recreation areas to satisfy the human requirements for relaxation, inspiration, and healthful enjoyment of the outdoors.

As we sit here today, I do not think there is a man in the room who doesn't want to carry out his full responsibility and do everything in his power to make this a great America to live in. On the other hand, I doubt whether there is a man in the room who can really comprehend not only the opportunities that are before us,

13

but the magnitude of the job. As Chairman of your Board, and
with your support, for without it nothing can be done, I hope to
lay before you various ways and means for your consideration
that will help advance our joint wishes, desires, and objectives.
I shall work very closely with your President, "Judge" Hella,
your Vice-President, Harold Dyer, and second Vice-President,
Lawrence Stuart. We shall try to mold together all park people
in other organizations, as well as our own, with one main objective
in mind, and that is to develop a park and recreational system
worthy of the American people. Let's all pledge ourselves to this
task and get on with the job.

꧁꧁꧁꧁꧁꧁꧁

Resolutions Adopted by the National Conference on State Parks at its 44th Annual Meeting, Morristown, N. J. September 20-25, 1964

FOLLOWING a discussion of Water Resources Planning, the two following resolutions offered respectively by Conrad L. Wirth and Edward J. Meeman were adopted:

THE National Conference on State Parks at its 44th Annual Meeting in Morristown, New Jersey, September 23, 1964, commends the Bureau of Outdoor Recreation of the Department of the Interior in undertaking with the aid and help of other co-operating agencies a study of the nation's remaining wild rivers. These wild rivers are an important element of natural environment and they must be considered in any comprehensive national parks and recreation plan for the nation as authorized by Congress.

The Conference by this resolution urges all its members and the various State and Federal Agencies charged with natural resources responsibilities to aid and assist the Bureau of Outdoor Recreation in every way possible.

The Conference also urges close cooperation of departments and agencies at all levels of Government in the preparation of sound, comprehensive state plans for parks and recreation, for these plans must be the basis of the national plan.

Further, we endorse the principle that planning for optimum use of rivers and other water resources, and of the related land resources, for all beneficial purposes should be done on a comprehensive and coordinated basis. Such planning will play an important role in the cultural, social and economic development of our nation and make it a more beautiful and enjoyable place for people to live.

THE National Conference on State Parks, at its 44th Annual Meeting in Morristown, New Jersey, on September 23, 1964, expresses its gratitude to the Corps of Engineers of the Army for their great contributions to outdoor recreation.

But the present fast-growing appreciation and recognition of the unique value of clear, free-flowing rivers for boating, fishing and

(*Continued on page 18*)

CONRAD L. WIRTH
Noted Park Authority, formerly Director of the National Park Service, U. S. Department of the Interior.

Chairman, Board of Directors, The National Conference on State Parks.

LAWRENCE STUART
Director, Maine State Park and Recreation Commission.

Second Vice-President, The National Conference on State Parks (Right).

DONALD B. ALEXANDER
Executive Secretary, The National Conference on State Parks (Left).

Photo by Chase Ltd., Washington 6, D.C.

NATIONAL CONFERENCE ON

U. W. HELLA
Director, Division of State
arks, Minnesota State Depart-
ent of Conservation.
*President, The National Con-
ence on State Parks.*

HAROLD J. DYER
Manager, Taconic State Park
Commission, New York State Con-
servation Department.
*First Vice-President, The National
Conference on State Parks (Left).*

Photo by John Lane Studio, Poughkeepsie
New York

BEN H. THOMPSON
Recognized authority in the selection and
ablishment of National Parks, Monuments,
toric Sites and Recreation Areas, who has
ently retired as Assistant Director for
source Studies, National Park Service.
*Treasurer, The National Conference on State
rks (Right).*

ᵀATE PARKS—OFFICERS 1964-66

Resolutions Adopted by the National Conference on State Parks

(Continued from page 15)

viewing requires some extraordinary action that might not be encompassed by the traditional procedures of the Engineers which served well in the past.

Congress has just created its first National Riverway, the Ozark National Riverway. For this to reach its full usefulness to the Nation, it is required that there be no damming, not only within the limits defined by the legislation but elsewhere in the vicinity. It is required that the Eleven Point and Current Rivers originating in Missouri, not be dammed. It is also required that the Buffalo River in Arkansas, which has been approved by the Advisory Board on National Parks, Historic Sites and Monuments, for designation as another National Riverway, not be dammed.

We see the need of emergency action. Therefore, we ask the Bureau of Outdoor Recreation to use its good offices, through Secretary Udall, to point this out to the Corp of Engineers through the Department of Defense.

Planning To Meet Open Space Needs

By HERBERT H. SMITH, President, Herbert H. Smith Associates,
Planning Consultants, West Trenton, New Jersey

I MUST start by saying to you that I'm extremely disappointed.
I had a carefully prepared, 15-page paper which would take
the better part of an hour to read, filled with details and statistics
and I'm sure exciting tidbits for you. Unfortunately, I have had
to tear it up since everything in it has already been said. The
two previous gentlemen have covered their material so thoroughly that I am afraid that you are going to be stuck with my
ad-libbing. In so doing, I speak from my experience as a planner,
and I would like to think, perhaps, as a man who is concerned
about the direction in which our society is going.

To begin, I want to ask you a question and I trust that from
the way in which it is asked, I won't tip you off too soon as to
what I feel the answer to be. The question is: In this day, in this
conference, in this period of our social development, with our
concern for open space, are we setting the stage for the demise
of *local* parks and recreational systems?

You will note on the program that I am supposed to talk
to you about county and local planning for park's open space.
Frankly, I find it extremely hard to distinguish between them as
I consider county development to be local. There is the further
difficulty that in the very short period of time alloted to me and
to us here this afternoon, it would be impossible to examine in
detail the full spectrum of the scope of the problems involved in
planning for open space at the county and local level. Furthermore, my assignment becomes next to impossible when we realize
that if we did nothing else for the remainder of the day but talk
about needed cooperation and coordination between Federal,
State, regional, county and local open-space programs, we still
couldn't solve the problem, but we certainly would be spending
our time on a very serious matter.

INSTEAD, however, let's talk for just a minute about needs. Dr.
Kent has given you some perhaps alarming, perhaps well-known,
statistics on population trends. We all know what is happening
in this country as a result of our booming population. Mr.
Stansfield has told you of the problems of the State of New
Jersey in facing a projected growth of from slightly over 6 million
to 20 million people. We, in the East, are finding the situation

19

such that it is almost impossible even to build enough roads to move the people around from one place to another. We are seeing our farm lands and our remaining open lands exploited each day— eaten up by the lava-like spread of urbanization.

As a matter of fact, what has been referred to as wall-to-wall urbanization, faces the State of New Jersey. We find ourselves stuck with many of the older urban areas and some pathetic old cities. Pathetic from the standpoint of their appearance and from the problems which they face in trying to conduct a municipal government in a state with an archaic and outmoded tax structure. And we find our people turning their backs on the mistakes of the past, choosing to ignore them and move out to the open countryside to make the same mistakes over again. We are an urbanized State which is going to have more and more of a problem in providing the amenities of life and the necessities of community organization. The State and the Federal Governments, together with the county and local governments, are going to be hard pressed to meet the needs for open space to serve these people. But what are these needs?

Are they the 100 acres per thousand about which Mr. Stansfield spoke? Are they 10 acres per thousand? Are they 200 acres per thousand? How can you define an intangible need? How do you define the kind of thing that can make the difference between a society beset with psychiatric problems and a sane and sensible social organization? How can we make the transition from the time when people expected that there would always be open land and open space provided somehow—they didn't know how—but provided, to a period of time when we must convince them that, if there is going to be open space, it must be planned and arranged for now?

There can be no question but that there must be a role for county and local government in meeting these needs. However, there must be an acceptance of the idea that there *is* a need before we spend too much time theoretically figuring out that 48 acres per 500 people is a desirable norm.

What *is* enough open space? I think only the people involved in a given area can determine what is enough regardless of the geographic size of the area or its total population. But on the other hand, look at the problem that the county and local governments are facing in providing any open space. The biggest hue and cry raised today is to educate children. The biggest demand for money in any tax-based State is for the purpose of providing education—and well that it is. But with the problem of increasing cost of education and providing the absolute necessities of life, such as the disposal of sewage, provision of water, the paving of streets and roads, the meeting of emergencies, and the paying of salaries, what is the local government situation?

UNFORTUNATELY, personally, I am very much afraid that when it comes to talking about recreation and open space, the attitude of local government (and I include counties in this category) is that it is something which the State and Federal governments ought to do "so we won't be bothered with it." This is true because, even though we are paying the taxes, it is far less painful if it comes from that source, and we don't have to stand up before irate but ill-advised taxpayers come election time and answer to those who oppose rising local tax rates. The facts of the matter are that if the irate electorate were convinced of the need, if they understood the problems, they would be irate because of the inactivity at the local level.

Now both Dr. Kent and Mr. Stansfield spoke to you about the various lines of responsibility of state and regional agencies for open space and coordination with Federal agencies. I think, however, that we do need to examine this need for coordination. Forgetting the distressing things I have said (and I hope that you won't), but assuming that they can be overcome, ask yourself the question of what kind of coordination is taking place between state, regional, county and local agencies for open space planning.

Is it, as is sometimes true in state highway departments, that the last people to find out where the exact alignment of a highway is are the planners and the local officials of the community through which it is going? Is it, as occurs so many times, a matter of individual jealousy of prerogative—that of "if we tell you what we are going to do at the regional level, you might sneak in and build the park or preserve the open space first?"

I THINK we should ask ourselves whether we are empire builders or builders of a society *with the sole purpose being for the betterment of that society*. Until we get that kind of enlightened leadership, that which insists upon coordination at all levels, we are never going to have a meaningful open space program in this country.

WHAT are some of these problems which face the local community in open space planning? First of all, there is the problem of advanced preparation. In many cases, we find municipalities where, even if the proper atmosphere existed to do something about advanced planning for open space, they would have difficulty doing so. This may result from a lack of availability of professional advice and consultation in knowing how to get started. It may also be the result of the inability of a local governing body to agree that something to be done some time in the future should be put down on paper so that people can be informed about it before it occurs. Unfortunately, we still have the attitude among many of our local governing bodies that the best way to get re-elected is to let the people of a community know as little as possible about what is going on.

There next follows the problem of dealing with exploitation and speculation—the real bugaboo of advanced planning. Every time you begin to organize a program, what can you expect? The minute you make a proposal you are going to find that some one, perhaps even a member of the governing body or a member of the planning board, who also happens to be operating in real estate, has picked up the option on all the land proposed for parks and open space. We are a nation of greedy, grabbing people—a fact I'm afraid we must face—and we must be prepared to expose this type of endeavor where it exists or we are never going to overcome it. As long as there is a lack of concern, and a lack of a desire to get involved, we are going to be robbed blind as we are day after day right now in the open space program and in the highway program where billions of Federal dollars are being expended.

We also have the problem at the local and county level of handling our built-up areas. What are you going to do about providing parks for Perth Amboy, New Jersey? What are you going to do about providing additional open space for Bayonne? What are you going to do about the areas which are having a struggle just to keep themselves financially solvent, just to keep an orderly system of government going? Are you going to move in and superimpose community change from the outside?

Are you going to create more resentment from residents of the less developed areas by encouraging the so-called "outsiders" from the built-up area to use a park away from their own community, thus causing them to lose that much more of a sense of belonging and a sense of being a part of a social structure? What interest do you think that a man in Hoboken, N. J., has in a park that is built 25 miles away from his community and how are you going

to get him to feel that it is his park? And we wonder why we have
the destruction and vandalism that we have in our park areas!

Then we have the problem of the semi-rural and rural local
areas. Even though we have our urbanization problems in New
Jersey, we do still have some rural areas. Did you ever try to go
into a community of 28 square miles, populated by 1,200 hardy
parochial souls with ample room to rattle around in, and tell them
that *now* is the time to set aside a 200-acre open space area? Come
with me some night and I will let you share the rail that we ride
out of town.

We have a paradox in New Jersey (and you may have it in
your own State) of the rural area where the property owner wants
to hold land, with low taxes, for speculation and accrued value.
He doesn't want to be told what it is going to be used for and he
doesn't want any big government coming in and taking it over at
what he considers to be less than the price he can get from it 20
years from now. And yet, we have nearby urban areas crying
out for open space and no place to get it. In other words, we must
find some way to induce a happy marriage between older urban
cities, booming suburbs and rural lands. No doubt it can be done
on paper but the real problem in making any proposal effective,
is to get it carried out.

Now this all boils down to the fact that Dr. Kent and Mr.
Stansfield, for whom I have the greatest respect, quite
honestly scared me in listening to them today. Dr. Kent is sincere
in intent in telling you that regional planning is the answer to
many of these problems and I agree with him. Don Stansfield has
it all worked out from a State standpoint of what we need (what
I need as a citizen of the State of New Jersey) and I am all for
him. I think it's fine, but there was one word missing in what
they both said. Outside of the reference to population and outside
of the mention of figures and statistics, they cause me some unrest
by not talking about *people*. They scared me by not saying
education, by not talking about concern, and by not talking about
the loss of identity of man as a person.

It is my humble, but earnest opinion, that the most detrimental
occurrence in this country in the past several years has been the
loss of identity of the individual and a feeling of being meaningful.
All of us as professionals and technicians are too ready to write
the individual out of the book as an obstacle standing in the way
of going ahead with what we know is needed. The individual,

himself, has grown accustomed to this and is becoming more ready to turn all of his prerogatives over to someone else. As a result we are losing the initiative, the drive, the desire at the local and county level. Oh, you can't see it *yet* at the county level, but believe me, if you rode the circuit with me every night of the week out in the backwoods of New Jersey and Pennsylvania and New York, you could see it at the local level—and to me it is hand-writing on the wall.

Certainly, we need to plan ahead for parks and open space. We need more development at the Federal level. We need a coordinated program at the Federal level—so we need the Federal level to tell the State levels what they are doing. We need more program at the State level—but we need the State level to tell the regional what they are doing and to know how to draw clear lines of responsibility. We need the region to bring the open space program into focus on a smaller geographical scale.

A ND we need the Regional, the State, and the Federal agencies to remember that the basic, fundamental precept of carrying out Government, of effectuating programs in this country, has been, for hundreds of years,—and we pray to God that it will remain—*that of the local grass root level.* That is my message which I hope that you will take back to your States this afternoon. Thank you.

Land and Water Conservation Fund Act
—Some Interpretative Remarks

By EDWARD C. CRAFTS, Director, Bureau of Outdoor Recreation,
Department of the Interior

WHEN Don Alexander asked me to speak to you about the
Land and Water Conservation Fund Act a few weeks ago, I
reminded him I had talked to the National Conference rather
recently at Illinois Beach State Park. His response was, "Now
with the passage of the Fund Act, you've really got something
to talk about."

It is true there is a lot to talk about, but it is also true that it
is too soon to answer a good many of your questions.

The Land and Water Conservation Fund Act, now known as
P. L. 88-578, is well designed legislation. Nevertheless, there are
many questions of interpretation as well as policy and operating
problems that must be resolved before the Act can become
effective next January 1. These questions deal with a multiplicity
of operating procedures, specific planning guidelines for States,
delegations of authority, user fee regulations, criteria for apportionment of funds between States and other matters.

First of all, I want to express my appreciation for the unwavering support of the National Conference on behalf of this legislation.

Credit for the legislation cannot be given to any one individual,
organization, or group. Its passage is the result of the valiant
and untiring efforts of members of both Houses of Congress,
Presidents Kennedy and Johnson, the Secretaries of the Interior
and Agriculture, the States including 43 Governors, numerous
organizations, and countless individuals. On the other hand,
there was imposing opposition to the legislation. But in the final
analysis, this was either satisfied or overcome.

Many of you are professionals in the park field. You are fully
aware that the demand for outdoor recreation far exceeds the
capabilities of the States, local agencies, Federal Government and
the private sector to meet that demand, and the Land and Water
Conservation Fund Act offers a major opportunity in that
direction.

President Johnson, in signing the bill, said that it "assures our
growing population that we will begin, as of this day, to acquire
on a pay-as-you-go basis, the outdoor recreation lands that tomorrow's Americans will require."

Wayne Aspinall in discussing the bill on the floor of the House said that in his judgment the bill was of greater significance to the whole of the American public of today and tomorrow than any measure likely to be reported by the Interior Committee to the House in a long time to come.

Senator Jackson in presenting the bill on the floor of the Senate said there was "desperate need" for its enactment.

With the enactment of the Organic Statute for the Bureau of Outdoor Recreation in May 1963, and now with the passage of the Land and Water Conservation Fund Act, the Bureau of Outdoor Recreation is in a position to carry forward an effective program in cooperation with States and Federal agencies in accord with the mandates of Congress and the recommendations of the Outdoor Recreation Resources Review Commission.

I know you are interested primarily in learning what the States must do to participate in this program and how soon moneys will be available for this purpose. The best way to try to answer some of your questions, perhaps, is to tell you what we plan to do between now and next January 1.

ORGANIZATION and Personnel: I have organized a "hard core" group of about half a dozen key Bureau personnel to determine the actions that must be taken, their order of priority, and to develop plans for their accomplishment.

I am personally devoting most of my time to getting the Act functioning by January 1. Probably there will be some reorganization of the Bureau of Outdoor Recreation within the next few months to recognize the need for additional top calibre leadership plus a small number of supporting personnel whose responsibility will be to carry through on the necessary pre-planning for both State and Federal aspects of the legislation.

Such reorganization and staffing as is done within the Bureau will have to be within the framework of existing budget limitations.

One of the duties of this "hard core" group will be to finalize for top-level review the Presidential and Secretarial regulations and orders necessary to implement the act.

INFORMATION and Meetings: We have already prepared and cleared for publication a brief summary pamphlet telling what the Act provides and answering certain of the most frequent questions. Copies of this pamphlet are available at this meeting for distribution. In due course, we shall prepare more complete descriptive material, operating instructions, and answers to the multitude of questions which will be posed.

In addition to the informational material, we are planning a series of several interpretative discussions and question-and-answer sessions on the Act.

Later this week, we are having an initial session with our Regional Directors whose responsibility will include the administration of the legislation within the States which fall within their areas.

In addition, in late October, we have invited, through the Governors, State representatives from all States to meet with us at Illinois Beach State Park for a two-day interpretative discussion of the bill. At that time, we shall learn many of the questions that are in your minds and we shall be able to give you such answers and interpretations as are then available.

Some of you doubtless will be designated by your Governors to attend the meeting of State officials in October. In some instances, the Governor may send the State officer already designated as official liaison with this Bureau. In other instances, the Governor may make one of the two designations required under the legislation and those individuals may attend in lieu of, or in addition to, the present State Liaison Officers. Letters to Governors and State liaison officials already have been sent.

We are also planning to meet in due course with concerned Federal agencies on the Federal aspects of the legislation, but such discussions will probably not come until November.

Likewise there will be discussions with various members of the Cabinet, with the Executive Office of the President, and the Recreation Advisory Council. Active consideration is also being given to creating an Advisory Board to the Bureau.

A fourth meeting that we have in mind is to meet with approximately 25 outside organizations which gave the greatest support for the Fund legislation and which have a continuing, vital interest in its practical and successful administration. These organizations will be of great help to us in raising questions, posing problems, and in offering suggestions. This meeting and discussion will likewise come sometime this fall at a date not yet set.

I am well aware that there may be problems of competition between State agencies, as well as problems of relationships between State and local agencies. But our dealings under the law will necessarily be with the State officials designated by the Governors.

POLICY Questions and Interpretations: The Land and Water Conservation Fund Act is pioneering, landmark legislation. As was pointed out during the course of the legislation through Congress, there are many questions that will be subject to administrative interpretation. Accordingly, we shall need to depend heavily upon legislative history and the advice obtained from knowledgeable groups.

We already have lists of about 100 basic policy questions, some 15 specific actions required by the Federal Government, and 8 required actions by States.

In the regulations that will be issued, I am sure that such matters will be covered as apportionment to the States, Federal user fees, the form of contract or agreement with the States covering State participation, requirements for an acceptable State plan, the content of applications for financial assistance for planning, acquisition and development, the mechanism for making Federal funds available to States and through them to political subdivisions of the States, cooperative relations with HHFA and other Federal programs and activities, type of reports required, auditing records, and so on.

I underscore for you the importance from your standpoint and ours of developing reasonable planning requirements for the States. We have sent to the States recently as a technical service a so-called "White Book" which outlines our concept of an ultimate overall, long-range, comprehensive, statewide out-door recreation plan.

We have also sent, at the same time, a more specific outline of the type of planning requirements for the Land and Water Conservation Fund Act. The two are not the same thing at all. The former is much more complete than the latter.

Planning requirements and an equitable apportionment formula between the States are two of the most significant matters with which we shall be dealing with the States. We would welcome suggestions with respect to both of these key policy issues.

You are aware, of course, that three-fifths of the moneys to be apportioned among the States shall be at the discretion of the Secretary and he is instructed to consider State population, use of recreation resources within the State by out-of-State visitors, and Federal resources and programs within the States in determining such apportionment.

There are no guidelines in the legislative history as to what weight is to be attached to these criteria or what other criteria may be used, except that it was indicated on the Senate side that in-State population is to be given primary weight.

Parenthetically, I might say we have assembled for the use of our own working group the complete legislative history of the bill, which is an imposing mass of documents and must be carefully scrutinized in connection with actions we take. There was much legislative history built on user fees, State apportionments, and the other key matters during the House and Senate debate, in addition to the hearings on the bill, the bill itself, and the Committee Reports. In all cases where it is clear, the language of the statute itself is controlling.

One device that may be of help to some States is a model State bill. Some States will need new legislative authority by the State legislature either to raise moneys or to permit the matching requirements that the Land and Water Conservation Fund Act requires. We shall soon send to the States a sample bill which may be helpful in this regard.

I am aware of criticism from some States about the lack of uniformity in Federal regulations relating to programs of Federal assistance to States and local agencies. This criticism has dealt with such things as inconsistencies in the administration of programs, duplication of audits of State records by various Federal agencies, and differences in degree to which States are given operating latitude.

Undoubtedly, some of this criticism is justified but some of it may not be. You are all aware of the fact that there are various Federal statutes, decisions, and regulations with which all Federal agencies must comply. The Act, itself, provides certain restrictions on the States and contains certain specific requirements. Although we have no alternative but to comply with all legal requirements, it will be my objective to administer this program so as to give the States the greatest possible amount of flexibility within the framework of the statute, legislative history, and other requirements of Federal law.

USER Fees and Other Federal Aspects: The problem of Federal user fees has been one of the most controversial features of the bill. There are many guidelines and criteria spelled out, not only in the legislation, but also in the Committee reports and in the Congressional debate.

We have, in progress at the present time, two special interagency groups working directly on the question of user fees and measurement of visitor use. Their purpose is to prepare reports suitable for presentation to the public, to the Recreation Advisory Council, and probably also to the Congressional Committees, and at the same time, to draft necessary Presidential and Secretarial regulations to put their reports and recommendations into effect.

In many respects, user fees are the most difficult aspect of the bill. One reason is the so-called automobile sticker which, once decided upon, has to be designed, printed, a price set, and arrangements made for its sale through chosen outlets—all by the first of the year.

I might say that we have commitments to discuss proposed policies and interpretations on user fees with both the President's Recreation Advisory Council and also with the concerned Congressional Committees prior to their instigation. Any system of user fees employed will not directly affect the States and is primarily a Federal question. However, we hope to benefit from the experience that several States have developed over the past several years, and what is done on Federal areas may indirectly affect State policies.

With respect to other Federal aspects of the bill outside of user fees, the principal questions will be the apportionment of the Federal share as between eligible Federal agencies and the projects for which these agencies intend to use the Federal moneys, if appropriated. I am quite sure there will be competition between Federal agencies for the limited funds available just as there will be competition between the States and within a State by its various agencies. The Federal role of the Bureau of Outdoor Recreation will need to be made clear in the Presidential regulations.

I AM most grateful that Congress in its wisdom saw fit to make the Act effective January 1 because there is so much preliminary planning that needs to be carried out.

Already we are receiving numerous inquiries as to whether funds may be available for this or that purpose, such as for the control of jelly fish or the development of Olympic training facilities, whether local governments can apply directly to us or whether they must go through the States, how individual State agencies can see that their needs are properly considered within a State, and so on. Numerous organizations which supported the legislation are now looking to us to make sure their particular interests are adequately cared for in the statewide outdoor recreation plans.

We feel in a sense like the student who has worked hard through school, is now graduated and finds that he has to work even harder as he moves into the world of reality.

I can assure you that we need your wholehearted cooperation, patience, and understanding. Many of the questions that are in your minds today, I am quite sure I cannot answer. However, six months from now we should be able to answer most of them.

It would be of help to us if you would send us your questions as they occur to you even though you do not receive a definitive reply. They will go on our ever-growing list of matters to be resolved before the statute becomes a workable reality and before it can serve the purpose for which it was conceived; namely, to help meet, within the next ten years, our tremendously growing demand for both land and water outdoor recreation resources.

Although all of the remarks that I have made here today have dealt with the Land and Water Conservation Act, I should put these in perspective and remind you that we still have our continuing responsibilities that have been initiated and carried out over the past couple of years stemming from the Bureau's Organic Act. These include matters such as promotion of coordination within the Executive agencies of the Government, serving as staff to the President's Recreation Advisory Council, carrying out the Congressional mandate to develop a nationwide outdoor recreation plan, technical services to the States in planning, numerous special area studies such as the North Cascades, Wild Rivers, and Lewis and Clark Trail, certain research activities, and cooperative endeavors with educational institutions.

I do not want to leave the impression that the Land and Water Conservation Fund Act now becomes the sole function of the Bureau of Outdoor Recreation.

Thank you for your help and we welcome your suggestions.

CPSIA information can be obtained
at www.ICGtesting.com
Printed in the USA
BVHW04*1421310818
526160BV00008B/36/P

9 780332 636887